America
From the Road

Reader's Digest

America
From the Road

The Reader's Digest Association, Inc.
Pleasantville, New York/Montreal

Project Editor: Carroll C. Calkins
Project Art Director: Judy Skorpil
Associate Editors: Noreen Church, Ben Etheridge
Research Editors: Shirley Miller, Mary V. O'Gorman
Copy Editor: Rosemarie Conefrey
Art Editors: Robert Grant, Gilbert Nielsen
Art Associate: Roger Jones
Picture Editor: Robert J. Woodward
Picture Researcher: Margaret Matthews
Assistant Artist: Renée Khatami
Editorial Assistant: Dolores Damm

Contributing Editor: Margaret Perry
Contributing Writers: Kent and Donna Dannen
Contributing Designer: Robert Bull
Contributing Artists: John Dawson, Howard Friedman,
        John Lind, Ray Skibinski
        Topographical maps drawn by Edes Harrison
        for the U.S. Geological Survey
Contributing Researchers: Mary Elizabeth Allison, Margaret Brawley,
        Mary Ann Hart, Eileen Hughes, Jozefa Stuart
Geology Consultant: Rhodes W. Fairbridge, Professor of
        Geological Sciences, Columbia University

Contents

How to Use This Book

Follow a complete tour, sample a section, or decide on your own which highlights you want to see

This book includes 125 loop trips that describe almost 1,500 of the most interesting, beautiful, historic, and scenic places in America.

The editors of this volume carefully researched the highlights in every state and laid out the tours. These were then checked (and revised when necessary) by travel experts in each state and, finally, *every mile of every route was test-driven* to ensure optimum accuracy.

Each of the 47 map pages includes from one to five color-coded tours. The highlights on each tour are numbered in a clockwise sequence, and the text describing the highlights has matching numbers color-keyed to the tour. Leader lines show the exact location of the highlights on the tour. In the occasional situations where the map does not clearly show the route to the highlight, further driving instructions are included in the text.

The routes are superimposed on standard road maps. The detail is such that you can easily find alternate routes to the points of interest if you choose not to drive the tours as indicated.

The main reason for the loop tours is to connect the highlights in an orderly and efficient way and to help you get to the greatest number of the most interesting places with the least expenditure of time, money, and gasoline. The loops provide an overview of an entire area and an accurate description of the roads you will travel.

We do not, however, mean to suggest that the highlights should necessarily be approached in the order they are presented here or, for that matter, that the loops should be followed at all.

You can make up your own tours by looking at the map, reading the description of the highlights, and deciding what you would like to see and how you would like to get there. You might also want to follow part of a tour as you drive from one area to another.

On the facing page is a reproduction of a map page with tours in Massachusetts and Connecticut and a short leg in New York State. The broad arrow overlays suggest some of the ways in which these tours could be adapted to suit your specific needs. If, for example, you are driving from Hartford, Connecticut, north to Vermont, you might choose to go up Interstate 91 and stop off at any or all of the highlights (numbers 14, 13, 12, and 11) on the eastern side of the green tour.

If you have more time, you could consider the many options for interesting stops at numbers 17 through 13 on the red tour and numbers 2 through 9 on the green.

The numbered and color-keyed highlights are easily found in the text, where you can read about them and decide which ones you would most like to visit. Note that captions for the illustrations are numbered to correspond with the appropriate highlight. By studying the maps in your chosen area, you will see that there are many ways to get to the various highlights. The purpose of this book is to help you decide which highlights you would like to see and then show you how to get to them.

The map pages, as mentioned, are standard road-map scale. This, for Connecticut–Massachusetts, is 9 miles (14 kilometers) to the inch. At this scale, these states cannot be completely shown on the page. Therefore, the position of the loops is indicated on a locator map adjoining each map page.

In many states the tours are too far apart to include on a contiguous map, and only the separate, relevant areas can be shown. Such is the case in New Mexico, whose four tours are in different parts of the state. On the New Mexico locator map reproduced below, note that the blocks showing the location of the tours are each of a different color. These colors match the corresponding routes outlined on the map page.

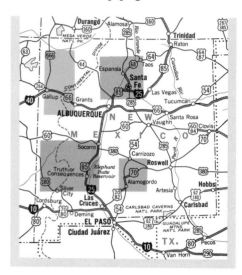

If you were planning a trip through New Mexico, for example, you could use the locator map to see which loops might be on your route and then check the map page and the text to see which of the highlights would interest you most.

The map of the United States, on pages 16 and 17, includes the Interstate Highway System and all major roads. It also shows the area covered by each of the three sections of the book: Eastern, Central, and Western. You will find this map helpful in determining the shortest and fastest way to get to the area you are interested in exploring.

You may want to consider flying to an area and renting a car to drive a loop or two. To help with this, we have indicated the towns where scheduled airline stops are made. The symbol for this and the other features of the map are shown on the legend facing the map pages.

If you are interested in camping, note that the state park and recreation area symbols indicate which ones have campsites. Note too that there is a symbol for points of interest. Many of these points are included on the tours, but there are many others within easy reach of the tour routes. These points are a further aid in choosing the tours that will be most interesting to you.

In planning the time to allow for your tours, keep in mind that the mileage scales, which are indicated on the legend, vary from map page to map page.

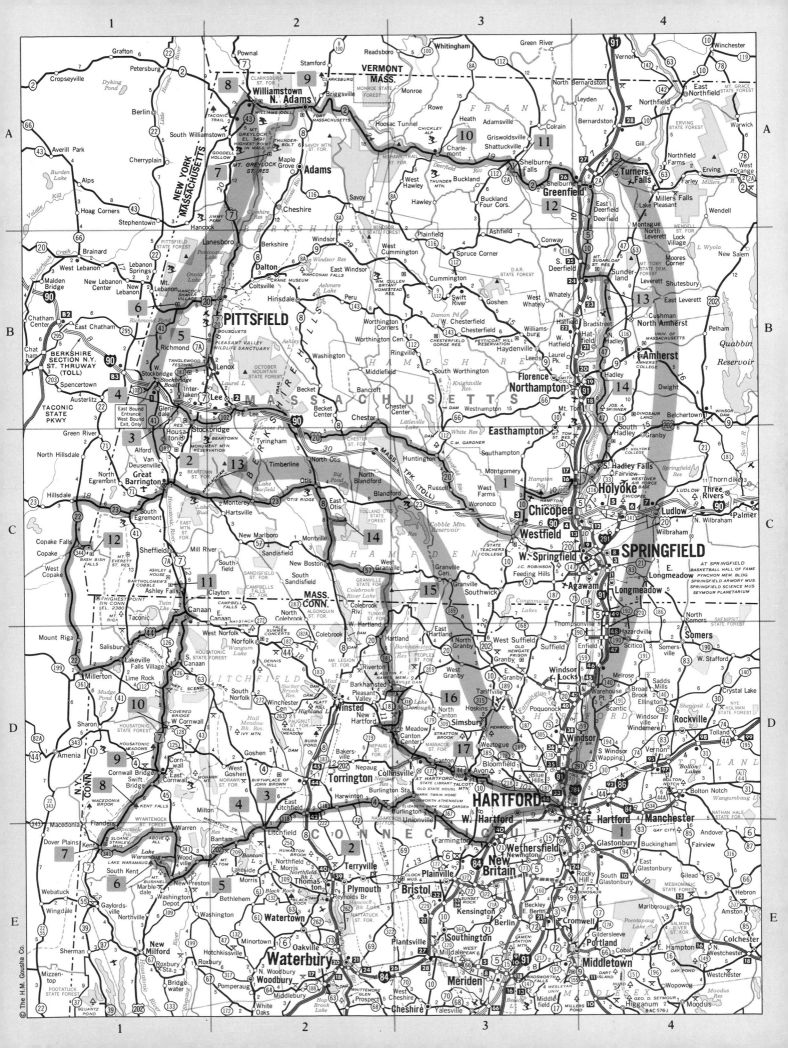

How Our Continent Has Moved

Knowing where America came from, and the time it took to get here, help us understand what we see from the road

When we behold the magnificence of snowcapped mountains, dramatic coastlines, and the subtle beauty of our countless hills, valleys, lakes, rivers, and streams, we are witness to the effects of a process only recently understood.

The theory of continental drift, illustrated below, was proposed in 1912 by the German astronomer and meteorologist Alfred Wegener.

Wegener proposed that the continents were all once joined in a single landmass, which he called Pangaea from the Greek for "all the earth," and that they drifted apart to create the Atlantic Ocean. His idea provoked violent controversy at the time, but today it is accepted by the scientific community, along with the concept of plate tectonics, which has to do with the mechanics of continental movement.

The drawing below left shows a section of Pangaea as it might have been some 300 million years ago. About 50 million years ago, a crack, now known as the central rift zone, developed. As molten lava poured through this rift, it was quickly cooled by seawater and formed the ocean crust. This process of seafloor spreading forced the opposing continental coasts apart at a rate of one or two inches a year, and is still going on. Over millions of years the crack became a valley, the valley became a seaway, and eventually the expanse of open ocean we know today.

As North America drifted west, it also moved north out of the hot, humid equatorial region and into the hot dry tropics and subtropics with a climate like that of the Sahara and the Persian Gulf region. The formations of red rock we see from New Jersey to Wyoming were developed in this era.

By 50 million years ago, as shown in the second illustration, the region of North America was in the temperate belt. At the same time, the continued widening of the Atlantic brought moisture and rain to the area of the Gulf of Mexico and the East Coast and started the luxuriant growth that we enjoy today.

In the last million years the continent moved far enough to the north to be exposed to the encroaching glaciers from the polar regions, which sculpted the coast of Maine, the valleys of New Hampshire and Vermont, the Great Lakes, and innumerable other scenic features of our northern states.

When the continents were still connected by land bridges, the most advanced creatures of the time (primitive reptiles) moved throughout the favorable climates of Pangaea, which accounts for the similarity of fossils found in Africa and the Americas. Further hard evidence of continental drift lies in the coalfields of West Virginia and Pennsylvania. Only a hot humid climate, like that near the equator, could develop the luxuriant growth necessary to create the deep layers of peat that with sufficient time and pressure are rendered into coal.

The incredible pressures that folded the crust of the earth to make the Cascade Range and the Rocky Mountains also rendered oil from the silt of ancient sea bottoms. Thus it is that the oil wells we see from the roads of Texas and Louisiana are reminders of the relentless forces of continents on the move.

300 Million Years Ago

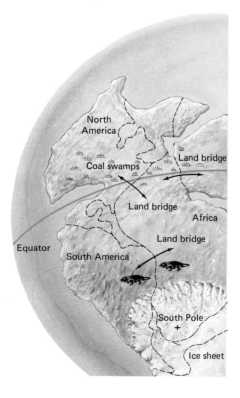

50 Million Years Ago

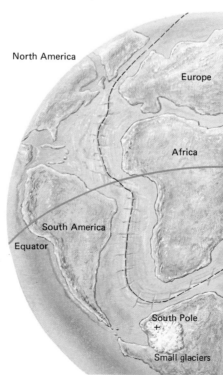

The Last 1 Million Years

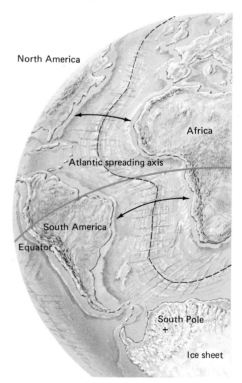

10

GEOLOGIC TIME CHART

Years Past	Era	Period	Epoch	Plants and Animals	Geologic Features
	CENOZOIC	Quaternary	Holocene	All recorded history	
			Pleistocene	Mammoths, bison, saber-toothed cats	Glaciers
		Tertiary	Pliocene	Ancestral bears, mastodons, hyenas	Start of Grand Canyon
			Miocene	Pigs, ancestral horses, four-horned antelopes	Volcanic activity in West
			Oligocene	Primitive dogs, giant rhinoceros, even-toed mammals	Great Plains develop
			Eocene	Grasses, odd-toed mammals, deer and squirrel ancestors	Coral reefs in Florida
65,000,000			Paleocene	Carnivorous mammals, hoofed mammals, insectivores	Coastal plains developing
	MESOZOIC	Cretaceous		Tyrannosaurus, Triceratops, sequoias, maples, Pteranodon, Andromeda	Rocky Mountains uplifting
		Jurassic		Stegosaurus, Brontosaurus, Plesiosaurus	Block tilting
225,000,000		Triassic		Cycads, early dinosaurs	Extensive deserts and red beds
	PALEOZOIC	Permian		Mesosaurus, ginkgoes	Appalachian Mountains fully developed
		Pennsylvanian		Insects, reptiles, conifers	Swamps of coal-forming plants
		Mississippian		Sharks, goniatites, crinoids	
		Devonian		Horsetails, tree ferns, amphibians	New England mountains build
		Silurian		Fish, cephalopods, sea scorpions, land plants	Shallow seas in Midwest
590,000,000		Ordovician		Echinoderms, corals, clams, snails	Adirondack Mountains rising
		Cambrian		Trilobites, brachiopods, graptolites	Appalachian trough develops
4,500,000,000	PRECAMBRIAN	Late		Flatworms, ancestral jelly fish	Extensive shallow seas
		Middle		Flagellates, sponges	Iron-ore formations
		Early		Bacteria, blue-green algae	Volcanic crust

■ = 100 million years

Time, in terms of geology, is all but impossible to fully comprehend. This is not surprising when we consider that current estimates put the age of the earth at about 4½ billion years and that all human history is included in just the past few thousand years. Occasional glimpses into the geologic past can be seen along the road, particularly on the Interstate Highways where steep cuts have been made to maintain an easy grade. Here you might see a succession of seabeds laid down over millions of years, solid rock that flowed up as liquid under unimaginable pressure, or cross sections of ancient lava flows.

Reading this geologic time chart from the bottom, we see that in the first 3.9 billion years, the Precambrian era, the early crust of the earth developed like slag in a blast furnace. The cooling iron core left a lighter residue to harden as the crust, parts of which we can see in the Adirondacks, Minnesota, upper Michigan, and the floor of the Grand Canyon. Each of the following periods, Cambrian through Permian, left distinctive fossils, such as trilobites, brachiopods, and other extinct representatives of the time that between 570 to 225 million years ago. In the Mesozoic era dinosaurs evolved and disappeared, and in the Cenozoic came the mammals, and finally, in the Quaternary, came the evolution of mankind.

Continental Cross Section

As the continent drifted, our scenery was being formed

According to geological evidence, the earth's crust that underlies most of the United States is in places 3½ billion years old. A few "windows," such as in the Grand Canyon and Minnesota and the Adirondacks, expose this ancient rock to view.

In the Midwest most of these rocks were laid down as sediments in shallow seas about 300 million years ago, as shown in the upper cross section. Note, too, that at this time our continent was still attached to West Africa. An earlier continental collision here led to the uplift of a mountain range of which today's Appalachians were the western foothills.

Fifty million years ago there was little change in the Midwest except for a general emergence of land from the shallow seas and some narrow seaways and gulfs around the ancestral Rockies, which were just beginning to rise up. The former mountains along the East Coast had eroded down to modest dimensions, such as we now see in the Blue Ridge.

On the West Coast at this time there was a dynamic situation. A slab of the Pacific Ocean crust was driving in under the edge of the continent, which was moving irresistibly to the west and north. The heat generated by these opposing forces melted the rock, which rose up as magma through fissures in the earth to create the volcanic mountains along the Pacific Coast, including Mount St. Helens—a dramatic reminder that powerful forces are still at work here. The Coast Ranges were also beginning to build up and fold as they slowly emerged from the sea.

At this time giant faults were breaking up the crust into blocks that would become the Sierra Nevada and depressed segments that were destined to be the Great Valley of California, the Salton Sea, and the Gulf of California.

Today's profile, illustrated here with a greatly exaggerated vertical scale to emphasize the various developments, still shows only local changes since its emergence from the ocean nearly 200 million years ago. To the east, beside the Atlantic Ocean, the roots of the earliest mountains are now covered by the young sediment of the coastal plain. Slightly inland, the Appalachians and the New England Province have been gently uplifted in broad domes. This slow uplift has given them the status of reactivated mountains. Likewise, to the west, the Rocky Mountains have also been reactivated, and important fault lines separate them from the low-lying plains of the Midwest.

An alternating series of ups and downs has created the Basin and Range Province, separated, in turn, by tremendous fault lines from the Sierra Nevada, which is the greatest uplift of them all.

Dividing the Coast Ranges longitudinally is the San Andreas Fault, the most remarkable fracture trace in the country. It is still highly active, moving many feet per century, not smoothly but in shattering jerks, as the western fringe of our continent drifts inexorably toward Russia and Japan.

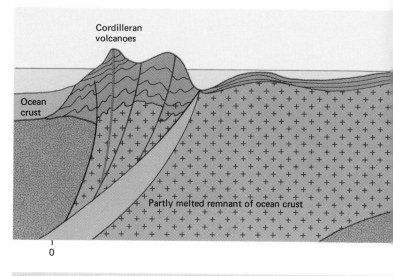

300 Million Years Ago

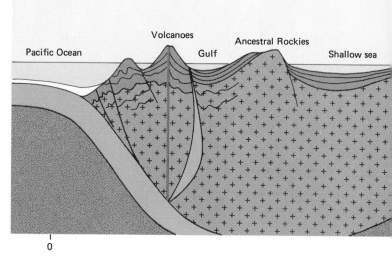

50 Million Years Ago

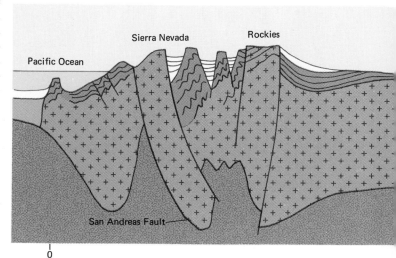

Today

12

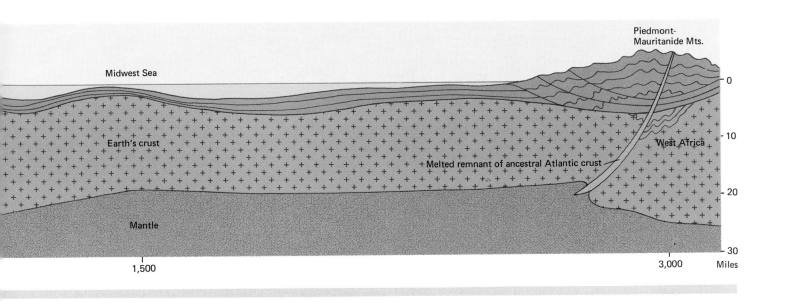

Midwest Sea

Earth's crust

Melted remnant of ancestral Atlantic crust

Mantle

Piedmont-
Mauritanide Mts.

West Africa

0

10

20

30

1,500

3,000

Miles

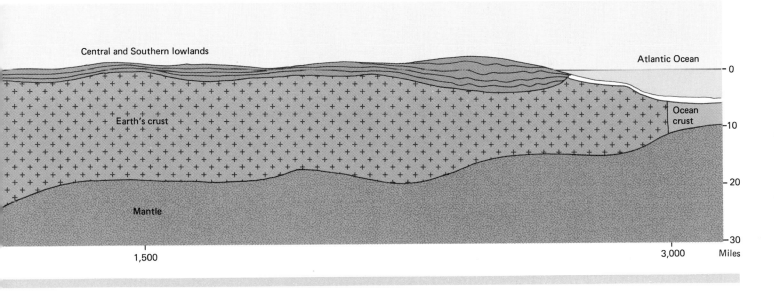

Central and Southern lowlands

Atlantic Ocean

Earth's crust

Ocean
crust

Mantle

0

10

20

30

1,500

3,000

Miles

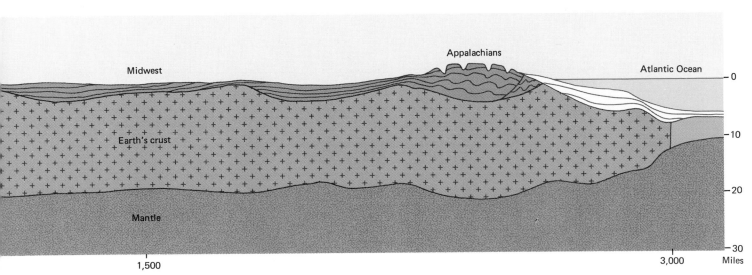

Midwest

Appalachians

Atlantic Ocean

Earth's crust

Mantle

0

10

20

30

1,500

3,000

Miles

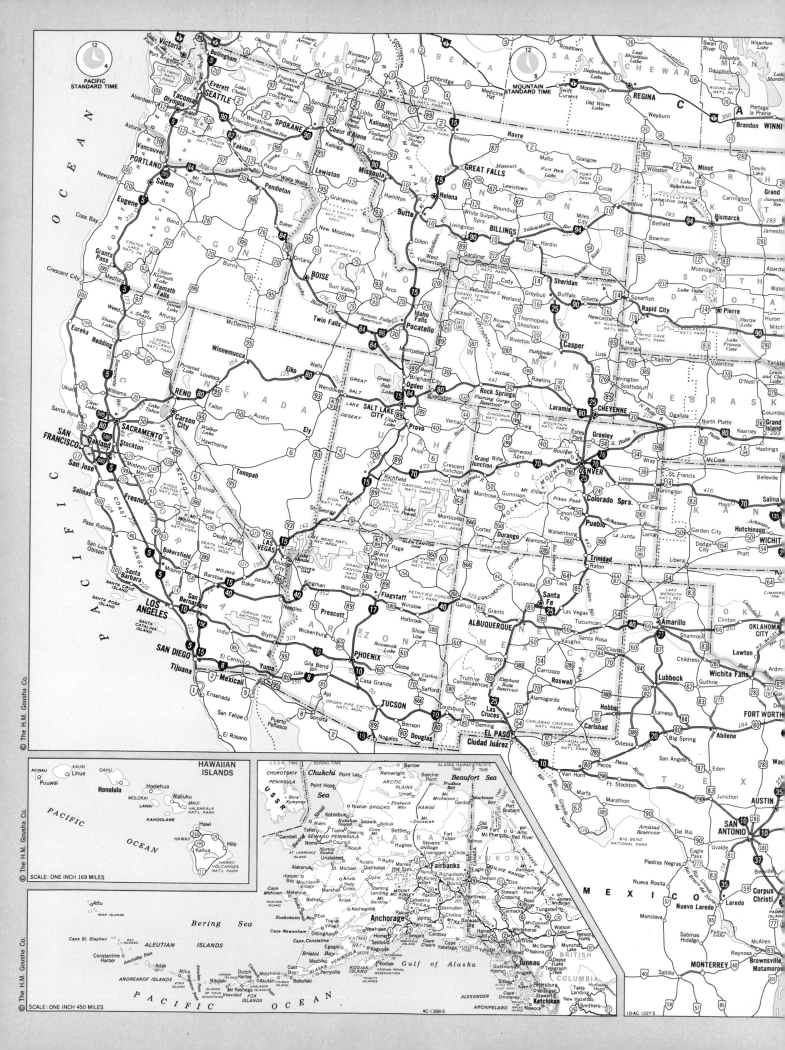

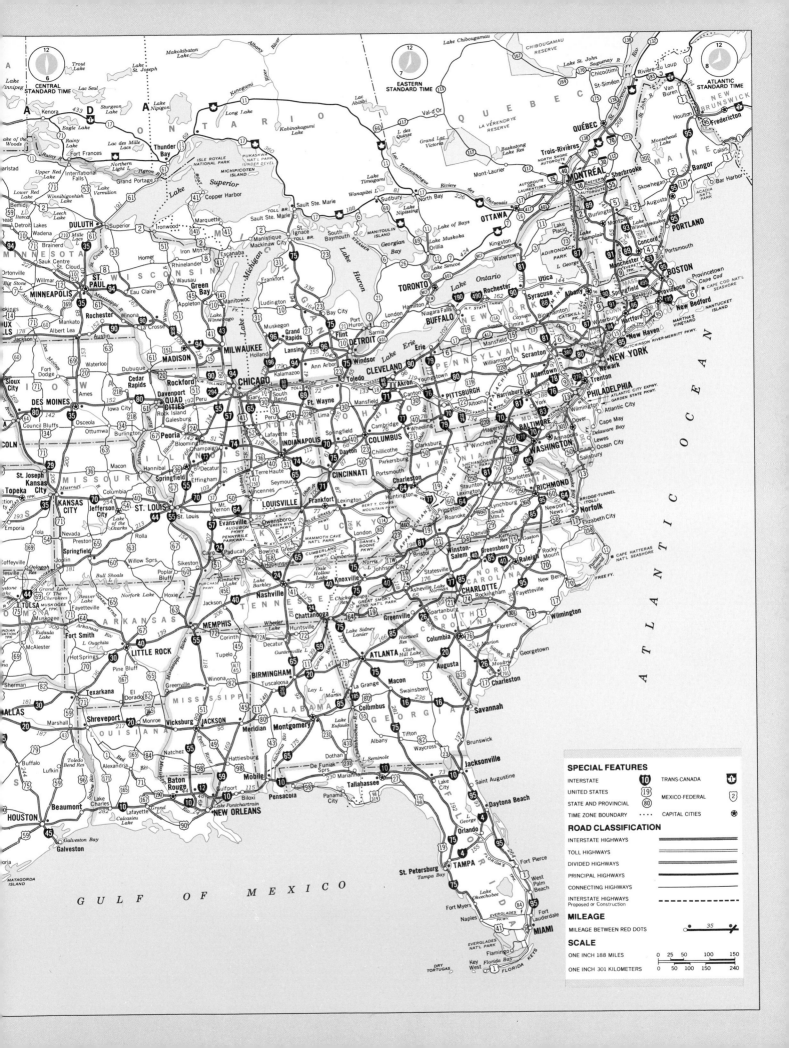

Exploring the Eastern States

Our longest coastline, greatest lakes, and oldest mountains offer surcease from the crowded cities

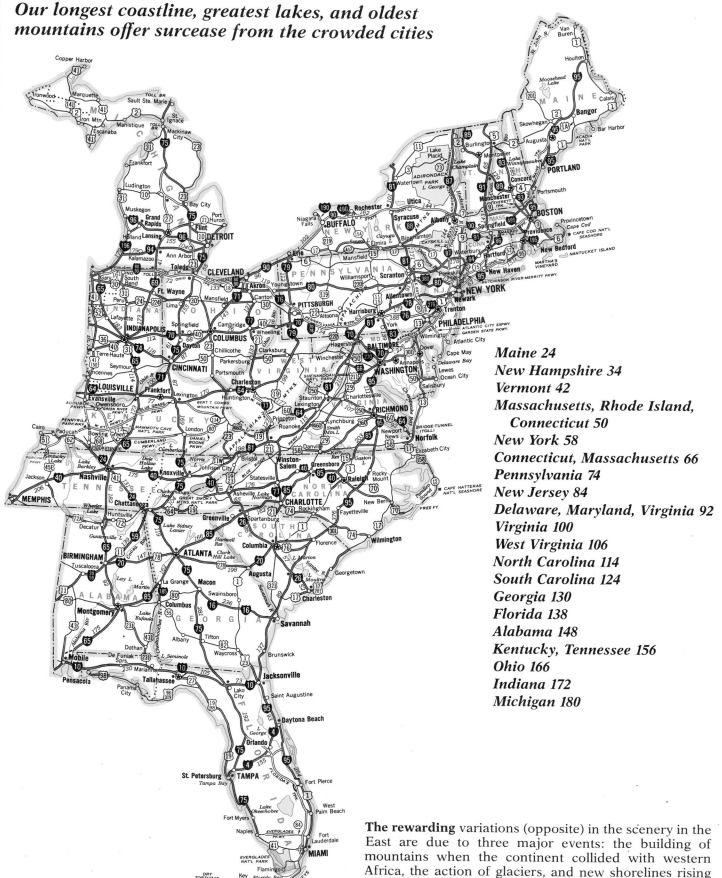

Maine 24
New Hampshire 34
Vermont 42
Massachusetts, Rhode Island, Connecticut 50
New York 58
Connecticut, Massachusetts 66
Pennsylvania 74
New Jersey 84
Delaware, Maryland, Virginia 92
Virginia 100
West Virginia 106
North Carolina 114
South Carolina 124
Georgia 130
Florida 138
Alabama 148
Kentucky, Tennessee 156
Ohio 166
Indiana 172
Michigan 180

The rewarding variations (opposite) in the scenery in the East are due to three major events: the building of mountains when the continent collided with western Africa, the action of glaciers, and new shorelines rising from the sea. The concentration of roads indicates the density of population today.

10-AC-1227-S

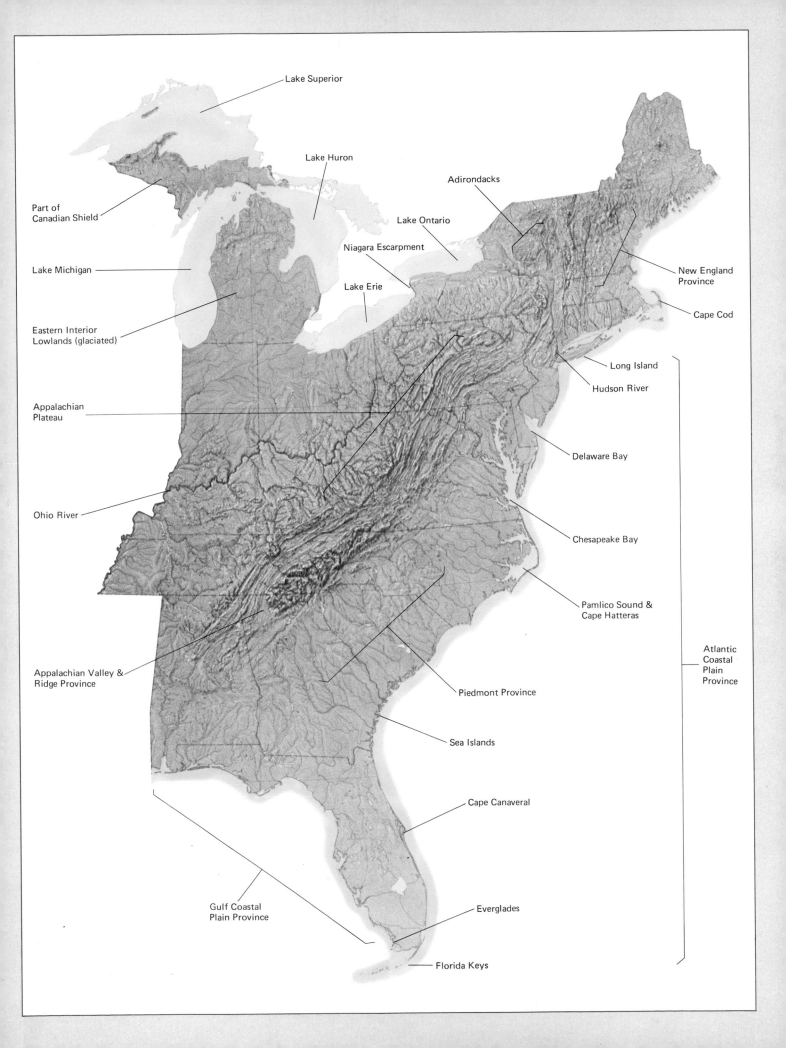

Lake Superior

Lake Huron

Adirondacks

Part of
Canadian Shield

Lake Ontario

New England
Province

Lake Michigan

Niagara Escarpment

Cape Cod

Lake Erie

Eastern Interior
Lowlands (glaciated)

Long Island

Hudson River

Appalachian
Plateau

Delaware Bay

Ohio River

Chesapeake Bay

Pamlico Sound &
Cape Hatteras

Atlantic
Coastal
Plain
Province

Appalachian Valley &
Ridge Province

Piedmont Province

Sea Islands

Cape Canaveral

Gulf Coastal
Plain Province

Everglades

Florida Keys

Plants, Birds, and Animals to Watch For

From the northern forests to the watery Everglades, there is a remarkable range of nature's works to see

Among the greatest natural displays in America is the autumn color of the northeastern hardwood forests. The most spectacular single tree at that time is the sugar maple, which has a spectrum of colorful leaves ranging from yellow through orange to scarlet. These same forests are also host to birch trees, with their startling white bark under a cool green canopy of foliage, and dogwoods, with their lovely white and pink flowers in the spring. Mountain laurel, rhododendron, and flame azalea are other native plants that add welcome highlights of color to the woods. The most unusual tree is the swamp cypress,

which sends up "knees" that serve to provide oxygen for the underwater roots.

Among the most interesting birds are the loon, the ibis, the wood stork, and the great blue heron. The moose and the black bear have things pretty much their own way in the north woods, and in the South the alligator is the unchallenged king of the swamps.

As for the denizens of the Atlantic shore, there is no question that the lobster is at the top of the list among connoisseurs of seafood. The eastern oysters, of which there are many kinds, are also highly regarded.

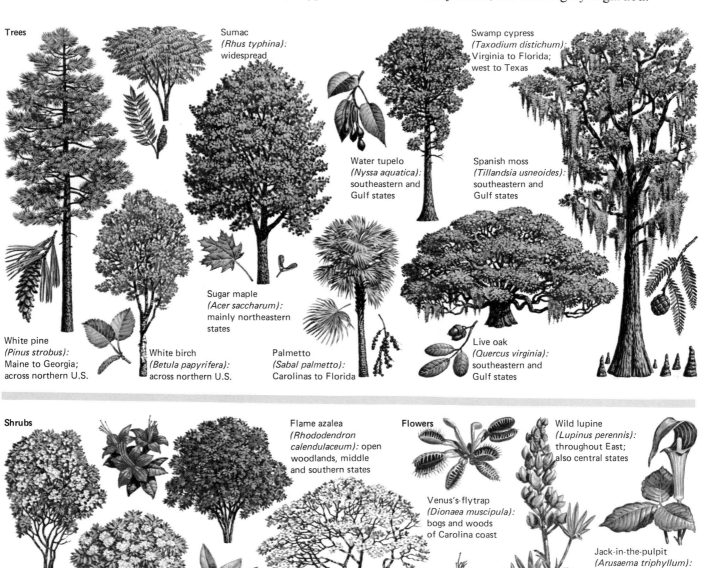

Trees

Sumac
(Rhus typhina):
widespread

Swamp cypress
(Taxodium distichum):
Virginia to Florida;
west to Texas

Water tupelo
(Nyssa aquatica):
southeastern and
Gulf states

Spanish moss
(Tillandsia usneoides):
southeastern and
Gulf states

Sugar maple
(Acer saccharum):
mainly northeastern
states

White pine
(Pinus strobus):
Maine to Georgia;
across northern U.S.

White birch
(Betula papyrifera):
across northern U.S.

Palmetto
(Sabal palmetto):
Carolinas to Florida

Live oak
(Quercus virginia):
southeastern and
Gulf states

Shrubs

Flame azalea
*(Rhododendron
calendulaceum):* open
woodlands, middle
and southern states

Flowers

Venus's-flytrap
(Dionaea muscipula):
bogs and woods
of Carolina coast

Wild lupine
(Lupinus perennis):
throughout East;
also central states

Jack-in-the-pulpit
(Arusaema triphyllum):
widespread in woodlands

Mountain laurel
(Kalmia latifolia):
woodlands, throughout
East; also Louisiana

Great laurel/rose bay
(Rhododendron maximum):
bogs and woods south
to Georgia and Alabama

Flowering dogwood
(Cornus florida):
throughout East; also
west to California

Pink azalea
(Rhododendron nudiflorum):
from Carolinas and
Tennessee northward

Moss campion
(Silene acaulis):
mountains, mainly
New England

20

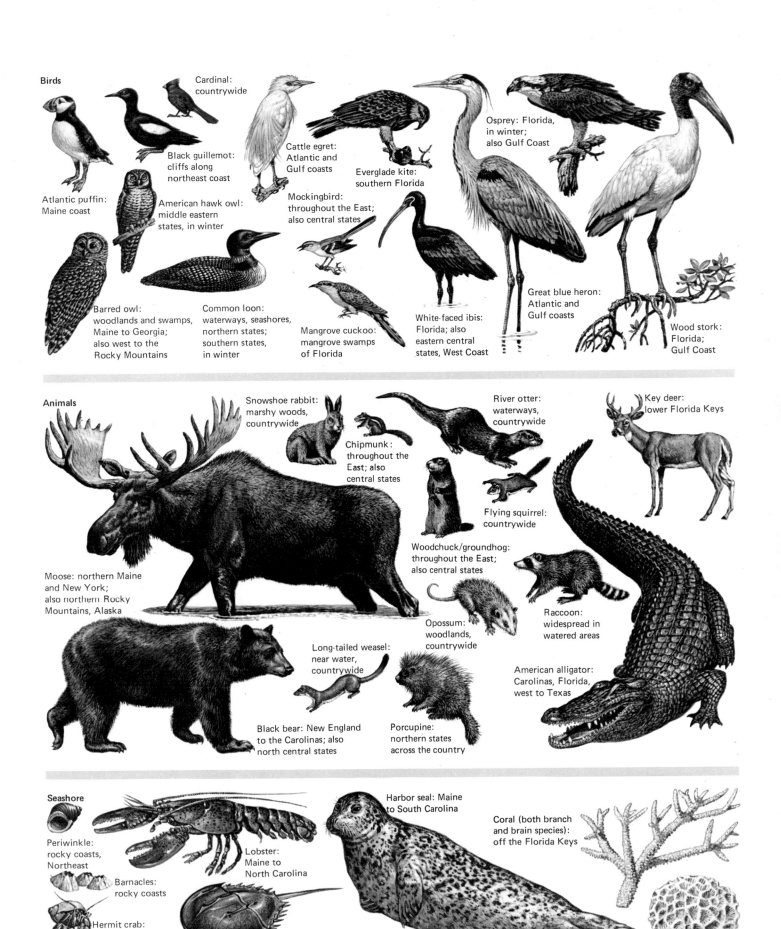

Birds

Cardinal: countrywide

Atlantic puffin: Maine coast

Black guillemot: cliffs along northeast coast

American hawk owl: middle eastern states, in winter

Cattle egret: Atlantic and Gulf coasts

Everglade kite: southern Florida

Osprey: Florida, in winter; also Gulf Coast

Barred owl: woodlands and swamps, Maine to Georgia; also west to the Rocky Mountains

Mockingbird: throughout the East; also central states

Common loon: waterways, seashores, northern states; southern states, in winter

Mangrove cuckoo: mangrove swamps of Florida

White-faced ibis: Florida; also eastern central states, West Coast

Great blue heron: Atlantic and Gulf coasts

Wood stork: Florida; Gulf Coast

Animals

Snowshoe rabbit: marshy woods, countrywide

Chipmunk: throughout the East; also central states

River otter: waterways, countrywide

Key deer: lower Florida Keys

Flying squirrel: countrywide

Woodchuck/groundhog: throughout the East; also central states

Moose: northern Maine and New York; also northern Rocky Mountains, Alaska

Opossum: woodlands, countrywide

Raccoon: widespread in watered areas

Long-tailed weasel: near water, countrywide

American alligator: Carolinas, Florida, west to Texas

Black bear: New England to the Carolinas; also north central states

Porcupine: northern states across the country

Seashore

Periwinkle: rocky coasts, Northeast

Barnacles: rocky coasts

Lobster: Maine to North Carolina

Hermit crab: along Atlantic Coast

Horseshoe crab: along Atlantic Coast

Harbor seal: Maine to South Carolina

Coral (both branch and brain species): off the Florida Keys

Machinery Worthy of Note

Along the road you can see some of what it takes to put milk, butter, and eggs in your local store

Milk, butter, and eggs are among the staples you can find in every grocery store and account for the great numbers and fascinating variety of bucolic scenes we encounter along the road. The hayfields, pastures, and all the equipment it takes to plow, cultivate, plant, and harvest; the silos and barns and outbuildings, not to mention the cows and poultry, are colorful evidence of what it takes to fulfill our needs.

There are still some traditional small farms where you can see a big barn with a hayloft, a silo for storing chopped corn (ensilage), and some sheds for equipment.

On larger farms you may also see gleaming silos of enameled steel. These are used to hold forage crops harvested while they still retain moisture, instead of allowing them to dry as hay. The chopped feed is blown in through the top and moved automatically out the bottom into the feed troughs.

On many farms the machines that make the familiar rectangular bales of hay are being replaced by equipment that rolls up large round bales that weigh up to 1,700 pounds. These are moved where needed by other machines. No hand labor is required.

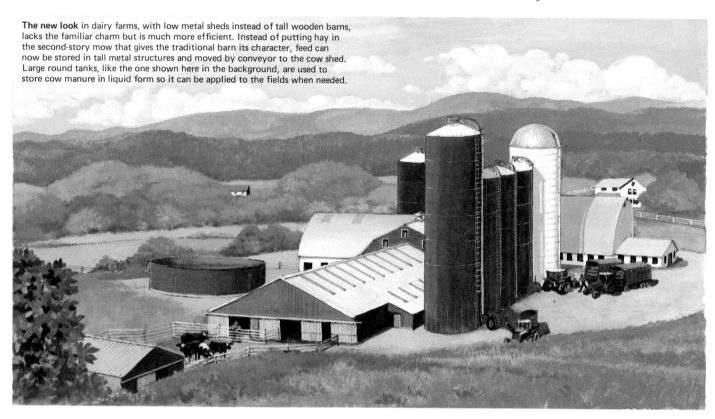

The new look in dairy farms, with low metal sheds instead of tall wooden barns, lacks the familiar charm but is much more efficient. Instead of putting hay in the second-story mow that gives the traditional barn its character, feed can now be stored in tall metal structures and moved by conveyor to the cow shed. Large round tanks, like the one shown here in the background, are used to store cow manure in liquid form so it can be applied to the fields when needed.

Mower-windrower cuts the hay and leaves it heaped in a narrow pile so it can be picked up by a bailing machine. Many farmers still use a mower to cut the hay and a windrower to line it up. This means the field has to be gone over twice. To save fuel and time, the newer equipment does both functions simultaneously.

Wherever you see the big round bales of hay in the fields, there will be machines like this. Hay is lifted from the windrow onto a conveyor, flattened into a mat, and rolled like a rug. When full size, it is automatically tied with twine.

If the bales you see in the fields are rectangular, watch too for the other equipment used to get the hay into the barn. There may be big loads of hay on a flatbed trailer behind a slow-moving tractor and, at the barn, a self-powered or tractor-driven conveyor to lift the bales into the loft. Off-season, between harvests, when you see this equipment in the barnyard, you will know what it is for.

Corn grown for feed is cut and chopped—stalks, leaves, cobs, and all—in the field and transported to the silo in a self-unloading wagon. The wagon has a conveyor in the bottom that feeds the corn into a blower, which lifts it up and drops it into the silo from the top. In the newer silos the blower system is built in.

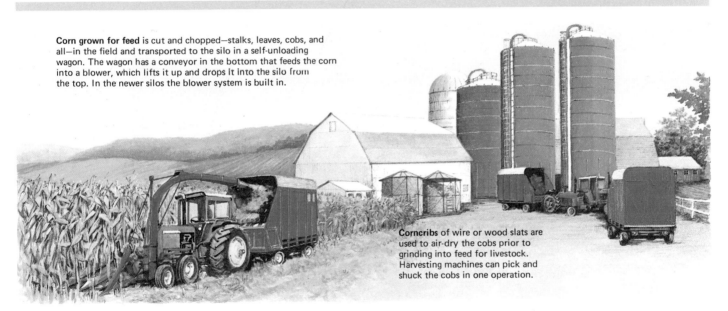

Corncribs of wire or wood slats are used to air-dry the cobs prior to grinding into feed for livestock. Harvesting machines can pick and shuck the cobs in one operation.

In egg- or broiler-producing areas, you see feed plants where all the scientifically balanced ingredients of chicken feed are combined before transport to the hoppers at the chicken house.

The chickens for commercial egg production are kept indoors and about the only clues to this activity are the grain hoppers and ventilating fans in the outside walls.

23

The Northeast Corner

In Maine the forces of the ice age are revealed in the lakes, mountains, valleys, and rugged coast

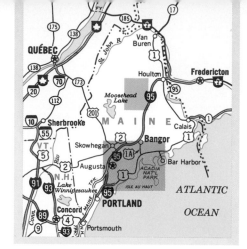

Following the retreat of the glaciers from this region, 10,000 to 12,000 years ago, the forests began to develop. In the early 1600's, when the British established a colony here, the land was almost completely forested and there were great stands of white pine trees more than 100 feet tall. In 1691 the crown decreed that all pines within three miles of the shoreline were reserved as masts for the ships of the Royal Navy. The mast pines are gone now, but Maine is still the Pine Tree State and more than 85 percent of the land is still forested. The vast forests, laced with rivers and studded with lakes, provide matchless opportunities for wilderness experience, and the rock-ribbed coastline is justly famous for its fishing villages, resort areas, and offshore islands.

This part of Maine, at the edge of a vast wilderness, reserves its greatest rewards for those with an appreciative eye for nature and the time with which to indulge it.

Baxter State Park is at the southern end of the Allagash Wilderness Waterway, a 92-mile corridor of woodland lakes and rivers where, for the most part, canoes are the favored mode of transportation.

The 200,000 acres that make up the state park were given to the people of Maine by former Gov. Percival P. *Baxter to serve as a wilderness area and wildlife sanctuary. The roads in the park are unsurfaced so as to have the least possible impact on the pristine environment.*

Of the 46 mountains here, the crowning glory is Mount Katahdin, which rises to a height of 5,268 feet. There are some 150 miles of trails in the park, many inviting picnic areas, and eight campgrounds. Reservations for camping space are recommended. For information, write to the Reservation Clerk, 64 Balsam Drive, Millinocket, Maine 04462.

1 Access from the south to Baxter State Park and Allagash Wilderness Waterway is through the town of Millinocket. If you are interested in learning about the process of converting wood into paper, stop in at the Great Northern Paper Company in East Millinocket to see about a tour of the plant.

From the road on a dike between Millinocket and Ambajejus lakes you can see the stumps and snags (called driki) of a drowned forest. This eerie scene of watery desolation was created by the rising waters behind a dam east of Millinocket on the Penobscot River. On a calm day the ghostly effect is doubled by reflection of the driki in the mirrorlike surface of the water.

2 Out-of-staters pay an entrance fee to Baxter State Park, and most people take the 50-mile Perimeter Road through the park to the gatehouse at the other end. Gasoline is not sold within the park; so check your supply before entering.

There is no road to the top of Mount Katahdin, "highest land" in the Algonquian language of the local Abnaki Indians. Only those with the stamina to achieve the summit by foot can enjoy the magnificent view.

The closest you can come to the summit by car is to take the eight-mile drive up to Roaring Brook campground. A short walk from here reveals fine views of the east face of Katahdin. Another short walk, along the trail to South Turner Mountain, leads to Sand Stream Pond, where you might see moose feeding.

This is not the place to drive if you are in a hurry. Take your time and enjoy the beauty of the wilderness. The unpaved roads are slippery when wet and dusty when dry. As for the surface, "washboardy" is the term backcountry drivers use.

2. Visitors can enjoy the unspoiled wilderness and 100-foot-tall pines of Baxter State Park by car or on foot, but Mount Katahdin—"highest land" to the Abnaki Indians—is explorable only on foot. Its summit is the end point for hikers of the 2,000-mile Appalachian Trail.

SPECIAL FEATURES

ROAD GUIDE	HIGHLIGHT	**1**
STATE PARKS	SCHEDULED AIRLINE STOPS	
With Campsites ▲ Without Campsites △	MILITARY AIRPORTS	
RECREATION AREAS	OTHER AIRPORTS	
With Campsites ▲ Without Campsites △	BOAT RAMPS	
SELECTED REST AREAS	COVERED BRIDGES	
POINTS OF INTEREST	PORTS OF ENTRY	
SKI AREAS		

ROAD CLASSIFICATION

CONTROLLED ACCESS HIGHWAYS   Divided **5** Undivided
(Entrance and Exit only at Interchanges)
Service Area   Interchanges

TOLL HIGHWAYS

OTHER DIVIDED HIGHWAYS

PAVED HIGHWAYS

LOCAL ROADS In unfamiliar areas inquire locally   Paved   Gravel   Dirt
before using these roads

MILEAGE

MILEAGE BETWEEN TOWNS 3 / 4   MILEAGE • 35 •
AND JUNCTIONS   BETWEEN DOTS

SCALE

ONE INCH 14 MILES   0   5   10   15

ONE INCH 23 KILOMETERS   0   5   10   15   24

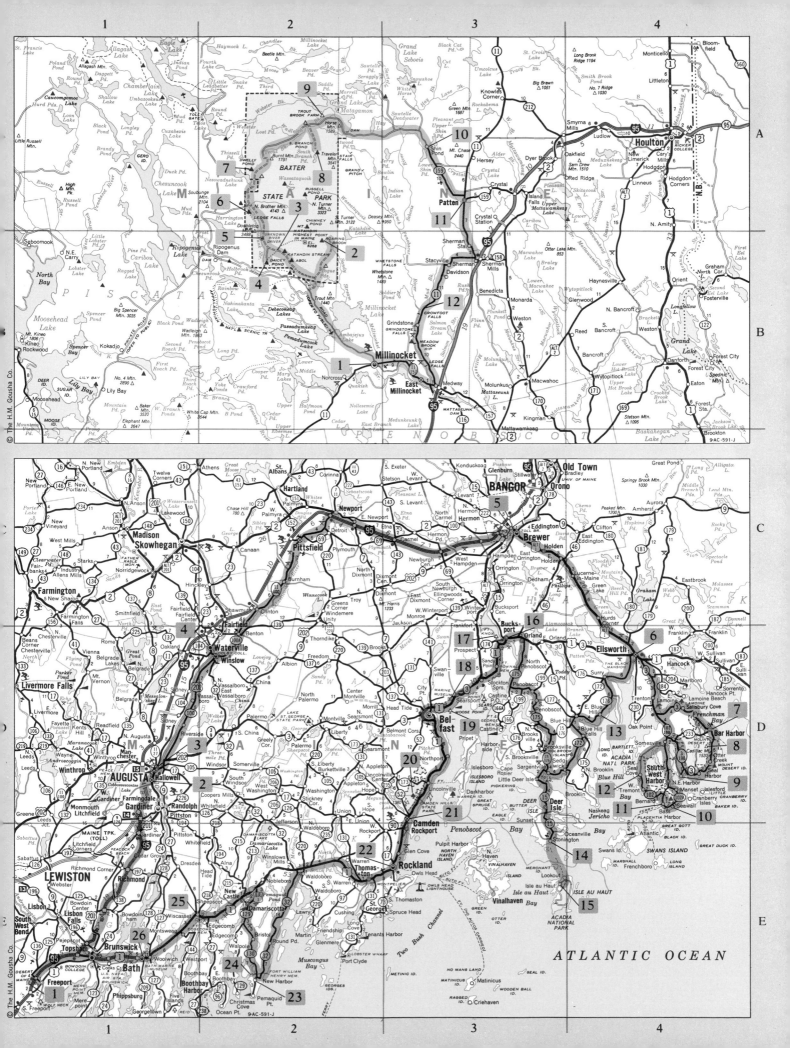

3 Although the roads may be narrow and rough for cars, they are easier for hikers than the trails. At a point about four miles from the park entrance, watch for the sign that shows where the Appalachian Trail joins the road. Stop for a moment, in the comfort of your car, and consider the impact of this junction on the "2,000 milers" who have walked this trail from Mount Oglethorpe in Georgia. Here in Baxter State Park the hikers get a pleasant 1½-mile stroll along the road before heading up slope for the final hard push to the summit of Mount Katahdin and the end of the Appalachian Trail.

hand (not to mention the back and knees) at paddling their own.

There are some pleasant walking trails in this vicinity, including one to Big Niagara Falls, somewhat smaller than its namesake but very attractive nevertheless.

Around the lake and on the trails you can see white pines (*Pinus strobus*), the state tree. These trees, however, are second- or third-generation offspring of the 100-foot giants for which the Pine Tree State was named in the mid-1800's. In fact, the early Mainers were so taken with the pine that they proclaimed its cone and tassel to be the state flower.

On such rocky streams as the Nesowadnehunk, which leads to the Penobscot River and the mills at Millinocket, there were frequent logjams. The river drivers would then go out on the jumble of logs with their pike poles and peaveys, break up the jam, and get the logs floating again. When a jam was suddenly broken, the movement of the logs was unpredictable, and men could be injured or killed. Since there was little time for the formalities of a funeral, river drivers were often simply buried beside the stream and their caulked boots were nailed to a tree. This marker, at the grave of an unknown logger, commemorates all those drivers who lost their lives on the Nesowadnehunk.

6 For a classic view, and perhaps a photograph, of a fast-moving mountain stream flowing over a slope of smooth rock, stop for a while at Ledge Falls.

It is not hard to imagine how in the days of the river drives logs could pile up in places like this and create dangerous problems for the drivers.

A few miles from here the road touches Nesowadnehunk Lake, the source of the stream. Some anglers say that of the 1,100 lakes in Maine where brook trout are found, this one provides the best fishing. The lake lies just outside the park, and at the jog in the road, which is also outside the park, there is a general store.

7 From the Perimeter Road, in many places, you can see great house-size boulders sitting incongruously in the deep woods. These are glacial erratics deposited here when the last of the great ice flows retreated.

At Dwelly Pond there is a campground and an inviting place for a picnic lunch. There are moose that also share this opinion, and you may be lucky enough to see them feeding in the shallows here.

The moose, largest of the deer family, is an impressive animal. A full-grown male can stand more than five feet tall and weigh up to 1,200 pounds. The great broad antlers may be as much as five feet across. At one time moose were hunted almost to extinction in Maine, but now, protected by law, there are an estimated 15,000 or more moose in the state.

4. Baxter State Park includes camping facilities, nature trails, and calm waters for canoeing. However, the ironically named Big Niagara Falls, the highlight of one walking trail, is a small but impressive rapids best enjoyed from the safety of the banks.

If you would like to sample a pleasant and relatively easy section of the trail, take a hike downhill to the west of the road.

4 The narrow road through the woods down to Daicey Pond parallels Nesowadnehunk Stream. At the pond is a campground with cabins, and there are also canoes for rent. On a placid pond such as this one, it is a good place for novices to try their

5 The Perimeter Road north of Daicey Pond turnoff also follows the rushing waters of the Nesowadnehunk. About 1½ miles up this road, watch for the white cross that marks the grave of the Unknown River Driver.

In the early days of logging in Maine, logs were frequently floated down the streams and rivers from the backwoods to the mills below.

8 For a few miles before the turn-off to South Branch Pond, the road follows the course of Trout Brook, another lovely, winding stream. The south branch of this stream leads to the pond, one of the most attractive sites in the park. The entry road drops down to the campground and to the pond in its scenic setting between two mountains. As an added attraction, canoes can be rented here.

Although the roads in the park may sometimes seem too narrow, especially when meeting another car, they make a minimum impact on the wooded setting. In places, birches with their gleaming white trunks line both sides of the road and spread their branches to form a leafy tunnel where only an eerie green light filters through.

9 Logging has been a major industry in Maine since the state's earliest days. There was once a logging operation at Trout Brook Farm, and artifacts from the logging era are on display here along with interpretive information. There is also a campground here.

10 Both Upper Shin Pond and Lower Shin Pond are popular with fishermen angling for the brook trout and landlocked salmon (the state fish) that thrive in these cold waters.

For an unsurpassed view of the many lakes and forests of the watery

5. Seen here against the backdrop of Double Top Mountain is the rock-strewn Nesowadnehunk, which was once a busy logging thoroughfare for Maine's important timber industry. Logjams en route to the mills downstream presented many dangers to the bold, brave men known as river drivers.

wilderness of northern Maine, you can take a ride in a floatplane based here on Shin Pond. From the air you begin to appreciate the extent of the forests of northern Maine and see how the Allagash Wilderness Waterway winds its course through this densely wooded land. Apparent in the Allagash is the remoteness and unspoiled beauty that holds such appeal for adventuresome canoeists and for nature lovers.

11 In Patten, The Lumberman's Museum is a collection of some 2,000 artifacts, including photographs and dioramas related to the logging camps, the sawmills, and related industries in Maine. The displays, from bunkhouse scrimshaw to a 20-ton steam loghauler, are contained in nine buildings that are museum pieces in their own right. Everything on display has been donated by people who think of the museum as a community project, the community being the state of Maine.

The museum is closed from mid-October until mid-May.

Just south of Patten the road tops a rounded hill, and suddenly you are faced with an unexpected 360-degree view of the countryside.

In the area around Sherman you can see potato fields that help to make Maine, along with Idaho and Washington, one of the three states that are the most bountiful producers of this essential tuber.

12 About 13 miles south of Sherman, where Mud Brook joins the East Branch of the Penobscot River, there begins an exciting stretch of white water. You can see Crowfoot, Moxie, and Ledge falls and another spot called Meadowbrook Rip. There are picnic tables along the river here, and depending on the season and flow of water, there may be canoeists or kayakers running the rapids.

Canoeing through Maine's wilderness

One of the best ways to enjoy the marvels of the wilderness is to take a canoe trip on the rivers and streams of Maine. Evolved from the Indian birchbark craft, today's lightweight canoes of fiberglass and aluminum can be handled easily with practice and care. The charm of a canoe is the way it glides noiselessly through the water, the only sound breaking the stillness being the gentle plash of the paddle. Below are four basic paddling strokes used in canoeing.

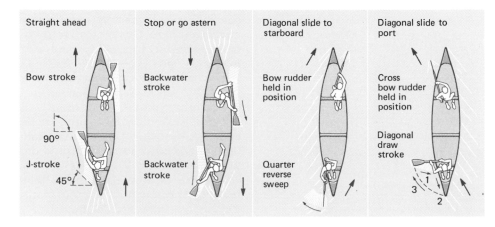

About 2,800 miles of shoreline in Maine are contained in a straight-line distance of only 230 miles. This is an impressive statistic, but more impressive is to see some of the ins-and-outs for yourself, as suggested on this tour.

Although the most dramatic scenery is on the coast, the Kennebec River valley has a charm of its own, as does Augusta, the state capital. For a charming anomaly in this heavily forested state, consider the barren dunes in the Desert of Maine.

1 The Desert of Maine is a fascinating landform that would seem more at home on Cape Cod, Massachussetts, or the Outer Banks of North Carolina than in this wooded, rock-bound state. But here it is, some 60 acres of dunes surrounded by typical Maine woodland and farms. This area was, in fact, a farm that was overcut and overgrazed. When the thin layer of topsoil eroded, the underlying glacial deposits of sand were blown and moved by the wind to create the dunes you see here today.

In the grains of sand are more than a hundred discernible shades of color. These are derived from the many kinds of rock picked up and pulverized by the glaciers and deposited here by the meltwater streams as sand. To the eye, the sand has a soft, pale beige color and a finer texture than beach sand.

2 Here on the Kennebec River is a charming reminder of the 19th-century river ports from which Maine-built ships once sailed to trading ports around the world.

The city of Hallowell was settled in 1754, the same year as Fort Western up the river at Augusta. Hallowell is known for its many waterfront antiques shops and the restoration and preservation of a number of handsome old homes by private citizens. The historic district has some 200 acres in all.

3 In Augusta, Maine's capital, the State House sits, predictably, on the corner of Capitol and State streets. The massive granite building, designed by Charles Bulfinch, was completed in 1832. It was later remodeled, but the impressive Bulfinch facade was retained. On the capitol grounds is the State of Maine Library-Museum-Archives Building, which features specimens of wildlife and minerals native to the state.

Fort Western on Bowman Street by the banks of the Kennebec has 18th-century period rooms, collections of military and naval items, early tools, and Indian relics. In 1625 the Pilgrims built a post here as a center for trading with the Indians. A fort was built in 1754, and in 1919 reproductions of the blockhouses and the stockade were added. Closed from early September to mid-May.

4 Colby College has a pleasant 600-acre campus on Mayflower Hill, which affords fine views of Waterville and Mount Blue to the west.

In the Bixler Art and Music Center is an excellent collection of paintings, including works by Pierre Auguste Renoir, John Singleton Copley, Gilbert Stuart, and Andrew Wyeth.

The college library has one of the best collections of Thomas Hardy's works in the United States.

Along Route 95 between Newport and Bangor is an admirable example of highway landscaping. The plantings of pine, spruce, and various hardwoods in the wide median strip are set out in attractive masses and textures amid sweeps of greensward.

5 Grotto Cascade Park in Bangor has as its centerpiece a 45-foot cascade, which is quite a respectable size for a man-made waterfall. This pleasant park also has a pool and fountain, footpaths, and floral displays.

Across State Street on the Penobscot River is the Bangor Salmon Pool, a natural pool where in May and June the salmon fight their way upstream to spawn in the river of their origin.

6 Although Ellsworth is the commercial center of an area devoted primarily to recreation, it does have a number of interesting buildings.

The federal-style Tisdale House on State Street, built in 1817 with Palladian windows and a cupola, has served as a public library since 1898.

The First Congregational Church is considered to be the best example of Greek Revival ecclesiastical architecture in Maine.

The most elegant house in town is the Black Mansion on West Main Street. The two-story brick home of modified Georgian design was built about 1802 for Col. John Black, a land agent. Three generations of his family have lived here. On a guided tour you can see period furnishings and a remarkably graceful spiral staircase. Closed from mid-October until June.

7 The town of Bar Harbor may seem rather more elegant than is fitting for the rugged character of the coast of Maine. But it was inevitable that shops and services would develop to cater to the tastes of those who come to enjoy one of the most inviting and dramatic landforms on the eastern seaboard.

1. The Desert of Maine is an intriguing geological phenomenon. Farmers once cultivated the land, which was atop a sandy glacial outwash. Deprived of the protective vegetation, erosion by the wind created a miniature Sahara in this formerly verdant landscape.

8. *Acadia National Park's Cadillac Mountain, highest point on the east coast, affords incomparable vistas of Bar Harbor, Frenchman Bay, nearby islands, and the Atlantic Ocean. The view here, across* Frenchman Bay, *shows Bar Harbor in the foreground and Schoodic Point in the distance. The park itself is a testament to the summer residents whose generous gifts created it in 1916.*

Although it is now a tourist town, it still retains some of the aura it had when it was a resort for the wealthy.

On a pleasant grassy knoll in the town is Bar Harbor Park, which provides an interesting view of Frenchman Bay, the spruce-covered Porcupine Islands, and Schoodic Point on the mainland to the east. From the city dock, adjacent to the park, there are boat tours of the harbor area and the nearby islands. On some tours there is a naturalist to describe the marine life in these waters.

8 In 1604 when Samuel de Champlain first saw this wooded island, its treeless granite mountaintops prompted him to call it the *Isle des Monts Deserts*, which has since been anglicized to Mount Desert Island.

There are many French names in this region, since the land was claimed by France before the British and then the Americans took it over.

Acadia, the name of the national park that covers more than 38,000 acres of the island, was the French name for their holdings on the eastern seaboard in the New World.

The literal highlight of the park is Cadillac Mountain, whose granite dome rises 1,530 feet above the sea. The paved road to the summit climbs steadily, with easy curves and a number of turnouts that offer vast panoramas of the ocean, coves, inlets, and islands below.

At the base of the mountain near Bar Harbor is Sieur du Monts spring and the Robert Abbe Museum of Stone Age Antiquities, where you can learn about the lives and times of the earliest inhabitants here. There is a nature center at the spring, a marshland environment, and gardens of wild flowers to admire. Starting with the Labrador tea in May, wild flowers bloom throughout the park until fall,

when the glow of goldenrod appears.

Along Ocean Drive, which follows the shoreline, are various turnouts with spectacular views of the bay and ocean. There is swimming at Sand Beach if you can brave the bone-chilling water. A favorite walk is along the Shore Path to Otter Point.

At Thunder Hole when the tide is right and the sea is running high, the water crashes into a narrow chasm, compressing the air to create the earthshaking boom for which the hole is named. In the tide pools along Ocean Drive you can see mussels, periwinkles, sea anemones, barnacles, and sea urchins in abundance.

In the park areas of the island are cool green forests and some 120 miles of hiking trails on and around the 18 hills and 27 lakes and ponds. Fifty species of mammals are in residence here, and some 275 species of birds have been sighted.

New England coastal creatures

Sea animals on the North Atlantic coast include: *orange-footed cucumber,* with tube feet and bushy tentacles; *crumb of bread sponge,* whose colonies spread over several feet; *green sea urchin; red common eastern chiton,* a primitive mollusk; and *rough periwinkle,* which eats algae.

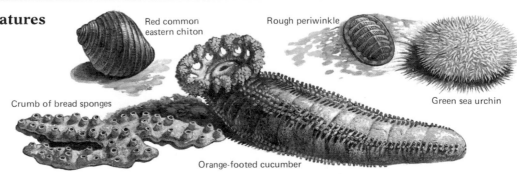

Red common eastern chiton

Rough periwinkle

Crumb of bread sponges

Green sea urchin

Orange-footed cucumber

14. Stonington's calm harbor has waterfront facilities that provide for the complete processing of fish—from sea to consumer. In addition to the highly-prized lobster, Maine's coastal waters produce a dozen-plus species of fish as well as other shellfish.

All who visit this incomparable preserve owe a debt of gratitude to the small group of wealthy summer visitors who donated more than 6,000 acres of land in 1916 to create the first national park in the East and the first to be created solely by private donations. More land was given over the years to bring it to its present size.

9 Northeast Harbor, at the mouth of Somes Sound, is a popular yachting center. At the municipal wharf, at the end of Sea Street, you can see more sailboats and other pleasure craft than workboats, which in Maine harbors is unusual.

There are cruise boats here to the offshore islands. On Great Cranberry, the largest of the five Cranberry Isles, are some 200 acres of bogs where this colorful fruit is harvested in the fall.

On Little Cranberry Island is the Islesford Museum, which has pictures, artifacts, and tools related to the development of these islands, as well as a fine collection of ship models.

In the summer, cruises to Baker Island feature a ranger-naturalist who identifies wildlife and explains the geological phenomena in the area. This scenic excursion is a favorite with photographers.

You again enter Acadia National Park on Sargent Drive north of Northeast Harbor on the shores of Somes Sound. The narrow road clings to the base of the cliff and has a welcome safety rail of granite blocks.

The narrow sound that cuts Mount Desert Island almost in half is one of the few fjords on our Atlantic coast. Fjords, which are gouged out by glacial action, are much deeper in the center, whereas inlets, which are created by the sea or rivers, are normally deepest at the mouth.

About 6½ miles south of Somesville on Route 102 is a turnoff to Echo Lake, which is the most popular place in the park to swim.

About four miles past Route 102-A at Seawall Campground is an inviting picnic area in a grove of pines overlooking a gravel bar and the rocky shore. The seawall here is not man-made; these boulders were placed here by the force of the ocean.

10 At the ranger station at Seawall Campground pick up a booklet describing the Ship Harbor self-guiding nature trail about a mile down the road. On this lovely walk along the shore of Ship Harbor, a typical rocky Maine coast inlet, there are markers keyed to the guide booklet. Along the trail you see not only the trees, shrubs, and groundcovers native to this area, but also the seaweeds that thrive in the shallows here.

11 Bass Harbor, as compared to Bar and Northeast harbors, is very much a working community. Here you see more lobster and fishing boats than pleasure craft.

The docks are frequently piled high with lobster traps and accented with the bright colors of marker buoys.

On the south side of town is a dead end road leading to Bass Harbor Head and the photogenic lighthouse there. Built on its rocky ledge in 1858, the light is 56 feet above sea level and marks the entrance to this well-protected harbor.

12 Seal Cove is another classic seacoast town with fishing and lobster boats moored in the harbor. The elegant shape of the workboats you see here and all along the coast of Maine are beautiful examples of form following function. These boats that look so serenely graceful at their moorings are remarkably seaworthy in the heavy weather offshore. Their shapes have evolved through centuries of working these waters where the ever-changing wind, weather, and waves are a constant challenge.

13 East Blue Hill is an attractive harbor with many sailboats and workboats at anchor. The town also supports a busy boatyard and is a pleasant place to wander around and soak up the Maine coast atmosphere.

On Routes 176 and 172 you can savor further elements of the Maine coast. Here are saltwater ponds, patches of woods, open meadows with outcrops of rock and glacier-strewn boulders, lobster traps and buoys, fishnets, weathered shingled barns and lobster shacks near rocky inlets, and on the horizon the reaches of the sea.

14 A narrow suspension bridge spans Eggemoggin Reach to Deer Isle, and Stonington is at its southern end of the island. This is a working town where the rhythm of life is geared to fishing, lobstering, and the cutting of stone. The granite from the quarries here and on the nearby islands is noted for its fine grain and its pinkish color.

The docks are often piled high with lobster traps. A stone jetty serves to calm the waters of the harbor, which is the home port for scores of lobster and fishing boats. Canning and packing facilities on the waterfront process the harvest of the sea.

Although the town is increasingly favored by artists and craftsmen, there are few concessions to the tourist trade. There is, however, a boat from here to Isle au Haut, an adjunct of Acadia National Park.

15 As the boat from Stonington threads its way through the scattering of islands to Isle au Haut, about five miles away, it is easy to understand why so many ships have been wrecked in these waters, especially when you consider the frequency of the dense Maine fogs.

About 3,000 acres of Isle au Haut are part of Acadia National Park. There are about 20 miles of trails through the woods, along the cliffs, and past the beaches and lakes on this relatively untouched preserve.

An interesting feature on the island is narrow Long Pond, with woodlands growing down steep banks to the edge of the pond's unusual amber-colored water.

Primitive campsites in the park are available by reservations only. Write Acadia National Park, Route 1, Box 1, Bar Harbor, Maine 04609.

16 The drive north on Route 175 to Bucksport winds through dense woodlands, rocky meadows, and along tree-lined inlets with occasional long views of Penobscot Bay to the west. There are weathered barns and neat white houses with the predictable stacks of wood, in amounts that vary with the season.

At Bucksport is a division of the St. Regis Paper Company, which offers tours of the plant except during fall and winter. Here you can learn how coated paper for magazines is made—from four-foot logs to the finished product. You may be surprised at the speed of the machines and the volume of noise that they generate.

17 In 1846, when it seemed that a dispute with Britain over our northeast boundary might escalate into warfare, it was decided to build a fort at the mouth of the Penobscot River.

While the military aspect of Fort Knox may be questionable (the fort was never used or finished), it is an engineering masterwork.

The circular stairs, curved brick arches, and massive walls made of granite from nearby Mount Waldo

are fine examples of stonecutting and construction in the days when most of the work was done by hand.

Named for Henry Knox, the distinguished Revolutionary War general and first U.S. secretary of war, this is one of the largest masonry forts in the nation. The name is not inappropriate, in that Knox, at more than 250 pounds, was the largest of George Washington's generals.

18 Searsport is one of the more than 20 towns on Penobscot Bay that helped make Maine the shipbuilding capital of America in the days of sail.

The Penobscot Marine Museum here memorializes this dynamic era. There are three 19th-century houses on the site with furnishings that reflect the taste of the many well-traveled shipmasters who hailed from Searsport. The museum complex also includes a Congregational Church, barns, a workshop, and an exhibit building. You can see a variety of Maine-built small craft, models of sailing ships, shipbuilding tools, navigational instruments, and examples of scrimshaw. The museum has an exceptional collection of marine paintings, many of which are commissioned ship portraits that were done at various ports of call. Closed from mid-October until early June.

Maine's favorite harvest from the sea

The Indians of the Northeast relished the lobster, and the taste for this succulent crustacean (*Homarus americanus*) continues unabated. Today the lobster reigns as one of our great delicacies and among the most expensive. The demand, however, threatens the supply of legal-size lobsters, which must be at least 3-3/16 inches from the eye socket to the end of the body (carapace).

Although traps are identified with a buoy painted a distinctive color and pattern, they can be lost in storms or dislodged by passing boats. Oil spills affect productivity, as does the taking of those too young to reproduce. Only state residents are allowed to fish for lobsters in Maine waters.

Lobster boat heads out by dawn's early light

Baiting the trap with fish

Hauling in the catch

Gauge indicates legal size

Claws are plugged or banded

19 Moose Point State Park is a lovely place for a picnic or a walk along a rocky beach where driftwood abounds. Some picnic tables are in the deep shade of tall conifers interspersed with white birch. There is also an open grassy area with picnic tables and a wide view of Penobscot Bay and long, narrow Islesboro Island to the south.

Should you want to visit Islesboro, there is a state ferry from Lincolnville Beach about three miles from the entrance to Camden Hills State Park. There are some large estates on the island, and in an old lighthouse is the Sailors Memorial Museum, where a collection of Maine-related nautical items is displayed.

20 Another inviting bayside picnic area is at Camden Hills State Park. There is a short drive east of Route 1 to parking places in the deep shade of the conifers that carpet the ground with their fragrant needles. A path to the water's edge wends its way for a hundred yards past rock outcrops covered with lichens and moss.

Seats and picnic tables on a low bluff offer sweeping views of the bay and a close-up look at the granite that dominates the rockbound coast of Maine. Just across Route 1 from this small seaside section is an entrance to the 5,000 acres of hills, valleys, and lakes that comprise the rest of Camden Hills State Park.

A toll road leads to the summit of Mount Battie, and at the tollhouse you can get a map and description of the many miles of varied hiking trails in the park.

The viewing platform on the stone tower at the summit of Mount Battie is about 800 feet above sea level and affords a fabulous 360-degree view. To the south is the town of Camden with its attractive harbor, white houses, church spires, and the masts of sailing craft seen against the green of the land and blue of the sea. To the east is an array of wooded islands scattered in Penobscot Bay, which blends with the Atlantic Ocean in the haze beyond the farthest islands. The next land due east is southern France, some 3,200 miles away.

The low-lying islands are of every conceivable size and shape, and the expanse of water reflects the ever-changing color of the sky, from slate gray to the deepest blue. Frequently, the wind is visible in riffled patterns on the surface of the sea.

The island view from the tower reveals the rocky bones of these low mountains showing through the thin cover of trees and shrubs.

On the paths around the tower are great outcrops of rock subtly colored by spreading lichens and patches of moss, with wild flowers in the crevices where soil has collected.

The park is closed for camping from the end of September until mid-May.

21 Along a seacoast noted for the charm of its towns and villages, Camden is one of the most attractive. Trees grow to the water's edge along the curving harbor, where sleek sailing craft and sturdy lobster boats are moored. Boatyards and marinas line one shore of the harbor; on the other are the public docks where windjammers tie up to take passengers on cruises of Maine waters.

On Conway Road off Route 1 is the Historic Old Conway House Complex, a national historic site. Here you can see a restored 18th-century farmhouse, a barn with tools, farm implements, carriages, and sleighs, and a blacksmith shop.

22 To judge from roadside evidence, it seems that Maine residents take remarkable pride in the places where they live. There is an historic precedent for pride along the coast.

20. The view southward from Camden Hills State Park encompasses the town of Camden and the park at the head of the harbor. Although it is a popular destination for tourists, Camden's well-pro-tected harbor helps the town to keep its traditional ties with the sea. In the mid-1800's Maine produced nearly a third of the ships built in that era, many of them the fastest craft afloat.

23. New Harbor lives off the ocean. Maine's thriving fishing industry supports the state's second most important business, which is food-processing. Contrary to the popular image, manufacturing is the backbone of Maine's economy.

Many of the ships from the yards of Maine were the fastest ever built. The clipper *Red Jacket*, built in Rockland in 1854, sailed from New York to Liverpool, England, in 12 days, a record never equaled by a ship under sail.

Rockland boasts an impressive collection of 19th- and 20th-century American paintings in the William A. Farnsworth Library and Art Museum on Elm Street. Here you can see works by Winslow Homer and three generations of Wyeths. In the adjacent Farnsworth Homestead, a Greek Revival mansion built about 1840, are handsome appointments and Victorian furniture.

The homestead is closed from October through May.

Pride of place is evidenced all along Route 1, where houses are freshly painted, usually white, lawns are kept mowed, and cordwood is stacked in straight ricks.

23 Along Route 32 on the way to New Harbor are lovely views of coves and inlets on the shore of Muscongus Bay. Just before entering the picturesque fishing village of New Harbor, the road skirts Long Cove and leads to Back Cove, where fishing boats and dories ride at anchor.

On the docks here the lobster traps, floats, nets, boxes, barrels, booms, and lifting tackle clearly identify this as a working port.

24 Where Route 32 joins Route 130 continue straight on to Colonial Pemaquid and Fort William Henry.

A settlement was established here in the early 17th century, and by 1630 a wooden fort was built for protection from pirates. This and a later fort were burned not by pirates but by Indians, and in 1692 the first stone fort in New England was built here. This too was destroyed by a combined force of French and Indians in 1696.

Archeologists have unearthed 14 foundations on this rewarding site and are still digging. The small museum has some 30,000 items found in the vicinity, including coins, tableware, and pottery.

The Fort William Henry Memorial is a reconstruction of the stone fort and also has a museum. The museums are closed from early September until the end of May.

25 As you cross the Sheepscot River at Wiscasset, you may see the hulks of the *Luther Little* and the *Hesper* grounded in the mud. These are the last of the more than 500 four-masted schooners that were built in Maine. It is also possible that the schooners' remains will not survive unless the money required to stabilize them can be raised.

In Wiscasset are a number of interesting houses of the federal and Victorian eras. On Federal Street at Maine is the Nickels-Sortwell House, an imposing three-story mansion built in 1807. It has Palladian windows and federal-style fanlights. The furnishings are of the period. Also on Federal Street is the old Lincoln County Jail, a sturdy granite structure that now impounds a collection of early tools and Americana.

26 Some shipbuilding is still done in Bath, but there was a time when more ships were built and launched here than in any other single port in the world.

Some of this history is recalled at the Percy & Small Shipyard on Washington Street. Nearby is the Maine Maritime Museum, an 1844 classical-style mansion that houses an extensive collection of marine memorabilia in its 32 exhibit rooms.

Many of the displays, including dioramas, photographs, and paintings, relate to the colorful days of shipbuilding industry here, which dates from 1632.

25. These two hulks whose days may be numbered are all that remain of Maine's once magnificent fleet of working four-masters. In times past, nearly every coastal and river town here included shipyards whose vessels sailed to distant ports.

Seeing the Granite State

Highlights of New Hampshire's rugged mountains, glacier-carved and clothed in forest green

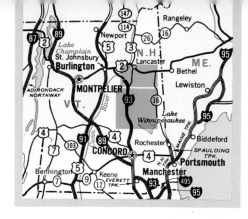

It can safely be said that there are no uninteresting views in New Hampshire. Along the roads from the White Mountains in the north to the Massachusetts border there are streams, lakes, gentle valleys, and peaceful villages to beguile the eye.

The colors of the foliage range from soft and varied greens in the spring through deep green in summer to blazing reds, oranges, and yellows in the fall. In winter the landscape is unified by an all-encompassing blanket of brilliant white.

The steep slopes and valleys of the White Mountains and the celebrated Presidential Range have long been revered. They draw multitudes of people each year, but they are still a wondrous, unspoiled wilderness. Their altitude is not great compared with the Rockies, but they stand formidably high above the surrounding terrain.

As you penetrate the heart of the mountains, great bare peaks, sometimes wrapped in clouds, rise all around you, and from the road you behold the drama of their great ridges and deep ravines. From the summit of Mount Washington, the highest point in New England, the world lies at your feet and you can easily share that euphoric sense of freedom and elation usually reserved for more intrepid rock-climbers and mountaineers.

1 Lancaster is beautifully situated at the confluence of the Connecticut and Israel rivers, with a border of low hills and a skyline of blue mountains. Chartered in 1763, the town has a number of marvelous old houses, including the Wilder-Holton House, the first two-story dwelling that was erected in Coos County. The 200-year-old house, built with sturdy shutters for protection against Indians, is now a museum of local history. It is closed from September through June.

East of Lancaster the road stays close to the Israel River, along which the lumber industry once flourished. Every turn of the road opens new vistas of peaks, ravines, and cascades. About midway between Jefferson Highlands and Randolph you can see Castellated Ridge, a reddish-brown granite formation that resembles the ruins of ancient battlements, slanting upward toward the summit of Mount Jefferson. Part of the road along this stretch is attractively lined with neat stone walls laboriously built by local farmers with the stones that were brought up to the surface by frost-heaving and had to be removed every year when the fields were plowed.

The town of Randolph became a center for mountain climbers in the

The Presidential Range

Eight presidents of the United States are memorialized in a 15-mile chain of New Hampshire mountains that has become known as the Presidential Range.

The practice of naming the mountains for the country's great leaders began before the federal government was established. In 1784 a group of scientists climbed the loftiest of the peaks and estimated it to be 9,000 feet high. (Its elevation is actually 6,288 feet.) These men are credited with first calling that peak Mount Washington, in honor of the general who led the colonial army to victory in the American Revolution.

According to the account of a local pioneer woman, Lucy Crawford, a party of distinguished visitors came to the vicinity of Mount Washington in 1820 "to ascend the mountains and give names to such hills as were unnamed." It is believed that Mounts Adams, Jefferson, Madison, and Monroe, all soaring more than a mile above sea level, were so designated on that occasion. It is not known when Mount John Quincy Adams was named.

In the southern part of the range, the name of Mount Clinton was changed to Mount Pierce in 1913, honoring New Hampshire's only native son to become president. And in 1969 Mount Pleasant became Mount Eisenhower. Whether Mount Jackson was named for the seventh president remains unknown.

To the west of the Presidential Range are peaks honoring Lincoln and Garfield. Mount Hayes, to the north, is not named for the president but rather for a former hotel proprietress in the area.

1860's and 1870's. Farmhouses were expanded into hotels and summer homes were built. Both local people and visitors developed trails fanning into the mountains to scenic spots, such as the Cold Brook Falls, and to summits in the Presidential Range. By 1912 there were 109 miles of trails within a five-mile radius of Ravine House, the farmhouse-hotel owned by one of the early trailblazers. Many of the early trails are still maintained; their starting point today is at the Appalachia parking lot on Route 2 in Randolph.

2 The Shelburne Birches are east of Gorham on Route 2. These beautiful white birches (*Betula papyrifera*), the official state tree, densely line the sides of the road for half a mile, and it is incredibly lovely to drive beneath their meeting branches. The grove is protected by the village of Shelburne as a memorial to its citizens who served in the two World Wars.

3 The Dolly Copp Campground, in the White Mountain National Forest, is one of the few places named in honor of New Hampshire's pioneer women. In 1831 Dolly Copp, a footproud young bride who had a fancy for dainty slippers and other finery,

---

SPECIAL FEATURES

ROAD GUIDE ▬▬▬	HIGHLIGHT	**1**
STATE PARKS	SKI AREAS	
With Campsites ▲ Without Campsites △	SCHEDULED AIRLINE STOPS	
RECREATION AREAS	OTHER AIRPORTS	
With Campsites ▲ Without Campsites △		
SELECTED REST AREAS	BOAT RAMPS	
With Toilets 🚻 Without Toilets 🚻		
POINTS OF INTEREST ▣	COVERED BRIDGES	

ROAD CLASSIFICATION

CONTROLLED ACCESS HIGHWAYS   Divided **5** Undivided
(Entrance and Exit only at Interchanges)   Interchanges

PAVED HIGHWAYS

LOCAL ROADS   In unfamiliar areas inquire locally   Paved   Gravel   Dirt
              before using these roads

MILEAGE

MILEAGE BETWEEN TOWNS   3 ⌣ 4   MILEAGE   • 35 •
AND JUNCTIONS   BETWEEN DOTS

SCALE

ONE INCH 9 MILES   0 1 2 3 4 5   10

ONE INCH 14 KILOMETERS   0 1 2 3 4 5   10   16

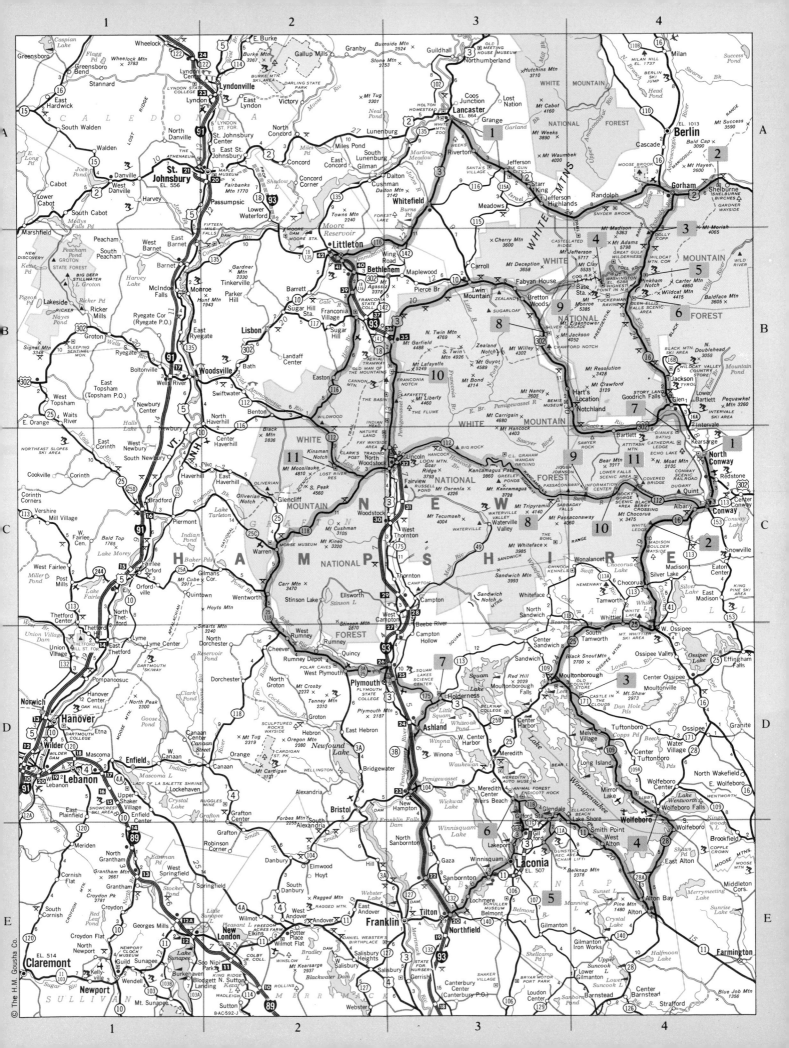

Mountain sandwort *(Arenaria groenlandica)*. Alpine azalea *(Loiseleuria procumbens)*.

Mountain cranberry *(Vacciniam vitis-idaea)*. Bluebell *(Campanula rotundifolia)*.

Cotton grass *(Eriophorum)*. Dwarf Cinquefoil *(Potentilla robbinsiana oakes)*.

4. *Masses of* Diapensia lapponica *(at left), found near the Mount Washington Auto Road at the edge of the Great Gulf, drift toward Mounts Adams and Madison. Other rare and fragile plants flourishing on the rocky plateau above the mountain's timberline are shown above. Among them the Dwarf Cinquefoil is unique to these slopes. The flowers are best seen in June.*

rode here on horseback from Bartlett, New Hampshire. For the next 19 years she and her husband lived on their farm here without any immediate neighbors. Dolly became a hearty, pipe-smoking character, but through the years she never lost her yearning for beautiful things and she became a skilled weaver and needleworker. In later years summer visitors came to her door to buy the fine linen and woolen articles she made.

The campground on the site of the Copp Farm, with picnic areas and tent and trailer sites amid meadows and forests, is popular with campers as well as with the local chipmunks, squirrels, raccoons, and birds that come here for scraps of food. At the entrance the stone terracing along the river is secured by gabions.

4 The turn onto the Mount Washington Auto Road is at an intervale (a low, flat area) known as Glen House, named after a popular hotel formerly at this site. The road zigzags back and forth for eight miles until it reaches the summit, and it is a breathtaking trip, especially if you are unnerved by high places.

The auto road has numerous turnouts where you can park and enjoy the scenery. From the Ledge, an eminence at the treeline halfway up the road, you can look down 1,500 feet into the extraordinary Great Gulf

Wilderness. The gulf, which was once nicknamed the Gulf of Mexico, is a forested basin approximately two miles long and a mile wide, excavated by glaciers in the last ice age and in earlier ones. Permits are required to enter the area. They can be obtained from the U.S. Forest Service, Gorham, New Hampshire 03581.

P. T. Barnum called the view from the top of Mount Washington "the second greatest show on earth." It is the highest peak in the Northeast (6,288 feet), and the vista from its bald summit makes you feel that you are on the top of the world. Spreading below you are the other massive peaks of the Presidential Range and the lesser ranges that roll into the horizon, their ridges falling away into valleys, ravines, and cirques. Brooks and cascades flash on the slopes, and lakes sparkle like scattered brilliants. Here and there little white villages are visible. The summit is often enclosed by clouds, but on a very clear day you can see for a hundred miles in any direction, a radius that includes the Atlantic Ocean to the east.

At the summit take time to visit the Mount Washington Observatory. This private research weather station is manned throughout the year, and its building, believed to be the strongest wooden building in the world, is bolted to the rocks and protected by stone "battlements" to withstand the battering winds that reach hurricane force on an average of one day out of two. The weather on the summit is about as dramatic as it is any place on earth. A wind velocity of 231 miles per hour, the highest that has ever been measured on land, was recorded here on April 12, 1934.

The toll road to the summit, completed in 1861 as a carriage road, climbs at a steady pace and it is amply wide. Automobiles have been ascending it ever since 1899 when F. O. Stanley chugged up the mountain in one of his own steam-driven cars. But if you prefer to leave the driving to someone else, you can make the round trip in a van operated by a guide who will comment on the scenery. Mobile campers are not permitted on the road. It is closed from late October to mid-May, and after dark in season.

There are also several trails to the summit, the shortest and most popular being the Ammonoosuc Ravine Trail. Hikers should keep in mind, however, that violent storms blow up in minutes, and a number of hikers have lost their lives as a result.

5   Two miles south of the Mount Washington Auto Road turnoff is the Pinkham Notch Camp of the Appalachian Mountain Club, which maintains about 370 miles of trails in the White Mountain area. Information about trail and weather conditions and entry permits—required for hikes in certain areas—can be obtained at this popular meeting place for backpackers. Guided overnight hikes can also be arranged.

Hiking on Mount Washington

Once the blanket of snow has melted in June, Tuckerman Ravine, a glacial cirque hollowed out of the southeast side of Mount Washington, is a spectacular destination for a hike. The Tuckerman Ravine Trail is a wide, evenly graded path built originally as a tractor route to camping shelters near the rim of the ravine. The trail leaves Route 16 at the Pinkham Notch Camp to enter the woods, and after about a quarter of a mile it crosses a bridge over the Cutler River. A few yards beyond the bridge a short side path leads to Crystal Cascade, one of the most beautiful in the mountains. The main path continues to the shelters. From there a narrower trail leads to a nearby ridge that gives magnificent views into the ravine and across the mountains. The round trip is five miles and takes about four hours.

6   Glen Ellis Falls is on the lower slopes of Mount Wildcat, within easy access of the highway. The crystal waters of Ellis River plunge from the edge of a cirque down a narrow rocky cleft. Grooves worn in the walls of the cleft cause the water to spiral as it tumbles. A long rustic path descends to a ledge where the water, a frothy column of white, falls 70 feet into a pool of green.

A lovely covered bridge crosses the Ellis River to Jackson, a mountain village whose magnificent setting and access to ski trails and scenic spots have made it a favorite tourist center.

7   Diana's Baths on Cedar Brook is an inviting place for a swim and a picnic. The brook flows down a gently sloping rock bed and falls into deep rock basins. The rock formations are worn so smooth by the stream that you can actually slide down them.

The baths are not easy to find: on Route 302 go 2.2 miles west of its junction with Route 16 and then turn south onto West Side Road. Follow that for 4.3 miles to a white farmhouse with a weathered barn, and then take a dirt road through the fields for a hundred yards to a barricade where there is a sign reading "Moat Mountain Trail." From there it is a 6- to 10-minute walk to the baths.

From the dirt road cutting through the fields to the baths you can see Cathedral Ledge, a striking cathedrallike arch formed by a semidetached bluff. Hiking trails lead to the ledge, but they are not well marked.

7. At Diana's Baths the granite has been shaped, smoothed, and polished by sand and pebbles carried down by the stream. Water seeping down from the bank streaks the rock.

8. *The silvery countryside at Bretton Woods shows the distinctive beauty of a New England winter. The weather observatory can be seen on the summit of Mount Washington.*

8 Silver Cascade, which is in Crawford Notch State Park, can be seen from the road. A small stream slides and leaps down the side of Mount Webster for 1,000 feet and then passes underneath Route 302. A dazzling streak of silver in the sunlight, the cascade is one of the loveliest sights in the White Mountains.

Sprawled on a plateau north of Crawford Notch is the village of Bretton Woods, where the United Nations Monetary and Financial Conference was held in 1944.

9 From Marshfield, the base station of the Mount Washington Cog Railway, coal-burning steam engines push passenger cars up to the summit of the great mountain. Each engine has a cog gear, a heavy toothed wheel, underneath, and each passenger car has two. The cogs mesh with a steel rack, which looks like a miniature ladder, bolted to the crossties between the two rails. Three miles of

this thrilling 3½-mile, 70-minute trip are on a trestle. The grade throughout averages 25 percent, a rise of one foot in every four, and one stretch, called Jacob's Ladder, has a grade of 37.41

percent, a rise of more than one foot in three. Built in 1866–69, this was the first cog railway of its kind in the world. It is closed from early October to the end of May.

10 Especially beautiful with its variety of dramatic natural wonders is the Franconia Notch State Park. The most famous of these wonders is the Old Man of the Mountain, whose sharp, craggy profile juts out from the shoulder of Profile Mountain 1,200 feet above Profile Lake. About 45 feet in height, the profile is formed by several random ledges of granite, and it is estimated to be about 200 million years old. In 1916 iron anchors were embedded in the forehead to help safeguard the face against the effects of frost and heat. First seen by white men in 1805, the profile has been immortalized by artists and writers, including Nathaniel Hawthorne in "The Great Stone Face," and it has been designated as New Hampshire's official trademark. The best vantage point for viewing it is from a place marked on the edge of Profile Lake, and the best time is about four in the afternoon.

At the side of the road in the park is The Basin, a beautiful granite bowl about 20 feet in diameter, filled with the clear icy waters of the Pemigewasset River. The bowl was carved over a period of thousands of years by stones and boulders trapped there and whirled by the force of the water crashing down from a falls. Above The Basin, footpaths wind into the woods along the sides of the lovely stream.

9. *The Mount Washington Cog Railway steam engines are tilted so that their boilers are level on the steep slopes, seen here in the distance. The engines back their way downhill.*

10. The Old Man of the Mountain was sculpted as melting snows seeped into cracks and joints on the cliff and then froze, flaking off stone and forming the planes of the face.

Close by is The Flume, a narrow chasm about 800 feet long with rock walls that rise 70 feet on each side. At the bottom of the fissure a stream splashes its way around the boulders in its path. Wild flowers and vines reach out from the crevices in the moist, mossy walls, and small trees arch across the slash of sky above. The narrowest part of The Flume is only 12 feet wide, and as you walk along the rustic boardwalk edging the brook in the cool depths, you sense the overwhelming power of the great dark walls that seem to close in on you. From the parking lot you can reach The Flume via a well-marked path through a growth of hemlocks, birches, and spruces or, if you prefer, you can take a bus most of the way.

Franconia Notch State Park offers picnicking, camping, hiking, swimming, and fishing. The facilities are closed from mid-October to late May.

11 Lost River Reservation at Kinsman Notch is a large, magnificent nature area owned and controlled by the Society for the Protection of New Hampshire Forests. Near the entrance there is a nature garden with more than 300 varieties of shrubs, flowers, ferns, mosses, and trees native to the region. There is also a nature museum with geologic displays, and a self-guiding ecology trail with a voice box that describes special features.

Among the scenic wonders at this reservation is the Lost River Gorge, a chasm in the Moosilauke River. Glacial action left a chaotic mass of huge granite boulders, overhanging ledges, and potholes, and for half a mile the river plays hide-and-seek as it winds through caves and past fantastic rock formations with such names as the Lemon Squeezer and the Guillotine until it emerges at Paradise Falls. Walkways and stairs enable you to walk, climb, crawl, and squeeze your way along the river's hidden course. It is an interesting and pleasurable way to explore the gorge.

Lost River Reservation offers other hiking trails, some connecting with the Appalachian Trail. There are also fishing, swimming, and camping facilities here. The place abounds with wildlife from small to large, and the air is filled with the spicy fragrance of balsam. The reservation is closed from mid-October to mid-May.

To the south of the rugged peaks of the White Mountains lies an inviting landscape of more gentle persuasion. Here are hundreds of tranquil lakes, their cool, clear waters contained by softly rolling ranges that are patched with forest and meadow.

From North Conway, where an old-fashioned railway offers you an excursion into the past, the route touches the northern tip of Lake Winnipesaukee near the Castle in the Clouds, one of the most unusual estates in the East. Skirting the edge of this sparkling lake, you pass through several villages with the peaceful charm of another era. A highlight is the Kancamagus Highway, a spectacular drive through the heart of the White Mountains.

1 The lovely village of North Conway, which sits in the curving valley of the Saco River, offers a fine view to the north of the great peaks of the Presidential Range rising majestically against the sky.

With fine ski areas nearby, the town is a busy one in the winter. In the spring, white-water adventurers come to try the waters of the Saco River. (Kayaks and canoes can be rented here.) However, in summer and early autumn the major attraction is the Conway Scenic Railroad. Departing from a hundred-year-old restored railroad station, you ride in an old-fashioned club car pulled by a puffing steam engine or an early-model diesel locomotive. The train, bound for Conway a few miles to the south, passes through forests, fields, and farms that have changed little in the last hundred years. The hour-long ride is a memorable excursion into the recent past. The railroad is closed from mid-October to May. From May to mid-June it is closed weekdays.

2 The sharp, rocky cone of Mount Chocorua, known as the Matterhorn of America, rises to a height of 3,475 feet and dominates the skyline to the west of the road. The summit provides marvelous views of the White Mountains to the north and the lake district to the south. Several trails lead up to the peak, including one that starts at White Ledge Campground. The hike is a long, demanding one, however, and the converging of the various paths at the top can be confusing when you start down.

Native American Names

Several mountains south of the Kancamagus Highway bear the names of former Indian leaders of the region.

One peak honors Passaconaway, a chieftain at the time of the Pilgrims' landing and among the first Indians to meet the white man. A wise, peace-loving man, Passaconaway united many tribes of central New Hampshire in the Penacook Confederacy in 1627, and until his death in 1669 he worked for friendly relations with the white settlers.

Another mountain commemorates Kancamagus, the grandson of Passaconaway, who became the third leader of the confederacy about 1684. He eventually became an uncompromising enemy of the colonists and led bloody raids against them. In 1691 the confederacy broke up and Kancamagus moved north.

A third peak is called after Paugus, a chieftain of the Pequawkets who lived along the upper Saco River. He also opposed the whites and led his people in the battle of Lovewell's Pond in the early 1700's.

The most legendary of all New Hampshire's mountains perpetuates the name of Chocorua, an Ossipee Indian who lived in the area about 1760. According to the story, Chocorua's feud with a white settler resulted in the Indian's death on the mountain's summit.

Two famous Indians from other parts of the nation are also honored here: Osceola, the leader of Florida's Seminoles, who died in prison in 1838, and Tecumseh, the great Shawnee who was killed in the War of 1812 while fighting for the British in the Midwest.

The most beautiful view of Chocorua is through the birches and pines edging Chocorua Lake, whose silvery blue surface mirrors the mountain in perfect clarity. In 1792 a visitor describing the scenery wrote that Chocorua "touches heaven." This majestic mountain has long been a favorite subject of artists and photographers. The bald ledges of the summit are covered with lichens, which after heavy rains change the color of the peak from grayish brown to silvery green.

3 Castle in the Clouds, the most lavish estate in New Hampshire, is the 1910 creation of Thomas Gustave Plant, who spent more than $7 million fulfilling his desire to see beauty wherever he looked. He bought 6,000 acres of woodland and imported workmen from Europe to build the castle of his dreams. Plant called his estate "Lucknow" after a castle in Scotland.

From the castle's spectacular site high in the Ossipee Mountain range, there are glorious views of the mountains, ponds, streams, and waterfalls that are right on the estate, as well as of Lake Winnipesaukee and the White Mountains in the distance. Some of these scenes are also depicted in the colorful stained-glass windows of the castle. There are tours of the mansion, garden walks, and also trails for hiking, riding, and snowmobiling. Western-style horseback rides with a guide through the Ossipee Mountains can also be arranged. The castle is closed from mid-October to May.

The largest of the state's 1,300 lakes is Winnipesaukee, whose sapphire waters extend for 27 miles in an irregular shape varying in width from 1 to 10 miles. The route shown here partially circles the lake, alternately hugging the shore and ascending the hills. From the hills you can see the beautiful, sprawling lake, which is studded with islands and rimmed with forests that recede toward the dusky blue ranges.

4 There are several resort villages on the bays of Lake Winnipesaukee, a few of which were settled two centuries ago as trading ports. An especially attractive community, which has retained much of its charm, is Wolfeboro. The village, named in honor of the British general James Wolfe, a hero of the French and Indian War, rises picturesquely up a hill from the waterfront.

5 The Gunstock Recreation Area, set in the midst of mountain peaks in the Belknap Range, has something to offer in each season, with skiing in the winter and hiking and camping in the spring, summer, and fall. In July there are several special attractions: pops concerts, a crafts festival, and a major gem and mineral show.

6 On the western shore of Lake Winnipesaukee is Weirs Beach. It takes its name from the fish traps (weirs) the Indians used to set in a channel here. Weirs Beach is the starting point for a number of excursion boats, including the Winnipesaukee steamer *Mount Washington* that takes you on a lovely 3¼-hour cruise among the islands. The lake is sparkling and crystal clear because of the enlightened environmental control practiced by the surrounding communities.

7 The Squam Lakes Science Center is located on a 200-acre national reserve between Squam Lake and Little Squam Lake. The name is a shortened form of the Indian word *asquam* ("water").

The science center offers ecology-oriented programs that are fascinating for everyone in the family. You can take field trips to streams, bogs, meadows, and forests to discover how plants, animals, and birds survive in their habitats, and you can see exhibits of local wildlife including raccoons, bears, deer, and bobcats. There is also a nocturnal exhibit on animal night life.

The center has a hundred-year-old steam-powered mill in operation, a windmill, a sap house for maple sugaring, and other demonstrations of

The Kancamagus Highway

Cutting through the heart of the White Mountains for 34 miles is the highest mountain highway in the Northeast, and one of the most scenic. From Lincoln it follows the branches of the Pemigewasset River and then climbs to the Kancamagus Pass at an elevation of nearly 3,000 feet. From there it descends along the Swift River to Conway. Along this route some of the grades are steep and difficult.

The Kancamagus Highway, which passes through heavy forest most of the way, is beautiful at all times of the year. But it is magnificent during the foliage season, which reaches its peak in this locale about the end of September. The glowing reds and yellows of the maples, birches, and beeches, intermixed with dark evergreens, spread up the great slopes until the firs and spruces take over, their crest of green seeming to contain the blaze below. Autumn's pageant in this vast mountain setting is overwhelming. There are overlooks where you can pause to enjoy the breathtaking panoramas.

How leaves change color

Although the range of hues in the colorful foliage of deciduous trees in the fall may summon thoughts of the rainbow, relatively few colors are involved. There are the greens of the chlorophylls, the yellow and orange tints of the carotenoids, and the reds and purples of the anthocyanins. Often they combine, creating bronzes and other glowing variations. The carotenoids are always present in the leaf, but they are masked by the chlorophylls during the growing season.

The anthocyanins develop as a result of chemical changes in the leaf as summer wanes, and the brighter the days at that time, the more brilliant will be the colors that they produce.

As the summer season ends, a random accumulation of cells of a corklike composition develops, creating an abscission layer at the base of the leaf stem. These cells act as stoppers, blocking the flow of fluids through the veins. In the deprived areas of the leaf the production of chlorophyll ceases, the green fades, and patches of other colors appear. When all of the veins are sealed off, the leaf falls.

Leaf cells

Chlorophyll

Carotenoid

Anthocyanin

Leaf stem

Abscission layer

man's use of natural energy and resources. At the entrance to the grounds in lilac time, there is a profusion of the fragrant purple blooms of *Syringa vulgaris*, which is the official flower of New Hampshire.

8 Sabbaday Falls is a short, easy walk from the highway. The cascades, falling in tiers down a narrow flume, were discovered on a Sabbath by early explorers. Later the walk to the falls became a favorite Sabbath Day outing—hence the name "Sabbaday." It is four-tenths of a mile from the road to the falls.

9 The Passaconaway Information Center features exhibits of the natural history and the settlement of the region. There is also a half-mile self-guided nature walk called the Rail 'N River Trail. The center is closed from the end of the foliage season in October to the end of May.

10 Another beautiful spot along the highway is the Rocky Gorge Scenic Area where the Swift River—living up to its name—crashes through a cleft it has worn in solid rock. Below this miniature canyon there is an attractive pond that can be reached by a short walk across a rustic footbridge and down a path.

11 The road to the Covered Bridge Campground crosses the Swift River through a renovated covered bridge, originally built in 1858, and winds through a grove of white birches. The campground is spacious, with trailer sites and a picnic area, and offers

opportunity for fishing and hiking.

Driving through the wilderness of the White Mountains, you soon understand why Justice William O. Douglas spoke of the "solace and comfort" the region offers to those who seek "refuge from civilization."

The Kancamagus Highway *a few miles east of Lincoln offers this view toward the hump of Mount Osceola. Trail entrances along the road lead to scenic spots in the forest.*

A State for All Seasons

Vermont is a rural landscape of changing colors that gloriously signal the time of year

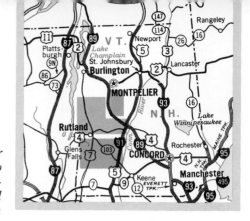

As the winter snow melts, springtime brings the excitement of white water and a countryside splashed with apple blossoms and wild flowers.

With summer the myriads of greens deepen and the velvetlike hillsides are strewn with red clover, buttercups, and daisies. The sunset silhouettes a mowing machine or a hay baler left in a field for another day.

From mid-September to mid-October the fiery yellows and reds of deciduous trees move up the mountain slopes, and the air is pungent with dry leaves and ripened crops.

When the leaves have fallen, snow blankets the rolling hills and mountains and the New England villages snuggled in their valleys. The world becomes blue and white with accents of dark evergreen and barn red.

The impact of seasonal change is heightened by the mountainous terrain. "The surface of Vermont is generally uneven," wrote a historian back in 1842. It is that "unevenness," so laconically stated, that provides such beauty from the road.

Driving up the Ottauquechee River valley and tracing the river almost to its source high in the Green Mountains rewards you with cascades and gorges, covered bridges, forest-hidden villages, panoramas of mountains, upland valleys, and meadows, and breathtaking views of some of Vermont's highest peaks.

At Sherburne Pass the road drops down the western slopes of the mountains into the narrow limestone Valley of Vermont with its famous marble quarries, crosses the Taconic Range, and then drops into the Champlain Valley. The road from Vergennes recrosses the Green Mountains via the Middlebury Gap and cuts through the favorite countryside of the poet Robert Frost. After following the course of the White River to the Piedmont, the route leads south toward Woodstock and through magnificent ski country with silvery lakes and ponds.

1 The Ottauquechee River flows gently below the covered bridge in the center of the restored mill village of Quechee, but less than a mile downstream it becomes a furious thing. Leaping over a 100-foot cliff at the head of Quechee Gorge, the river rages and roars between the schist walls of the mile-long chasm. The narrow fissure, called Vermont's Little Grand Canyon, and the state's most remarkable natural wonder, was carved out about 15,000 years ago when glaciers of the Great Ice Age covered the land. As they melted, powerful streams dug channels beneath the ice sheets.

From the bridge spanning the gorge on Route 4, you can look down into its depths and see the river seething 165 feet below. Gradually the gorge melts into the hills, and the river is again subdued.

2 The road winds along the river through hilly dairy country to Woodstock. The village, nestled in a bowl of green rimmed by forested hills, is considered to be one of the loveliest in America, with its handsome late 18th- and early 19th-century frame

and brick houses. Although it is both a resort and an art center, Woodstock is still unspoiled. A stroll past Woodstock's beautiful green, its appealing shops, and its fine old houses makes a pleasurable outing and gives you the feeling of the scale of an old New England town. An unexpected attraction here is the Norman Williams Public Library, which houses a choice collection of Japanese art.

3 Just off the route and south of the Calvin Coolidge State Park is the small town of Plymouth, the home of Calvin Coolidge. The size of the village has not changed since Coolidge's childhood, and the post office is still in the general store, as it was when Coolidge's father was both storekeeper and postmaster. It is in this small, serene village surrounded by mountains that the former president asked to be buried. The little house where Coolidge was born, the homestead where he was sworn in as president by his father on August 3, 1923, the white frame church he attended, and a barn housing the Farmers' Museum are now part of a national historic landmark. It is closed from mid-October to June.

1. Quechee Gorge, viewed here from the bridge, is a corridor carved through schist.

SPECIAL FEATURES

ROAD GUIDE	HIGHLIGHT **1**
STATE PARKS — With Campsites ▲ Without Campsites △	SKI AREAS
RECREATION AREAS — With Campsites ▲ Without Campsites △	SCHEDULED AIRLINE STOPS
	OTHER AIRPORTS
SELECTED REST AREAS — With Toilets ⊠ Without Toilets ⊠	BOAT RAMPS
POINTS OF INTEREST ⊠	COVERED BRIDGES

ROAD CLASSIFICATION

CONTROLLED ACCESS HIGHWAYS (Entrance and Exit only at Interchanges)   Divided **5** Undivided

OTHER DIVIDED HIGHWAYS

PAVED HIGHWAYS

LOCAL ROADS In unfamiliar areas inquire locally before using these roads   Paved   Gravel   Dirt

MILEAGE

MILEAGE BETWEEN TOWNS AND JUNCTIONS 3 / 4   MILEAGE BETWEEN DOTS 35

SCALE

ONE INCH 9 MILES   0 1 2 3 4 5 10

ONE INCH 14 KILOMETERS   0 1 2 3 4 5 ...... 10 16

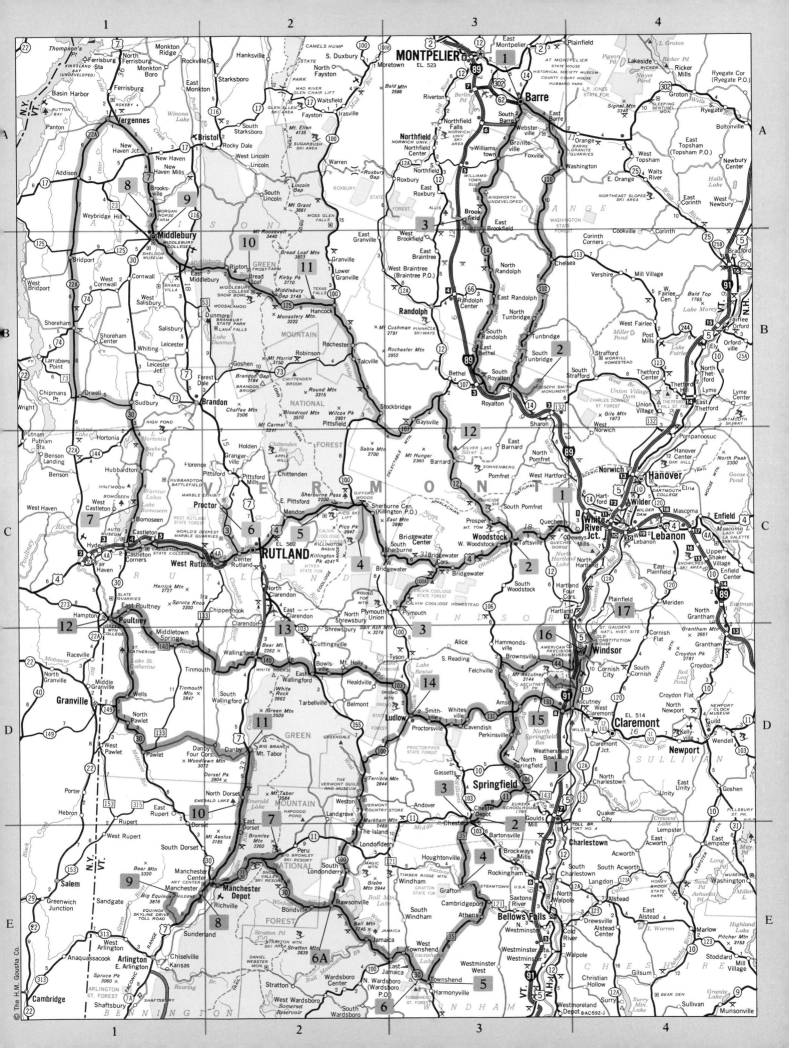

7. *Glacially formed valleys and winding streams established the pattern of settlement in Vermont. The streambeds became the routes for trails and roads, and the rich alluvial soil became farmland, as exemplified in this countryside west of Rutland.*

4 Killington Peak can not be seen from the road as you ascend the Ottauquechee River valley toward the crest of the Green Mountains—the forested hills walling the narrow valley block it from view. But Killington, the second highest peak in Vermont (4,241 feet), should not be missed.

During the summer and winter seasons, weather permitting, you can take a 3½-mile aerial ride to the summit on the Killington Gondola Tramway. Another way to reach the top is to take the chair lift from the base of the mountain at the end of Killington Road. (The lift is not operated in the spring, and in winter it is reserved for skiers.) The turn onto Killington Road is opposite Bill's Country Store on Route 4, about five miles west of the gondola base.

Killington's bare, rocky peak affords magnificent views of five states and Canada. The view may have been the inspiration for the state's name: it is claimed that in 1763 the Reverend Samuel Peters climbed the peak and, looking out upon the vast landscape, called it Verd-Mont "in token that her mountains and hills shall be ever green." Some hold, however, that it was from Stratton Mountain to the south that the Reverend Samuel Stratton named the state.

5 Sherburne Pass is one of the few notches in the spine of the Green Mountains. There are places to park for day hikers. It is a short climb to Deer Leap Overlook, which provides fine panoramic views. Just to the north is Gifford Woods State Park with picnicking and camping facilities and foot trails. A virgin stand of sugar maple *(Acer saccharum),* Vermont's official state tree, and some of the state's oldest trees are found in Gifford Woods.

Beyond the pass the land falls away sharply into a fertile valley coursed by Otter Creek and rises again on its western side in the Taconic Range. Otter Creek, the longest river within Vermont, flows northward to Lake Champlain, a travel route long favored by the early Indians.

6 The town of Proctor is right in the heart of marble country. So much of the place is built of marble, including an impressive bridge, that it gleams a spectral white.

The marble deposits were formed by tiny marine creatures that lived in the inland sea that covered the area 400 to 700 million years ago. As they died, their shells of lime sank to the bottom, mixing with mud. Gradual changes within the earth crystallized the sediment, hundreds of feet thick, and thrust it upward, literally forming mountains of marble.

The exhibit of the Vermont Marble Company (sold in the 1970's to a Swiss corporation) is closed from the end of October to the end of May. Another attraction here is the Otter Valley Railroad, which offers an hour-long ride in old-fashioned cars up steep grades to old quarry sites with splendid mountain views. It is closed from the end of October to the end of May and on weekdays from then to July 1.

7 Crossing the valley from Rutland and driving through Castleton, noted for its Greek Revival-style houses, you come to Lake Bomoseen. Nearly eight miles long, it is the largest natural lake within Vermont and the center of a resort area. The lake, fringed with cedars and surrounded by forested mountains, is a beautiful setting for a day of boating (rentals are available) and swimming or fishing for trout, pike, and bass.

In the Champlain Valley the scene is pastoral with hayfields and cornfields bordered with elms and birches; to the east are undulating hills and to the west the violet profile of the Adirondacks. Going toward Middlebury you pass through rich pastureland tinged in summer with red clover, the state flower. This is one of the state's most prosperous dairy regions. Most of Vermont's cattle are Holsteins, but here also are Jerseys, Ayrshires, and Guernseys.

8 Just north of Middlebury is the Morgan Horse Farm with about 70 registered Morgans and a statue of the stallion Justin Morgan (named after its owner), the progenitor of the breed. This horse, which died in 1821, was probably part Arabian. Smallish, lively, and stylish, Morgans are favored for riding and driving, but they are sturdy enough for farmwork. Vermont has decreed the Morgan the official state animal, and the farm is now a national historic site with guided tours, a slide-tape show, and a picnic area. It is closed from November to May.

9 Sheltered by the slopes of the Green Mountains, Middlebury is an attractive college town with a park-like campus and one of the best examples of church architecture in New England. Built in 1806-09, this Congregational Church has a fine Palladian window over the entrance and a graceful 136-foot tower. The Sheldon Museum in Middlebury is a restored brick house dating from 1829, with black marble fireplaces and 19th-century furnishings. It also has a collection of curios reminiscent

Making maple sugar

The term "sugaring" is from colonial times when maple sugar rather than syrup was the principal product. The season arrives in Vermont between late February and late March, before the new buds of the sugar maples begin to swell. Internal pressure causes the nutrition-bearing sap to flow when the tree is tapped. A mature tree can give 8 to 15 gallons per taphole without being harmed.

In the sugarhouse the sap is boiled down in evaporating pans, often over a wood fire. It takes 24 to 40 gallons of sap to make a gallon of syrup.

of life in early Vermont. It is closed from mid-October to June.

Also in Middlebury is the Vermont State Craft Center at Frog Hollow, south of the bridge on Frog Hollow Road. The center has studios for resident craftsmen who display and sell their work and that of others. It is closed in January. A restored stone mill next to the center adds to the rustic charm of the place.

Route 125 east is a pleasant road winding through a forest with the Middlebury River alongside. The road is also known as the Robert Frost Memorial Drive, celebrating the poet who made his summer home in this area until his death in 1963.

10 Just north of the road east of Ripton is the Robert Frost Wayside Area, and near it is the Frost farmhouse. South of the road, the Robert Frost National Recreation Trail leads through woods lit by shimmering aspens and through fields with blueberries and beaver ponds, all described in his poems.

11 The Texas Falls Recreation Area is to the north of the road as you descend toward Hancock. A trail follows a moss-edged flume through the woods to the falls, one of the most beautiful in the state. Cascading down a rocky gorge, the water flings itself into a basinlike pool. Sunlight shooting through the overhanging trees dapples the pool with bright green, and the water seems to dance over a bed of emeralds.

South of Hancock the road accompanies the fast-flowing White River, where an angler may catch rainbow and brook trout.

12 Nearing Woodstock, you pass Silver Lake, its white sand bottom returning the sunlight as a sheet of silver. There are lovely wooded roads in the vicinity of Silver Lake, and Silver Lake State Park offers camping, swimming, and picnicking. Nearby is the village of Barnard, where a few writers, including Dorothy Thompson and Sinclair Lewis, found seclusion.

8. On its home farm the Morgan is trained for show in manners, boldness, and speed.

On this interesting and scenic one-day outing you will see great quarries of granite, rustic villages, a floating bridge, and, on all sides, the peaceful valleys and wooded hills of Vermont.

1 The discovery of the bustling town of Barre in the midst of Vermont's peaceful hills is something of a surprise, but the place has its own interesting character as the locale of the world's largest granite quarry. Because of the granite's flawless texture and attractive off-white and soft blue-gray shades, it excels as stone for monuments.

Granite is the principal material of the earth's crust. At a depth of 10 miles or more, the once-molten rock formed crystals as it cooled—glasslike quartz, milky feldspar, and spots of black ferromagnesian minerals. Only where the crust has been uplifted during mountain-building can granite be seen at the surface.

A pinnacle on the brink of Barre's Rock of Ages quarry gives a spectacular view of granite miners 350 feet below carving out gigantic blocks with special jet-channeling flame machines, and a tour of the huge

Craftsman Center allows you to see artisans turning out finished products. The center is closed weekends.

2 The road from Barre to South Royalton passes rustic villages in a deep river valley walled in by rugged mountains. A two-mile drive along a country road near South Royalton leads to Sharon, where there is a 360-acre sanctuary in memory of Joseph Smith, founder of the Church of Jesus Christ of Latter-day Saints. This was his birthplace, and in the midst of the peaceful grounds rises a tall granite monument commemorating him. The shaft proper is a 38½-foot monolith quarried at Barre.

3 Brookfield offers the special opportunity to drive across Sunset Lake on a floating bridge, the only one of its kind in Vermont. The original bridge, built in 1819, floated on wooden barrels. In 1936 the citizens of Brookfield were offered a conventional bridge, but they rejected it: they had always had a floating bridge and they saw no reason to change. In 1978 the 320-foot bridge was reconstructed for the seventh time. The deck now rests on polyethylene barrels held by wooden racks.

Here is an easy introduction to the varied aspects of the "Green Mountain State." On these roads you will be rewarded with a unique combination of rural charm and gentle scenic beauty accented, in the towns and small industrial centers, with evidence of Yankee ingenuity, craftsmanship, and hard work.

1 Springfield is a fine old town that spreads up the steep hillsides rising from the river. From the road through the narrow valley you can see the brick-walled machine shops typical of New England's turn-of-the-century industrial towns. One such, by the waterfall on the Black River, has a plaque reading "The Fellows Gear Shaper Company 1918." In the era of the burgeoning automobile industry, the machines made here for cutting and shaping gears were in great demand. The Fellows Corporation, now located upstream, is still famous for the manufacture of these machines. This and other Springfield precision machine shops welcome visitors by appointment.

2 The road through the uplands from Springfield to Chester passes the mill of Green Mountain Cabins, Inc., where spruce is hand-peeled, sawed, and notched to make custom versions of the old-time log cabin. Much of the machinery and activity can be seen from the road on a weekday, but it is also possible to take a tour of the facility.

3 Chester is a lovely little town with beautifully restored 19th-century homes and a charming inn on the village green.

One mile north of the green on Route 103 (North Street) is the Stone Village at Chester Depot. This cluster of beautiful old houses and the church are distinguished by the gray-green gneiss used in their construction. The buildings add to the charm of Chester and to the appreciation of the effort and craftsmanship required when working with stone. This metamorphic rock, quarried in the nearby hills and brought to the site by teams of oxen, was formed about 400 million years ago by the uplift and folding of the ridge of the Green Mountains. Extreme compression deep within the earth altered the original rock formations and rear-

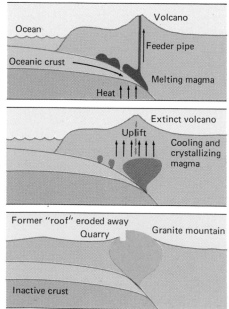

1. When one continental plate pushes over another, the combination of pressure and heat causes the lower plate to melt. Masses of molten magma form and rise into the overriding plate, and often erupt as volcanoes. In this case, after the assumed eruptions, the magma cooled and hardened into a domelike intrusion of granite, revealed after millions of years of erosion.

Evolution of the covered bridge

The techniques used in building barns were adapted for the construction of covered bridges in the early 19th century. The single kingpost, the queenpost, and the cross-braced Warren truss were all used. The spans of these early bridges were limited because the horizontal timbers had to reach from one bank or pier to the other.

To construct longer spans, bridge builders later designed new trusses that distributed the load and made it feasible to use spliced timbers. The sturdy, economical, and easily built Town lattice truss bridge, using spliced stringers and short timbers, was the most popular in Vermont. The bridges were covered to increase their longevity by protecting the trusses and flooring against the destructive effects of weather. The Scott Covered Bridge, built at Townshend in 1870, has a Town lattice span of 165.7 feet, the longest single span of this type in the state. Although Ithiel Town claimed his bridge could be "built by the mile and cut off by the yard," some designers, including Burr and McCallum, introduced an element of horizontal thrust for added strength, as shown below.

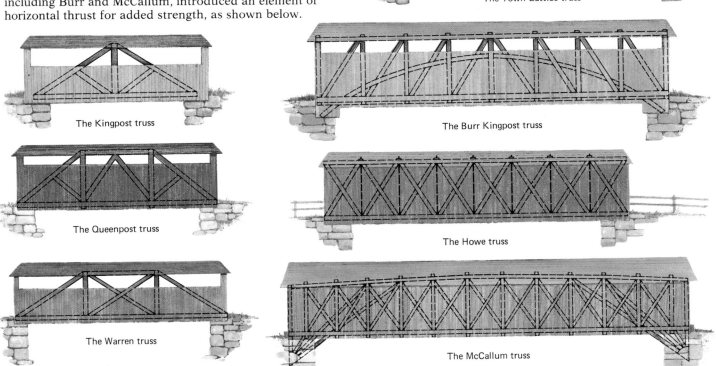

The Town Lattice truss

The Kingpost truss

The Burr Kingpost truss

The Queenpost truss

The Howe truss

The Warren truss

The McCallum truss

ranged the mineral crystals, creating light and dark layers. The last ice sheet pushing south scraped the soil off the top of the ridge and left the range's bedrock exposed.

4 An unblemished gem in its setting of wooded hills, Grafton is a materialization of everyone's dream of an unspoiled New England village. This is due in part to a faithful restoration of its post-Revolutionary houses and shops. Turn west off Route 35 to find the loveliest of its frame houses, the pristine churches, the beautiful Grafton Tavern (built in 1801), the village store, the old post

office that is now a museum, and the Grafton cheese shop where you can buy some locally made cheddar.

Traveling south, you notice the rocky streambed along the side of the road, a reminder that in this hilly country streams were often the guidelines when roads were built.

5 Snuggled among rocky hills is the small village of Townshend with its smooth, level green contrasting sharply with the rugged landscape. On the green is the Congregational Church, which was built in 1790 and is one of the most photographed structures in New England. Also no-

table is the Town Hall with its columned portico and clock tower.

Spanning the West River in Townshend is the Scott Covered Bridge. Built in 1870 in a Town lattice design, it has three spans and an overall length of 276 feet. Contrary to popular belief, bridges were not covered to keep off snow; in fact, in the days of the sleigh, tollmen had to shovel snow onto the floor of covered bridges to enable sleighs to cross. The enclosures were built to protect the timbers from the alternating and destructive effects of moisture and hot drying sun.

6 A road crossing the top of the Townshend Dam takes you over to the Townshend Dam Recreation Area. Whether your preference is white water, smooth lake water, or simply fishing off a bank, you will find it here. Many kinds of boats, from kayaks to sailboats, are available for rent. Close by are the Townshend State Forest and the Jamaica State Park with campsites, picnic areas, and a beach for swimming. Jamaica is a small, quiet village that comes to life in May when the National Canoe and Kayak Championship Races are held on the West River. The campgrounds in the state parks and recreation areas are closed from mid-October to the end of May.

6A An alternate drive is Route 100, often described as one of the most beautiful in the United States. It follows the West River past South Londonderry, with its lovely red brick church, to Weston, a small, beautifully restored town banked all around by forested mountains. Weston is especially known for its classic, shaded green bordered by stately houses, its summer theater, and the Vermont Country Store. The road north of Weston, ascending a long grade, offers superb views of the hills and valleys so typical of the state.

7 South of Bromley Mountain the Long Trail follows the highway for 300 or 400 feet before it branches into the woods toward the summit. Big Bromley (3,260 feet) is popular with skiers, and the lodges offer all the expected amenities. Thrill seekers, young and old, may want to try the Bromley Alpine Slide: sitting in a bucketlike wagon with a brake lever, you weave down a 4,000-foot-long track through wooded slopes and hillside meadows with glorious views of mountains and valleys. But have warm clothes on hand: the temperature can plummet to 50°F in July. The slide is closed from the end of October to the end of May and during bad weather.

8 Manchester is a cosmopolitan town with an aura of wealth. It has been an elegant resort for more than a century, and among those who visited frequently were Mrs. Abraham Lincoln and Mrs. Ulysses S. Grant.

On Route 7 south you will see a blend of historic colonial buildings and modern summer houses with white pillars, manicured lawns, and marble sidewalks canopied by elms. The mineral springs of Equinox House rivaled those of Saratoga's spas in bygone days, and they are still in operation. Manchester has a

6. *Swollen by the spring thaw, the West River at Jamaica swirls around rocks, and attracts white-water enthusiasts like this contestant negotiating one of the gates in a kayak race.*

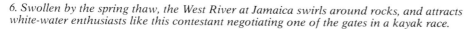

8. *Manchester's Congregational Church, built in 1871, and the old Courthouse, renovated in 1849, face the village green.*

number of attractions, including the Southern Vermont Art Center, an art gallery, and the American Museum of Fly Fishing.

9 Overshadowing Manchester is Mount Equinox (3,816 feet), the highest peak in the Taconic Mountain range. Take the Skyline Drive, a short toll road winding through a hardwood forest to the summit, for sweeping views of the Green Mountains, the Berkshires, and New York State. The Skyline Drive is usually closed from the end of October to May.

10 Emerald Lake (also known as North Dorset Pond) is indeed an emerald color on a sunny afternoon. Emerald Lake State Park encompasses 430 acres of inviting fields and wooded hills with many secluded campsites, foot trails, a picnic area, boat rental facilities, and a beach for swimming.

11 Danby is an attractive, small community lying in a sheltered valley. Its prosperity can be attributed to marble quarrying, dairying, and, to some extent, the sale of antiques. Nearly every parlor and barn seems to have been converted into an antiques shop.

The road west winds around mountains that give way to upland farm country and bucolic scenes of cornfields and grazing cows. The land seems lost in time, and must look much as it did 100 years ago. The village of Pawlet, with its restored millpond and waterwheel, is typical of the picturesque places to be found throughout Vermont.

12 Poultney, settled more than 200 years ago, is a neat, unpretentious place with slate-roofed houses and an exceptionally attractive post office built (1962) of slate—an appropriate material to use in the center of Vermont's slate industry. Poultney drew many workmen from the slate quarries of Wales. Curiously, the slates of Vermont, Pennsylvania, and Wales were all formed about 450 million years ago, originally as muds on the seafloor of an ancestral Atlantic. Long before continental drift separated the continents, that sea was just a narrow trough.

The Two Editors' Inn on Poultney's Main Street honors Horace Greeley and George Jones. In 1826 Greeley, a 15-year-old lad from New Hampshire, came to nearby East Poultney to work as an apprentice on the weekly gazette, where Jones, a local youth, was employed. Later Greeley became the founder of *The New York Tribune*, and Jones the cofounder of *The New York Times*.

As you approach the ridge of the Green Mountains you pass through Wallingford, a gracious village with a broad main street flanked by splendid homes with columned porches and neatly trimmed lawns.

13 The Long Trail crosses Route 140 about three miles east of Wallingford. There you can park your car and hike in some of Vermont's wildest country to make your personal discoveries of wild flowers, a ruffed grouse startled in the undergrowth, crystal streams, and shining ponds cupped in hollows.

14 (See also 6A on page 48.) Unlike so many of Vermont's villages with their traditional white frame houses and churches, Ludlow is a place of red brick. Driving through the town you see not only brick houses but also the red brick Black River Academy from which Calvin Coolidge graduated in 1890. The building is now a museum of local history and a national historic site. It is closed from mid-October to late May.

15 Mount Ascutney (3,144 feet) rises to form a prominent landmark in the Connecticut River valley. Surprisingly, this peak is not part of the Green Mountains, which were formed by an upthrusting of the earth's crust. It is, instead, a monadnock, formed by the erosion of all the land that once surrounded it. From the mountain road a ¾-mile foot trail leads to the summit, which provides vistas of some of New England's best scenery. Ascutney State Park has camping and trailer sites, nature trails, and picnic areas.

The Long Trail

In 1910 a group of Vermonters who wanted "to make the Vermont mountains play a larger part" in people's lives founded the Green Mountain Club to develop a hiking trail. Twenty-one years later the Long Trail was completed, a 260-mile footpath skimming over the major peaks of the Green Mountain range the length of Vermont.

Vermont's rolling countryside, viewed by Benton MacKaye from the top of Stratton Mountain in 1900, also inspired the idea for the Appalachian Trail, which now runs from Maine to Georgia. The two trails are one between the Massachusetts-Vermont border and Sherburne Pass.

Today thousands of people hike these trails and the numerous side trails that so intimately reveal the wilderness of Vermont.

The Long Trail skims over Pico Peak at an elevation of 3,957 feet near Sherburne Pass.

When General Lafayette, the French hero of the American Revolution, visited the United States in 1824-25, the local people eagerly rushed to complete a road and build a hut on the top of Mount Ascutney where they might entertain him and impress him with the view. The general arrived in Windsor on June 28, 1825, but he failed to make it up the mountain.

16 At Windsor, in a public tavern, a group of delegates met on July 8, 1777, and adopted the constitution of the Free and Independent State of Vermont. The document was the first in the country to outlaw slavery and to reject property ownership or specific income as a voting requirement. The tavern, now relocated and called Old Constitution House, is cherished as the birthplace of Vermont, and is maintained as a historic shrine and museum. It is closed from mid-October to the end of May.

Windsor is also distinguished in the industrial history of Vermont. Anyone interested in hand and machine tools will be fascinated by the American Precision Museum on South Main Street (closed from mid-October to the end of May). The building itself was erected in 1846 as the most modern armory of its time, and it is now a national historic landmark.

17 The short drive to Cornish, New Hampshire, just across the Connecticut River from Windsor by way of the longest covered bridge in the United States, leads you to Aspet, the home, studios, and gardens of Augustus Saint-Gaudens (1848–1907), one of America's greatest sculptors. In order to escape the hot and humid New York City summers, he rented the mansion in 1885, remodeled it, and turned it into his permanent home. Other artists followed his lead, and Cornish became well known as an art colony. The estate was designated a national historic site in 1965. Saint-Gaudens enjoyed developing the elaborate gardens, where copies of his most famous works are now displayed. And from his porch he loved to watch the spectacular sunsets behind Mount Ascutney.

The sunsets can still be spectacular, and as you drive through Vermont's beautiful rolling countryside back to Springfield, you may hope that nothing here will ever change.

New England Sampler

From scenic coastal headlands to rolling wooded hills and the birthplace of the Revolution

Included here are roads in the states of Massachusetts and Rhode Island, as well as the eastern part of Connecticut. In this historic region, which abuts the rocky shores of the Atlantic, Narragansett Bay, and Long Island Sound, much of America's seagoing heritage was established.

Here too textile and leather goods manufacturing began in the 1700's.

Beginning at Concord—the starting point of the American Revolution—the drive takes us north through Wilmington and Andover to Haverhill on the Merrimack River, then east to Newburyport and Ipswich and on to the edge of the Atlantic where it washes the shores of Cape Ann.

The cape is composed of an ancient granite, formed deep down in the earth about 300 million years ago. It is a sliver of the earth's crust that was originally part of northwest Africa.

The road from Swampscott across to Concord cuts through an area of soft rocks in what is called the Boston Basin, which was formed by an ancient ice age about 450 million years ago, at a time when the basin was attached to Morocco.

1 Concord, the 17th-century town where the first hostilities of the American uprising took place, was home to such famous American authors as Henry David Thoreau, Ralph Waldo Emerson, Louisa May Alcott, and Nathaniel Hawthorne. Although Concord was settled in colonial times, the dominant architecture today, including the homes of several of these authors, is that of the more elegant Victorian era.

About a mile north of town toward Bedford, a great marshland and forest sliced through by the Concord River provides a sanctuary for animals as well as for nesting and migratory birds.

The marshland occupies depressions in the Boston Basin that were scoured out by the last glaciation. As the ice melted, it left lakes that slowly became filled with sediment and peat. Early settlers were attracted by the rich blackish soil.

With trails for walking and bicy-cling, the Great Meadows National Wildlife Refuge offers an unusual opportunity to observe much of the wildlife indigenous to eastern Massachusetts, including muskrats, raccoons, rabbits, white-tailed deer, chipmunks, and short-tailed and long-tailed weasels, as well as turtles, frogs, and the big brown bat.

The Dike Trail, a 1½-mile loop, has two blinds and an observation tower where photographers and bird-watchers can see the wild creatures. Nesting boxes for wood ducks are placed in the marshes, which are edged with cattails and the purple spikes of loosestrife in midsummer.

2 Wooded, winding roads lead northward toward Andover. Just south of the town is the Harold Parker State Forest, a 3,400-acre parkland that has camping facilities, picnic grounds, and at one of the ponds a swimming beach with lifeguards in attendance. Besides a series of hiking trails, the park has an area set aside for trail bikes. The trails are used in the winter for such sports as snowmobiling, cross-country skiing, and snowshoeing. The trails are all well marked.

A fish hatchery is maintained at one of the park's ponds. The others, where fishing is allowed, are stocked with bass, trout, pickerel, and hornpout, all raised in the hatchery.

Small animals are plentiful in the forest, from raccoons and chipmunks to rabbits and minks. And the birds include owls, wild geese, cardinals, woodpeckers, and the chickadee—the official state bird.

South of Haverhill the road goes through the colonial town of North Andover and then climbs along a winding, hilly stretch of farmland. At Haverhill, on the Merrimack River, farms and factories blend. The steep wide streets are lined with stately Victorian homes and a few remaining American elms. Although it has been struck by the Dutch elm disease and is fast disappearing, the American elm (*Ulmus americana*) is still the official state tree.

In a small park at Main and Water streets there is a statue of Hannah Dustin, who was captured by Indians in 1697. According to local lore, she later escaped and returned to Haverhill carrying the scalps of her captors.

Following the wide, placid, tree-bordered Merrimack River, the road crosses and recrosses the river as it winds toward the Atlantic coast, where the river empties into the sea.

3 The Salisbury Beach State Reservation, a strip of coast bordering both river and ocean, includes beaches, sand dunes, and long stretches of salt marsh. Surf fishing and swimming are permitted, and camping facilities are provided in a large fenced area upriver from the Atlantic shore.

Quite separate is an amusement area on the ocean just beyond the entrance to the reservation.

A short drive through a sandy landscape takes you to Newburyport. High Street, a wide main thoroughfare of the town, follows a ridge a few blocks in from the water. Its large handsome mansions were built by shipbuilders and shipowners during the early 1800's.

The waterfront, part of the old town that is being restored, changes slowly as it approaches Plum Island. Fishing sheds and old shops give way to salt marshes bordering the mouth of the Merrimack.

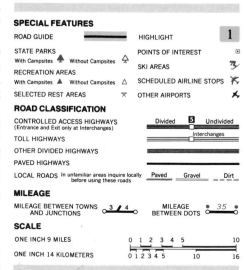

SPECIAL FEATURES

ROAD GUIDE ▬▬▬   HIGHLIGHT **1**

STATE PARKS   With Campsites 🌲   Without Campsites △   POINTS OF INTEREST ⊡

RECREATION AREAS   With Campsites ▲   Without Campsites △   SKI AREAS 🎿   SCHEDULED AIRLINE STOPS ✈

SELECTED REST AREAS ⋈   OTHER AIRPORTS ✈

ROAD CLASSIFICATION

CONTROLLED ACCESS HIGHWAYS (Entrance and Exit only at Interchanges)   Divided **5** Undivided

TOLL HIGHWAYS   Interchanges

OTHER DIVIDED HIGHWAYS

PAVED HIGHWAYS

LOCAL ROADS In unfamiliar areas inquire locally before using these roads   Paved   Gravel   Dirt

MILEAGE

MILEAGE BETWEEN TOWNS AND JUNCTIONS 3 • 4   MILEAGE BETWEEN DOTS • 35

SCALE

ONE INCH 9 MILES   0 1 2 3 4 5   10

ONE INCH 14 KILOMETERS   0 1 2 3 4 5   10   16

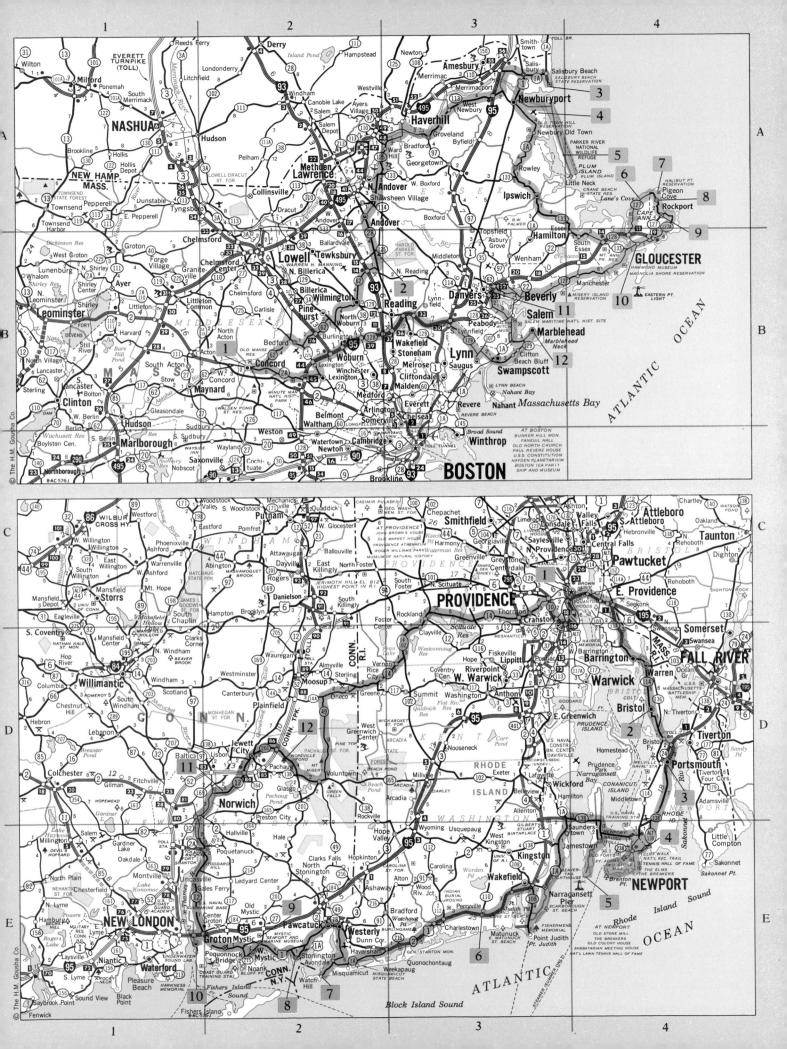

4 Just before the bridge to Plum Island, there is a small, one-story red-and-white building, with a fleet of small airplanes parked along the edge of a wide, open field. Two wind socks and an east-west runway announce that it is indeed an airfield. Short flights over Newburyport and Plum Island are available daily year-round, as weather permits. One of the sight-seeing planes is a classic open-cock-pit biplane, a Curtiss Travelair built in 1927 and maintained in top condition.

5 Sand dunes, salt- and freshwater marshes, tidal waters, and six miles of sandy ocean beaches make up the 4,600 acres of the Parker River

semipalmated sandpiper, herring gull, and ring-necked pheasant. The mowed salt marshes provide feeding and resting areas for waterfowl and shore birds.

Surf fishing is popular at the refuge, and boardwalks give easy access from parking lots to the beach.

Square wooden boxes on stilts—traps to catch the buzzing, biting green-head flies that appear in swarms in mid-July—are placed along the edge of the marshes. The flies are attracted by the dark color and warmth of the boxes, and are then trapped by a fine wire-mesh V-shaped screen inside.

6 From Ipswich to Essex and on to Cape Ann, the road meanders along the coast. It winds through the summer-resort town of Annisquam, and climbs northward to Lane's Cove, a wide, almost circular bay bordered by wooded bluffs—a sight as startling in its sudden appearance as in its beauty. A rocky path leads down to a half-moon gravel beach that is a popular place for swimming.

Where the cove comes into view, the roadway has been widened to provide a stopping place from which to view the water, woods, rocks, and sky—a beautiful sight at sunset.

7 A short drive beyond Lane's Cove, in Pigeon Cove on the northern tip of Cape Ann, there is a wide rock ledge known as Halibut Point, a state park. According to local lore, its original name was Haul About Point—the end of the cape where sailing vessels had to "come about" to make for the safety of the harbor.

From a small parking lot off Gott Street a 5-minute walk through a patch of woods takes you to the point, which is a perfect place for a picnic. In the rock's tide pools you can see periwinkles, dog whelks, sea anemones, sea urchins, crabs—both the little green and the hermit crab—starfish, and many varieties of seaweed.

8 As you drive down a hill along the coast toward the center of Rockport, Cape Ann's most picturesque village, you will come to the New England Lobster Company on the left. A narrow driveway leads out to the end of the strip of land called Pigeon Cove Wharf, where the lobster plant has its small building. Several sheds for lobster pots line the roadway along the wharf, which is protected from the sea by a 30-foot breakwater built of huge rocks.

The New England Lobster Company processes as much as 1,500 pounds a day of this tasty crustacean.

Visitors are invited to see the plant and to watch the unloading of the lobsters brought in by local fishermen. If some unusual sea creature finds its way into the lobster pot—perhaps a horseshoe crab or a big bullhead—it is exhibited in a tub of seawater.

9 Before leaving Rockport, be sure to visit the harbor to see the weather-beaten wharf that has been

7. *Groups of schoolchildren gather to observe marine life in the tide pools on Halibut Point, where large slabs of rock surfaced (exfoliated) along fracture lines created 350 million years ago as the intrusion of granite slowly cooled on this northern point of Cape Ann.*

National Wildlife Refuge, which occupies most of Plum Island. The dunes, made up of saltwater sands, were created from the sandbars washed up by the sea after the last glacial time, about 5,000 years ago.

Along Hellcat Swamp Nature Trail, where there is an observation tower and blind, many kinds of animals, such as rabbits, foxes, skunks, weasels, muskrats, and deer, make their homes along with hundreds of species of birds, such as the black duck,

The coastal town of Ipswich, a favorite summer resort, was one of the shipping and industrial centers of early America. Although lace was its first manufactured product, today the town turns out electronic parts. The old village green is surrounded by houses dating from the 17th and 18th centuries—among them the Whipple House (1640) and the Heard House, which is now a museum of objects from the days when America was engaged in the China trade.

9. In Rockport's harbor the red fishing shed called Motif No. 1 is such a well-known landmark that it was rebuilt after storms destroyed it in 1978.

painted by artists more often than any other single object anywhere. It turns up in paintings found in all parts of the world, and has come to be known in Rockport as Motif No. 1.

Rockport and Gloucester are joined by a winding, windswept drive called Atlantic Road. Here many large summer homes, built on hillsides, overlook the ocean and the great stretch of rugged coast known as Bass Rocks.

10 As you approach Gloucester harbor, the road winds through a little peninsula known as Rocky Neck, where artists and fishermen have settled along the narrow streets. There are also many restaurants.

The harbor and its many sailboats are watched over by the "Gloucester Fisherman," a famous bronze statue set up as a memorial to all the Gloucester fishermen lost at sea.

Just beyond the harbor, a medieval castle was built on a cliff at the water's edge by the late John Hays Hammond, Jr. Inspired by his many years of travel in Europe, he built the castle in 1928 and filled it with his priceless collection of medieval furniture and art. The 100-foot Great Hall houses an 8,600-pipe organ.

The castle is at 80 Hesperus Avenue, just off Route 127. Closed in winter except on weekends.

11 In the colonial town of Danvers is a handsome mansion called Glen Magna, on Ingersoll Street just off Route 1. Originally a farmhouse, it was rebuilt by Mrs. William Endicott in the early 1800's. Its formal garden is planted with a profusion of perennials and annuals, with flowers in bloom from spring through autumn. The garden is enhanced by an 18th-century teahouse, a national landmark that is closed except on the first weekend in July. The garden is closed from mid-October to mid-May.

The historic seaport of Salem is famous for its House of Seven Gables, which sits at the edge of the harbor, and its Witch House, so-called because it was the home of Magistrate Jonathan Corwin during the witch hunt days of 1692, when more than 200 people arrested as "witches" were brought to the house for pretrial examinations.

12 Marblehead, once a part of Salem, lies at the end of a rocky headland jutting into the Atlantic across from Salem's harbor.

It was originally called Marble Harbor because its cliffs looked like marble from the sea. Actually, the rock here is a spectacularly banded gneiss of quartzited mica-rich layers. The harbor is a relic of a former landscape only partially affected by the last ice age. The old valleys were overwhelmed by the rising sea as the ice melted.

The town has one of the busiest ports for pleasure craft on the Atlantic coast today. The streets are narrow, and the houses crowding the roadway mostly date from the 17th and 18th centuries, giving the little town a quaintness almost unsurpassed on the eastern seaboard.

The town hall of Marblehead, called Abbot Hall, houses one of America's best-known paintings—"The Spirit of '76." Also known as "Yankee Doodle," it depicts two drummers and a fife player, with the American flag flying, leading a group of soldiers into battle. The artist, A.M. Willard, used his young son as a model for one of the drummers.

From Marblehead and Swampscott the route back to Concord goes through Lexington, where a large monument on the village green honors the eight Minutemen who lost their lives early in the morning of April 19, 1775, when the British opened fire.

10. Keeping nets in good repair is a never-ending chore of the Gloucester fishermen, who brave the Atlantic Ocean's weather in both summer and winter as they pursue their trade.

Rhode Island's license plates are labeled "The Ocean State" with good reason. *Its many harbors, islands, bays and inlets, and its sparkling sandy beaches combine to create a splendid and diverse landscape that is almost entirely dominated by the sea.*

The drive along the state's byways, from the capital city of Providence to the coastal towns of Newport and Jamestown, westward to Watch Hill and on through the seaside villages and farmlands bordering eastern Connecticut, is one of ever-changing beauty both natural and man-made.

Connecticut's coastline with its colonial seafaring villages of Stonington, Mystic, and little Noank—hardly changed from its earliest days—offers a picturesque drive that follows the many coves and inlets of the Atlantic shore, a popular vacationland.

As the road winds its way back toward Providence, through miles of forested hills, it comes full circle at the outskirts of the city.

1　Whether you travel by train or by car, the first sight that greets you as you approach Providence is the state capitol, the handsome Rhode Island State House, standing in its landscaped grounds on Smith Hill.

One-Day Side Trip

Windswept and still unspoiled, Block Island lies 12 miles off the southern coast of Rhode Island. Ferries to the island leave from Providence (a 4-hour sail) during the summer, and from Galilee near Point Judith (1¼ hours) all year long. Cars can be taken if reservations are made in advance. Several round trips are made daily, depending on the weather.

The road from Old Harbor, where the ferry docks, to Mohegan Bluffs is fine for bicycling or hiking—a three-mile route along the southeast coast that offers a dramatic view. These bluffs, of sand and boulders left by melting glacial ice, were eroded to form cliffs when the ocean returned to the region 12,000 years ago.

Bicycles and mopeds can be rented in Old Harbor, and bathing facilities are available at Block Island State Beach, a wide stretch of sand about a mile north of town.

The 19th-century structure has a freestanding marble dome and is surrounded by cupolas at each corner of the main building. Atop the dome stands the bronze "Independent Man," symbolizing the individuality that has been attributed to Rhode Islanders since colonial days, when Roger Williams founded Providence. For having dared to challenge church power and champion Indian rights, Williams was banished to the wilderness by the Puritans of the Massachusetts Bay Colony in 1635.

Guided tours of the statehouse are given twice a day. Closed Saturdays, Sundays, and holidays.

2　In the colonial town of Bristol the wide main street of modest mansions is lined with trees as old as the town itself. Here are the homes of the sea merchants, some of whom made great fortunes in the slave trade prior to the American Revolution.

At the north end of town, off Route 114 on Hope Street, are two tall stone gateposts, each topped by a replica of a prancing bull. This is the entrance to Colt State Park, a part of the Colt family estate. Here are fields, picnic grounds, salt marshes, and beaches for swimming or walking along Narragansett Bay. A superb scenic drive follows the edge of the bay.

As you leave Bristol and cross Mount Hope Bay on the short Mount Hope Bridge (a toll bridge), you come to the island of Rhode Island, for which the state is named. This island is still sometimes called Aquidneck, its original name.

3　Portsmouth at the north end is as green and wooded as the landscape you have just left. Off Route 114 on Cory's Lane are the Green Animals Topiary Gardens, a collection of shrubs and trees pruned to resemble animals—among them an elephant, a lion, and a tiger—as well as arches, spirals, cones, and many other forms. Trees in the gardens include the red maple (*Acer rubrum*), the state tree.

The gardens are closed from September 30 to May 1 except on weekends in October.

As you approach the Atlantic Ocean, the green rolling farmlands gradually give way to rocks and sand. Along the coast are great outcroppings of hard stone that was folded and metamorphosed about 350 million years ago. This part of the country originally lay along the shore of Morocco and became welded onto eastern North America before the Atlantic Ocean was formed, about 150 million years ago.

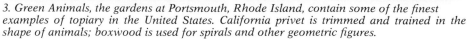

3. Green Animals, the gardens at Portsmouth, Rhode Island, contain some of the finest examples of topiary in the United States. California privet is trimmed and trained in the shape of animals; boxwood is used for spirals and other geometric figures.

4. Newport's Cliff Walk curves along the Atlantic shoreline over rocks and through brambles. The 19th-century owners of the shorefront "cottages" tried to keep this stretch of coast for themselves, but the courts ruled that local fishermen must have free access to the sea. Fish of record-breaking size, including striped bass and blackfish, have been caught off these rocks.

4 The rugged coast at Newport, with its cliffs and its wild, windswept waterfront, appealed in particular to 19th-century millionaires, many of whom built mansions of unbelievable magnificence along the craggy shore.

With pounding waves on one side and the mansions on the other, the Cliff Walk, a national recreational trail, follows the coast for three miles, starting at Newport's Memorial Boulevard and ending at Bailey's Beach.

Along the way a stairway known as Forty Steps leads down a steep cliff to the water's edge. In places, as the path climbs over the rugged landscape, the trail can be difficult, and in a high wind even dangerous, but the view from Cliff Walk of both land and sea is spectacular.

The harbor on Narragansett Bay looks much as it did in the 18th century when it was a busy seaport. With its restored houses on a hillside overlooking the water and a series of wharves leading to the docks, it is still a bustling port. Sailboats, motor launches, dredgers, and naval ships come and go through Newport's waters, and as long as the winners of the America's Cup continue to prefer these waters, this most prestigious race will begin here.

On Bowen's Wharf, which survives from colonial days, and on several of the other wharves there are craft shops, boutiques, and small restaurants for both indoor and outdoor dining. Here too is the frigate *Rose*—a replica of a 24-gun British ship.

4. The Gothic Room of Marble House, the mansion built in 1892 for Mr. and Mrs. William K. Vanderbilt, is dominated by an enormous fireplace with a delicately carved facing. The matching chandeliers are bronze, and some of the furnishings are original.

5 As soon as you cross Narragansett Bay to Conanicut Island, turn down into Jamestown and look back. Here you will get the full impact of the size and handsome lines of the Newport suspension bridge. Almost 2½ miles long, it soars to a height of 400 feet. The bridge was built in 1969 to replace the Newport Ferry.

The road continues on down to the end of the island, where Beavertail Lighthouse sits atop a huge outcropping of rock, warning all seagoing traffic to stay clear. The great shelves of stone whose long flat layers are warmed by the sun and washed by the tides are popular with fishermen and picnickers from early spring to November.

After crossing the Jamestown Bridge—an old structure that looks like an Erector Set creation—the road to Point Judith follows along the western shore of Narragansett Bay, a rolling, wooded countryside.

Along the way is The Towers, an arched building spanning the road, all that remains of the once-popular Narragansett Pier Casino designed by Stanford White.

At the end of the peninsula stands the Point Judith Lighthouse, an octagonal brick structure that was built in 1816 to warn ships away from the rocky shore, and has served as a working beacon ever since.

6 Westward along the coast the scenery changes from sand and open pastureland to long stretches of woodland. A well-marked country road to the right leads to the town of Perryville—a mere crossroads—and the Perryville Trout Hatchery.

When the lane becomes a cow path and you think you have lost your way, drive on over a small log bridge and between two stone pillars into what seems to be a private dooryard. The hatchery is down the hill beyond a small parking lot.

Here rainbow and brown trout and Atlantic salmon are raised. A pond near the entrance holds hundreds of fish, all eager for the handfuls of feed that visitors can buy for five cents from an old-fashioned gum-ball machine. An attendant will answer your questions about fish and fishing in Rhode Island. Sixty ponds and streams throughout the state are stocked with fish from this hatchery in time for the annual trout season.

7 The 19th-century summer resort of Watch Hill was built on a series of bluffs and winding roads that follow the Atlantic coast just south of Westerly, much in the manner of Newport's Ocean Drive. The mansions,

however, are more modest. The little town boasts an antique merry-go-round called the Flying Horse Carousel, which has been a Watch Hill landmark for more than a hundred years. The horses are fine examples of the wood-carver's craft.

8 Stonington is one of the prettiest colonial villages on the Connecticut coast. Its green, surrounded by buildings dating from colonial times, is only a step away from the harbor, a wide port that served the sea captains of whaling ships and cargo vessels during the 1700's and 1800's. It is filled with pleasure craft today.

9 On the Mystic River just upstream from the historic town of Mystic is the Mystic Seaport Museum. This re-creation of a maritime village includes harborside buildings, small houses, a church, shops, and, docked at the waterfront, the last of the wooden whaling ships, *Charles W. Morgan.* The seaport is closed Christmas and New Year's days. Also worth a visit is the excellent aquarium nearby.

Beyond Mystic the tiny, hilly town of Noank, a charming fishing village, spreads upward from the sea.

5. Beavertail Lighthouse marks the entrance to Narragansett Bay. The rocks, sloping into the sea, provide access to the surf where fishermen try their luck.

10 Groton, the center of the submarine-building world, lies at the mouth of the Thames, pronounced just as it is spelled.

Docked here at 359 Thames Street is the World War II submarine U.S.S. *Croaker*, which is open to visitors daily. Closed Christmas and New Year's days.

The road northward along the Thames River winds through wooded hills where white oak (*Quercus alba*), Connecticut's state tree, grows. The river, far below, comes into view as woods give way to grassy fields.

11 As you come down a steep hill into the town of Norwich, a long sweep of 19th-century factory buildings greets you. With the old red bricks glowing in the sunshine, it is a handsome sight as well as a reminder of times gone by. The buildings are still used for manufacturing, for storage purposes, and for other business activities.

As you enter Norwich, turn north on Broadway and follow the signs to Mohegan Park and its Memorial Rose Garden on Mohegan Road. There are some 2,500 plants on display, including virtually every known rose variety. A festival is held in Norwich each year for 10 days in June and July when the plants are in bloom. The park features a children's zoo, a pond with swimming facilities, and several picnic areas.

12 Hopeville Pond State Park, a recreational park with campgrounds and a pond for swimming and fishing, has many acres of woodland. The park has a short nature trail as well as a section of the so-called Blue Trail, which is one of a network of trails through Connecticut that can be hiked for as far as you wish. All kinds of wildlife common to Connecticut can be seen here, including deer, foxes, rabbits, grouse, ducks, bluejays, robins, and, in winter, hundreds of Canada geese.

Nearby, along the wooded winding road, the Pachaug State Forest also offers facilities for camping, swimming, and picnicking.

Northward along Route 49 from Voluntown, the land slopes gently upward to a wide plateau of pastureland. Along this road is a succession of neatly maintained dairy farms. Barns, silos, milking sheds, and acres

9. *The 1841 whaling ship* Charles W. Morgan *is docked at Mystic Seaport. Visitors who go belowdecks marvel at the limited space in which sailors spent years at sea.*

and acres allotted to field corn indicate that the soil and climate here are ideal for the herds of Guernsey, Jersey, and Holstein cattle that you may see in the pastures and barnyards along the road.

At the top of the rise, before turning eastward onto Route 14, you will pass a bright red farmhouse on the left. With barns and milking sheds to match and a gravel courtyard bordered by beds of brilliant flowers,

Ekonk Hill, as it is called, is one of the prettiest sights along the way. Fantail pigeons, turkeys, peacocks, and cochin hens are kept together in a large chicken yard near the entrance gate.

After several miles of wooded roads, reservoirs, and ponds, and not a vestige of village or town, signs of civilization begin to appear, and the tall white dome of the Rhode Island State House once again looms on the skyline in the distance.

10. *Four firing chambers fill the aft torpedo room of the U.S.S.* Croaker, *the ship that is part of Groton's Submarine Memorial on the shores of the Thames River.*

Two Facets of New York

In the Adirondack wilderness and the Finger Lakes pastoral valleys there is pleasure enough for all

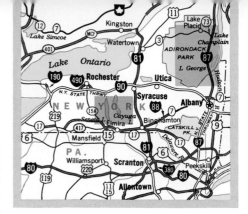

In the northern mountains of New York, where some of the highest peaks of the eastern United States soar above the ridgetops, there are miles of trails for skiing, facilities for camping in the wilderness, remote towns and villages, and many spectacular drives.

The Finger Lakes region, a gentler landscape of rolling farmlands and quiet waters, offers splendid scenery and dramatic waterfalls among its wooded hillsides.

The Adirondack Mountains are an awe-inspiring region of rugged ridges, heavily wooded valleys, and countless lakes and streams. Here are some of the highest peaks in the northeastern United States, outranked only by those of New Hampshire's stately White Mountains.

This untamed wilderness, where the rising morning mists tinge the mountain tiers with the sheen of gunmetal blue, is a land of the black bear, the beaver, the coyote, and the loon. It is also a land whose geology is exceptionally well exposed for all to see.

In past geologic ages the region was covered by at least three seas. Some 10,000 years ago the meltwaters of a mile-thick ice sheet formed the Champlain Sea. Present-day Lake Champlain is a lingering remnant of those icy waters.

1 Saratoga Springs on the southeastern fringes of the Adirondacks became a fashionable spa in the mid-19th century when wealthy families were drawn here by the supposed curative powers of its mineral waters. Many elaborate mansions were built around the springs, hotels lined Broadway, and during the "season" from June to the end of August, the town was a scene of social splendor.

Today the hotels and large mansions have almost completely disappeared, but visitors to Saratoga Spa State Park can taste the waters, relax in the naturally carbonated baths, enjoy the many nature trails either on foot or on bicycle, picnic in the well-kept park, and in winter follow the cross-country ski trails that wind through the wooded countryside.

Here is the Saratoga Performing Arts Center, an imposing building that is known as the summer home of the Philadelphia Orchestra and the New York City Ballet Company, and the historic Saratoga Racecourse, which dates back to 1865 when a group of well-known sportsmen including Leonard W. Jerome and Cornelius Vanderbilt formed the Saratoga Association for the Improvement of the Breed of Horses. The course, one of the oldest and

Classical Names

New York State holds first place among the states of the Union in the number of ancient names given to its cities and towns.

The naming of these towns in the so-called classical belt was no accident. A three-member board of state commissioners met in New York City on July 3, 1790, charged with the task of naming several parcels of land near Cayuga Lake that were to be given to Revolutionary War veterans.

Names of England's kings and their queens had already been widely used, as had those of our own war heroes and generals. With the well-established city of Troy on the Hudson to the east and Seneca Lake nearby, the board's decision was to continue the use of classical names in the area.

Writers of the ancient world are represented by such place-names as Ovid, Homer, Cicero, and Tully (as Cicero was also called). Names taken from historic towns, some Greek and some Roman, include Athens, Marathon, Corinth, Rome, Syracuse, Carthage, and its neighbor Utica.

There are at least two islands represented—Corfu and Ithaca; such Roman statesmen as Camillus, Cincinnatus, Cato, Marcellus, and Manlius; and at least one character from mythology—Aurora, goddess of the dawn.

Regions of the ancient world, such as Attica and Macedon, are included. The town of Arcade has the title of a Roman architectural design. And to round out the list, a city near the shores of Lake Ontario is called Greece.

finest thoroughbred racetracks in the United States, is open for four weeks in August.

The Saratoga Harness track is another popular place for visitors, who can see these horse-and-sulky events from April to November and on every weekend during the months of December and January.

2 About three miles west of Saratoga Springs is the Petrified Gardens, a fossil bank containing the petrified remains of plants from the floor of a shallow sea that covered the Adirondack region in the Cambrian geological age (about 500 million years ago). So far as is known, this is the largest formation of this kind outside of northern Asia.

Here too you can see potholes cut into the rock by the action of swirling stones set in motion by glacial meltwaters thousands of years ago. These grinding stones can be seen lying at the bottoms of the potholes. The Petrified Gardens are closed from mid-September to June.

3 As the road winds westward toward Great Sacandaga Lake, you come upon a well-preserved old mill and a millrace with a dam nearby. Beside the interesting mill is a small

SPECIAL FEATURES			
ROAD GUIDE	▬▬▬	HIGHLIGHT	**1**
STATE PARKS		POINTS OF INTEREST	⊡
With Campsites ▲ Without Campsites △		SKI AREAS	🎿
RECREATION AREAS		SCHEDULED AIRLINE STOPS	✈
With Campsites ▲ Without Campsites △		OTHER AIRPORTS	✈
SELECTED REST AREAS		BOAT RAMPS	◄
With Toilets ⨉ Without Toilets ⨉			

ROAD CLASSIFICATION

CONTROLLED ACCESS HIGHWAYS — Divided **5** Undivided
(Entrance and Exit only at Interchanges) — Interchanges

TOLL HIGHWAYS

OTHER DIVIDED HIGHWAYS

PAVED HIGHWAYS

LOCAL ROADS In unfamiliar areas inquire locally before using these roads — Paved — Gravel — Dirt

MILEAGE

MILEAGE BETWEEN TOWNS AND JUNCTIONS 3 ⁄ 4   MILEAGE BETWEEN DOTS • 35 •

SCALE

ONE INCH 14 MILES   0   5   10   20

ONE INCH 22 KILOMETERS 0   5   10   20   32

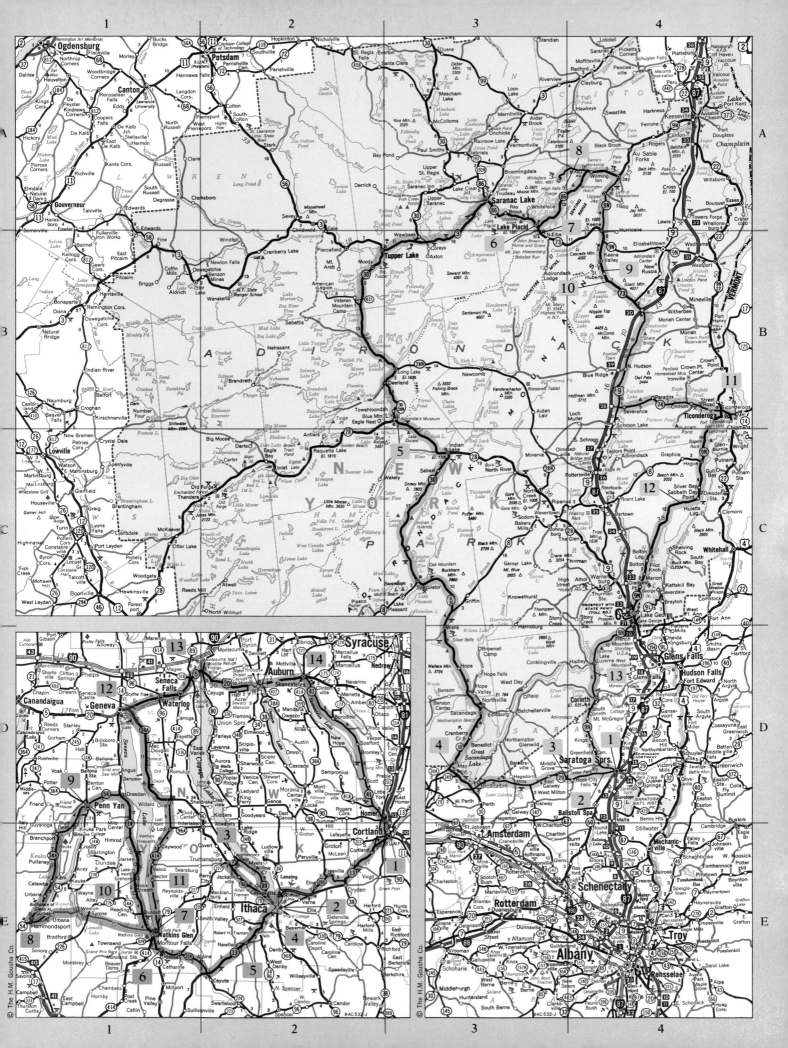

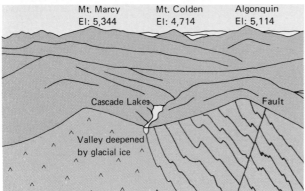

Mt. Marcy El: 5,344   Mt. Colden El: 4,714   Algonquin El: 5,114

Cascade Lakes   Fault

Valley deepened by glacial ice

The peaks of the mighty Adirondacks form an imposing skyline, with the Great Range in the far distance, Mount Marcy, New York State's highest peak, Mount Colden, and Mount Algonquin, the state's second highest peak, all visible in this aerial view. The Cascades Lakes, situated in a valley that was deepened by glacial ice millions of years ago, can be seen far below the road from Keene to Lake Placid, which follows the ridge.

The mountains here are the eroded roots of an ancient mountain chain. Perhaps 30,000 feet of material has been removed during an erosion that has been going on, with some interruptions, for 1½ billion years. This ancient mountain system was once the site of two crustal plates that collided and crushed the ocean sediments between them. You can see the folded and faulted crumpled rocks (metamorphic, that is, altered by heat and pressure) depicted on the right side of the diagramatic profile. On the left you see some igneous rock, the anorthosite, that was the result of ice melting at the base of the mountains. Today it is nicely crystalline rock and is made up almost entirely of feldspar.

parking space for those who would like to stop and look at these relics of a century gone by.

4 Just beyond Broadalbin, a small town settled by a group of Scots in 1810, Route 30 turns north along the west side of Great Sacandaga Lake and soon enters the 6-million-acre Adirondack Park, which includes 2½ million acres of state forest preserve.

All along the drive, as it wanders northward from the entrance to the park, there are campgrounds and trailer sites on the shores of Great Sacandaga Lake.

From the town of Wells to Speculator, the winding way follows the banks of the boulder-strewn, meandering Sacandaga River. The town of Speculator, known as a ski resort and for its many snowmobile trails, is located at the northern end of long, narrow, mountain-rimmed Lake Pleasant, where ice skating and ice fishing are excellent.

The stretch of road running along the Sacandaga River is dominated by

Wallace and Hamilton mountains rising to the west and Buckhorn to the northeast. Although these mountains are some 2,000 feet lower than the so-called High Peaks farther north, they mark the beginning of the rugged topography characteristic of the Adirondacks.

5 The indoor-outdoor Adirondack Museum at Blue Mountain Lake chronicles man's historical relationship to the mountains and the wilderness. A relief map of Adirondack Park and several dioramas are on display, plus an unusual collection of photographs, paintings, and prints that visually reconstruct and detail the character of life in these mountains during bygone days.

The museum has 18 buildings, each one displaying a different aspect of 19th-century life. One building has logging equipment, another shows the techniques and tools for ice cutting. An old blacksmith shop has been restored and set up in its own house. There are exhibits of several

kinds of horse-drawn vehicles, including an old Concord coach. Under a plexiglass dome there is a 19th-century racing sloop.

The roadway from Long Lake to Tupper Lake passes through majestic wilderness, the road often no more than a narrow corridor walled in by towering white pine and spruce. The increasing density of pine, spruce, and hemlock, to the exclusion of some of the hardwoods prevalent at the southern boundary of the park, signifies the beginning of a northern climax forest. Here in the northern Adirondacks such a forest consists largely of American hemlock, white pine, red spruce, white spruce, yellow birch, white birch, sugar maple (*Acer saccharum*), the official state tree, and beech. In summer these wooded mountains combine every shade of green in their display; in the fall the brilliant colors of the changing foliage is dramatic.

The understory of the forest includes spruce, striped and sugar maple, and wild cherry, all shade-tolerant species that grow well in the thin dappled light that penetrates the dense canopy of the tall trees.

The town of Tupper Lake, a small resort community not quite a hundred years old, is popular in winter for its ski trails through the nearby mountains, and in summer for free swimming in Little Wolf Lake, where a lifeguard is on duty. There is also hunting, fishing, and mountain climbing nearby.

Saranac Lake during the late 19th century became known as a health center for those suffering from lung disorders. Today it is a popular resort for both summer and winter sports. During the winter of 1887 Robert Louis Stevenson spent some time here in the clear mountain air, and his cottage is open to visitors.

6   The town of Lake Placid, sheltered by Whiteface Mountain, is spread along the waterfront of Mirror Lake, a miniature version of the larger lake for which the resort town is named.

Lake Placid itself, veiled by early morning and evening mists, and in the clutch of dramatic mountains, is surpassingly romantic. As its name suggests, it is as quiet as a reflecting pool most of the time.

Hour-long boat trips put out several times a day during the summer and fall, circling Lake Placid and passing many of the palatial so-called camps that were built at the turn of the century.

The Winter Olympics were held at Lake Placid in 1932 and again in 1980. Many of the facilities and structures built for the first event, and used continuously ever since, were refurbished for the 1980 games.

7   John Brown's Farm, the simple homestead of the fervent abolitionist who led the historic pre-Civil War raid on Harpers Ferry, has been restored and furnished much as it was more than a hundred years ago.

From the site of the farm you can see the two enormous Olympic Ski Jumps towering in the distance.

A particularly intriguing part of the Adirondacks lies along Route 86 as it follows the West Branch of the Ausable River, one of the most challenging trout streams in America. Certain stretches of the river can be fished

only by special permit. Fishing is by fly and lure; the use of any kind of bait fish is prohibited.

8   At Wilmington Notch you can see the awe-inspiring High Falls Gorge. Here a combination of glaciation and later erosion by the Ausable River has created a spectacular sight. The water, cascading in thundering silver leaps, has cut through the remarkable rectangular joints and slabs of Cambrian sandstone to expose the ancient anorthosite bedrock of the Adirondack Dome.

The gorge is surrounded by a veritable garden of lichens and unusual plants, such as the Lapland rosebay, a flowering shrub that resembles the rhododendron.

9   About two miles south of Keene Valley on Route 73 is the slender, silvery ribbon falls of Roaring Brook, on the lower flank of 4,627-foot Giant Mountain. The creek bed of bare rocks above the falls was scoured of vegetation by a huge 1963 landslide.

There is a parking area and a bridge over the brook. From here a half-mile trail leads to the top of the 600-foot falls, a walk that should not be attempted alone or without wearing sneakers or hiking shoes.

10   About a mile south of the Roaring Brook Falls you come upon a small but beautiful tree-lined body of water called Chapel Pond. Awesome cliffs rise from the far shore of the pond, and if you are lucky you will see climbers scaling these heights.

Chapel Pond is an excellent trout pool and a perfect place to canoe, enjoy a picnic lunch, and take a cool, refreshing dip.

5. The old blacksmith shop at the Adirondack Museum dates from the 1860's. The museum buildings are spread over 30 acres on a hilltop overlooking Blue Mountain Lake.

11. The cannon of Fort Ticonderoga were trained, as shown at right, to cover a bend in the waterway that leads from Canada to New York. Demonstrations of firing are given daily in midsummer, and visitors are sometimes invited to aim the guns.

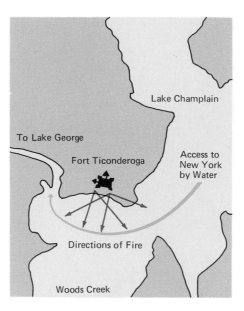

Lake Champlain

To Lake George

Fort Ticonderoga

Access to New York by Water

Directions of Fire

Woods Creek

11 Fort Ticonderoga, a restored fort of the French and Indian War period, is situated on a promontory dominating the channel where Lake George drains into Lake Champlain. The stone of which the fort was built was quarried by the French from the hilltop where the fort stands.

The fort's guns, one of which is still in place, commanded commerce moving from Lake Champlain into Lake George. Lake Champlain's narrow channel lies below you as you stroll through the fortress and about its battlements. Closed from mid-October to mid-May.

12 About 16 miles south of Ticonderoga on Route 9N there is a marvelous vantage point from which to see Lake George. Although the lake has been the scene of a great deal of heavy commercial development along its southern reaches, from Bolton Landing to the town of Lake George, this particular northern portion is relatively untouched and suggests what the entire lake was like in its unspoiled state.

13 A view of the Hudson River occurs about a mile south of Lake Luzerne. The stream makes a broad, lazy bend about two miles above Corinth, a town on the river's bank. Throughout this stretch of the drive, before the Hudson is joined by the Mohawk and other tributaries, you see the river in surroundings that reflect its wilderness origins.

North-central New York State is known as the Finger Lakes region. According to legend, the long, slender bodies of water that give it the name are the imprint left by the Creator's hand when He pronounced a benediction on a favored land.

Geologists claim that the lake beds were made by glaciers that retreated about 14,000 years ago, leaving their meltwaters in the deeply scoured out depressions.

Some of the finest upland scenery in the East is found in this part of the state. It is a region of year-round beauty, from early spring through the chromatic splendors of autumn and the snows of winter. The rolling, forested countryside is graced with many lakes, waterfalls, and gorges.

Here too are the fields and pastures of prosperous dairy farms, orchards in perfect patterns, great stretches of lakeside slopes covered with well-tended vineyards, and wineries ready to offer visitors a sample of the hillsides' bounty.

1 Cortland has retained much of the quaint flavor of its early days. In 1791 white settlers came here to farm the rich fields and fish the lakes and streams. Many handsome buildings put up in the 19th century to accommodate the town's expanding industries have withstood the test of time and are still in use today as factories for such products as fishing lines and industrial hardware.

The Cortland apple was named for Cortland County.

From Cortland to Ithaca there are lovely sweeping views of pastoral valleys, with rolling fields of corn, oats, and other crops stretching to a horizon of forested ridges. The sight of silos, corncribs, and a fascinating variety of farm machines and equipment is further evidence of a bounteous land.

2 Ithaca is the site of Cornell University, whose campus of manicured lawns, stately trees, and handsome buildings is situated on the heights overlooking the lake immortalized by the Ivy League school's well-known song, "Far Above Cayuga's Waters."

The countryside around Ithaca is filled with streams, gorges, and more than a hundred waterfalls. You can see many of these by following the

13. From the road near Lake Luzerne you may see the brilliantly decorated airships during the Hot Air Balloon Festival, held in September at Glens Falls 10 miles to the east.

7. *The Vista, one of the falls in Watkins Glen, is brightened in spring by shrubs clinging to the rocks. The gorge was named for Dr. Samuel Watkins, who discovered it in 1788.*

Just west of Odessa on Route 224 there is a breathtaking panorama of Catherine Valley off to the south.

6 At the head of Main Street in the village of Montour Falls stands She-quaga Falls, whose tumbling waters fill the business district with the incessant music of nature. The falls flows into a magnificent two-mile gorge called Havana Glen, the original name of the settlement, where 37 waterfalls cascade through the ravine. The public is invited to camp, picnic, and enjoy the cascades.

The Museum Room at the rear of the town's library displays ancient fossils and prehistoric Indian artifacts found in the region.

7 The town of Watkins Glen, known for its unusual gorge, is at the southern end of Seneca Lake. During the summer, sight-seeing cruises leave daily from the municipal dock for a sail through the scenic waters of the lake.

The Watkins Glen Grand Prix Racecourse, established in 1948 and reconstructed to its 3⅓-mile configuration in 1971, is the scene of major events in American and international automobile racing.

One of Watkins Glen's major products is salt, which is mined along the

Circle Greenway, a well-planned footpath and a bicycle path that traverses the city. In the spring the city, known as New York State's forsythia capital, is a riot of yellow, and during the summer the fields are filled with wild flowers, including violets, wild roses, buttercups, clover, and Queen Anne's lace.

Ithaca has a boat-launching site at the Allen H. Treman Marina State Park that provides an entranceway to the lake for waterskiing and sailing. In these waters, fishing for landlocked salmon, trout, and bass is especially good.

3 At Trumansburg, about eight miles north of Ithaca on Route 89, is Taughannock Falls. Its waters plunge over a 215-foot precipice and then flow on to join adjacent Cayuga Lake. This is the highest straight drop of any natural waterfall east of the Rocky Mountains.

The waterfall is most impressive in the spring and after a heavy rain. In

the autumn, when there is less water, an eerie quiet fills the gorge as a moving curtain of mist lightly blows across the precipice and partially screens it from view.

4 Buttermilk Falls, situated in a scenic state park of the same name on the outskirts of Ithaca, is a series of rapids and cascades along Buttermilk Creek, which drops some 500 feet as it flows through the rocky landscape. These falls with their airy, delicate quality have a unique and charming character.

In the park there are facilities for camping and swimming, as well as two hiking trails.

5 The small town of Newfield, southwest of Ithaca, has the only authentic covered bridge in the Finger Lakes region. The bridge spans West Branch Creek in the center of town. Built in 1853 and restored in 1972, the old structure is still in use and traffic still moves as slowly across it as it did in the horse-and-carriage era.

Into Another World

Watkins Glen's narrow, 1½-mile gorge is one of the most impressive natural wonders of the eastern United States. Chiseled into the mountainside by the erosive forces of a glacial meltwater torrent, the gorge contains a series of spectacular cataracts, caverns, and grottoes in a deep, serpentine canyon sloping down from a steep cliff.

The gorge is located in the Watkins Glen State Park, just west of the center of the town. From the main entrance you can climb up through the entire length of the canyon, about 500 feet, on a network of natural stone paths and bridges that blend into the canyon walls.

For a less strenuous tour, you can take a taxi to the upper entrance and walk downhill to the main entrance.

The glen's 19 waterfalls have been given such imaginative names as Diamond, Rainbow, and Minnehaha. Behind Pluto Falls there are ice age potholes, scoured out by glacial boulders carried by swirling waters.

8. A 1918 Curtiss Jenny biplane opens an airshow at Hammondsport by swooping in to cut a ribbon stretched across the airstrip on 10-foot poles placed about 50 feet apart.

shores of the lake. Wells are drilled, some as much as 1,800 feet deep, and then filled with lake water. The resulting brine is brought up to the surface and evaporated to produce the salt.

The drive to Hammondsport over well-marked backcountry roadways passes through the village of Weston, where Waneta and Lamoka lakes almost meet. Both lakes offer excellent fishing, particularly for bass. At North Urbana there are marvelous vistas of Keuka Lake and its vineyard-lined shores.

8 Hammondsport is the commercial center of the New York State wine industry. It is the home of Taylor and Great Western wineries, both located on the west side of town. The wineries offer tours that include lectures on old and modern winemaking methods, plus a sampling of their products.

Hammondsport prides itself on having been the scene of pioneer aviation in the early 1900's. It was the birthplace of Glenn Hammond Curtiss, the aviation pioneer whose flying machine *June Bug* made one of the earliest powered flights, taking off from Hammondsport on July 4, 1908.

The Curtiss Museum in Hammondsport, at the corner of Main and Lake streets, contains memorabilia of the early days of flying and provides an intriguing nostalgic experience for anyone with an interest in aviation. The museum is closed Sundays except in July and August, and from November through April.

9 Penn Yan—whose curious name is the result of a compromise by the town's early settlers, who were Pennsylvanians and New England Yankees—is rich in architectural styles of an earlier time. Fronting its few main business streets are well-maintained 19th-century red brick commercial buildings. Contrasting with these is the Birkett Mills Building, a massive 19th-century clapboard structure that still houses the world's largest producer of buckwheat products. Through the years Penn Yan's factories have produced boats and buses, and have processed the grain, grapes, and other fruits and vegetables that are grown on the farms of the surrounding countryside.

Every year on the Saturday before Labor Day the residents of the area gather on the shores of Keuka Lake and, carrying on an old Indian custom, light flares in thanksgiving for their bountiful crops.

10 Glenora Wine Cellars is one of the smaller wineries of the Finger Lakes country. This company produces award-winning vintages by the old-fashioned hand-picking methods now largely abandoned by the bigger vineyards. Visitors are welcome from May to November to taste the wines and see the presses and fermentation

9. Vineyards on the hillsides around Keuka Lake, not far from Penn Yan. The grapes are gathered by a harvester that strips the vines and sends the fruit through a chute into the adjacent tractor-drawn container.

13. The Montezuma Wildlife Refuge (right) serves as a resting and feeding area for migrating water birds. Here a flock of Canada geese, which have nesting grounds in the refuge, fly across the marshes. A great blue heron (above) wades through the waters on its constant search for food.

equipment. In early and mid-fall you can watch the workers harvest and press the grapes and prepare the must—juice before it is fermented.

11 A few miles north of Watkins Glen on Route 414, in the midst of the fruit-growing belt, is Hector Falls. It is partially screened from the road by foliage in summer, but is well worth a stop and a closer look. The water cascades down a series of wide terraces, about a dozen in all, to create a lovely sight and the natural music that is heard only when water tumbles over rocks.

Between Ovid and Geneva there is a broad open valley where much of the region's grain and feed crops are grown. Here are acres upon acres of soybeans, oats, alfalfa, corn, and sunflowers, arranged as precisely as the squares of a checkerboard.

12 As the road approaches Geneva, it passes over the Seneca-Cayuga Canal, a branch of the Erie Canal system, which connects the Great Lakes at Buffalo with the Hudson River at Albany. The completion of this system in the first quarter of the 19th century encouraged the rapid settlement of the nation's Central Plains by providing access to eastern markets. This canal, connecting Seneca and Cayuga lakes, tied the Finger

Lakes to the Erie system and brought prosperity to this region throughout the 19th century.

Stop for a moment when you get to the end of Route 96A and look across Seneca Lake to the town of Geneva. The view on a smaller scale is strikingly similar to the one from across Lake Geneva of the famous Swiss city for which this town was named.

13 Montezuma National Wildlife Refuge consists of a vast tract of marshland and wilderness totaling more than 6,000 acres. There is a five-mile self-guided automobile route on the preserve's well-maintained gravel roads.

Observation towers along the way offer views of the marshlands, where the great blue heron and many kinds of waterfowl can be glimpsed as they fish, hunt, feed, and raise their broods. More than 235 different species have been observed at Montezuma, and among the songbirds is the bluebird, the official state bird.

The bald eagle, which was in danger of becoming extinct, has been introduced to the refuge. On one observation tower there is a closed-circuit television set connected by cable to a bald eagle's nest. On weekends and on holidays in the spring and the early summer, visitors can have a

close-up view of the eagles' fascinating family life.

Birding is best from March through November. The peak migrations of waterfowl occur in mid-April and early October.

While the preserve is a bonanza for the serious birder, it also offers a great deal for the casual visitor. Few sights are so thrilling as the common one here of a giant, chesty great blue heron lumbering low in the air, or the rarer one of a glimpse of a bald eagle flashing its white head and tail as it dives into marsh grass to catch a fish with its talons.

14 Skaneateles (scan-ee-*at*-el-es), a charming old resort town at the northern end of the lake bearing the same name, has an unspoiled waterfront. Two lakeside parks afford a splendid view of the slender lake reaching into the distance. When the wind shifts to the southeast, whitecaps pile up in a spray of mist along the shore.

A rich dairy-farming region stretches along Route 41 from Borodino almost to Cortland. Large cow barns, towering concrete silos, corncribs, cattle at pasture, and wide fields of corn, oats, red clover, alfalfa, and hay make this a memorable scene of pastoral prosperity.

Southwestern New England

Small farms, villages, and rolling uplands between the Connecticut River valley and the Berkshires

Here in western Massachusetts and Connecticut, where the Berkshires blend with the Litchfield Hills, the boundary between the states is imperceptible. This entire region is a favored place with its village greens, steepled churches, and shining lakes, ponds, rivers, and waterfalls. In spring the foliage is a dozen shades of green, which turn to a darker, unified color in summer. In the fall the area shares with the rest of New England the glorious reds, oranges, and yellows of the hardwood forests that clothe the peaks and valleys, and in winter the color scheme is almost entirely white.

This is a prosperous area, and there are more art galleries and craft and antiques shops than one would expect to find in so rural a setting. People are drawn from nearby cities to the relative peace and quiet of this countryside, and considering the density of the surrounding population, the towns and villages have been remarkably successful at maintaining the qualities of life that attracted people to this charming part of New England in the first place.

This route includes sections of the two major drainage systems in western Massachusetts and ascends to the highest point in the state. The rich alluvial soil of the Connecticut River valley supports prosperous tobacco farms, while the winding, rockbound Housatonic is a favorite of canoeists and fishermen.

The southern connector between the two valleys threads its way gently through the rounded hills, but the other link is the mountainous Mohawk Trail, anchored on the west by the lofty height of Mount Greylock, whose summit affords spectacular views of the surrounding countryside.

1 If you happen to be in the Holyoke area on a warm sunny day, Hampton Pond State Park with its curving sandy beach is an excellent place for a swim. There is also a pleasant picnic area set in a grove of stately pines, birches, oaks, and hemlocks, and fishing in the pond is reported to be good.

2 Even if this is your first visit, the village of Stockbridge may seem familiar. It has the same neat, clean, orderly, and settled character that tends to evolve in small towns where families live for generations in a place in which they take pride. The illustrator Norman Rockwell lived and worked here, and many of the places and people in the area were models for his famous *Saturday Evening Post* covers and other works.

3 In the village of Glendale is Chesterwood, the home and workplace of the sculptor Daniel Chester French. The estate includes some 150 acres of woodland and affords lovely views of the Berkshires. French created more than 150 works, the most famous of which is the "Seated Lincoln" at the Lincoln Memorial in Washington, D.C. In the studio here are plaster casts of this superb sculpture. There are other works on display in a barn gallery and beside a nature trail that winds through the woods.

4 The Berkshire Garden Center at the junction of Routes 183 and 102 is a charming, unexpected oasis in a busy setting. Footpaths lead to the gardens of herbs, roses, and wild flowers and the beds of bulbs and perennials. There are also demonstration gardens of vegetables and grains and a display of window gardening ideas. The plants are labeled for easy identification, and you can gather a lot of interesting information in a short time here.

On the way to Lenox you pass Tanglewood, the summer home of the Boston Symphony Orchestra. If you can work it into your schedule, it is a memorable experience to hear this great orchestra in such a pleasant, informal setting. For those who are passing through, it is a good idea to find out when concerts are scheduled. For an hour or so before and after there is too much traffic for Routes 183 and 7 to bear, and it is best to take Route 41 instead.

5 To get to the Pleasant Valley Wildlife Sanctuary, watch for West Dugway Road on the west side of Route 7 about 2½ miles north of its junction with Route 183. True to its name, this 680-acre preserve is a pleasant place to visit. There are some seven miles of trails through woods and fields and past swamplands and streams where you may see beaver at work. More than 180 species of birds have been sighted here. Bird walks and other guided tours are offered by appointment.

The Trailside Museum has live displays of reptiles, mammals, amphibians, fish, and insects.

6 The side trip to Shaker Village at Hancock is about a 10-mile round trip, and if you are interested in the culture and lifestyle of these remarkable people and the exceptional quality of all their works, a visit here is time well spent. Nineteen of the 20 buildings are open and furnished as they were in the days when this was a thriving community. Of particular interest is the round stone barn, an ingenious example of functional design. All through the village you can see tools and artifacts all created in the elegantly straightforward designs for which the Shakers were renowned. At the visitor center there is a display gallery of Shaker drawings and paintings and a small cafeteria that offers light lunches. Closed from November until June.

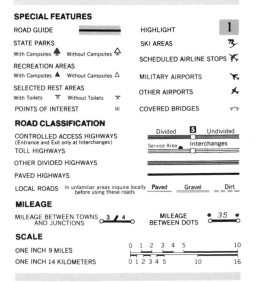

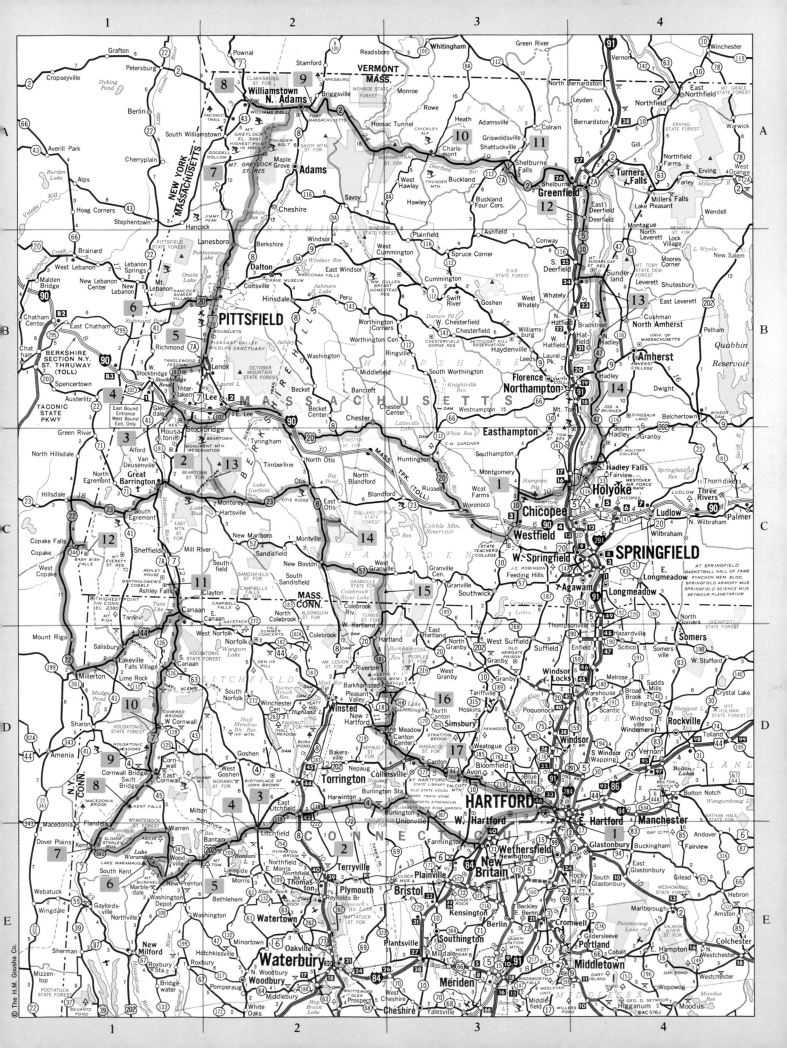

7. *From the summit of Mount Greylock, Saddle Ball Mountain, to the west, is seen with a partial cloud cover. Saddle Ball, at 3,238 feet, is the second highest peak in Massachusetts. Both mountains have excellent trails for cross-country skiing.*

7   About 1½ miles north of Lanesboro watch for the turnoff to Mount Greylock State Reservation. Before driving the 8½ miles to the summit, you may want to stop at the visitor center to see the displays that will help you identify the trees, animals, birds, moths, and butterflies (more than 30 kinds) indigenous to this area. You can also pick up a map that shows the campgrounds, picnic areas, roads, and hiking trails in the reservation.

The steep, curving road to the mountaintop passes through a typical eastern hardwood forest that includes ash, beech, maple, oak, and birch in addition to such evergreens as pines, spruce, and hemlock. In some sections on the way up, the birches with their gleaming white trunks line the road and their spread-ing branches arch across to make a veritable tunnel of green.

The summit of Mount Greylock, at 3,491 feet, is the highest point in the Berkshires. From the 90-foot granite War Memorial Tower, weather permitting, you can see a panorama of forested peaks and mountain ranges in five states, including Mount Monadnock in New Hampshire and the Catskills and the lofty Adirondacks in New York.

The winds at the summit can be fierce, as indicated by the twisted and stunted evergreens that manage to survive here. At lower elevations, where they get more protection, the trees assume their natural symmetrical form. From the road as it winds its way down the north side of the mountain, there are further spectacular views to be enjoyed.

8   If you are interested in seeing a quintessential New England college town, a side trip to Williamstown and the Williams College campus is worth your while. Tours of the campus can be arranged at Mather House.

The Sterling and Francine Clark Art Institute on South Street has, in addition to an excellent general collection, an outstanding group of paintings by 19th-century French artists, including Renoir, Corot, Degas, Monet, Toulouse-Lautrec, and others.

9   On the outskirts of North Adams, about a half-mile north on Route 8, is the Natural Bridge, which was carved by erosion from marble created when this area was covered by seas some 550 million years ago. As the glaciers receded about 13,000 years ago, the melting waters scoured out a chasm 60 feet deep and 475 feet long, leaving the bridge that spans the chasm at a point where it is about 30 feet wide at the top. The area is closed from November until June.

10   The Mohawk Trail (Route 2) is named for the Indians who first used the east–west passes through this mountainous country. It is now a delightful scenic drive with spectacular panoramic views from various switchbacks at the western end and more intimate wooded scenes where the road parallels the boulder-strewn Deerfield River as it wends its way toward the Connecticut River. The dense woodlands here in the Berkshires make this a favorite route in the fall when the foliage of the hardwoods is a blaze of color. There are also many stands of birch whose white trunks contrast dramatically with the background of other hardwoods and evergreens.

Anyone interested in covered bridges should not miss the picturesque Bissell Bridge, just north of Charlemont where Route 8-A crosses Mill River.

11   An old trolley bridge across the Deerfield River at Shelburne Falls has been lined on both sides of its 400-foot length with colorful flowers. It is a pleasant stroll across the footbridge, and a short distance downstream there is a series of three cataracts with pools and potholes carved by glacial meltwaters grinding hard pebbles, such as quartzite, against the softer bedrock.

12 To tour The Street in Deerfield, the mile-long thoroughfare laid out in the 1660's, is to appreciate the elegant proportions, functional designs, and careful detailings of the best of 18th-century residential architecture. The earliest of the dozen houses open to the public dates from 1717, and all the houses that have been built since then are in character with the original structures. This national historic landmark is a functioning community, and the homes are occupied.

13 The road between Sunderland and Hadley takes you through the heart of one of several tobacco-growing areas in the broad fertile Connecticut River valley. In summer the fields are covered with panels of white or bright yellow netting supported on posts. The shade is needed to grow the kind of leaves that are used for the outer wrapping of cigars.

As the leaves mature, they are picked one by one, and in the fall they are hung to cure in the handsome long, low, ventilated barns that you see in the fields.

14 From Route 47 a steep, narrow, winding but well-surfaced road leads through groves of white birch and other native hardwoods to the summit of Mount Holyoke in Joseph Allen Skinner State Park. Although the summit is less than 900 feet above sea level, there are spectacular views of the surrounding countryside, and on a clear day the horizon is 70 miles distant. The tall bluffs of Mount Tom can be seen to the west, as well as the meandering course that the Connecticut River has carved on the floor of the valley. Hikers might enjoy sampling the steep section of the Metacomet–Monadnock trail that cuts through the park.

The Litchfield Hills are noted for an abundance of lakes, reservoirs, streams, rivers, and waterfalls. There are covered bridges and nature preserves and, all along the way, pleasant roads to drive.

Although the farms are fewer than before, as evidenced by the stone walls marking off neat rectangles in the woods that have grown up where pastures used to be, this is still farm country. Along the roads you can see stands with fresh flowers, fruits, and vegetables for sale in their season.

1 Elizabeth Park in Hartford, the capital of Connecticut, is the site of the first municipally owned rose garden in the United States. Here, at the junction of Prospect and Asylum avenues, are more than 1,000 different varieties among the 14,000 rose plants to be seen. The park also includes a complex of four greenhouses and masses of annuals and perennials.

The Wadsworth Atheneum at 600 Main Street boasts a remarkably varied collection of art displayed in 47 galleries. Both the quantity and quality of the paintings, sculpture, furniture, and other objects here are exceptional, and for any one interested in the visual arts the museum is well worth a visit. Closed Mondays and some major holidays.

On the way out of town, at the junction of Farmington Avenue and Forest Street, you can see the Mark Twain and Harriet Beecher Stowe houses. The Twain house is a handsome three-story red brick Victorian Gothic residence with an upstairs deck that some observers have likened to the deck of a Mississippi River steamboat. The Stowe house, of simple Victorian design, is where the famous author of *Uncle Tom's Cabin* lived and worked.

2 The Congregational Church in Harwinton was gathered in 1738. The current building, a fine example of a classic New England meetinghouse, replaces the church that burned in 1949. Some of the stones in the nearby graveyard date back to 1700.

3 The charming old town of Litchfield, founded in 1719, has wide tree-lined streets and many handsome and historic houses, some of which date from the 1700's. The historic district around the village green

Tobacco-growing in New England

The alluvial deposits of sandy loam flanking the Connecticut River and the long New England growing season are ideal for tobacco. Some varieties are grown in the open (top). Others are shaded by netting (above). While plants are small, they are held upright by strings attached to the wire mesh that holds the netting. Leaves are harvested individually and hung for air-curing in barns with slats that can be opened for ventilation, as shown at right. Shade-grown tobacco has soft and pliable leaves, used as the outer wrapper in making cigars.

and along North and South streets is worth investigating on foot.

The houses, in colonial and federal style, were built when Litchfield was an important stop on the New Haven–Albany and the Boston–Hartford stagecoach lines. To see an interior typical of the late 18th century, you can visit the Tapping Reeve House on South Street (closed from mid-October until mid-May). Adjacent to the house is the one-room office of Judge Tapping Reeve where, in 1774, he started the first law school in America.

When water power was developed and railroads were built along the Housatonic and Naugatuck valleys, both traffic and industry bypassed the town and it was spared the benefits of industrialization—for which we can be thankful today.

There are 10 churches in the town. Gathered in 1721, the First Congregational Church on the Green has a double-octagon steeple that stands out as a superb example of the early American style.

4 About 2½ miles west of Litchfield watch for Bissell Road and the entrance to the White Memorial Conservation Center and the White Memorial Foundation. The entry drive is through an imposing alley of maple trees and is flanked by a superb stone wall of New England dry-wall construction.

The museum has interpretive exhibits; live owls, reptiles, and other animals on display; and a bird-observation blind. There is also a remarkably complete butterfly collection. Closed Mondays.

There are inviting picnic areas here as well as trails winding through this 4,000-acre lakeshore sanctuary. The trails lead to meadows, ponds, streams, and marshlands bordering Bantam Lake and provide a leisurely, intimate view of the myriad facets of nature in a delightfully unspoiled state. Within easy range of the museum parking lot you can see most of the trees and shrubs native to the Litchfield Hills area, including some lovely stands of mountain laurel (*Kalmia latifolia*), the Connecticut state flower.

5 Although the name Mount Tom State Park suggests the uphill hike and distant views to be had from the top of Mount Tom (elevation 1,291 feet), a delightful surprise in this park is a small, sparkling lake in a densely wooded setting. At lake's edge there are picnic tables and firepits for cooking. Small sailboats and canoes can be launched from the grassy shores, and there is an excellent swimming area with a sandy beach and bottom. This can be a refreshing stop on a hot day.

Classic symbol of New England

Longmeadow, Massachusetts, Meeting House (1767)

Southhampton, Massachusetts, Congregational Church (1786)

Hampton, Connecticut, Congregational Church (1754)

Abbington, Connecticut, Congregational Church (1751)

The steepled churches of early America have become symbols of the villages and towns that are nestled in the hills of New England. Rising above the treetops, these sparkling white spires are often the first sight travelers have of a town.

Four elements, with many variations and combinations, traditionally comprise the steeple: a tower, usually square and sometimes faced with a clock; a belfry, an open structure where the church bell is hung; the lantern, a windowed section for dispatching signals, such as the one that sent Paul Revere on his famous ride to Lexington; and a slender spire topped with a weathervane. According to legend, the cock, which tops many a church spire, symbolizes Christ's prediction that Peter would deny Him at cockcrow.

The steeple of the Warren, Connecticut, Congregational Church (left) is the epitome of the so-called wedding-cake design that became popular in the 1800's.

The mile-long trail to the top of the mountain is a comfortable one-hour hike up and back on an abandoned wagon trail or a narrow footpath. At the summit there is a 40-foot lookout tower of stone and cement.

6 To reach Lake Waramaug State Park, watch for the hard turn to the north onto Route 45 at New Preston, and then for the left turn to go around the lake. The road along the lakeshore is twisting and narrow, and the driver should leave to the passengers the attractive views of the lake and the quaint summer cottages beside the road. Cars with trailers should not take this road but continue on Route 45 to Warren.

Inside the park the picnic tables are nicely spaced along the shore, and there are changing rooms convenient to the sandy beaches. By July the water is usually warm enough for comfortable swimming.

Some fishing is done from the shore, but the most successful anglers bring their own boats or canoes.

A dense stand of stately maples offers welcome summer shade and in the fall becomes a brilliant blaze of color against the bright blue skies.

Watch for the handsome white church with its octagonal steeple on the hillside at the junction of Routes 45 and 341. On Route 341 a mile or so west of the junction there is an outcrop of rock about 100 yards long on both sides of the road. This is a hard schist, about 500 million years old, that forms a belt running from northeast to southwest and terminates in New York City.

7 In driving through the town of Kent, it seems proper to slow down without quite realizing why. There are, to be sure, lovely old houses along the highway, and right beside the road is one of the most attractive carpenter Gothic churches in all of New England. But there is also something more—or less. It soon becomes apparent that this town enforces an enlightened ordinance regarding advertising signs. The necessary signs for the stores, restaurants, and real estate offices are here, but they are unobtrusive and attractive. You have to slow down to see and read them, and it is interesting to see how much this one feature adds to the charm and tranquil appearance of the town.

8. *The waters of Kent Falls, in the early morning sunshine, splash over the ledges of the lower cascades. The falls is formed by Kent Falls Brook, a small stream that rises at Forestell Pond a few miles to the east and joins the Housatonic River.*

Among the many 19th-century iron smelters in Connecticut, there was one here in Kent, and the ruin still remains. It is about a mile north of Kent Center on Route 7 at the site of the Sloane-Stanley Museum. Here, in a replica of a colonial barn, a gift of the Stanley Tool Works, is the Eric Sloane collection of more than 500 early American hand tools and implements. Mr. Sloane, a distinguished artist and writer, has displayed the tools in relation to the work that was done with them. Adjacent to the museum is the Noah Blake House, a reproduction of a primitive cabin that dramatically illustrates the meager amenities of pioneer life in New England.

8 The largest waterfall in the state, and one of the most attractive picnic areas, is here at Kent Falls State Park. The 200-foot falls is a series of cascades tumbling over broad rock ledges. From the steep wooded path that leads to the top of the falls, you can look down into the pools and potholes carved into the horizontal surfaces of the rock by the irresistible force of the flowing water. The music of the falls varies from the relative quiet of the summer dry season to the fortissimo of the heavy runoffs in spring and, to a lesser degree, in fall. The autumn is also the time to enjoy the colorful foliage that flanks the water here and, of course, covers the heavily wooded hills all through this part of Connecticut. The broad expanse of lawn is a natural habitat for the omnipresent Frisbee and its devotees.

To the west of the road about a mile north of Kent Falls there is a good view of a typical New England hardwood forest blanketing the hills.

9 Housatonic Meadows State Park, bordering the gently curving tree-fringed Housatonic River, is a lovely retreat deeply shaded with red pines. There are campsites and picnic tables here and hiking trails with scenic views of the river. During the season you may see fly fishermen practicing their graceful art, and if you have the gear, you may want to try for some trout yourself; for this is one of Connecticut's most popular streams for fishing.

The camping area here is about a mile north of the south entrance to the park. Farther north on Route 7 there are places with canoes for rent. The Housatonic is popular with canoeists and kayakers, and in good

developed for covered bridges in the 19th century. For more on this subject, see page 47.

The rapids just below the bridge is rated as a Class III. If you are here as canoeists or kayakers are going through, you can vicariously share a little of the excitement.

Driving through the town of Canaan, keep an eye out for the handsome old railroad station on the west side of the road. It is typical of the graceful design of these structures in the days when, for many communities, the railroad was the primary link with the rest of the world.

11 Bartholomew's Cobble Reservation is just north of the Connecticut line. Watch for the road to Ashley

different kinds grow here. With some 500 species of wild flowers and about 100 different trees, shrubs, and vines, the Cobble is a varied and colorful natural rock garden.

Here you can see all stages in the development of plant life. There are lichens, the first living plants to appear on earth, as well as many mosses and ferns, all of which helped to create a thin layer of soil on the rock in which other plants could establish themselves. The slopes now support handsome stands of white pine, hemlock, red cedar, white birch, and oak.

This is a lovely place to walk. There are short hikes on the rocky cobble and a trail along the banks of the Housatonic where there is a classic oxbow lake (called Half River), which was created when the river meandered from an earlier course through the alluvial plain. The river with its adjacent marshes attracts waterfowl, and the Cobble, with its many plant communities, attracts more than 250 different kinds of birds.

For more ambitious hikers there is a one-mile trail to a high pasture on Hurlburt's Hill and a rewarding view of the Housatonic Valley to the north.

Picnicking is allowed in the Cobble, and there is a small museum of natural history. Among the useful pamphlets for sale here is a guide to an interpretive trail on which much can be learned about the nature of this environment.

Even for people without a special interest in plants or birds, the rocky sculptured outcrops of weathered rock, the small cliffs, steep slopes, patches of meadow, and the winding river make the Cobble a refreshing and memorable place to visit.

12 Bash Bish, the intriguing name of a mountain, a brook, and a waterfall, comes from an Indian word for the "sound of falling water." The falls is in Massachusetts near the state line, but the easiest access is from Taconic State Park in New York. In addition to the falls, which is reached by a pleasant 15-minute walk on a wide, graveled pathway starting at the parking area, the park is popular for picnicking, camping, and hiking. The forest is laced with hiking trails, many of which are blazed. A trail map is available at park headquarters.

The falls splashes its way down a

10. The covered bridge at West Cornwall, which opens onto the main street of the little village, is framed in autumn with brilliant foliage that blends perfectly with the weathered rust-red of the structure. Along the narrow village street are several antiques shops.

weather you may see them on the river. Rapids are graded on a scale of Class I to Class IV, and along this stretch of the river most of the rapids are graded as I and II and a few as III. This is enough to make the runs interesting but not too frightening.

The rental places provide instruction, guided trips, and delivery and pickup of passengers and canoes.

10 The covered bridge that crosses the Housatonic to the village of West Cornwall is of Town lattice construction and has served here since 1837. The design was developed by Ithiel Town and was one of the most popular of the various trussing systems

Falls and the signs to the reservation.

A cobble, in the language of the pioneer settlers, is a rocky knoll or crest, and this one is composed of marble and quartzite and rises 75 to 100 feet above the nearby Housatonic River.

As the marble and quartzite here weather and leach out, they create a range of soil conditions that support a remarkable number of different plants in this relatively small area. Marble gives the soil an alkaline balance, while the quartzite makes it acidic. Ferns, in particular, are very sensitive to a subtle acid-alkaline balance of the soil, and more than 40

11. This is one of the small rocky cliffs of marble and quartzite in Bartholomew's Cobble. In the foreground are clusters of wild flowers, sheltered by nearby trees.

narrow chasm filled with great chunks of fallen rock. This gorge is another dramatic relic of the tumultuous meltwaters of the dying ice age that covered escape channels in this landscape about 14,000 years ago. At the lip of the falls, before it plunges into the pool below, a craggy monolith splits the stream in two to make a double cascade.

13 The white birch is one of the glories of the New England woods, and you drive through a lovely stand on Blue Hill Road on the way to Beartown State Forest.

Just three miles from Route 23, this densely forested, mountainous reservation seems much more remote than you would expect it to be. The sense of solitude is further increased if you spend a half-hour or so on any of the many hiking trails in the area. There is a pleasant picnic area, and Benedict Pond is popular for swimming. Should you want to sample a section of the Appalachian Trail, there is access here. Trails in the park are not only used for hiking but for horseback riding and in the winter for snowmobiling.

14 As you drive through the town of Otis, watch for the First Congregational Church with its handsome columned belfry. The church was organized in 1779, and this building was dedicated in 1815. About four miles south of town on Route 8, watch for the entrance to Tolland Otis State Forest. There are picnic areas with tables and fireplaces, as well as camping sites. There is also a swimming beach with lifeguards. The swimming is in the Otis Reservoir, which was built in the 19th century to maintain the water level in the Farmington River. In that era a constant flow was needed to drive the waterwheels of the many mills along riverbanks. As electric power became available, the water-driven mills were abandoned, and today the chief value of the reservoir is for recreation. A boat-launching ramp is open year-round, and fishermen come here for the bass, crappies, trout, bream, and pickerel.

15 Along Route 8 between Otis and New Boston, you may want to take advantage of the roadside picnic places on the banks of the Farmington River.

About five miles after the turn onto Route 57, keep an eye out for the sign to Granville State Forest. A narrow winding road follows a rocky stream through a dense woodland to the forest. Camping is allowed on one side of the stream and picnicking on the other.

The junction of the Granville Forest road and Route 20 may be confusing if the road sign at that point is missing. If you do not get to Hartland, Connecticut, and the junction of Route 181 within three miles, you are going the wrong way.

16 Back in Connecticut, the road to Barkhamsted Reservoir crosses Seville Dam with its picturesque slate-roofed round stone tower. There is a lovely view here looking north over the reservoir to the low New England hills on the horizon. Below the dam is Lake McDonough, which has an excellent swimming beach, bathhouses, and boats for rent. Beside the road to the beach there is a superb rock garden in the ideal setting of a natural outcrop. There is also a picnic area carpeted with fragrant needles from the grove of tall pines.

17 Among the many beautiful white wooden churches in New England is the Congregational Church at Avon with its 32-light windows and attractive applications of gingerbread. It is on the northwest corner of Routes 44 and 10.

12. The wide, shallow pool that sparkles at the bottom of Bash Bish Falls delights young swimmers, as picnickers settle on the gravel bank to enjoy the dappled sunlight and sounds of the falls. Winding through Bash Bish Falls State Forest are several riding trails.

Diversity in Pennsylvania

A blend of history and industry amid fertile farmlands, rugged mountains, and peaceful valleys

The three tours in Pennsylvania are all rewarding but in such different ways that they could well be in three different states. In the northwest corner are the broad sandy beaches of Lake Erie; in the Poconos you can see a mountainous landscape of trees, forests, and lakes; and the southeastern section is an inviting area of gentle farmlands and famous historic places.

The distinctive character of the northwest corner of Pennsylvania is established by its 63 miles of oceanlike shoreline on Lake Erie, rolling farmlands, extensive vineyards, winding rivers, narrow lakes, and more than half a million acres of deep woods in the vast Allegheny National Forest. At Sheffield, in the heart of the preserve, is a ranger station where you can get maps and information about the dozens of campsites that are scattered throughout the forest.

1 A typical drive through these spectacular woods is the one west from Sheffield to the Hearts Content Recreation and Scenic Area. An un-numbered road off the main street in Sheffield goes immediately over a little bridge, then forks to the left and begins to climb. This narrow, picturesque country lane with a bumpy surface is little traveled, and traffic is no problem. Almost at once you enter into a deep and delightful forest through which you travel for about 20 miles—to Hearts Content and beyond. At the recreation area are parking places, several campsites, a shelter, and a trail through some of the scenic area.

Four or five miles beyond the recreation area and you are back on a surfaced road. Soon the forest begins to thin. There are clearings here and there, but little of the land is under cultivation.

2 Tidioute Overlook appears with little warning, other than the Forest Service sign with its yellow lettering on a brown board. There are two trails accessible from the small parking area. One leads to the Valley Overlook and the other to the Town Overlook. The first is just a few steps to the right and provides a majestic view through the trees of the great Allegheny River where it forks and runs between steep wooded banks. Only a scattering of farms on the opposite shore reveal the presence of man in this seeming wilderness. From Town Overlook, about a quarter of a mile down the trail to the left, another bird's-eye view reveals the little town of Tidioute with its tiny white and red houses lining the riverbank. You can also make out a little iron bridge over the river to the western shore. You will cross this one-lane bridge on your way into Tidioute.

3 Between Pleasantville and Titusville are Oil Creek and Oil Creek Valley, where this valuable resource was first commercially produced in the United States by drilling. Edwin L. Drake made the initial strike in August 1859. This led in the 1860's to a boom in this quiet Pennsylvania valley that was comparable to a gold rush. The discovery of oil in this area changed the face of America forever and was the basis of some of the greatest fortunes known to man.

Drake's lucky strike on the bank of Oil Creek is commemorated at Drake Well Memorial Park, which features a fascinating museum and a replica of

2. Tidioute Overlook, in the mountains above the Allegheny River, was named for the little town that was first settled by members of the Harmony Society in the early 1800's.

SPECIAL FEATURES

ROAD GUIDE ▬▬▬	HIGHLIGHT	**1**
STATE PARKS With Campsites ♣ Without Campsites △	SKI AREAS	⩔
RECREATION AREAS With Campsites ▲ Without Campsites △	SCHEDULED AIRLINE STOPS	✖
SELECTED REST AREAS	OTHER AIRPORTS	✖
With Toilets ✖ Without Toilets ✖	MILITARY AIRPORTS	✖
POINTS OF INTEREST ◙	INFORMATION CENTER	✪

ROAD CLASSIFICATION

CONTROLLED ACCESS HIGHWAYS
Interstate interchange numbers are mileposts.   Divided **5** Undivided
Interchanges

TOLL HIGHWAYS

OTHER DIVIDED HIGHWAYS

PAVED HIGHWAYS

LOCAL ROADS In unfamiliar areas inquire locally   Paved   Gravel   Dirt
before using these roads

MILEAGE

MILEAGE BETWEEN TOWNS 3 ◢ 4   MILEAGE ● 35 ●
AND JUNCTIONS   BETWEEN DOTS

SCALE

ONE INCH 12 MILES   0   5   10   15
ONE INCH 19 KILOMETERS 0   5   10   15   24

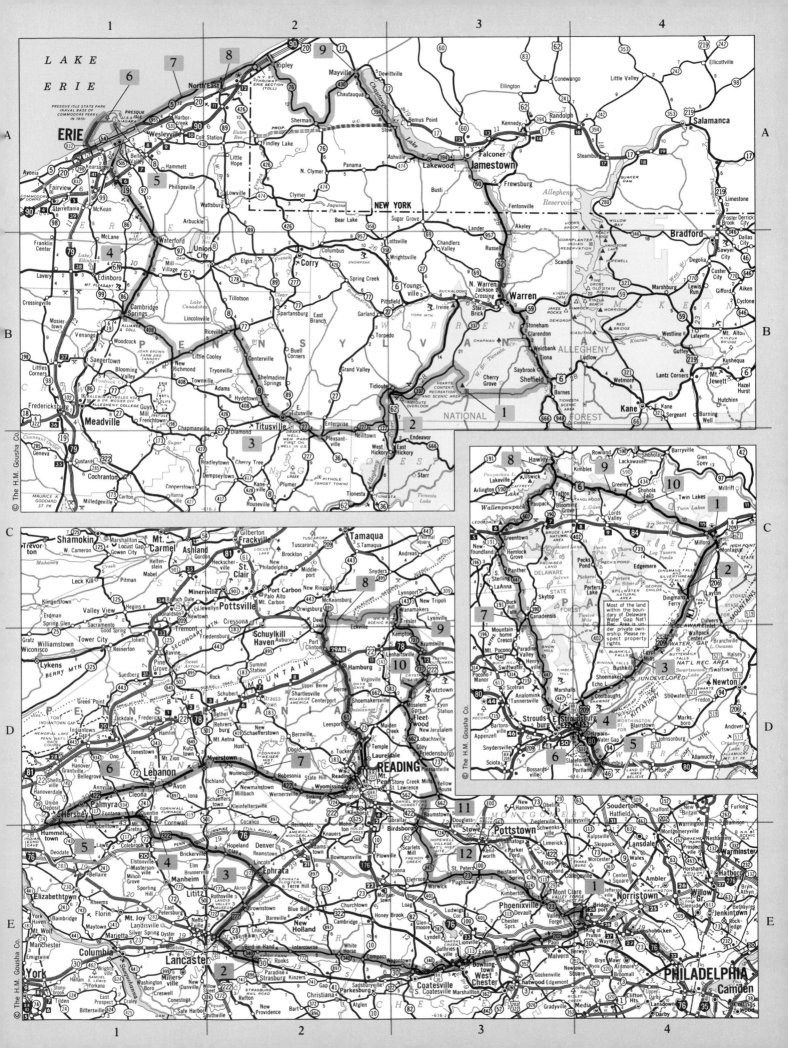

3. *Rolling farmlands border curving Oil Creek. A replica of Drake's first well, called Drake's Folly by the local villagers before the strike was made, stands near the original site.*

Drake's well. The museum has a fine display detailing the discovery of oil and a research library on the history of oil. Oil was originally sought only for lighting purposes to replace whale oil, which was becoming increasingly hard to get. Later it was used for lubrication, but it was not until the turn of the century that the automobile and the internal-combustion engine established the future of the oil industry. The exhibit traces the dramatic rise and fall of a long list of Pennsylvania towns whose fortunes waxed and waned with the flow of oil. Pithole, one of the most famous, once had a population of 15,000, but the town was in existence for less than two years. A short drive takes you to this ghost town. All there is to see is the outline of the streets, a museum, and a visitor center.

4   The town of Waterford was the site of Fort Le Boeuf. This had been by turns a French, an English, and an American fort and trading post in an area that was the American frontier throughout the 18th century. The English and French zones of influence overlapped in this territory, and Fort Le Boeuf's chief claim to fame was that in the winter of 1753 George Washington, then a young major on the staff of the British governor of Virginia, was sent there with a message for the commander of the fort challenging the presence of the French in Pennsylvania. The French refused to budge, and the confrontation expanded (as the English had probably intended) into the French and Indian War. Washington's mid-winter journey was a long and difficult one, handled, obviously, with a considerable amount of courage and initiative. The complete story is told in a delightful modern museum located where the fort once stood. The exhibits provide an excellent background to the French and Indian War and the early fur trade. At the site there is also a statue of Washington as he appeared in his early days.

5   Route 19 is a fast approach to Erie. As it enters the city it becomes Peach Street and leads to the heart of the downtown area. State Street is two blocks to the right, and as you approach the Lake Erie waterfront, turn onto State. At the foot of it, at the edge of the harbor marina, sits the flagship U.S.S. *Niagara*. This was the brig Comdr. Oliver Hazard Perry sailed when his little fleet defeated the British in the Battle of Lake Erie during the War of 1812. The *Niagara* was eventually allowed to sink. But heeding the admonition of Perry's battle flag, "DON'T GIVE UP THE SHIP," she was hauled up again in 1913 for the centenary of the battle, and the present ship was reconstructed on the salvaged keel timbers of the original. She is a sturdy, two-masted square-rigged warship that now sits high and dry on concrete pilings. You can walk around her decks and see exhibits showing how the guns worked. But, rather disappointingly, there is no access to the quarters where the crew lived belowdecks.

6   Erie's most outstanding attraction is Presque Isle State Park. Presque Isle means "almost an island" in French, a name given by the first explorers, and that is just what this lovely place is. It is a long hook of land stretching out into Lake Erie, one side of it facing back toward the city across Presque Isle Bay, the other fronting the waves of this immense lake. A circular drive (25 miles per hour is the maximum speed) takes you along the south side of Presque Isle, with a series of magnificent views of the city's waterfront, past the Perry statue and Misery Bay, where the ship *Niagara* was sunk. There are ponds and lagoons for fishermen here, woodland trails, and, along the north shore, a string of fine swimming beaches. The lake is not tidal but the waves, sometimes lashed by winds, are reminiscent of the sea.

7   Route 5 out of Erie to the east is an attractive drive lined with pleasant houses with lawns and trees set well back from the road. Although the lakeshore is only a hundred yards or so away, it is screened from view. One of the few opportunities to see what the lakeshore looks like along most of its southern reaches is provided at Shades Beach. This is a small Erie County park that has boat-launching ramps, parking, and a food concession. The lake here is lined by steep wooded slopes, and it is an ideal spot for fishing or for simply contemplating the restless waves in the foreground and the serenity of the distant horizon.

8   Back on Route 5 you begin to notice a new crop on each side of the road. The low green staked bushes on these gently rolling slopes are vineyards, and for the next five miles, to the New York State border and a bit beyond, the vineyards are an ever-present sight. These are Concord grapes, for the most part, and the region is the largest Concord grape growing area in the world. The first hint of their presence are the roadside stands selling grapes and grape juice. Wine is the more important business, however, and for those who did not know that Pennsylvania had its own small but thriving wine industry, this is the place to find out. The family-run Mazza Vineyards, located in the town of North East, offers tours of their small, attractive winery. Mazza produces 15 to 20 varieties of both sweet and dry red

and white wines and some champagne. Like the few other Pennsylvania winegrowers, the Mazza family must use grapes grown in Pennsylvania and make no more than 100,000 gallons a year.

Also in North East is Penn-Shore Vineyards, which produces 11 table wines and 2 kinds of sparkling wines—champagne and sparkling burgundy. Tours and tastings are offered. Closed Sundays.

Presque Isle Wine Cellars, the third winegrower in the town and a leading supplier of both grapes and equipment for amateur winemakers, produces red, white, and rosé table wines. Here too tours are offered, and picnic facilities are available on the grounds. The tour includes a brief wine-tasting session, and you may buy a bottle to take home. Closed Sundays and Mondays.

9 You soon leave the lake and its vineyard-clad shores and head into farm country, leaving the panoramic views of Lake Erie behind you. When you leave Sherman on Route 430 East, you will be driving on a fine wide road that rises and falls like a roller coaster through dairy country to Mayville at the head of Chautauqua Lake. This lake is long and graceful, curving delicately between gently wooded hills for nearly 20 miles to the southeast.

The short steep drops around the edge of the lake are the old beach lines left behind as the volume of the lake diminished after the last ice age.

At the water's edge you come upon Steamboat Village, which during the summer offers steamboat trips along the lake four times a day on weekdays and six times a day on weekends. The boat is the *Chautauqua Belle*, styled to resemble the steamboat that plied the lake in the 19th century. It is an ideal and relaxing way to see the lake. Four miles south of the town of Mayville is Chautauqua itself, famous as the home of the Chautauqua Institution, which offers an extensive program of seminars, guest speakers, and dramatic and musical events during the summer months. Not much of the lake is visible for the remainder of the journey down to Jamestown, except where the road rises to afford an occasional glimpse.

Ten thousand years ago retreating glaciers left the Pocono Plateau a scenic terrain of mountain ridges, narrow valleys, canyons, waterfalls, and tranquil lakes.

The verdant glacial valley in northeastern Pennsylvania where the Pocono Plateau meets the Delaware River is among the most picturesque terrain in the state. The high bluffs of the Delaware Water Gap, with awe-inspiring waterfalls cascading down the sheer escarpment, is the region's best-known landmark.

The drive through this impressive landscape follows the Delaware in Pennsylvania, crosses briefly into New Jersey for a dramatic view of the water gap, then returns to Pennsylvania and goes through unspoiled forest preserves, past roaring streams and waterfalls, and along the shores of Wallenpaupack, the Pocono's largest lake.

1 Milford, a town settled in the 1730's by Thomas Quick of Holland, is the site of the Pinchot Institute for Conservation Studies. Gifford Pinchot, the respected forester for whom the institute was named, was one of the first persons in the United States to advocate planned conservation. He was governor of Pennsylvania from 1923 to 1927 and from 1931 to 1935. His home, Grey Towers, is now the headquarters of the institute.

Built in 1886 in the style of a 15th-century French château, the house has three round, cone-capped 66-foot towers. The grounds attract many visitors during the autumn for the foliage display.

About a mile south of Milford a sheer escarpment rises up on the west side of the road. The top of the cliff marks the height of the land in this area before the ice age glaciers gouged out much of the bed of the present-day Delaware River. Evidence of vast rock slides down the wall of the escarpment reveals the force of erosion that has been at work since the local glaciation ended.

The deep valley of the Delaware River and Water Gap has an interesting history, paralleled by that of many other rivers crossing the Appalachians. Before the geological uplift of the mountains there was a lazy, sluggish river meandering across an almost flat plain. About 100

million years ago this zone of the earth's crust began to arch up. Slowly the riverbed cut lower and lower, superposing itself on the deep structures in the rock.

Almost immediately south of Milford, glimpses of the Delaware River first come into view, a narrow ribbon of blue water on the east side of the highway. The river flirts with the road for the entire drive along Route 209.

2 Both Dingmans Falls and Silver Thread Falls are near the village of Dingmans Ferry in a small, wooded section of the Delaware Water Gap

2. Silver Thread Falls drops down a cliff of sandstone in a gorge and into Dingmans Creek, a tributary of the Delaware.

National Recreation Area. A 15-minute shady walk takes you from the entranceway to both falls. In July masses of rhododendrons fill the area with brilliant blossoms.

Silver Thread Falls drops for more than 100 feet in a narrow torrent down a sheer rock face; Dingmans Falls is a broader cataract, cascading down eroded stairways of rock. Both waterfalls are examples of "hanging tributaries," which are waterfalls created by erosion of the main valley. Here the glacier that gouged out much of the bed of the present-day

Formation of the Delaware Water Gap

Some 100 million years ago the Appalachian Mountains were leveled by the forces of erosion, leaving a flat, tropical plain through which a mature river meandered. Fifty million years ago, relieved of the mountains' weight, the earth's crust had slowly risen, and the river had cut a gorge through the uplift. The climate was subtropical, and there were forests of oak, beech, maple, and other deciduous trees. About 20,000 years ago the land formation had been somewhat smoothed by the passing of the latest glacier. The river, still in its original configuration and strengthened by melting ice, cut an even deeper gorge. Today you see the gorge and the ridge of Kittatinny Mountain as they were left by the last glaciation.

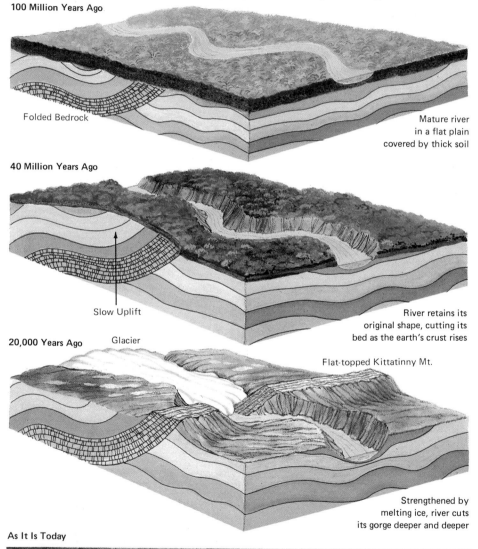

100 Million Years Ago

Folded Bedrock

Mature river in a flat plain covered by thick soil

40 Million Years Ago

Slow Uplift

River retains its original shape, cutting its bed as the earth's crust rises

20,000 Years Ago   Glacier

Flat-topped Kittatinny Mt.

Strengthened by melting ice, river cuts its gorge deeper and deeper

As It Is Today

Delaware River left its ancient tributary streams cut off, or hanging, at the edge of the cliff above. To rejoin the river, the old tributaries must now plunge down the face of the cliff to the valley floor.

The visitors' center in the recreation area has a display of the glacial geology of the Delaware Valley.

The Delaware is one of the most popular canoeing rivers in the eastern United States. The trip from Milford to the Delaware Water Gap 35 miles away can be made in two days. Rental canoes are available all along the river. Most outfitters will arrange to meet canoers at a designated point downstream and will fetch them and their canoes back by van or truck.

3 Bushkill Falls, locally called the Niagara of Pennsylvania, is actually a series of several waterfalls in a natural wooded setting. A network of safe catwalks, suspension bridges and steps provides a pathway along the walls of the gorge and over the foaming silver torrents. The walkways blend into the natural rock contours and forest foliage and give breathtaking close-ups of the spectacles of nature within the park. The air resounds with the cacophony of water crashing down rugged chutes of rock.

By following the well-marked trails and catwalks, it is possible to see the falls from several different levels—at the top, where the main falls plunges over the edge of the precipice, at several midpoints toward the base of the canyon, and at the bottom of the gorge, where the waters finally run still in quiet pools and streams.

There are picnic grounds, nature trails for hikers, and scenic overlooks of distant ridges and valleys.

Like Dingmans and Silver Thread, these falls are also hanging tributaries. The park is closed from November through March.

One mile south of the small town of Bushkill (Dutch for "little river") is the Pocono Indian Museum, which traces the history of the Delaware Indians back for thousands of years. The displays here include their tools, weapons, and other artifacts that were found in these mountains.

4 The Delaware Water Gap is one of the best known scenic features of the Middle Atlantic states. The gap marks the place where the Delaware

River breaks through a solid wall of mountain on the Pennsylvania-New Jersey border.

Our route through the gap includes a series of scenic water-level parking areas that afford the best possible views of this natural wonder, from both the Pennsylvania and New Jersey sides of the river.

As you cross the Delaware into New Jersey for a view of the Pennsylvania side of the gap, there is an exit on the left that takes you to the Kittatinny Point Information Station. National Park Service ranger-naturalists are on duty during the months of July and August at the visitor center, where audiovisual programs are given.

The Park Service naturalists lead canoe trips on the river during July and August. They give instruction in river-running and other skills necessary for the safe handling of the craft. Advance reservations are necessary.

The drive east affords a clear view of Mount Minsi on the Pennsylvania side of the gap. A parking area on the left side of the highway offers an opportunity to enjoy the view.

5 The toll bridge from Columbia, New Jersey, to Portland, Pennsylvania, a town founded in 1845 by James Ginn of Portland, Maine, provides an excellent panoramic view of the gap, including the mountains on both sides of the river.

6 As you drive north along the river you come upon a parking area on the left side of the road. A second overlook is located on the right side of the road about two miles beyond the first. From both of these there are clear views of Mount Tammany rising 1,600 feet on the New Jersey side of the river. Immense slides of weathered rock from the sheer vertical face of Mount Tammany are visual evidence of the ongoing processes of erosion, which have given the gap its present contours. Most of the giant boulders were wedged off the escarpment by freeze-and-thaw action, which was vigorous just after the glaciers retreated and continues each winter in a minor way.

Stroudsburg and East Stroudsburg are both popular gateways to the Poconos. They are divided by Brodhead Creek, named for Daniel Brodhead who established a Moravian mission

8. Lake Wallenpaupack, 13 miles long, is known for its excellent fishing. Along its shores is an 80-acre forest preserve with two miles of hiking and skiing trails.

for the Indians on the creek's west bank in 1752.

7 Buck Hill Falls is among the best known in the Poconos and is managed as part of the famous old resort hotel, the Buck Hill Falls Inn, which has manicured lawns, bowling greens, tennis courts, and rolling fairways on the golf course.

The falls itself is in an idyllic glade filled with giant hemlocks (*Tsuga canadensis*), the official state tree, tulip trees, birches, and great stands of rhododendrons. A series of man-made walkways lead along the rocky walls of the gorge to the stream at the top of the precipice and to the plunge pool at the base of the cataract. Closed during the winter.

The drive north to Newfoundland is through a landscape of streams, ponds, and unspoiled second-growth forest. Most of the trees of the present-day Poconos are no more than 70 years old. The original forest found by the first settlers was cleared by 19th-century lumbering interests and by tanneries, which used the bark of hemlocks for the tannic acid needed for tanning leather.

8 The finest view of Lake Wallenpaupack, the largest body of water in the Pocono Mountains, is from the grassy earthwork dikes at the northeastern head of the lake. Paths lead from several small parking areas up onto the shoulder of the earthworks for a view of the extensive white-capped reaches of the mountain-enfolded lake. The lake, with some 52 miles of shoreline, was created in 1924, when the Pennsylvania Power and Light Company completed a dam across Wallenpaupack Creek.

The lake is surrounded by privately owned cottages, several hotels and motels, and four lakeside camping grounds. Boats can be rented at several so-called landings.

9 From Lake Wallenpaupack east toward the town of Milford, the drive goes through unspoiled marsh and forest land, where blue herons, ducks, and other waterfowl are commonly seen from the road.

Some of the drive is through a Pennsylvania state forest. About 10 miles from Lake Wallenpaupack the road runs through State Game Land, which is open to the public for seasonal fishing and hunting. Hunting licenses are accompanied by a booklet that has complete information about dates, limits, and types of weapons allowed. At certain times of year bow-and-arrow hunting is allowed, as is muzzle-loading, especially for deer. The abundant game includes ring-necked pheasants, wild turkeys, and ruffed grouse, which is the official state bird.

10 Shohola Falls Water Fowl Management Area is a remarkably pristine wilderness park. It is but a short walk through a wooded area from the parking lot to a placid, tree-lined lake. If you have a canoe, this is a perfect place to use it. The perimeters of the lake are marshland and provide a haven for such waterfowl as geese, ducks, coots, and woodcocks.

Well-marked trails lead across a meadow into a glen where the roaring waters of Shohola Falls drop down a steep staircase of eroded rock to a gorge below. One of the best-kept secrets of the whole Pocono region, the Shohola Falls Recreation Area is both the perfect place to stop for a half-hour's walk through the woods to the falls, or to spend an entire day canoeing, picnicking, and fishing.

Like the glorious quilts of the Amish, Pennsylvania is a colorful combination of harmonious contrasts. Since this nation's earliest days Pennsylvania has been a manufacturing and commercial center rich in coal and other industrial resources; yet its good earth has also been fertile and abundantly productive. Beyond the centers of industry and commerce there are fields of amazing peace, tended by some of the gentlest folk on the face of the earth. Eastern Pennsylvania fairly bristles with commemorative monuments and historical sites.

1 Among the most famous historic places is Valley Forge, now a national historical park. It is a beautiful area with grassy hillsides, groves of trees, and lovely views of the Schuylkill River.

In these pleasant surroundings it is hard to imagine the privations endured by Gen. George Washington's battered army in that difficult winter of 1777-78. Some 2,000 men became sick and died here, but the perseverance of the survivors has become legendary. By spring, thanks to their faith in Washington and their strict training by the iron-willed Baron von Steuben, the army was ready to fight

1. Several of the 900 log huts that were built at Valley Forge have been restored.

the British to a standoff at Monmouth Courthouse in New Jersey.

Visitors today can see the house where Washington made his headquarters and inspect the log huts that the soldiers occupied. Reconstructed forts, original entrenchments, the grand parade ground, and well-placed monuments and markers all help to impart the spirit that pre-

vailed during the struggle for independence. A visitor center provides information and literature about Valley Forge, and there are several picnic areas available. The park is closed on Christmas Day.

Route 340, west of Valley Forge, winds its way through typical dairy country. This is grazing land where clusters of cattle, mostly Holsteins and Guernseys, feed when the fields are green. Soon the fields become smaller, the farms closer together, the buildings tidier and more pristine. Tobacco, corn, and wheat flourish here in the rich soil. Hex signs, those colorful designs that are put up on barns to bring prosperity to the farm, begin to appear, signaling that you are entering the land of the Pennsylvania Dutch. These signs are often created just to catch the eye of the tourist. The commercialism of the antiques shops, farmers' markets, buggy rides, quaint motels, family-style restaurants, and other tourist attractions centered around the little towns of Intercourse and Bird in Hand can be misleading. The quiet, devout, hard-working Amish people do live here. You can see them black-garbed and wide-hatted, shopping in the small towns.

Hex Signs

The Pennsylvania Dutch people, being both religious and superstitious, began years ago to decorate their barns with so-called hex signs to give thanks for the goodness of the earth and to bring good luck to the farm. The word "hex" comes from *hexe*, German for witch.

Designs are said to have various meanings. Below from left, the distlefink calls for good fortune, rain drops for a plentiful rainfall, double rain drops and star for good luck, hearts and six-petaled tulip for love, and stars and closed tulip for fertility.

The Pennsylvania Dutch

These people are descendants of German-speaking religious sects who came to Pennsylvania in the 17th and 18th centuries to escape religious persecution. The name "Dutch" is a misspelling of *Deutsch*, the German word for that language.

The largest of these various religious groups are the Mennonites and the Amish.

The Amish use only horses for farming and transportation, and have no electricity or telephones (but use public phones for business). Men and boys dress in plain black clothes and wide-brimmed hats. The married men have beards but no moustaches. The women wear long, brightly colored dresses covered with dark capes and aprons, and white prayer caps, with black bonnets over them when outdoors.

The Mennonites, who are more liberal, also dress plainly, but use electricity and phones and drive cars. The men are clean-shaven and wear plain dark clothes. The women wear long plain dresses and small white caps.

The Amish and Mennonites take no oaths, believing only in the rule of God. The Amish are not allowed to hold public office or marry outside their faith.

The Pennsylvania Dutch, who own some of the finest farmlands in the southeastern part of the state, harvest their crops with old-fashioned horse-drawn reapers. All through this rolling countryside you can see the beautifully proportioned architecture, the farm wagons, black buggies, and plain dress favored by these Plain People, who have chosen to live close to the land that provides them with almost all their simple needs.

2   There are several places that demonstrate the Amish way of life. One of the most interesting and authentic is the Amish Farm and House, a replica of an Old Order House Amish home and farmstead. The so-called House Amish, unlike the Church Amish, always held their religious services in a member's home. The stone house, which was built in 1805, is filled with furniture and fixtures of the era. A tour of the farm provides a vivid picture of a way of life that dates back to the 1600's.

Besides the Amish, the several religious sects who live in this countryside include the Mennonites, the Schwenkfelders, and the Dunkers, who were so named because they believe in a baptismal ritual of total immersion.

All the Pennsylvania Dutch prefer to earn their living from the land, and because of their devout and simple way of life, they are known as the Plain People.

3   Members of a German Protestant monastic order built the medieval-style buildings of the Ephrata Cloister on Zion Hill in the mid-18th century. During the Revolutionary War wounded patriots from the Battle of Brandywine were nursed here.

Conrad Beissel, the German Pietist mystic who founded the order, was also a composer, and it is his music that forms the basis of the religious drama *Vorspiel,* performed on Saturday evenings from late June to Labor Day in the cloister setting.

3. Guides at Ephrata Cloister, in hooded costumes like those the members of the order used to wear, demonstrate basket weaving and the use of old garden tools.

4 As you drive west through this wooded country, watch for the signpost to Cornwall Furnace. On the road you journey through several communities of look-alike, 19th-century stone houses that are reminiscent of the old miners' cottages in Cornwall on England's southern coast.

On the south side of the road is the mammoth Cornwall iron-ore open-pit mine, worked for nearly 200 years and at one time the largest iron mine in the New World. The iron ore, deposited in a 450-million-year-old geological formation, can be traced from New England to Alabama. The Cornwall mine was flooded in the great hurricane of 1972 and now looks like a huge sunken lake.

The Cornwall Iron Furnace, a short distance away, is a magnificently preserved (and partly reconstructed) furnace, dating from 1742. The vast furnace, built in the Gothic style, produced cannon for the Revolutionary War and remained in use until 1883.

5 Here in the rolling farm country typical of southeastern Pennsylvania is Hershey, one of the most remarkable examples in the United States of a one-industry, one-company town. Everything in the town, including the lampposts on Chocolate Avenue that are shaped like the Hershey Kisses, is a reminder of the company and its chocolate products. There is a great deal to do and see, and, of course, a Hershey hotel and a motel in which to stay. Chocolate World is a brilliantly designed exhibit in which viewers ride on moving cars past animated re-creations of all the steps involved in the making of chocolate, from cocoa bean to candy bar.

Hersheypark is an elaborate fun fair; at ZooAmerica, animals and plants are exhibited in simulated natural settings; Hershey Gardens offer six "theme" gardens and are especially notable for their extensive collection of beautiful roses, which cover an entire hillside.

6 If you are interested in food, you may want to sample the celebrated bologna of Lebanon. Weaver's Lebanon Bologna plant just outside the town is one of the places where it is made and is well worth a visit. Beef is coarsely ground and seasoned with spices from a secret family recipe.

The mixture is then forced into casings and is hung for days in wooden smokehouses over smoldering hardwoods. The delicious smoky aromas are mouth-watering, and tasty samples are offered. The product is sold on the premises.

7 The Conrad Weiser Historic Park is the well-kept wooded setting for the handsome, simple stone house that Weiser built in 1729 and enlarged in 1751. The house has been restored and now displays furnishings and fixtures dating from the mid-18th century. As a boy, recently arrived from Germany with his family, Weiser became the adopted son of

6. Lebanon bologna, prepared as it was in the 1700's, is cured in rustic smokehouses over slowly burning wood fires.

an Iroquois chief. His knowledge of the Indians' language and customs served him well, and in his later years he was known as "ambassador" to the Iroquois Indian nation.

8 With 2,000 acres, the privately endowed Hawk Mountain Sanctuary is one of the finest wildlife refuges in the country and was the first sanctuary in the world to provide protection for migrating hawks, eagles, and other birds of prey. The impressive Sanctuary Headquarters with its

cavelike entrance is a large museum with splendid displays of bird life, a fine selection of bird guides, and an active bird-feeding station outside the picture windows. A well-marked hiking trail wends through wooded knolls to two magnificent overlooks. The path to South Lookout is a five-minute walk. A more difficult 30- to 45-minute hike over rocky ground is rewarded by a spectacular 70-mile view from the 1,500-foot elevation of the North Lookout. Below, spread out to the south, is the "Great Valley" of the Appalachians, which can be followed from the middle Hudson Valley in New York State all the way to Georgia.

The Appalachians have a distinctive, truncated look, famous to geologists the world over. Originally they were much higher, like the Alps, but over millions of years they became eroded to a flat so-called peneplain. Later these mountains were arched up again, and river gorges were cut through, leaving the flat-topped ranges as visual testimony of that old peneplain.

From early September to late November, the North Lookout is a superb vantage point from which to see the southward migration of hawks and eagles, soaring on powerful wings along the sharp outline of the Kittatinny Ridge of the Appalachians. In the fall, a naturalist on duty is available to help you to understand and appreciate the significance of this unique preserve. All plants and animals within the sanctuary are protected by law and they must not be disturbed.

9 The little town of Kempton is the headquarters for the Wanamaker, Kempton & Southern Scenic Rail Road steam engines and passenger cars. The trains, complete with whistle blasts and clanging bell, take the Hawk Mountain Line, a spectacular meandering route through woods and along the banks of Maiden Creek to the hamlet of Wanamaker and back again. There is a shop that sells antiques at one end of the run and a trackside picnic grove with inviting nature trails. Kempton boasts a farm museum in an old barn (open Sundays year-round and also on Saturdays during the summer) and a hotel that serves remarkably generous

8. As many as 15,000 birds of prey have been counted at the Hawk Mountain Sanctuary during the fall migration. Here a broad-winged hawk soars past the South Lookout.

lunches. The W.K.&S. operates on weekends only. Closed from November to early April.

As you drive by the cornfields that edge right up to the highway, watch for the birdcagelike structures called corncribs in which cobs are stored for use as livestock feed. Soon you are traveling in wilder, uncultivated land. This is limestone country, and over the eons water seeping through the porous stone has hollowed out a number of spectacular caverns. This 500-million-year-old limestone belt can be seen, here and there, from New Jersey to Virginia.

10 Crystal Cave has been a tourist attraction ever since it was discovered in 1871. The cave has exquisite stalactite, stalagmite, and dripstone formations, which are artfully enhanced by special lighting effects. The 35-minute tour is preceded by an informative slide show explaining the history of cave formation. The cave is situated in a 125-acre park that includes picnic areas, hiking trails, a restaurant, a gift shop, a miniature golf course, and facilities for other family activities. The cave is closed from December to Washington's Birthday.

Onyx Cave, a few miles to the southwest, is a smaller cave. Guided tours through its striking geological formations are available.

11 Near Yellow House you find the Daniel Boone Homestead. The homestead was built on the site of the log cabin in which the celebrated frontiersman was born to a Quaker family in 1734; the family moved to North Carolina when Daniel was 15. Some of the foundation of the original cabin, and its spring, remain. Boone's father probably built part of the 18th-century farmhouse that stands here now. It is carefully furnished and equipped in the style of the day, and from the outstanding guides you can learn a great deal about 18th-century country living. Nearby are other buildings of the period restored to their original condition and also a museum where the exhibits include a leather shoulder bag that belonged to Daniel Boone. From spring to fall, organized youth groups can make arrangements to "rough it" overnight in a wayside lodge provided for this purpose.

12 Hopewell Village is a splendid restoration of an early 19th-century iron-smelting community, including several original buildings. The village is traversed by the original millrace, which still turns a waterwheel of the kind that was used to drive the bellows for the iron-making furnace. The charcoal hearth where the fuel for the furnace was made, the sheds where the charcoal gatherers emp-

tied their loads, the houses where the workers lived, and the casting house where the pig iron was poured can all be seen here. The ironmaster's home, "the Big House," is an expression of middle-class gentility in the wilderness. The workers' homes, the lofty barn, the blacksmith shop, the company store, and, above all, the great furnace contribute to an understanding of the social and economic dynamics of a typical 19th-century industrial village.

Although Hopewell was productive from 1771 to 1883, the height of its prosperity was reached in the mid-1830's. In 1853 an anthracite-burning furnace was built, but Hopewell could not compete with other anthracite furnaces located nearer to their markets in the growing cities. Today it is a beautifully preserved relic of early industrialism, made all the more poignant by its idyllic setting. Hopewell is surrounded by French Creek State Park with its nature trails, camping grounds, and picnic facilities. The village is closed on Christmas and New Year's days.

As you leave the woods of French Creek State Park, you may wish to visit the charming village of St. Peters. The buildings here are much as they were in the 19th century, and this is a pleasant place to stroll past antiques and craft shops.

Variety in New Jersey

From the lakes of the northern hills to the sandy Atlantic shores, the scene is ever-changing

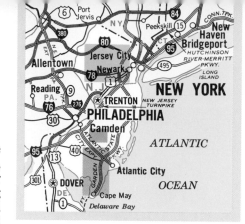

Long, narrow, S-shaped New Jersey, with the Atlantic Ocean on the east and the Delaware River along its western border, is known as the Garden State. Despite the concentration in the northeast of oil refineries, chemical plants, factories, and research laboratories, much of the state is indeed a garden, a combination of wooded hills, fertile farmlands, and areas of wilderness where the natural environment has been preserved.

Historic sites scattered throughout the state are reminders of colonial days and battles of the Revolution.

Starting at the city of Newark, settled in 1666 by a small group of Puritans and now grown into one of the most important industrial centers in the nation, this tour follows a trail of history as it winds through the hills of the northern part of the state.

From West Orange, where Thomas Edison lived and worked, to Morristown, one of Gen. George Washington's headquarters during the Revolutionary War, and westward almost to the Delaware Water Gap, the route passes many lakes and small towns.

1 On the outskirts of Newark are Branch Brook Park and its extension, which have become famous for their outstanding collection of flowering Oriental cherry trees. From late April more than 2,000 of these colorful trees put on a brilliant display that lasts about three weeks.

Included are both the single- and double-blossom varieties, as well as the so-called weeping cherries, a combination that produces a splendid array of colors ranging from white through deep violet.

Walking trails and roadways thread their way through the plantings and lead to tempting places for picnics.

2 As you leave the park, turn west on Park Avenue and continue for about three miles to West Orange. Here is the Edison National Historic Site, a complex of buildings that includes Thomas Alva Edison's main laboratory, several smaller laboratories, a museum, and a replica of Black Maria, as the first motion picture studio was called. The name derived from the black tar paper that covered its walls. This strange structure was open to the sky, and as the sun

moved, the building was turned by the cast and crew to catch the light for the camera.

Half a mile away, on a hilltop in Llewellyn Park, is Glenmont, the handsome, 23-room Victorian mansion that was home to the Edisons for 44 years. Surrounded by grounds landscaped with shrubs, trees, gardens, and sweeping lawns, Glenmont remains as it was when the Edisons lived here. Guided tours of the mansion are given except on Mondays, Tuesdays, and holidays. Tickets are available only at the laboratory.

3 Northfield Avenue, as it heads west, becomes Route 508. On the south side of the road is South Mountain Reservation, an expanse of ravines and natural woodlands just two minutes away from traffic, towns, and industrial sites. Here on 2,048 acres are walking trails, bridle paths, and inviting picnic grounds with fireplaces. A path leads to the top of Washington Lookout, an escarpment from which it is believed American spys kept watch of British maneuvers during the Revolutionary War.

At Northfield the tour turns to the south on Route 527, which is called

1. Oriental cherry trees in full bloom form clouds of soft pink along the Second River at Branch Brook Park Extension. The floral display lasts for as long as three weeks as the several different varieties come into bloom.

SPECIAL FEATURES

ROAD GUIDE	━━━━	HIGHLIGHT	**1**
STATE PARKS		POINTS OF INTEREST	
With Campsites ♠ Without Campsites △			
RECREATION AREAS		SCHEDULED AIRLINE STOPS ✈	
With Campsites ▲ Without Campsites △			
SELECTED REST AREAS ✕		OTHER AIRPORTS ✈	

ROAD CLASSIFICATION

CONTROLLED ACCESS HIGHWAYS
Interstate interchange numbers are mileposts.

TOLL HIGHWAYS

OTHER DIVIDED HIGHWAYS

PAVED HIGHWAYS

LOCAL ROADS In unfamiliar areas inquire locally before using these roads   Paved   Gravel   Dirt

MILEAGE

MILEAGE BETWEEN TOWNS   3 4   MILEAGE   35
AND JUNCTIONS   BETWEEN DOTS

SCALE

ONE INCH 7 MILES   0 1 2 3 4 5   10

ONE INCH 11 KILOMETERS 0 1 2 3 4 5   10   16

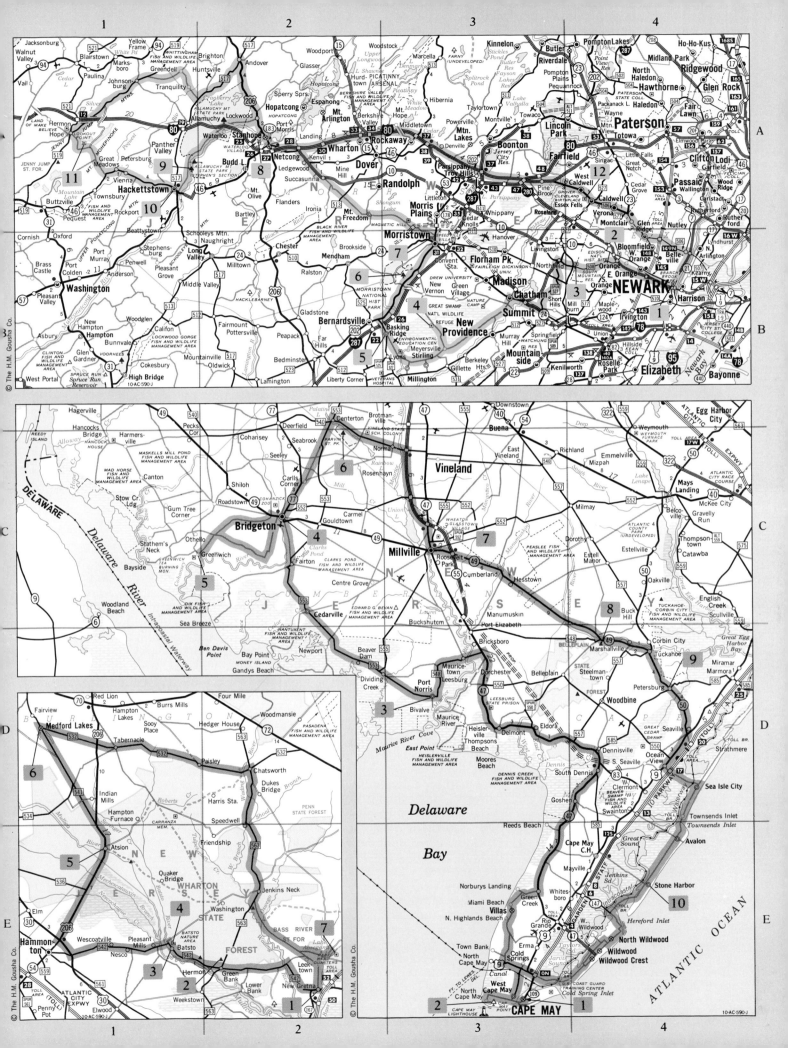

Red-headed woodpecker

White-breasted nuthatch

Male eastern bluebird

Snowy egret and young

Green heron

Great horned owl

4. A short boardwalk extends over a marsh of the Great Swamp National Wildlife Refuge. Roadways also traverse the area. Some of the 200 kinds of birds found at the refuge are shown at right.

Kennedy Parkway, and winds through woodlands and rolling hills between attractive residential areas.

4 From the colonial town of Chatham, where Washington and his army kept the British at bay, Fairmont Avenue runs southwest to Meyersville and the entrance to the Great Swamp National Wildlife Refuge. This 6,500-acre expanse, once part of a prehistoric lake carved out by receding glaciers 16,000 years ago, includes several kinds of habitats—forested swamps, meadowlands, and marshes filled with cattails.

The refuge, a favorite haunt of bird-watchers, includes one of the state's largest breeding areas for bluebirds. More than 200 species of birds, such as the mocking bird, mourning dove, green heron, Canada goose and the rarely seen snow goose, and the red-headed woodpecker, have been spotted here. Several kinds of mammals and an impressive variety of turtles, frogs, and nonpoisonous snakes also make their home in the swamp.

Dry woodland paths lead through the refuge. Nearby county education centers offer guided trail walks and classes in natural sciences.

On the way to Basking Ridge, an attractive colonial town, the road passes several horse farms.

5 The Basking Ridge Presbyterian Church, a square red brick, white-pillared building dating from the early 1800's, was founded by a group of Scottish settlers in 1717. The small churchyard cemetery, sheltered by a huge white oak tree said to be more than 500 years old, has headstones dating back to 1736. Here is the grave of Polly Kinnan, an early settler who was captured by Indians, sold into slavery, and finally rescued and brought back to the town.

6 Morristown National Historical Park, which commemorates the part played by the town in the Revolutionary War when Washington and his army were encamped here, is divided into three sections that are scattered through the town. Jockey Hollow, the area where 10,000 soldiers camped during the winter of 1779-80, is located on a quiet, narrow road just to the west of Route 202, south of the center of Morristown.

Here is the Wick House, home of Henry Wick, a prosperous farmer who turned his home over to Gen. Arthur St. Clair and his officers. The restored house is furnished with pieces dating from the late 1700's. Apple orchards and an herb garden entice visitors during the spring.

At 230 Morris Avenue stands the Ford Mansion, also part of the historical park. This elegant residence, built in 1774 by Col. Jacob Ford, Jr., a prosperous colonial iron and munitions manufacturer, became General Washington's headquarters during the winter of 1779–80.

The mansion has been preserved with many of its original furnishings intact. Adjacent to the building is a museum with a collection of Revolutionary War memorabilia.

All buildings of the park are closed on Thanksgiving, Christmas, and New Year's days.

7 Just north of Morristown green is Speedwell Village, a reconstruction of a 19th-century settlement. This was the site of the Arnold Jacobs homestead and ironworks, built during the latter part of the 18th century.

Early in the 19th century Stephan Vail took over the ironworks, turned it into a foundry, and produced various kinds of machinery.

On display are wooden patterns used in the manufacture of engine parts as well as models of the early telegraph apparatus, which Vail's son worked on with Samuel F. B. Morse. Closed from November to April.

8 Waterloo Village, a restored colonial town, is now a national historic site. The Andover Iron Forge, built here on the Musconetcong River in 1763 by two Tories, was confiscated during the Revolution for the production of cannonballs. Restored buildings include the Methodist Church and the Stagecoach Inn and Tavern. Closed Mondays and from January to Easter.

9 South of Waterloo is the Stephens Section of Allamuchy Mountain State Park, known for picturesque Saxton Falls and the rushing waters of the Musconetcong River. A guard lock from the old Morris Canal, a waterway that carried shipping during the last century from the Delaware River to the Hudson River, is located at the side of the falls. Trout fishing is excellent in the swift-moving waters of the river, and there are camping sites and picnic grounds.

10 The Charles O. Hayford State Fish Hatchery, located at Hackettstown, breeds rainbow, brown, and brook trout, and stocks striped bass, tiger muskellunge, and largemouth bass. Group tours of the hatchery can be arranged by appointment.

11 As the road goes through Great Meadows, it twists among the hills and climbs to the entrance to Jenny Jump State Forest, an area of some thousand acres that has been set aside for the conservation of water and timber, with one section open for recreation. A winding road leads to a lookout where there is a fine view of the Delaware Water Gap 12 miles to the northwest.

Northeast of Hope the road follows along a stream. This is a scenic road with vistas of the valleys to the east as it passes farmhouses and ivy-covered cottages and goes through some almost forgotten villages.

Cranberry Lake borders the road on the west, and soon Lake Lackawanna comes into view. Lake Hopatcong, New Jersey's largest lake, has become so popular that cottages for both year-round and summer living seem to fill every hillside along its wooded waterfront. At Hopatcong State Park are barbecue grills, benches, and tables for picnickers, and a sandy swimming beach.

12 At Caldwell is the birthplace of Grover Cleveland, who became the 22nd and the 24th president of the United States. The simple clapboard house where he was born on March 18, 1837, served as the manse for the Presbyterian Church while the Reverend Richard Cleveland, the president's father, was pastor. The restored building contains several pieces of furniture that belonged to President Cleveland. Closed on Mondays and Tuesdays.

One of the unusual features of New Jersey is the Pine Barrens, a wilderness area that extends through most of the lower half of the state. Once the bottom of an ancient ocean, the sandy soil and dunelike landscape are a testimony of the last glacial melting. The ice front reached a line across central New Jersey, but south of it the meltwater carried streams of sand and gravel. Before the warm climate returned, the sands were blown up into extensive desert dune formations. The landscape is now a combination of sand and marsh, forested mostly by pitch pines and scrub oaks.

So close to the surface is the water table in this wilderness that rivers have risen through the sandy soil, forming bogs, lakes, and slow-moving shallow streams. And so flammable is the forest growing in the dry sandy soil that, despite the abundance of water, fires have occurred so often through the ages that all plants that could not adapt to the frequent burning over have been eliminated. The flora that has survived sprouts anew each time it is seemingly destroyed, sending up shoots from the roots and stumps that the fires could not kill.

From New Gretna, a 19th-century town on the eastern edge of the Pine Barrens, the road passes historic settlements as it circles this landscape.

1 When New Gretna was settled early in the 1800's, it was, according to legend, named New Gretna Green after the famous Scottish town where marriages can be easily arranged. The settlers apparently intended to establish a similar convenience here, but New Jersey laws did not permit such a procedure, and the "Green" was dropped from the name. Today the town serves primarily as the gateway to the Pine Barrens.

Shortly after leaving New Gretna, you drive over a narrow wooden bridge to a stretch of marshlands filled with pond lilies, cattails, and tall grasses, surrounded by forest.

The Pine Barrens, so named by the early colonists because they believed it to be unfit for farming, is a sandy pine-covered wilderness of 3,000 square miles.

With much of it now preserved as state forest, the area is known not only for the pitch pine, white cedar,

8. The general store at Waterloo Village, built in 1831 on the banks of a canal, has been restored and is once again offering an array of merchandise, just as it did during the 19th century. On sale are candy sticks, cornhusk dolls, and other such treasures.

1. The Pine Barrens, bright green in early spring, is known for its many wild orchids, including the dragon's mouth (top), the yellow-fringed (center), and the grass pink, shown here in its white phase.

red maple, red oak (*Quercus rubra*), the official state tree, and scrub oak trees that thrive here, but for its wild flowers, including more than 20 varieties of orchids. Pickerel, catfish, and pike perch swim in the streams, and herons, egrets, migrating waterfowl, and many kinds of songbirds, including the goldfinch, the state bird, live in the forest along with opossums, raccoons, white-tailed deer, and gray foxes.

The town of Green Bank, on the southern edge of Wharton State Forest, was settled in 1697 by a group of Swedes led by Eric Mullica. Although Mullica later left the settlement, he gave his name to the nearby river, one of the longest in the Pine Barrens.

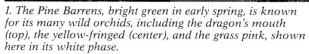

Wharton State Forest, a wilderness of woods and water, is laced with sandy roads that lead to the area's many campgrounds, picnic sites, lakeside cabins, and boat rental centers. Fishing and hunting in season are permitted in the forest, and with more than 60 miles of rivers and streams, the area attracts many canoe enthusiasts.

3 The road follows the Mullica River as it goes westward to Historic Batsto Village, which was settled in 1760 by Swedes from Delaware.

The little 18th-century village, whose name probably comes from a contraction of *badstuga*, Swedish for "bathing place," has been restored almost to its original condition.

The Batsto colonists, like many others of the time, were attracted to the Pine Barrens because of the iron-ore bogs and the seemingly endless supply of lumber in the area. Iron-ore furnaces and forges sprang up during the 18th century along the riverbanks in this wilderness, and for almost a hundred years these so-called fur-

nace towns flourished, producing kettles, stoves, nails, and other equipment needed by the colonists, and furnishing firearms and ammunition for the American Revolutionary War.

After coal was discovered in Pennsylvania and started to replace lumber as fuel in the early 1800's, the furnace towns of the Pine Barrens began to decline. With the exception of Batsto Historic Village, hardly a trace of these once-prosperous villages can be found today.

At Batsto the ironmaster's mansion sits on a knoll overlooking the millpond, with the post office, the general store, the blacksmith shop, the gristmill, and other village buildings clustered nearby. The sandy narrow main street continues on the other side of a wooden bridge across the Batsto River, a stream dammed by the settlers to form the pond for their grist and lumber mills, and here there are the workers' cottages, now restored. Guided tours of the town and several of the buildings are available.

4 The Batsto Nature Area, a short walk from the village, is a 150-acre wildlife preserve that includes most of the plants indigenous to the Pine Barrens. Here along the well-marked trails you can find arbutus, beach, or false, heather (*Hudsonia*), bearberry, mountain laurel, several kinds of fern, including the four-foot Virginia chain fern, and many kinds of orchids, all growing among the scrubby oaks and pines.

The Batona Trail, a 41-mile hiking path that wanders through both Wharton and Lebanon state forests, has camping sites along the way. Permits for camping, which are required, are available at the Batsto Visitor Center. The trail can be picked up at several points, including the Batsto Fire Tower.

To the west, through Pleasant Mills and Wescoatville, there are peach and apple orchards where you may pick your own fruit, acres of both wild and cultivated blueberry bushes, and occasional vegetable farms with roadside stands offering the produce of the fields. Tomatoes, which thrive in the Pine Barrens soil, are particularly plentiful here.

The road north goes through open farmlands in the scrubby woods and miles of marshlands filled with cran-

3. *The ironmaster's mansion at Batsto Historic Village, originally constructed in 1766, was remodeled several times. The last additions, including the tower, were made in 1878. The mansion is being restored and furnished to reflect the elegance of past eras.*

passes farmhouses, with horses (the state animal) quietly grazing in the grassy forest-edged fields.

6 Medford Lakes is also a summer resort, where water sports are popular. Here the forest surrounds the water so closely that the lakes are not visible from the road. A short spur road, however, takes you to the beaches and the fishing area.

At Medford Lakes the turn onto Route 532 is not marked and can easily be missed. Watch for the Settler's Inn at the fork of the road.

Tabernacle Road, Route 532, takes you to Chatsworth through several small residential communities. Turning south, you once again enter the wilderness of bogs and woods where wild flowers, among them the purple violet, the state flower, grow beside the road. The roadway crosses and recrosses small streams carrying an occasional canoe enthusiast.

7 Just east of Leektown, watch for the signs to Bass River State Forest. Lake Absegami, a short drive from the entrance, has wide sandy beaches, tree-shaded picnic tables, barbecue grills, and a boat-launching ramp.

berry bogs, which produce one of the area's most important crops. The berries at harvesttime carpet the bog waters with great patches of red, as the fruit is floated to a conveyor belt for removal to packing plants.

5 Atsion Lake, across the road from a now-vanished furnace town called Atsion—the ironmaster's mansion is all that remains—is a popular summer resort with a wide sandy beach, picnic grounds, and facilities for swimming and boating.

On the way to Medford Lakes, a pretty country road winds through cornfields and orchards in a wooded landscape. The flat countryside slopes gently downward as the road

Growing cranberries

Cranberries were enjoyed by both Indians and Pilgrims, and today are used for juice, relish, and sauce, and are as traditional as turkey for Thanksgiving dinner. The plants, which are grown in bogs, form dense ground covers about a foot high and produce their flowers and fruits on upright stems. In the spring the plants are pruned with a machine that has comblike blades. At harvesttime, after the bog has been flooded enough to just cover the plants, the berries are removed from their stems by machines with rotary beaters and floated to the edge of the bog, where a power-driven conveyor belt loads the fruit onto trucks that carry it to processing plants.

Rotary beater

Floating berries to shore

Loading berries on a conveyor belt

From the southern tip of New Jersey, where one of the nation's best-known and oldest seaside resorts hugs the coastline of both the Atlantic Ocean and Delaware Bay, to the inland forests, lakes, and streams, this part of the state is a mixture of sand and sea, fishing villages, historic towns, and open rural countryside.

Here in South Jersey, as the area is often called, you find quiet communities and the extensive farmlands where the state has gained its rightful reputation as one of the richest fruit- and vegetable-producing areas in the East. With the surrounding water and the cooling breezes, this is a land quite different from the industrial north.

1 Cape May, the narrow strip of New Jersey that stretches southward between the Atlantic Ocean and Delaware Bay, was settled by whalers from New England in the early 1600's. When the whales began to disappear from the local waters before the American Revolution, the people of the town that had grown up on the tip of the cape began to open their homes to visitors, thus starting the tradition of seaside tourism for which Cape May is famous.

These early tourists, attracted by miles of wide sandy beaches, mild weather, and sparkling ocean waters, arrived by boat and, later, as the popularity of the area increased, by train. Sprawling frame hotels, their wide porches facing the ocean, sprang up along the waterfront during the next hundred years, enticing not only business tycoons and their families but also prominent public figures, including five U.S. presidents.

The seaside town expanded as its reputation spread, until the disaster of the "Great Fire" in 1878 destroyed almost every building in town.

As Cape May City was rebuilt, elaborate homes and luxurious hotels, most of them trimmed with the intricate jigsaw work called gingerbread or carpenter's lace that was popular in the Victorian era, replaced the old structures and created a seaside resort of unusual distinction. In 1976 the town was designated a national historic landmark.

Many of the restored homes are now guesthouses and, along with the rambling old hotels, offer accommo-

dations in keeping with the character of the town. One of the handsomest of the guesthouses is the Mainstay Inn, an elegant Victorian mansion that survived the Great Fire. Tours of this and of several other restored homes are offered during most of the year. Self-guided bicycle tours and guided walking tours of the city's historic district are available.

1. The Pink House, one of the best known of Cape May's Victorian houses, was built in 1879. The carpenter's lace trim is an exuberant example of handsaw work.

2 Cape May Point, on the Delaware Bay side of the peninsula, is a quiet summer colony. Unlike the sandy beaches of Cape May City, here there is a rocky shore with stretches of sand dunes and beach grass. Sunbathing, fishing, and shelling are especially popular in this area.

Cape May Lighthouse, which has been standing on the point since 1859, is adjacent to Cape May Point State Park, a small wildlife refuge and nature preserve that offers picnic grounds and seaside nature trails.

Here on the shores of Delaware Bay the renowned Cape May diamonds, semiprecious stones of quartz that have been smoothed and polished by the sand and waves, are often found. Here too is the New Jersey terminal of the Cape May–Lewes, Delaware, ferry, which operates between the two states several times a day.

3 Port Norris and the nearby fishing town of Bivalve are known for their crops of oysters, harvested from the waters around the mouth of the Maurice River. In these towns you can find fishing sheds, small cottages, and several informal restaurants where you can sample the local oysters and crabs.

4 Bridgeton, on the Cohansey River, was founded by Quakers in 1686, and for the next hundred or so years was known for its glass manufacturing plants.

Although the town today has food-processing plants and clothing manufacturing establishments, as well as glass bottle factories, Bridgeton still retains the atmosphere of a small town. In the residential section there are fine examples of colonial, federal, and Victorian homes. Guided walking tours are available here.

The Woodruff Indian Museum, in the Bridgeton Library, has a collection of Indian tools, pots, pipes, and artifacts from this area that date back as far as 10,000 years.

5 Greenwich is a small, picturesque 18th-century town on the Cohansey River. All during the 17th and 18th centuries the town was a busy port, and many of the homes and other buildings from that time are intact today. The Richard Wood Store, on Bacons Neck Road, was built in 1795 and is still operating as a retail shop. The nearby mansion, built in the same year for Richard Wood, is open to visitors from April to November.

Greenwich was the site of a tea-burning incident in 1774, when the captain of the brig *Greyhound*, which had been turned away at Philadelphia, sailed up the Cohansey and stored his cargo of tea in the home of a Tory sympathizer. When the townspeople learned of it, they staged an "Indian" dance, raided the house, and burned the tea.

6 On the way to Parvin State Park you drive through flat farmlands, with fields of corn, soybeans, and vegetables crops on each side of the road. The park, with its thousand acres of forest land, includes two lakes and was the site of a prisoner of war camp during World War II. Today it is a popular vacationland, with pleasant facilities for swimming, boating, fishing, picnicking, and camping. A group of small cabins on the shores of Thundergust Lake are available for rent.

One section of the park is maintained as a natural area for such wildlife as white-tailed deer, opossums, foxes, and raccoons. During the migrating season, from mid-April to mid-May, and from mid-August to early October, the forest is alive with songbirds, including the eastern goldfinch, the state bird. Eight miles of well-marked trails wind through the woods.

From Centerton to Vineland and then south to Millville, the route goes through the heart of New Jersey's famous farmlands. Tempting stands along the road offer fresh local fruits and vegetables in season.

7 Millville is on the southern end of Union Lake, making it an ideal summer vacation spot for those who enjoy swimming, boating, and fishing. The town grew up around an iron foundry and a glass factory. At the Victorian village of Wheaton in Millville you can visit a reconstructed glass factory and watch a glass-blowing demonstration. Also at the village are a restored schoolhouse, a railroad station where you can buy a ticket for a short ride on an old-fashioned train, and the Wheaton Museum, which has a large collection of early American glass. The village is closed on New Year's, Easter, Thanksgiving, and Christmas days.

6. Baby white-tailed deer, like the one-week-old fawn shown here in a wild flower meadow, are a seasonal addition to the natural area at Parvin State Park.

About four miles east of Millville is The Holly Farm, a 16-acre tract planted with some 4,500 holly trees of several different varieties. Holly from this grove is shipped to all parts of the United States during the holidays.

8 Shortly after you cross the Tuckahoe River you come to the northern edge of Belleplain State Forest. Lake Nummy within the preserve has fine beaches with bathhouses and lifeguards, picnic groves, and camping sites. Nearby there are horses for those who wish to explore the riding trails that wander through the thick stands of spruce, hemlock, and pine. There are also nature trails.

9 At the small farming community of Petersburg is the northern end of the Great Cedar Swamp. Buried within the swamp waters lies an ancient forest of fallen cedar trees. In colonial days these trees were "mined" and used for shingles. The water-cured wood was so durable that the shingles were almost indestructible. Although cedar logs are still buried there, they are no longer of commercial value and are left completely undisturbed.

As you approach the sea, you begin to notice the salt air breezes. At Townsends Inlet a high narrow bridge takes you across to the shore road. With the Atlantic Ocean surf on the left and the calm marshy waters of the inland waterway on the right, the view as you cross the bridge is spectacular. Ocean Drive follows a string of islands to the south.

10 The Stone Harbor Bird Sanctuary is an area of scrubby cedars, holly trees, and bayberry thickets. Some 6,000 birds spend the summer here.

Also found here is the cattle egret, a native of Africa that made its way to this continent only about 30 years ago. Unlike the other egrets, which feed in the water on fish, the cattle egret searches for insects that have been stirred up by cattle. They can often be seen feeding on the backs of grazing livestock.

As you continue southward you come to several turnoffs to the beaches.

10. The loons, grebes, herons, and ibises that summer at the Stone Harbor Bird Sanctuary feed in these nearby marshes, viewed from the Wetlands Institute tower. The best time to see them is before sunset as they return to their nests.

Delmarva and More

Bountiful waters, sandy shores, and a full measure of farmlands studded with historic landmarks

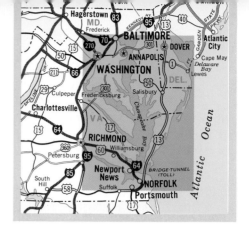

The Delmarva Peninsula, *between Chesapeake and Delaware bays and the Atlantic Ocean, includes most of Delaware and the Eastern Shore of Maryland and Virginia. This area, as well as that on the western shore of the Chesapeake, has some of the finest farmlands on the East Coast. The region also abounds with sandy beaches, salt marshes, harbors, coves, and inlets, providing splendid vacationlands for untold thousands as well as ideal habitats for a multitude of bird and animal life. The surrounding waters are abundant with some of the world's finest seafood, including Chincoteague oysters and the famous Maryland blue crabs.*

Evident in this countryside is the quiet atmosphere that has always prevailed in the area. The small towns and villages, the seaports and farming communities have changed relatively little since the 18th century, when many of them were founded.

Also on this tour are places where the first colonists settled and our future government was formed.

1 Baltimore, Maryland's largest city, has been an important seaport since the 18th century, when tobacco crops from nearby plantations and grain from the fields to the west were shipped from its harbor to all parts of the world. Today the harbor is still one of the busiest in the United States.

The area surrounding the Inner Harbor, which has been squared off and bordered by parks and promenades, marks the hub of the city's cultural and commercial activities. Buildings clustered around the waterfront include the Maryland Science Center, the Aquarium, the Baltimore Maritime Museum, and the pentagonal tower that houses the World Trade Center. Permanently docked in the harbor and open to visitors (except from October to May) is the frigate U.S.S. *Constellation,* the oldest ship in the U.S. Navy, which was launched in Baltimore in 1797. There are also tour boats from the Inner Harbor that will take you to Fort McHenry.

Fort McHenry, named for a Marylander who was an aide to Gen. George Washington, is a national shrine and monument set in a tree-shaded park. It still guards the entrance to Baltimore's harbor as it did on the night of September 13, 1814, when Francis Scott Key saw the red glare of the British bombardment. The 30- by 42-foot 15-star, 15-stripe flag that "was still there" the next morning—the inspiration for Key's "The Star-Spangled Banner"—was made by Mary Pickersgill for Fort McHenry. A replica of it still flies over the fort today.

As you enter the park, which can be reached by way of Key Highway and Fort Avenue, you come first to the visitor center, where a 15-minute film depicting the famous battle is shown. The fort is closed on Christmas and New Year's days.

2 Annapolis, Maryland's capital and the home of the U.S. Naval Academy, is a handsome city with much of its colonial heritage still intact. The imposing brick State House, built in 1772, dominates the city from its hilltop park in State Circle. Serving

2. Skipjack oyster dredgers race during the annual Chesapeake Appreciation Days to symbolize the era when old-time bay watermen raced to reach port first and claim the highest prices for their catch. The 19th-century craft are indigenous to the Chesapeake. By law, only sailing vessels are allowed to dredge for oysters in the bay.

SPECIAL FEATURES			
ROAD GUIDE	━━━	HIGHLIGHT	1
STATE PARKS			
With Campsites ▲ Without Campsites △		SCHEDULED AIRLINE STOPS	✈
RECREATION AREAS			
With Campsites ▲ Without Campsites △		MILITARY AIRPORTS	⚞
SELECTED REST AREAS	✕	OTHER AIRPORTS	✕
POINTS OF INTEREST	⊡	BOAT RAMPS	◢

ROAD CLASSIFICATION

CONTROLLED ACCESS HIGHWAYS (Interstate interchange numbers are mileposts.) Divided **5** Undivided

TOLL HIGHWAYS   Interchanges

OTHER DIVIDED HIGHWAYS

PAVED HIGHWAYS

LOCAL ROAD In unfamiliar areas inquire locally before using these roads Paved Gravel Dirt

MILEAGE

MILEAGE BETWEEN TOWNS AND JUNCTIONS 3 ⊿ 4   MILEAGE BETWEEN DOTS ● 35 ●

SCALE

ONE INCH 18 MILES   0 5 10   20

ONE INCH 29 KILOMETERS   0 5 10   20 32

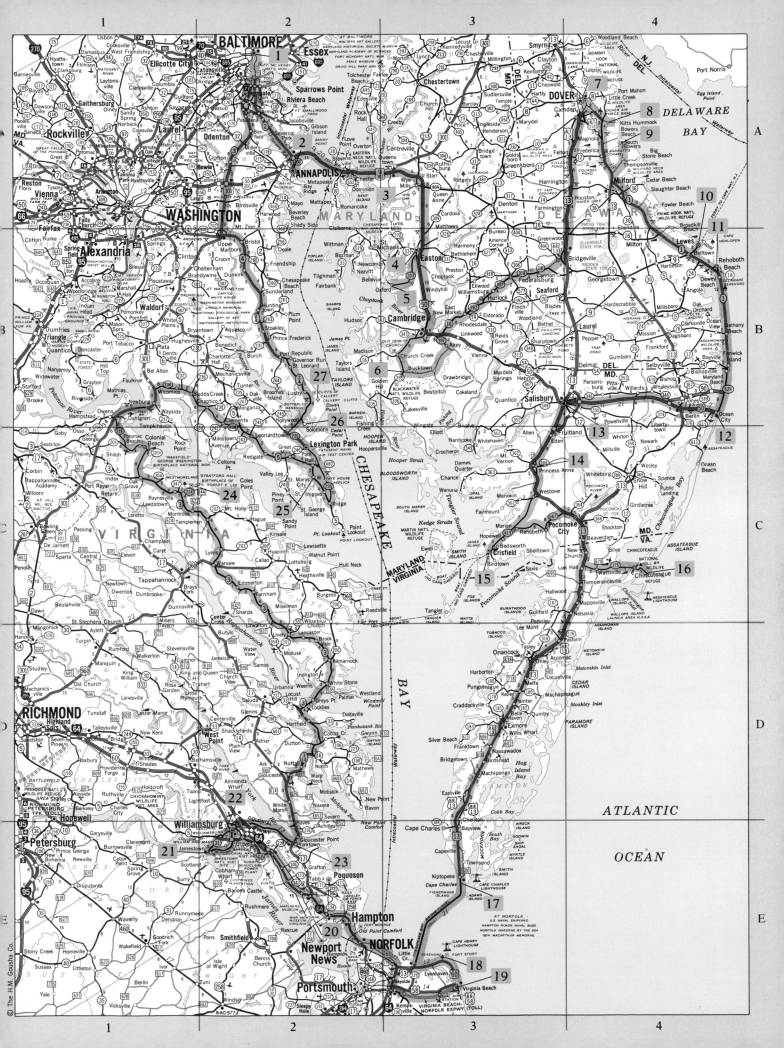

today as Maryland's capitol, the historic structure was used as the U.S. Capitol from November 1783 to August 1784. Guided tours are given daily except on Christmas Day.

Annapolis is a delightful place to walk. The narrow streets, many of them with well-restored 18th-century houses, fan out from State and Church circles at the top of the town. The National Historic Landmark District, often called a museum without walls, includes several handsome colonial buildings open to visitors. The Paca House, one of the loveliest, and its 18th-century gardens have been faithfully restored.

Market Space, lined with shops and tempting restaurants, faces the town's harbor, one of the most popular ports for pleasure craft along the Atlantic coast. Sight-seeing tours of the harbor and the surrounding waters are given daily during the summer and on weekends in May and September.

As soon as you cross the twin-spanned Chesapeake Bay Bridge (officially, the William Preston Lane, Jr. Bridge, named for a Maryland governor), which rises to a height of 186 feet above the main shipping channel to Baltimore harbor, the landscape changes. Here on the Delmarva Peninsula, the countryside is flat, with miles of level farmlands, salt-water marshes, tidal rivers, and brackish streams and inlets. The tidelands are a paradise for the coastal ecologists and geomorphologists.

3 The colonial village of Wye Mills developed around a gristmill that ground flour for Gen. George Washington's army. The mill still produces flour and cornmeal.

Here too is the Wye Oak, a white oak said to be some 450 years old. The white oak (*Quercus alba*) is the official tree of Maryland.

4 Near the headwaters of the Tred Avon River is the town of Easton. Here in 1682 a small group of settlers put up a plain wooden meetinghouse, which is still in use. A little brick courthouse, built in 1712, was replaced in 1794 by a large brick building that is used today as the Talbot County Court House. It is situated on Washington Street in a park of carefully tended lawns, gnarled cedars of Lebanon, and boxwood plants.

A Sail to St. Michaels

The cruise boat *Annapolitan* sails across the Chesapeake on all-day excursions from Annapolis to St. Michaels, a charming colonial town on Maryland's Eastern Shore.

At St. Michaels you can visit the Chesapeake Bay Maritime Museum, a complex of 12 buildings grouped around a parklike green.

Also at the museum is the old six-sided Hooper Strait Lighthouse, standing on its stilts at the river's edge. Anchored nearby is a Chesapeake Bay skipjack, used by bay watermen for oyster dredging.

A walk around St. Mary's Square will take you through the little town's most picturesque section, where you will see one of the best collections of 18th- and 19th-century houses on the Eastern Shore.

While you are here, be sure to sample the area's famous steamed blue crabs at one of the town's small but enticing restaurants.

Cruises do not run from Labor Day to Memorial Day except on weekends in September and May.

Wide, shady streets, handsome 18th- and 19th-century houses, and a quiet atmosphere make Easton one of the area's most attractive towns.

3. The Wye Oak, some 95 feet tall, is one of the largest white oaks in the United States.

5 Route 333 leading to Oxford, one of the most interesting colonial towns on the Eastern Shore, winds through rural countryside to the Tred Avon River. The town, just upstream from the bay, was designated an official port of entry in 1694 and for many years rivaled Annapolis as the busiest port in the Maryland colony.

The tree-lined main thoroughfare, with its handsome restored houses, leads to the waterfront. There you can find the dock of the little Tred Avon Ferry, which connects Oxford with Bellevue across the river.

Along the road to Cambridge there is a series of dairy farms and great stretches of fields planted with corn, potatoes, and soybeans. Chicken farms also are found here, and you can see red-tailed hawks circling endlessly overhead, perhaps with an eye out for a stray hen.

A well-paved country road meanders through flat open countryside to the little crossroads of Church Creek, where the productive farmlands give way to salt marshes and untouched wooded wilderness.

6 The entrance to Blackwater National Wildlife Refuge, which is easily missed, is on the east side of the road. The visitor center with its wildlife displays is well worth a visit.

The five-mile Wildlife Drive takes you through the refuge and along the edge of the marsh to an observation tower overlooking the Blackwater River and the surrounding bogs.

During the migrating season, which begins in September and reaches its peak by late November, as many as 100,000 Canada geese on their way south come here to rest and feed. Some 15,000 of them stay for the winter, returning in spring to their nesting grounds in Canada.

Among the other birds found at the refuge are bald eagles and red cockaded woodpeckers, both endangered species, whistling swans, ducks, loons, herons, egrets, vultures, gulls, and a long list of songbirds, including the Baltimore oriole, the state bird. Other wildlife found in the refuge include foxes, deer, otters, muskrats, and the Delmarva fox squirrel, an endangered species.

The visitor center is closed on Christmas Day and on weekends from Memorial Day to Labor Day.

Bucktown Road, leading away from the refuge, is a twisting country route past planted fields, patches of woods, and occasional farmhouses. As the route turns northeast and leads into Delaware, you drive past small towns, manufacturing centers, food-processing places, farming communities, and chicken farms.

A chicken, in fact, is Delaware's official state bird—the Blue Hen chicken, a breed that supposedly produces fine gamecocks.

7   Dover, the capital of Delaware, was planned by William Penn in 1683. He chose this name for the town because of his fondness for Dover on England's Channel coast.

Dover's historic Green, where the 18th-century Old State House still stands along with several other 18th- and 19th-century buildings, brings to the town a distinctive dignity and charm. The nearby complex of government buildings on Capitol Square blends attractively with the old houses on the Green.

South of Dover, the road passes the Dover Air Force Base, headquarters for the shipping of military cargo and home of the largest U.S. Air Force wing of C-5 aircraft.

8   Just beyond the base, on Kitts Hummock Road, you come upon the restored John Dickinson Mansion, a lovely old brick building. It was the plantation home of Samuel Dickinson, whose son, John, became known as the Penman of the Revolution because of the vast number of articles and pamphlets he wrote espousing independence for America.

The mansion grounds are planted with a variety of trees, including the American holly (*Ilex opaca*), the state tree. Closed Mondays and holidays.

9   Delaware's Island Field Museum at South Bowers was inhabited by Indians of the Middle Woodland Period. These Indians traded with tribes as far away as the Great Lakes, exchanging shells from the Atlantic Ocean for stone objects and other goods. Exhibits include Indian burial sites dating from A.D. 740 and a collection of artifacts that were found in the region.

As the road continues southward toward the town of Lewes (pronounced *loo*-is), it once again traverses the flat, cultivated croplands

6. A great blue heron takes shelter beside a clump of marsh grass at the Blackwater Wildlife Refuge during a spring rainstorm.

so characteristic of the Delmarva Peninsula. Interspersed among the fields are vegetable- and chicken-processing plants, making the area an important East Coast source for these products.

10   Settled by the Dutch in 1631, Lewes was the first colony in Delaware. "Delaware's Plymouth," it is sometimes called. Its harbor on Delaware Bay is protected by the sand dunes of Cape Henlopen to the east.

Cape Henlopen State Park is a sandy hook of land known for its so-called walking dunes, which form and re-form as the seasons change.

Swimming, picnicking, camping, boating, and surf fishing are all popular here, and there are bicycle paths, two nature trails, and a fishing pier in the park. Kite-flying contests are held here every year on Good Friday.

11   South of Lewes is the fashionable resort town of Rehoboth Beach. Although in the mid-19th century it was the site of a Methodist Camp Meeting, the area soon became popular with vacationers.

Rehoboth Beach is known for its wide, sandy beach and its boardwalk where several luxurious hotels face the ocean. The city is virtually deserted from September to May, except for an occasional homeowner who ventures to the shore during the colder months.

The road south goes through the Delaware Seashore State Park, a narrow eight-mile-long strip of sand and marsh that separates the Atlantic Ocean and Rehoboth Bay.

12   Crossing into Maryland, you come to Ocean City, at the end of a narrow coastal barrier strip. It is the state's only resort on the Atlantic coast. Here you come upon a wide, three-mile-long boardwalk that follows the superb beach of sparkling white sand. Deep-sea fishing is a favorite sport off this shore, with white marlin the favorite catch.

10. American beach grass is planted in rows to stabilize the sand dunes at Cape Henlopen State Park. The lighthouse in the distance marks the entrance to Delaware Bay.

95

16. On Assateague Island a pond reflects the scrubby vegetation typical of the area. The wild ponies that graze here are frequently seen from the main road and from the island's winding drives. The annual roundup is shown above.

13 Although the town of Salisbury was settled in the early 18th century, hardly a trace of the city's early days exists because of two devastating fires, one in 1860 and a second in 1886.

One fine example of architecture from the past is the Poplar Hill Mansion at 117 Elizabeth Street, which dates from 1800. Closed except on Sundays from 1 to 4 P.M.

14 About 13 miles south of Salisbury is Princess Anne, a charming little town of white colonial houses with picket fences and boxwood-bordered gardens.

The Teackle Mansion was built by Littleton Teackle, an associate of Thomas Jefferson. The building was copied from a Scottish manor house and is now on the National Register of Historic Places. Closed except on Sundays from 2 to 4 P.M.

15 Crisfield, near the tip of Maryland's Eastern Shore, is an old fishing village of wharves, fish-processing plants, and small, undistinguished-looking restaurants that serve delectable dishes of locally caught seafood. The town is best known as the gateway to Maryland's Smith Island and Virginia's Tangier Island in the Chesapeake Bay.

A few almost-forgotten villages—Hopewell, Marion, Rehobeth—are scattered along the winding road from Crisfield to Pocomoke City, a processing and shipping center for the nearby farmlands.

As you cross into Virginia, you begin the drive down a narrow sandy stretch of the Delmarva Peninsula, which tapers to an end at Cape Charles, about 60 miles to the south.

This is an appealing area of small coastal towns, on both ocean and bay, where summer visitors come for the beaches, the harbors, the yacht

Cruise to Smith Island

Cruises to Smith Island, 12 miles offshore, leave from Crisfield every day at 12:30 P.M.

Capt. John Smith discovered the little island in 1608 and gave it his name. About 50 years later, in 1657, a group of English settlers came here, and today most of the island's 800 or so inhabitants are direct descendants of the original settlers.

Fishing, with one or two exceptions, is the only industry. So peace loving are these people whose lives are ruled by wind and wave that there is no need for a local government, a police department, or a jail.

The three villages—Ewell, where the boat docks, Rhodes Point, and Tylerton—have remained almost unchanged for the last hundred years.

Meals are served, family style, at three places on the island, and the abundance of seafood found in local waters is reflected in the menus that are offered.

The cruise does not run from October to May.

basins, and the fleets of fishing boats ready to take passengers for a day's excursion to offshore waters.

16 Barrier islands built of sand thrown up by Atlantic storms are strung all along the Atlantic coast here. These are fragile ecologic environments that could be easily washed away. Two of the best known are Chincoteague and Assateague, which are located at the end of a 10-mile stretch of winding, paved highway that crosses marshes, bridges, and causeways and goes through a desolate tidal landscape.

Chincoteague, closer to the mainland, has been known for its abundance of shellfish and other seafood since the early 1600's. The little town is mainly involved in the harvesting and packing of shellfish. Chincoteague oysters, which have brought fame to the island, are considered to be among the finest in the world.

A popular annual festival here is the so-called Pony Penning, when the wild ponies on Assateague are herded across the narrow channel to Chincoteague. Here they are penned, and some of the foals are sold at auction. The following day the herd is driven back to Assateague, where these handsome buff-colored, black-spotted ponies roam free.

The ponies are thought to be descendants of a herd of horses that was being taken to Peru by a Spanish galleon several hundred years ago.

The ship was wrecked, and the horses swam ashore and survived. They are small because for centuries their diet has consisted entirely of salt-marsh grasses.

Along with the ponies on Assateague, there are ducks, snow geese, herons, egrets, and ibis. When these fly north for the summer, shorebirds predominate.

Also found here are the helpful small white cattle egrets that perch on the ponies and dine on bothersome bugs.

On Assateague are herds of white-tailed deer, otters, muskrats, and sikas, small oriental elks that were introduced to the island several years ago.

Well-marked drives circle ponds and coves, skirt the marshes, and wind through the woods. There are also bicycle paths, guided nature walks, and bridle paths.

17 At Cape Charles, on the southern tip of Virginia's Eastern Shore, you come to the Bay Bridge-Tunnel, a 17.6-mile-long complex that crosses the outer part of Chesapeake Bay. The ramp onto the bridge turns sharply to the right, giving you an opportunity to see the long expanse of raised roadway that seems to stretch across the water into space. When the bridge comes to a shipping channel, the road drops down into a tunnel, then returns to the surface and continues over the water. There is a second tunnel at the point where the route swings southward, and at its exit you can stop for a snack, to fish, or to admire the view.

18 At Seashore State Park, hardwoods and a mixture of pines fill the forests, and along the watery marshes there are stands of bald cypress draped with Spanish moss and ringed with cypress knees—so called because of their buttresslike stumps. Several of the 58 different kinds of oak varieties that grow in Tidewater Virginia are found here.

An abundance of wildlife inhabits the park, including songbirds, otters, muskrats, and white-tailed deer. Raised boardwalks thread through the woods and along the bogs. Camping, picnicking, boating, and fishing are permitted.

From the park you can see the first U.S. lighthouse, an octagonal tower built on top of the tallest dune on Cape Henry to warn ships away from the treacherous shoals.

19 Virginia Beach, with a shoreline extending along the Chesapeake and the Atlantic, has 28 miles of wide, sandy coastline. The town's two-mile boardwalk, the surf, the nearby camping sites, the boat-launching ramps, and the fishing tempt vacationers all year long.

On Pleasure House Road, on the west side of the town, is the Adam Thoroughgood House. Built in 1636, this simple structure is said to be the oldest brick house in America. At the back of the house is a formal kitchen garden where boxwoods edge the beds of herbs. The house is closed on Mondays and on Christmas and New Year's days.

20 The city of Norfolk is situated on one of the world's great natural harbors. Here the waters of the James, Elizabeth, and Nansemond rivers flow into the Chesapeake, forming the channel of Hampton Roads. In these waters the famous battle between the *Monitor* and *Merrimac* took place in 1862.

The city, settled in 1682, has been an important seaport since colonial times. Today it is the headquarters of the U.S. Navy's Atlantic Fleet.

The Norfolk Botanical Gardens, known as the Gardens-by-the-Sea, are a 175-acre area of plantings that include thousands of camellias, azaleas, rhododendrons, perennials, and roses. Some 150 species of birds, including the cardinal, the state bird of Virginia, have been spotted here.

20. Azaleas border winding paths through the pine groves in the Gardens-by-the-Sea. They bloom in early spring, when the white dogwood adds its flowers to the annual spectacle.

21. The replica of Fort James at Jamestown Festival Park, built on a bank overlooking the James River, includes some 20 buildings. Stocks, in foreground, were used for discipline.

Small boats carry visitors along a network of canals that winds through the gardens, and motorized trams take passengers along the 12 miles of roadway.

In April there is an annual Azalea Festival, when a queen, usually the daughter of an internationally prominent diplomat, is crowned.

21 Jamestown, the first permanent settlement in the New World, was founded in 1607 by 104 adventurous souls who arrived on the swampy banks of the James River after a long voyage from England on three tiny ships—the *Discovery*, the *Godspeed*, and the *Susan Constant*.

Under the leadership of Capt. John Smith, the colonists formed the first democratic government in America and erected the first statehouse.

The colony survived until 1699, when, after several seasons of crop failure and disease among the colonists, a general revolt divided the community. Malcontents burned much of the town, and the government was removed to Williamsburg.

Today all that remains of the first American settlement is the old church tower and the foundations of several of the buildings. The Jamestown Island Park preserves these vestiges of the original colony. The park, which extends from the information center to the banks of the James River, is closed on Christmas and New Year's days.

About a mile before you reach the original site is the Jamestown Festival Park. Here replicas of the three ships that brought the original colonists are anchored in the James. Nearby a primitive village has been built to show the kind of settlement these first adventurers lived in. Closed Christmas and New Year's days.

22 Williamsburg is undoubtedly one of the nation's best known and most beautifully reconstructed and restored colonial towns. At the eastern end of the town was the Capitol, where George Washington, Thomas Jefferson, George Mason, Patrick Henry, and the other giants of their generation met. On the Palace Green was the stately Governor's Palace. Both buildings have been reconstructed on their original sites, along with some 50 other buildings, all returned to their original appearance by the Colonial Williamsburg Foundation.

At the information center tickets to the buildings are available. Buses leave every few minutes from the center, stopping at the various buildings and exhibit areas throughout the historic district.

23 The drive along Colonial Parkway from Williamsburg to Yorktown meanders through woods, which are spectacular in spring when the dogwood (*Cornus florida*), the official state tree, is in bloom. On a cliff overlooking the York River is the town where, on October 19, 1781, the British general Charles Cornwallis surrendered and the hostilities of the Revolutionary War ended.

In the old part of this charming town, the site of the famous Yorktown siege, is the Grace Episcopal Church, a small building constructed in 1697 of marl, a combination of limestone and oyster shells. It has been preserved, as have many small white clapboard houses on the narrow streets nearby. The church and sev-

22. The gardens behind the Governor's Palace reflect the formality of those in 18th-century England. Topiaries along the central path create an elegant *allée*. Flower beds provide seasonal color, such as this spring show of bulbs. In the cabinetmaker's workshop demonstrations of colonial woodworking skills are given by experts who have been trained in this craft. Thirty-six different colonial crafts are shown in the exhibit area.

eral of the houses are open to visitors. The houses, however, are closed during the winter.

The site of the battle of Yorktown is now a national park. Tours of the battlefield leave from the National Park Service Visitor Center. The center is closed on Christmas Day.

The Yorktown Victory Center, at the opposite end of town, is a large brick complex overlooking the York River. It was built to commemorate the great events that led to the creation of the United States. Among the displays are a museum of the history of the area, a film telling the story of the great struggle, and a re-creation of a colonial street. There are nature trails, picnic areas, and a replica of an 18th-century army camp in the woods overlooking the river. Closed on Christmas and New Year's days.

24 On the Potomac is Stratford Hall Plantation, built by Thomas Lee in the 1720's. Here Robert E. Lee, commander-in-chief of all the Confederate armies, was born.

The Great House, as the main building has always been called, and its several dependencies have been carefully restored, the gardens brought back to their original beauty, and the stables and barns put into working condition.

Although open to visitors as a historic shrine, Stratford Hall is also once again a working plantation, with a herd of Black Angus cattle and several horses. Corn, grain, sorghum, and other crops are grown in the fields, and the gristmill that Thomas Lee installed on the bluffs overlooking the Potomac is again producing flour and cornmeal.

The southwest dependency contains relics found on the plantation. Some of these belonged to early Indian settlers; others were dug from the 15-million-year-old Miocene compaction of Stratford's "clifts"—the bluffs along the river.

Just beyond Stratford Hall is Wakefield, the birthplace of George Washington. Nothing of the original plantation—then called Pope's Creek Plantation—remains, but a typical colonial farm has been constructed on the point of land where the Washington home stood. Wakefield is now a national monument. It is closed on Christmas and New Year's days.

Shellfish of the Chesapeake

Some of the finest shellfish in the United States is found along the shores of Maryland and Virginia. Here in Chesapeake Bay and the immediate offshore waters, the salt water from the sea and fresh water from the rivers blend to create a remarkably productive environment for mollusks and crustaceans.

The blue crab, a member of the family of so-called swimming crabs, is the most important of the commercial crustaceans and is usually served steamed. The common oyster, best known of the bivalves, has brought fame to Chincoteague Island, where it is abundant. Two kinds of clams are found in these waters—the soft-shell kind, which is small, delicate, and usually eaten raw, and the quahog, or hard-shell clam, the one used in clam chowder. The edible blue mussel, found on rocks and wharf pilings, is an important part of the Chesapeake commerical catch.

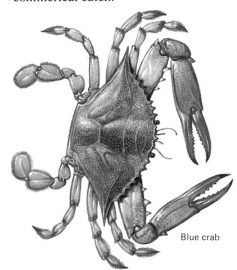
Blue crab

Common oyster

Soft-shell clam

Quahog, or hard-shell clam

Blue mussel

The drive north, across the Potomac to Newburg, Maryland, is a scenic one of gentle, rolling hills and forests. As the road turns south in what is called Southern Maryland, it goes through the state's major tobacco-growing area. Here are the carefully cultivated fields, the curing barns, and the machines that plant and harvest the crops.

25 St. Mary's (now called St. Marys City) was Maryland's first settlement and first capital. Although nothing of the original town remains, the old State House has been reconstructed near its original foundation, and Trinity Church, which dates from 1829, is built with the bricks of the old State House. The State House is closed on Mondays from November to April and on Christmas and New Year's days.

26 As you cross the Governor Thomas Johnson Bridge, a high structure spanning the Patuxent River, you suddenly see the picturesque fishing village of Solomons far below on a small island just upriver from the Chesapeake. A right turn from the bridge takes you over a causeway to the village. Solomons is known for its fleets of fishing boats and for the abundance of seafood found in its waters.

The Calvert Marine Museum in the old Solomons School House has exhibits featuring the local maritime history, several kinds of fishing boats, and displays of local fossils. The museum is closed on Thanksgiving, Christmas, and New Year's days.

27 About a mile south of Lusby, on the shores of the Chesapeake, is Calvert Cliffs State Park, which has clay bluffs that rise as much as 120 feet above the bay. These are formations from the Miocene epoch and are filled with marine fossils. Many visitors come to search the beaches for fossils, but digging on the cliffs is not permitted.

At Upper Marlboro, where Route 4 joins U.S. Route 301, are the Marlboro tobacco sheds. Tobacco auctions are held here from mid-April through June. Visitors are invited to attend and hear the auctioneers' musical lingo as one of the most important crops grown around the Chesapeake Bay is sold to buyers from all over the world.

Beauty on the Blue Ridge

Virginians revere the Blue Ridge Mountains and the lovely valleys on either side

In the Shenandoah Valley are the Luray Caverns, well known for the splendor of their limestone formations. To the southwest are Virginia's rolling farmlands and fruit-growing country, which gradually give way to high peaks and ridges as you continue toward North Carolina and an area of almost unpopulated mountain wilderness.

The Blue Ridge Mountains hold much of America's history in their wooded terrain. Early pioneers made their homes in these hills, leaving their imprint on such historic places as Culpeper, Charlottesville, and Front Royal.

The Blue Ridge Parkway south of Roanoke weaves through the gently rolling hills and grassy meadows of the Blue Ridge Plateau, a highland rich in natural beauty and pioneer history. Numerous scenic overlooks marked by parkway mileage posts present magnificent vistas of seemingly endless lowlands, valleys, and mountains. Frontier museums along the way offer a sample of pioneer life.

At Laurel Springs, North Carolina, the parkway climbs into higher elevations, revealing spectacular views and popular recreational areas. Near Doughton Park the route swings northward to the beautiful Virginia state parks and the farmlands in the Jefferson National Forest.

1 At the southern end of the Shenandoah Valley, between the Blue Ridge Mountains and the Alleghenies, lies the city of Roanoke. Because of the rapid progress it made after World War II, Roanoke is called the Star City of the South. This is symbolized by a 100-foot-high neon star atop nearby Mill Mountain. Also found here are a wild flower garden and a children's zoo where the animals live in Mother Goose Land.

The Roanoke Valley overlook, on the west about six miles along the parkway, offers a fine view of the city of Roanoke.

2 The area known as Smart View is named for its "right smart view" of the pastoral lowlands and valleys that skirt the Blue Ridge foothills. A picturesque roadway leads uphill from the parkway to what once was the Trail family's home, a one-room cabin built of hand-hewn logs in the 1890's. Typical of much earlier frontier housing, the chimney is constructed of stones and red clay that was gathered from nearby slopes. Hiking trails wind through meadows and forests veiled with a profusion of wild flowers a good part of the year; the adjacent picnic area is set in a bower of flame azaleas and dogwood (*Cornus florida*), the state tree. The lilting warble of a variety of songbirds, including the meadowlark, the crested flycatcher, and the state's official bird, the cardinal, enhances this 500-acre natural sanctuary.

Of the several scenic overlooks between Smart View and Mabry Mill, the one at Milepost 168 is particularly interesting. Here from a ridge on Rocky Knob Mountain you can see a broad sweep of the Blue Ridge crest: from this great divide, the waters flowing west find their way into the Gulf of Mexico; streams running east cascade down the Blue Ridge and flow on to the Atlantic.

3 Set in an idyllic clearing on the mossy banks of a stream-fed pond, Mabry Mill is a superb example of the kind of multipurpose industry that

1. From the overlook atop Roanoke Mountain, on the Blue Ridge Parkway, the view sweeps across the town of Roanoke nestled in a wide basin. Beyond are the Allegheny Mountains whose more distant ranges form a soft wash of blue fading into the sky.

SPECIAL FEATURES

ROAD GUIDE	HIGHLIGHT	**1**
STATE PARKS With Campsites Without Campsites	SKI AREAS	
RECREATION AREAS With Campsites Without Campsites	SCHEDULED AIRLINE STOPS	
SELECTED REST AREAS	OTHER AIRPORTS	
POINTS OF INTEREST	BOAT RAMPS	

ROAD CLASSIFICATION

CONTROLLED ACCESS HIGHWAYS Interstate interchange numbers are mileposts. Divided **5** Undivided Interchanges

OTHER DIVIDED HIGHWAYS

PAVED HIGHWAYS

LOCAL ROADS In unfamiliar areas inquire locally before using these roads Paved Gravel Dirt

MILEAGE

MILEAGE BETWEEN TOWNS AND JUNCTIONS 3 4 MILEAGE BETWEEN DOTS 35

SCALE

ONE INCH 18 MILES 0 5 10 15

ONE INCH 29 KILOMETERS 0 5 10 15 24

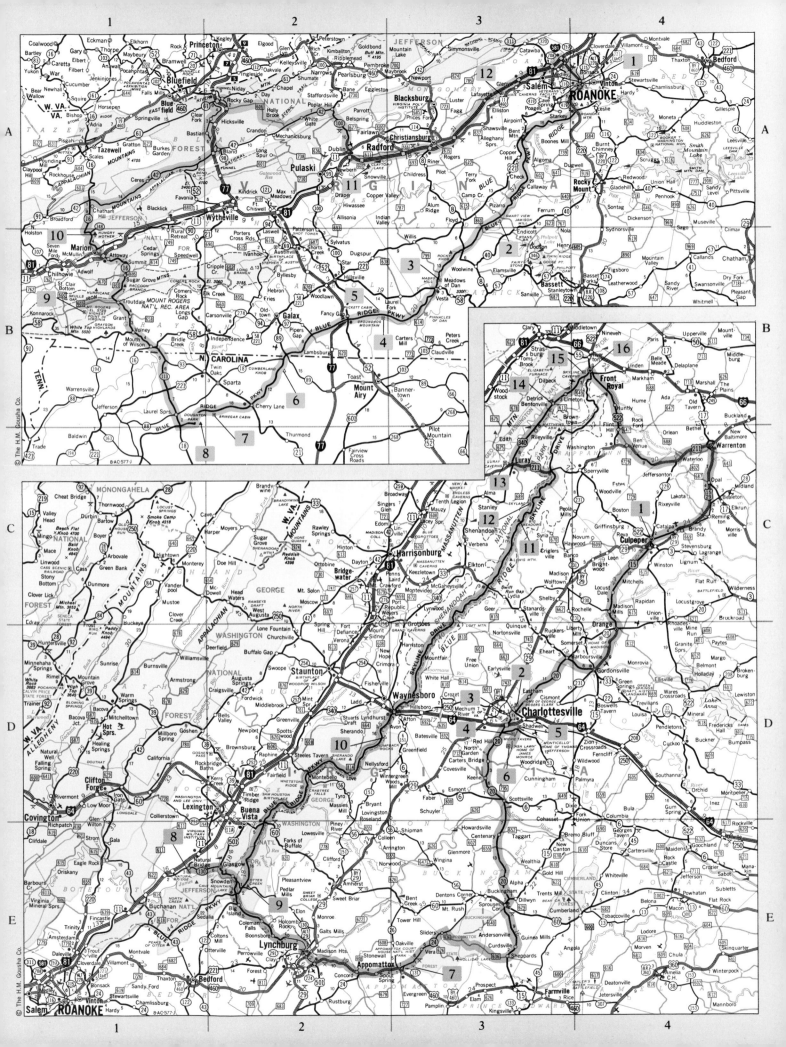

was indispensible to mountain people's survival. From 1910 to 1935 E. B. Mabry served his neighbors with a combination grist and saw mill, a blacksmith shop, and a reputation as the "man who could fix most anything." The old mill wheel still grinds corn and buckwheat, and a smithy works the forge. On weekends during October you can see sorghum molasses and apple butter being made. Placards along a self-guiding trail illustrate other pioneer enterprises, including shoemaking and soapmaking. A National Park Service restaurant features pancakes made from the mill-ground flour.

4 Groundhog Mountain was named in honor of these once-shy forest creatures. However, groundhogs quickly multiplied and grew fat on the abundance of vegetation that sprang up after settlers cleared the mountain slopes for farming. Now these animals prefer to burrow near their food supply and, nibbling away, are a more common sight along the parkway's roadside than on Groundhog Mountain.

The mountain's tower—a wooden lookout designed to resemble an old

3. The overshot waterwheel at Mabry Mill was a source of power as water flowed from a storage pond through a sluice into the vanes around the wheel. The water then tumbled into the holding pond. The lower section of the mill housed a jointer and a jigsaw.

tobacco-drying barn—provides a magnificent view of the plateau and Piedmont. Groundhog's 3,030-foot summit also features an exhibit of three types of traditional fences— snake, buck, and post-and-rail—that border some pastures in the region.

5 Less than a mile from the entrance to Groundhog Mountain's summit is the road to Puckett Cabin,

home of Mrs. Olena Hawks Puckett from 1865 until her death in 1939 at the age of 102. A skillful midwife, Mrs. Puckett is credited with having successfully delivered more than a thousand babies during her career. Ironically, not one of her own 24 children lived past infancy. This one-room cabin stands as a monument to her courageous spirit and devotion.

Rail fences

To enclose 10 acres of farmland with a rail fence took about an acre of forest. But these fences were popular with Virginia's settlers who had an abundance of timber to be cleared. They built most of their fences with chestnut; for the rails, tree limbs and logs were cut to length, usually 11 feet, and split with a sledge and wedge. Round poles were also used. Three types of fences used in Virginia are shown here. The rarest of these today is the buck, which was used on ground too rough and uneven for other fencing; the most

commonly seen in the Virginian countryside is the snake: this zigzag fence was lavish in its use of wood, but it was quick to build, and easy to take down and move. Snake fences were often braced against wind with a pair of cross stakes set at the corners, or locks. The most practical, and the most laborious, fence to build was the post-and-rail. The posts had to be slotted for the rails and set deep in the ground, and the rails had to be tapered at the ends to interlock. This fence made the most efficient use of the timber.

The buck fence, made by bracing short, heavy rails against each other, lent itself to very rough land.

The zigzagging snake fence was easiest to put up or take down; it also required the most timber.

The straight post-and-rail fences were both sturdy and economical, but time-consuming to build.

The parkway continues to ramble through picturesque farmland, apple orchards, and dense hardwood forests that are illuminated in early June by the blooms of countless white rhododendrons.

From an overlook at Milepost 202.8, just beyond Fancy Gap, Mount Airy, site of the largest open-face granite quarry in the United States, is revealed in the distance.

The mountain country becomes higher and more sparsely settled when you cross the border into North Carolina. Near Lowgap the roadside is carpeted with galax, "glory groundcover of the Appalachians." The shiny, heart-shaped leaves of this evergreen are favored by florists for wreaths and decorations. In June and July the forest's floor has patches of its tiny white flowers.

6 Cumberland Knob Recreation Area, a forested hilltop, is a delightful place to stop for a picnic and take a leisurely walk through the woods that are brightened in season by clumps of flowering rhododendron.

7 Brinegar Cabin is a beautifully maintained homestead that was built from scratch almost a hundred years ago by Martin Brinegar and his wife, Caroline. In addition to the cabin, barn, shed, and springhouse, there is a well-tended garden showing some of the crops that were cultivated by mountain pioneers. These include rye, wheat, buckwheat, corn, potatoes, turnips, and sorghum. Weaving demonstrations are given on Caroline's four-poster loom.

8 Just 2¼ miles south of Brinegar Cabin is the entrance to Doughton Park, 6,000 acres of Blue Ridge natural splendor that provide lodging, camping facilities, numerous hiking trails, and streams for fishing. The unpainted wooden lodge buildings with sloping roofs and wide overhangs covering the verandas seem to blend with the rural setting. A trail leads to the Candill Cabin, a typical mountain home built about 1865 by Martin Candill, who cleared his own land and farmed in this then-remote place for some 20 years.

The road back into Virginia passes through several small towns where commercial signs are a sharp contrast to the rustic simplicity of the Blue Ridge Parkway.

9 One mile north of Troutdale is a turnoff to Mount Rogers, which at 5,729 feet is the highest peak in Virginia. Its summit may be reached by a three-mile hiking trail. There are several campsites tucked into the foothill forests, making this an especially peaceful place to spend the night or to stop for a picnic.

10 Hungry Mother State Park, a 2,180-acre natural preserve, offers boating, fishing, and swimming on a man-made lake with six miles of shoreline. Twelve miles of footpaths are designed for leisurely walks as well as for more rugged hiking. Riding horses are also available. Tent and trailer campgrounds, rental cabins, and several picnic areas make this an ideal place for a family vacation.

Fine views of the surrounding countryside can be seen from the crest of Mollys Knob, the mountain where, legend has it, Molly Marley collapsed after wandering in the woods for days having escaped with her child from their Indian captors. The child found his way to a group of houses but could only say "hungry mother." When the search party found Molly, she was dead.

Hugging a wall of sienna-colored rock, the road beyond Hungry Mother commands a breathtaking view of the valleys below and their distant Appalachian frame. The descent from the mountain leads into the Jefferson National Forest.

8. At Doughton Park a Virginia snake-style fence zigzags across a meadow. Among the most picturesque features of the Blue Ridge countryside are the miles of rail fences that bound fields and pastures and blend with the mellow beauty of the highlands.

11 Claytor Lake State Park is just southeast of Dublin, home of the annual Pulaski Old Time Bluegrass Fiddlers Convention held in July.

Featuring a 21-mile-long lake created in 1939 when a dam was built here for hydroelectric power, the park has a campground, cabins, and a marina and appeals to fishermen as well as to water-skiers and swimmers.

12 Formed over millions of years by the constant dripping of calcareous water, the rock formations in Dixie Caverns have strange and fantastic shapes. Reflections in the still waters in the cave serve to double the impact of the fascinating forms. Guided tours are conducted seven days a week year-round in a constant subterranean temperature of 54° F.

The caverns area, offering complete camping facilities, is adjacent to the Roanoke River and some of the finest fishing in Virginia.

5. *The classical symmetry and fine proportions of Monticello make the house seem larger than it is. Its interior is both elegant and personal. The gardens have been restored in accordance with Jefferson's plans, which were complete with lists of plants for each bed.*

On this tour *you sample the best of three worlds: there are the eastern foothills of the Blue Ridge Mountains and the historic city of Charlottesville and its environs; then comes Shenandoah National Park with the winding Skyline Drive and its ever-changing views of the Virginia countryside; and in the lovely rural setting of the Shenandoah Valley there are dramatic caverns to be enjoyed.*

1   In 1777 men from Culpeper and its environs were among the first to march to Williamsburg and join the fight for liberty. In the Civil War, Culpeper seesawed as a military headquarters for one side or the other. The Cavalry Museum on Main Street commemorates the Battle of Brandy Station, the largest cavalry engagement in that war. The Information Center on Main Street is a charming verandaed building built in the mid-1700's, and the County Courthouse is an interesting blend of classical revival, Georgian, and Victorian styles.

2   A house much like the original has been moved to the site where George Rogers Clark was born in 1752. Furnished and equipped to represent that pioneer era, the cabin shows the austerity of frontier life and reminds us of Clark, a vigorous hero of the Revolutionary War. He and a hardy band of about 175 backwoodsmen captured Forts Kaskaskie and Sackville, established by the British to control passage on the Ohio

and Mississippi rivers. The taking of these forts opened the Northwest Territory, an area that included the present states of Ohio, Indiana, Illinois, Michigan, and Wisconsin.

3   Much of the character of Charlottesville stems from the University of Virginia, of which Thomas Jefferson was the founding father.

Jefferson himself designed the "Academical Village," which opened in 1825 and around which the university still centers. His masterpiece here is the Rotunda, based on the Pantheon of Rome. After a disastrous fire in 1895, the structure was rebuilt and the shape of the dome was altered. In 1974 the Rotunda was restored to its original form.

4   Michie Tavern is perhaps worthy of the cliche "steeped in history." The original house was the boyhood home of Patrick Henry, the firebrand of the Revolution. Patrick's father sold the place to John Michie, who turned it into a popular tavern. Presidents Jefferson, Madison, Monroe, and Jackson were guests here.

The building, moved to this site in 1927 and greatly expanded, now houses a superb collection of pre-Revolutionary furnishings and artifacts. Also of interest are the outbuildings, including a kitchen, a smokehouse, a springhouse, and a gristmill that dates from 1797.

5   Few houses are so closely identified with their owner as is Thomas

Jefferson's Monticello. He leveled the top of his hilly domain and started to build in 1769. During the next 40 years, as time would allow, he built, revised, and rebuilt until he attained the perfection that is Monticello. The one oddity about its design is the steep, narrow staircases.

Many of the ideas incorporated into the place were acquired in France, but the whole is unmistakably Jeffersonian–a remarkable expression of his good taste, sense of proportion, and inventiveness.

6   When James Monroe resigned from Congress in 1786 and returned to Virginia to practice law, he chose a building site near the home of his good friend Thomas Jefferson. But Monroe soon returned to public life. While he was minister to France (1794–96), Jefferson and James Madison watched over the construction of Monroe's house, which he named Highlands. (A later owner renamed it Ash Lawn.)

Monroe lived here with his family for more than 20 years. The house has many of their furnishings and reflects their refined but simple tastes. There are splendid boxwoods in the garden and a fine statue of Monroe.

7   The best way to get to Appomattox Court House National Historic Park is to return to Route 20 and head south. The park commemorates the place where the Civil War ended. Twelve buildings and sites have been restored or reconstructed to resemble their appearance in 1865 when, on April 9, Gen. Robert E. Lee surrendered the Army of Northern Virginia to Gen. Ulysses S. Grant. The focal point is the McLean House, where the surrender was formalized.

A fascinating feature of the park is the living-history demonstrations. An appropriately uniformed impersonator of a soldier from one of the armies gives a first-hand account of his impressions and feelings on that fateful day. These remarkably touching performances bring one about as close as possible to the reality of the war between the states.

On Route 501 beyond Boonsboro the road begins its ascent through the foothills of the Blue Ridge Mountains. Along the road the kudzu vine blankets the landscape, imparting an eerie, other-world look.

8. *Taller than Niagara Falls, Natural Bridge is ranked among the natural wonders of the world. From the road on top of the arch you can watch Cedar Creek running quietly through the limestone gorge and the majestic formation carved by its incessant flow.*

8   To get to Natural Bridge, cross the Blue Ridge Parkway and continue about seven miles; then take Route 130.

As a young surveyor in the 1750's, George Washington was one of the earliest admirers of this imposing limestone formation, which stands 215 feet high and spans a chasm 90 feet wide. Thomas Jefferson was inspired to buy a 175-acre tract that included the bridge, and many of his friends visited here.

9   Back on the Blue Ridge Parkway, at the Otter Creek Visitor Center, you can get literature about the parkway, the Shenandoah National Park, and the Skyline Drive, as the road through the park is called.

Nature trails through the woods are mapped and color-coded on a signboard.

10   At Humpback Rocks is an interesting reconstruction of a mountain farm. A self-guiding trail leads past split rail fences, a cabin, and outbuildings—all typical of Appalachian hand-hewn construction. The handmade tools and farm implements testify to the ingenuity and hard labor required to wrest a living from this hilly land.

11   The early settlers grazed their cattle at Big Meadows, a large, natural clearance in the woods. Today it is a favorite stopping place for tourists. The visitor center presents a slide show on the relationship of man and nature in the Blue Ridge Mountains. Nature trails and wild flower paths fan out from the center and the attractive lodge.

12   Skyland, so called because at 3,680 feet it is the highest point on the Skyline Drive, is a good starting point for a hike along part of the Appalachian Trail. From Skyland's lodge the trail leads to Little Stony Man Cliffs, where there are fine views of mountains, cliffs, and distant hills. There are also riding trails and a stable of horses here.

13   From the junction with Route 211 you can continue north on Skyline Drive or, for a change of scene, head west down into the Shenandoah Valley and the Luray Caverns.

The caverns are a series of vast chambers with an amazingly baroque conglomeration of stalactites, stalagmites, pillars, flowing ribbons, mantles, and draperies, all mirrored by quiet pools of water. Guided tours follow easily walked paths. In one large room an organ console activates mallets that strike some of the stone formations. Reverberating, the stones produce the full range of the chromatic scale so that music can be played.

14   The South Fork of the Shenandoah River is a favorite place for canoeing. You can find canoe rentals west of Bentonville on Route 613 and south of Front Royal on Route 340.

The Thunderbird Museum and Archaeological Park features artifacts created by Indians who lived in this area some 10,000 years ago. A slide show illustrates the culture of these prehistoric people. Five miles of nature trails lead to ancient sites, one of which is an active dig where you can see archeologists at work. The museum is closed from mid-November to mid-March.

15   The Skyline Caverns are noted for the profusion of snow-white flowerlike calcite clusters on the limestone walls and ceilings. There is also a 37-foot waterfall in the cave and a crystal-clear stream stocked with trout. The indirect lighting is planned to show to best advantage the formations of flowstone.

16   Front Royal is the northern entry to Shenandoah National Park and the Skyline Drive. In the town, on Chester Street, is the Warren Rifles Confederate Museum, where you can see a collection of firearms and other memorabilia of the Civil War.

On Route 522 a few miles south of Front Royal you may be surprised to spot some zebras grazing in a pasture. The road here passes part of the Smithsonian Institution's Conservation and Research Center, a 3,200-acre annex to the National Zoological Park in Washington, D.C. The center is not open to the public, but exotic animals can frequently be seen from the road.

The Hills of West Virginia

These lovely mountain ranges extend into Maryland and Virginia, to the benefit of all

West Virginia is aptly called the Mountain State. There are more high mountains here—the average elevation is 1,500 feet—than in any other state east of the Mississippi, and the Allegheny ranges of the Appalachian Mountains cut rugged ridges across the state's eastern third.

While the terrain produces few crops except in the Greenbrier River valley, West Virginia's mountains contain vast deposits of coal, oil, and natural gas, which have long contributed to the state's economy.

To balance the ravages of mining, more than a million acres of land have been set aside to preserve its beauty and to provide recreation in forest areas where camping, fishing, hunting, and boating are popular.

Here in the northern reaches of Virginia, West Virginia, and a corner of Maryland, there are poignant reminders of the Civil War. There is also superlative scenery. In this wooded countryside, with its lakes, caverns, dramatic rocky escarpments, and mountaintops from which there are magnificent views, there are a number of state parks that are renowned for their recreational opportunities.

1 An aspect of most Civil War battlefields is the incongruity of the silent beauty of the setting and the thundering horror it commemorates, and Antietam is no exception. Here on some 800 acres of parklike land are eight miles of winding road from which you can see the plaques, monuments, and the deceivingly picture-pretty cannon.

In one bloody day of fighting—September 17, 1862—more than 23,000 casualties were sustained here. There was no winner on that awful day, but since the Union forces stopped the Southerners on their push to the north, foreign diplomatic recognition of the Confederacy was forestalled.

At the visitor center a short slide show explains these battles and their significance. Here too is a museum of uniforms, weapons, and artifacts. Tape recordings keyed to locations on the drive through the battlefield are also available.

2 At Harpers Ferry the sense of being in a special place begins as soon as you leave Route 340. You follow the shallows of the Shenandoah River past the ruins of the Savery Mill to the town with its narrow streets and its many handsome stone

and brick buildings perched on the steep hillside.

Although this is a national historical park with some two dozen buildings administered by the Park Service, it is also a town of private homes and stores. The architecture is remarkably homogeneous. The oldest building in town is Harper House, built between 1775 and 1782 and now restored with period pieces. Most of the other buildings here were built within the following 100 years.

The town is probably best known as the site of abolitionist John Brown's unsuccessful attempt to capture the federal armory here in 1859. The raid, the trial, and Brown's subsequent hanging presaged a time of trouble. The town was occupied at various times by both sides during the Civil War, and severe flooding in the late 1800's all but ended the life of the community.

But today a renovated Harpers Ferry is thriving. The architecture, the exhibits, and the living history

SPECIAL FEATURES

ROAD GUIDE	HIGHLIGHT **1**
STATE PARKS With Campsites ⛺ Without Campsites △	SKI AREAS
RECREATION AREAS With Campsites ▲ Without Campsites △	SCHEDULED AIRLINE STOPS
SELECTED REST AREAS	OTHER AIRPORTS
POINTS OF INTEREST	BOAT RAMPS

ROAD CLASSIFICATION

CONTROLLED ACCESS HIGHWAYS
Interstate interchange numbers are mileposts.

Service Area   Interchanges

TOLL HIGHWAYS

OTHER DIVIDED HIGHWAYS

PAVED HIGHWAYS

LOCAL ROADS In unfamiliar areas inquire locally before using these roads   Paved   Gravel   Dirt

MILEAGE

MILEAGE BETWEEN TOWNS AND JUNCTIONS   3 ⁄ 4   MILEAGE BETWEEN DOTS   ● 35 ●

SCALE

ONE INCH 15 MILES   0   5   10   15

ONE INCH 24 KILOMETERS   0   5   10   15   24

2. Located at the juncture of the Potomac and Shenandoah rivers, Harpers Ferry was an important link between the Ohio Valley and the East. It also gained importance as an arms-producing center—which is one reason why abolitionist John Brown came to town.

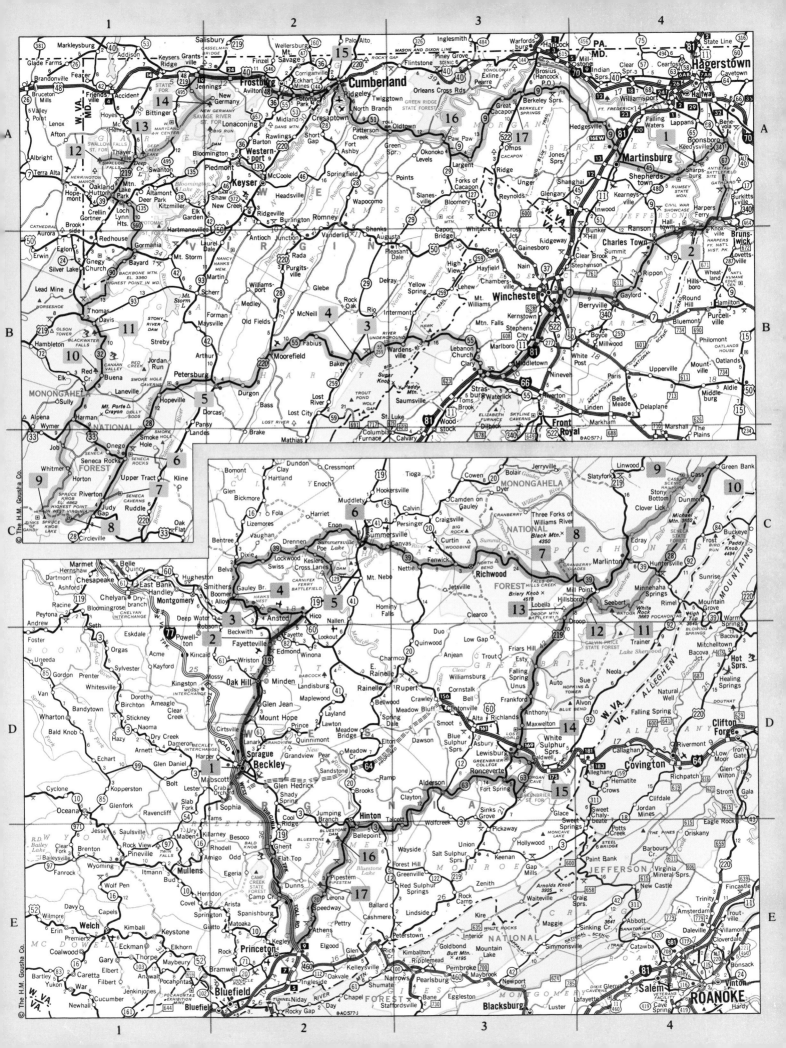

6. *While not characteristic of the craggy, dramatic terrain of the Potomac Highlands, this formation, known as Seneca Rocks, is particularly noteworthy for its almost primordial appearance—an ancient sculpture profiled against the heavens.*

and audiovisual presentations here all contribute to making this a fascinating place to visit.

3 Lost River is a pleasant little stream where you cross it on Route 55 just west of Wardensville. But about a quarter-mile upstream it does the disappearing act that accounts for its name.

To see where the river goes underground, you can walk down the trail on the west side of the bridge to where the river loses itself amid a great pile of rocks, goes under Sandy Ridge, and appears again two miles downstream, where it becomes the headwaters of the Cacapon River.

4 About five or six miles west of Lost River on the north side of the road you can see a bank of reddish-yellow rock. This formation is Oriskany sandstone, which is a rich reservoir for natural gas in West Virginia. The name Oriskany comes from Oriskany Falls, New York, where this distinctive sandy formation was first noticed. Of Devonian age, about 400 million years old, these sands were originally the beachline of the ancestral Appalachians. The sands are so porous that they make excellent storage reservoirs for natural gas.

At Moorefield, on Route 220, the tall concrete towers of a feed mill stand as a dramatic reminder that this area is called the Poultry Capital of West Virginia. This modern computerized mill mixes up to 40 ingredients to produce feed for chickens. Such products as corn, soybean meal, meat, fish, gluten, limestone, salt, calcium, various vitamins, and trace elements, as well as day-old bakery goods, are mixed in proportions that are scientifically balanced. There are specific feeds for starting the chicks, for their fast growth, and for fatting and firming. The laying hens are given a special diet to promote egg production.

5 Smoke Hole Caverns are so called because it is said that the early Indians and the white settlers who came later used the caves to smoke their meat in order to preserve it.

The largest chamber here, nearly as high as the Big Room in New Mexico's Carlsbad Caverns, is famous for its countless number of stalactites. The cave also has the longest ribbon stalactite in the world. Closed from mid-November until March.

6 Route 28 south of Smoke Hole Caverns follows the South Branch of the Potomac River and is flanked by farmsteads and low-lying hills. It comes as a dramatic surprise to see a jagged knife-edged escarpment of rocks protruding from the side of a rounded hill. These are the Champe Rocks. Even more dramatic, five miles farther on, is the great gray mass of Seneca Rocks etched against the sky.

This formation of Tuscarora sandstone rises to a height of 960 feet and is only about 15 feet wide at the top. There is a pathway to the summit, from which there is a magnificent view. The face of the escarpment is a favorite of rock climbers, who earn their view the hard way. At the visitor center there are excellent displays explaining the geological development of this entire area.

7 Seneca Caverns delve to an underground depth of 165 feet. Throughout these limestone caves are stalactites and stalagmites that create an endless panorama of fanciful shapes. Among the most striking rooms here are the Great Ballroom, the Council Room, and Fairyland chambers. Favorite formations are Niagara Falls, the Statue of Liberty, and the Fruit Chimney.

8 Upon returning to Route 28 from Seneca Caverns, you must decide whether to take the gravel road to Spruce Knob and Spruce Knob Lake or go back to Seneca Rocks and take paved Route 33 west to Harman. If the weather is good, the Spruce Knob trip is recommended for the inspiring views to be had from this, the highest point in West Virginia.

If you opt for the view, head south on Route 28 and watch for the Spruce Knob sign about two miles down the road. The dirt-and-gravel Forest Service road winds steadily upward, and after about eight miles you come to the turnoff to Spruce Knob.

The spruce trees and other native vegetation on Spruce Knob are stunted and misshapen by the severity of the wind and cold on this exposed hilltop with an elevation of 4,863 feet. On a clear day the view from the observation tower is seemingly endless, and you can count as many as nine mountain ranges in the distance.

9 A good gravel road curves down through the forest to Spruce Knob Lake, where there is a picnic ground and camping area. This is a lovely little lake where boating is allowed and trout fishing is considered to be

excellent. The lake is surrounded by woodlands, and it is not unusual to see white-tailed deer in the area.

The unpaved road going north from the lake wends its way uphill and down dale through the forest following the course of Dry Fork River. You see signs for hiking trails along the way, and if some exercise is in order, you might want to sample a section of one.

After about 12 miles the gravel road becomes blacktop, but it is still very narrow, so do not expect to drive fast.

10   The 6,000-acre Canaan Valley State Park is a favorite West Virginia recreational area. Here there is golf, tennis, swimming in a heated pool, many fishing streams and ponds, and miles of hiking trails. The altitude here is about 3,000 feet above sea level, which helps keep the area cool in summer.

There is also an ice skating and ski area. In summer the chair lift is used for easy access to the summit of Weiss Knob, from which there are spectacular views.

A large lodge provides accommodations, and there are also cabins and campsites within the park.

11   Blackwater Falls State Park is best known for its dramatic 60-foot waterfall on Blackwater River and

11. The Blackwater River roars downward through a 10-mile series of rapids and falls. It drops 1,350 feet on this tumultuous run.

the deep wooded canyon through which the river runs.

Along the edge of the half-mile-wide canyon there are easily accessible observation points, and at the falls there are stairs and boardwalks leading to the rocky splash pool at the bottom. The nearby Falls of Elakala, spanned by a wooden footbridge, is a gentler cascade flowing over a picturesque outcrop of rock.

Park accommodations include a lodge, housekeeping cabins, and a tent and trailer campground. There is a large lake for swimming, a stable with horses to ride on a bridle path, and miles of hiking trails. On the trails, through stands of red spruce, hemlock, black cherry, and rhododendron, you might see deer or wild turkeys, and in the springtime there are bountiful displays of wild flowers.

12   A look at the map shows that both Routes 219 and 90 head north toward Swallow Falls State Park. Route 219 is somewhat faster, but the route marked on the map is more scenic. It follows the North Branch of the Potomac River through dense woods to Gormania, where it crosses the river and swings north into Maryland. Here the road reaches a high plateau and seems to skim along the top of the world.

The four falls in the park can all be seen on an easy half-hour hike. Swallow Falls is the highest, and the water flowing down the stairsteps of its textured rock face makes a satisfying sound. A highlight of Muddy Creek Falls is the swinging bridge that hangs above it.

There are more than 10 miles of trails in the park, some through a virgin forest of tall conifers.

13   Deep Creek Lake State Park has about a mile of shoreline on a lake created as part of a hydroelectric project. Boating and fishing are popular here, and there are marinas with boat rentals. Swimming is good, and lifeguards are on duty on the sandy beach during the summer. There are campsites and a shady picnic area. A naturalist occasionally leads walks on the nature trail.

14   It is a pleasant surprise when the road to New Germany State Park breaks out of its forest setting to an open area of ridgetop farms.

In the park there are picnic tables in the deep shade of the pines and hemlocks and a small, still lake with a beach for swimming. The lake is stocked with trout, and rowboats are available. Along the various hiking trails in the park you may see deer, grouse, and wild turkeys.

15   As Route 48 East drops down Savage Mountain, you can see some fine long views of Maryland's hills.

In Cumberland, after turning south

10. The Canaan Valley State Park is located in this gentle valley, where various wildlife like the deer shown here make their home. Named for the Biblical land of Canaan, the area also has a large and popular vacation resort lodge, campsites, and rental cabins.

on Route 51 and going through the railroad underpass, watch for the turn into the North Branch of the Chesapeake & Ohio Canal National Historical Park.

Here you can see the old lock, a towpath, a dry-docked barge, and a dry channel of this historic canal, as well as a water-filled section and a tollhouse. You can pick up a folder with a map that shows the 184 miles of canal right-of-way and towpath between Cumberland and George-town in Washington, D.C. The pamphlet also includes a capsule history of the canal.

16 One of the most challenging aspects of building the C & O Canal was the construction of a tunnel at Paw Paw, West Virginia.

Most of the local people here in the 1830's were farmers and tradesmen. They were not much interested in digging a 20- by 25-foot hole more than 3,000 feet long through a mountain of rock, and Welsh miners and other immigrants were brought in to do the work with pick and shovel and black blasting powder. To see the tunnel now in its pleasant setting, it is

hard to imagine the labor it involved.

Easier to imagine (quite modern in fact) is that the project, begun in 1836, was not finished until 1850 and that it exceeded its estimated cost by 300 percent.

Watch for the sharp turnoff to the tunnel area about a half-mile west of the bridge across the Potomac at Paw Paw. It is an easy walk to the tunnel from the parking area.

17 On Route 9 at the Prospect Point turnoff, just west of Berkeley Springs, there is a view worth stopping to see. The vista is of broad valleys, the tree-lined Potomac River, and low ranges of wooded hills rising behind the scattering of white buildings in the village far below.

Berkeley Springs State Park is a health spa in the center of town. The warm springs here have been popular since the mid-18th century and were a particular favorite of George Washington's. The waters are piped to bathhouses and used for a variety of health treatments. There is a pool for swimming in the reputedly beneficial mineral waters. The pool is closed from Labor Day to Memorial Day.

The southwestern part of West Virginia lies in the heart of the largest bituminous coalfield in the world. The many mines that can be seen from the road between Beckley and Summersville attest to the immensity of this natural resource.

Along this entire drive the ancient rolling mountains are constant companions, standing in quiet contrast to the open meadowlands where today's highlanders, as the West Virginians call themselves, make their homes.

1 Although the city of Beckley was established in 1838 by Gen. Alfred Beckley when he came "west" to raise cattle, it was not until the 1890's, when coal mines in the surrounding hills were opened up, that the little village began to grow.

Beckley sits on a high plateau in the midst of deep valleys and densely wooded hills. It serves as a center for the more than 200 small mining and farming communities scattered throughout the nearby mountains.

The Beckley Exhibition Mine, in the town's New River Park, offers a rare opportunity to see a coal mine. Here you can board a remodeled motorized coal car at the adit, as the mine's entrance is called, and ride into the mine's underground passageways. At stops along the way guides explain the entire workings. The mine is closed from the end of October to May.

The road from Beckley winds through the mountains, passing a few farms and white, steepled churches. Just beyond Fayetteville it crosses the New River on the New River Gorge Bridge, the world's longest steel arch, which spans the gorge at one of its widest points.

2 One mile north of Fayetteville, just east of the bridge in Canyon Rim Park, is a scenic overlook. Here a wooden walkway leads down to a platform poised on the edge of the gorge, affording a sweeping view of the bridge and of the river almost a thousand feet below.

The New River, which runs some 320 miles from its source in the Blue Ridge Mountains of North Carolina to join the Gauley River in West Virginia, is considered to be the world's oldest river.

Because of treacherous shoals, this

17. From Prospect Point Overlook, which is a promontory above a turn in the Potomac River, views of West Virginia, Pennsylvania, and Maryland can be seen. In the distance is the village of Great Cacapon, near Berkeley Springs.

1. *Classical in design, with an airy elegance, the New River Gorge Bridge was completed in 1977. At 1,700 feet, its only rivals among steel arch bridges are New Jersey's Bayonne Bridge (1,652 feet) and, in Nova Scotia, Sydney Harbor's 1,650-foot span.*

17-mile section of the New River, as it raccs through the deep, rocky gorge, provides some of the most exciting white-water rafting in the East, ranking, according to some experts, with the float trips on the Colorado and Snake rivers. Numerous raft trips originate at various sites in the area.

3 Hawks Nest State Park is located on top of a cliff that soars 585 fcct above the New River Gorge. Named for the fish hawks that used to nest on the rocks here, the 276-acre park has facilities for tennis, boating, fishing, and picnicking and offers several hiking trails. A small museum displays Indian and pioneer artifacts.

From a modern lodge perched at the edge of the gorge, an aerial tramway descends to a marina on a quiet section of the New River below. Here rowboats and paddleboats are available for leisurely exploring of the shores. The view from the tramway is especially appealing in late April when the cloudlike flowers of the silver bell trees and the lavender spikes of the wild lupines appear throughout the canyon.

The tramway is closed from the end of October until April.

About a quarter of a mile west, the Hawks Nest Overlook provides a broad panorama of the gorge. Nearby is a double-truss steel railroad bridge across the New River. In this region railroads are used extensively to haul coal, usually following the easy grades of the rivers that have cut through the various mountain gaps.

Hiking trails into the park are well-marked at this overlook.

As the road continues, it follows the river and winds along the mountain ridges, here clothed with oak, beech, hickory, and evergreen trees, and occasionally drops into the lush valleys where the sugar maple (*Acer saccharum*), the state tree, flourishes.

4 The little town of Gauley Bridge was the site of Civil War skirmishes during which the Union forces gained control of what was then western Virginia.

The Gauley Bridge, built with continuous steel girders, spans the mouth of the Gauley River, which joins here with the New River to form the Kanawha River.

Route 39 follows the Gauley and the railroad, and passes many working coal mines typical of those that are scattered all through this area. Eighteen miles beyond the Gauley River Bridge you can get a particularly good view of a conveyor belt loading coal onto railroad cars.

5 The Carnifex Ferry Battlefield was the site of a Civil War confrontation that took place on September 10, 1861, between Union forces under Gen. William S. Rosecrans and Confederate forces under Gen. John B. Floyd.

The Patteson House, which was situated between Union and Confederate lines, has been restored and is now a museum containing Civil War relics. Picnic areas and hiking trails are further attractive features here.

6 The road to Summersville winds through the Appalachian highlands, passing many small towns and villages tucked into the hillsides.

Summersville was taken in 1861 in a surprise attack by Confederate forces led by a 20-year-old spy named Nancy Hart. Nancy was caught and jailed by Union troops, but managed to escape and return to the Confederate lines with vital information.

Summersville Lake, south of town, provides excellent fishing, boating, waterskiing, and swimming. Like most of the lakes in West Virginia, this one is formed by a dam. Nevertheless, it has an unusually natural appearance. The Appalachian Mountains rise around the lake, and early morning mists give a soft quality to the surrounding hills.

The Monongahela National Forest is comprised of about 846,000 acres of the Allegheny Mountains. Within its borders are many recreation areas, each with its own assortment of facilities, including swimming beaches, trout streams, picnic groves with fireplaces, and camping sites.

The forest is laced with roadways that wind through the wooded hills, offering views of some of the highest mountain peaks in the East. Miles of hiking trails penetrate areas of scenic beauty here.

7 An excellent opportunity to enjoy a hiking adventure is at the Falls of Hills Creek. From the parking area there is a ¾-mile trail through a dense, wet forest of red oak, red spruce, black cherry, and white ash, interspersed with rhododendron (*Rhododendron maximum*), the state flower, which brightens the hillsides with drifts of white blooms in May.

The trail leads some 250 feet down a steep ravine to a series of three waterfalls. Lower Falls, which drops 63 feet, is the highest in West Virginia. The trail can be slippery in wet weather, and the uphill walk is strenuous. You should allow at least an hour for the round trip.

Sundew

Pitcher plant

Butterwort

Wild orchid

8. *A gift of the ice age, Cranberry Glades' bogs are the southernmost ecological refuge for some animal and plant species native to the Arctic and other northern regions. But as the bogs slowly dry out, botanists predict that the surrounding birches and red spruces will take over these open glades.*

8 Cranberry Glades, a landscape that resembles a northern bog, or muskeg, harbors plants and animals that are seldom found this far south.

Boardwalks through the glades permit close inspection of wild flowers, trees, and shrubs without disturbing the delicate plantlife. Here in the spring you can see such beauties as painted trillium, pink lady's slipper, marsh marigold, and hepatica. During the summer and fall there is Indian pipe, tall meadow rue, Joe-Pye weed, white aster, and the carnivorous sundew and pitcher plant.

Two kinds of cranberries grow here, amid red spruce, alder, various grasses, and sedges, as well as mosses, lichens, and other plants found in the northern tundra.

The Cranberry Mountain visitor center, three miles to the south, provides maps of the glades and the national forest lands as well as information regarding guided tours and nature study programs. Bicycle and hiking trails give access to wilderness areas where motorized vehicles are prohibited.

Along Route 39 open meadows stretch upward to low forested hills, and wherever the fields have not been recently cultivated, a profusion of wild flowers adds color throughout the summer months.

Just south of Marlinton is the Pocahontas County Historical Museum, a small 1904 house that contains Indian relics and pioneer artifacts relating to the history of the county.

9 The Cass Scenic Railroad provides a glimpse into West Virginia's past, when lumbering was a booming industry. Restored logging cars powered by the original steam locomotives climb 12 miles through the scenic Allegheny Mountains to the summit of Bald Knob, the second highest peak in the state. The views from the train are breathtaking in clear weather, but even on a cloudy day it is worth the trip to Cass just to see the old engines billowing with steam in this historic setting.

The "ole-time logger" is powered by a shay, a steam engine in which each wheel is geared separately. This makes it possible for the train to negotiate steep grades and sharp turns.

The railroad trip, which takes 4½ hours, is not available on Mondays and from November to Memorial Day, and runs only on weekends during October.

10 The National Radio Astronomy Observatory at Green Bank has some of the world's largest radio telescopes. The Appalachian heights in

9. *As proud as when they helped haul 2 billion board feet of timber down from the mountain forests, the splendid locomotives of the Cass Scenic Railroad now take visitors on a 4½-hour trip that is rich in nostalgia and visual treats.*

this area provide an ideal environment for radio astronomy because the mountains act as a natural shield from man-made radio noise. Guided tours of the facilities are available.

11 Watoga State Park is the largest park in West Virginia. A lumber mill near the park entrance indicates that loggers are still at work in the hills of the region.

A narrow road through the park follows Beaver Creek, one of the tributaries of the Greenbrier River, which defines the park's western boundary. The river's shallow meanderings have created many sandbars and islands, thus inspiring the name *Watoga*, which means "river of islands" in Cherokee.

Park facilities include hiking and riding trails as well as tennis, swimming, fishing, and boating. During the summer the park naturalist gives lectures and conducts tours explaining the plant and animal life found here. The wildlife includes raccoons, wild turkeys, rabbits, quail, grouse, woodchucks, and white-tailed deer.

The dense forest disappears on the outskirts of Seebert, a small town on the park's western border.

12 At Hillsboro is Stulting House, birthplace of Pearl Buck, the American author who for many years lived in China with her missionary husband and who became famous for her novels about Chinese life. The house, built in the 1850's by Dutch immigrants, has been restored and contains exhibits of rare autographed books and other memorabilia related to the author.

13 The most significant Civil War battle in West Virginia took place on Droop Mountain on November 6, 1863. Union troops led by Gen. William W. Averell defeated a Confederate army commanded by Gen. John Echols. This was the last important Southern opposition in the state. A museum here houses pertinent artifacts. Nearby is a lookout tower that commands a magnificent view of the vast Greenbrier Valley.

The road between Droop Mountain and Lewisburg winds along mountain ridges and then descends slowly into the Greenbrier Valley. Throughout the area there are widely spaced dairy farms, signaled by their large double silos and their immense fields of corn. The entire gently rolling valley is a rich agricultural resource of the state and contrasts dramatically with the rugged wooded mountain terrain just to the north.

14 The Lost World Caverns are part of a system of underground limestone caves in West Virginia. An unusual array of shapes and colors has been created here by the stalagmites and other formations. There are several stone "waterfalls" in the cave, and the main room is known for its terraced, pedestallike stalagmites.

15 A travertine formation in the shape of an enormous pipe organ gave Organ Cave its name. The formation, almost 40 feet high, rings with musical tones when tapped with a wooden mallet. Also within the cave are beds of petrified sponge and a templelike structure with a golden hue. The cavern was used as a refuge by Confederate Gen. Robert E. Lee's forces during the Civil War. A natural limestone formation in the cave resembles General Lee.

17. The area that is now Pipestem State Park was once the purview of nomadic Indian tribes who often hunted here.

On the stretch of road between Alderson and Talcott the sandbars and islands so characteristic of the Greenbrier River are plainly visible.

Near the town of Talcott are the Chesapeake and Ohio Railway's Twin Big Bend Tunnels. It was in the construction of the first of these tunnels, in 1872, that John Henry became famous. The huge black steelworker, so the legend goes, could work his way through the rock with the help of his enormous steel hammer faster than the new-fangled steam-driven steel drill. The ballad that tells of John Henry's feat, a song now known around the world, was sung by the workers as they labored. The ballad was never actually written, it just evolved, and today there are more than a thousand verses and some 300 tunes for the song, many of which have never been published.

16 Bluestone State Park, along the shores of the Bluestone River, is a short distance from the Bluestone Dam. Information about the three nature trails through the wilderness is available at the dam. The park also offers a wide range of recreational facilities, including pools and bathhouses and camping areas. One section of the park is set aside for a cluster of cabins that can be rented. There are launching ramps for those who bring their own boats.

17 Pipestem State Park is so named because of the hollow-stemmed shrub *Spiraea alba* from which the Shawnee Indians and early settlers in this area made stems for their pipes. The bowls were made of clay, which was expensive; if one could not afford it, a corncob was used.

The park has two modern lodges, one on a ridgetop that offers a sweeping view of the mountains, the other accessible only by a tramway that carries you down a cliff to the bottom of Bluestone Gorge.

There are also two golf courses, indoor and outdoor swimming pools, riding and hiking trails, and camping grounds.

The town of Princeton is a prosperous farming and mining community. It was named in honor of Hugh Mercer, an early settler here and a general in the Revolutionary War who was killed in the Battle of Princeton, New Jersey.

North Carolina

The historic sites of the Old North State blend gracefully with the scenic hills and seashore

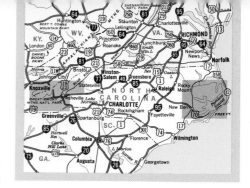

With the Atlantic Ocean to the east and the Great Smoky Mountains to the west, North Carolina has a remarkable assortment of terrains and climates; of wilderness, forests, and salty sea breezes.

Many early colonists settled in this part of America, and their imprint can be found today in the historic towns and villages and the preserved landmarks all through the state. One of the handsomest is Tryon Palace at New Bern, which dates from the 1700's. Its gardens, like many others in the Carolinas, have been restored to their original elegance.

The two wings of this butterfly-shaped route incorporate the southwestern segment of the Blue Ridge Parkway, one of America's loveliest and most carefully planned scenic roads. Running 469 miles from Shenandoah National Park in Virginia to Great Smoky Mountains National Park in North Carolina and Tennessee, the parkway crests the great ridge that rears up from the Piedmont to the east and south and marks the beginning of the wide, westward-spreading Appalachian system. This swooping double loop takes in the highest and ruggedest section of the parkway, as well as the majestic Great Smokies themselves.

1 Once called the City of Temples, Asheville with its steepled silhouette rose from the hills like a man-made echo of nature's beauty. The skyline still has its drama, but as in other American cities many of the most interesting buildings have been razed to make way for urban renewal.

One remnant of the past, at 48 Spruce Street, is the family residence of Thomas Wolfe, who offended his neighbors by revealing their foibles in *Look Homeward, Angel* and subsequent novels. The Wolfe home is open to visitors.

2 Going north toward Weaverville, keep to the business route (not the bypass), and you find signs to the Zebulon B. Vance Birthplace State Historic Site on Reems Creek Road. In addition to the two-story homestead, visitors can see a cluster of reconstructed log buildings that typifies a mountain farm of the 1800's, including a springhouse, slave house, toolhouse, loom house, smokehouse, and corncrib. A small visitor center and museum houses exhibits on the life and career of Zebulon B. Vance, governor of North Carolina during the Civil War, who was born here in 1830. After the Civil War, Vance served nearly four terms as a U.S. senator from North Carolina.

As Route 19 heads due east, it climbs into the western foothills of the Blue Ridge. The wooded hills, whose fall colors are brilliant in mid-October, are checkered with small patches of corn, tobacco, and pastureland, and tobacco-drying sheds with widely spaced plank sides for air circulation are a common sight. Lumber trucks are frequent and sometimes intimidating companions on the highway.

The countryside becomes woodsier and wilder as you proceed to the intersection with the Blue Ridge Parkway, which has been named a national park.

3 At Linville Falls Recreation Area trails lead through forests of Carolina hemlock, oak, birch, black gum, and rhododendron to spectacular overlooks of the upper and lower falls of the Linville River and the steeply cut Linville Gorge. The Linville Gorge Wilderness Area is a breathtakingly rugged terrain with cliffs that plunge nearly 2,000 feet from the crest of the Blue Ridge to the Catawba Valley below.

4 To learn more about the geology of the mountains and their mineral content, you may want to stop at the Museum of North Carolina Minerals at Gillespie Gap, which is run by the

3. Linville Gorge is an area of untamed nature that can provide a considerable physical challenge even to experienced hikers. Trails leading to and from the gorge are often steeply graded. Passage is slow, but the scenery makes it worthwhile.

SPECIAL FEATURES

ROAD GUIDE ▬▬▬	HIGHLIGHT **1**
STATE PARKS With Campsites ▲ Without Campsites △	SCHEDULED AIRLINE STOPS ✈
RECREATION AREAS With Campsites ▲ Without Campsites △	MILITARY AIRPORTS ✈
SELECTED REST AREAS ⤬	OTHER AIRPORTS ✈
POINTS OF INTEREST ⊡	MAJOR MTN. ROADS ▬▬
SKI AREAS 🎿	CLOSED IN WINTER Closed in Winter

ROAD CLASSIFICATION

CONTROLLED ACCESS HIGHWAYS (Entrance and Exit only at Interchanges) Divided **5** Undivided
Interchanges

OTHER DIVIDED HIGHWAYS

PAVED HIGHWAYS

LOCAL ROADS In unfamiliar areas inquire locally before using these roads Paved Gravel Dirt

MILEAGE

MILEAGE BETWEEN TOWNS AND JUNCTIONS 3 ⁄ 4   MILEAGE BETWEEN DOTS ●⊸ 35 ⊸○

SCALE

ONE INCH 18 MILES 0 5 10 20
ONE INCH 29 KILOMETERS 0 5 10 20 32

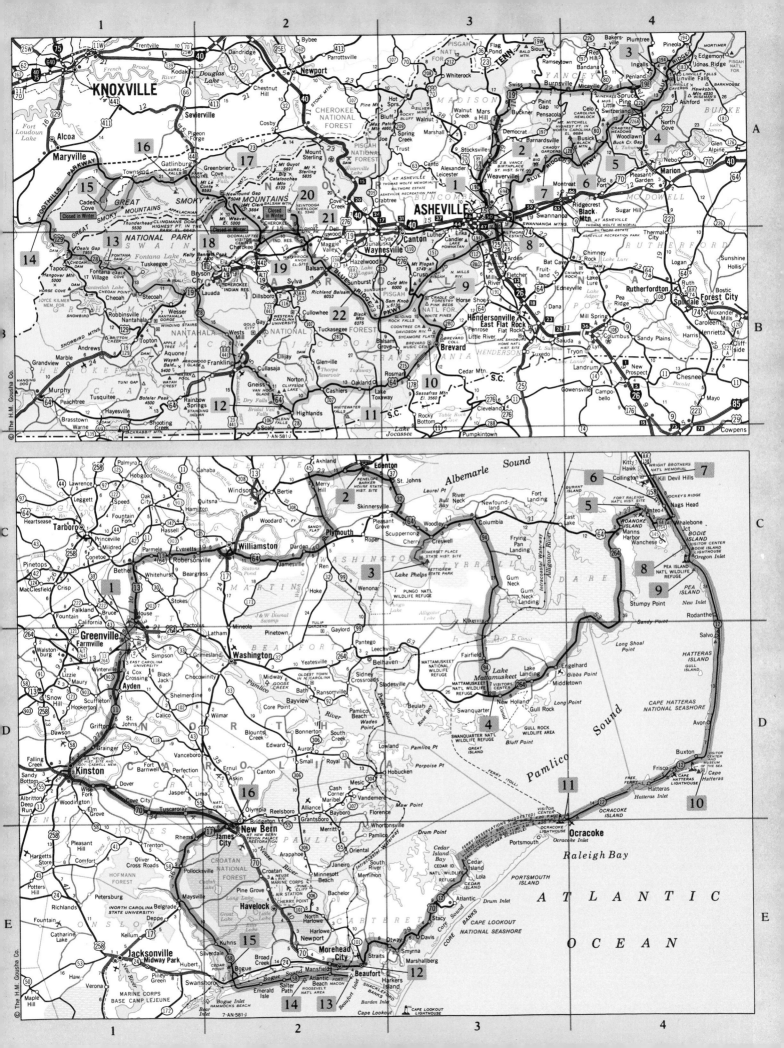

National Park Service. North Carolina is remarkably rich in rocks and minerals, with more than 300 varieties that include many precious and semiprecious stones. The museum tells the story of how these mineral resources have been used both by the early Indian inhabitants and by modern settlers of the area.

South of the museum the parkway becomes increasingly hilly and winding, and occasionally passes through picturesque tunnels. Woodchucks (locally called whistle pigs) feed along the verges of the road undisturbed by passing traffic, and red hawks and black ravens soar above, making lazy circles in the sky. Rhododendrons and hardwoods are common along the roadside.

5 Crabtree Meadows Recreation Area is a well-developed stopping place with a coffee shop, gift shop, service station, campground, and other amenities, as well as beautiful nature trails and an amphitheater. From spring well into summer these mountain meadows are a riot of wild flowers, and the adjoining oak–hickory forest is filled with rhododendron, mountain laurel, dogwood, and flame azalea.

Proceeding along the parkway, you soon see the Black Mountain Range, which includes Mount Mitchell, the highest peak east of the Mississippi. This section of the parkway is particularly notable for the profusion of laurel and rhododendron that lines both sides of the road.

6 Route 128 winds upward to the summit of 6,684-foot Mount Mitchell, named for the Reverend Elisha Mitchell, who first measured the peak in 1835 and subsequently fell to his death on its slopes while attempting to substantiate his findings. Mount Mitchell's broad dome is an austere world with a harsh climate. The red spruce and Fraser fir that cloak its sides are bent aslant from the constant pressure of the wind, and many of them have been killed in their unending struggle with temperature and weather. Snow falls on Mount Mitchell from October to May, and winter temperatures of −20 to −25°F are not uncommon. Even in summer picnickers are urged to bring warm clothing. You may want to climb the observation tower by Dr. Mitchell's gravesite. From here, you may be able to see the Great Smokies, 75 miles due west. Facilities within Mount Mitchell State Park include picnic and camp grounds and trails, accessible from mid-May to mid-October, and a rustic mile-high restaurant. A nature museum was scheduled to open in 1981. The road to the summit may be closed in winter.

7 Craggy Visitor Center has exhibits of local shrubs and flowers and a self-guiding nature trail.

Through a tunnel and about three miles south is the turnoff to Craggy Gardens Picnic Ground. Here a trail winds from the beautifully situated picnic grounds to part of the gardens themselves. These damp highlands are aburst with a variety of flowering trees, shrubs, and wild flowers from May to September.

The parkway curves down to the plateau where Asheville is situated and then ascends again to skirt the summit of Mount Pisgah. From an overlook there are superb views of range upon range.

8 To see the Biltmore Estate, leave the parkway at Milepost 85 and turn right on Route 25, which soon becomes Hendersonville Road, and then bear left at McDowell Street. The entrance to the house and gardens is on the left through the imposing stucco-and-brick lodge gate, 3.7 miles from the parkway. A three-mile approach road winds through elaborately landscaped grounds to Biltmore House itself.

Now a national historic landmark, Biltmore was the last of the great mansions constructed in various parts of the eastern United States by the flamboyantly wealthy Vanderbilt family. It was built by George Washington Vanderbilt, grandson of the "Commodore," Cornelius Vanderbilt, and was completed in 1895. Designed by Richard Morris Hunt in the style of a 16th-century French château, Biltmore was the focus of an estate that encompassed 125,000 acres. The gardens were laid out by Frederick Law Olmstead. Much of the estate was in forest, and Mr. Vanderbilt pioneered the first forestry school in America. (See highlight number 9.)

The house and grounds, which beggar description for grandeur, are closed on Thanksgiving, Christmas, and New Year's days.

7. Scenic extravaganzas are almost commonplace along the 469 miles of the splendid Blue Ridge Parkway. This overlook south of Ashville offers a sweeping expanse of western North Carolina's noble high country with its dense forests set against broad-peaked mountains.

climb through the Pisgah National Forest, part of which was once included in the huge Vanderbilt estate. Seven miles beyond the river the parkway passes through a triple tunnel at Ferrin Knob, one of many tunnels on this section of the route.

9 Route 276 snakes down the side of the ridge through beautiful pine and hardwood forest in a series of hairpin turns that are startling after the smooth curves of the parkway, and after four miles reaches the Cradle of Forestry in America. Turn left into the visitor center.

This is the Biltmore Forest School, where Dr. Carl A. Schenck, brought from Germany by George Vanderbilt to manage the forests on the Biltmore Estate, taught apprentice foresters 12 months a year from 1898 until 1909. When the school closed its doors in 1913, it had graduated about 300 foresters. The doctor and his students lived simply, sleeping in primitive cabins. After morning lectures they went into the field to practice Dr. Schenck's theories of forestry.

A milc-long national recreation trail makes a loop through the "campus" to the schoolhouse, commissary, living quarters, and other buildings complete with the old furnishings, utensils, gear, and the personal memorabilia of the students.

The high country of western North Carolina is renowned for its waterfalls because its multitudinous streams and rocky ledges so often combine to create soothing and refreshing cascades and water slides. There are many pleasant places to pull off the road and rest. Approximately 3.4 miles below the Cradle of Forestry there is a parking area at Sliding Rock. Here Looking Glass Creek flows swiftly over a huge, smooth rock where bathers can slide into the deep pool below.

Another two miles brings you to Looking Glass Falls, on the left, where the creek plunges gracefully, misting the growth of mosses and ferns on the pool ledge.

The landscaped gardens, woods, and meadows of Biltmore provide a stunning contrast to the wild natural beauty of the Blue Ridge and the Great Smokies.

The parkway southwest of Asheville sweeps across the French Broad River (so named because it flows westward into territory once controlled by France) and begins to

8. After much searching, the late George Washington Vanderbilt chose this location near Ashville for a baronial estate. Biltmore House's 250 rooms include the huge 70-foot-high Banquet Hall, a 20,000-volume library, and the imposing 75-foot-long Tapestry Room.

10　The resort town of Brevard is the site of the world-renowned Brevard Music Center, which each year from July to mid-August offers to 325 carefully selected youngsters a 6½-week course of musical instruction combined with a music festival of symphonic concerts, grand operas, musicals, and choral concerts that feature outstanding guest artists. The picturesque grounds of the music center are on the west edge of town.

11　About 18 miles west of Brevard the road crosses Toxaway Lake on a small concrete bridge, where there is a rough pulloff area to the right. Below this bridge and stretching away to the south is a striking vista of Toxaway Falls, where the waters of the lake flow over a huge mass of rocks formed like domed steps to splash into a pool below. Here bathers can slide down the rock face into the pool. A very rough trail leads from the west end of the bridge to the foot of the falls.

12　The route leads on to Highlands, a charming resort and at 4,118 feet the highest incorporated town in the East. It is at the center of what natives call Land of the Waterfalls, and their appellation is well supported. As you follow Route 64 toward the northwest, you soon encounter Bridal Veil Falls on the right and shortly thereafter Dry Falls on the left. At Bridal Veil you can drive your car behind the sheet of descending water. At Dry Falls you can look through to the beautiful, fast-flowing Cullasaja River, which cuts a steep-sided rocky gorge through which the road passes.

The town of Franklin is the center of the Cowee Valley ruby mines, and as you follow Route 28 north you pass the Gibson and Shuler mines. There is a small admission fee at each mine, which entitles you to a bucket of gravel in which you *might* find a ruby.

About 14 miles north of Franklin you begin to notice startling examples of the encroaching kudzu vine, which covers trees, banks, power lines, and guard rails like an all-engulfing green menace, as the road rises, dips, and curves through impressive rocky ridges and cliffs.

13　Watch for the Fontana Dam access road on the right. The road leads 1.2 miles to the dam itself—at

15. Black bears, often seen in the Great Smokies, are engaging but dangerous, especially when tempted with food.

480 feet the highest dam east of the Rockies. The TVA dam backs up the Little Tennessee River to form 30-mile-long Fontana Lake, where fishing and boating are available. You can drive to the powerhouse, where the big generators can be seen in action. The access road continues across the top of the dam (as does the Appalachian Trail) to parking areas on the other side that provide excellent views of Fontana Lake and the face of the great dam.

Some sections of the road to the northwest dip and curve along the ridgeline in a series of hairpin turns. But careful driving and a relaxed attitude can make it an exhilarating rather than a tiring stretch. There is a rough turnoff where you can stop to shake out the kinks and enjoy the spectacular views of Calderwood Lake at the same time.

14　The Foothills Parkway, which lies in Tennessee beyond Great Smoky Mountains National Park, was planned to provide views of the Smokies from points previously inaccessible by car. When the weather is right, it succeeds magnificently. Parking areas are numerous, and some seven miles from the entrance is Look Rock, where there is a campground, a picnic area, and an obser-

vation tower, which can be reached by a climb from the parking area.

Leaving the Foothills Parkway and continuing on Route 73 toward Townsend, you see places where road construction has exposed rock bedding planes that show a stratified dolomite rock. Remember that no gasoline is sold inside the park.

15　For a more intimate acquaintance with Appalachia, take the time for a visit to Cades Cove. White settlers first reached the cove, a broad, level area rimmed by ridges, in 1818, and a small farming community grew. Cades Cove is now a fascinating museum of restored old buildings that depict the hard life of an isolated mountain people. An 11-mile paved road loops around the village. There are also trails for hiking and riding and horses for hire.

To reach Cades Cove, which is within Great Smoky Mountains National Park, take the Rich Mountain Road at Townsend. (If this is closed for the winter, take the Laurel Creek Road, which turns west off Route 73 two miles within the park bounds.)

Returning to Route 73, you enter beautiful Little River Gorge, where rocky overhangs seem scarcely to allow room for the passage of your car. Many pulloffs afford an opportunity to explore the river's cascades, including The Sinks, a series of steep rapids and deep pools.

16　Not far from The Sinks is the turnoff and parking area for Laurel Falls on the north. A paved 1.3-mile trail leads to these popular falls, whose abundant flow of water testifies to the fact that the Great Smokies receive quite a bit of rain.

Near the junction of Routes 73 and 441 are the park headquarters and the Sugarlands Visitor Center, where you can see a short film on the park and exhibits on the natural history of the Smokies.

Route 441, a transmountain highway, twists and turns as it follows the West Fork of the Little Pigeon River up into the evergreen-covered peaks. Often in summer the air seems smoky—hazy with heat and vapor from trees or with actual mist. Other days can be crystal clear. But there is plenty to see in either case: the tree-cloaked mountains; the picturesque twin peaks called the Chimney Tops, which loom up on the right; The Loop, where the highway passes under and then over itself in its steep climb; an occasional family of black bears foraging at the roadside; and in season blooming mountain laurel. And finally, at 5,048 feet, is Newfound Gap itself.

17 There is a limit to what can be said about views, and on this drive that limit must be tested again and again. From the overlook at Newfound Gap, on the border of Tennes-

with strong feeling—whether exhilaration, awe, reverence, or deep calm.

18 There is an equally variable and equally inspiring view from Clingmans Dome, at 6,642 feet the highest peak in Great Smoky Mountains National Park and the third highest in the East. The Dome, with its strikingly designed modern observation tower, is reached by a seven-mile spur road from Newfound Gap. (The road is closed in winter.) On a clear day, corners of Georgia, South Carolina,

tor an opportunity to see how the southern Appalachian settlers lived virtually off the land until the early part of the 20th century. A self-guiding tour booklet explains the details of farm life and the functions of various buildings and tools. Indigenous crafts and skills are demonstrated by park employees.

20 Leaving the park at the Cherokee entrance, turn east onto the Blue Ridge Parkway. This is the highest and wildest part of the parkway, and it is sometimes closed in winter. The slopes above and below the road bristle with dead evergreen trees (many killed by the balsam woolly aphid, which penetrates the bark and needles and sucks out the nutrients). Outcrops of red and gray rock, partly covered with lichen, reveal the underlying gneiss and schist structure of the mountains.

About 10 miles along the Blue Ridge Parkway, turn north onto the Heintooga Ridge spur road and continue 1.3 miles to Mile-High Overlook for a breathtaking view of the Smokies. A campground and picnic area lie six miles farther up the spur.

21 Waterrock Knob Overlook provides some of the most spectacular views on the entire Blue Ridge Parkway. A half-mile-long side road leads off the parkway to the overlook, which has an elevation of 5,718 feet. Here is a 360-degree panorama of the misty mountains, dark forests, and twisting valleys that comprise the Southern Highlands. Informative schematic drawings in exhibit panels identify the peaks of the Great Smokies to the north and west, the Blue Ridge and Cowee ranges to the south, Mount Pisgah to the east, and the Great Balsam Range of which the Knob itself is a part. A trail leads to the top of the Knob.

22 Proceeding from one wild vista to another, at Richland Balsam Overlook you reach the highest point on the parkway—6,053 feet. Because of the altitude, the forests on the mountain have the same characteristics as those found in Canada, hundreds of miles to the north. A self-guiding nature trail leads from the Haywood Jackson parking area, less than half a mile farther on, through a growth of Fraser fir and red spruce reminiscent of the great north woods.

17. At Newfound Gap on the crest of the Smokies, the air is cool, clouds often lie in the gaps between the mountains, and the vegetation is more appropriate to the Northeast. Adding to the other-worldly effect are spruce–fir forests, relics of the ice age.

see and North Carolina, the mountains and ridges stretch in all directions. At any season and in any weather, at any time of day, the changing mood and gigantic scale of this panorama inspires the viewer

and Virginia are visible from here. There is a self-guiding nature trail through the moody spruce–fir forest.

19 At the Oconaluftee Visitor Center there is a completely restored pioneer farmstead that gives the visi-

This area has appeal for anyone who *loves fishing, swimming, sunning, beachcombing, or bird-watching. The roads are rarely more than a few miles from water, be it ocean, bay, river, lake, or swamp. This is land formed from alluvial deposits carried down by the many rivers from the mountains and the Piedmont and worked over by the waves and alongshore currents. The broad rivers in this flat area open into wide bays, seemingly guarded from the ocean's encroachment only by the narrowest wisp of barrier beach. The beaches are thrown up by the waves, but the forceful flow of the fresh water in the rivers partially stabilizes the barriers and keeps open most of the outlets to the sea. The bays, which contain both salt and fresh water, are a breeding ground for such delectable shellfish as crabs, oysters, and scallops.*

1 Greenville is the second largest center in the state for the processing and marketing of tobacco. From July to November the warehouse auctions are in full swing; if you would like to attend and listen to the calls of the auctioneers, you are welcome to do so. At the Tobacco Farmers' Show in mid-November you can also see the processes and machinery used in the industry. A pleasant place for an outing is the Greenville Town Common, a public park on the bank of Tar River.

Along Routes 13 and 64 the land is a mosaic of tobacco, corn, peanut, and soybean fields; the patches of pine forests are also harvested, as the logging trucks testify.

Between the pleasant river village of Plymouth and the coastal town of Edenton, the road crosses estuaries of the Roanoke River delta and spans the wide Chowan River. Driving along, you begin to realize what a watery domain this is.

2 Edenton, on Albemarle Sound, was incorporated in 1722, and it is truly an amalgam of architectural styles, ranging from the Jacobean, as exemplified by the Cupola House, through Georgian, federal, Greek Revival, and Victorian. The Chowan County Courthouse on Broad Street is the oldest courthouse in the United States in continuous public use.

The federal-style Barker House, built about 1782 and moved to its parklike waterfront setting in the 1950's, is now home to a museum and a visitor center (closed Mondays and Thanksgiving, Christmas, and New Year's days). Here you can get a guidebook showing the locations of the fine, old buildings in the town and in Chowan County, or embark on a two-hour guided tour of Edenton's historic district.

The demanding process of growing tobacco

North Carolina grows more flue-cured tobacco than any other state in the Union. The designation "flue-cured," borrowed from the old term for the curing process in heat-controlled barns, actually refers to a variety of the species of *Nicotiana tabacum* that produces a mild, light tobacco.

The tiny tobacco seeds are spread over plant beds in winter and protected with plastic sheeting. After 6 to 10 weeks the rooted plants are transplanted in the fields. Many growers now use irrigation to improve the yield of the plant and the quality of the leaves. They also remove the tobacco flower to divert energy into leaf development. When mature, the plants are from four to six feet tall, with leaves up to three feet long and half as wide.

The lower leaves ripen before the upper ones, and so the harvesting is done in stages. The leaves are sorted and graded, mainly by color, and suspended in racks in bulk-curing barns where humidity-controlled, heated air is evenly distributed. The curing, which takes three or four days, turns the leaves the desired golden brown. The tobacco then goes to the warehouses for auction. Buyers age tobacco for several years before manufacturing the final product.

Tobacco flower

Mature plant

Protected seedlings

Transplanting

Harvesttime

Bulk-curing barns

4. Although Lake Mattamuskeet is the state's largest natural lake, the water is remarkably shallow, averaging two feet in depth. The lake is a national wildlife refuge for migratory waterfowl and certain endangered species. There are also special fishing areas.

[3] The route south from Creswell to Pettigrew State Park cuts through coastal swamp, and the road is edged with drainage ditches that hold standing water. In the midst of this area lies spring-fed Lake Phelps, the discovery of which, in 1755, led to the development of the marshlands into huge, prosperous plantations.

At Pettigrew State Park, which includes parts of the old Collins and Pettigrew plantations, you can tour the restored Somerset Place, the elegant mansion built by the Collins family about 1830, and stroll down tree-bordered lanes to the gardens and outbuildings. (Closed on major holidays.) Camping, hiking, boating, and fishing are also enjoyed here.

[4] Mattamuskeet National Wildlife Refuge is famous for its whistling swans. During November and December as many as 25,000 of them congregate here. Also here for the winter months are many thousands of Canada geese and ducks. In the spring and summer osprey nest in the cypress trees. There are herons and egrets, and in winter the southern bald eagle and the even more rare golden eagle may be seen. The refuge has a foot trail and a short auto loop, and permits nonmotorized boats.

As you head toward the ocean, pine woodlands, which include longleaf pine (*Pinus palustris*), the state tree, become more swampy and pond pine and saw grass more frequent.

[5] Between the marshy mainland and the sandbars of the Outer Banks lies small Roanoke Island, chosen by Sir Walter Raleigh (on the basis of favorable reports) to be the site of England's ill-fated first colony in America.

The visitor center at Fort Raleigh National Historic Site has displays relating to the landing of the settlers here in 1585 and to the colony's mysterious disappearance soon afterward. In summer a musical drama about the Lost Colony is effectively staged at an outdoor theater overlooking Roanoke Sound near the presumed site of the settlement. You can also see the reconstruction of the fort the colony had built and follow a nature trail to a pleasant point for a view of the sound.

It is just a short walk from the historic site to the serenely beautiful Elizabethan Gardens, developed and maintained by the Garden Club of North Carolina. There is something in bloom here year-round, but the most colorful displays are mid- to late April, when azaleas are ablaze amid flowering dogwood (*Cornus florida*), North Carolina's state flower, and flowering bulbs carpet the ground. In midsummer roses, gardenias, magnolias, crape myrtle, and flowering annuals are at their best. The gardens are closed from December to March.

[6] Driving north from Whalebone Junction on Bodie Island, you can take either Beach Road 158, which

5. Adjacent to the presumed site of the Lost Colony founded on Roanoke Island, the Elizabethan Gardens are a lovely memorial to those settlers who, in dramatist Paul Green's words, "walked away through the dark forest into history."

edges the Atlantic Ocean, or Bypass 158. Numerous crossroads connect them, and near Nags Head the roads almost merge.

Jockey's Ridge State Park, at Nags Head, is an area of shifting sands and dunes with no vegetation at all. A 30-minute walk from the parking lot takes you to the top of Jockey's Ridge; nearly 100 feet high, this is the largest dune on the east coast. From its crest are fine views of sound, beach, and ocean. Dune climbing, hang gliding, and sand skiing are popular activities here.

7 People usually think of Kitty Hawk as the place where the Wright brothers made their first powered flights, on December 17, 1903, but that actually took place a few miles south at Kill Devil Hills, where the steady winds provided lift and the sands a soft landing. In the three preceding summers Frank and Orville Wright carried out nearly 1,000 glider flights here, learning to keep aloft their fragile craft of cloth, wood, and wire.

The Wright Brothers National Memorial Visitor Center has a reproduction of their first powered flying machine, and it is awe-inspiring to see. (The original is in the Smithsonian Institution.) At the site are markers showing the distances of those four history-making flights. Near the field are two weathered-looking clapboard buildings, reconstructions of their 1901–03 camp and workshop and their 1903 hangar. Close by is the Wright Monument, a granite pylon rising from the top of Kill Devil Hills, from which the Wrights launched glider flights. The dune has been planted with grass to keep it from being blown away by driving winds.

8 For 70 miles—from Whalebone Junction to Ocracoke Inlet—the Cape Hatteras National Seashore presents a dramatic landscape of pale golden sand beaches, surf, dunes, marshes, and maritime forest. To learn about facilities in the park, stop at the small information center at Whalebone Junction. There are five Park Service campgrounds; in addition, privately operated campsites and modest accommodations can be found in the eight villages along the road.

For a swim or a lunch at a shaded picnic table, take the spur road to Coquina Beach, one of seven beaches

in the park posted with lifeguards in summer. Near the parking lot is Sand Castle, a nature center for children with programs on sand painting and marine life. A short distance away you can see the hull of a ship that was wrecked here in 1921. Park only in designated areas to avoid getting stuck in soft sand.

Returning to the highway, look for the turnoff to Bodie Island Lighthouse (1872), one of several that have operated on the Outer Banks for more than a century to warn ships away from the dangerous shoals. The Bodie Island Visitor Center, also located here, has exhibits related to the history of the lighthouse and to the story of duck hunting. On the grounds are a self-guiding nature trail and a bird observation platform. A campground is close by.

Stretches of the road on Bodie Island are bordered with thickets of yaupon, wax myrtle, groundsel, and southern bayberry. So dense are these shrubs that they seem ready to overtake the road if given a chance. In places the thickets open upon marsh dotted with hammocks, knolls or small islands tufted with trees. Flamingos and other wading birds may be seen as they seek food in the shallow water.

8. Distinguished by its horizontal bands of black and white paint, Bodie Island Lighthouse is easily identified by day.

9 From Bodie Island the highway curves like a white ribbon across the blue waters of Oregon Inlet to Hatteras Island, the north end of which was once separated by an inlet and known as Pea Island. A midway point in the Atlantic flyway of migrating birds, this area was set aside in 1938 as the Pea Island National Wildlife Refuge. It is a favorite wintering spot for snow geese, and enormous flocks of them sometimes line the road. With its varied environment, the refuge attracts more than 260 species of waterfowl, shorebirds, wading birds, and songbirds. Among those commonly seen during most of the year are the glossy ibis and certain herons, terns, and egrets.

At the refuge headquarters you can pick up a listing of the birds found here season by season. For bird-watching, take the foot trail encircling North Pond Lake to one of the two observation platforms. Other pleasures that are permitted within the refuge limits are crabbing along Oregon Inlet and surf fishing.

10 Just east of Buxton on Hatteras Island turn south off Route 12 to reach the Cape Hatteras Lighthouse. The tallest brick lighthouse in America, it stands sentinel at Diamond Shoal, which reaches 10 miles into the ocean and has been the scene of more than 100 wrecks. The climb up 268 steps to the lighthouse platform (175 feet above the sea) is worth it for the spectacular view of the Cape, known as the Graveyard of the Atlantic, where the ocean waters churn above the shoals. The exhibits at the Cape Hatteras Visitor Center have as their theme the history of shipwrecks along here.

The maritime forest that you pass between Buxton and Frisco is the largest on the Outer Banks. A foot trail winds among its gnarled and twisted loblolly pines and live oaks, their leaves thick and leathery to withstand the salt spray. The forest is a welcome retreat from sun and surf, and its tangled growth provides a refuge for wildlife.

Beyond the town of Hatteras is the dock for the free ferry to Ocracoke Island. Ferries run every 40 minutes from mid-April through October, and every hour on the hour the rest of the year. The ride takes 40 minutes.

10. *A stray, weather-warped tree adds to the wild beauty of Cape Hatteras. Visible in the distance is the edge of a maritime forest that grows densely to within a mile of the ocean before it thins out and yields the coast to brush and dune grasses.*

11 Ocracoke Island has a special appeal. The town, which suggests a New England village with a semitropical air, sprawls around Silver Lake, which was created when the U.S. Navy widened and deepened Cockle Creek for a harbor during World War II. Dominating the village is the picturesque Ocracoke Lighthouse, built in 1823. Ocracoke is a pleasant place to linger and slow down, stroll the narrow streets, ride a bicycle, and enjoy the peace of its uncrowded, secluded beaches.

A main feature of the island is the semiwild Ocracoke ponies (believed to be descended from Spanish mustangs stranded here in the 16th century). From the road you can see the remnant of the once-great herds of these small horses, still living in a natural state but in a fenced area. The island is also steeped in the lore of the pirate Blackbeard, whose hideout this was and who was killed on Ocracoke Inlet in 1718.

You should make a reservation (well in advance in summer) for the 2½-hour ferry ride from Ocracoke to Cedar Island. The moss-draped pines and oaks of Cedar Island and the adjacent mainland are a refreshing sight after the treelessness of most of the national seashore. Water and prairies of marsh grass are also much in evidence, and fishing and crabbing boats are tied to wharves alongside the highway.

12 Beaufort, the third oldest town in North Carolina and once a flourishing seaport, has a charming historic district on the waterfront with close to 85 oak-shaded houses and public buildings from the 1700's and 1800's. In the center of the district is a small complex of restored buildings that you can tour with a costumed hostess. The restoration includes houses built in the old style of the Bahamas, plus the Carteret County Courthouse (1791), which displays its original 13-star flag, the jail with living quarters for the jail keeper, and a quaint little apothecary shop. The headquarters for the Beaufort Historical Association is in the complex. Closed Thanksgiving and Christmas days.

A step away is the Hampton Mariners Museum, which focuses on boatbuilding, navigation, and seacoast ecology. You can see early sailmakers' and boatbuilders' tools, navigational instruments, models of sailing vessels, seashells, fossils, and waterfowl decoys. But the museum is not just of the past, for it has a summer program with courses on the construction of indigenous types of wooden boats (visitors can watch).

13 A causeway from Morehead City leads to Bogue Banks, on the eastern tip of which is Fort Macon State Park. Fort Macon, built between 1826 and 1834 to guard the port of Beaufort, has a moat (now dry) and casemates opening onto a central parade ground, and is considered to be an unusually fine example of 19th-century military architecture. The fort was garrisoned off and on from 1834 to 1862, when it was taken by Union forces. It was again manned during the Spanish-American War and in World War II. Closed from Labor Day to June. The park has picnic grounds and a fine beach.

14 The Marine Resource Center is at the Theodore Roosevelt Natural Area, a state park. A half-hour walk on the nature trail provides a sampling of local ecological features, including saltwater marsh, freshwater pond, maritime forest, and pine-covered hammocks.

15 The semiprimitive campground at Cedar Point, in the Croatan National Forest, is in a lovely clearing among pines, oaks, and sweetgums on the banks of the White Oak River. Boating, fishing, and exploring along a nature trail are to be enjoyed here. The swamps and forest are the habitat of waterfowl, swamp birds, fiddler crabs, and other wildlife.

The bogs are also the home of five kinds of insectivorous plants, including a rare species of Venus's-flytrap (*Dionaea muscipula*), pitcher plants, sundews, butterworts, and bladderworts. The last are floating plants buoyed by inflated leaves (bladders) that also trap small aquatic animals and the larvae of mosquitoes. A note of caution—do not stray from the trail to search for the plants because alligators also live in the swamps.

16 New Bern, the second oldest town in North Carolina, has a concentration of handsome Georgian-, federal-, and Victorian-style houses and public buildings. At the Chamber of Commerce on Broad Street you can get a map for a walking tour that includes many of them.

But the crown jewel of New Bern is Tryon Palace. The magnificent Georgian building was finished in 1770 and became the seat of government and residence of colonial Gov. William Tryon. It later served as North Carolina's first state capitol. In 1798 a fire destroyed all but the basement and the two wings. Governor Tryon's detailed inventories of his furnishings, the original architectural plans, and some research have made possible the meticulous reconstruction of the palace and the extensive gardens, also of 18th-century English design. The guided tour takes about two hours. The palace is closed Thanksgiving Day, December 24–26, New Year's Day, and on all Mondays except national holidays.

South Carolina

The coastal plain, the Piedmont, and the Blue Ridge province provide engaging changes of scenery

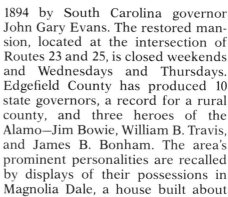

Gentle echos of the Old South ring down through the scenic wooded hills, beside the many lakes, and across the fertile plantation lands of the Palmetto State.

In the city of Charleston you can enjoy the epitome of civic grace and charm, and at nearby Middleton Place is one of America's most beautiful gardens.

On the seaward side are inviting islands, and inland are superb wildlife preserves to explore and enjoy.

Tiny churches, old homesteads, and wooded hills are the recurrent theme of this rolling loop through the South Carolina Piedmont.

Lakes provide occasional vistas of water, while a number of towns and sites are reminders of the area's history. But most characteristic are the weathered farmhouses and barns, many engulfed by kudzu vine, others tilting and slanting in aged eccentricity, which give this countryside a picturesque quality.

1 Located virtually at the geographical center of the state, Columbia, the capital of South Carolina, was partially destroyed by Union troops at the close of the Civil War. It has been rebuilt into a proud, broad-avenued city on a hill. The building that serves as the capitol and state-house is a handsome derivation of the U.S. Capitol in Washington, D.C. Other points of interest in Columbia include the Governor's Mansion and the President Woodrow Wilson Boyhood Home.

2 Heading west from Columbia, the highway soon brings you to Lexington and to the Lexington County Museum, located on the south side of Route 378 at Fox Street. The simple, two-story frame farmhouse was built in the early 1800's and was the home of state senator John Fox. Representing a small, mid-19th-century landholding, the museum has furnishings handmade of local wood and artifacts typical of the region and the period. It is closed Mondays and on Sunday mornings.

As you continue westward, you drive through farmland dotted with peach orchards and fields of soybeans. Signs show a number of access roads to Lake Murray and to picnic areas and boat-launching ramps. Just two miles east of the junction with Route 121 at Saluda, a modern Milliken textile plant makes a striking contrast with the abandoned farmsteads scattered through the countryside.

3 Edgefield, a county seat, has several historic buildings and homes. Among them is Oakley Park, built in 1817 and presented to the county in 1894 by South Carolina governor John Gary Evans. The restored mansion, located at the intersection of Routes 23 and 25, is closed weekends and Wednesdays and Thursdays. Edgefield County has produced 10 state governors, a record for a rural county, and three heroes of the Alamo—Jim Bowie, William B. Travis, and James B. Bonham. The area's prominent personalities are recalled by displays of their possessions in Magnolia Dale, a house built about 1800. Open by appointment.

The road, as you drive toward Clarks Hill Lake, cuts through banks of red clay and passes weathered old farm buildings. For a short interval the handsome white rail fences of a prosperous farm provide a snappy contrast.

4 From Modoc, take Route 28 south to the Clarks Hill Dam, which forms one of the nation's largest man-made lakes. Completed in 1954, the dam backs up the waters of the Savannah River for 40 miles, creating a sportsmen's paradise with innumerable lovely inlets, coves, and islands. Near the dam are several picnic grounds, a boat ramp, and a place for swimming. The huge dam and its powerhouse are fascinating in their own right.

4. In a state that has no large natural lakes, the Clarks Hill Dam creates an important recreation area. It is also part of a network of dams—among them, the Hartwell and the Richard B. Russell—essential for both flood control and electric power output.

SPECIAL FEATURES

ROAD GUIDE	HIGHLIGHT **1**
STATE PARKS With Campsites ▲ Without Campsites △	SCHEDULED AIRLINE STOPS ✗
RECREATION AREAS With Campsites ▲ Without Campsites △	OTHER AIRPORTS ✗
SELECTED REST AREAS	MILITARY AIRPORTS ✗
With Toilets ✗ Without Toilets ✗	BOAT RAMPS ◢
POINTS OF INTEREST ⊞	INFORMATION CENTER ✪

ROAD CLASSIFICATION

CONTROLLED ACCESS HIGHWAYS — Divided **5** Undivided
Interstate interchange numbers are mileposts. — Interchanges

OTHER DIVIDED HIGHWAYS

PAVED HIGHWAYS

LOCAL ROADS In unfamiliar areas inquire locally before using these roads — Paved — Gravel — Dirt

MILEAGE

MILEAGE BETWEEN TOWNS AND JUNCTIONS 3 ▲ 4 — MILEAGE BETWEEN DOTS ●—35—●

SCALE

ONE INCH 18 MILES 0 5 10 20

ONE INCH 29 KILOMETERS 0 5 10 20 32

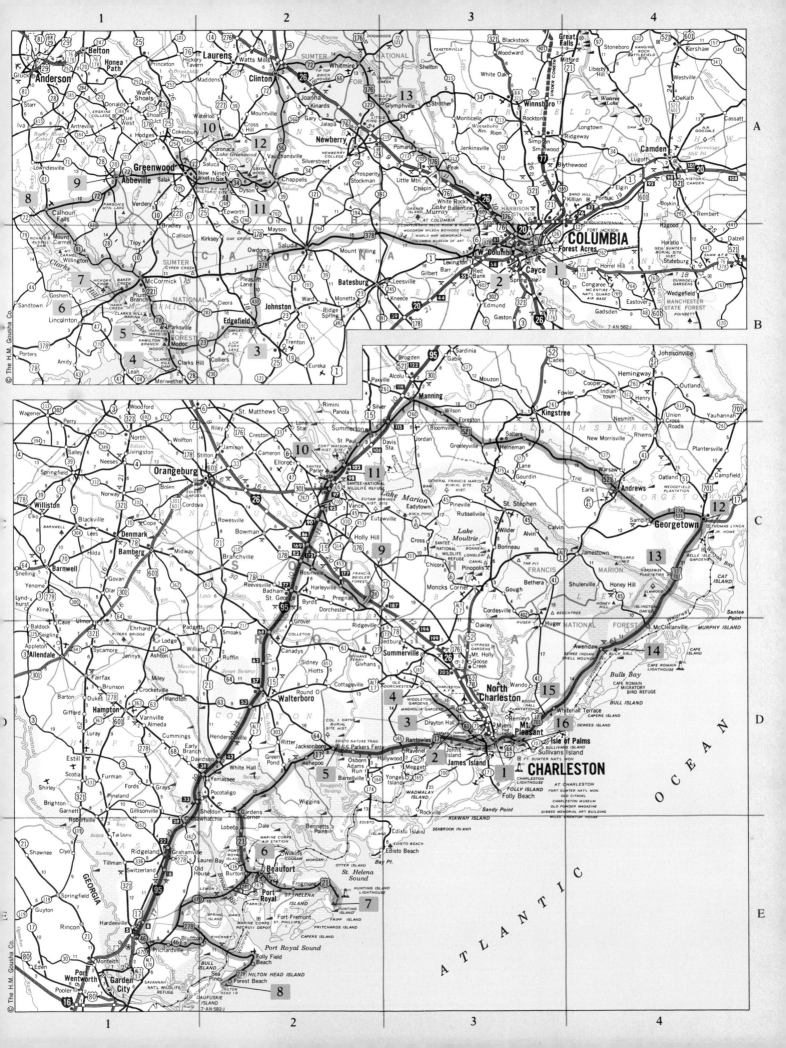

5 Returning to Modoc, continue north for 1.7 miles to Hamilton Branch State Park. Pleasantly situated on a wooded point, the park offers campsites, three picnic areas, and fishing. Just two miles farther north, a roadside park provides excellent views of the lake. Following the road along the lakeshore, you notice a commercial woodyard and a large lumber mill.

6 At McCormick, turn west onto Route 378 and continue for about four miles to Baker Creek State Park, another lakeside spot in rolling, wooded terrain. Here you can play miniature golf, rent a paddleboat, or enjoy an outdoor playground in addition to such standard park activities as picnicking, boating, fishing, and camping.

7 Six miles farther west on Route 378 is the turnoff to Hickory Knob State Resort Park, which provides comfortable accommodations in handsome, modern cabins or in a lodge, once again in a beautiful, wooded lakeside setting. There are also campsites, a nature trail, and a multitude of recreational facilities for everyone in the family.

8 About four miles north of Mount Carmel, turn west onto a narrow road leading to the Richard B. Russell Dam overlook, which offers a splendid view of the dam.

9 Abbeville, founded in 1758, was the birthplace of Vice President John C. Calhoun. An early cultural and commerical center, the town was a witness to many historic events in the Revolutionary War and the Civil War. The historic section of Abbeville,

13. Cottontail rabbits inhabit Sumter National Forest, nesting and nurturing their young in hidden hollows.

which centers around the city square, has been charmingly restored. Among the places to see is the Opera House, which was built about 1807. By appointment you can visit the Burt–Stark House where the War Council of the Confederate forces concluded that the South's cause was hopeless and agreed to disband the army. The County Museum, housed in a former jail, contains interesting local memorabilia.

10 Six miles north of Greenwood are the gardens of the Park Seed Company. The trial gardens and the floral displays are outstandingly beautiful, especially in midsummer when they are featured at the South Carolina Festival of Flowers held in Greenwood. Guided tours are given weekdays. Closed weekends and holidays and the last week of July.

11 From the junction of Routes 34 and 248, follow the signs south to Ninety Six National Historic Site. An early crossroads settlement that became an important military objective during the Revolutionary War, Ninety Six fell into obscurity and decay in the early 19th century.

Two village sites dating from the French and Indian War and fortifications built during the Revolutionary War are being excavated and restored by the National Park Service. The unusual name is said to refer to the distance in miles from an Indian village that was well known in colonial times. Displays and a loop trail to the settlements and redoubts give fascinating insights into the history of the region.

12 Backtracking and continuing toward Lake Greenwood, take a two-mile detour north on Route 702 to Greenwood State Park. Situated on two points in the lake, the park provides a wealth of recreational facilities amid beautiful pine groves.

Reflecting the foundation of the region's economy are the sawmills, woodlots, and soybean fields that flank the road en route to Clinton. Now an attractive town and the site of Presbyterian College, Clinton was described in 1865 as "a mudhole surrounded by barrooms."

13 Turning southeast toward Columbia, the loop takes you through part of the Sumter National Forest where there are several small recreation areas. Especially appealing is Molly's Rock Picnic Area, a quiet, secluded spot with sheltered picnic tables by a pond. A short distance away is a large rock where, legend has it, a little girl named Molly used to sit and talk to the wild creatures of the woods. To reach the picnic area, watch for the intersection of Routes 176 and 121. Continue southeast another two miles to Forest Service Road 387; turn left and drive another half mile.

Between Molly's Rock and Columbia pines and oaks line the road. In this deep country setting is Pomaria, which, with its roadside park, epitomizes the small rural southern town.

12. An occasional deciduous tree on the shore of Lake Greenwood signals the gentle approach of autumn, an enjoyable time of year for camping, boating, and hiking here in the Piedmont. A cluster of picnic tables visible among the pines invites the passerby.

This romantic loop takes you through a land of moonlight and magnolias, Spanish moss and cypress swamps, and the grand plantations of the Old South. Many plantations and homes, more than 200 years old, still convey the gracious and quiet charm of a way of life enjoyed in the early days of the state of South Carolina.

Strung along the Atlantic coast are islands, famed of pirates and blockade runners, that have become a vacationland almost unsurpassed.

1 The vibrantly gracious, beautiful, and aristocratic city of Charleston, always a spirited center of culture, commerce, and class, serves to epitomize our vision of the Old South.

You can easily spend days exploring the city's large historic district with its charming 18th- and 19th-century houses, the restored City Market, the museums, and the colorful port.

The Charleston Visitor's Information Center at 85 Calhoun Street is the best place to go for maps and for help in arranging tours by foot, car, bus, or horse-drawn carriage. You can also take a boat tour to see Fort Sumter in Charleston Harbor. It was at Fort Sumter that the first shot was fired in the Civil War.

Before heading down the coast, take the time for a short drive up Ashley River Road (Route 61) to see one of the finest examples of early Georgian architecture in America—Drayton Hall. Not far beyond are two unusually beautiful and interesting plantation gardens.

2 About nine miles from downtown Charleston is the entrance to Drayton Hall, a plantation home built between 1738 and 1742. The stately red brick building, which commands sweeping grounds edged by majestic live oaks, is now a property of the National Trust for Historic Preservation. Since the house has never been modernized, it is a pristine example of early 18th-century architecture. It is noted for its bald cypress paneling, exceptional wood carving, and fine ornamental ceilings. Closed Thanksgiving, Christmas, and New Year's days.

3 Just west of Drayton Hall is the entrance to Magnolia Plantation and Gardens. The gardens, begun in the 1680's in a formal French style, were

4. A national historic landmark, the landscaped gardens of Middleton Place lay wild and untended for five decades after the Civil War. In 1916 a direct descendant of Henry Middleton began the loving restoration, exemplified by the serene Rice Millpond (above).

redesigned in an informal arrangement in the 1820's and remain as such today. Paths wander through the 500 acres of lovely shrubs and trees. The gardens have colorful blooms for much of the year and are vivid with flowering azaleas and camellias in the spring. The plantation house is also open to visitors.

4 In striking contrast to the latter is the elegant formality of the gardens of Middleton Place. The oldest, and among the most beautiful, landscaped gardens in America, these were designed with a symmetry and elegance that reflect English and French models. The gardens were laid out in 1741 and, according to family legend, required the labor of 100 slaves for 10 years to complete. Among the features of a self-guiding tour are an octagonal sunken garden, camellia *allées*, sculptured terraces that lead down to twin lakes contoured like butterfly wings, and one of the largest known specimens of a

flowering crape myrtle tree. In the house are family portraits by Benjamin West and period furnishings.

5 Returning to Charleston and veering south on Route 17, you cut through wide saltwater marshes and tidal rivers and then cross the Edisto River. Half a mile farther, on the north side of the road, is a turnoff for the Edisto Nature Trail. A well-marked path leads through a typical Carolina Low Country forest setting, with loblolly and slash pines, and past an abandoned road and canal and a deserted homesite. The stop provides a pleasant 20-minute walk.

Route 17 continues through vistas of tidal marshes, crossing the Ashepoo and Combahee rivers. Approaching the Combahee, you notice examples of the low, tree-covered elevations called hammocks that dot the tidewater flats.

6 At Gardens Corner, follow Route 21 south to Beaufort. Penetrating its commercial periphery, you

8. In addition to being a resort capital, Hilton Head Island is a sports paradise. The famous Heritage Golf Classic and the CPC (Colgate-Palmolive Company) International are held here. The tennis clubs boast world-class pros among their members. Other pleasures to be enjoyed here are sailing, fishing, biking, riding, and loafing on the long beaches of white sand.

find at the heart of this charming little city beautiful old pre-Revolutionary homes, narrow streets shaded by live oaks trailing Spanish moss, and the seven-acre Henry C. Chambers waterfront park, which has parking space near the historic district. Visit the Chamber of Commerce offices at 1006 Bay Street for information on houses and museums to see.

7 Sixteen miles east of Beaufort lies the dramatically windswept beach of Hunting Island State Park. Thick, subtropical woods march to the sea's edge, where pine and palmetto (*Sabal palmetto*), the state tree, fall victim to the storm waves of the Atlantic, occasionally littering the sand with debris. A 136-foot-high lighthouse, open to the public, gives broad vistas of the ocean and the coastal plain.

On the west side of the island an elevated boardwalk extends into the salt marsh, providing a fine opportunity to observe wildlife, including swarms of tiny fiddler crabs that scuttle beneath the walk at low tide.

The park offers rental cabins as well as a store and complete camping and picnicking facilities.

Backtracking, follow Route 170 southwest from Beaufort. After five miles or so the road crosses the Broad River. Just across the river is a roadside rest area in a grove of pines and palmettos that provides a splendid view of the sweep of marsh and river. Continuing through a scenic wooded area, turn east on Route 278 to reach Hilton Head Island.

8 One of the largest sea islands on the Atlantic coast, Hilton Head has also become one of the nation's most luxurious resort areas. It boasts huge residential "plantations," or private resort developments, plus many hotels, restaurants, and shopping complexes, and virtually every kind of recreational activity.

Despite this extensive development, nature lovers can still enjoy the island. Points of interest are the Sea Pines Forest Preserve and the Whooping Crane Pond at Hilton Head Plantation. For more details,

stop at the information center just before crossing the bridge from the mainland to the island.

Leaving Hilton Head, the loop takes you to Hardeeville and then heads north through a heavily forested landscape interspersed with riverside swamplands.

9 To find the Francis Beidler Forest, exit from Route 95 onto Route 178. About seven miles east of Harleyville, turn onto Route 28, a paved, northbound road. Continue another four miles to a dirt road that leads you to the entrance of this unique and lovely nature sanctuary.

Managed by the National Audubon Society, Francis Beidler Forest contains the largest remaining virgin stand of tupelo and cypress trees in the world. Here a 1½-mile boardwalk winds through Four Holes Swamp, where sparkling-clear pools and black-water sloughs are overhung by towering trees. In the silence of this forest, broken only by the sudden scurry of a lizard or another wild creature, the visitor seems carried back in time. The wildlife here includes deer, bobcats, opossums, red-shouldered hawks, owls, herons, turtles, and alligators. Exhibits in the visitor center tell more about local flora and fauna. Closed Mondays.

10 Return to Route 95 and drive north to Exit 98. About 1½ miles west on Route 6 is the entrance to Santee State Park and its unique Vacation Village. Beautifully situated on the shore of Lake Marion, the park offers a wonderful array of recreational opportunities, nature trails, and facilities for camping and picnicking. In the village are 30 strikingly designed cabins that can be rented by the day or week at reasonable rates.

11 Across Lake Marion is the Santee National Wildlife Refuge, where as many as 20,000 Canada geese may winter from September into March. A nature trail with interpretive signs and an observation tower introduce you to their habitat. (No picnicking is allowed here.) Within the refuge is the site of Fort Watson, a British outpost during the Revolutionary War, which was built on an Indian mound that still remains. The refuge is closed after dark and on major holidays.

12 From Manning, a flat, straight road runs through pine groves to the coast. Georgetown, the third oldest city in South Carolina, is the seat of what was once the most productive rice-growing county in America. For 200 years, from the beginning of the 1700's to the 1900's, life in this section of Low Country depended upon and revolved around that one crop. The Rice Museum in Georgetown vividly illustrates the story of a one-crop society, its rise, and its decline. The museum is housed in the picturesque old Market Building on Front Street. It is closed on major holidays.

13 A drive of another 12 miles through piney woods brings you to the turnoff for Hopsewee Plantation. With its serene white frame house on the banks of the North Santee River, this is a typical Low Country rice plantation of the early 18th century. A stroll on the grounds beneath magnolias and live oaks draped with Spanish moss provides a soothing interval in the day. Closed on holidays.

14 About eight miles south of the small town of McClellanville, a sign indicates the turnoff for Buck Hall

11. Colonies of white ibis, a beautiful wading bird, spend all but the winter months at Santee National Wildlife Refuge.

Recreation Area, a pleasant camp and picnic ground on the site of an old plantation overlooking the Intracoastal Waterway. The waterway and the marshes and small islands beyond form a lovely backdrop for this agreeable setting.

15 Just off the highway a few miles north of Charleston is Boone Hall Plantation. A land grant dating from 1681, Boone Hall was once a cotton plantation of some 17,000 acres. Today it is most famous for its spectacular and romantic ¾-mile Avenue of Oaks, often seen in television shows and motion pictures, including *Gone with the Wind.* The lovely plantation house underwent an extensive restoration in 1935. For the undertaking, old bricks made on the plantation were used as well as flooring and woodwork from the original mansion. Flanking the house are formal gardens rich with camellias and azaleas. Also preserved are the boat dock, the slave quarters, and other buildings that were important in plantation life. Closed Thanksgiving and Christmas days.

16 For a dramatic change, stop to see the World War II aircraft carrier U.S.S *Yorktown*, which is permanently moored at Patriots Point in Mount Pleasant just south of Route 17. Not only does the *Yorktown* serve as a fascinating self-contained display and a museum of naval air memorabilia, but its flight deck—one of the highest points for miles around—provides a magnificent unobstructed view of the city of Charleston and Charleston Harbor, with Fort Sumter in the distance.

15. Boone Hall, called America's most photographed plantation, was seen not only in Gone with the Wind, *but also in* Sweet Bird of Youth *and* Ada. *Walt Disney Studios filmed here twice, and Alistair Cooke shared a visit with viewers of the* America *TV series.*

The Empire State of the South

Georgia was the undisputed leader of the agricultural empire in the antebellum South

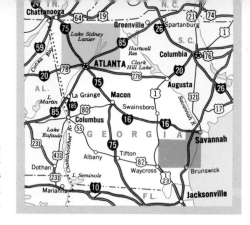

With its reminders of a pioneer past, its gracious old mansions in the romantic setting of magnolias and azaleas, and its modern cities, Georgia is a pleasing blend of the traditional and the contemporary.

Scenically, the state offers a surprising variety, from the mountains, lakes, and waterfalls of the Appalachian range in the north, through the Piedmont Plateau, to the coastal plains and marshes of the south.

From Atlanta, Georgia's strikingly modern capital, this tour takes you into the mountainous pioneer territory near the northern border, with its country music festivals and a fairy-tale copy of a Bavarian village. Leaving this land of misty blue ridges and crystal lakes, the route wends its way south to the Piedmont.

1 The vital, sophisticated city of Atlanta has appropriately chosen as its symbol the phoenix, the mythical bird that rose from its ashes. In 1864, because it was the transportation and supply center of the Confederacy, the town was almost completely destroyed by Union troops under Gen. William T. Sherman. The burning of Atlanta is depicted in a painting with a circumference of 400 feet. The canvas, completed in 1886, is on display in Grant Park as part of the Cyclorama, a sight-and-sound show on this phase of the Civil War.

The city today has some impressive modern buildings and many plazas and parks with fountains, contemporary sculpture, and flowering trees and shrubs. Part of the city that was reconstructed at the end of the Civil War was covered over by a system of viaducts in the 1920's. Now restored and known as Underground Atlanta, the area provides a 19th-century setting for artists' studios, boutiques, cafés, and nightclubs.

North of Atlanta's suburbs the road passes through partially wooded countryside with occasional farms. Here and there the land is mantled by the kudzu vine (*Pueraria thunbergiana*), which turns road banks into mysterious green grottoes and trees into fantastic shapes. The purple-flowering vine, brought from Asia in the 1870's and planted around porches and along road banks, has taken hold of much of the southern countryside and has caused much damage and destruction.

2 Kennesaw Mountain National Battlefield Park is the site of General Sherman's victory over Confederate Gen. Joseph E. Johnstone, which was a decisive turn in Sherman's thrust

1. Rapidly growing kudzu completely covers trees, which then die for lack of sunlight.

toward Atlanta. A museum at the visitor center displays guns and uniforms of the Civil War and shows a slide program on Sherman's Atlanta campaign. Here too you can get a map for a self-guided automobile tour of the park and the earthworks and battle sites.

The park's four hiking trails, all of which include some climbing, range in length from 2 to 16 miles, and cross hills wooded with poplars, sweet gums, birches, dogwoods, persimmons, azaleas, and rhododendrons.

3 On a small plain in the Etowah Valley are some of the largest ancient Indian ceremonial mounds in the East. The mounds and a fortified village were built by the Etowahs, who occupied the site between A.D. 1000–1500. The Indians carried soil in baskets to construct the mounds, the largest of which is 63 feet high. Steps or a ramp led to the tops of these earthen platforms where, it is believed, the Etowahs built temples of wattle and daub for religious festivals and burial ceremonies.

The villagers, who may have numbered several thousand, farmed in the valley, hunted in the hills, and fished in the Etowah River, which flows past the mounds. Today only the soft, rushing sound of the river breaks the silence here.

The Etowah Mounds Archeological Area is now a national historic landmark. A museum displays artifacts found here. Closed Mondays and Thanksgiving and Christmas days.

4 The restoration of New Echota, on a plain three miles east of Calhoun, is a poignant reminder of the tragic expulsion of the Cherokees from land that was recognized as theirs by several treaties with the United States. New Echota had been the capital of the Cherokee Nation from 1825 to 1838, when the people were forced to move out of Georgia, the village was razed, and the grounds were taken for farmland.

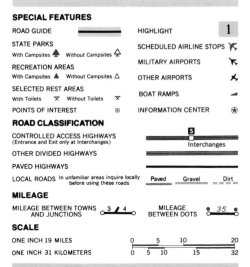

SPECIAL FEATURES		
ROAD GUIDE ▬▬▬	HIGHLIGHT	**1**
STATE PARKS		
With Campsites ⛺ Without Campsites △	SCHEDULED AIRLINE STOPS ✈	
RECREATION AREAS	MILITARY AIRPORTS ✈	
With Campsites ▲ Without Campsites △	OTHER AIRPORTS ✈	
SELECTED REST AREAS	BOAT RAMPS ◢	
With Toilets ✕ Without Toilets ✕		
POINTS OF INTEREST ▣	INFORMATION CENTER ✳	

ROAD CLASSIFICATION

CONTROLLED ACCESS HIGHWAYS
(Entrance and Exit only at Interchanges)   Interchanges

OTHER DIVIDED HIGHWAYS

PAVED HIGHWAYS

LOCAL ROADS In unfamiliar areas inquire locally   Paved   Gravel   Dirt
before using these roads

MILEAGE

MILEAGE BETWEEN TOWNS   3 4   MILEAGE   35
AND JUNCTIONS   BETWEEN DOTS

SCALE

ONE INCH 19 MILES   0   5   10   20
ONE INCH 31 KILOMETERS   0   5   10   15   32

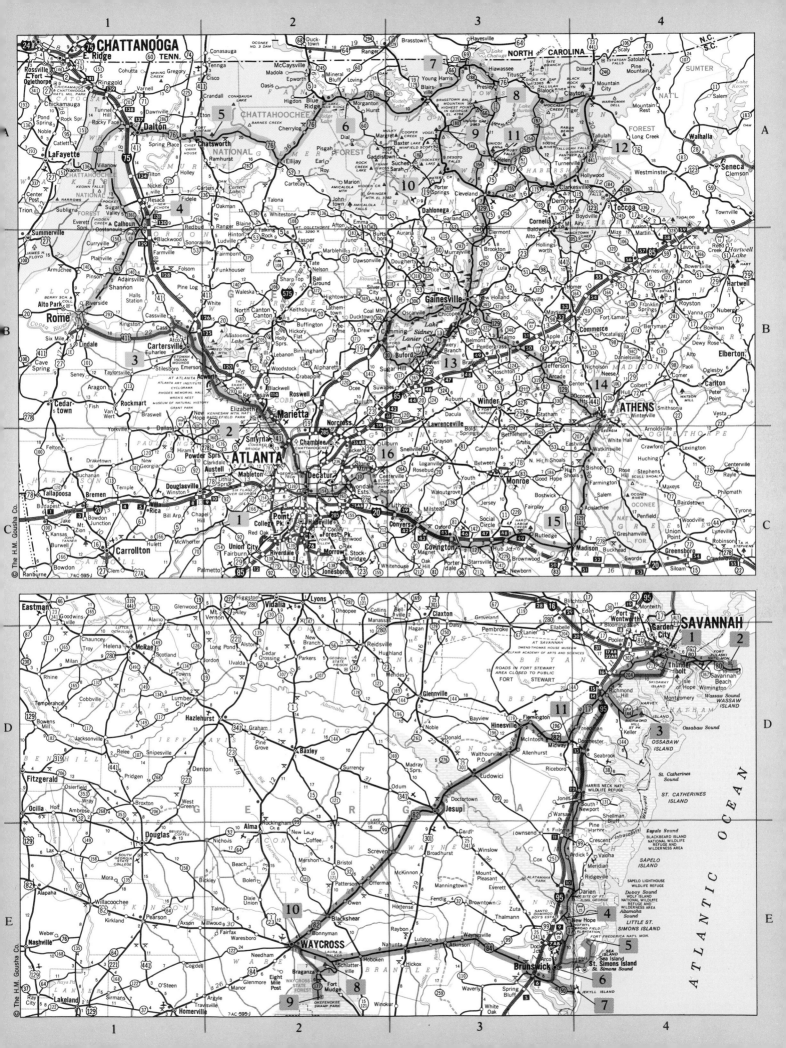

8. In spring the slopes of Brasstown Bald Mountain are vibrant with blossoming flame azaleas (Rhododendron calendulaceum) (top); rhododendrons (above, left); American mountain ash (Sorbus americana), which is festooned in autumn with bright red berries (above, center); and mountain laurel (Kalmia latifolia) (above, right).

At New Echota the Cherokees had published a newspaper in English and Cherokee, using the Cherokee syllabary developed by Sequoyah in 1815-17. Replicas of the printshop and the Cherokee courthouse have recently been constructed on their old sites. The restoration also includes the home of a missionary to the Indians at New Echota and a Cherokee-built tavern brought here from another place. The buildings are closed Mondays and Thanksgiving and Christmas days.

Leaving the farmland of the river valleys and the vast fields of soybeans and corn, the road cuts into the mountains of the Chattahoochee National Forest. This lovely wooded area, known as Georgia's pioneer territory, is filled with quail, wood ducks, deer, and other game. Occasional clearings reveal small upland farms and provide sweeping views of ridges and valleys.

5 Rising abruptly to an elevation of 2,954 feet, Fort Mountain looms above the attractive village of Chatsworth at its base. The steep road up the mountain provides dramatic views of both the village and the surrounding countryside. A short hike from the parking lot near the top brings you to the summit and to the ruins of an 855-foot-long serpentine stone wall. Its origin and purpose are a mystery, but archeologists are inclined to believe the wall was built by Indians centuries ago, possibly for religious ceremonies.

Fort Mountain State Park is a beautiful recreation area with tent and trailer sites, cottage and boat rentals, picnic grounds, hiking trails, and a lakefront beach for swimming.

East of Fort Mountain the road runs along the crest of Cohutta Mountain, providing magnificent views of the valleys on both sides, and then descends into a lush plain with apple orchards and meadows through which Turniptown Creek and other streams flow. Across the eastern horizon you can see the scalloped silhouette of the Blue Ridge Mountains' southern range.

6 Nestled in the mountains is Lake Blue Ridge. Formed by a TVA dam across Toccoa River at an elevation of nearly 1,700 feet, the clear blue waters of the lake spread through the hollows among the forested slopes, creating a shoreline 65 miles long. Waterfront campsites with a public beach and a boat ramp are maintained by the U.S. Forest Service at Green Creek and at Morganton Point. The lake offers superb fishing for pike, bass, crappies, and catfish.

In northeastern Georgia you are in the land of country biscuits, smokehouse ham, fruit cobblers, and boiled peanuts. Road signs advertise fiddle music and square dancing, barbecues, craft fairs, and the annual sorghum festival held at Blairsville on two weekends in October.

Between Blairsville and Young Harris you drive through a narrow valley with meadows and cornfields divided by the steel-blue ribbon of Butternut Creek. The views across the valley, as the road ascends the mountains from Young Harris, are among the loveliest in the state. As many as seven ridges can be seen, their soft blue silhouettes receding into the distance.

7 For several miles the road skirts Lake Chatuge, a large body of water on the border of Georgia and North Carolina. An extraordinarily beautiful lake, its still, glassy surface reflects the smoldering blue peaks rising from its shores. Cottage and boat rentals can be found in the vicinity of Hiawassee; there are also camping grounds and picnic areas on the lakefront and beaches for swimming.

8 With an elevation of 4,784 feet, Brasstown Bald Mountain is Georgia's highest peak. From the observation deck at the summit the panorama is a vast one: you can see four states, and on a clear day the skyline of Atlanta is visible.

The Cherokee name for the mountain was *Itse'yĭ,* "Place of Fresh Green," and in the spring it is just that: a burst of fresh greens mingled with flowering rhododendron, mountain laurel, and mountain ash. But the region is appealing year-round, and under winter snows it is a place of enchantment.

The cry "Thar's gold in them thar hills" referred to the 1828 discovery of gold at Dahlonega, about 25 miles from Brasstown Bald Mountain, in Cherokee territory. The exhibit hall at the visitor information center on the mountain presents the story of the 1828 gold rush and the seizure of Cherokee land.

The center also has excellent exhibits on the natural history of the region and presents a captivating slide program on the flora and fauna of the mountain in the four seasons. The center is closed from mid-December to mid-March, and on weekdays from mid-March to May and early November to mid-December.

A road leading up to a large parking lot below the summit is open year-round, weather permitting. From there a small bus takes you the last few hundred yards to the top, unless you prefer the paved but steep footpath. There are hiking trails on the mountain, and there is a picnic area near the parking lot.

9 A waterfall on the west side of the highway marks the location of Vogel State Park. From the entry gate an attractive driveway, giving views of the water through the trees, descends to Lake Trahlyta. The lake is sheltered by the hills rising around it, and its white sand beach makes it an especially inviting place for a swim.

In addition to picnic areas, there are trailer sites and rental cottages. Fishing is permitted, and there is a trail for hikers. Other trails, including the Appalachian Trail, can be found outside the park.

All the roads in northeast Georgia offer magnificent scenery, and one of the more spectacular stretches is Route 129, which cuts through Neels Gap, a high, narrow pass on the shoulder of Blood Mountain.

10 De Soto Falls Recreation Area is a secluded haven for camping or a day's outing. From the parking lot a short footbridge crosses a rippling brook to paths leading to the upper, middle, and lower falls. It is a steep climb of nearly three miles to the upper falls, but only 0.3 of a mile through the woods to the lower one. Here the brook splashes down the mountainside over tiers of mossy rock, its course half hidden by clumps of tall rhododendrons.

The falls are named after Hernando de Soto because, according to legend, a piece of armor believed to belong to the Spanish explorer or one of his men was found here.

11 In 1969 the citizens of Helen decided to improve the appearance of their community, and because of the mountain background, they chose to model it on an alpine village. Cobblestone streets and Bavarian-style building facades gaily painted in pastel colors give the place a story-book charm. The transformation of the old lumber mill town has lured visitors ever since to its Bavarian restaurants, lodges, candy kitchens, and craft and toy shops.

About a mile northeast of Helen are the Anna Ruby Falls, a double waterfall in a wilderness whose beauty is enhanced by azaleas, rhododendrons, and dogwoods.

The hilly countryside around Helen and Sautee is lovely, with trout streams flanked by fields of grasses and wild flowers that even in autumn display a remarkable palette of pinks, reds, violet, salmon, yellow, and gold. Unsuitable for cultivation, this part of Georgia specializes in the production of broilers. Everywhere there are the uniformly long, narrow sheds in which several hundred million chickens are processed annually.

The road north winds steadily upward through aromatic forests, skirts Lake Burton, and then ascends even more steeply, with sharp, blind turns. This is one of the highest stretches of road in the state, and the scenery it offers is superb.

11. Falling in harmony in the wild disarray of a wooded setting are the twin cascades of the Anna Ruby Falls. Picnic facilities are nearby.

12 Heading south from Clayton, the highway hugs the rim of Tallulah Gorge, a 600-foot-deep slash in the earth that is believed to be the oldest natural gorge in America. At the bottom of its sheer, forested walls you can see Tallulah River and shimmering Tallulah Lake.

Gradually the mountains give way to rolling hills with apple and peach orchards. In early May clouds of pale pink and white blossoms fill the landscape, and in summer fruit stands appear along the roadside.

13 The Lake Lanier Islands at the southern end of Lake Sidney Lanier are managed by the state as a family recreation area. This beautiful cluster of islands offers a variety of water sports for vacationers of every age, as well as golf, tennis, and riding. The islands, which are connected to the shore by causeways, have trailer sites and cottage and houseboat rentals. From the highways encircling the lake there are access roads to other waterfront recreation areas with picnic grounds and campsites.

The lake was created in 1957 by the damming of the Chattahoochee River at Buford and was named for a well-known poet of the 19th century and one of Georgia's favorite sons.

14 Famous for its antebellum mansions with their formal boxwood gardens, Athens is called the Classic City of the South. The A. P. Dearing House on South Milledge Avenue and the University President's House on Prince Street are two of the finest examples of Greek Revival architecture in the country. Among Athens' other notable buildings are several found on the campus of the University of Georgia.

The Athens Welcome Center is located in the city's oldest dwelling, the Church-Waddel-Brumby House on East Dougherty Street. A splendid example of federal architecture, it was built in 1820 and restored in 1971. Available here is a brochure for a self-guided driving tour to discover "Athens of Old."

15 The town of Madison is an architectural gem that narrowly escaped destruction in the Civil War. Chartered in 1809, it flourished as a stop on the stagecoach road between Charleston and New Orleans, and in 1864 the publication *Harper Weekly*

16. *The Stone Mountain Memorial Carving is one of the largest pieces of sculptural art in the world. The niche containing the mounted figures of the three Confederate heroes is the size of a city block. Despite the gigantic scale of the carving, its sculptors gave it fine details, depicting harness buckles, finger creases, and strands of hair. Work continued sporadically for nearly 50 years before the project was completed in 1970.*

called it the "most picturesque town in Georgia." Yet later that year Madison was slated to be burned to the ground by General Sherman on his march to the sea. It was spared only because of an eloquent plea by one of its citizens, Sen. Joshua Hill, who had opposed secession and who was a friend of Sherman's brother.

Much of Madison is now a national historic district, and more than 90 of its buildings are included in the National Register of Historic Places. Invitingly small, the town can best be seen by taking a leisurely stroll along its shaded sidewalks. An imposing red brick courthouse with white Corinthian columns dominates the central square, and most of the landmarked houses are only a few blocks away. A few Victorian houses of the 1880's, with lacy gingerbread, provide a pleasing contrast to the older residences. Among other notable buildings are the Presbyterian Church, which was constructed in the 1840's and has Tiffany stained-glass windows, and the 1895 Romanesque Revival schoolhouse, which is now a museum and the home of the Madison-Morgan Cultural Center.

16 The great gray dome of Stone Mountain rises against the skyline and overlooks Atlanta. This is the largest exposed mass of a single kind of granite east of the Mississippi River. It is 825 feet high and is about 285 to 294 million years old.

You can ride the gondola of a skylift to the top, where there is a museum and an observation tower. For hardy hikers, there is a steep 1½-mile trail up the mountain.

A monumental carving on the face of the mountain honors the Confederate heroes of the Civil War, President Jefferson Davis and Gens. Robert E. Lee and Stonewall Jackson. The relief is so deep that a car could be driven on the back of the representation of Lee's horse, Traveller.

On its 3,200 acres, Stone Mountain Park has camping facilities, picnic areas, and a working antebellum plantation. There is a river cruise on a stern-wheeler, as well as walking trails and displays of wild flowers, which include the Cherokee rose (*Rosa laevigata*), the state flower. A seasonal highlight is the Yellow Daisy Festival held here when the Confederate daisy blooms in the fall.

Along this stretch *of the Atlantic coast you can visit Savannah, one of America's loveliest cities, and the "Golden Isles of Georgia," which are justly famous for their well-tended wooded seclusion and broad sandy beaches.*

The route inland takes you through some historic towns and vast plantings of pine forest, and then touches the northern edge of Okefenokee's watery wilderness.

1 It is a tribute to the foresight of Gen. James Oglethorpe and William Bull that the street plan they laid out for Savannah in 1733 still functions so well. Even with the necessary one-way traffic, the streets, interspersed with parks and verdant squares, are a pleasure to drive and to walk.

The town was the capital of the Georgia Colony from 1733 until about 1778, and the wealth and status of its residents was an inducement to excellence in architecture. This precedent was followed throughout the first half of the 19th century, when cotton was king and Savannah was a thriving port. Factors' Walk with its iron bridges is a reminder of that era, and the inviting new Riverfront Plaza is reminiscent of the past.

The streets of the Historic District are literally lined with more than 1,100 restored 19th-century homes and commercial buildings of architectural and historical distinction. This is the largest Historic District in the United States, and many of the homes are open to the public. At the visitor center on West Broad Street you can get an excellent map with suggested tours.

2 Route 80 as it approaches Fort Pulaski National Monument on Cockspur Island is flanked by salt marsh studded with islands of pine and live oak. The Savannah River is shielded from view, and ships seem to be steaming through a sea of grass.

The moated fort with its thick masonry walls is a quiet, orderly place and has grassy mounds, a parade ground, 19th-century cannon, and handsome arched gun rooms. From the parapet are lovely views of the Savannah River and the marshland surrounding the island.

In this peaceful setting it is hard to imagine the chaos of April 10, 1862, when the newly developed rifled cannon fired by the Union forces on Tybee Island a mile away pierced the seven-foot masonry walls of the fort. This historic step in the escalation of weaponry rendered obsolete the concept that masonry was impregnable. The Union troops who captured the fort repaired the damage, but some of the more than 5,000 shots fired can still be seen in the walls.

Some of the officers' quarters have been refurbished and furnished in keeping with the Civil War period. And there are exhibits pertaining to the lives of soldiers in the fort.

There are places for picnicking and walking trails. Nearby Tybee Island offers swimming at Tybee Beach and a museum with interesting displays related to the Civil War and the early history of the area.

3 The live oak (*Quercus virginiana*), the state tree, and various pines are the trees most common to the Georgia coast. In Richmond Hill State Park the oaks are festooned with Spanish moss, and the dense stands of pines have carpeted the pathways and picnic area with their fragrant needles. This pleasant park also has camping facilities, swings, and a boat-launching ramp.

Adjacent to the park is Fort McAllister Historic Site. This fort, along with Fort Pulaski and others, was meant to protect the town of Savannah from attack by sea. The fortifications here were of earth, not masonry, and in 1863 they held up under the heaviest shelling that the Union gunboats could deliver. But late in

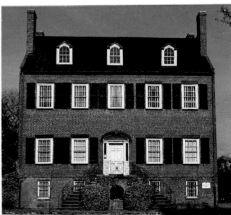

1. This vista of Savannah's Forsyth Park (left) speaks of more formal times. The park, set out geometrically around this 1858 fountain, contains a Confederate monument and a Fragrant Garden for the Blind. The Davenport House (above) was built in 1815–20 and has fine examples of federal-style elements. Double, curving stairways guarded by delicate iron railings lead to an entrance crowned with a graceful fanlight. The house was badly neglected until an extensive restoration was undertaken in the early 1960's.

5. Great egrets hunt for food among the placid Marshes of Glynn near Brunswick. At one time these birds were hunted for their silky plumage. Eager milliners paid a high price, and the wildfowl nearly vanished. These egrets seem alert but unafraid.

1864 the fort was taken from the land side by a division of Gen. William T. Sherman's army. In the museum are Civil War artifacts and displays explaining the battles fought here.

Route 17 has wide, grassy shoulders lined with oaks and pines, but vistas of salt marshes and waterways appear near Darien. Fishing boats berthed in the Darien River are a reminder of the excellent seafood to be had along the Georgia coast.

4 After crossing the Altamaha River, keep an eye out for the turnoff to the Hofwyl Broadfield Plantation. The plantation's pastoral setting recalls the peace, quiet, and unhurried pace of the rice-planter's life. A map available at the plantation's visitor center outlines a walking path from which you can see the dikes, canals, fields, and freshwater marsh required for the cultivation of rice. The house has furnishings of the era. The machinery, outbuildings, fences, gates, and animals here help to authenticate the plantation atmosphere.

5 The straight, flat causeway connecting St. Simons Island and Sea Island to the mainland crosses the vast meadowlike expanse of the Marshes of Glynn, the largest salt marshes on the Atlantic seaboard. In this evocative setting, one can see what inspired Georgia poet Sidney Lanier to immortalize the marshes in one of his works: "A league and a league of marsh-grass, waist high, broad in the blade,/ Green, and all of a height and unflecked with a light or a shade,/ Stretch leisurely off, in a pleasant plain,/ To the terminal blue of the main."

The islands are models of controlled landscaping and meticulous maintenance. Oaks, pines, and a scattering of palmettos flank the roads, and in places you drive through veritable tunnels of green created by oaks and Spanish moss overhanging the road. An historic highlight on St. Simons is Fort Frederica, established in 1736 by Gen. James Oglethorpe. Britain, France, and Spain claimed

the land here, and Spanish soldiers made an attempt to capture it in 1742 but were defeated in the Battle of Bloody Marsh.

In the visitor center is a diorama of the area as it was when the fort was fully manned. The area is now a national historic monument, and tours and living history demonstrations are available year-round.

On the road to the fort you can see the handsome latch gate and entry to Christ Church, a charming wood Gothic structure built in 1884.

Sea Island is, if possible, even more neatly tended than St. Simons. Sea Island Drive is considered one of the most beautiful streets in the nation.

6 Brunswick is not only the gateway to the "Golden Isles of Georgia" but also a major port for shrimp boats. When the boats are in, usually in the afternoon, the dockside scene is a fascinating tangle of nets and a seeming forest of booms and masts silhouetted against the sky. Here too are the packing plants where shrimp and crabs are packed and processed. To get to the docks, turn off Route 17 and follow Route 25 (Gloucester Street) north. A good viewpoint is at the foot of this street.

7 From the parkway to Jekyll Island the marshes seem to extend to infinity, a sweep of subtle colors ranging from green to brown. Their

6. The masts, lines, and hoisting equipment on these shrimp boats may seem to be a confused muddle, but the gear is efficiently organized to bring in large catches.

vastness gives this area an other-world quality—all so fresh and clean.

The first left turn after crossing the parkway starts you on a clockwise tour of the island. To learn about "Millionaire's Village" and the houses you can visit there, stop at the Macy Reception Center, which is the first house on the right. The Jekyll Island Club was founded in 1886 as an exclusive retreat for some of the richest families in America. It is said that the members of the club once controlled one-sixth of the world's wealth. A chapel and seven of the vacation "cottages" are open to visitors. There are picnic sites on the island, a campground, and, on the ocean side, some nine miles of sandy beach.

Leaving the coast, Route 84 west cuts a straight swath through miles and miles of tree farms.

8 After passing Schlatterville, take Route 177 south to Laura S. Walker State Park. Here in the needle-carpeted groves of pine are picnic areas with tables and firepits, campsites, and a playground. There is also a swimming pool and a small lake.

On the way to Okefenokee Swamp Park are more forests of tall pines. In some areas the trees have cans attached near their base to collect the resin, which is distilled to make turpentine and is also used for rosin.

9 Step into a flat-bottom johnboat at Okefenokee Swamp Park and within two minutes you are totally immersed in a strange and fascinating new environment.

There is an engaging sense of adventure in this immediate transition from the world of the familiar to a primeval watery wilderness virtually unchanged in thousands of years. Here in a setting of cypresses, oaks, grasses, shrubs, and vines, every waterway mirrors the towering trees and looks like every other. It is easy to see how one could quickly become lost in this swamp, which encompasses 681 square miles.

In addition to the boat ride, there is a winding nature trail on a raised boardwalk, with signs identifying plants and trees.

The Interpretive Center, the Ecology Center, the Serpentarium, and the Pioneer Island museum are all handsomely designed and are well worth visiting.

10 In Waycross take Route 82 north for about two miles to North Augusta Street and the Okefenokee Heritage Center. The center, which commemorates the life of the area at the turn of the century, has a display on the forest industry, the Heritage Farm, a printshop typical of the late 1800's, and an exhibition center. A

9. The mirroring waters of the dreamlike Okefenokee Swamp move sluggishly among broad-leaved plants. The Indian name means "land of trembling earth," so called because of the swamp's floating vegetation. Many kinds of reptiles, birds, and mammals dwell in the swamp, and they often can be seen at close range from the boats and boardwalks here. Sunning himself (right) is Oscar, king of the local jungle, who measures over 14 feet from stem to stern and weighs an estimated 650-700 pounds.

highlight here is *Old Nine*, a 100-ton 2-8-2 steam engine, with a baggage and passenger cars and a caboose. The train stands beside a railroad station dating from about 1912.

11 Driving east to Midway you see feed mills, egg co-ops, and supply houses related to the poultry business that flourishes in this part of Georgia.

And the miles of tree farms that you see along the road are evidence of the many lumber and turpentine industries in this region.

At Midway is the Congregational Meeting House, which was built in 1792 to replace an earlier structure (from about 1756) destroyed in the American Revolution.

The museum adjoining the meetinghouse is a raised cottage typical of this part of the South. The furnishings and exhibits are of the colonial period, and the documents commemorate the remarkable number of outstanding public servants who were members of the Midway Church and Society.

A Land Like No Other

Florida is an exotic world of living coral reefs, cypress swamps, palm trees, and sandy beaches

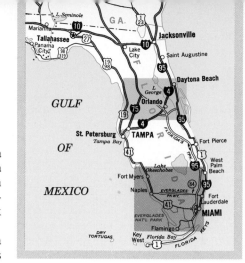

Often called America's Great Escape, Florida is much more than an endless vacationland as it stretches southward between the Gulf of Mexico and the Atlantic Ocean. Its citrus groves, cattle ranches, and many farms furnish much of the nation's food, its forests contribute to the world's wood and paper supply, and the great wilderness areas at the southern tip of the peninsula provide a unique environment for untold numbers of animals, birds, and plants.

Important as Florida's agriculture is to the welfare of the state and the economy of the country, tourism continues to be the major industry here. The wintertime climate lures northerners with the promise of sunny skies, wide sandy beaches, and some of the world's finest fishing.

Florida's wildlife refuges and forests also attract visitors who come to enjoy the tropical and subtropical vegetation and the great marshes and grasslands of the Everglades.

These tours, past sandy coastlines and offshore coral reefs, midland lakes and gardens, and acres of junglelike wilderness, reveal the essence of this remarkable state.

Central Florida *with its farmlands, cattle ranches, hardwood forests, thousands of lakes, gently rolling hills, and mile upon mile of citrus groves has long had a permanent population of well-established families, but until recently there have been few tourists.*

Today this scene is changing as visitors come from far and near to see the wonders of Walt Disney World and to enjoy the crystal-clear waters of the many natural springs here and the pleasant parklike surroundings that are being developed.

1   Orlando, the metropolis of central Florida, has within its borders some 80 lakes and about 50 parks, making it one of the state's prettiest towns. It also serves as a shipping center for the fruits and vegetables grown nearby.

2   To the southwest of Orlando, just beyond the city limits, is Sea World, a well-landscaped 135-acre park featuring marine exhibits. There are trained dolphins and other sea mammals, Adelie penguins, and a man-made tide pool where you can inspect such creatures as sea anemones, starfish, and crabs without risk of getting your feet wet.

The star of Sea World is Shamu, a trained killer whale. Shamu performs in a stadium that seats 3,000, showing off his handsome black-and-white markings as he goes through his routine, which is called "Shamu Goes to College." Among the many tricks of this four-ton mammal is jumping over a rope stretched across his pool several feet above the water's surface. The splash he creates when he falls back into the water always astonishes his audience. He responds to such signals as a nod and a raised arm, and is rewarded with food, a back scratching, or simply a "good job."

3. Cinderella's Castle, focal point of Walt Disney World's Magic Kingdom, serves as an entrance to the area called Fantasyland.

The killer whale, actually a large dolphin, is so called because it feeds on large fish such as salmon and tuna, and occasionally attacks sea lions, seals, and smaller dolphins. This mammal has never been known to attack humans.

Sea World is also a wildlife rehabilitation center with facilities for treating injured animals and birds, and has a highly trained team on call day and night, with all necessary gear ready, to rescue beached mammals.

From Sea World's observation tower you can see the entire park and the surrounding fields and pine forests. Picnic areas are provided nearby.

3   Walt Disney World, a few miles south of Sea World, is Florida's most popular amusement park. The 43-square-mile complex includes not only the Magic Kingdom with its towered and turreted castle and its multitude of attractions, but also a complete resort area with three hotels, several restaurants, golf courses, and tennis courts.

SPECIAL FEATURES		
ROAD GUIDE	HIGHLIGHT	**1**
STATE PARKS	POINTS OF INTEREST	
With Campsites ▲ Without Campsites △	SCHEDULED AIRLINE STOPS	✈
RECREATION AREAS	MILITARY AIRPORTS	
With Campsites ▲ Without Campsites △	OTHER AIRPORTS	
SELECTED REST AREAS	BOAT RAMPS	
With Toilets ✗ Without Toilets ✗		

ROAD CLASSIFICATION

CONTROLLED ACCESS HIGHWAYS
(Entrance and Exit only at Interchanges)

TOLL HIGHWAYS

OTHER DIVIDED HIGHWAYS

PAVED HIGHWAYS

LOCAL ROADS In unfamiliar areas inquire locally before using these roads   Paved   Gravel   Dirt

MILEAGE

MILEAGE BETWEEN TOWNS AND JUNCTIONS   3 / 4   MILEAGE BETWEEN DOTS   • 35 •

SCALE

ONE INCH 19 MILES   0   5   10   20

ONE INCH 30 KILOMETERS   0   5   10   20   32

5. *Citrus groves, such as this one of orange trees, extend almost endlessly through central Florida. Other fruits grown here include grapefruit, lemon, kumquat, and tangelo. Occasionally, as shown, trees have fruits and flowers at the same time.*

Disney World is built around Bay Lake, which has facilities for camping, four miles of beaches for swimming, several different kinds of boats for rent, and fishing privileges.

On Bay Lake's Discovery Island, which you can reach by side-wheel steamboat, there is a sanctuary for more than 400 kinds of colorful birds, such as flamingos, peacocks, swans, cranes, and cockatoos. Here too are plantings of bamboo, palm trees, orchids, and passion flowers and stands of moss-draped cypress trees.

A 7,500-acre wildlife refuge, developed partly to preserve the natural beauty of the landscape, offers information on the various techniques of land conservation.

4 In the neighborhood of Disney World is Circus World, a Ringling Bros. and Barnum & Bailey entertainment park where you can observe animal acts and performances by tightrope walkers and trapeze artists, in an atmosphere reminiscent of the Big Top and the traveling circus. If you are adventurously inclined, try your skill at walking a tightrope, swinging on a trapeze, and staying atop an elephant as it lumbers around the circus ring.

As the road turns north toward Clermont, the rolling hills dotted with scrubby pines give way to the dark green, patterned landscape of citrus groves. Florida's groves are mostly here in the center of the state, where the necessary days of sunshine can usually be depended upon. The fruit must mature on the tree because, unlike many other crops, citrus fruit does not continue to ripen after it has been picked.

5 One mile north of Clermont is Florida Citrus Tower, a 226-foot-high structure with an observation deck from which you can see 2,000 square miles of citrus groves. The neat rows of green are frequently broken by the bright blue of the sky reflected on the countless lakes in this area.

The road westward goes through the gentle hills of central Florida, with citrus groves all along the way.

6 At Weeki Wachee Spring, 12 miles from the Gulf Coast, there is an auditorium 16 feet below the ground, where an underwater ballet is featured. The swimmers control their breathing and use concealed air tubes so efficiently that they can perform for 45 minutes without returning to the surface.

Boats accommodating 85 passengers take visitors on cruises along the Weeki Wachee River through the lush green foliage of a tropical rain forest to a nature park. Here you can walk on the paths that wind through the grounds. Trained parrots and cockatoos display their skills, and owls, hawks, eagles, and falcons put on aerial shows, catching their prey on the wing and returning to the trainer's gauntlet.

7 About five miles before you come to Homosassa Springs, watch for the signs to Chassahowitzka National Wildlife Refuge. This is a 29,698-acre area where there are many kinds of wading birds and several varieties of small animals, including otters, bobcats, raccoons, and rabbits. Hunting during the waterfowl season and fishing are permitted, and there are facilities at the refuge for boating.

The name of the refuge comes from the Hichiti Seminole Indian language and means "pumpkin opening place." Pumpkins were a major food crop for these and other native Indians who lived in this area and worked these fertile fields for hundreds of years before the white man came. To preserve their crops of pumpkins, the Indians opened and dried them, and they chose the site of the refuge for this important task.

8 The placid waters of the Homosassa River and the surrounding landscape were also known to the Indians many centuries ago. In their language Homosassa means "place where peppers grow."

In 1846 David Levy Yulee, one of Florida's first two U.S. senators, established the first white man's settlement with a 3,000-acre plantation and sugar mill on the banks of the Homosassa River. All that remains is the ruins of the sugar mill, surrounded now by a small park with picnic tables among the palm, magnolia, and moss-draped live oak trees.

Homosassa Springs, the source of the river, is called Nature's Giant Fishbowl. Some 6 million gallons of clear springwater gush up every hour. With a depth of 55 feet and a year-round temperature of 72°F, the springs attracts more than 34 species of both fresh- and saltwater fish. The saltwater species swim upriver to get warm whenever the Gulf waters become too cool for their liking.

An underground observatory with three-inch-thick glass windows provides an unusual close-up view of the marine life in the springs.

At the park entrance, boats are available for a short cruise to a nature area, where geese, ducks, swans, alligators, otters, squirrel monkeys, and a hippo make themselves at home. Visitors are invited to feed the tame deer and sea lions. This nature area is also accessible by car.

Fishing is popular in the Homosassa River, with mangrove snapper, redfish, and sheepshead the usual kinds to be found during the winter months. Guides are available.

At the park museum there is a glass wall through which visitors can view temple, burial, and refuse mounds, and there are trails through the park for a closer look at the entire site.

10 Moss-covered live oaks, pines, and citrus trees, all typical of central Florida, dominate the landscape along the road to Dunnellon. This town was once the heart of a limestone-mining area, where much limestone rock and phosphate were discovered. The fishing here is famous. The bass in the Withlacoochee and Rainbow rivers are said to be the largest in the world.

Eastward toward Ocala is an area renowned for its thoroughbred horse farms. Along this route the beautiful

graze on the banks. Monkeys, now native, swing through the vines. Clearly seen through the "floor" of the boat are hundreds of colorful fish as they thread through underwater plants gently waving with the currents. The fish follow along with the boat, hoping for a crumb or two.

A 100-acre park of lawns shaded by tall live oaks and pines and gardens of bright flowering plants border the springs, the source of the river. Demonstrations are given at the Reptile Institute, and there is a special area where children can pet deer and other gentle animals.

12 The Ocala National Forest is a 366,000-acre stretch of wilderness known for its great stands of sand pine (*Pinus clausa*), the only tree that grows large enough in dry sandy soil to be used commercially. In the less arid parts of the forest there are longleaf and slash pines, scrub oaks, and hickory trees, with tall palms and other tropical vegetation along the many winding streams and more than 600 lakes. Miles of hiking trails wander through the forest.

Here too you can find the mockingbird, Florida's official state bird, and the so-called scrub jay, a close relative of the blue jay but without the familiar crest. This jay prefers to live in scrub oak forests and is found almost nowhere else but in this part of Florida.

Once out of the forest, at Altoona, you are again flanked by the precise green rows of the citrus groves, and you can see processing plants along the way, particularly at the towns of Umatilla and Eustis.

Tavares (pronounced tu-*vair*-eez) is the seat of Lake County, which has some 2,500 lakes, many of them depressions or sinkholes caused by the dissolution of the limestone bedrock. When rain is falling, it picks up carbon dioxide from the atmosphere to form a weak acid that attacks limestone. It works infinitely slowly, but over thousands of years the acid water seepage excavates channels and caverns. During the ice age the sea level was 400 feet lower than it is today, and the endless network of holes reached that much lower. Today the system constitutes a vast underground reservoir of immense value to the people of Florida.

10. Many of Florida's stud farms, such as this at Ocala, are known for the excellence of their thoroughbred racehorses. Some farms also serve as winter quarters for thoroughbreds and their trainers from Virginia, Kentucky, and other states to the north.

9 The Crystal River State Archeological Site is a 14-acre park containing the most important pre-Columbian Indian mounds in Florida, dating from about 200 B.C. This area was an Indian ceremonial center for some 1,600 years. The artifacts found in the more than 450 burial sites indicate that these Indians traded with tribes north of the Ohio River.

green pastures provide grazing for more than 8,000 horses on some 200 farms. Visitors are welcome at many of the farms.

11 Near Ocala is Silver Springs, one of the best known of Florida's many natural-springs parks. Here glass-bottom boats cruise along the tranquil Silver River, where giraffes, rhinos, and other African animals

The Florida Keys

These islands are remnants of a barrier reef that once extended almost the length of what is now Florida. Thousands of years ago as the sea level rose, the reef grew upward, and a lagoon filled with a white mud called oolite was formed. This happened several times along the Florida coast, the last time 125,000 years ago. During the last ice age the sea level fell about 400 feet, killing the corals and isolating the reef. About 6,000 years ago the melting of the ice brought the sea level back almost to the ancient level, and the dead reefs now form the row of islands that we call the Keys.

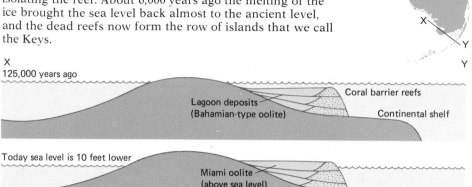

X
125,000 years ago

Lagoon deposits
(Bahamian-type oolite)

Coral barrier reefs

Continental shelf

Today sea level is 10 feet lower

Miami oolite
(above sea level)

13 The Dora Canal (formerly called the Elfin River) runs through the western part of Tavares. Giant moss-draped cypresses form a canopy over the canal.

You can cruise at your leisure through this green-dappled waterway, either in your own boat or in one you can rent at Tavares. The sportswriter Grantland Rice once called this charming canal the "most beautiful mile of water in the world."

A scenic drive takes you to Mount Dora, where a "mountain," which is actually a bluff 184 feet high, overlooks Lake Dora. This bluff is the southern extremity of what was the tip of the continent millions of years ago when the sea level was much higher and water covered most of the state. South of this point the geology changes. The entire southern section of Florida is built on the remains of a platform of ancient coral reefs.

Washed by the warm ocean current from the Caribbean, southern Florida is an ideal spot for corals to grow. The reefs have been building up here for several million years. Between cold phases of the ice age, they built up a few feet higher than the present sea level, and today you can see the old corals in any of the several roadside quarries along the way to Key West.

14 About 14 miles east of Mount Dora a well-marked road turns south to Wekiwa Falls, the world's largest flowing well. Immense casings have been installed to direct the 72 million gallons of water that spring forth daily into the pool below. The park that surrounds the falls has facilities for swimming, boating, camping, and picnicking.

The Auto-Train

Between Florida and Virginia, the Auto-Train Corporation offers transportation for passengers and their cars. Such amenities and facilities as dining cars, club cars, movies, lounge chairs, bedrooms, drawing rooms, and staterooms are available on the train.

The terminals are at Lorton, Virginia, a suburb of Washington, D.C., and at Sanford, Florida, 20 miles north of Orlando. Trains leave daily in each direction at 4 P.M., arriving the next morning at 9 A.M.

East of Sanford, the southern terminus of the Auto-Train, our route follows the state's flat lowlands.

15 Merritt Island National Wildlife Refuge, on Merritt Island, encompasses some 140,000 acres of saltwater lagoons, mangrove and grass marshes, upland woodlands, citrus groves, and miles of sand dunes.

There are numerous hiking trails as well as roads from which you may catch glimpses of manatees, alligators, sea turtles, muskrats, raccoons, marsh hares, and perhaps a white-tailed deer or wild boar.

On the north side of the road, not far from the wildlife refuge headquarters, is the ranger station for the Canaveral National Seashore, one of the few remaining wilderness areas on Florida's Atlantic coast. On the beaches here you can swim, sun-

15. Treelike yuccas, called Spanish bayonets, are shown here on sand dunes at Cape Canaveral with beach sunflowers in the foreground and seagrapes in center background. These yuccas grow as much as 25 feet tall, have leaves 2 feet long and 2 inches wide, and bear clusters of waxy creamy-white flowers that are succeeded by green seed pods.

16. Spacecraft Apollo 16, lifting off from Cape Canaveral in 1972. Rocket firings always attract thousands of spectators.

bathe, and fish, all within sight of the launch gantries and assembly buildings of the Kennedy Space Center.

16 From Titusville, Route 1 takes you to Route 405, which leads eastward to the Kennedy Space Center's Visitor Headquarters. Here there are displays of hardware that has been to outer space, rocks from the moon, interpretive movies, and buses to carry you to the launch sites on nearby Cape Canaveral.

At these sites the various exhibits include a full-scale model of a lunar module, a lunar rover, a model of Skylab Space Station, and the Vehicle Assembly Building, where there is an authentic Apollo/Saturn V launch vehicle poised outside.

17 Port Canaveral, an easygoing fishing and industrial town south of the space center, has curio shops and excellent seafood restaurants in among the shipyards and fish-processing plants. In the port you can see the picturesque shrimp boats, "shrimpers," and trawlers as they return from the Atlantic with their catch. You may also sight the stark black hulls of the U.S. Navy's nuclear submarines, which come to port here to be refueled and rearmed with nuclear-tipped Polaris missiles.

Here at the southern tip of Florida you can enjoy the coastline of both the Atlantic Ocean and the Gulf of Mexico and, between the two, the vast wilderness of the Everglades National Park with its alligators, flamingos, and anhingas and its fascinating array of plants.

On the Atlantic side, not far from the luxuries of Miami Beach, is a primitive coral reef to explore. On the Gulf, at Naples, is a famous collection of exotic plants and birds, and farther north the beaches of Sanibel and Captiva islands are famous for the variety of seashells to be found.

1 Miami Beach, on the Atlantic coast (usually referred to as the East Coast), is perhaps the most popular of Florida's many resort areas. The 7½-mile-long island is separated from the mainland and the city of Miami by Biscayne Bay, which the Spaniards named for their own Bay of Biscay. A series of causeways now connects the beach to the mainland.

In the early 1900's when John S. Collins of New Jersey set out to turn the island into a residential paradise, Miami Beach was a wilderness of sand dunes, mangroves, and scrub palmettos. The first bridge to the area was constructed in 1913 and from then on the island began to emerge as a wintertime retreat.

Today palm trees and Australian pines shade the streets, and a long chain of ornate hotels facing the Atlantic borders the sandy beaches.

2 The parks and beaches of Key Biscayne, reached by causeway from the mainland, offer some of the finest ocean swimming and fishing to be found in the Miami area.

Here at Crandon Park there are bathhouses and rows of cabanas, skating rinks, a golf course, a marina, and a small amusement park. Farther down the key, the Bill Baggs Florida State Recreation Area has facilities for picnicking, fishing, and swimming. The Cape Florida lighthouse, a historic structure that was built in 1825, still stands, and the lighthouse keeper's residence has been completely reconstructed.

3 In Miami, on the shores of Biscayne Bay, there is a re-creation of an Italian Renaissance palace built in 1912–17 by the late James Deering. Although the palace is Venetian in design, Mr. Deering gave it the Spanish name of Vizcaya, after the Basque province on the Bay of Biscay.

The elaborate 70-room mansion, filled with priceless antiques, faces the bay, and just offshore a breakwater in the form of a sculptured stone barge guards the waterfront. The barge, with its planters full of flowering shrubs, fountains, and trees, and with statues representing the joys and woes of the sea, is a bit of fantasy in the azure waters of the bay.

Vizcaya's acres of formal gardens, with their intricate parterres, fountains, sculpture, quiet reflecting pools, and shaded walks, are considered among the finest in America.

3. Gardens at Vizcaya, a Venetian-style mansion in Miami, have parterres of low-growing, carefully clipped boxwood. Elaborate stonework, with a wide stairway, formal pools, fountains, and statuary, serves as an entranceway to the mansion's gardens.

The Rare Plant House at the Fairchild Tropical Garden

Water lily

Hibiscus

Bird-of-paradise

Orchid

Water hyacinth

4. Many rare and tender plants, such as the tropical water lily and orchids, are kept in the Rare Plant House at the Fairchild Garden. Others—the hibiscus, water hyacinth, and bird-of-paradise, also grown at this garden—thrive in their outdoor setting. Water hyacinths threaten to clog the waterways, but these invasive plants are controlled by the herbivorous manatee.

Mr. Deering's family retained the mansion until 1952, when Vizcaya became the Dade County Art Museum. Closed on Christmas Day.

From Miami south to Coral Gables the road parallels the shores of Biscayne Bay, which is hidden from view by a series of large estates. Poinciana, banyan, and palm trees, including the sabal plam (*Sabal palmetto*), the state tree, shade the drive and fringe the beaches. For those tempted by the surf and sea, swimming facilities are available at the Matheson Hammock Park beach on Old Cutler Road.

4 The Fairchild Tropical Garden, named for David Fairchild, one of America's best known plant explorers, is the largest tropical botanical garden in the United States. The garden is especially noted for its palm collection, which includes more than 500 species of this vast family of plants. Here too are bromeliads, the ancient fernlike cycads that were known to the dinosaurs, silk-cotton trees, lipstick trees, the cannon ball tree from South America, and many different kinds of vines and ground covers. The Rare Plant House contains an orchid collection and other plants, such as the breadfruit tree, that are extremely sensitive to cold. There is also a magnificent hibiscus collection, with blossoms that range from brilliant scarlet to white.

Visitors can ride through the garden on a motorized tramcar as a member of the staff comments on the plants to be seen along the way.

5 Nearby, at 11000 South Red Road, is the Parrot Jungle, an area situated on a natural hammock. A winding path penetrates the thick groves of live oak and cypress trees, some of which are festooned with orchids. Hundreds of macaws, cockatoos, parrots, and other exotic birds fly free. Here too are exhibitions that demonstrate the remarkable adaptability of the performing cockatoos and parrots.

6 In a natural rainforest area, a bit farther south, is the Monkey Jungle. Here in 1933 some monkeys imported from Asia were set free as an experiment in the transplanting of animals to western tropics. Not only did these creatures survive, they flourished in their new home, chose a leader, and set up their own kind of structured society. They have adapted so well that now they are considered to be a native American species.

The monkeys roam free in their habitat. The visitors are protected by screened-in walkways that meander through the forest.

The landscape changes as it approaches the Florida Keys. Marshes, grassy plains, and mangroves stretch southward to the sea, with little or no evidence of civilization.

The Keys are a series of coral reef islands strung out westward in an arc from the southern tip of Florida's Atlantic coast to the Gulf of Mexico.

7   Key Largo, 28½ miles long, is the largest of the group and closest to the mainland. Off its shores are the Key Largo Coral Marine Sanctuary and also the John Pennekamp Coral Reef State Park, which was the first undersea park to be established in the continental United States.

Named for a Miami newspaper editor who was influential in establishing the park, this undersea "garden" extends for some eight miles from the shoreline to the continental shelf.

The fragile reefs are made up of limestone formations produced by saltwater organisms, particularly coral, which is a soft-bodied creature with a stony skeleton. At least 40 species of coral and hundreds of kinds of tropical fish and plants inhabit the park, the most extensive and luxuriant living coral reef on the North American coast.

You can take a 2½-hour cruise on a glass-bottom boat to view the undersea park. The narrow channels leading to the reef are lined with red mangroves, which help to protect the island from storms and provide a habitat for all the many kinds of fish that live among the roots.

At park headquarters on Key Largo there are facilities for camping, swimming, and picnicking. Canoes, paddleboats, sailboats, motorboats, and scuba-diving and snorkel equipment can be rented.

8   The Everglades National Park, a 2,000-square-mile wilderness at the southern end of Florida, is a region of freshwater marshy grasslands, hardwood hammocks, and an occasional stand of cypress that harbors such diverse and interesting wildlife as otters, deer, Florida panthers, bobcats, and manatees. Here too are crocodiles and alligators. This is one of the few places in the world where they live in the same environment. Among the many colorful tropical birds in the area is the anhinga, a large bird with a snakelike neck. This

A school of French grunt

A school of yellowtails with snappers

Snorkelers at the John Pennekamp Coral Reef State Park

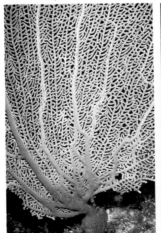
Fan coral

Giant sea anemone   Coral polyps, extended

7. *The Pennekamp reef has 40 species of coral, including the fan coral, which is popular with collectors, the giant sea anemone, and the coral polyp, a compound animal with tentacles that surround a tubelike mouth. Fish find refuge among the coral branches.*

8. *The anhinga, shown drying its wings, feeds on fish underwater in sloughs like the one above. During summer rains, waters in the Everglades rise and wildlife range into remote areas. In winter they come to the shrinking pools for food and water.*

fascinating creature feeds underwater, and when it emerges it perches on the bank or on a low branch to adjust its body temperature to the air and to let its wings dry before it can fly again.

The headquarters of the Everglades, which became a national park in 1947, is 12 miles west of the town of Homestead. A naturalist is on duty at the visitor center to answer questions about the unique ecosystem of the Everglades and the myriad plants, animals, birds, and fish it supports. Maps of the area are also available.

Two trails start at the Royal Palm Hammock: the Anhinga Trail, which leads through the Taylor Slough to ponds where alligators, turtles, and many kinds of birds can be seen; and the Gumbo-Limbo Trail, which wanders through a hardwood hammock. Along this shady walk you can see more than 75 different plants, including the tree for which the trail is named. The gumbo-limbo (*Bursera simaruba*) is distinguishable by the reddish color of its peeling bark.

The road to Flamingo, at the southern end of the Everglades, crosses the park through more than a hundred different kinds of grass and ground cover. Here you can see beard grass, saw grass (really a sedge), three-awn grass, coinwort, marsh fleabane, love vine, and creeping Charlie.

Among the inviting trails along the way is one through a dense hammock of palm and mahogany trees, air plants, and many kinds of orchids; and another through a typical mangrove forest.

9 At Flamingo there are campgrounds, a motel, a restaurant, several hiking trails, boat tours, picnic areas, houseboats for rent, facilities for fishing, and some of the most spectacular sunsets to be seen in Florida. The information center has an exhibit of the wildlife to be found in this area.

The best time to see the wildlife in the Everglades is in winter, during the dry season. When the water is low, the animals and birds seek out

Skimming the Sea of Grass

About 13 miles along the Tamiami Trail is the Coopertown Airboat Ride. Here you can take a trip through the grassy glades on one of these flat-bottom, shallow-draft boats, which can accommodate 8 to 18 passengers. You sit no more than a few inches above the sea of grass, while an accompanying guide offers a running commentary on the different kinds of bird and plant life to be seen along the way.

The airboat is driven by an airplane propeller attached to the rear of the boat and is steered by an airboat rudder.

At several points along the trail, airboat rides without commentary are offered. Most of these are run by the Seminole Indians, whose ancestors have fished these waters since the early 1850's when they sought refuge here rather than submit to the forced march west from their tribal lands in Georgia. Many of these rides start at small Indian villages, where souvenirs are sold.

the small lakes and ponds along the hiking trails. During the summer there are hordes of mosquitoes, and an insect repellent is necessary.

From Florida City, Route 27 leads northward to the Tamiami Trail, which crosses the peninsula from Miami to Naples. Alongside this section of our route, for its entire length, is a canal that was dug to supply fill for the roadbed. The fresh water of the canal is popular with local fishermen. The trail is fringed on its north side by the tall, graceful Australian pine (*Casuarina equisetifolia*), which is not a true pine. It is also called the horsetail tree because of its long needles. This tree was imported from Australia, and despite its usefulness as a windbreak, the National Park Service is trying to eradicate it because of its rampant growth.

10 The waters from Lake Okeechobee flow through Shark Valley into the Shark River, named for these predators that occasionally come to feed at the river's mouth, which is in the Gulf of Mexico.

You can take a two-hour tour with a commentator on a motorized tramcar through the valley's freshwater sour-grass prairie, a seemingly endless region where a few inches of very rich soil covers a bedrock of limestone some 12,000 feet deep.

The tram stops at an observation tower from which many kinds of wildlife can be seen, particularly in winter. Among them are alligators, white-tailed deer, raccoons, opossums, otters, black vultures, and great blue herons.

11 At the Western Water Gateway to the Everglades National Park, on the Waters of Ten Thousand Islands, is the quiet fishing village of Everglades City. The islands in the waters here are hammocks created by the mangrove trees, and because new islands are constantly being formed, it is impossible to tell just how many there are. Fishing is excellent in the sheltered island waters, where there are 50 species of fish. Here too one can see pelicans skimming the water in formation as they hunt for food.

Several boat tours are available. The Mangrove Wilderness Trip is a 2½-hour sail through this natural habitat of birds and animals; the Ten Thousand Island Trip is a 1½-hour exploration of many of the islands and beaches, with a brief stop along the way for shell collecting.

An Evening Bird Tour, 1½ hours long, is offered during the winter and is a chance to watch thousands of birds in their evening flight to roost.

12 Naples, on the edge of the Big Cypress Swamp, is known for its 1,000-foot fishing pier and its beautiful palm-shaded public bathing beach that stretches for seven miles along the warm waters of the Gulf.

Here too is a 200-acre botanical-zoological park called the Caribbean Gardens, where Jungle Larry's African Safari is located. In this park, exotic plants, colorful birds, and unusual animals create a setting similar to a true tropical jungle.

13 In 1894 at Estero a religious cooperative community that was known as Koreshan Unity was established. The Koreshans were as dedicated to their work as they were to their beliefs. They established citrus groves and grew fine fruits and vegetables. They published a weekly newspaper, a monthly magazine, and several religious tracts. They also believed in reincarnation and, like the Shakers, practiced celibacy. Just as with the Shakers, their numbers decreased and the community, now called Koreshan State Historic Site, was given to the state of Florida by the last surviving member of the cult.

14 Both Sanibel and Captiva islands, which are connected to the mainland by causeways, have some of the finest beaches in the world and are known by collectors for the

hundreds of kinds of shells to be found here, including left-handed welks, spiny periwinkles, junonias, cockles, and coquinas. The islands serve as barriers against storms and the strong currents that flow into the Gulf of Mexico through the Yucatan Channel and emerge into the Atlantic through the straits of Florida. Storms and ocean currents combine to carry the shells for many miles and deposit them on the beaches.

15 At Fort Myers, on the Caloosahatchee River, Thomas A. Edison established his winter home. Situated in a botanical garden, the home and his personal laboratory, left just as they were when he died, are open to

11. The crocodile, above, unlike its close relative, the alligator, shown at right, has a narrow snout and teeth that protrude when its mouth is closed. Although both animals live in warm coastal streams and feed underwater, they must come to the surface for air.

visitors. The large museum on the grounds contains an outstanding collection of Edison's experiments and inventions.

Along the road from Fort Myers to Lake Okeechobee you can see cattle ranches with herds of Brahmans, Charolais, and Charbray, and miles and miles of citrus groves, which give way to fields of sugarcane and watermelon as the road approaches Clewiston, a small town on the shores of the lake.

16 Known as America's Sweetest Town, Clewiston is the headquarters of the United States Sugar Corporation, the largest sugar company in the continental United States. During the harvesting season, from November to April, the company's mill produces 1,312 tons of sugar daily.

The Clewiston harbor and marina is a popular center for boating and fishing on Lake Okeechobee. For a view of the harbor, turn north at the center of town. The road parallels the lake, but because of the Herbert Hoover Dike, built in 1933, the lake is not visible.

Between Clewiston and South Bay there are more than a quarter of a million acres of sugarcane planted in what is considered to be some of the richest soil in the world.

Such vegetables as tomatoes, lettuce, string beans, sweet corn, radishes, broccoli, and cabbage—32 varieties in all—are also grown here. During the winter months the town of Belle Glade sends out as many as 33,000 railroad carloads of vegetables to various parts of the country.

17 Pahokee State Recreation Area on the east side of Lake Okeechobee offers the only view from the road of this enormous freshwater lake. The small park has facilities for picnicking at the lakeside.

From South Bay southward the road again cuts through vast fields of sugarcane and acres of what seems to be beautifully tended lawn. The grass is grown by sod farmers, who cut it into squares, stack it up, and ship it to all sections of the United States to produce instant lawns.

At Pennsuco the road meets the Florida Turnpike, which takes you back to the town of Sweetwater and eastward to Miami.

Through Time and Space

Alabama takes you from the past into the future, and from the earth's interior into the world of outer space

From the depths of its caverns where prehistoric man worshiped to the modern research centers where scientists seek to unravel the mysteries of the universe, Alabama brings together the old and the new. Once known as the Cotton State, its cotton fields now lie at the door of some of the largest industrial complexes in the world, and pastoral serenity exists in the shadow of impressive man-made structures.

In the caverns of Alabama you can explore unique realms of splendor that have long been places of mystery. Not far from them is the National Aeronautics and Space Administration's Marshall Space Flight Center, where you can walk through a world of spaceships, rockets, and shuttles.

Other natural and man-made wonders to be seen on this tour are one of the deepest canyons and the longest natural bridge east of the Mississippi River, an enchanting grotto that was the lifework of a monk, and the magnificent dams and lakes created by the Tennessee Valley Authority.

1 Overlooking Birmingham from the top of Red Mountain is a statue of Vulcan, the mythical god of fire and the forge. The 55-foot-tall figure—the largest ever made of cast iron—stands atop an observation tower in Vulcan Park as the symbol of the iron and steel industry that has made this city

famous. But Birmingham is known also for its great modern civic and medical centers, its art museum, its antebellum houses, and its botanical gardens. The downtown area is open and gracious, with small parks and many buildings that retain the charm of the 19th century.

2 A scenic drive leading off the highway winds through low, wooded mountains to Rickwood Caverns. The great, gnarled limestone stalactites and stalagmites in these caves began to form 2 million years ago, and they are still forming. Ducking stalactites, you walk through a series of corridors and chambers to a pool 35 feet wide and 59 feet deep. Here naturalists, diving to the bottom, have found salamanders, frogs, and transparent fish that have adapted to the cavern's total darkness.

A twisting, mile-long path descends 175 feet below ground level, and you have to watch your step, but the discovery of this mysterious inner world is worth the venture. Children are allowed to explore by themselves in the deepest chamber, known as the Diamond Room because of its glittering walls and ceilings.

The caverns are closed from November to March (except for visits by appointment) and on weekdays in spring and autumn. Rickwood Caverns State Park offers camping, picnic, and play areas and hiking trails through the woods.

3 The Ave Maria Grotto is located on the beautiful grounds of the St. Bernard Abbey, just east of Cullman. Nestled on a sheltered hillside amid flowering trees and shrubs are dozens of miniature representations of ancient Jerusalem and Rome, St. Peter's Basilica, Lourdes, the Spanish missions of the American Southwest, and other famous places, as well as Biblical scenes and statues of saints. They are the lifework of Brother Joseph Zoetti, a Benedictine monk who died here in 1961.

Brother Joseph drew mainly upon photographs for architectural guidelines, and used cement, limestone, marble, cold cream jars, seashells, beads, playing marbles, prisms, and bits of tile for his materials. Pieces were sent to him from people all over the world. His creations are remarkable for their detail, imagination, beauty, and charm. The few simple tools he used are displayed in a gift shop at the entrance.

West of Cullman you pass through pleasant, hilly countryside with hayfields and poultry and cattle farms, and then enter Bankhead National

3. The representation of Jerusalem at the Ave Maria Grotto includes the Temple, the Cenacle, where the Last Supper was held, the Fortress of Antonia, and the tomb of Lazarus. In the background is a grouping of Roman landmarks.

SPECIAL FEATURES

ROAD GUIDE	━━━	HIGHLIGHT	**1**
STATE PARKS		POINTS OF INTEREST	⊞
With Campsites 🌲 Without Campsites ⬘		SCHEDULED AIRLINE STOPS	✈
RECREATION AREAS		OTHER AIRPORTS	✗
With Campsites ▲ Without Campsites △		BOAT RAMPS	◄
SELECTED REST AREAS ✗			

ROAD CLASSIFICATION

CONTROLLED ACCESS HIGHWAYS
Interstate interchange numbers are mileposts.

OTHER DIVIDED HIGHWAYS

PAVED HIGHWAYS

LOCAL ROADS In unfamiliar areas inquire locally before using these roads — Paved   Gravel   Dirt

MILEAGE

MILEAGE BETWEEN TOWNS AND JUNCTIONS 3 ╱ 4   MILEAGE BETWEEN DOTS ● 35 ●

SCALE

ONE INCH 17 MILES   0   5   10   20
ONE INCH 27 KILOMETERS 0 5 10   20   32

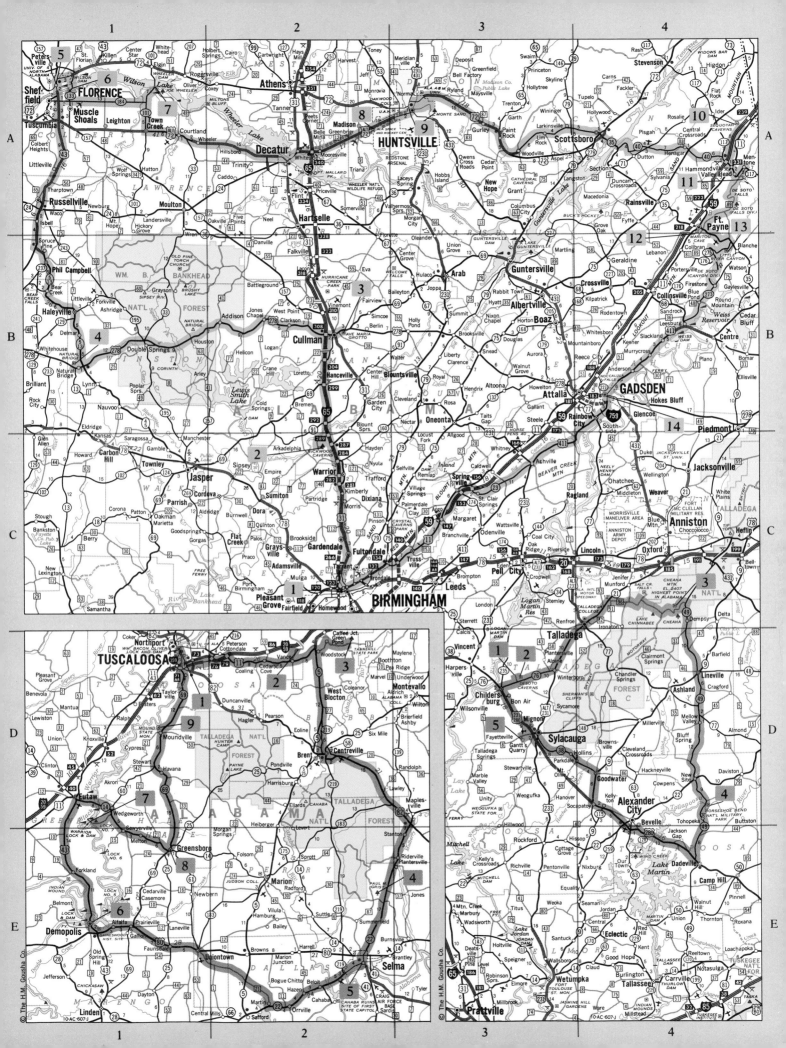

Forest, where uncounted brooks tumble beneath a canopy of oaks, sweet gums, and southern yellow pines (*Pinus palustris*), one of four pines listed as the state tree.

In this part of Alabama an occasional road sign indicates that you are in the Free State of Winston. The people of Winston County opposed Alabama's secession from the Union in January 1861, and argued that if a state could secede from the Union, a county could secede from a state. They remained Unionists until the governor ordered their punishment as traitors.

4 Arching 60 feet overhead and dwarfing the nearby trees is the awesome Natural Bridge of Alabama. The longest natural bridge east of the Mississippi River, it has two spans, the larger of which is 148 feet long and 33 feet wide. The bridge was created by a stream that cut its way down over a period of several million years and washed away the soft shale underlying a sandstone deposit formed some 200 million years earlier. The iron-rich crust adds strength to the formation.

A short walk through a profusion of wild ferns and mountain laurels encircles the cavernous space beneath the bridge. There are also two short nature trails—one ascends the rock formation beyond the bridge and the other leads to Indian rock shelters. Close by a stream flowing through the park grounds are picnic tables and swings, shaded by sycamores, beeches, giant wild magnolias, and Canadian hemlocks.

Bordered by woodlands, fields, and ponds, the road north winds through hills and then makes a dramatic, arrow-straight descent toward Russellville, providing a superb view of a broad plateau and distant hills.

5 Florence, a large modern city with some noteworthy Victorian architecture, has several places of interest, including the restored log cabin where W. C. Handy, the "Father of the Blues," was born in 1873, the Handy Museum, and Pope's Tavern.

The tavern, a lovely white-painted brick house with a long veranda, was built in 1811 as a stopover on an old stagecoach route known today as Hermitage Drive. Now the building is a museum with furnishings, kitchen

4. Natural Bridge soars magnificently above magnolias, beeches, and sycamores. The smaller span of the bridge branches off the main arch in a Y-formation.

equipment, tools, and firearms that give you a vivid picture of bygone days. The tavern is closed Mondays.

6 To reach Wilson Dam from Pope's Tavern, continue along Hermitage Drive and then follow Route 133 east. Built in 1918–24 by the U.S.

Army Corps of Engineers, Wilson Dam became the cornerstone of the Tennessee Valley Authority's system, and it is now a national historic landmark. The dam is 4,541 feet long and 137 feet high, making it the highest of the dams on the main stream of the Tennessee River. It boasts the highest single-lift lock in the United States, with a maximum lift of 100 feet, and its hydroelectric generating capacity is the greatest of all the TVA dams. Visitors are welcome at the huge, immaculate hydroelectric plant at the south end of the Wilson Dam.

7 The Wheeler Dam, almost the twin of the Wilson Dam, also has an impressive hydroelectric plant that may be visited. Wheeler Lake and Wilson Lake, created by the dams, are popular recreation areas. The Joe Wheeler State Park, which has two areas on the north side of the Tennessee River and one on the south, offers a motel resort, rental cottages, campsites with utilities, picnic areas, a marina, and a wide variety of recreational activities, including golf and water sports.

Bordering the Tennessee River is a network of high-tension power lines serving gigantic industrial complexes that have been built in the midst of the valley's cotton fields and dairy farms. The state's northern cotton belt stretches to the horizon, and in October the landscape on both sides

8. The Apollo-Saturn V rocket in the Alabama Space and Rocket Center is similar to the one that sent men to the moon. The first stage of the rocket, with its five liquid fuel engines, is 138 feet long. The rockets to the right were forerunners in the U.S. space program.

of the road is stippled with the fluffy white balls bursting from their cinnamon-brown pods.

8 There is nothing to compare with the Alabama Space and Rocket Center at Huntsville. It is one of the world's largest space museums, and it is, in a single word, staggering. To see the small Apollo command module with its charred heat shield, the fragile, spidery-looking lunar landing vehicle, and the training versions of the lunar roving vehicle (which was left on the moon) is a memorable experience. Stretched horizontally on the ground is an Apollo-Saturn V moon rocket similar to the ones that sent astronauts into space. As long as a football field, it suggests a skyscraper lying on its side, and the thought of launching something so enormous seems preposterous.

At the museum you are in a world of spaceships, rockets, and shuttles. There are dioramas of space life and many participating experiences that allow you to take your place in a module, flip switches, and feel that you are journeying among the stars. There is more than enough here to keep a family interested for hours.

You can also take a two-hour guided bus tour of the adjacent Marshall Space Flight Center of the National Aeronautics and Space Administration, where scientists and astronauts are working on our future space programs. Both the museum and the research center are closed on Christmas Day.

9 From the 1,600-foot summit of Monte Sano Mountain and roadside lookout points in Monte Sano State Park there are magnificent views of Huntsville, the lush Tennessee Valley, and the foothills of the Appalachian Mountains. The lovely, wooded park has rental cottages, camping and picnic areas, and hiking trails.

As you continue eastward the land becomes increasingly mountainous, and the scenery is splendid. Nearing Scottsboro, you see its church spires and majestic Guntersville Lake from the top of a ridge. One blue ridge after another unfolds before you, revealing the undisturbed serenity of the intervening valleys where jet black cows graze in emerald green meadows—an hour away and worlds apart from NASA's Space Center.

10 When you enter the Sequoyah Caverns, through the side of a rock bluff, it is to step into a magical world. The caverns' rock formations are delicate in color and shape, and many suggest minarets, castles, and ancient cities. Small, still lakes mirror these scenes, creating an illusion of limitless depth and extent so convincing that you cannot believe you are looking into water until you plunge in a finger. Known as the Looking Glass Caverns, these are considered to be among the most beautiful caverns in the world. It is an easy, 45-minute walk through the caverns, and where there are steps, there are also ramps for wheelchairs.

In the secluded adjacent area are a trailer campground, hiking trails, a playground, and fenced meadows where white deer and buffalo graze.

11 De Soto State Park, which stretches for 40 miles along the Little River on the spine of Lookout Mountain, is an unspoiled wilderness with forests, streams, waterfalls, and canyons. The park offers a resort lodge and restaurant, a campground, a tent site, cabin rentals, a picnic and play area, and nature trails.

One of the most dramatic displays of water in the park is De Soto Falls. In a wooded setting, the West Fork of the Little River flows over a dam and then catapults over two wide ledges, dropping 100 feet into a large pool partially walled in by the rock cliffs. If you are sure-footed, you may want to follow a path skirting the pool for the best views.

12 A beautiful drive down the western slope of Lookout Mountain brings you to Manitou Cave at Fort Payne, a few miles outside the park. Once a religious center of the Cherokee Indians, the cave became the South's first tourist attraction in 1878, with 10-cent tours by torchlight. In the 1890's fashionable balls were held

11. De Soto Falls, on a fork of the Little River, is the largest of the park's 15 waterfalls, many of which are along wooded trails. The Little River, formed by springs, is the only river in America whose entire course is on a mountain.

by candlelight in the largest chamber, a room 96 feet long. A railroad spur brought people from Fort Payne to the cave. Manitou Cave is closed weekdays from early September to the end of May.

Modern Fort Payne charmingly recalls its boom times with a red brick opera house bearing the date 1889, a city park with an old-fashioned bandstand, and an imposing Romanesque railroad station built in 1891.

13 Little River Canyon in De Soto State Park is one of the deepest and largest gorges east of the Mississippi River, with a maximum depth of 600 feet and a length of approximately 16 miles. At the north end of the canyon, Little River Falls makes a magnificent display. The 60-foot-high falls can be seen from the east side of the canyon, reached by a bridge near the junction of Route 35 and the Rim Parkway.

Little River Canyon Rim Parkway, a two-lane blacktop road with one-lane bridges, hugs the precipitous western wall. The curves are sharp, the grades steep, and the views into the canyon spectacular. After following a long U-shaped course around Bear Creek Canyon, which joins the larger canyon, the road forks. At this junction a sign instructs drivers with unreliable brakes or with "pull-behind" vehicles to proceed on Route 176, an easier route that veers away from the canyon and cuts through the forest to Route 68. From the junction the Rim Parkway continues south for another 11 miles in a series of hairpin turns and descends to the mouth of the canyon where the Little River quietly flows into Weiss Lake. Here the road is not much more than a lane, and it passes under a railroad trestle with a low and narrow clearance. (There is a bypass for large vehicles.) The road then improves and traverses a pleasant valley to Route 68 and Leesburg.

14 Noccalula Falls is in Gadsden's large municipal park. A small stream flows over a wide, curved ledge of rock and falls 90 feet into a beautiful round pool. Poised above the pool is a graceful bronze statue of Noccalula, the daughter of a Cherokee chieftain. According to legend, she was in love with a man of her own tribe, and rather than marry the Creek Indian to whom her father had promised her, she took her life by jumping into the pool at this site. Petroglyphs found on nearby rocks support the story.

Other features at Noccalula Falls Park are the botanical gardens, famous for their azaleas, a century-old covered bridge, and the Pioneer Museum, a small village of furnished, 200-year-old log cabins. There are also campgrounds and picnic and play areas in groves of dogwood.

This outing exemplifies the variety of Alabama's scenery and history. It includes a visit to a mid-19th-century gristmill, an excursion to an "onyx" cavern, a drive to the top of Alabama's highest peak, a tour of the site of a battle that launched a future U.S. president into national prominence, and a stop at a great marble quarry.

1 Settlers began to trickle into the Childersburg area in the early 1800's, attracted by the superior stands of longleaf yellow pine found here. Childersburg's growth as a lumbering center led to the construction in 1867 of the Kymulga Grist Mill, about five miles east of Childersburg. From Route 76 take Route 36 north to the intersection with Route 46; continue across the railroad tracks to the mill.

The weathered appearance of the mill belies its sturdy structure of great, hewn timbers, one of which runs the 60-foot length of the building. One of the oldest water-powered gristmills in Alabama, it has three underwater turbines and five massive sets of stones that could grind 3 million pounds of wheat and corn in a year. You can see the mill in operation on Saturdays, and buy some stone-ground wheat flour or a sack of corn-meal with a local recipe for corn bread.

The mill, on Talladega Creek, is adjacent to a dilapidated covered bridge of Town lattice design. Both are national historic landmarks.

2 Upon entering the De Soto Caverns you find yourself in a breathtaking cathedrallike room known as the Kymulga Room. The lofty ceiling and walls glow with rich, subdued colors, and 30-foot-long golden draperies hang in luxuriant folds. The drapery is actually composed of free-hanging translucent sheets of cave onyx, an elegantly banded variety of travertine. In fact, the cavern is almost entirely of this stone, which began to form 60 million years ago. You can see cave onyx formations still growing.

The caverns were used for tribal ceremonies by the Creek Indians at the time of Hernando de Soto's visit in 1540. Today concerts are given in the Kymulga Room; the acoustics are excellent because the irregular surface gives resonance but no echo. There are wooded picnic and camping grounds nearby. The caverns are closed in December and January, and on weekdays in February, March, October, and November.

As you head northeast the land becomes hillier. Hayfields and forests spread over the slopes, and primroses and black-eyed Susans brighten the roadside in summer.

2. The Kymulga Room in De Soto Caverns echoes with history. An Indian burial ground 2,000 years ago, it has also been a shelter for pioneer traders, a source of bat guano used by Confederate soldiers in making gunpowder, and during Prohibition, a speakeasy.

3. From the summit of Cheaha Mountain there are often lovely views of cloud strata floating over the valleys below. In the fall the foliage is a tapestry of glowing colors. The ridges here in the Talladega National Forest are a continuation of the Appalachian chain.

In a relatively small area here you can experience the major characteristics of central Alabama. There are the green wooded hills of the Talladega National Forest and its environs, the productive Black Belt soil, and a number of handsome homes built when cotton was king and the riverfront towns were prosperous shipping centers. Surprising highlights are an unusual rock garden and some impressive examples of ancient Indian mounds.

1 As the capital of the state from 1826 to 1846, and the home of the University of Alabama since 1831, Tuscaloosa has become the beneficiary of an architectural and social heritage beyond the scope of most towns of its size.

On the university campus, which is noted for its beauty, there are two superb examples of the Greek Revival style of architecture: the President's Mansion and the University Faculty Club.

There are many handsome houses of various styles to be seen along the oak-lined streets. Among those that

3 In the Talladega National Forest you make a serpentine, 10-mile climb to the top of Cheaha Mountain. Route 96, a narrow but excellent blacktop road, winds through fragrant woods of long-needled pines and oaks and crosses several small, cascading streams.

Rising 2,407 feet above sea level, Cheaha Mountain is Alabama's highest peak (Cheaha is an Indian word for "high"), and the panorama from the observation tower at the top is splendid. Cheaha State Park, which covers the wooded crest and upper slopes of the mountain, has a modern resort lodge, rental cottages, and campsites. Other attractions are hiking, swimming, and fishing.

4 Driving through the carefully tended grounds of Horseshoe Bend Military National Park, you find it hard to believe that this was the setting for the final defeat of the Creek Indians by Gen. Andrew Jackson on March 27, 1814. The museum at the visitor center graphically outlines the strategy of each side, and a diorama vividly presents the climactic battle at the Barricade. You can follow the course of the battle on a marked road tour. The park also has hiking trails, paved paths for wheelchairs, and a picnic area.

Continuing from Horseshoe Bend, you traverse rich farmland and then cross the northern end of Lake Martin. The arms of the lake reach into low wooded hills filled with azaleas, and the shady inlets are noted for their bass and catfish.

5 The quarries of Sylacauga, known as Marble City, have supplied the creamy white rock for many notable buildings, including the U.S. Supreme Court in Washington, D.C.

To reach Gantt's Quarry, the industrial center of Sylacauga's three marble companies, turn west onto Route 8 at its intersection with Route 280, and then turn south when you cross the second set of railroad tracks. The yards are white with marble dust, and the air thick with it. Great mounds of marble chips and powder resemble artificial ski slopes. The pulverized marble is added to cattle feed as a source of calcium, to paint and rubber as a whitener and toughener, and to many other products, including cosmetics. An open quarry is visible through a fence at the side of Quarry Road; nearby there is a marble finishing plant with a shop for visitors.

1. A handsome brick structure built in 1835, the Battle-Friedman House has square, stuccoed columns and a colonial doorway.

are open to the public are the Gorgas House on the campus, the Battle–Friedman House and the Friedman Memorial Library, both on Greensboro Avenue, and the restored Old Tavern on Capitol Square. The architecture of the picturesque inn, built in 1827, shows a French influence.

2 On Route 11 watch for the turn-off to Bama Scenic Rock Gardens. The sign is at Vance, just past the marker for Mile 101. The gardens are a fascinating geologic phenomenon in an unexpected place. An exposed table of limestone has been eroded by the rain and running water to create gullies, ledges, steep ravines, caves, named for the Tannehill Furnaces, a major producer of armaments for the South during the Civil War. Although the furnaces were destroyed by Union raiders in 1865, the iron industry that developed later in nearby Birmingham has its roots in the technology developed at Tannehill. One of the plant's original furnaces has been park is a remarkable reminder of Alabama's pioneer heritage.

Back on Route 5 heading south, the drive on the gently undulating road is a pleasant one, passing small farms with cattle grazing in green pastures. The green contrasts with the rich red of the clay soil revealed by the embankments where the grade cuts

In the realm of King Cotton

Alabama is one of the nation's major producers of cotton, with 320,000 acres devoted to the crop. In late June great expanses of the state are covered with its deep green foliage and creamy white blossoms. Turning a deep pink, the blossoms fall off, leaving the green bolls, or seedpods. Masses of soft fibers growing from the seeds in the pods cause the pods to burst open in early autumn, revealing fluffy white balls (shown at right). Then cotton-picking machines harvest the crop, and gins separate the seeds from the fibers. The ginned fiber, which is called lint, is pressed into 500-pound bales and wrapped for shipment, and the seeds are processed into oil and meal. Seeds to be reserved for planting are delinted and treated with a fungicide and a purple dye for easy identification.

In early autumn the fields of cotton are ready for harvesting.

Dyed cotton seeds

Young cotton plant

A cotton blossom

Green cotton boll

Mature cotton

pockets, and potholes. There are walls covered with fern and patches of lichen, and brilliant green moss thrives on the surface of the porous rock. Rain and groundwater are naturally acidic and tend to erode limestone more readily than they erode other rock.

A walkway of pebbled concrete, with bridges and steps, leads through this unusual landscape studded with pines, oaks, and a few dense stands of bamboo. The walk through the garden takes about half an hour.

3 The sign to Tannehill State Park is just south of the junction of Routes 11 and 5. The drive of about five miles to the park follows a ridge flanked by small farmsteads. Some signs simply say Tannehill Trail, but they lead to the 1,000-acre preserve. The park is reconstructed beside the riffles of a mill creek, and a nearby museum features tools and equipment related to the making of iron and steel.

In a lovely wooded setting near the furnace are some 20 pioneer homes moved here log by log and stone by stone from their original rural locations. This section of the park also includes campgrounds, a picnic area carpeted with the fragrant needles of the surrounding pines, and a restaurant in a rustic log building.

A short walk, or a ride on a miniature train, leads to the site of a 19th-century farmstead with its dairy farm, sorghum mill, and blacksmith shop, and to working reconstructions of an early-day water-driven gristmill and cotton gin that were located here on Tannehill Mill Creek. All in all the through the rolling terrain. This red soil is due to a long history of rock weathering under subtropical conditions and the oxidating of the iron content. The oxide is a rusty red.

4 The Paul M. Grist State Park is a pleasant place to stop for a respite, a picnic lunch, and, perhaps, a little exercise. There are hiking trails, a playground, and tennis courts. The 1,000-acre lake edged with heavy stands of pine and oak offers swimming, canoeing, boating, and fishing.

5 The hills are heavily timbered in this part of Alabama, close by the Talladega National Forest, and on the road to Selma you may see logging trucks on their way to the sawmills.

Selma is an old river town, and in the steamboating days it was a busy shipping point. The cargo was mostly bales of cotton produced in the plantations that abounded on the Black Belt, so called for a 30-mile-wide swath of rich dark soil that crosses Alabama and swings northwest from here into the state of Mississippi. The most interesting part of town is along Water Avenue, where the old commercial buildings still stand with cast-iron posts supporting verandas over the sidewalk. The historic district also has fine examples of antebellum and Victorian residences.

About 18 miles southwest of Selma watch for the turn onto Route 21 to Uniontown. This two-lane road cutting right through open fields of the rich Black Belt soil provides intimate views of rural Alabama. There are prosperous farmhouses as well as unpainted shacks, and on all sides is the fertile black soil that yields bumper crops of soybeans and corn.

When Route 21 seems to come to a dead end, make a right turn to reach Uniontown and Route 80.

6 There are echoes of the antebellum South in the handsome storefronts of the business district of Demopolis, as well as in two notable homes you can visit here.

Before the Civil War there were great plantations in this area, and both Gaineswood and Bluff Hall were built for prosperous planters.

Gaineswood, a national historic landmark, is dramatically situated on Route 43 just 0.2 of a mile north of Route 80. It was designed by the owner, Gen. Nathan Bryan Whitfield, and built under his close supervision from 1843 to 1861. The elegantly proportioned, beautifully detailed 20-room Greek Revival-style house has the original furnishings.

Bluff Hall, next to the Civic Center on North Commissioners Avenue, was built in 1832 for Francis Strother Lyon. The design was originally federal, but about 1850 a columned portico was added to give the house the Greek Revival look that was fashionable at the time. The furnishings are primarily Empire and Victorian.

Just north of Demopolis are signs pointing to various small parks, including Lock Four, Runaway, Birdseye, and Backbone Branch, all of which are pleasant places for a picnic lunch. Particularly attractive is Damsite Park, on a bluff overlooking the Black Warrior River just east of Eutaw on Route 14. It has picnic tables in a grove of oak trees.

7 Warrior Lock and Dam has a pleasant picnic area in addition to the neat and orderly site and the lock itself, which has appeal for anyone interested in the mechanics and techniques of river navigation. Although there is not a lot of traffic on the river, the locks are in operation and you might well be there when a boat goes through.

8 Because Greensboro was a cotton center and of limited strategic value during the Civil War, it was spared by Union troops and it still boasts a remarkable number of interesting antebellum and other 19th-century buildings. There are cottages with gingerbread fretwork trim, carpenter Gothic and Victorian houses, and Greek Revival mansions.

At the end of Main Street is Magnolia Grove, a lovely Greek Revival mansion set among some magnificent specimens of evergreen magnolia (*Magnolia grandiflora*). Built about 1838, it is now a state shrine and open to the public.

There are other lovely houses on Main Street, as well as on South Street and on Tuscaloosa Street.

9 The entrance drive from the main gate of the Mound State Monument to the archeological museum wends its way between massive grass-covered mounds that rise steeply from the level plain, once the central plaza. The imposing scale of these mounds still conveys the sense of mystery and awe that was probably intended when this ceremonial city was built by Mississippian Indians some 600 to 800 years ago. There are 20 flat-topped earthen structures here, the largest of which is more than 60 feet high. These Indians did not employ the wheel, had no draft animals, and their only tools were made of stone, shell, and wood. When you realize that all the earth in these mounds was transported by hand in baskets, the work involved seems overwhelming.

The mounds were built as platforms for buildings. On top of the largest one, there is a reconstruction of a temple and a representation of a religious ceremony, all modeled on the best archeological evidence available. There are other representations of Indian life in the small reconstructed village on a bluff overlooking the Black Warrior River.

In the museum, which features an impressive collection of artifacts found on the site, there are also two burial pits that show more than 50 skeletons exactly as they were interred centuries ago. An audiovisual presentation explains the Moundville site, the history of its excavations, and the culture of this vanished people.

3. A path bordering a creek in the lovely rustic setting of Tannehill State Park brings you to the John Wesley Hall Grist Mill and Cotton Gin. The mill, with its overshot waterwheel, is a reconstruction of the original, which operated from 1867 to 1931.

Kentucky and Tennessee

From the Appalachians to the Mississippi are historic shrines, superb state parks, and inviting waterways

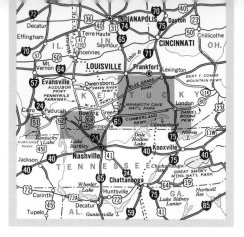

Kentucky and Tennessee lie between the northern states of Illinois, Indiana, and Ohio and the Deep South states of Mississippi, Alabama, and Georgia. The landscapes and the citizens of the two states share characteristics of both the North and the South. In the east fir trees cling to rugged Appalachian ridges where independent mountain men remained loyal to the Union during the Civil War. In the west great groves of cypress trees stand amid the marshes and swamps of Mississippi bottomlands where wealthy cotton planters and landowners once took up arms for the Confederacy.

This short tour touches interesting aspects of four states. It includes a lake in Tennessee where waterfowl abound and bald eagles may be seen. After a ferryboat ride across the Mississippi, the tour leads through "the boot heel of Missouri," which boasts some of the richest farmland in the United States, to the junction of the Ohio and Mississippi rivers. In Kentucky on bluffs above the high-water mark of the Ohio are ceremonial mounds built by pre-Columbian Indians, and farther south is a Civil War battlefield with fine views of the Mississippi River. Kentucky and Tennessee are similar enough ecologically to have the same official state tree, the tulip poplar (Liriodendron tulipifera).

1 During the bitter cold winter of 1811-12 a series of earthquakes, called the New Madrid Quakes and the longest ever recorded east of the Rockies, rocked the central Mississippi Valley. Thousands of acres along the Mississippi were inundated by floodwaters, covering the land to a height of 20 feet, and Reelfoot Lake was born. As the waters receded, a ridge was left that separated the lake from the river. In 1914 the state of Tennessee gained control of property around the lake through court action and preserved the area for recreational use and wildlife management. Finally, in 1973, Reelfoot Lake State Resort Park was established.

The fishing is excellent and popular at Reelfoot Lake. Large catches of crappie, bream, and largemouth bass are common. Rental boats, tackle, and bait are available.

A special attraction at Reelfoot is its great flock of wintering bald eagles, which usually numbers more than 100. From December to March the park naturalist conducts daily eagle tours, but you are quite likely to see them on your own by driving slowly around the lake along Route 21. Reelfoot Lake is also famous for its great flocks of wintering ducks and other waterbirds. In the fall, duck hunters from all over the South and Midwest converge on the lake. The park offers camping facilities and hiking trails.

2 The Hickman Ferry carries not only cars but trucks across the Mississippi River every day between 7 A.M. and 6 P.M. The trip takes 15 minutes. If you do not see the ferry when you arrive at the landing, flip over the sign to signal the captain that you are waiting for a ride.

After you disembark from the ferry, Route 77 takes you north through some of the finest farmland in the United States. The six small flatland counties that form what is known as the boot heel of Missouri account for some 40 percent of the state's total agricultural output while comprising only about 10 percent of its area. The deep topsoil here was laid down over the millennia by Mississippi floodwaters. Local farmers say they know the area was once a great cypress swamp because plows frequently strike the tops of ancient buried cypress trees. Proud residents have dubbed the area the "hub of American agriculture," bragging that it produces corn as good as Iowa's, wheat as good as Kansas's, cotton as good as Mississippi's, and crops of soybeans second to none.

1. Bald cypress trees, so named because they lose their needles each fall, are reflected in the waters of Reelfoot Lake.

SPECIAL FEATURES			
ROAD GUIDE	━━━━	HIGHLIGHT	**1**
STATE PARKS		SCHEDULED AIRLINE STOPS	✈
With Campsites ▲ Without Campsites △		OTHER AIRPORTS	✈
RECREATION AREAS		BOAT RAMPS	⊿
With Campsites ▲ Without Campsites △		COVERED BRIDGES	⌒
SELECTED REST AREAS ⊼		INFORMATION CENTER	✳
POINTS OF INTEREST ⊡			

ROAD CLASSIFICATION

CONTROLLED ACCESS HIGHWAYS
(Entrance and Exit only at Interchanges)

TOLL HIGHWAYS

OTHER DIVIDED HIGHWAYS

PAVED HIGHWAYS

LOCAL ROADS In unfamiliar areas inquire locally before using these roads   Paved   Gravel   Dirt

MILEAGE

MILEAGE BETWEEN TOWNS AND JUNCTIONS ○3╱4○   MILEAGE BETWEEN DOTS ●—35—●

SCALE

ONE INCH 20 MILES   0 5 10   20

ONE INCH 32 KILOMETERS   0 5 10   20   32

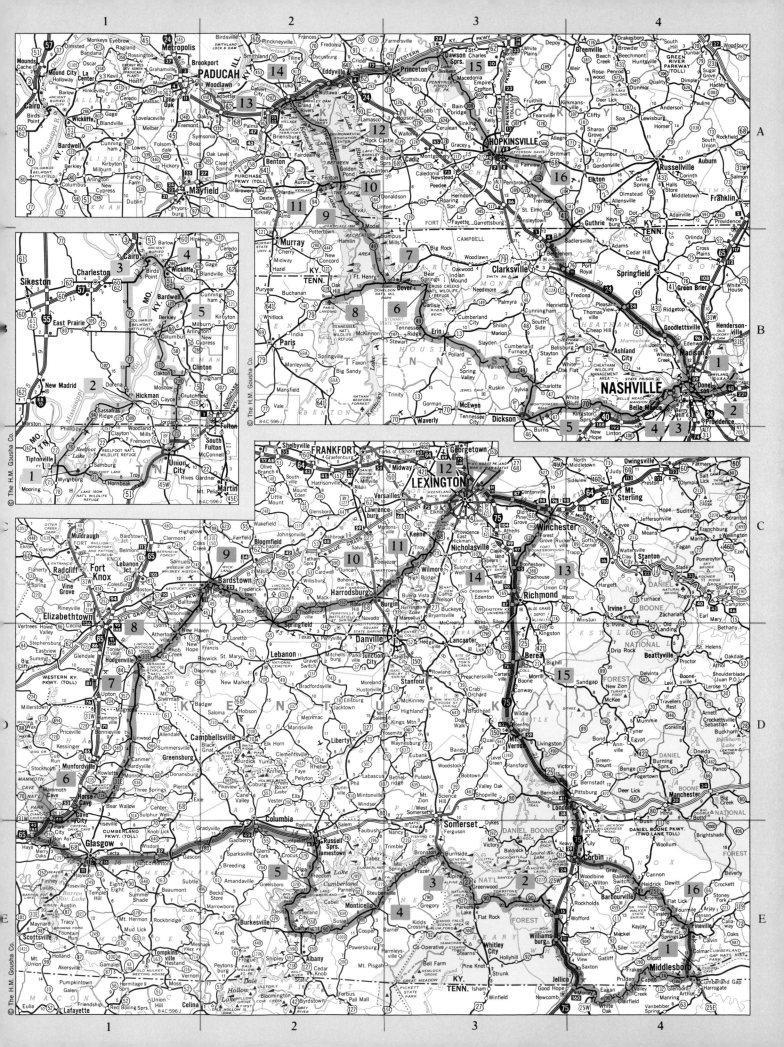

3 Early 19th-century land promoters had high hopes for the city of Cairo, Illinois, because of its commanding location at the junction of the Ohio and Mississippi rivers. Today, however, it is simply a quiet river town completely surrounded by a levee system that gives it the appearance of being a walled city. Shade trees line pleasant residential streets on which Italianate Victorian mansions stand alongside simple frame cottages. The brick facades of many buildings in the business district of the town remain much as they were in the 1880's.

Magnolia Manor, built by a wealthy local miller who supplied the Union Army with hardtack during the Civil War, was the scene of a reception for former President Ulysses S. Grant and his wife in 1880. It is now a museum open to the public.

The city was named by an early settler who thought the area resembled Egypt. Even today the lower tip of Illinois is called Egypt or Little Egypt by local residents.

4 At Wickliffe, Kentucky, which is just over the Ohio River bridge from the town of Cairo, are bluffs that rise well above the river's high-water mark. Here, about 1,000 years ago, Indians lived and built large earthen mounds to serve as temples, burial and ceremonial sites, and residences. At Ancient Buried City, several of these mounds have been carefully excavated so that artifacts and human remains lie just as they were when they were uncovered. The pottery, jewelry, and tools buried with the dead suggest to archeologists that these mound-building Indians were a prosperous, sophisticated, and knowledgeable group of people. Conducted tours of the excavations at Ancient Buried City are available.

5 Located on high bluffs, 156-acre Columbus–Belmont Battlefield State Park offers splendid views of the Mississippi River. A well-marked historical trail winds through earthworks built to protect Confederate artillery. Civil War and Indian artifacts are displayed in a museum that once served as a Confederate Army infirmary. Four stone shelters provide pleasant picnicking sites. Other park facilities include a campground and a children's playground.

1. Six white columns of modified Corinthian design, supporting a dentil-trimmed cornice, form the facade of Andrew Jackson's tree-shaded Hermitage. Lights frame the doorways on the wide galleries that run across both levels of the two-story mansion.

There is a rewarding variety of experiences to be enjoyed here in southwestern Kentucky and central Tennessee. Near the city of Nashville, the acknowledged capital of country music, is the stately home of Andrew Jackson as well as two other plantation houses reminiscent of the opulence of the antebellum South. Also on the tour in Tennessee are a wildlife refuge and a restored Civil War fort.

Land Between the Lakes, created by dams of the Tennessee Valley Authority, is a recreation area about 8 miles wide and 40 miles long that crosses the Tennessee–Kentucky border and has varied highlights in each state. Both states have developed superb resort parks, and five of them are included on this tour.

1 The Hermitage, the stately white-columned home of Andrew Jackson, has been meticulously restored and maintained. The house and grounds appear today very much as they did in 1845 when Old Hickory, the seventh president of the United States, died here in retirement.

Visitors can see the original French wallpaper hung in the entrance hall in 1836 and the "Eighth of January mantel" in the dining room, carved by a soldier who fought under Jackson at the Battle of New Orleans on January 8, 1815. The soldier worked on the mantel only one day each year,

on the anniversary of the battle, finally presenting the completed piece to Jackson in 1839 after 24 days' work. Beside the mansion is the formal garden Jackson created for his beloved wife, Rachel. In one corner of the garden, shaded by hickories and magnolias, is the tomb where Rachel and Andrew Jackson are interred. Closed on Christmas Day.

2 Opryland, U.S.A., an outstanding family entertainment park, offers five musical theme areas and 12 fully staged live productions featuring a wide range of American popular music—gospel, country, bluegrass, Dixieland jazz, folk, riverboat, showboat, and disco. Closed from November through March.

Also located at Opryland is one of the world's largest broadcast auditoriums, the home of the internationally famous *Grand Ole Opry*. The oldest continuous radio program in the United States, *Grand Ole Opry* has never missed a weekly broadcast since November 1925.

3 Completed in 1853, Belle Meade was once the mansion of a 5,300-acre plantation and a showplace of central Tennessee. Now only a 24-acre remnant of land remains here on Harding Road, but the house has been restored to its original antebellum splendor.

Belle Meade Stud, as the plantation was once called, was the first and probably the finest horse farm of its time in America. Descendants of the outstanding thoroughbreds raised at Belle Meade include the great Secretariat. A huge carriage house at the rear of the mansion contains a collection of old carriages. The plantation is closed Thanksgiving, Christmas, and New Year's days.

4   Less than two miles south of Belle Meade is Cheekwood, a magnificent private estate that in 1959 became the home of the Tennessee Botanical Gardens and Fine Arts

Center. The mansion has several galleries where works of art from private collections and traveling shows are displayed. The grounds feature superb formal gardens, greenhouses that contain year-round displays of exotic flowers, and beautiful wild flower trails. The mansion and its gardens are closed on Christmas Eve afternoon and Christmas Day.

5   The iron ore in Dickson County was largely exhausted nearly a century ago and with it the iron industry, but the remains of an old furnace and

traces of ore pits can be found within 3,782-acre Montgomery Bell State Resort Park.

This well-maintained resort park is typical of the excellent parks of this kind that are so popular in both Tennessee and Kentucky. It offers, at reasonable prices, a full complement of recreational facilities, including an inn, a swimming pool, vacation cottages, campsites, boating and fishing on Acorn Lake, picnic pavilions, an 18-hole golf course, lighted tennis courts, and a 19-mile network of hiking trails.

6   The 9,600-acre Cross Creeks National Wildlife Refuge stretches for 11 miles along both sides of Barkley Lake on the Cumberland River. A mixture of marsh, croplands, woodlands, and impounded waters provides an ideal habitat for migratory waterfowl. Come between late September and March and you can see large flocks of wintering ducks and Canada geese. If you are fortunate, you may also glimpse a southern bald eagle, the only endangered species presently using the refuge. Summer residents include Canada geese and wood ducks.

7   Fort Donelson was built to protect the Confederate gun batteries on the Cumberland River from land attack. That Confederate troops fought hard before surrendering this key outpost to the Union is affirmed by 670 Union graves at Fort Donelson National Military Park and Cemetery. Visitors can tour the restored fort with its earthworks and gun batteries and in summer can watch uniformed interpreters conduct rifle- and cannon-firing demonstrations. The fort is closed on Christmas Day.

8   Paris Landing State Resort Park is a gem of the Tennessee park system. A spacious inn has beautiful views of Kentucky Lake. A campground complete with centrally located bathhouses is ideal for family camping. Among the park's recreational facilities are an Olympic-size public pool, a challenging 18-hole golf course, and tennis and basketball courts. The marina rents fishing boats and outboard motors.

9   At the Homeplace-1850 the Tennessee Valley Authority has reconstructed with painstaking accuracy a typical southern family farm of the

4. At Cheekwood, ancient boxwood hedges surround the rectangular stone-edged pool. A small iron-railed terrace, whose double stairway leads to the lawn, provides a view across the garden to a similar platform and two reclining lions, which form a gateway to the Mustard Meadow beyond. The tall spruce trees are reflected in the pool.

9. The farmhouse at Home Place-1850, an original 19th-century log structure surrounded by a weathered board fence, has a dogtrot connecting two sections of the house. The porch, supported by a single long log, protects a woodpile; rain barrels stand nearby.

1850's. Staff members carry on household activities and farm chores in the main cabin and the 14 outbuildings, which include barns, corncribs, and a springhouse.

10 For up-to-the-minute, detailed information about the extensive recreational opportunities at Land Between the Lakes, stop at The Golden Pond Information Center.

The area known as Land Between the Lakes is a 170,000-acre peninsula about 8 miles wide and 40 miles long nearly surrounded by two large manmade lakes. Administered by the TVA as an outdoor recreational unit and demonstration area, it contains no private land holdings, no motels, hotels, or gas stations—just nature study facilities, historical reconstructions, campgrounds, day-use areas, several miles of gravel roads crisscrossing hilly, hardwood forest lands, logging areas, croplands, and a 158-mile system of backpacking and day-hiking trails. There is such an abundance of wildlife in Land Between the Lakes that hikers are almost bound to sight waterfowl, wild turkeys, birds of prey, deer, beaver, or other animals.

This unique multiple-use region is considered by many to be one of the best places in the United States to hunt, fish, hike, ride, study nature, camp, and enjoy the great outdoors.

11 The emphasis is on tennis and boating at 1,400-acre Kenlake State Resort Park, one of the most popular resorts in the Kentucky state park system. Eight hard-surface tennis courts are available day and night. In addition, guests may enjoy a nine-

10. The male wild turkey, a bronze-colored, bald-headed fowl, spreads his tail to display his plumage. These handsome birds are abundant in the Land Between the Lakes.

hole golf course, a riding stable, and a beach and bathhouse. The lodge and efficiency cottages provide overnight accommodations. A wooded campground overlooks the lake.

12 A focal point of activity at Land Between the Lakes is the 5,000-acre Environmental Education Center. Here visitors can enjoy an audiovisual presentation and numerous exhibits on the natural history of an area once occupied by Indians, ironworkers, and moonshiners. Indian artifacts and Civil War mementos are also on display. Interpretive nature trails range from a ⅓-mile paved walking trail suitable for handicapped people in wheelchairs to a five-mile motor trail. Skunks, raccoons, white-tailed deer, and fallow deer are frequently observed at a wildlife observation station. Empire Farms, a 120-acre demonstration farm, stages craft programs that allow visitors to participate in such activities as broom making, sheepshearing, spinning, weaving, and sorghum molasses making.

13 Kentucky Dam Village State Resort Park was the first major state park on Kentucky Lake, and it remains one of the best. A lodge, housekeeping cottages, a marina, a swimming pool, tennis courts, an 18-hole golf course, and a beach-bathhouse complex are all located within walking distance of one another. Adjacent to the 1,200-acre park is the largest state-owned boat dock complex in the Kentucky park system. Boats, from 14-foot fishing skiffs to 50-foot houseboats, can be rented.

14 Serving as a gigantic spigot, the 8,422-foot Kentucky Dam controls the flow of the Tennessee River into the Ohio. Completed by the Tennessee Valley Authority at a cost $118 million in 1944, the 20-story-high dam created the largest man-made lake in the East by backing up the Tennessee River across the western tip of Kentucky and almost the entire width of Tennessee. The huge storage capacity of Kentucky Lake allows TVA engineers at the Kentucky Dam to cut back or temporarily turn off the flow of water from the Tennessee River as flood crests pass on the Ohio or Mississippi. You can turn off Route 62 at the eastern end of the dam and visit the powerhouse and the locks.

15 Pennyrile Forest State Park is a 15,000-acre preserve, the largest in the Kentucky state forest system. It contains a 435-acre resort park whose facilities include a comfortable lodge, housekeeping cottages, and camp-sites. A 55-acre lake on the grounds has a sand beach, a bathhouse complex, and rental boats. A nine-hole golf course and a stable of riding horses are located here. Closed from November through May 26.

16 Long before you reach it on Route 68, you can see the 351-foot obelisk across the level farmland outside Fairview.

The Jefferson Davis Monument, erected between 1918 and 1924, marks the birthplace of Jefferson Davis, the only president of the Confederate States of America. An elevator carries visitors to the top of the monument for fine views of the Todd County countryside. In a 20-acre park surrounding the monument stands a replica of the two-room log cabin in which Davis was born on June 3, 1808.

1. There are sweeping views of the Cumberland Gap from Kentucky's Pinnacle Overlook. Seen here from the slope above are the rounded viewing platform and, in the distance to the left, the little town of Arthur, Tennessee. Fern Lake in Kentucky is at the right.

Following the course of history for a way, this tour starts at Cumberland Gap, the first gateway to the trans-Appalachian West, and includes three of Kentucky's outstanding resort parks. At one of them you may see a moonbow in the mist of a cataract, and at Mill Springs is one of the largest waterwheels in the world.

At the western edge of this circuit is Mammoth Cave with more than 200 miles of underground passageways. You can also see where Abraham Lincoln was born and where he spent his early boyhood. Daniel Boone, the famous Kentucky pioneer, is commemorated at a rebuilt fort, and at Berea College the various handicrafts developed in the Appalachians are still carried on.

1 Drive west to Cumberland Gap from Virginia, and you understand why this famous pass became the gateway to the trans-Appalachian West. The Cumberland Mountains form a mighty, seemingly impenetrable wall.

The first European to discover the gap was Dr. Thomas Walker, a physician and surveyor. He took an Indian trail through the gap in 1750 and returned with tales of a bounteous country beyond. In 1775 Daniel Boone and a party of woodsmen blazed a trail through the Cumberland Gap into the region known as Kaintuckee, a land of plentiful game and well-watered, fertile soil.

Today Cumberland Gap National Historical Park, with more than 20,000 acres, is one of the largest historical units in the national park system.

The visitor center near the north entrance to Cumberland Gap provides a fine introduction to the park.

A Walk to Hensley Settlement

At Hensley Settlement you can enjoy a restored pioneer community similar to those founded by the early settlers of Kentucky and experience a living bit of our frontier past. It is reached by a pleasant four-mile hike up the Chadwell Gap Trail. Maps are available at Cumberland Gap Park Headquarters.

Sherman Hensley and his family established the settlement in 1903. Soon others followed, and a small community of scattered log cabins grew up. There were no roads, electricity, or other conveniences. The settlers cleared and plowed the land with hand tools and mules. They split oak and chestnut rails for fences and hewed their cabin logs with adzes and broadaxes.

Prior to World War II the settlement grew to about 100 people, but in the postwar years it was gradually abandoned. Since 1965, 25 of the nearly 40 buildings have been restored by the National Park Service. Farmer-demonstrators live in the settlement year-round, working the fields with horse-drawn equipment.

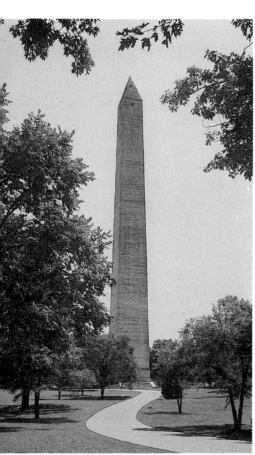

16. In the Jefferson Davis Monument, the tallest cast concrete structure in the nation, is a bas-relief likeness of this hero.

Museum exhibits and a slide show highlight the wildlife, geology, and history of the area.

Cumberland Gap National Historical Park offers nearly 50 miles of excellent hiking trails. More than 125 species of birds are known to be residents of or visitors to the park, including the blue-winged warbler, the marsh hawk, and the endangered bald eagle. Wild flowers bloom from March to October, and there is a large population of mammals, including gray squirrels, chipmunks, raccoons, and white-tailed deer.

2 Fifteen of Kentucky's state parks are classified as "resort parks." They offer reasonably priced rooms, food, and a variety of recreational facilities, which include tennis courts, swimming pools, riding stables, and golf courses. As one of the showplaces in the state park system, 1,794-acre Cumberland Falls State Resort Park in the heart of Daniel Boone National Forest boasts all of these amenities, except for a golf course.

At the falls for which the park is named, the waters of the Cumberland River thunder over a semicircular, 68-foot-high bluff in a seething 150-foot-wide curtain of water. Mist created by the rushing water constantly floats in the air and is responsible for the only known moonbow in the Western Hemisphere. If you are lucky enough to be visiting on a clear night when the moon is bright, you can see a luminous white arch extending downstream from the base of the falls.

In addition to the resort facilities at the park, there are two campgrounds and 15 miles of hiking trails.

3 General Burnside State Park is named for Ambrose E. Burnside, who held eastern Kentucky for the Union in 1863. The 400-acre park is

situated on land that was once known as Bunker Hill. When the Cumberland River was impounded in 1950, Bunker Hill became an island and was dedicated as a state park. The park has a large campground with a beach, an 18-hole golf course commanding pleasant views of the surrounding hills, and fine picnicking facilities. Nearby, Burnside Marina on the mainland rents fishing boats, tackle, and houseboats.

Just north of the marina, where the Cumberland River and its South Fork join, the great impoundment called Lake Cumberland begins. Steep cliffs of flat-lying sandstone sedimentary rock about 300 million years old that are topped by hardwoods wall this fjordlike section of the lake.

4 The hamlet of Mill Springs was first settled in 1770 by pioneer hunters and later became a Civil War battleground. A gristmill for the milling of corn and wheat was first built here in 1827 below springs flowing from a hillside. This mill burned and was rebuilt at least twice before the existing structure was erected in 1877. In 1908 a huge, 40-foot overshot steel waterwheel, one of the largest of its kind in the world, was installed.

5 At the end of the winding five-mile entrance to Lake Cumberland State Resort Park there is one of the most beautifully situated, best-equipped resort complexes in the Kentucky park system.

Two lodges contain 88 well-appointed rooms; in addition there are housekeeping cottages scattered among the trees and a camping area. Also on the grounds are tennis courts,

2. Cumberland Falls, famous for its moonbow, also produces a rainbow, as shown here, when the sun and mist are just right. The falls, located on the Cumberland River, can be seen from an observation point on a nearby bluff. Within the park are several hiking trails.

a nine-hole golf course, two swimming pools (one Olympic size), a miniature golf course, a riding stable, and nature trails. But perhaps the most popular of all the facilities at the park is the boat dock. Here you can rent a variety of craft, from a small sailing or fishing boat to a 58-foot houseboat.

During your stay at Lake Cumberland State Resort Park, keep some nuts or popcorn handy to feed the wildlife. No one knows exactly how the large populations of apparently friendly deer, raccoons, woodchucks, gray foxes, squirrels, and skunks became established, but an astonishing number of mammalian freeloaders materialize around dinner time behind the lodges and near the campsites. These animals are accustomed to people, but you should remember that they are wild nevertheless and should never be handled.

white, and purple displays of dogwood, shadbush, and redbud. In the autumn the hardwood trees are ablaze with reds and brilliant golds.

Some 300 million years ago a succession of shallow seas covered the Mammoth Cave area. The deposits of shells and ooze and sand left by these ancient seas hardened into limestone and sandstone layers. Eventually the earth's crust shifted, the land rose, and the seas drained away. Rains fell and rivers formed. Wind and water eroded many layers of sedimentary rock. Mildly acidic groundwaters working their way through fractures in the rocks slowly dissolved the limestone around them to create sinkholes and chambers. Working horizontally along the boundaries between the soluble limestone and the impervious shales, tunnels and passageways were formed. Much of the groundwater in the Mammoth

longest known cave system on earth.

More than 200 miles of Mammoth's passages have been explored. Among the cave's outstanding features are a rotunda as large as New York's Grand Central Station; a three-mile-long passage, aptly called Broadway, wide enough to accommodate a four-lane highway; gypsum "flowers," deposits of calcium sulfate resembling petals or needles; and Frozen Niagara, a majestic travertine formation.

7 The Abraham Lincoln Birthplace National Historic Site is located where Thomas Lincoln settled in December 1808 with his pregnant wife, Nancy Hanks. She gave birth to her second child, Abraham, in a one-room cabin on February 12, 1809.

Fifty-six steps, one for each year of the Great Emancipator's life, take visitors up to the imposing granite monument that encloses the cabin.

8 At Knob Creek stands Lincoln's Boyhood Home, a reproduction of the cabin where young Abe lived from age two until he was almost eight. It contains the simple tools and rustic furniture that might have been found in the original homestead. The cabin is closed from November through March.

9 Settled in 1775, historic Bardstown is the hub of Kentucky's bourbon industry. At the Barton distillery on Barton Street you can tour bottling facilities in operation and visit the company's Museum of Whiskey History, which contains a collection of whiskey industry artifacts.

On Stephen Foster Street stands charming Old Talbott Tavern, probably the first hotel west of the Alleghenies. Established in 1779, its doors have been open ever since. Andrew Jackson, Henry Clay, and William Henry Harrison all stopped here.

Also on Stephen Foster Street is the oldest cathedral west of the Alleghenies, St. Joseph's Cathedral, built between 1816 and 1819 by the bishop of the Bardstown See, Benedict Joseph Flaget.

The most popular summer attraction in Bardstown is *The Stephen Foster Story*, a lively two-hour musical production based on 50 of Foster's most familiar songs. It is staged daily (except Mondays) from mid-June through the day before Labor Day in an amphitheater on the grounds of

6. The Onyx Chamber of Mammoth Cave glows with a golden-amber light. Tours of the cave are offered throughout the year, some of them only an hour long, others lasting for almost a day. Walkways are smooth, but all the trails include steep stairways.

6 As you drive from the entrance of Mammoth Cave National Park to the visitor center, you pass through a maturing forest of shagbark hickory, beech, sugar and red maples, white ash, black gum, and sycamore. In spring patches of mountain laurel brighten the forest beneath pink,

Cave area eventually flowed into the Green River. As the river continued to cut deeper into its limestone bed, the surrounding water table dropped and Mammoth's upper passages drained. The result today is a series of at least five overlapping, interconnecting cave levels that forms the

11. Craft demonstrations are given in the red brick Bretherens' Shop (top), which is part of the East Family Complex at Pleasant Hill. The matching spiral stairways (above) are a feature of Central Hall, a building that today serves as a restaurant and inn. Vegetables and herbs are used in dyeing yarn at demonstrations during special events held at the village.

rodsburg in 1774, building five or six cabins near "a boiling springs." After helping to quell a Shawnee uprising, Harrod and his men brought their families to live with them in 1775 and built a fort on high ground.

Today the early history of Harrodsburg, the oldest permanent settlement in Kentucky and the first English outpost west of the Alleghenies, is commemorated by Old Fort Harrod State Park. On the grounds are a reproduction of the fort built by Harrod and his settlers; a pioneer cemetery with a number of interesting gravestones; The Lincoln Marriage Temple, housing the cabin in which Abraham Lincoln's parents were married; the Mansion Museum, containing mementos from the various periods of Kentucky's history; and the Old Fort Amphitheatre, where during summer months *The Legend of Daniel Boone* is staged.

11 Pleasant Hill is a meticulously restored Shaker village preserving 27 superb 19th-century buildings. Pleasant Hill was founded in 1805 by three farmer converts after Shaker missionaries visited Kentucky. By 1820 it was a self-sufficient, prosperous farming community of some 500 souls. Strict laws of chastity kept the sexes apart. Men lived in the right-hand side of a dwelling, women in the left-hand side, and each group had its own entrance.

On a self-guided tour you can visit the various village buildings, including the Information Center, containing exhibits on the history of Pleasant Hill; the 40-room Centre Family Dwelling House with more than 1,600 authentic Shaker artifacts; the Meeting House, where the Shakers performed the spirited dancing that gave them their name; and the Cooper Shop with its barrel- and cask-making demonstrations. There are also frequent demonstrations of spinning, weaving, broom making, and cabinet-making.

12 The road from Pleasant Hill to Lexington takes you into the heart of Kentucky's fabled bluegrass country. As you near the city's outskirts, you see white board fences enclosing the manicured bluegrass pastures in which some of the world's finest horses are raised. One of the best places to begin your visit to the inner

My Old Kentucky Home State Park. The 235-acre park was established in 1922 to preserve Federal Hill, the stately 1818 brick home of the John Rowan family. Here Stephen Collins Foster of Pittsburgh composed the beloved ballad "My Old Kentucky Home" while visiting his Rowan cousins in 1852. The park has campsites, a picnic area, and a nine-hole golf course.

10 A young Pennsylvanian named James Harrod, together with a party of 31 adventurers, established Har-

bluegrass country is the Kentucky Horse Park on Iron Works Pike.

The park is situated on 1,032 acres, most of which were once part of the celebrated Walnut Hall Stud Farm. Among the 23 new structures and 14 renovated buildings are a visitor center featuring an orientation film on horses and a two-story museum tracing the history of the horse.

On a guided farm walking tour, you are likely to see a farrier fitting shoes and grooms tending various types of horses, for the park is a working farm as well as a tourist attraction.

You can ride a horse or pony in the park or tour the grounds in a horse-drawn vehicle. Special events are scheduled frequently in the dressage and jumping rings and the show arena, as well as on the half-mile track, the polo field, and the steeple-chase and cross-country courses.

When you leave the park, make a left turn and drive east along Iron Works Pike for a short self-guided auto tour of the area's fabulous horse farms. Beyond the park grounds on the left is Walnut Hall. It specializes in French Charolais cattle and in standardbreds for harness racing.

The drive continues on Iron Works Pike across Russell Cave Road. After Kenny Lane, you pass the elaborate gates of Spendthrift Farm, famous for its great stallions, including Nashua, Affirmed, Seattle Slew, and Majestic Prince.

Make a right turn onto Paris Pike and drive past Walmac Farm with its two beautiful mansions, one columned and the other Tudor. Here too is the Kentucky Horse Center. The 270-acre center is devoted to the training and sale of horses. On the grounds are two large barns with 600 stalls, a mile-long outdoor track, and a ⅝-mile covered all-season training track. A multimedia presentation dramatizes the life of a racehorse.

13 The centerpiece of Fort Boonesborough State Park is a replica of the fort built on the banks of the Kentucky River in 1775 by Daniel Boone and a group of about 80 pioneers. Cabins in the fort are furnished as they might have been in Boone's time. Craftsmen in costume demonstrate such pioneer skills as quilting, spinning, weaving, dyeing, soap making, candlemaking, and basket weaving.

Also in the fort are a working forge and a small museum. A modern camping area near the Kentucky River provides fully equipped sites. At the river you can swim at a fine sandy beach. A stern-wheeler excursion boat, the *Dixie Belle*, takes one-hour cruises several times a day. The park is closed from September through April.

14 White Hall State Shrine preserves the home of Cassius Marcellus Clay (1810-1903), a founder of Berea College and a fervent opponent of slavery. Built in 1799, the mansion was originally a three-story Georgian structure. The Italianate addition now forming the larger portion of the house was added during the 1860's while Clay was serving under President Lincoln as minister to Russia.

from the Greater Appalachian region without regard to color or economic means. Berea charges no tuition fee but expects all students to work in one of the student craft industries or service organizations.

Campus tours leave hourly in summer from the information center and twice a day in other seasons from the Boone Tavern Hotel. Visitors can talk to student craftsmen and see them working at the Demonstration Center and craft workshops. Finished products are sold at the Log House Sales Room.

Wilderness Road, a perennially popular historical musical, is presented each summer evening, except Sundays, in a beautiful outdoor setting at the Indian Fort Theatre in College Forest just south of town.

12. *In the bluegrass countryside there are many privately owned horse farms that have produced outstanding racehorses. This one, on the outskirts of Lexington, is typical of the white-fenced pastures where foals grow strong on the abundant grasses.*

Costumed guides conduct tours through the house, which contains many original pieces of furniture and fascinating memorabilia of Clay's life and times. Closed from September through March.

15 Berea is considered by many to be the crafts capital of the southern Appalachians. At the center of town is the tree-shaded, 140-acre campus of Berea College. Founded in 1855 by abolitionist preacher John G. Fee with the support of Cassius Marcellus Clay, the college's central purpose has remained the same for more than 100 years: to educate able students

16 At Pine Mountain State Resort Park, the Mountain Laurel Festival is held annually in late May.

An abundance of wild flowers and a splendid display of blooming laurel make this park especially appealing in spring. In addition to the well appointed lodge, there are one- and two-bedroom cottages and several efficiency cabins available for rent between April and mid-November. Other park facilities include horseback riding, day-hiking trails, a nine-hole golf course, a 35-acre lake where boating and fishing are permitted, and a campground.

Beautiful and Diverse

The engaging landscapes of Ohio include the rocky shores of Lake Erie, broad valleys, and steep hills

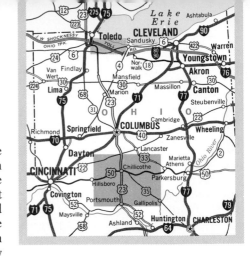

To the ancient saw of Ohio being round on both ends and high in the middle, you might add "and wet all over." The commerce of the northern part of the state is dominated by Lake Erie, reached via the St. Lawrence Seaway. On the southern edge, the Ohio River and its tributaries provide routes for the Mississippi–Missouri system of riverways, which transports three to four times the tonnage of the Panama Canal. This water-transport network has helped to make Ohio a major manufacturing state.

Water strongly influences the countryside as well. Glaciers planed most of the state nearly flat and left behind rich soil. Heavy rainfall established dense forests here, bane and blessing to post-Revolutionary War pioneers, who converted the forests to fields. Today, outside the cities, most of Ohio presents a picture of lush farmland.

Glaciers did not reach the southern part of the state, however. This hilly area remains heavily wooded, with state and national forest land and many state parks.

The northern area is dominated largely by Lake Erie. Its history of War of 1812 skirmishes contrasts with the now long tradition of peace between the United States and Canada. Natural history also is interesting, with long-legged wading birds and geese at Ottawa National Wildlife Refuge Complex and Crane Creek State Park. Many recreational facilities are located along the lake and on lovely South Bass and Kelleys islands. Winding through vineyards and peach and apple orchards, the route leads inland to spring-fed lakes and pools where waterfowl are abundant.

1   One of the reasons for the U.S. declaration of war against England in 1812 was a desire to annex Canada. This extension of U.S. borders seemed to be a relatively easy undertaking while the British were fighting for survival against Napoleon. During the campaign against the British in Canada, Gen. William Henry Harrison constructed Fort Meigs on the Maumee River.

A fine replica of Fort Meigs, the largest military reconstruction in America, stands on the site of the original. Relics in the museum-fort explain events of the War of 1812 and some of the gloomy aspects of the fight here. To reach the site, exit from Interstate 475 at Route 25 and follow the Fort Meigs signs.

2   A century ago 75 miles of marsh alive with wildlife stretched between Sandusky, Ohio, and Detroit, Michigan. Since then drainage and development have left less than 5 percent of this Black Swamp. A remnant of this marsh is in the Ottawa National Wildlife Refuge Complex. Here nature lovers with binoculars can observe a great variety of birds, including egrets, Canada geese, and possibly a bald eagle. White-tailed deer and small wild animals can also be seen. There are seven miles of self-guided trails, with four loops designated for the observation respectively of mallards, yellowlegs, swans, and blue herons. The entrance to the refuge from Route 2, which is well marked, warns you of a goose crossing.

3   The habitat at Crane Creek State Park is similar to that of the national wildlife refuge, and in spring and fall it abounds with migrating birds of various species. The park is oriented for family enjoyment: in addition to a nature trail through swamp and forest, there are roads that allow some viewing of wildlife from cars. Crane Creek also has a viewing tower, a pond frequented by water birds, and a migratory bird center with exhibits of decoys and mounted birds of the area.

4   Nine-acre Catawba Island State Park is linked by causeways to the mainland. The large fishing pier and the picnic area overlooking the lake and harbor are the park's main features. Boating is also popular.

In summer South Bass Island can be reached by auto ferry from Port Clinton, an hour-and-15-minute trip that brings you to the quaint village of Put-in-Bay, or from Catawba Island, an 18-minute ride leaving you at Lime Kiln Dock. The island has buses, tour trains, and bicycle rentals, so you do not need to bring your car.

The island is a colorful place to explore or to spend a day fishing. There are also campgrounds and picnic areas cooled by lake breezes.

Fly in a Classic Plane

The airport at Port Clinton is the only place in the United States where you can board the legendary *Tin Goose*, the all-metal trimotor airplane developed by Henry Ford in 1926. At the grand speed of 85 miles per hour you can take a 20-minute sight-seeing trip over the area. Reservations are required. Call the airport at 419/734-3149.

Comdr. Oliver Hazard Perry selected Put-in-Bay as an anchorage for his small fleet in the summer of 1813, the second year of the War of 1812. From here he sailed on September 10 to battle the British for control of Lake Erie. Perry reported his victory to General Harrison: "We have met the enemy, and they are ours."

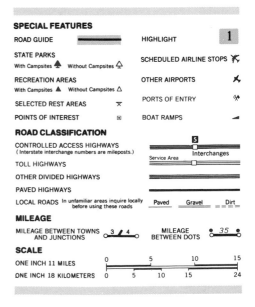

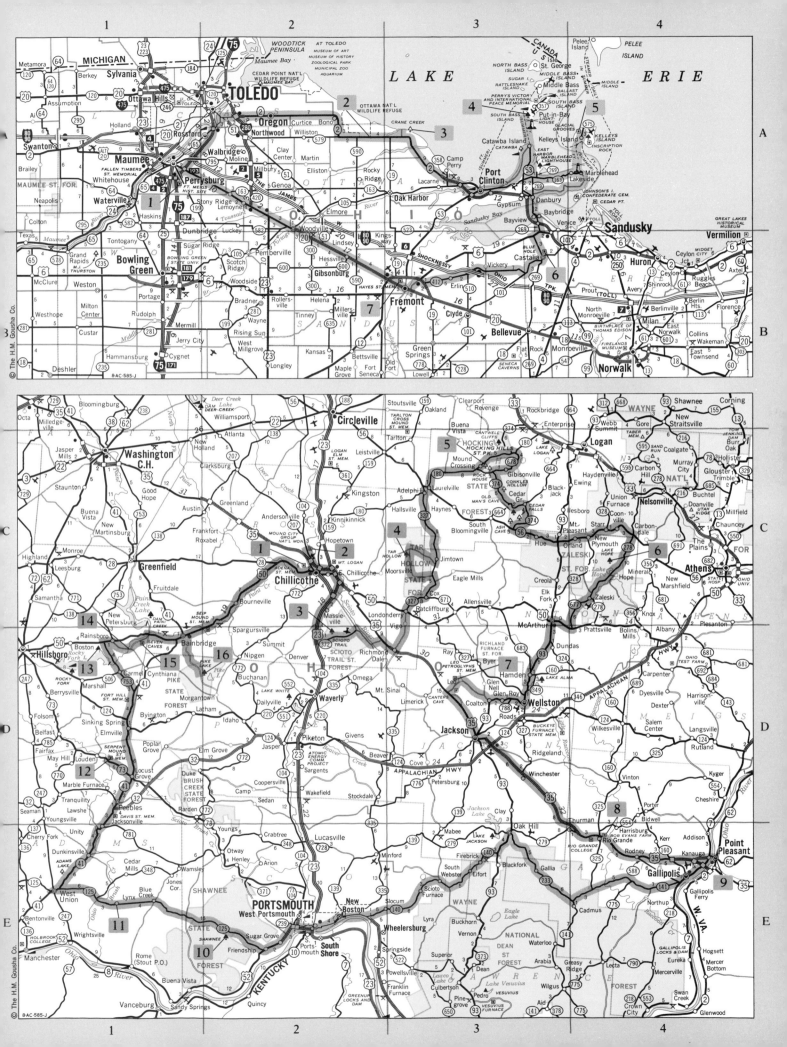

A 352-foot-tall granite column at Put-in-Bay commemorates Commander Perry's victory. It also stands for the resolve between the United States and Canada to maintain a peaceful border. An elevator carries visitors from the rotunda to the top for a wide look at Lake Erie and its islands and shoreline.

After returning to the mainland, take the scenic drive out Marblehead Peninsula. Along the road are a number of colorful harbors and extensive orchards. The peninsula is infamous as the most dangerous point on Lake Erie for ships. Gales that sweep unobstructed for some 200 miles from Buffalo push 10- to 12-foot waves ahead of them to pound this rugged coast. At the tip of the peninsula stands Marblehead Lighthouse, the oldest continuously used lighthouse on the Great Lakes and considered to be the most picturesque.

5   Kelleys Island, a smaller and quieter version of South Bass Island, is also reached by ferry in the summer. For your visit, it is suggested that you leave your car at the dock in

4. The Marblehead Lighthouse has stood sentinel since 1821 on the rockbound shore of Marblehead Peninsula.

Marblehead. Taxis and bicycle and golf cart rentals are available for sight-seeing, but it is easy to walk to most places.

In addition to the lovely 750-acre Kelleys Island State Park, which offers a variety of outdoor recreational activities, there is an incredible set of glacial grooves, the most impressive example of such phenomena in the world. Some of these grooves are 15 feet deep and up to 300 feet long, gouged into limestone about 25,000 years ago by harder rocks carried within a continental ice sheet.

6   Blue Hole is a beautifully landscaped artesian spring in Castalia. The pond's clear, deep blue water bubbles up from a limestone formation 65 feet below the surface, but the source of the water is still a mystery.

Devoid of free oxygen, the water is aerated by artificial waterfalls and by a waterwheel. With oxygen thus supplied, the cold water (its temperature stays about 48°F) can support a population of various kinds of large trout. Since fishing is not allowed, the trout are not afraid to surface for food and are easily observed. Displays explain their life cycle. Nearby, in a pleasant, open grove, is a picnic area with a playground.

In a village park setting, one block farther along Route 101, is a much larger pond, connected to the Blue Hole by an underground passage. Because it never freezes, the pond swarms in winter with mallards and other species of ducks. Protected here, they have become relatively tame. A smaller population remains to nest in the summer, when you can see lines of ducks and ducklings parading past street signs marked "Duck Crossing."

7   Spiegel Grove was the home of President Rutherford B. Hayes. The grounds of the 25-acre Hayes State Memorial are beautifully landscaped with trees and shrubs that accent the Victorian elegance of the mansion. The iron gates at the six entrances to the estate stood at the White House during Hayes's administration. The interior of the mansion is furnished as it was when the former president and three-time Ohio governor lived here. A memorial museum displays mementos of the Hayes family.

To reach Spiegel Grove, follow Route 412 to Route 6 and then turn east. This road becomes Hayes Avenue and leads to the mansion.

5. Resembling a deeply channeled toboggan course, the extraordinary glacial grooves on Kelleys Island intrigue scientists. Of special interest are the striae, or scratches, along the grooves' limestone walls, made by debris carried by a glacier as it moved across this region. By plotting the orientations of hundreds of such striae on a regional map, geologists established that the glacier had flowed from central Quebec.

3. *Stewart Lake, cupped at the base of gently rounded hills in Scioto Trail State Forest and removed from the roar of traffic, offers serenity, seclusion, and idyllic year-round beauty. A walk-in primitive campground is at the upper end of the lake.*

Natural beauty abounds *in the peaceful countryside of southern Ohio. Tucked among the hills and woodlands are lakes, gorges, waterfalls, cliffs, and unusual rock formations. Scattered through this region are mounds built by a long-vanished Indian people whose complex culture continues to mystify us.*

1 In Chillicothe, look for road signs to guide you to Adena State Memorial, or go to the visitor center for directions. This buff sandstone mansion was begun in 1807 by pioneer Ohio statesman and governor Thomas Worthington, and was considered to be one of the finest homes in the West. Both the house and the grounds have been restored.

The view from Adena of the Scioto River and the sunrise over Mount Logan inspired the design of Ohio's state seal. Mount Logan was named in honor of a famous Indian warrior who lived in the area in the 1770's.

2 Mound City Group National Monument is a necropolis—a city of the dead—built with Stone Age tools by Hopewell Indians between 1,800 and 2,000 years ago. These people honored the elite of their dead by erecting large earthworks to contain their cremated remains, along with material goods meritorious for workmanship and artistry. A variety of trade items was also included.

Encircled by earth walls 3 to 4 feet high and 3,000 feet around are 23 mounds, 22 of which are reconstructions on their original sites. Many of the artifacts excavated by archeologists are on display in the visitor center, which also has a viewing platform and a recorded description of the exhibits.

A self-guiding trail through the grounds and into one of the burial mounds adds information about the life and customs of these people. The visitor center is closed on Christmas and New Year's days.

3 At the entrance to Scioto Trail State Forest and Park, a monument erected in 1842 commemorates a colorful frontier hermit, William Hewitt. After living for 14 years in an isolated cave, Hewitt died in 1838, reportedly from trying to eat three dinners one after the other!

The forest road climbs to the top of a ridge where a 60-foot fire tower, built in 1925, rises above oaks, maples, and hickories for a view sweeping over 200,000 acres.

Other features of the park are Stewart and Caldwell lakes, where hiking, camping, fishing, and boating are popular pastimes. There are no roads to Stewart Lake; if you hike in, take drinking water.

Traversing rich bottomlands, the route winds toward Tar Hollow State Forest and Park. Since the narrow valley floors provide only small patches of tillable land, squatters in the early part of this century used the bottomland to grow corn, and increased the value of their crop by converting it to moonshine.

4 Turning into the Tar Hollow State Forest at Clark Holly Road, you climb to the crest of a ridge. Here a right turn twists through a leafy green tunnel of trees. After continuing three miles along the ridgeline, you then descend to the 15-acre Pine Lake, popular for swimming, boating, and fishing for catfish, largemouth bass, bluegill, and panfish. For hikers the park has several trails, including the 21-mile Logan Trail and a segment of the statewide trail system, the Buckeye Trail.

Pine tar, which Ohio pioneers used as a liniment and as a lubricant for wagons and machinery, gave Tar Hollow State Forest and Park its name.

5 Outstanding in Ohio scenery are the six units of Hocking Hills State Park, each unique in charm and character. Dominating the park is the Black Hand, a sandstone formation with deep gorges, high cliffs, dramatic overhangs, and spectacular falls for the waters flowing from Hocking River and Salt Creek. Black Hand is named for a black hand painted by Indians on a sandstone cliff east of Columbus. It is believed that the hand pointed toward a source of flintstone.

5. *A scenic trail leads to the Lower Falls (top) in the quiet woods of Hocking Hills State Park. Eastern hemlock, mountain laurel, Canada yew, and many kinds of wild flowers such as the lady's slipper orchid flourish in this vacationland wilderness. Also found here are several species of animals, including the gray fox (above left) and the red fox (right).*

At Cantwell Cliffs, trails wind through narrow passageways between vertical cliffs. The corridors and rock shelters here were formed by erosion along vertical cracks in the stone.

Erosion along joints also created Rock House. This straight, natural corridor, about 30 feet wide, 25 feet high, and 200 feet long, runs along the wall of a cliff. Light enters the "house" through seven tall "windows" formed by erosion along cracks in the wall.

Conkles Hollow may be the most dramatic gorge in the area. A half-mile long and 200 feet deep in places, it is shaded both by its high cliffs and by heavy vegetation. You can find plants left from a cooler, subglacial climate growing here. The gorge is dangerous, and hikers are advised to stick to the trails.

Old Man's Cave, the largest and most popular site in Hocking Hills,

has falls, cliffs, potholes, and caves—rock shelters where the softer part of the Black Hand eroded away from beneath a harder overhanging cap.

Trails and roads lead from Old Man's Cave to Cedar Falls, where a shallow basin has been ground out by sand and boulders carried by the tumbling water.

Ash Cave is the largest rock shelter in Hocking Hills—100 feet deep and 700 feet wide—and it is evocative of a cathedral in its mood and its acoustics. Especially lovely is the echo in the cave of a waterfall plummeting over the cave's rim. The cave is named for the ashes left here from Indian bonfires.

6 Lake Hope is a 120-acre reservoir built as a work project in the 1930's. Popular with boaters and swimmers, the lake is in a setting of lovely rounded hills clothed with a mixed forest of deciduous and evergreen trees, particularly impressive in

fall. A lodge overlooking Lake Hope is crafted of various types of Ohio sandstone, with rippled flagstone on walkways and drain covers.

A 20-mile backpacking trail beginning at Hope Furnace, a quarter of a mile from Lake Hope, winds through Zaleski State Forest and provides some of the state's finest hiking. Common here are sightings of deer, wild turkeys, ruffled grouse, pileated woodpeckers, and cardinals. Only the chimney is left standing at Hope Furnace, an old iron-ore smelter.

7 At Leo Petroglyphs State Memorial you can see carvings made by Indians in a sandstone ledge 700 to 900 years ago. In addition, the memorial offers the delights of an uncrowded park. Below the pavilion protecting the glyphs is a deep gorge with rock shelters and lush vegetation. A nature trail marked with interpretive signs runs through the gorge and around the rim.

To reach the memorial, follow County Road 28, which passes through picturesque rural countryside, for about 5½ miles. Then continue on County Road 29 for about 200 yards to an unpaved road that leads to the petroglyph site.

8 The 1,100-acre Bob Evans Farm, family headquarters for a restaurant chain, is a fascinating place to see. Among the attractions are a wildlife pen for the rehabilitation of injured or orphaned deer, birds, and other wildlife; a farm museum displaying implements of the past; a gristmill and a windmill; three century-old log cabins; and a half-mile nature trail. Horses and canoes may be rented, and wagon tours of the farm are offered in summer.

9 Overlooking the confluence of the Ohio and Great Kanawha rivers at Point Pleasant, West Virginia, is Tu-endie-wei Park, a place of historical significance.

This point of land is indeed pleasant with lawns and trees, a large battle monument, and a picturesque log tavern built in 1796 and now restored with colonial furnishings. It was anything but pleasant on the morning of October 10, 1774, however, when the confederated Shawnee tribes, led by Chief Cornstalk, crossed the Ohio River and attacked the settlement of colonists. In anticipation of trouble,

1,100 Virginia militiamen were encamped here at the time. Suffering heavy losses after three days of fighting, the Shawnees retreated, their power broken.

Sometimes called the first battle of the Revolutionary War, the conflict at Point Pleasant freed the colonists of their worries about Indians and encouraged them to defy British law forbidding settlement of Indian lands to the west. The small park is closed from November to April.

10 Signs mark the spur roads to Roosevelt and Turkey Creek lakes in Shawnee State Park. Campgrounds, boat ramps, a deluxe lodge, and rental cabins make this park a popular goal for Ohio vacationers. Trails penetrate the deep woods, dimly lit by sun filtering through the leaves.

Now 60,000 acres in size, Shawnee State Forest was established in 1922 with 5,000 acres of land devastated by poor foresting practices and fire. Today the dense forest is a testimony to the productive potential of Ohio's humid climate when encouraged by sound environmental policy. Scattered among the wide variety of hardwoods grown here are the Ohio buckeye (*Aesculus glabra*), the state tree, which grows along streams, and the yellow buckeye, which is found halfway up the hillsides.

11 Lynx Prairie is a vestige of the unique grassy environment formed here at least 11,000 years ago as a peninsula of the western prairies.

To reach the prairie, turn north on Tulip Road and park near the East Liberty Church cemetery. The preserve is south of the cemetery and is accessible through an opening in a stand of trees. Until you reach this trail head, poison ivy and myrtle are far more common than grass under foot in the woods, but you are soon in the open where tall prairie grasses and wild flowers shine in the sun on a bright summer day. The path continues through a forest, a swamp, and other remnant prairies, passing a waterfall and rock outcrops.

Driving north from West Union, you follow one of the oldest roads in Ohio. Zane's Trace was hacked from the wilderness in 1797 and became a stage road that connected Wheeling, West Virginia, with Limestone (now Maysville), Kentucky.

12 Serpent Mound is the most famous of the mounds constructed by prehistoric Indians. One of the largest effigy mounds—mounds in the form of animals or other objects—it represents an uncoiling serpent with its mouth open, according to current interpretation.

Archeologists believe the Serpent Mound had religious significance. It is presumed to have been built by the

12. Serpent Mound extends for almost a quarter of a mile from its oval, hinged mouth to its coiled tail. Excavations show that stones had been placed as a guideline in building the form with its seven sinuous curves. Serpent symbols are also found in other ancient Indian art.

Hopewell Indians, who flourished in Ohio and neighboring states from 1000 B.C. to A.D 700.

Farther along this route, at Fort Hill State Memorial, is an earth-and-stone wall with a circumference of 1⅝ miles and a height of about 5 feet, also constructed by the Hopewell Indians. Encircling a hilltop, the wall may have been built to protect a ceremonial site.

13 Rocky Fork Lake, a 2,800-acre reservoir, comprises most of Rocky Fork State Park. Popular with water sports enthusiasts, the park also provides three miles of paths, which originate at North Shore Road south of Route 50. Century-old McCoppin's

Mill operates on Rocky Fork Creek below the dam.

14 At the crossroads in Rainsboro, take Barrett's Mill Road to Barrett's Mill, where a covered bridge crosses Rocky Fork Creek. This charming bridge was built in the 19th century and has recently been renovated.

15 Seven Caves Park is three miles east of the covered bridge. It contains limestone caves, dramatic cliffs along the narrow gorge of the creek, handsome hemlock and oak forests, and an unusually large population of pileated woodpeckers. Paths and overlooks make this beautiful park easy to explore.

16 On the eastern edge of Bainbridge, a well-marked turn leads through five miles of scenic farmland and forested hills to Pike Lake State Park in Pike State Forest. The lake is a pretty site for fishing, boating, swimming, picnicking, and camping. A highlight is a display of native wildlife, including friendly white-tailed deer and an albino raccoon named Ralph. Five or six miles of hiking paths loop through the park.

In the Hoosier State

Indiana is an engaging blend of industry, forests, waterways, farmlands, and friendly small towns

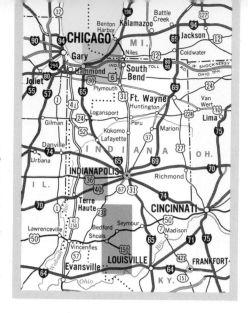

Hoosiers tell two stories to explain their nickname. According to one, the name stems from pioneer days, when Indiana settlers would ask the people moving on west, "Who's yer?" ("Who are you?") Another version has it that Samuel Hoosier, an Indiana canal builder, preferred to hire Indiana men, who soon became known as Hoosiers. In any event, the name is still used today.

Indiana ranks among the most scenic states in the country. Between its borders—marked by Lake Michigan on the northwest and the Ohio River on the south—lies the beauty of lush forests, rolling countryside, and well-kept farmsteads. Although its bustling steel mills, coal mines, and oil refineries dominate the economy, much of Indiana is still rural, with farmlands and forests covering 74 percent of the area.

You do not need to drive far to realize you are in the Midwest's Corn Belt. On a quiet byway on a warm summer night, if you stop and listen you might even hear the crackling sound of the corn as it grows. In the fall and winter you might still see corn tied in shocks in a barren or snow-covered field.

Nearly as many acres of Indiana's farmland are planted with beans as with corn. "Beans," as the farmers call them, are soybeans, a low-growing, bushy, broad-leaved legume crop from which soybean meal is made. The meal is used mainly for livestock feed and as a raw material in various manufactures.

You are sure to see the state's chief bean consumers, beef and dairy cattle and poultry. Hogs too are bean-eaters. The 6 million or so corn-fed hogs raised annually in Indiana also get a soybean supplement.

The Lake Michigan shoreline of northern Indiana and southwestern Michigan is a broad strip of sand constantly whipped by the wind and the waves of the lake. Depending upon weather, the beach vegetation, the dunes, and the shoreline advance and retreat. Where you remember picnicking or climbing a dune one summer may not be recognizable the next.

In Michigan the coastal region is relatively flat, with sandy beaches and dunes. There is a sharp contrast between this region and the rich farmlands in the southern part of the Lower Peninsula. The contrast is also striking in Indiana, where the coastal plain is known as the Calumet region. Driving south from the lake, you soon enter the area Hoosiers call the central till plains, the beginning of the North American prairie's great western sweep and one of the most fertile farming regions in the world.

Indiana's 45-mile lakeshore is the state's playground. It is also a productive industrial area, housing the steel mills, oil refineries, and various factories of Gary, Hammond, Whiting, and East Chicago.

1 Indiana Dunes State Park and Indiana Dunes National Lakeshore straddle Route 12 as it arcs northeastward along the southern shore of Lake Michigan. The National Lakeshore Visitor Center, about three miles east of the intersection of Routes 12 and 49, is a good starting point for the exploration of the area. Excellent maps and brochures describing the unique ecology of the Indiana dunes are available at the center, and there are informative exhibits and a slide show.

You can drive directly to the beach, using one of several roads within the park. But you may prefer to leave your car in one of the many parking lots in the park and walk along one of the short trails that wind up the dunes through the cottonwood trees, marram grass, and low bushes. This is one of the few places in the country where you come across southern dogwoods, northern tundra bearberries, prairie wild flowers, and southwestern cacti growing side by side.

As you draw near the summit of the dunes, Lake Michigan stretches out below you for as far as the eye can see. It may be blue and placid with sunlight playing over its calm surface, or it may be gray and stormy with whitecaps pounding onto the beach.

The geological history of the Indiana dunes area was changed dramatically by the last ice age. About 10,000 years ago a warming climate melted the glaciers that covered all of Canada and many of our northern states. A drastically altered landscape emerged from beneath the ice. The Valparaiso Moraine, a long, low, natural dike, stretches across northwestern Indiana. This ridge of gravel, silt, and boulders, left by melting ice about 9,000 years ago, formed the southern shore of a lake much larger than present-day Lake Michigan. Over the centuries that followed, the waters of the lake slowly receded, exposing immense deposits of quartz sands and gravel that have since been covered with the topsoil you see on these rolling hills.

Three things gave birth to the huge dunes that are now along the lake: a plentiful supply of sand, a steady northwesterly wind blowing across the lake, and the beach vegetation. As the wind carried the sand up from the

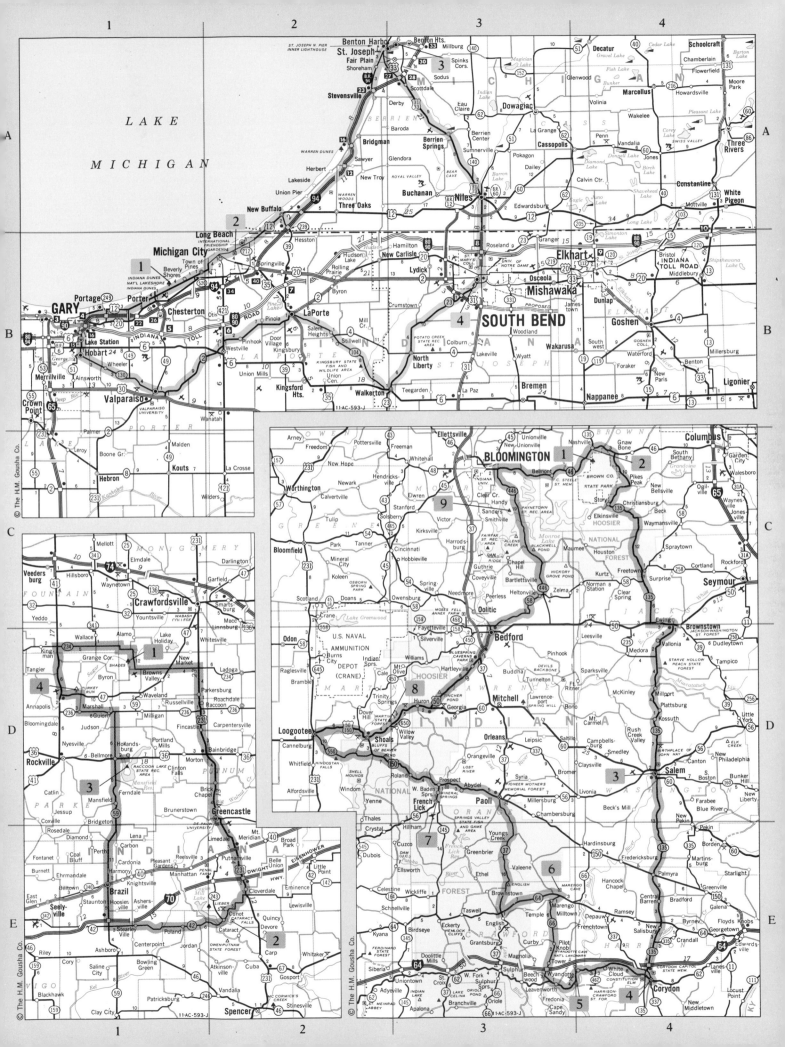

beaches, the vegetation that developed on the dunes helped to block the wind and allowed the sand to accumulate.

The protected lowlands behind the dunes form a natural water basin. In the 1700's, French trappers and Indians canoed on a narrow, 45-mile waterway behind the dunes. Today you can find moss-filled bogs, ponds, and swamps here that attract a variety of wildlife, including snow buntings, deer, raccoons, opossums, salamanders, and harmless hognose snakes.

1. The couple exploring a part of the Indiana Dunes State Park help to illustrate the height of the hills. These inland, or back, dunes are sufficiently stabilized to support plant life. Lakefront, or active, dunes are newly formed and ever-changing.

There is a campground in Indiana Dunes State Park and several commercial campgrounds are nearby. Picnic areas, snack bars, rest rooms, and parking lots are located throughout the 20-odd square miles of the state and federal lands.

Just before the route leaves the national lakeshore, it passes Mount Baldy, an active dune moving southward. On many days you can see the northwest wind picking up sand from the face of the dune and dropping it in the protected area behind the dune. The oak woodland that lies in the path of the slowly shifting dune is gradually being buried. In some places the sand has reached the lower branches of the trees.

2 In Michigan City, about 2½ miles north of the intersection of Routes 12 and 35, Liberty Trail leads south through a pleasant residential area to the International Friendship Gardens. There are 100 acres of formal gardens here, which include flowers representing 65 countries. During the summer you can stroll leisurely along the garden paths and enjoy the beauty and variety of the flowers, plants, and trees. Numerous species of birds are attracted to this idyllic setting.

Continuing northeastward into Michigan, you quickly leave behind the industrial pockets of Indiana's Calumet region but not the breathtaking vistas of Lake Michigan. Warren Dunes State Park, about halfway between Michigan City, Indiana, and Benton Harbor, Michigan, provides another pleasant access to the dunes and beaches bordering the lake. The park has facilities for picnicking, swimming, and camping.

3 The lake cities of Benton Harbor and St. Joseph share a scenic harbor at the mouth of the St. Joseph River. Both municipalities have public parks with beaches and fishing piers on their respective sides of the deepwater inlet.

St. Joseph was the site of Fort Miami, erected in 1679 on the bluffs overlooking the harbor and Lake Michigan by the French explorer Robert Cavalier, sieur de La Salle. The fort, which served as a French trading post, was destroyed only a few years after it was built. In 1700 a new fort and a Jesuit mission were constructed on the site, but in 1763 the Indian chief Pontiac razed the fort and struck the French colors. The site is now marked by a large stone monument in Lake Bluff Park.

In the summer Lake Bluff Park comes alive with fairs, tours, ice cream socials, and concerts hosted by local residents. If you are fortunate enough to come across one of these homespun functions, be sure to see if any of the ladies' organizations is selling homemade jams, jellies, and preserves. If so, when winter comes you can enjoy a pleasant reminder of this fruit-growing region.

On the way south toward the Indiana border there are well-tended gardens, truck farms, and orchards. As you near the state line, the landscape becomes more typically midwestern, with increasing acreage planted with corn, soybeans, and fruit trees.

4 In 1679 La Salle saw what is now Indiana from the St. Joseph River and was impressed by the beauty of its "prairies, streams, rivers, fish, game..." The route follows the river valley upstream to South Bend. Here, at the Century Center on St. Joseph and Jefferson streets, you can enjoy a spectacular view of the St. Joseph River as it rolls over a dam and down a spillway just beyond a 38-by-130-foot window in the Great Hall.

During the summer you can take a more intimate look at the St. Joseph River and enjoy a picnic at Island Park, accessible by a footbridge over the White Water Rapids.

The center's Discovery Hall, a 12,000-square-foot gallery, includes the Studebaker Historic Vehicle Collection, which traces the development of American four-wheel transportation from the 1830 Conestoga wagon to the 1963 Studebaker Avanti. Also on display are four presidential carriages, including the one in which President Abraham Lincoln rode to his fate at Ford's Theatre, an assort-

2. The beautiful International Friendship Gardens have as their theme the nations of the world and their people. Within the garden complex is the Symphony Garden Theater, which honors world-famed musicians. The theater has a stage large enough for a symphony orchestra.

ment of military vehicles, and Raymond Loewy's controversial aerodynamic design for the Studebaker of the 1950's, which started the American car toward a more streamlined appearance.

Off Route 31, just north of South Bend's city limits, is the University of Notre Dame. Highlights on this wooded campus, which has two lakes and some 500 varieties of trees, are the Sacred Heart Church and its carillon (the oldest such set of bells in North America), the Administration Building with its gold-leafed dome, and the Snite Museum of Art. Inquire at the main gate for the "Campus Guide and Map." Guided tours are available here during the summer months.

Going west toward Lake Michigan, you may be surprised to see long pipes slowly turning on fields of corn and spraying a constant fall of life-giving water. This area is one of the most fertile corn-growing regions in the country. The land is productive enough and level enough to justify the considerable investment required for self-moving irrigators. Corn yields average a little over 100 bushels per acre annually. La Salle could not have foreseen that irrigation would be necessary in the cornfields, but he anticipated Indiana's rich bounty when he wrote these words more than three centuries ago: "Those lands surpass all others in everything . . . so beautiful and fertile . . ."

Indiana's central till plains, in the watershed of the Wabash River, include fertile farmlands, forests, and typical small midwestern cities, such as Greencastle and Brazil. The term "till" comes from the geologists' name for the heavy clay soils left by the ice age glaciers and leavened by the loess of a yellowish silt blown by the wind from the retreating glaciers.

State parks in this area have preserved the rugged natural landscape, the virgin woods, the waterfalls, and the mineral springs. Dating from the horse-and-buggy era, there are many covered bridges that span the deep ravines.

1 As Route 234 heads eastward toward Shades State Park, it descends into the deep, wooded Sugar Creek Valley, one of the most picturesque places in the state. This area is a good example of what Hoosiers refer to as unspoiled "original America." As the road nears the valley floor, look for a hillside spring in a small clearing. Here, as a reminder of earlier times, there is a cup hanging on a branch, inviting the traveler to drink the clear water that springs cool and sweet from the earth.

A half-mile farther east the route skirts Deere's Mill Covered Bridge. Built in 1878, the bridge is closed to vehicular traffic but may be crossed on foot; it leads to a canoe-launching site on Sugar Creek. The bridge is part of Shades State Park. The entrance to the park is located on the right side of the road a few miles farther along the route.

The park has facilities for canoeing, canoe and backpack camping, picnicking, fishing, and hiking. (Swimming is strictly prohibited because of Sugar Creek's treacherous currents.) The park offers almost 15 miles of hiking trails, with a broad range of difficulty and length. Several of the trails wind through deep sandstone gorges and virgin forests and pass cold mineral springs and slender waterfalls. Other trails climb to natural lookout points. After only a short time on these quiet trails it is easy to understand why Hoosiers bought and paid for this 3,000-acre park with a statewide public subscription.

From Shades State Park the route meanders south through Putnam County's rich farmland. In Greencastle, the county seat, the route passes the courthouse square, the Midwest's

1. Canoeists on this curve in Sugar Creek keep a wary eye out for rocks that have fallen from the adjacent cliffs. Note the trees and shrubs growing wherever they can take hold on the layered limestone embankment in the background.

equivalent of New England's village greens. South of Greencastle the highway crosses Routes 40 and 70, two of the important thoroughfares that have contributed to making Indiana "The Crossroads of America." Farther south the route enters the northwestern corner of central Indiana's hill country, or Hoosier Hills as local residents call it.

2 The largest waterfall in Indiana—Cataract Falls—is nestled in the woods of the Lieber Recreation Area, reached by going west from Cloverdale on Burma Road. Rangers will provide directions to the waterfall, which plummets into the southern end of Cataract Lake. Flowing briskly by the tulip trees (*Liviodendron tulipifen*), the state tree, the waters of Mill Creek leap over a series of high rocks and then tumble into the 1,500-acre lake. You can get an impressive view of the falls from a shaded picnic pavilion and picnic grounds at the water's edge. Another scenic overlook is at the opposite end of the lake at Cataract Dam.

Cataract Lake is a pleasant place for boating (rentals available), fishing, waterskiing, and swimming. The 8,063-acre recreation area also has facilities for campers and hikers.

Northwest of the Lieber Recreation Area the route passes through Brazil, the county seat of Clay

2. Mill Creek tumbles down a series of limestone terraces to form Cataract Falls. The covered bridge with its shingled roof and unusually long span was built in 1876. Thanks to regular maintenance, it still serves as a pedestrian entrance to the town of Cataract.

County, famous for its rich deposits of clay used in ceramic products. (Drivers of recreation vehicles must detour around the railroad bridge in Brazil, which has a clearance of only 10 feet.) Hoosiers have given the names of foreign countries, such as Peru, Holland, and Morocco, to many of their communites. The surrounding area of strip coal mines is called the Brazil Block District because coal from this region usually breaks into almost perfectly rectangular blocks.

In the farming region north of Brazil you may see huge wheeled tanks crossing the cornfields. These tanks are filled with anhydrous ammonia, a form of nitrogen that is liquified under high pressure. As the tanks move through the fields, the nitrogen is injected underground by knifelike blades. The nitrogen, a basic plant nutrient, greatly boosts corn yields.

3 Most of the Raccoon Lake State Recreation Area, just east of Bellmore off Route 36, is located on a large peninsula enclosed by the horseshoe-shaped lake. Here you can camp, swim, hike, rent a boat, waterski, and fish for crappies, walleyes, bass, catfish, and bluegills. The 2,600-acre park is one of the newer properties in the Indiana Department of Natural Resources system, and much of its woodland is young second

4. A narrow footbridge crosses a creek on Bear Hollow Trail at Turkey Run State Park. Sycamore, black walnut, and sugar maple trees tower above the park's terrain. The overhanging ledge (lower right) suggests occasional higher waters.

growth, which provides an interesting contrast to the virgin forests found in many of the other parks. Although new, the forests are filled with native wildlife, including raccoons, white-tailed deer, and cardinals (the state bird).

4 As the route heads north, it again descends into the cavernous, rugged valley of Sugar Creek. Turkey Run State Park was named for the flocks of wild turkeys that once lived here. The spectacular cliffs of Turkey Run are composed of Mansfield sandstone, so named for the Indiana city. The sandstone formations began as sand deposits, left by flowing waters, which evolved into sedimentary rock through a process of pressure and cementation. But it was the last ice age that was responsible for the formations seen today.

During the ice age the park was covered by the glaciers. As the ice melted, boulders of sandstone were carried downstream by the icy waters, cutting away and shaping the Sugar Creek streambed and the Turkey Run canyons. You can still pick up these water-smoothed rocks, a heritage from the ice age, along the shores of Sugar Creek.

There are 14 miles of trails, ranging from rugged to easy and from half a mile to three miles long, that allow the hiker to explore the canyons, woods, and streams of Turkey Run. Several of the trails are the byways Miami Indians followed some 300 years ago. Turkey Run also offers a look at our pioneer heritage. There is a log cabin museum, a settlers' church, and two covered bridges. Hoosiers call this area "the covered bridge capital of the world." There are frequent guided tours to the covered bridges in the summer.

Visitors who want to enjoy the wilderness during the day but relax at night can rent rooms at the Turkey Run Inn.

Soybeans, the world's most versatile crop

The soybean plant is a valuable livestock feed, either when green or when silage. The bean itself is used to make salad oils and oils for margarine, shortening, cleaning compounds, paint, ink, linoleum, and plastic. Soybean meal, a by-product of the oil making process, is an excellent high-protein feed and is also used in making dozens of products from adhesives to waterproofing materials. In all, soybeans are used in more than 100 different ways. Since they are legumes, plants that develop nitrogenous nodules on their roots and hence add to the fertility of the soil, soybeans are often rotated with other crops, most often corn.

Plant of yellow soybean

Mature beans

Root nodules

Sowing seeds

Cultivating the field

Ready for harvest

Harvesters at work

This tour leads through the rolling woodlands and fertile farmlands of south-central Indiana. Along the way you can see Indiana's largest state park, largest cave, largest lake, and oldest seat of government.

1 Brown County State Park, the largest state park in Indiana, is nearly 25 square miles of woodlands, hills, hollows, lakes, rushing streams, sandstone ravines, and quiet meadows. It is one of the most beautiful parks in the Midwest and one of the easiest to enjoy from the road. Winding through the park are 27 miles of paved roads that pass 15 scenic overlooks, two artificial lakes, a covered bridge, and a fire tower.

Except in winter, you are sure to see a soft blue haze hanging over the woodlands. This is caused by sunlight acting upon the moisture released into the air by the dense vegetation.

A map of the park is available at the entrance gatehouses. If you enter through the north gate, you cross the north fork of Salt Creek on one of the park's landmarks, a covered bridge said to be the oldest timber bridge in the state.

The colorful foliage for which this area is famous reaches its glorious

5. *Standing on the edge of a shallow trench, a figure is photographed in the Valley of the Shades section of Wyandotte Cave.*

peak in the second or third week of October when the leaves of red oak, locust, beech, sassafras, maple, birch, and other trees take on the bright hues of autumn.

Those who venture beyond the paved roads can enjoy 10 miles of hiking trails, 45 miles of bridle paths, several campgrounds, picnic areas, and a swimming pool. Fishermen can try for bass, catfish, and bluegills at Lakes Ogle or Strahl.

In your wanderings may see several of the park's long-term residents, including blue jays, juncos, whippoorwills, white-tailed deer, raccoons, gray squirrels, and perhaps a pileated woodpecker or even a wild turkey.

2 Nashville, just outside the boundaries of Brown County State Park, is the county seat. This small town was little known until paintings and drawings by visiting artists publicized the natural beauty of these environs, and visitors and summer residents began to arrive.

Nashville has only about 600 permanent residents and about 55 original old log cabins still stand. Get a *Brown County Almanack* from the Chamber of Commerce to use as a guide to explore art galleries, antiques shops, restaurants, museums, a reptile institute, and a display of John Dillinger memorabilia.

3 On East Market Street in Salem, a museum, a library, and the restored birthplace commemorate Salem's most famous son, John Hay. He was private secretary to Abraham Lincoln and secretary of state for Presidents William McKinley and Theodore Roosevelt. The small dwelling where Hay was born on October 8, 1838, was built in 1824 as a schoolhouse and is one of the oldest brick structures in the town.

4 In 1816 pioneers used the native limestone quarried south of Salem to construct the state's first capitol, which still stands in the village square in Corydon. The two-story structure has walls more than two feet thick.

After Indianapolis became the state capital in 1825, the original capitol served as a county courthouse for many decades. In 1929 restoration was begun, and today the structure looks much as it did when this town was the seat of state government.

5 West of Corydon the route descends into the rugged hills and hollows of the Ohio Valley. In places the craggy limestone bluffs protrude overhead. At the Wyandotte Caves

7. *Fishermen, ankle-deep on the upper ledge of Hindostan Falls and also working the shallows downstream, are hoping to catch some of the wide variety of fish, including white perch and catfish, for which the East Fork of the Little River is noted.*

the limestone has been hollowed out over millions of years by acidic water seeping through cracks that were gradually enlarged into serpentine channels. Wyandotte Cave is the biggest cave in Indiana and one of the most important in the United States. Some 25 miles of known passageways wind beneath the surrounding hills. The cave contains one of the largest underground rooms in the world, measuring about a half-mile in circumference and 200 feet in height. Inside the cave Monument Mountain, the largest underground mountain known, stands 140 feet high.

Prehistoric peoples mined flint for weapons in the cave, and during the War of 1812 miners employed by the fledgling American republic extracted saltpeter to make gunpowder to use against the British. Shortly before the war, William Henry Harrison, then governor of the Indiana Territories and later president of the United States, visited the cave and scratched his initials on a wall.

Just a stone's throw away is Little Wyandotte Cave, thought to be an extension of the larger cave. There are daily tours through both caves.

6 Another limestone cavern at 75-acre Marengo Cave Park offers a mile of underground passageways running through a forest of slender, fragile stalagmites and stalactites.

Northwest of Marengo the route leaves the rugged limestone bluffs and valleys and enters the rolling plains of Orange County. In the Pioneer Mother's Memorial Forest, part of the Hoosier National Forest, there are stands of black walnut trees, the most valuable hardwood in the state.

7 In the early 1700's, a French trading post set up shop about two miles south of Prospect. For centuries before, the mineral springs and salt licks in this area attracted many animals. The odd name, French Lick, reflects the history of the place. Today tourists come "to take the waters" at the posh hotel that is the mainstay of the community. Pluto Water, which comes from the local springs, is marketed worldwide.

West of French Lick and south of Route 550 is the Hindostan Falls State Fish and Wildlife Area, with facilities for boat launching, picnicking, camping, hiking, and fishing.

8. *Above: A once-active limestone quarry near Bedford is now a catch basin for rainwater. Stone from this quarry was used in New York's Empire State Building. Beyond the trees is a stacking yard filled with limestone blocks ready for cutting and finishing. Left: In an active quarry in the same area the blocks are being cut by channeling machines mounted on tracks. They cut a two-inch channel in the stone to whatever depth is required. The blocks are then lifted out by derricks and stored in the yard. Compared to other building materials, natural stone requires relatively little energy (fuel) to process.*

8 At Martin State Forest, where wheat, corn, and hay crops once grew, you can now see thick stands of coniferous and deciduous trees. This 10-square-mile park has a fire tower, hiking trails, and facilities for picnicking and primitive camping, as well as good fishing spots.

Just south of Bedford the route passes a turnoff to Bluespring Caverns Park, another small limestone cave open to visitors. Quarrying limestone is the major industry in Bedford. Stone from local quarries was used in the Empire State Building in New York City and in the Federal Triangle in Washington, D.C.

9 Northeast of Bedford the highway mounts the crest of a wooded hill from which you can see the shimmering waters of Monroe Lake, the largest lake in the state.

This immense body of water is a joint flood-control project of the Indiana Department of Natural Resources and the U.S. Army Corps of Engineers. The lake behind the 1,350-foot-long earth-and-rock dam across Salt Creek has an indented shoreline measuring nearly 150 miles. You can get maps and information about the lake at the Paynetown State Recreation Area, one of nine recreation areas on the lake's shores.

The Two Faces of Michigan

The state's two peninsulas, the Upper and the Lower, are separated by the Straits of Mackinac

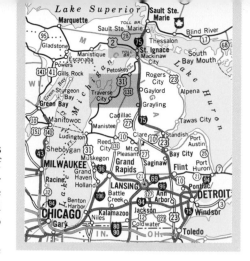

Michigan's coastline, washed by four Great Lakes, is longer than the Atlantic coast from Maine to Florida. Within two peninsulas—the Lower, called the Mitten because its shape is mittenlike, and the Upper Peninsula, known as the U.P.—there are some 11,000 inland lakes and 36,000 miles of rivers and streams, most of them unpolluted and alive with game fish.

Water is only part of the story, for the state of Michigan has sand dunes rising hundreds of feet above the lakes, rich fruit-growing farmlands, and forests of hemlock, oak, elm, maple, and—representing the state—white pine (*Pinus strobus*).

It was this lush beauty and the bountiful resources that lured millions of Germans, Scandinavians, and Dutch to Michigan's shores during the 1800's.

Today Michigan is one of the most industrialized states in the nation, but despite its many factories and extensive commercial areas, this land, almost entirely surrounded by water, remains rich in natural beauty.

The Upper Peninsula, a wilderness area shaped roughly like a triangle, stretches from Lake Michigan to the shores of Lake Superior. Although the origin of Michigan's nickname, The Wolverine State, has been lost in legend—not one wolverine has ever been found in the state, so far as is known—the name has remained.

This great expanse of rolling woodlands is known for winter sports and for hunting, fishing, and wilderness trekking.

From the northeastern tip of the triangle, where Sault Ste. Marie presides over the Soo Locks, to the little town of St. Ignace on the Straits of Mackinac, the coast, where much of Michigan's early history took place, is bordered by Lake Huron, the third of the Great Lakes that surround the Upper Peninsula.

1 According to Michiganites, the only place in the United States where you can see the sun rise over one Great Lake (Huron) and watch it set on another (Michigan) is Mackinaw City, a small town at the northern tip

of the Lower Peninsula. The town is located at the southern end of "Mighty Mac," the awesome, five-mile-long bridge that spans the Straits of Mackinac (pronounced *mack*-in-awe) and connects the two parts of the state.

In 1715 on this strategic point the French built Fort Michilimackinac as a headquarters for the thriving trade they were conducting with the local Indians. The fort, which was transferred to the British in 1761, has now been completely restored. On Memorial Day weekend an annual pageant reenacts a 1763 attack by Indian raiding parties against the British. The Indians always win.

Historic Mackinac

Mackinac Island, a speck of land barely measuring two by three miles in the deep blue waters of the Straits of Mackinac, is almost as unspoiled as it was when the first Europeans arrived here some three centuries ago. The cannon still boom at the island's fort, you still must get around either by bicycle, by horsepower, or by shanks' mare, and a blacksmith still uses a glowing forge to fashion the horseshoes and wagonwheel rims that are needed on the island.

In 1817 John Jacob Astor established a trading post on the island for his prosperous American Fur Company. As the number of beaver, whose pelts were a major part of the fur trade, slowly declined in Michigan's forests, the island became a vacation spot.

Today the island is still popular with visitors, who either take the half-hour sail by ferry from Mackinaw City or arrive by chartered air taxi from St. Ignace.

The island has several inns, including the elegant Grand Hotel, which is said to have the longest porch in the world. Tours of the island include its wave-sculptured cedar-fringed shoreline.

Visitors return year after year, but only after they have sampled the delicious product of one of the many renowned fudge shops on Huron Street are they considered to be true "fudgies," as the islanders like to call visitors.

In the Old Mackinac Point Lighthouse, which is now a museum, there are exhibits that re-create the maritime history of the straits and nearby waters.

Heading north between sky and water on the soaring Mackinac Bridge, you enter a world of forests and lakes, the Upper Peninsula.

2 St. Ignace, the small port on the north shore of the Straits of Mackinac, was founded more than 300 years ago by Father Jacques Marquette, the Jesuit missionary and explorer. Father Marquette's old mission church is now a museum containing several mementos of the famous cleric, whose grave is in the churchyard.

The drive westward from St. Ignace along the southern shores of the Upper Peninsula abounds in unexpected scenic overlooks, picnic tables shaded by fragrant pines, and secluded pebble beaches along Lake Michigan's dark blue waters. The road winds through the forests past hidden coves and deserted bays. The

SPECIAL FEATURES

ROAD GUIDE	▬▬▬	HIGHLIGHT	**1**
STATE PARKS		SCHEDULED AIRLINE STOPS	✈
With Campsites ⛺ Without Campsites △		MILITARY AIRPORTS	✈
RECREATION AREAS		OTHER AIRPORTS	✈
With Campsites ▲ Without Campsites △			
SELECTED REST AREAS	✕	PORTS OF ENTRY	⊶
POINTS OF INTEREST	▣	BOAT RAMPS	⊿
SKI AREAS	⅔	INFORMATION CENTER	⊛

ROAD CLASSIFICATION

CONTROLLED ACCESS HIGHWAYS
Interstate interchange numbers are mileposts.   **5**   Interchanges

OTHER DIVIDED HIGHWAYS

PAVED HIGHWAYS

LOCAL ROADS In unfamiliar areas inquire locally before using these roads   Paved   Gravel   Dirt

MILEAGE

MILEAGE BETWEEN TOWNS AND JUNCTIONS 3╱4   MILEAGE BETWEEN DOTS •—35—•

SCALE

ONE INCH 17 MILES   0   5   10   20

ONE INCH 27 KILOMETERS   0   5   10   15   32

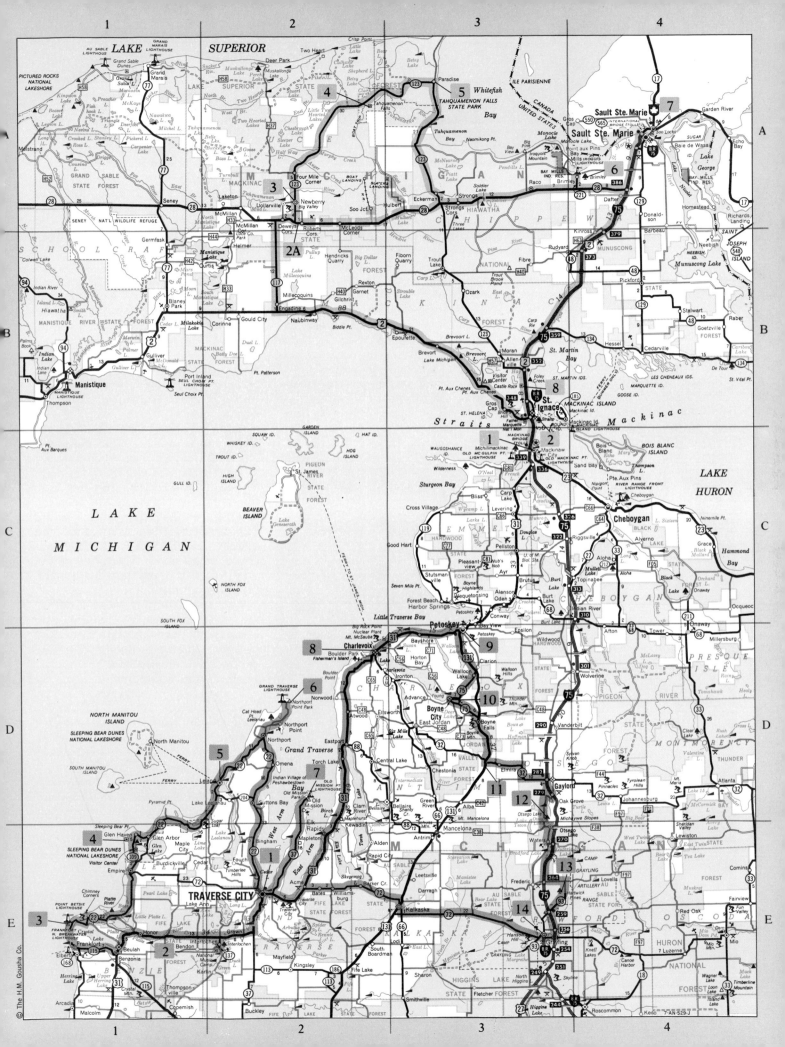

scenery in this area, which is part of the Hiawatha National Forest, is much as Longfellow described it in his epic poem "The Song of Hiawatha."

At Pointe Aux Chenes (French for "Point of Oaks") there are beaches and picnic groves along the shore and a visitor center where information about the area is available.

2A From Route 28 a well-marked two-mile road to Soo Junction heads north, taking you through a dense cedar swamp to a parking area and a small depot. This is the departure point for a 6½-hour round-trip journey called the Toonerville Trolley and Boat Trip to the Tahquamenon Upper Falls, a spectacular cascade on the Tahquamenon River.

Penetrating a wilderness accessible by no other means of transportation, the narrow-gauge railroad goes through forests of maple, spruce, pine, aspen, and oak trees as it winds north to the river, where you board a boat for the falls. A guide comments on the wildlife to be seen—deer, porcupines, raccoons, ruffed grouse, woodcocks, and hundreds of species of birds—as you cruise through the remote landscape. The trip does not run from October to mid-June.

A similar trip to the Tahquamenon Upper Falls leaves from Slater's Landing, off Route 28 about 10 miles north of Hulburt. This 4½-hour round trip, known as the Tom Sawyer River Boat and Paul Bunyan Timber Train, begins on a sight-seeing boat that travels through the upper reaches of the Tahquamenon. About midway to the falls the passengers are transferred to a rubber-tired timber train and transported to within a three-minute walk of the falls.

On this tour a guide also comments on the flora and fauna and gives a history of the Tahquamenon River.

The tour does not run from mid-October to Memorial Day.

3 The town of Newberry is located in a forested recreation area that is popular in winter because of its toboggan runs, cross-country skiing, and snowmobile and snowshoeing trails.

4 Tahquamenon (pronounced tah-*kwa*-meh-non) Falls State Park is hidden among the rolling, pine-covered hills along the shores of Lake Superior's Whitefish Bay. Running through the park is the Tahquamenon River, a meandering, tree-lined waterway that was made famous by Longfellow as the riverbanks where Hiawatha built his canoe.

At the awesome Upper Falls of the river, in the heart of the park, the stream thunders over a ledge some 200 feet wide and about 50 feet high. When the sunlight catches the roaring stream, you can see the deep tea color of the water, the result of tannic acid leached from leaves and pine needles along the river's twisting course. Walkways, with observation platforms along the way, lead to the brink of the falls.

With four camping areas, a nature preserve, backpacking and cross-country ski trails, and facilities for fishing, canoeing, and swimming, Tahquamenon Falls State Park serves as an all-year vacationland.

5 Paradise, a small resort town on Whitefish Bay, has sandy beaches fringed with pine and birch trees, campgrounds, miles of hiking trails, and superb fishing in the nearby Tahquamenon River and its tributaries.

Boats and canoes can be rented in Paradise, and for fishing in the Queen of Lakes, as Lake Superior is often called, guided trips are available.

An alternate drive terminates at the junction of Routes 28 and 123. (See 2A on this page.)

6 From the excellent sandy beach at Brimley State Park on Whitefish Bay you can swim, or wade, in the lake's chill waters and watch the ore boats as they pass the rugged hills of Canada on the horizon. The park also has facilities for camping, picnicking, boating, and fishing.

4. The forests around the Tahquamenon Lower Falls (above) frame it with brilliant foliage in autumn. Native here are the female woodcock (far left), shown protecting two baby chicks that are barely visible to the left of her head, and the chipmunk (left), emerging from its burrow in the forest floor.

The Soo Locks

Four parallel locks, which allow shipping to pass from Lake Superior to lower-level Lake Huron and back, form the Soo Locks. They link the United States with Canada and, via the St. Lawrence Seaway, with ports all over the world. Of the different types of vessels that make use of the locks each year, several are freighters large enough to carry more than 68,000 tons of cargo. The U.S. Army Corps of Engineers has operated the system toll free since 1881.

Freighter leaves MacArthur, one of the Soo locks.

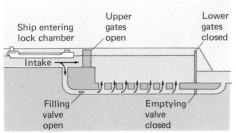

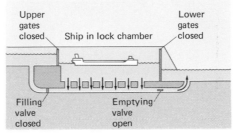

Just east of Brimley, Route 28 crosses the Waiska River, which flows north into Lake Superior. Local canoe enthusiasts enjoy paddling down this stretch of the river to the lake and along the shore to the park. The waters of Lake Superior are known to be rough at times but are usually calm during the summer.

7 Sault (pronounced soo) Ste. Marie was founded by Father Marquette in 1668. The Soo, as it is called by local residents, is situated on the southern banks of the St. Mary's River, a narrow stretch of water connecting Lake Superior on the west with Lake Huron on the east.

Waterfalls (*sault* in French) gave the city part of its name. These falls, tumbling down from Superior into Huron, are bypassed today by the famous Soo Locks, the four sets of locked channels that form an important link in what is called the St. Lawrence River System.

You can watch the locking operation from covered observation towers as Great Lakes ore boats and freighters, as well as "salties" from ports around the world, navigate the narrow channels.

Visitors can take a two-hour boat trip through the locks, or board the rubber-tired tourist "train" for a tour of the historic city.

At the visitor center, in Fountain Park along St. Mary's River, there is a working model of the locks. The center is closed from November until mid-May.

South of Sault Ste. Marie the road runs through the rolling eastern edge of Hiawatha National Forest. Roadside restaurants in this part of the state serve delicious pasties, copies of the traditional Cornish pasties of southwest England and one of the lesser-known delights of this section of the world.

Pasties are as different as the cooks who concoct them, but generally they are a hearty mixture of onions, potatoes, carrots, and chunks of beef baked in a thick envelope of yeast bread. A pasty, steaming hot, can chase the chill of the coolest U.P. evening. They can also be eaten cold for a picnic lunch.

8 In Hiawatha National Forest is Castle Rock, a spectacular cliff from which you can see the waters of Lake Huron, with Mackinac Island in the distance. The Straits State Park on the shore of Lake Huron has a fine sandy beach, camping and trailer sites, and picnic groves.

From Traverse City, on the west coast, to the top of Michigan's Mitten, there are fruit-growing farmlands, popular vacation areas, and wooded rolling hills and valleys filled with lakes and streams.

Lake Michigan's meandering shoreline, with thousands of coves and inlets and miles of sandy beaches, entices vacationers, who come to swim, fish, and sail on the quiet waters of the many bays.

Along the shores of Grand Traverse Bay, where the climate is tempered by the bay's protected waters, orchards fill the countryside. Cherry trees blossom from April well into May, putting on an almost unsurpassed springtime show.

The waters of the inland countryside are popular with fishermen and canoe enthusiasts, and backpackers and campers come to enjoy the lush beauty of the densely wooded hills.

1 Traverse City, an early frontier mill town, is known today as the Cherry Capital of the World. The lakeshore port, located at the southern end of Grand Traverse Bay, is surrounded by rich fruit-growing farmlands that produce some 100 million pounds of cherries annually.

Cherry trees, more than a half-million of them, turn the town and surrounding area into a magnificent park during blossom time. In many of the local orchards you can pick your own fruit.

At Traverse City's Clinch Park, on the shores of the bay, there is a zoo of animals and waterfowl native to Michigan, a museum of Indian and pioneer artifacts, a swimming beach, and a marina.

2 The community of Interlochen is the site of the National Music Camp. Hundreds of young people from all over the country spend the summer studying music, drama, and the dance with world renowned artists, who come here to teach and concertize. From late June to mid-August public concerts are given by both students and artists.

3 Frankfort, a port city on the shores of Lake Michigan, is surrounded by hills that overlook Betsie Lake, known locally as Betsie Bay. Nearby is historic Point Betsie Lighthouse. Built before the Civil War, this

183

4. *Sand dunes meet moody clouds over Lake Michigan on an autumn day at Sleeping Bear Dunes National Lakeshore. Blown by winds, the dunes constantly encroach upon the land. A bold shelter belt of trees protects a lone farmhouse from shifting sands.*

is one of the oldest still-working beacons on the Great Lakes. Tours of the picturesque structure, which is a popular subject for both painters and photographers, are available on holidays and weekends.

4 Although Sleeping Bear Dunes National Lakeshore stretches along Lake Michigan for 31 miles, from just north of Point Betsie to Good Harbor Bay, the section where Sleeping Bear Dune itself is located is three miles north of Empire. One mile north of Route 22, on Route 109, is the park's visitor center.

The name of the park, and that of the largest dune, comes from a Chippewa Indian legend that tells of a mother bear and her two cubs that tried to swim across Lake Michigan. As the cubs began to lag behind, the mother bear climbed up on shore to wait for them and soon fell asleep. She sleeps there still, as Sleeping Bear Dune. The cubs are are still offshore, transformed into North Manitou and South Manitou islands.

The dunes consist largely of wind-blown debris left by the immense glaciers that scooped out the lake basin more than 15,000 years ago. Although constantly changed by wind and wave, the sands are the habitat of a variety of wildlife, including porcupines, deer, foxes,

snowshoe hares, skunks, and more than 200 species of birds. The park is popular with fishermen, lured by the park waters, which abound with rock bass, bluegill, perch, and trout. Every fall the run of coho salmon, which school near the mouth of streams, entices anglers from near and far.

You can drive across the sands along the 7½-mile Pierce Stocking Scenic Drive, through an area where camping facilities, picnic grounds, and several miles of hiking trails are available.

5 Fishtown, on the waterfront at the small town of Leland, is one of the most interesting, and easily missed, pockets of local color in all of Michigan. Here there are weathered smokehouses and fishing huts, huddled between the shores of Lake Michigan and Lake Leelanau's swift outlet, which leaps over a spillway and enters Leland harbor.

If you pick your way among boat moorings, drying nets, the boxes of freshly caught fish, dozing sailors, and pole fishermen lining the boardwalk, you can sample fresh-smoked whitefish, perch, or lake trout at one of the many fish markets.

6 Leelanau State Park, at the tip of the Leelanau Peninsula, which separates Grand Traverse Bay from Lake Michigan, offers good views of

both bodies of water and of the Grand Traverse Lighthouse, a structure built in 1852.

At the Leelanau State Park there are several camping sites and a sandy swimming beach.

Old Mission Peninsula, a narrow spine of land that divides Grand Traverse Bay, is a colorful patchwork of summer cottages, farms, forests, vineyards, orchards, and meadows squeezed between two shorelines dotted with wave-ripping, rocky outcroppings and quiet, secluded coves.

About midway along the 17-mile-long peninsula, you can taste some of the Chateau Grand Travers Winery's prize-winning vintages and see the vintner and oenologists at work. The entire peninsula is blessed with a growing season surprisingly long for an area this far north. Wild flowers sometimes bloom in December.

7 At the north end of the peninsula is Old Mission Lighthouse, built in 1870. This sentinel is exactly halfway between the North Pole and the Equator.

America's Emerald Isle

The town of Charlevoix, on the eastern shore of Grand Traverse Bay, is the departure point for Beaver Island, a bit of land 13 miles long and 6 miles wide some 32 miles offshore. This charming little island has often been called America's Emerald Isle because of the Irish fishermen who settled here in the late 1800's.

Before the Irish came, the island was the home of a group of Mormons who declared the island a monarchy. It was ruled by a self-proclaimed king named James Jesse Strang. King Strang reigned from 1850 to 1856, when his assassination abruptly ended the monarchy. There is a local legend that says the king's downfall was sealed when he issued a royal proclamation ordering all women, including his own several wives, to wear bloomers.

Today Beaver Island is a fishing and sailing center and a quiet vacation retreat. Most of the permanent residents are descendants of the original Irish families.

Beaver Island is accessible by car ferry from mid-April to December. The trip takes about 2½ hours, and reservations are necessary.

The road goes back down through the peninsula to the southern end of Great Traverse Bay. As you drive northward along the bay's eastern shore, you have a fine view of the Old Mission Peninsula.

8 The resort town of Charlevoix was once a bustling port of entry, with several lumber mills in the surrounding countryside. The town straddles a strip of land between Lake Michigan and Lake Charlevoix, and is known today for its beaches, campgrounds, picnic areas, and its many connecting waterways.

The drive from Charlevoix to Petoskey, a resort town on the shores of Little Traverse Bay, is one of Michigan's most scenic. During the spring the meadows along the road are carpeted with wild flowers, and parks on the shores of the bay offer facilities for picnickers and campers in groves of birches and pines.

9 Petoskey is a center for salmon fishing, sailing, swimming, picnicking, and camping, and serves as a shopping center for the many nearby vacation communities.

Petoskey State Park, 2½ miles north of town on the shores of the bay, has a mile-long sandy beach where visitors like to hunt for Petoskey stones, which are wave-polished agate pebbles and much prized by rock collectors.

10 Boyne City, at the east end of Lake Charlevoix, and the nearby town of Boyne Falls are the hubs of a skiing and outdoor recreation area known as Boyne Country. The area abounds with small lakes, streams, pine and birch forests, and neat farms on a rolling landscape that is punctuated by knobs of rounded glacial hills. Here too are old lumber centers that are now ghost towns.

11 One mile south of the junction of Routes 32 and 131, at a sign indicating the entrance to Jordan Valley State Forest, a gravel road heading west leads to Deadman's Hill. From the cliff, named when a young teamster was killed while working on a precipitous slope, there is a splendid view of the Jordan River valley and the dense forests of pines and hardwoods hundreds of feet below. The mounds, grooves, and depressions here were sculpted by Michigan's ice age glaciers.

9. *Subtle hues and bewitching patterns make Petoskey stones well worth finding. The Petoskey is Michigan's state stone.*

12 Seven miles south of Gaylord, a small town in the heart of potato-producing farmlands, is Otsego Lake State Park, on the southeast shores of Otsego Lake, which is famous for perch, bass, tiger muskies, and pike. There are sandy beaches and bathhouses along the lakeshore.

If you are lucky, you may catch sight of a flock of whistling swans or see cormorants diving for fish.

13 A few miles east of Route 75, Hartwick Pines State Park, a 9,221-acre area within the Au Sable State Forest, has an 85-acre tract of virgin white pines and hemlocks, the only remaining stand of such virgin growth in Michigan. The patriarch of this secluded living monument is a 300-year-old, 155-foot white pine known as the Mighty Monarch. Self-guided nature trails and the park's logging museum offer a close look at this bit of Michigan natural history.

Hartwick Pines State Park has facilities for boating, fishing, and picnicking, as well as campgrounds.

14 Grayling is a center for canoeing and fishing. The old mill town's half-dozen or so canoe rentals can furnish boats and equipment. Experienced canoeists take part in an annual July race on the Au Sable River that starts at Grayling and ends 240 miles away at Lake Huron.

From the town of Grayling the road winds westward past dairy farms and cornfields and through rolling woodlands on its way to the waters of Lake Michigan's Grand Traverse Bay.

12. *Lilies that would delight the eye of an impressionist painter speckle the marshy rim of Otsego Lake, whose name comes from the Iroquoian word for "rock site." A boat regatta and a fireworks display take place on the lake every July 3rd.*

Exploring the Central States

The Great Plains, rolling hills, and a network of streams and rivers leading to the Gulf Coast

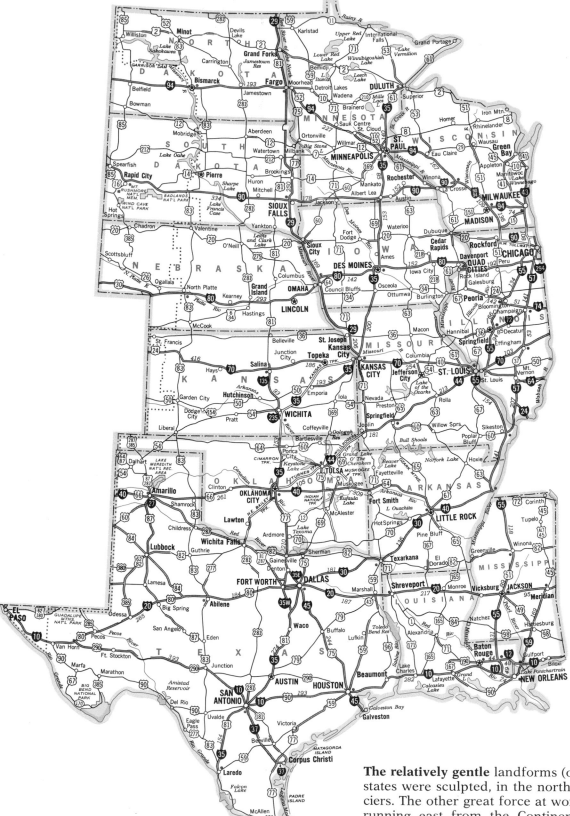

The relatively gentle landforms (opposite) of the central states were sculpted, in the north, by the retreating glaciers. The other great force at work is erosion by waters running east from the Continental Divide. The great outwash plains and the many waterways are the most obvious effects of ice age melting.

10-AC-1227-S

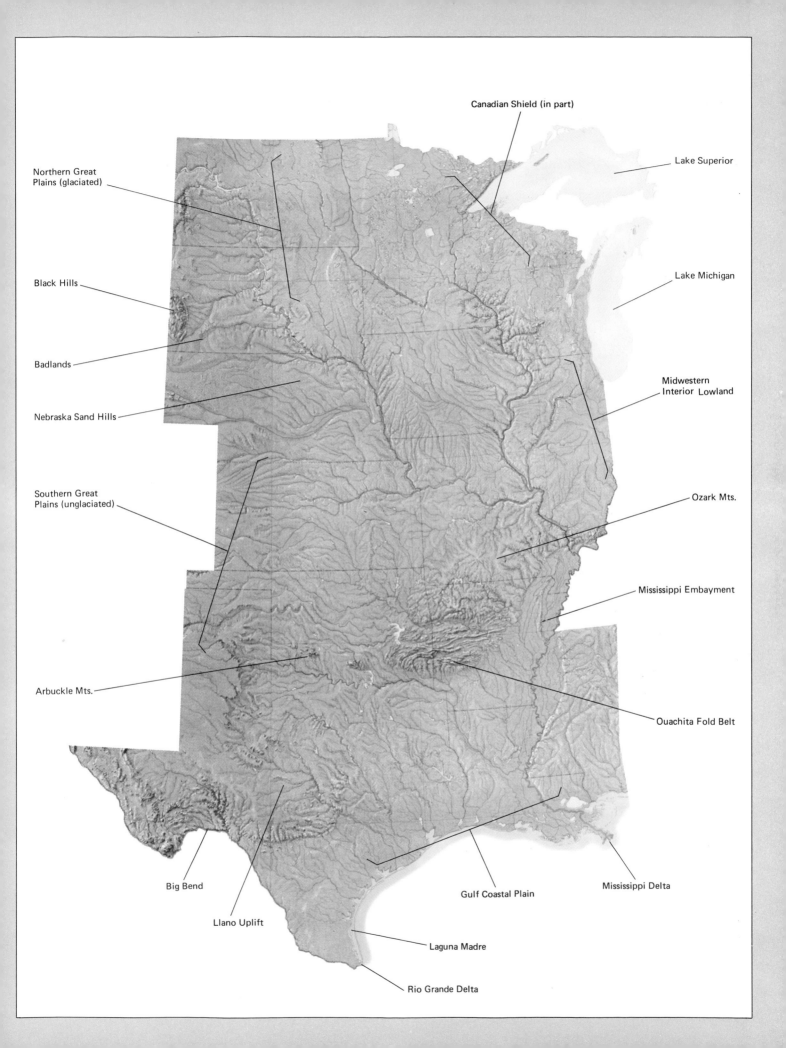

Canadian Shield (in part)

Lake Superior

Northern Great
Plains (glaciated)

Lake Michigan

Black Hills

Badlands

Midwestern
Interior Lowland

Nebraska Sand Hills

Ozark Mts.

Southern Great
Plains (unglaciated)

Mississippi Embayment

Arbuckle Mts.

Ouachita Fold Belt

Big Bend

Gulf Coastal Plain

Mississippi Delta

Llano Uplift

Laguna Madre

Rio Grande Delta

Plants, Birds, and Animals to Watch For

There are lovely trees and flowers and interesting animals, but it is the birds that are most unusual

All the birds illustrated here are a delight to ornithological enthusiasts. Of particular interest is the whooping crane, a magnificent large bird once on the verge of extinction and now slowly increasing in number. It has chosen as its wintering ground the vast coastal area of Aransas National Wildlife Range on the Gulf coast of Texas.

Among the unusual animals to watch for along the highways and byways of the central states are the armadillo, the peccary, the pronghorn, and the jackrabbit with its distinctive ears and remarkable running speed.

A jack at full tilt can get up to 45 miles per hour. Nutria, beaver, and muskrats stay near the rivers, streams, and ponds. The prairie dog towns are not difficult to spot in the open land, and bison are seen on their special preserves. Squirrels abound in the forests, and the bobcat is a wary denizen of the deep woods.

Most of the land in the central states has been cleared for farming, but there are forest plants and animals still to be found in the Ozark Mountains of northwest Arkansas and in the wooded ravines of the South Dakota Badlands.

Trees

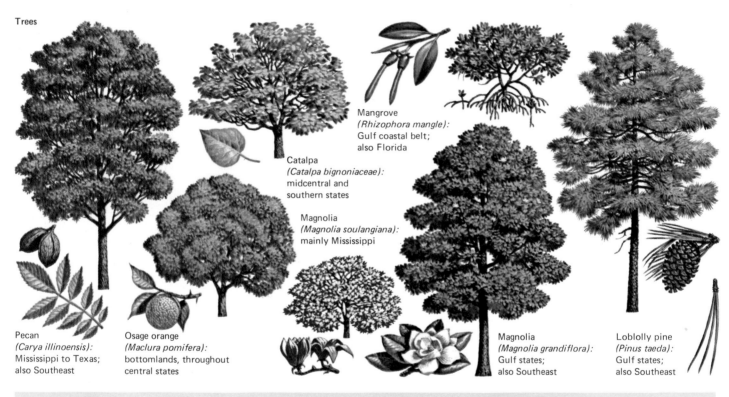

Mangrove
(Rhizophora mangle):
Gulf coastal belt;
also Florida

Catalpa
(Catalpa bignoniaceae):
midcentral and
southern states

Magnolia
(Magnolia soulangiana):
mainly Mississippi

Pecan
(Carya illinoensis):
Mississippi to Texas;
also Southeast

Osage orange
(Maclura pomifera):
bottomlands, throughout
central states

Magnolia
(Magnolia grandiflora):
Gulf states;
also Southeast

Loblolly pine
(Pinus taeda):
Gulf states;
also Southeast

Shrubs and Flowers

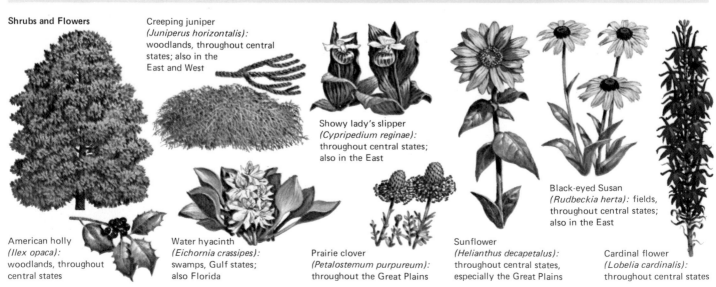

Creeping juniper
(Juniperus horizontalis):
woodlands, throughout central
states; also in the
East and West

Showy lady's slipper
(Cypripedium reginae):
throughout central states;
also in the East

Black-eyed Susan
(Rudbeckia herta): fields,
throughout central states;
also in the East

American holly
(Ilex opaca):
woodlands, throughout
central states

Water hyacinth
(Eichornia crassipes):
swamps, Gulf states;
also Florida

Prairie clover
(Petalostemum purpureum):
throughout the Great Plains

Sunflower
(Helianthus decapetalus):
throughout central states,
especially the Great Plains

Cardinal flower
(Lobelia cardinalis):
throughout central states

Birds

Greater prairie chicken: prairies, Dakotas south to Oklahoma

Burrowing owl: southern prairies; also in the West

White-tailed hawk: southern Texas; also in Southwest

Anhinga: swamps, ponds, Gulf states

American kestrel: open prairies; also in the East

Roseate spoonbill: Gulf Coast

Louisiana heron: Gulf Coast

Whooping crane: Aransas National Wildlife Refuge, Texas

White ibis: swamp forests, Gulf states

Snowy egret: Gulf Coast; also Carolinas, Florida

Upland sandpiper: throughout central states

Animals

Nine-banded armadillo: Mississippi to Texas; also Alabama

Bobcat/wildcat: lower Mississippi Valley into Texas

Bison/buffalo: national wildlife refuges, north central plains; also Montana, Alaska

American beaver: prairies

Javelina/ collared peccary: southern Texas; also Arizona, New Mexico

Prairie dog: mainly central Texas

Jackrabbit: Nebraska to Texas; also in the West

Coypu/nutria: swamps, Gulf states

Gopher: prairies

Pronghorn, or American, antelope: deserts, west central states; also California, Oregon

Muskrat: swamps, Gulf states and elsewhere in U.S.

Franklin's ground squirrel: prairies

189

Engineered to Feed the World

The farm machinery and related facilities on the Great Plains are wonders of efficiency and design

The pioneers who broke the sod of the Great Plains, struggling with a single-furrow plow pulled by a team of oxen, would be astonished to see 16 furrows plowed at one pass of the field. They would wonder too at the vast grain elevators rising dramatically against the horizon. These imposing structures are, in effect, monuments to the efficiency of the men and machines who carry on the tradition of farming here.

From early spring until late fall you can see machines, such as those shown here, as they prepare the soil and plant, cultivate, and harvest the crops.

Tremendous power is required to drive these machines, and a remarkable generation of tractors has been developed to do the job. The driver sits in a comfortable, adjustable seat in an acoustically designed, air-conditioned cab with a radio for entertainment. The work, however, still goes on from dawn to dusk (and with headlights, even longer), as it did for those who first farmed this fertile land. No matter how sophisticated the machines, a farmer's work is still dictated by such natural forces as pests, disease, and the ever-changing patterns of the weather.

Just one of this assembly of gigantic concrete towers can hold as much as 40,000 bushels of grain. The primary crop is wheat, but oats and rye are also stored. The grain is brought from the fields by truck at harvesttime and taken away as needed by the specially designed freight cars to be transshipped to markets all over the world.

Combines are so called because they combine in one operation the cutting of the crop and the separation of the final product from the stems, stalks, or vines. Combines are used for grains of all kinds, as well as for corn and soybeans. In order to harvest vast acreages in the minimum time that the crops are at their proper stage of ripeness, combines often work in formation, as shown.

A plow like this can make as many as eight furrows at one time. Tandem hookups can make even more. Tremendous horsepower is required, which accounts for the gigantic tractors you see in the fields and in the equipment salesyards.

Disking is done to break up the clods after plowing. In the fields you see disks ganged up in different conformations, depending on the type of soil. The disks are also varied, with edges to match soil conditions.

Grain crops, such as wheat, barley, and flax, are planted with a "drill" like this. The seed is in the horizontal boxes, and in some models fertilizer can be applied simultaneously. Four 10-foot drills can sow a 40-foot swath.

When the soil is ready, planting begins, and there are machines for every job. A corn planter like this sows 12 rows at once. Some models handle up to 40 rows in one swath and can also apply fertilizer, herbicides, and pesticides.

A corn combine can move steadily through a field as it cuts the rows of corn, separates the cobs from the stalks and leaves, strips the kernels from the cobs, and delivers the cleaned grain to an internal holding tank. When the tank is full, a truck pulls up alongside, and the grain is automatically transferred. At harvesttime, you can see these trucks on the road.

The Marvels of Minnesota

In a land of lakes, forests, and iron mines, you can also see the source of America's mightiest river

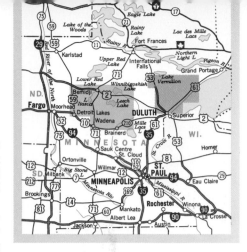

Tall trees and tall tales abound in this land sprinkled with thousands of lakes, said to be the hoofprints of Babe the Blue Ox, which aided the legendary lumberjack Paul Bunyan. But the real giants that shaped Minnesota's landscape were continental ice sheets. Glaciers up to 10,000 feet thick exerted 150 tons of pressure on each square foot of land across which they flowed, scraped, and gouged. When the glaciers retreated, they dumped their huge loads of debris in various shapes and contours across the land; the resulting deposits of soil produced a magnificent forest land, much of which still remains wooded in the north.

The first migrants into this virgin landscape were the ancestral Indians, nearly 11,000 years ago. The next visitors were perhaps a small band of Vikings, about 600 years ago. In recent history the fur traders, the famous French voyageurs, came here to deal with the Chippewas and were followed by lumberjacks and iron miners. Today as tourists enjoy the state's natural beauty, the romance and legends of this wet, wooded land seem almost believable.

Visitors to Minnesota's state parks require an annual windshield sticker or a daily permit. Both can be purchased at entrance stations to all the developed state parks.

Paul Bunyan's trade dominates the north woods of Minnesota, but numerous glacial lakes also make this the land of fishermen. Abundant and varied wildlife dwell in these forests, which for centuries kept secret the location of the Mississippi River's headwaters, now surrounded by Itasca State Park.

1 In Brainerd the name of Paul Bunyan has been given to an area devoted to the task of producing trees rather than consuming them. The Paul Bunyan Arboretum is located west of the Mississippi River on Seventh Street, N.W.

A relatively new arboretum, the Paul Bunyan also has nature trails, hiking and cross-country skiing paths, and wildlife feeding stations.

Roads through the arboretum pass flower gardens and plots of different types of grasses, which are tested here for their suitability to this soil and climate.

The artful blend of wild and managed nature produces sights of joy and wonder: a spiderweb glistening in the dewy morning sun; a white-tailed deer flagging its long tail as it bounds into the pines; the delicate color and fragrances of blooming fruit trees.

The Minnesota "Gold" Rush

Wild rice, an aquatic grass that yields a much sought edible grain, grows in such abundance in the waters of Minnesota's shallow lakes that "ricers," as the harvesters are called, flock to the area in great numbers when the valuable crop is ripe.

The highly nutritious grain, often called false oats, is harvested by hand. Canoes, whose size is limited by law, skim the waters and glide through the 10-foot-tall light green grasses. They are propelled by navigators who stand in the stern, pushing the craft with a forked pole.

The harvester sits in the bow of the canoe and uses two dowels as flails. These too are limited in size by law. With one flail, clumps of grass are bent into the boat. With the other, the seed heads are beaten from their stalks.

After the harvested rice has been lightly toasted, hulled, and winnowed, it is carefully packaged and sent off to market.

2 The heavily developed recreation land around Gull Lake includes Lumbertown, U.S.A., a replica of an 1870's Minnesota village. Salvaged old buildings have been assembled here to portray life on the Minnesota frontier. A riverboat cruises past an old-time lumberyard and the lodge of the state's first lumberjack, the beaver. A frontier bank, homes, a barber shop, a school, a furniture factory, a maple sugar plant, an undertaker's parlor, a railroad depot, a livery stable, and a blacksmith shop are among the 26 restorations.

3 Leech Lake, third largest in the state, is backed up behind moraines, natural ridges of earth and rock deposited along glacier edges about 11,000 years ago. Glacial erratics, rocks carried here by conveyor belts of ice, are obvious along roads near the lake. Presumably not named by the local chamber of commerce, Leech Lake is far more pleasant than it sounds. About 615,000 walleyed pike, Minnesota's tasty state fish, are estimated to inhabit the waters here.

Another delicacy provided by nature is wild rice, a water grass harvested from boats, mainly by the Chippewas of Leech Lake Indian Reservation.

The Medicine Rite Indian burial grounds is an interesting site in Chippewa National Forest on the detour to Stony Point. In keeping with the Chippewa custom, plank houses are built above the graves; they present a lovely picture in the dark woods.

Stony Point, a very pleasant campground and recreation area managed by the Forest Service, features boating, fishing, and walking the Stony

---

SPECIAL FEATURES

ROAD GUIDE	HIGHLIGHT	**1**
STATE PARKS	SKI AREAS	
With Campsites ⛺ Without Campsites △		
RECREATION AREAS	SCHEDULED AIRLINE STOPS	
With Campsites ▲ Without Campsites △		
SELECTED REST AREAS ⊼	OTHER AIRPORTS	
POINTS OF INTEREST ⊞	BOAT RAMPS	

ROAD CLASSIFICATION

CONTROLLED ACCESS HIGHWAYS (Entrance and Exit only at Interchanges)	Interchanges
OTHER DIVIDED HIGHWAYS	
PAVED HIGHWAYS	
LOCAL ROADS In unfamiliar areas inquire locally before using these roads	Paved Gravel Dirt

MILEAGE

MILEAGE BETWEEN TOWNS AND JUNCTIONS 3 / 4	MILEAGE BETWEEN DOTS 35

SCALE

ONE INCH 18 MILES	0 5 10 15 20 25
ONE INCH 29 KILOMETERS	0 5 10 20 30 40

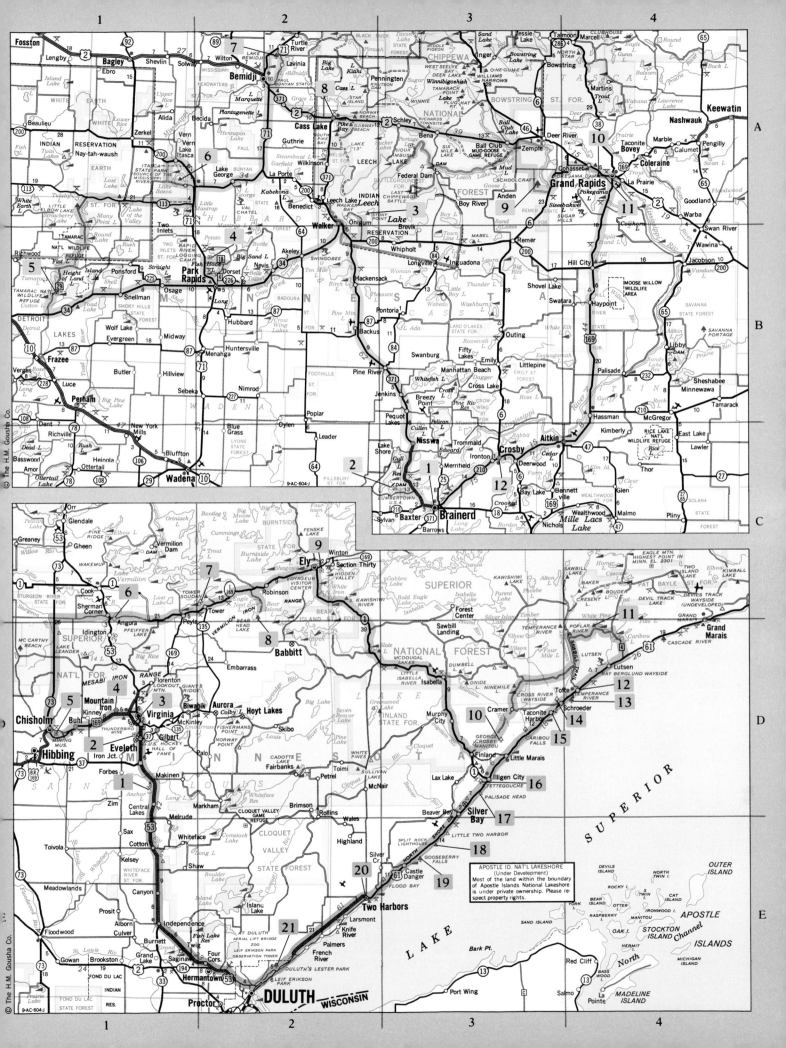

Point Trail. The history of white settlement at Leech Lake is preserved in the Cass County Historical Museum and the adjacent restored log schoolhouse along Route 200 in Walker.

4   Before reaching Park Rapids, turn right onto County Road 4 and follow the signs to Rapid River Logging Camp. This restoration of an early lumber operation features a working sawmill complete with the

Road 18 to circle Fish Hook Lake. Several small parks along the shore are good places to watch for the common loon, Minnesota's state bird. Its eerie wailing, laughing cry is likely to be heard in the early morning.

5   To reach the Tamarac National Wildlife Refuge, turn right at the junction of Route 34 and County Road 29 and drive eight miles. Conifers to the north, hardwoods to the

6   Itasca is the second largest and the most visited of Minnesota's state parks. At the South Entrance begins Park Drive, lined with large red pines (*Pinus resinosa*), the state tree, alternating with lakes. Beyond the developed service area around the East Entrance, Park Drive reaches Lake Itasca, hemmed by forest greenery.

A highlight along the lake section of Park Drive is Preacher's Grove, a virgin stand of magnificent red pines. At the base of their trunks are "catfaces," scars from past forest fires. Ironically, these fires benefit red pine by clearing the ground of underbrush for the germination of new pines. Beyond Preacher's Grove is Peace Pipe Overlook, an outstanding viewpoint of Lake Itasca.

Not to be missed is the Mississippi River headwaters. Just beyond the park's North Entrance road an interpretive center explains the history and significance of the spot. From the center, a short, easy path leads to a small footbridge spanning the Mississippi, here only a brook, and on to the lake outlet. Visitors frequently use stepping stones or wade across the "Father of Waters."

Beyond the headwaters the road becomes unpaved Wilderness Drive, an appropriately named one-way road. Along the way a very short trail leads to the largest living red and white pines in Minnesota and possibly in the world. Back on Park Drive, take the East Entrance to Route 71.

7   The scenery opens up a bit as farmlands alternate with forests. Piles of glacial erratics in the fields proclaim the difficulties involved in plowing land overlain by moraines. The early Scandinavian farmers, however, were accustomed to dealing with this obstacle because similar boulders were scattered across their native land in just the same way.

A statue of Paul Bunyan stands beside that of Babe the Blue Ox on the shore of Lake Bemidji. Continue on through town and stay on Old Route 71 to Bemidji State Park.

Virgin red pine forests and magnificent sugar maples keep Bemidji similar to the way it looked when traders and lumberjacks first entered the area. There is a pleasant self-guiding nature trail along the lakeshore to Rocky Point Overlook.

6. *Lake Itasca, source of the Mississippi River, spills over rocks in the foreground to send its waters on a 2,552-mile journey to the Gulf of Mexico. Pine trees stand guard at the shoreline. The lake provides a beach and boat landing for Itasca State Park.*

scream of a steam whistle and the scent of freshly sawed pine. To maintain equipment and provide shoes for huge draft horses, logging camps had a blacksmith shop, which is present here along with many artifacts from Minnesota's timber-cutting past. A lumberjack mess hall serves food to visitors.

Several marked trails through the woods surrounding the camp follow the bank of the Potato River, passing old locks and dams. Along a self-guided nature trail is the showy lady's slipper (*Cypripedium reginae*), the state flower.

When leaving the lumber camp, turn left and continue along County

south, and tallgrass prairie to the west contribute to the wildlife mix. The refuge was established as a shelter for flocks of migrating birds, and spectacular wood ducks nest here in large numbers, as do eagles and ospreys.

Glaciers left 25 lakes and numerous bogs and swamps in more than a third of the refuge's 42,725 acres. The balance contains forests, through which wind 35 miles of roads dotted with historical markers. They indicate old thoroughfares, a Chippewa burial ground, Indian mounds, and remains of logging operations. Hiking trails also penetrate the deep, green woods, and fishing is permitted at some lakes.

8. The bald eagle, America's national emblem, stretches its seven-foot wingspan as it hunts for fish in Chippewa National Forest. In the view at left, the eagle's sharp gaze, beak, and talons can be seen.

8 Cass Lake is in the midst of one of the densest populations of nesting bald eagles in the United States, excluding Alaska. The bald eagle's success in Chippewa National Forest is largely due to an abundance of fish, the bird's main food, and to many undisturbed nesting sites in tall trees.

You can identify a mature bald eagle by its large size and familiar white head and tail. Birds less than four or five years old may be as big as the adults, but they lack the white coloring. In flight all eagles can be recognized by the flat way they hold their wings. Eagles and their protection are explained in displays in the forest headquarters lobby.

To reach the headquarters, turn right from Route 2 onto Route 371 in Cass Lake. A right turn three blocks later is marked by a sign. The three-story headquarters, one of the world's largest log buildings, was constructed in the 1930's and is a fine example of logger craftmanship as formerly practiced by Finnish immigrants.

9 Signs direct motorists through rolling farmland to Schoolcraft State Park, located along the Mississippi and named for the discoverer of the headwaters. As agent for the Chippewas, Henry Rowe Schoolcraft recorded many of their customs, legends, and history. From Schoolcraft's work, poet Henry Wadsworth Longfellow gathered the material for his epic, "The Song of Hiawatha."

The 133 acres of Schoolcraft State Park contain virgin stands of red pine, even though the area was heav-ily logged in the early part of this century. Less massive but equally impressive are the yellow lady's slipper orchids that grow on the lawn in front of the park office. A self-guided nature trail loops through forests. Other paths run along swamps and beside the main channel of the Mississippi, already a good-size river.

When leaving the park, turn left and continue on County Road 74 to another left onto County Road 65. Turn left again onto Route 6.

10 A U.S. Army Corps of Engineers dam is the center of Pokegama Lake Recreation Area. This concrete dam, built in 1903, replaced the rock-and-timber dam built in 1884 to help control water levels on the Mississippi. During the heyday of lumbering, loggers floated timber past the dam in a log sluice (which still remains) on the way to sawmills downstream.

The recreation area features boating, camping, fishing, and picnicking.

11 A mile beyond Pokegama Dam, signs lead to the Forest History Center. Snuggled in an attractive second-growth forest along the Mississippi, the center is reached by a short path that leaves most aspects of modern living behind.

The 105-acre center, developed by the Minnesota Historical Society, features the buildings of a logging camp staffed by costumed guides. Equipped with many logging artifacts, the center uses carefully produced replicas to interpret the lumber industry of the 1890-1920 era.

The multiuse of the forest today is scheduled to be included in the center's story, along with aspects of Indian, logger, and settler history.

About 10 miles beyond Lake Pokegama the land beings to flatten, and forests are replaced by dairy farms. The Mississippi, with almost no grade to give it cutting power, meanders in great oxbow bends across this plain.

12 There had to be a lot of magnetic iron formation around Crosby, federal surveyors reasoned in 1859, because their compasses were thrown off. But all the bedrock was buried under 150 feet of glacial drift. Not until 1903 was the Cuyuna iron range discovered. Ore here was first taken out of underground mines and later from open pits. The pits are now full of water, and the piles of red waste rock stand as reminders of the activity here.

The state purchased the defunct Croft Mine in 1978 and opened the mine's surface operation to the public in 1980 as an historical park. The mine's 117-foot-high stack is a landmark; signs direct you to the site from the park in the middle of town.

The making of an oxbow lake

In a process called meandering, geologically mature rivers like the Mississippi wind through flat plains, as shown in the sketches below, eroding the riverbank on the outside curve, where the water flows faster, and depositing sediment on the inside curve. Eventually, the meanders become so exaggerated that the river cuts across the loop, leaving an isolated bend with a body of water called an oxbow lake.

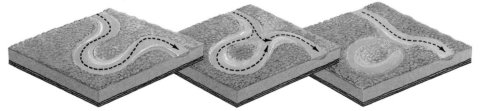

Iron mining is a prominent feature of the Mesabi and Vermilion ranges along the north shore of Lake Superior, where scenic contrasts are provided by idyllic woodland lakes and gorge-cutting waterfalls.

Wildlife varies from moose sloshing through glacier-formed lakes and swamps to hawks sailing the ridgelines above Lake Superior.

1 From Duluth, Route 53 is the straight and easy way north into the iron range forests and lakes west of Lake Superior, past swamps, tree farms, beaver workings, and forests where light-barked aspen and birch trunks contrast with large, dark evergreen trees.

Anchor Lake Tourist Information Center, in a lovely picnic area, offers brochures and exhibits about the Arrowhead region. Above the center a short pleasant walking trail reaches an overlook of Anchor Lake before looping back through a picturesque birch woods.

2 Hockey fans may wish to pause for a while at Eveleth and visit the United States Hockey Hall of Fame. An eight-minute slide show, a collection of hockey mementos, and photos honor notable players and explain the origin of the game.

3 A quarter of a mile north is a left turn to the Thunderbird Mine, identified on a hillside by a large Ford Motor Company emblem. Most of the iron derived from the mine's taconite ore is used by Ford in the steel for cars. Drills for dislodging the ore, huge shovels, and removal trucks can be seen on a one-hour free bus tour of the mine. The tours leave from the parking lot at 10 A.M. and 12:30 P.M. There are no tours from Labor Day until mid-June.

A highlight of the Virignia–Eveleth area is Mineview in the Sky above Route 53. This observation platform, atop a huge red pile of mine waste, overlooks the colorful open pit of the nearly three-mile-long Rouchleau Mine Group in the Mesabi Range iron formation. The original purpose of the station was to enable pit foremen to observe the entire mine.

4 Iron of the Mesabi Range was first discovered in 1890 at Mountain Iron. The original mine, now a water reservoir for Minntac operations, has been designated a national historic landmark, and an overlook is located near the town's post office.

The current Minntac Mine operation here annually produces 61 million tons of taconite, which is ground and magnetically separated from waste sand to yield 18 million tons of ore containing about 65 percent iron. A free 90-minute bus tour of the mine and plant leaves every hour on the half-hour from 9:30 to 4:30 daily, except from mid-August to mid-June.

5 A castlelike gate leads to the Minnesota Museum of Mining with its replica of an iron mine and various mining memorabilia and exhibits.

A half-mile along Route 169 brings you to the Iron Range Interpretive Center, poised on the edge of a huge man-made canyon of the abandoned Glen Mine. By means of innovative exhibits and programs, the center ties together the story of iron mining and of the multicultured immigrants who wrenched the red ore from the ground. Ethnic variety is emphasized in a kitchen and art center, as well as in recordings of old immigrants telling of their experiences in a new land. Outside the museum a nature trail highlights the way nature recaptured the red pit of the Glen Mine.

North of Chisholm, Route 73 leaves the narrow band of the Mesabi Range, crosses the Laurentian Divide, and reenters the woodlands, soon penetrating Superior National Forest. Three million acres of public forest are a mixture of birch, aspen, pine, and spruce.

6 After traveling 0.4 of a mile beyond the post office in Angora, note on the right the patterned rocks of the ancient Vermilion gneiss. A mixture of sedimentary rocks was crumpled and changed by heat and pressure some 2.7 billion years ago when they were uplifted. These "basement rocks" are among the oldest in the world and underlie all other rocks everywhere. The Laurentian, or Canadian, Shield (represented in the United States only in the Lake Superior region) is the largest area where these ancient rocks lie on the surface.

7 Tower Soudan State Park offers a unique experience, an underground mine tour. Visitors are provided with a hard hat. You should provide your own jacket, since mine temperature is constant at 52° F.

3. *Man has worked on nature for nearly a century to produce this moonscape. It is the Rouchleau Mine on the Mesabi iron range, operated by United States Steel and its predecessors since 1893. The pit, which yields rich ore, is four-tenths of a mile wide.*

9. *Skirting the water lily pads of Fenske Lake, present-day canoeists in a handsomely decorated boat follow the Echo Trail in the Boundary Waters Canoe Area. Indian birchbark canoes as well as* the fur-laden craft of French traders navigated this same route hundreds of years ago. They too must have noticed the beauty of the water, pines, flowers, rocks, and sky.

Riding the elevator cage that once carried miners into the state's deepest iron mine, you drop nearly 2,400 feet below the surface in three minutes. Down on the 27th level, a guide who worked the mine before it closed in 1963 explains what the labor was like. Since the guide is almost certain to lace his talk with technical terms, it is best, preceding the tour, to see the 10-minute movie that explains how the mine worked.

An aboveground highlight is the engine house with a cable and electric lift used to lower and raise the elevator. The clanging of bells, whirring of cables, and spinning of dials are impressive. Outside note an open-pit mine sliced into the hill, where the rubble of glacial till is easy to distinguish from bedrock. Five miles of trails wind among other pit mines in the 1,200-acre park.

Surrounding the iron deposits are beds of very hard Ely greenstone, among the oldest rock in Minnesota. A greenish rock often decorated by pretty patterns, Ely greenstone is relatively easy to identify and can be seen in road cuts near the state park.

8 The seven-mile road to the more than 4,000-acre Bear Head Lake State Park passes lovely Eagles Nest Lakes

Numbers 3 and 4. Both Bear Head and Eagles Nest were gouged from bedrock by glacial action. Road cuts reveal unsorted accumulations of boulders within the glacially deposited dirt that today supports a deep, dark coniferous forest.

Logging and forest fires consumed most of the woodlands within park boundaries in the early decades of this century. Today many charred pine stumps still line hiking trails, but abundant rains have restored the forest to much of its former glory. Deer and moose inhabit the woods and swamps.

9 A half-mile beyond Ely, outfitting point for trips into the Boundary Waters Canoe Area, is the Voyageur Visitor Center. Exhibits and audiovisual programs at this Superior National Forest facility show the local wildlife and tell the story of French fur traders, Indians, miners, and loggers. Particularly impressive is a large birchbark freight canoe like those that hauled trade goods to the Indians and returned downriver with beaver pelts for shipment to Europe. A half-mile nature trail loops through the forest surrounding the visitor center, which is closed from mid-September to mid-May.

Through carefully managed natural forests and tree plantations in Superior National Forest, Route 1 twists its way to a bridge over the Stony River. Below the bridge the water runs over the ruins of a dam, a reminder of former logging practices in this area.

At the beginning of this century timber camps along the Stony River contributed significantly to the state's lumber production. Trees were cut down and dumped in the river to be sluiced and rafted to sawmills. Log dams were built to maintain a high water level. After the forest was used up, most of the Stony River watershed became part of Superior National Forest, and the tree cover was restored. Today the forest once again provides vital wood products, but on a managed, sustained-yield basis.

10 Watch for moose in the open swampy areas between Isabella and Finland and along Blesner Creek between Finland and George Crosby Manitou State Park. Also present are white-tailed deer, one of the main prey of timber wolves. Since wolves are quite shy, you are unlikely to see them. But if you backpack along the 20 miles of trail, you may hear the howling of a wolf chorus.

Crosby Manitou is for those who like to hike and escape crowds. Trails that are described as rugged climb the "back" side of the hills above Lake Superior's north shore. Biting insects can be even more rugged; insect repellent is a necessity. However, the views from the hilltops and along the watercourses are ample compensation for minor tribulations.

Beyond the park, living tunnels of hard-maple branches arch the unpaved road, adding further variety to the mixed conifer–hardwood forest. The maples are impressive on Heartbreak Hill. At the top a sign explains the problems that the steep grade caused for the loggers.

Beyond a crossing of the Temperance River a left turn leads along an improved though still unpaved road to Forest Road 164 and a white pine blister rust research area.

11 Winding along ridgelines past beaver ponds, the route presses on through the woods toward the Poplar River. Ely greenstone and pink granitic rocks add color and bumps to the road, making sure that you drive slowly enough to enjoy the scenery. Turn right onto County Road 4, which descends for three miles to pavement. A mile farther on is your first view of Lake Superior.

Encompassing about 32,000 square miles, Lake Superior is the largest area of fresh water in the world, and its deepest point is 688 feet below sea level. More than 11,000 cubic miles of rock were scoured out by the ice age glaciers. However, it is called Superior because of its uppermost position among the five Great Lakes. The 80-mile drive south along the shore to Duluth has the well-deserved reputation of being one of the most scenic roads in America.

12 Tofte was settled in the 1890's and grew to be an important boat landing and a commercial logging and fishing settlement. The remains of the town's old concrete pier still jut into the lake but now serve only as a landing place for gulls.

The rounded mass of Carlton Peak, the highest point on the north shore, rises 1,529 feet above the lake.

13 The Temperance River State Park owes its name to a play on words. Most streams entering Lake Superior are nearly closed by bars of

gravel and sand dropped by water that loses velocity as it enters the lake. The bars are shaped by the lake's waves. Although such a bar can be seen at the mouth of the river today, you must deduce that there was none in 1864, when the river was named, hence the title Temperance.

Trails from the large roadside parking lots of the park lead downstream to the lake and upstream to various points of interest. The gorge of the Temperance River, where it is crossed by the highway bridge, is very narrow and was formed by several stream-worn potholes in the basalt lava flow breaking through their walls and coalescing. Upstream from the bridge, Hidden Falls is nearly concealed in a gorge overhung by vegetation and hard lips of rock undercut by the sand-laden water.

13. Bunchberries bloom in late May with clusters of flowers surrounded by petallike bracts (above). In fall edible red berries appear (left).

Trails bordered by wild flowers, such as red columbine and bunchberry, climb through the woods above Hidden Falls along the edge of a deep pothole gorge in which more waterfalls swirl and plunge. After rain, the water may be brown with runoff from upland swamps contain-

ing decaying tamarack needles. Eroded soil from the clay banks above the river also adds its color.

14 A mile from the Temperance River a marked road cuts left to Father Baraga's Cross. This gray granite emblem stands at the mouth of the Cross River on the site where a pioneer missionary landed his canoe to escape a Lake Superior storm. A very beautiful falls foams over a massive basalt lava flow just upstream from the highway bridge over the river. Here several giant potholes have been ground out of the rock by the swirling water.

15 At Taconite Harbor, watch for a large but inconspicuous sign after the third railroad overpass above Route 61. The sign indicates a left turn to an observation stand, from which you can watch the process of transferring the taconite from trains to ore carriers. More than 50,000 tons of taconite pellets can be loaded in four hours, to be transported to steel mills along Lake Superior. The observation stand, maintained by the Erie Mining Company, also displays samples of taconite pellets for a closer look. Gulls make a fierce racket, competing for attention with the ore boats and the ducks in the harbor.

16 Tettegouche River State Park, formerly called Baptism River State Park, boasts some of the finest scenery in Minnesota. From the upper parking lot, an easy path skirts cliff tops to Shovel Point and Little Palisades. These 170-foot precipices were formed by wave action on reddish rock called felsite porphyry, which originally was a volcanic lava. From the lower parking lot a trail leads to the mouth of the Baptism River. Upstream, the Baptism forms the highest waterfall in Minneosta.

17 A wayside rest sign indicates a left turn up a steep road to the top of Palisade Head. This 350-foot-high felsite lava promontory presents an excellent view of Shovel Point. At some places between these buttresses, waves have eroded caverns that perforate the cliff.

A communication tower rises from the top of Palisade Head. Local legend maintains that Indians in canoes below competed to see who could shoot arrows to the top of the precipice, but that few succeeded.

17. The coastline of Lake Superior yields many compelling sights, but few are as dramatic as this sheer drop to the lake's north shore at Palisade Head. Pieces of felsite lava from the bluff line its base, and a thin layer of soil supports a crown of trees.

18 Split Rock Lighthouse State Park is the most famous point on the north shore. At the turn of the century the water below Split Rock's anorthosite cliffs was dangerous to bulk iron-ore carriers, whose compasses were affected by the metallic rock formations in the area. In 1907 Congress appropriated $75,000 for a lighthouse and fog signal. Completed three years later, the lighthouse was the highest in the world, with a beam visible for 22 miles. The opening of the North Shore Road in 1924 made Split Rock accessible, and the striking octagonal structure has since drawn a great many visitors.

By 1969 electronic navigation equipment had made the lighthouse obsolete, but it is now being restored to its pre-1920 appearance by the Minnesota Historical Society. Exhibits and guided tours explain the day-to-day life of the keeper.

Trails radiate from the large parking lot to various overlooks along the 100-foot-high cliff and to the lakeshore below. A turnout about a mile southwest of the entrance to the park presents a distant dramatic view of the lighthouse as well as a plaque explaining the local geology.

19 The visitor center at Gooseberry Falls State Park sits to the right of the highway just before it bridges the Gooseberry River. A self-guided nature trail, the Voyageur Trail, begins at the center, and other trails loop through the park's woods to scenic overlooks. The mouth of the river is a good place to look for Lake Superior agates, Minnesota's gemstone.

From the parking lot beyond the bridge, trails lead for a short distance to the Upper Falls above the bridge and to the Lower Falls below.

20 In Two Harbors a sign indicates the turn into a historical museum, located at a city park from which you can watch ore boats in Agate Bay being loaded with taconite. Burlington Bay, the second harbor, has a boat landing and a campground. A lighthouse marks the harbor entrance. Beside the Lake County Historical Society Museum stand a locomotive, a wooden ore car, and a caboose, artifacts of early iron-mine railroading.

Beyond Two Harbors, signs lead to Lake Superior Scenic Drive, which runs past antiques and craft shops and marinas for about 20 miles along the lakeshore to Duluth.

21 At Duluth's Lester Park along Route 61, signs indicate a turn onto Seven Bridges Road and the Skyline Drive. Seven Bridges Road climbs via interesting old stone bridges over Amity Creek to the crest of Hawk Ridge and to panoramic views of Duluth and its harbor.

The Skyline Drive is marked with signs along the shoreline of ancient Lake Duluth, a mammoth body of water of which Superior is a remnant.

Wave action on Lake Superior has formed the Duluth harbor behind the protective sand spit of Minnesota Point, which is visible from Skyline Drive. This excellent protection so close to the Mesabi iron range has made the harbor one of the largest in the United States.

Skyline Drive passes through Hawk Ridge Nature Preserve, one of the best spots in the world for hawk-watching. Almost 71,000 hawks have been counted in migration along the ridge from mid-August through December. Reluctant to cross Lake Superior, the birds are funneled along the ridge by updrafts formed when lake winds strike the hills along the shore. West winds and clear skies can send thousands of hawks per day along the ridge in mid-September. It is one of nature's most spectacular wildlife displays.

199

America's Dairyland

Wisconsin's crops and cattle thrive on rolling hills and lowlands watered by its lakes and rivers

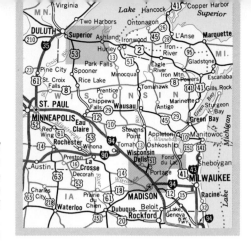

Legend says the word *Wisconsin* comes from an Algonquian word meaning "meeting of the waters." Although the true origin of Wisconsin's name is in doubt, it is certainly a state with an abundance of water—14,957 lakes, 7,400 rivers and streams, and 500 miles of shorefront on Lakes Superior and Michigan.

Superior, the westernmost, largest, and deepest of the Great Lakes, is a vital link in the waterway that connects America's heartland with the East. The first Europeans to see Wisconsin—French explorers, missionaries, and fur traders—came by water to the northern shores of the state. British traders followed them through the Great Lakes, and later, farmers from New England and New York came by way of the Erie Canal and Lake Michigan. In the 1840's steamboats brought the first European settlers to the lake ports of Milwaukee, Racine, and Kenosha. The Mississippi River brought miners to the rich lead deposits in the southwest corner of the state, as well as the speculators, tradesmen, and farmers who settled along the river.

Wisconsin's lakes and streams, like the Great Lakes themselves, are a legacy of the ice age glaciers that ground across this section of North America for thousands of years until the earth's temperature warmed up again about 10,000 years ago. These immense sheets of ice also left a thick blanket of fertile glacial soil. To this day Wisconsin is an important farm state and the nation's foremost producer of milk, butter, and cheese. The hayfields that seem to stretch endlessly on the horizon are responsible for making the state the nation's number one hay producer. This crop is converted by millions of contented cows into some 21 billion pounds of milk annually. Small wonder that the state is called America's Dairyland.

The state is also called the Badger State, but not for the reason you might think. While badgers may still be seen at night along country byways, it was the lead miners who built badgerlike houses in mudbanks during the lead rush of the 1820's that earned Wisconsin this sobriquet.

Winding east from the thriving inland seaport of Superior, Route 13 brushes near the very edge of Superior's deep blue waters. In places this country road climbs over high glacial hills and dips into valleys with rushing streams, most of which leap over picturesque waterfalls on their way to join the lake. Looking northward on the horizon, you may catch a glimpse of a Great Lakes ore boat or freighter low in the water with its heavy burden. From Bayfield the silhouettes to the east are shaped like ships, but are many times larger. These hazy blue shapes are Wisconsin's Apostle Islands, 22 wind- and water-sculptured bits of land beckoning campers, hikers, sailors, and fishermen.

Turning inland at Ashland, on beguiling Chequamegon Bay (often thought to be the "shining Big-Sea-Water" of Longfellow's well-known poem "The Song of Hiawatha"), the road leads through the heart of Chequamegon National Forest, a stronghold of towering balsam, oak, birch, pine, aspen, and spruce trees. Within its boundaries you might see a deer drinking at one of the forest's many trout streams.

North of Hayward, the Eau Claire lakes are the center of a fisherman's paradise where muskies (the muskellunge is the official state fish), bluegills, and perch are abundant.

1 Residents of Superior are fond of saying that theirs may not be the world's largest city, but that it is the city of the world's largest grain elevators, iron-ore docks, and coal-shipping terminal—and all on the world's largest body of fresh water. You can marvel at these wonders from vantage points on Barkers Island at the eastern outskirts of the city. From the island you can see the city's busy docks; the ships called lakers, which can measure 1,000 feet in length; freighters from the world's most distant ports of call; and the waterfront of Superior and of Duluth, Minnesota, across Superior Bay.

You can get an even closer look at this bustling transportation hub from the deck of one of the excursion boats that leave the island for two-hour

trips several times a day, except in winter when the lake may be frozen to a depth of several feet.

The S.S. *Meteor*, the only remaining whaleback freighter in the world, is permanently moored at the island and is now a maritime museum that offers tours daily during the summer. The ship's unique design, with sides that curve over the top to meet a narrow deck, was used for a fleet of 43 ships in the late 1800's. Most of the ships, which plied the lakes with cargoes of ore, sand, gravel, grain, coal, oil, and, eventually, automobiles, were launched in Superior. The *Meteor*, the only survivor, was used initially to carry iron ore. The ship has most of her original fittings and contains displays of Great Lakes memorabilia, such as several artifacts recovered from the bottom of the lake. On the wharf there is a display of the lake's aquatic life.

If you want a look at the landlubber's side of this historic region, a few blocks away from the waterfront you can meander through a restored 42-room 1890's mansion, modeled on a

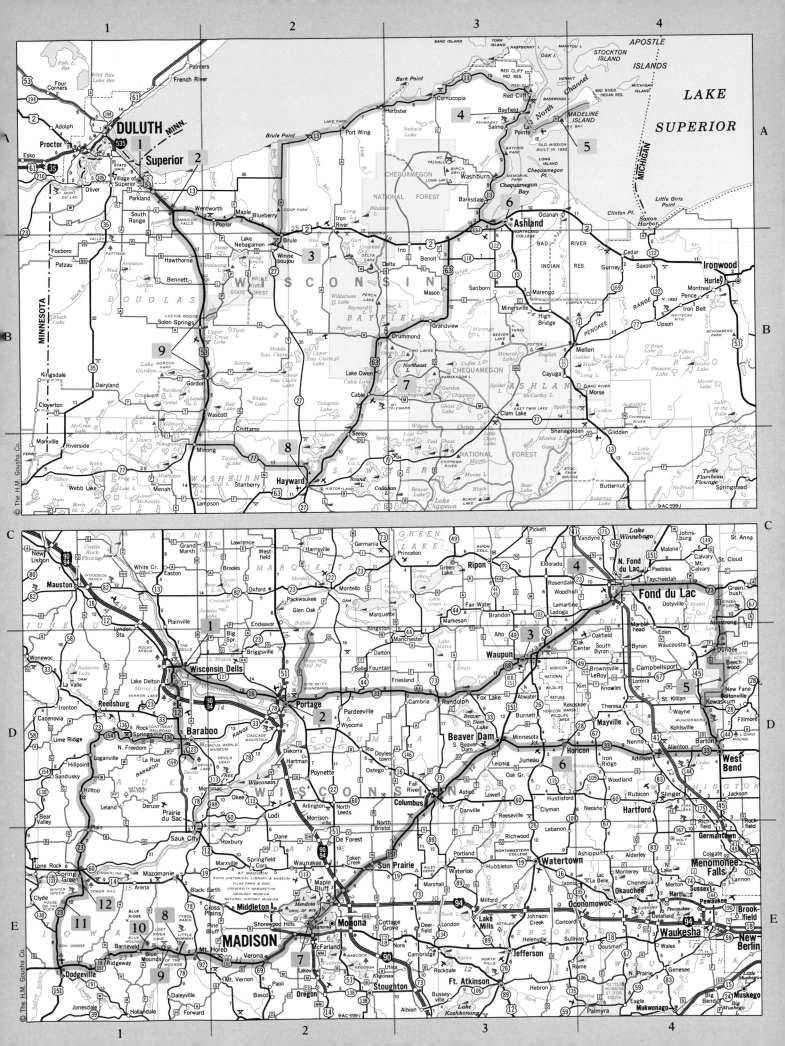

château near Paris. The mansion, which has been turned into a museum and the home of the Douglas County Historical Society, is closed Mondays and holidays, and in January and February.

2   Southeast of the city is a region of gently rolling woodlands and farms, crossed by many rushing streams and rivers on their way to the lake. At Amnicon Falls State Park, the Amnicon River crosses a steplike break in the 600-million-year-old red sandstone bedrock that forms the geologic foundation for most of this region. This immense fracture runs across Douglas County, but nowhere is it more strikingly exposed than here where the river descends the escarpment in shimmering cascades.

Hiking trails wind along the narrow stream and through a covered bridge to a small island below one of the most picturesque of the falls. Facilities for picnicking and camping are provided, and fishing is popular, particularly in the spring when lake walleyes ascend the stream to spawn. Entrance to Amnicon Falls State Park (and to most of Wisconsin's state parks and forests) requires a permit, which can be bought from the ranger on duty. The park is closed from November through March.

3   The trout in the Brule River, known as the River of the Presidents, have attracted famous anglers since President Ulysses S. Grant tried his luck here in the 1870's. Other national leaders who have fished in this stream are Presidents Calvin Coolidge (whose summer White House was located nearby) and Dwight D. Eisenhower and, recently, Vice President Walter Mondale. The fly-fishing season begins in April, and every year several trout are landed that tip the scale at 10 pounds or more.

Brule River State Forest straddles the stream for some 30 miles, from its headwaters at the Upper St. Croix Lake north to the Brule's mouth on Lake Superior. The river is a temptation for white-water canoeists and kayakers, since it has some of the most exciting runs in the Midwest. One long stretch is also suitable for novice and intermediate paddlers. Winter brings cross-country skiers to traverse many of the 200-odd miles of well-marked trails in the forest.

2. Dislodged rocks from the escarpment in the background add to the rugged beauty of Amnicon Falls.

4   On Route 13, the picturesque lake coves and inlets of the Bayfield Peninsula border a typical section of the great north woods. When you see road signs advising that you are subject to the tribal laws of the Red Cliff Indians, you know you are on their reservation, on the northern tip of the peninsula. Bayfield, a small fishing and tourist village on a cove of the North Channel, is a gateway to Wisconsin's spectacular Apostle Islands archipelago. The village, a quaint jumble of docks, fishermen's warehouses, craft shops, cheese stores, fish stores, restaurants, and residences, fills the natural amphitheater surrounding the harbor. If luck is with you, you might be in town the first week in October for the Apple Festival and a taste of the best of the local homemade apple pies. Another tasty time to visit is late in June when the boiling kettles of the Fish Festival spread their appetizing aromas.

You can plan your trip to the Apostle Islands at the National Park Service's headquarters in the old County Courthouse. Twenty of the 22 islands are part of a national lakeshore. Like most of Wisconsin's terrain, these rustic, remote, and unspoiled islands were created in the ice age by glaciers that piled up a thick blanket of rocky debris on platforms of sandstone bedrock. Since then, the elements have sculpted the islands into a fan-

tasy world of red sandstone cliffs, inlets, bays, and sandy beaches.

During the summer, boats leave Bayfield daily for a variety of narrated trips through the islands lasting from a couple of hours to all day. Shuttle ferries take campers, hikers, bird-watchers, swimmers, beachcombers, and picnickers to Oak and Stockton islands. On Stockton, you can swim and walk on one of the most attractive beaches on all the Great Lakes—and certainly the noisiest. Its singing sands literally squeal under your feet. Water-taxi service from Bayfield takes the more adventurous day-trippers and campers to several of the smaller islands where camping is permitted, but which have no cleared campsites or trails.

5   Madeline Island, the largest of the Apostles, is not a part of the national lakeshore but is one of the most popular destinations.

The 14-mile-long island is located 2.6 miles (15 minutes) off Bayfield and is served hourly by car ferries that are large enough to carry trailers and motor homes. From about New Year's Day until spring there is a road across the ice, and you can drive from Bayfield to La Pointe, the island's port, which has about 150 year-round residents. This part of the lake is usually the first to freeze and the last to thaw.

On the island there are about 45 miles of road (mostly paved) winding along the beautiful coastline. You can explore the island for several days; there are several motels as well as campsites at Big Bay State Park and the municipal park. Five miles of hiking trails wind along the lagoon behind the 1½-mile-long Big Bay Beach and the eroded sandstone cliffs at the picnic grounds at Big Bay Point.

An historical museum lies just uphill from the La Pointe ferry dock. A half-mile south of the dock is an Indian burial ground where small wooden structures were built to house the spirits of the dead.

Some of the buildings in Bayfield and in Washburn, to the south, may remind a few travelers of home. Many of the public structures are built of the distinctive sandstone from the same Wisconsin quarries that supplied the material for the famous brownstones of New York and Boston at the turn of the century.

5. At Big Bay State Park on historic Madeline Island, a thin layer of soil on red sandstone more than 500 million years old supports dense forests of white pine, birch, spruce, and cedar. The shallow-rooted trees are frequently blown over.

6   Ashland, at the head of Chequamegon Bay, offers yet another pleasant access to the fishing, boating, and swimming facilities of Lake Superior. The Chamber of Commerce office at 111 West Front Street has information about tours through an American Can Company paper mill and the Munsingwear Company, both located here. In early January sled dogs come to town with their masters for the annual dog sled races.

7   Southwest of Ashland the route crosses what residents call the Great Divide. North of this ridge, which Route 63 crosses at Drummond, all the runoff flows into the Great Lakes. On the south side the drainage system leads to the Mississippi. Not far east of Cable, Mount Telemark rises steeply against the horizon. This is a popular ski-resort area with superb downhill runs and several cross-country trails. In season you can also sail, waterski, cycle, ride horseback, and play golf and tennis here.

8   To stand in the world's only four-story-high concrete, steel, and fiberglass fish is an unusual experience. This 140-feet-long version of a leaping muskie is a major attraction of the National Fresh Water Fishing Hall of Fame in Hayward. The fish houses a museum, and the observation gallery is in its mouth. In June, during the annual Muskie Festival, you might also get to see some of the big ones firsthand. In the museum and nearby buildings there are more than 100 antique outboard motors,

200 mounted species of fish, and other fishing memorabilia. Here too the world records for freshwater sport fishing are documented.

At Historyland, just east of town, you can see how Wisconsin residents lived in an earlier age. Historical displays include a logging camp and a Chippewa Indian village. Indians from all over the United States attend

the All Tribes Powwow, held on July 4 each year, to sing traditional music and to dance. Later in the month lumberjacks convene here for the annual World Lumberjack Championships, to test their skills in sawing, logrolling, chopping, and tree-climbing competitions. A paddle-wheel steamboat, the *Namakagon Queen*, leaves Historyland hourly on river cruises. Canoeists can have a more intimate river experience on the Namekagon, one of the nation's first designated wild rivers. The Chamber of Commerce office at the intersection of Routes 27 and 63 can give you the locations of several canoe liveries and outfitters.

9   Going north toward Superior from Minong, Route 53 crosses through some of the best boating, fishing, and hiking (or in winter, cross-country skiing and snowmobiling) country in the state. Here nearly 200 miles of rivers and some 75 lakes are easily accessible. Some of the finest facilities can be found in the Brule River State Forest Annex at Gordon and in the Brule River State Forest, whose southwestern gateway is just north of Solon Springs.

8. World Lumberjack Championships at Historyland. Above: Springboard, wedged into notch, is used for footing. First man to chop through log wins. Top right: Sisters compete in championship log-rolling contest. Bottom right: First man who cuts three slabs, each two inches thick or less, with a chain saw wins.

203

In southwestern Wisconsin you can see countryside that was not touched by the ice age glaciers, and this is a rarity in the Badger State. Nevertheless, this sizable pocket, which geologists call the Driftless Area, was indirectly shaped by the glaciers. Their rushing meltwaters helped to carve the Wisconsin River valley, the rock palisades and gorges of the Wisconsin Dells, and various distinctive landforms in the region. East of the Driftless Area, in the region of Kettle Moraine State Park, the glacial landforms have a completely different character.

1 The spectacular scenery of the Wisconsin Dells began to take shape even before the ice ages. Millions of years ago this part of North America

1. The layered sandstone of Grotto Rock, mirrored here on the dark blue waters of the Wisconsin River, is a typical formation of the Lower Dells. In the background is one of several modern sight-seeing boats that cruise these waters.

lay at the bottom of an immense inland sea. Sand and other bits of rocky detritus washed into the sea and hardened over thousands of years to form thick beds of layered sandstone. Long after the sea retreated, immense sheets of ice ground their way south covering much of the continent, but left this part of the sandstone bedrock unscathed as a rocky island in a sea of ice. As the earth's

climate slowly warmed, the glacial meltwater surged over the Driftless Area, carving out the Wisconsin River valley and the astonishing rock formations at the Dells. The bizarre shapes evolved as the relatively soft layers of rock eroded more quickly than the harder parts. In some places the monoliths are so top-heavy that they look as if they might topple into the Wisconsin River's deep blue waters.

A hydroelectric dam, dating back to 1909, divides the Dells region into the Upper Dells, where the river squeezes past towering cliffs and gradually widens to a broad lake, and the Lower Dells, a narrow, deep valley. The Dells are one of the Midwest's most popular attractions, and they can be enjoyed in a variety of

ways. Not only are there motor launches, ducks (amphibious vehicles), a narrow-gauge railway, and single-engine seaplanes, but also an immense gondola that rises on a 335-foot steel tower. The free Chamber of Commerce guide, *Dells Territory*, is available at most of the businesses along Broadway in the town of Wisconsin Dells, and provides a concise listing of these and other facilities.

2 The Wisconsin River, which is a tributary of the Mississippi, became a vital transportation link as Europeans started to migrate to Wisconsin some three centuries ago.

The Fox River provided another access to the wilderness for trappers and hunters, but goods had to be hauled a short distance overland between the two rivers. This portage gave the community its name, and today Portage residents proudly call their town "the point where the North begins." You can follow the scenic Fox River on County Route F.

Route 33 east leads to the restored Old Indian Agency House, built in 1832. From this point you can see the canal linking the Fox and Wisconsin rivers. The Agency House is closed from November through May.

A few years earlier, in 1828, Fort Winnebago was built under the supervision of a young West Point graduate, Lt. Jefferson Davis. The original log cabin where the fort's surgeon held office hours still stands. There is also a restoration of a garrison school that was used in the mid-1800's.

3 Along the road leading to Waupun, the rolling countryside presents fine vistas of some of the richest farmland in America. In the summertime the fields are mostly covered with corn, the nation's most valuable crop, stretching in green and golden-tasseled carpets for as far as the eye can see. The signs in the cornfields identify the brand of seed that has been planted and the cryptic numbers identify the variety of hybrid. This is for the benefit of local farmers who are potential customers for seed corn. In Waupun, at Shaler Park on North Madison Street, is the first bronze casting of James Earle Fraser's famous statue "End of the Trail." If the Indian on horseback looks familiar, it is because the artist also designed the Indian Head nickel.

4 In the early 19th century French traders named Fond du Lac "end of the lake," to describe the city's position at the lower tip of Lake Winnebago. Today you can enjoy the lake at a municipal park, which has canoe rentals and facilities for boating and picnicking, as well as a children's playground and a "petting" zoo. The strong European influence on this part of America is evident in the

Deciphering a glacial landscape

Much of Wisconsin's countryside was shaped by the action of ice sheets during the Pleistocene era. The remnants of such action, as shown in the sketch below, include *cravasses*—great chasms created by glacial action; *moraines*—rippling hills of debris left by melting ice; *drumlins*—long wedged-shaped deposits of glacial debris; *eskers*—long winding ridges of gravel left by meltwaters of the retreating glacier; *kettles*—depressions formed when lumps of ice remained as the glacier melted away; and *kames*—cone-shaped mounds left by meltwaters that deposited gravel into ice holes.

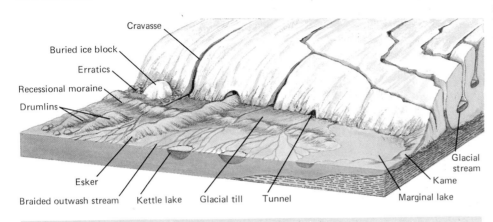

Episcopal Cathedral of St. Paul the Apostle, an impressive Gothic edifice located on West Division Street. Life-size wood carvings of the Apostles made in Oberammergau, Germany, and the stained-glass windows, the murals, and the cloister garden reflect strong ties to European customs, art, and craftsmanship.

In comparison to the European influence is the straightforward expression of frontier life that is found at the historic Galloway House and Village, located at 336 Old Pioneer Road. In this living museum are a restored 30-room Victorian mansion and a pioneer settlement complete with working gristmill and printshop.

5 Driving east toward Kettle Moraine State Forest (Northern Unit) in the vicinity of Dundee, the landscape is an outstanding example of the awesome power of Wisconsin's glaciers. Here you can see moraines, low, rippling hills of boulders, gravel, and clay deposited by the retreating ice; kettles, hollows left by great chunks of ice imbedded in the earth; kames, conical hills formed by streams washing gravel into ice holes; and eskers, serpentine gravel ridges deposited by the retreating glaciers torrential meltwaters.

The forest is part of the Ice Age National Scientific Reserve, and maps and other information about the area are available at the headquarters, about four miles south of Dundee on County Route G. There is also an Ice Age Interpretive Center a quarter of a mile south of Dundee on Route 67.

The well-marked auto tours help illustrate the vivid contrast between this glacial area and the Driftless Area at Wisconsin Dells. A wide variety of wildlife may also catch your eye. In the spring you may see a violet or a robin, the state flower and bird. In the fall, which starts early here, the sugar maple (*Acer saccharum*), the state tree, stands out in shades of brilliant red. Facilities for hiking, camping, picnicking, horseback riding, and boating—and in the winter, cross-country skiing and snowmobiling—are located throughout the forest.

6 Continuing south and west, the route leads through Horicon, at the southern tip of the Horicon Marsh Wildlife Area. Until the mid-19th century this great marshland on the headwaters of the Rock River was teeming with fish, beaver, and muskrat, and produced bountiful amounts of wild rice. On a major flyway for migratory waterfowl, the area was visited by ducks and geese in flocks so large that they darkened the sky. In 1846 an earthen dam, built to harness the waterpower of the river, flooded the area, and much of the wildlife moved on. The dam was opposed by many people, and in 1869 it was taken down. The area began to revert to marshland, and in the late 1930's the state and federal governments bought land to set aside as a reserve. Today it attracts nature lovers from all over the country, especially in the fall when thousands of Canada geese stop here on their annual migration south. Visitors can see much of the wildlife up close from well-marked hiking trails.

Route 151 going southwest toward Madison passes through rich farmland and extensive dairyland typical of Wisconsin.

6. *Although the Horicon National Wildlife Refuge was intended primarily as a stopping place for migrating Canada geese, shown here resting on the refuge marsh, it has proven to be beneficial to other waterfowl and wildlife.*

7 If you have never been to Madison, you are in for a pleasant surprise. As you approach through the outskirts of the city, the usual clutter of office buildings and businesses seems to melt away when you catch sight of the gleaming white granite dome of the capitol directly before you. In the center of the Capitol Park on a hill dominating the city, the capitol has an observation deck below the dome that affords striking views of Lake Mendota to the north and Lake Monona to the south. The dome is capped by Daniel Chester French's gilded bronze statue "Forward," which personifies the state's one-word motto. Tours of the capitol are conducted several times a day year-round. The observation deck is closed in winter.

Madison's twin lakes, with waterfowl, swimmers, water-skiers, fishermen, and the billowing colorful sails of fleets of sailboats, are unexpected here in the political center of the state. A few blocks west of the capitol, at the edge of Lake Mendota, is the campus of the University of Wisconsin, said by many to be one of the most beautiful in the Midwest. Campus tour maps and parking information are available at the Park Street entrance to the Memorial Union. Traveling along Observatory and Willow drives affords remarkable views of the city and its colorful lakefront parks. At the U.S. Forest Products Laboratory on University Avenue and Walnut Street, the only federal lab of its kind, you can take a tour and see scientists working to develop new products that can be made from wood.

8 In the rolling farmland and the forests around Mount Horeb, a winding country road turns north from Route 18–151 and leads to the sheltered glen of Nissedahle (Norwegian for "Valley of the Elves"). The name was chosen by Isak Dahle, who was raised in Mount Horeb, made his fortune in the insurance business in Chicago, and bought the farmstead of Osten Olson Haugen, a Norwegian immigrant who settled on the land here in 1856. Dahle, a knowledgeable and discriminating collector, restored about a dozen of the original log buildings and made this picturesque place his summer home. The pioneer homestead, with its outstanding collection of early American and Scandinavian antiques, was later opened to the public as Little Norway. The buildings include a log farmhouse, a barn, and a summer cottage, all displaying fascinating household items from a bygone era.

Little Norway's centerpiece is the Norway Building, a model of a 12th-century Norwegian stave church, carved by hand in Norway and reassembled in the United States for the World's Columbian Exposition, which was held in 1893. The church, once displayed in Paris, was built so it could be taken apart and reassembled. However, the last team of carpenters to do this accidentally switched some parts. If you have sharp eyes, you might be able to spot the mistake when you see the interior. If not, ask one of the costumed tour guides.

9 One of the most dramatic features of the Driftless Area is the Cave of the Mounds. In 1939 quarrymen blasting in the limestone bedrock of Blue Mounds were amazed to discover a vast cavern system that had lain undetected for centuries. Such limestone caverns are particularly rare in a state where much of the landscape was altered by glaciers. The cave, now open to the public, has some dozen large rooms dramatically lighted for daily tours. On October 31, Halloween, there are special tours with the lights turned off and the guides masquerading as creatures of the night. Closed on major holidays.

10 You can get a good overview of the Driftless Area at Blue Mound State Park (closed November to May), a mile north of the village of Blue Mounds. Here on a thick deposit of Niagara limestone, the same kind of 400-million-year-old rock that forms the ledge of Niagara Falls, are two observation towers at an elevation of 1,716 feet. This is the highest point in southern Wisconsin. On clear days you can see the capitol dome gleaming in the sunlight some 22 miles to the east. The park also has facilities for nature hiking, picnicking, and camping, and for swimming in a large, heated outdoor pool. The roller coasterlike roads that twist

Making Swiss cheese—a fine art

For more than 500 years the making of wheel Swiss cheese has remained unchanged. With knowledge gained from years of experience and careful training, the cheese maker chooses the right milk, the correct amount of "starter" (whey containing rod and coccus bacteria) and rennet (an enzyme used as a coagulant), and the exact moment for each step in the procedure. All this is part of the great tradition developed in the land for which the cheese is named.

So-called grass milk, produced while the cattle are grazing, produces the finest cheese. Fodder milk, produced in winter, does not give the same high quality.

After being clarified, which removes 10 percent of the cream, the milk is heated in huge copper kettles, the whey (liquid) and the curd (solids) are separated, and the curd is placed in a round mold. After 24 hours it is put into a salt solution, where it remains for three days. It is then removed, placed in a large round wooden form, and for one week kept in a cellar at a temperature of 45°F.

During the next six weeks, while the cheese is being cured at a temperature of 77°F, the "eyes" are formed by propionic acid created by the bacteria. Finally the wheels are stacked and left for at least six months to age.

The resulting Swiss cheese wheel, weighing approximately 200 pounds, required some 2,500 pounds of milk and called for more expertise, more time, and more effort than of any other kind of cheese made in America.

A cheese harp, a device with wire strings, is used to separate the curd and the whey.

8. Top: On the roof of the Norway Building, dramatic dragon heads with tongues of fire guard against evil spirits. Above: The colorful master bedroom displays unusual mementos and antiques of the pioneer period. In the kitchen the cast-iron cookstove, beautifully embellished with acorn motifs, has a reservoir for warm water. Note, too, the wood box.

tacular views of the surrounding terrain. The house and adjacent attractions, including a large collection of mechanical music-makers and a street of shops recalling the gaslit era of the 1800's, are open to the public. Many of the features here are of particular interest to families traveling with children. Closed from December until April.

12 Just south of Spring Green is Taliesin, the home and studio of Frank Lloyd Wright, one of America's best-known architects. Watch for the sign to Frank Lloyd Wright Buildings. Mr. Wright, who died in 1959 at the age of 89, spent his boyhood years near here in the rolling hills of southern Wisconsin. The landforms and wide horizons of the area are said to have greatly influenced the design of his "prairie style" houses in the early 1900's. In turn, the advanced ideas in these structures became a major influence on modern concepts of residential design.

Here on 700 acres of farmland is the Frank Lloyd Wright Foundation school, where students come from far and near to study architecture. Tours are available in summer when the staff and students return from their winter sojourn at Taliesin West near Scottsdale, Arizona.

North of Spring Green, the rugged rocks and rills give way to a more gently undulating landscape where the countryside abounds with cornfields and hayfields, herds of Holstein cattle, dairy barns, and silos.

through the Driftless Area toward the Wisconsin River valley are in dramatic contrast to the flat expanses where glaciers prevailed.

11 The House on the Rock is built on and into one of the Driftless features: a 59-foot chimney rock overlooking the Wyoming Valley. Begun in the 1940's as an artist's private home, the house now has 13 rooms built on many levels around and through the rock itself. There are enormous fireplaces, interior waterfalls that splash into pools, and spec-

The curd, in the "dipping" cloth, is hoisted from the whey, which is left in the kettle.

After being dropped into a round mold, the curd is pressed to remove excess whey.

The wheels of Swiss cheese are aged for six months at a temperature of 40° F.

207

Essence of the Midwest

There is beautiful scenery in Iowa, but most typical of the state is its amazingly productive farmland

Iowans claim that their state's name is derived from a Siouan word meaning "beautiful land," and beautiful it is. Continental glaciers deposited tons of earth that combined with prairie grass, creating extraordinarily fertile soil. Hard-working people transformed the land into a meticulously cared for grid of farms that produces more food than any other state except California. Areas formed by early glacial deposits and erosional patterns of the rivers are in contrast to the flat fields formed by later glaciation, where corn, soybeans, and hay are now grown.

Throughout the state, many of Iowa's original settlers preserved various aspects of their ethnic heritage. This variety of cultures adds further interest to experiencing Iowa from the road.

From scenic and historic sites in Dubuque, Iowa's oldest city, this route heads south to the Victorian Gothic architecture of New Melleray Abbey, a Trappist monastery.

Nestled in a pleasant valley, the Manchester Fish Hatchery is one of the oldest trout hatcheries in America, and Backbone State Park is the oldest state park in Iowa. Iowa history and culture is recalled at Fort Atkinson, Spillville, and Decorah, and the Yellow River State Forest marks the beginning of spectacular scenery typical of land along the upper Mississippi River.

1 Built along the bluffs of the Mississippi River, Dubuque is the oldest city in Iowa. French Canadian Julien Dubuque settled here in 1788 to exploit local lead mines.

These mines were the reason for the shot tower here, one of only a few remaining in the United States. Located beside the river on Fourth Street, the nine-story stone-and-brick tower was built in 1856. To make shot, lead was melted at the bottom of the tower, drawn to the top, and poured through a perforated vat to divide it into drops. As the drops fell they took on a spherical shape, which was solidified by the cold water in a tub at the bottom of the tower.

The Fourth Street cable car, which dates from 1893, runs from Cable Car Square, an area of boutiques and art shops, to Fenlon Place, at the top of a bluff that overlooks the city and the Mississippi.

High above the Mississippi on the north end of Dubuque is 164-acre Eagle Point Park. A sign on Route 3 indicates a turn on East 20th Street to the Eagle's Point Bridge to Wisconsin, which is also the way to the park. Two-tenths of a mile from the highway, East 20th Street divides at a Y-junction. Go left to Rhomberg and proceed for a mile and a half, where a sign points to the park. On the way to the park entrance you pass the Mathias Ham House Museum, an interesting and varied exhibition of the region's early history.

Eagle Point Park presents a panorama of the Mississippi River and three states—Iowa, Illinois, and Wisconsin. You may see towboats guiding barges through Lock and Dam Number 11. Many picnic sites are scattered among the shade trees of this bluff-top city park. In summer colorful flowers are displayed in long ledge gardens.

1. Like figures on a wedding cake, statues decorate the brick-and-stone Dubuque County Courthouse on Central Street.

2 New Melleray Abbey is a monastery community of about 50 Cistercian monks. Abundant fields and orchards are cared for by the monks, who view manual labor as part of their spirituality. Another important part of the community's spiritual life is assembling several times daily to chant the Divine Office, a service comprised primarily of psalms, hymns, and Bible readings. The monks' Trappist dedication to silence limits the amount of talking during many of their daily activities.

Trappists welcome visitors to hear their singing during their frequent daily services.

3 The Basilica of St. Francis Xavier in Dyersville is one of the most imposing Roman Catholic churches in America. Completed in 1889, the huge church was a monumental achievement for its builders, who used only ropes and pulleys to lift the stone for the basilica's 212-foot spires. The sanctuary's elaborate ceiling was painted by a sister and brother team from Wisconsin.

In recognition of the church's magnificent Gothic architecture, Pope Pius XII in 1956 granted it the rank of minor basilica, of which there are only 26 in the United States.

SPECIAL FEATURES

ROAD GUIDE	▬▬▬	HIGHLIGHT	**1**
STATE PARKS With Campsites ▲ Without Campsites △		SKI AREAS	𝄃
RECREATION AREAS With Campsites ▲ Without Campsites △		SCHEDULED AIRLINE STOPS	✈
		OTHER AIRPORTS	✈
SELECTED REST AREAS	✕	BOAT RAMPS	◢
POINTS OF INTEREST	⊡	INFORMATION CENTER	⊛

ROAD CLASSIFICATION

CONTROLLED ACCESS HIGHWAYS Interstate interchange numbers are mileposts.	**5** Interchanges
OTHER DIVIDED HIGHWAYS	
PAVED HIGHWAYS	
LOCAL ROADS In unfamiliar areas inquire locally before using these roads	Paved Gravel Dirt

MILEAGE

MILEAGE BETWEEN TOWNS AND JUNCTIONS	3 4	MILEAGE ● 35 ● BETWEEN DOTS

SCALE

ONE INCH 14 MILES	0	5	10		20
ONE INCH 22 KILOMETERS 0	5	10	20		32

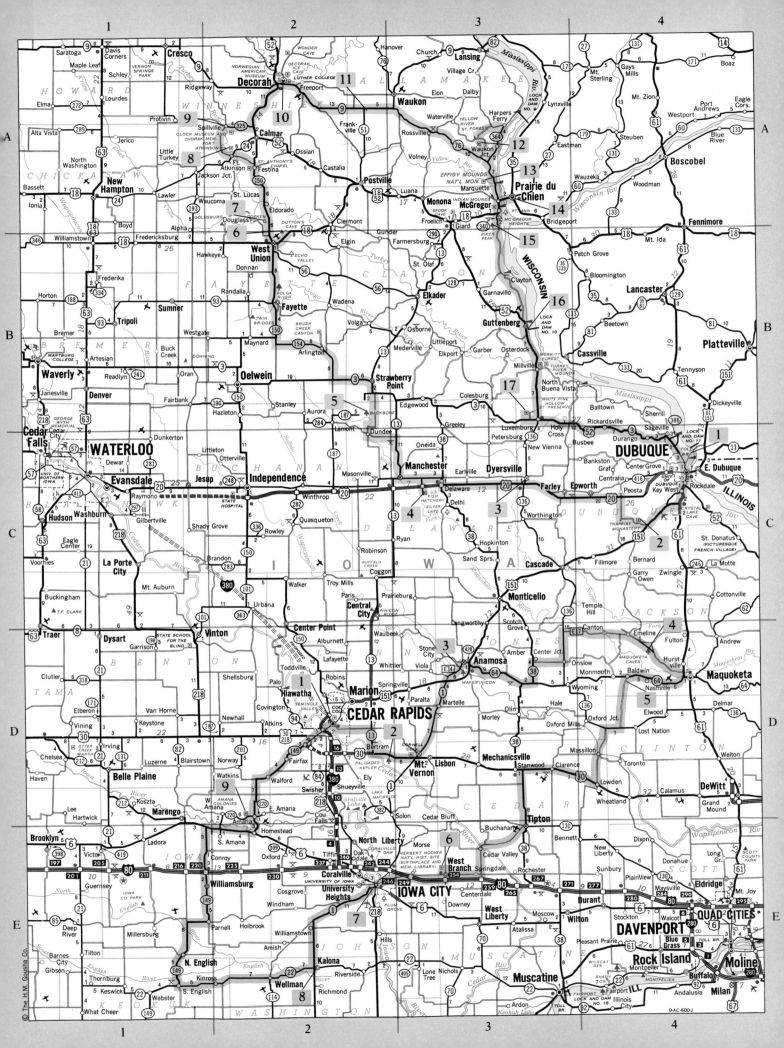

7. *Eldorado, the very model of a midwestern village despite its exotic name, is caught in a timeless moment under the Iowa sun. The view is from hilltop Goekin Park, a roadside rest and picnic ground north of West Union. The white-painted houses and the bountiful farmland seem to promise that at least a part of America is somehow immune from the harsher winds of change.*

4 Established in 1897, the Manchester Fish Hatchery is one of the oldest in America. Its brick buildings and concrete raceways lie in a lovely shaded hollow where the huge brood trout, which supply half a million eggs each year, are easy to see.

Thirteen streams in four counties throughout northeastern Iowa are stocked from this hatchery with trout of catchable size. These streams are replenished at least once a week.

5 Backbone State Park includes 1,600 acres of natural beauty around a high ridge crested by vertebralike boulders. The backbone is almost surrounded by the Maquoketa River, which flows southeast along the slightly more than quarter-mile length of the ridge before cutting through a saddle and flowing in the opposite direction. On the eastern side of the backbone the river is dammed, forming a 85-acre boating and fishing lake.

The cliffs of Backbone are popular with rock climbers, who may be seen practicing on some of the more precipitous places. Stony ledges covered with vines, and wild flowers enhance the beauty of the park's hiking trails. A fish exhibit has display ponds, and there is a popular nine-hole golf course and public country club adjacent to the park.

6 Three miles east of West Union a sign along Route 18 indicates a left turn onto a gravel road leading to Dutton's Cave Park. Lovely, well-shaded lawns surround picnic sites. Tree-arched grass trails lead along a spring-fed stream to Dutton's Cave, which was created in the cliff as limestone was dissolved.

7 Goekin Park, a pleasant picnic stop, sits on a hilltop and boasts a particularly fine view of typical Iowa farmland. Below the hill is the village of Eldorado, a classic picture of rural midwestern America. Church steeples rise above neat homes and a patchwork pattern of farmlands.

8 The road to Fort Atkinson is marked by an inconspicuous sign along the road to Spillville.

Fort Atkinson was built in an existing 40-mile-wide strip of neutral ground for warring Sauk-Fox and Sioux Indian tribes. It eventually became a reservation for the Winnebagos, enemy of both tribes.

In 1840 the U.S. government built a fort here to protect the Winnebagos. Fort Atkinson was constructed of locally quarried fossiliferous limestone. When the Winnebagos were relocated in 1849, the army left the post.

A barracks of the fort is now a museum, which tells the story of the fort's history and purpose.

9 Retaining its Czechoslovakian heritage, Spillville is built around a charming public square that features a World War I memorial bandstand.

In 1893 the famous Czech composer Antonín Dvořák spent the summer here while putting the final touches on his *New World Symphony.* Dvořák played some of his other compositions on the organ at St. Wenceslaus Church in the village. Picturesque Riverside Park has a memorial to the composer. This is also a nice place to do some trout fishing.

10 Decorah is a lovely, predominately Norwegian-American town built in a unique setting. Continental glaciers crossed this land but left few remains of their passing. The topography was shaped by the upper Iowa and Mississippi rivers and their tributaries, exposing layers of sedimentary rock along valley walls. Highlights of the geological phenomena include an unusual ice cave, Dunning's Spring, and Wonder Cave.

Vesterheim, a Norwegian-American museum, has excellent collections of ethnic furnishings, folk art painting, costumes, toys, tools, church furnishings, and other artifacts. It also has several restored buildings, including an old mill that houses an exhibit of Norwegian pioneer industry, a blacksmith shop, and numerous structures typical of Norwegian-American architecture. The last weekend in July is the Nordic Fest, an impressive Norwegian-style celebration.

The beautiful valley setting of Decorah's Fish Hatchery, which exhibits fish in rearing ponds, draws many visitors who are not anglers. There is, however, good trout fishing from a stocked stream on the grounds.

In the area of Decorah you can see barns built about a century ago by Norwegian immigrants in a style typical of mid-19th century barns in their native Norway. They feature a dormer in the middle of the roof above a large door approached via an earth ramp. Usually the foundation is made of limestone blocks.

11 Many dairy cows graze alongside Route 9. Black-and-white Holsteins are the most common, but Guernseys, Jerseys, and Brown Swiss are also seen.

A little more than 13 miles from Decorah, Ludlow Community Dairy, Inc., which produces fine Cheddar cheese, welcomes visitors. Morning is the best time to go. Milk trucks make their rounds at dawn, returning with rivers of milk to convert into cheese.

To reach Ludlow, turn south on Route 51 and drive for 0.2 of a mile. Turn east on a gravel road and drive for a short distance.

12 A gravel road to Yellow River State Forest is indicated by a sign 11.6 miles southeast of the junction of Routes 9 and 76. You enter the Paint Creek Unit of the forest about one mile later, as the road descends into a woodsy hollow.

The 4,000-acre Paint Creek Unit of Yellow River State Forest has a wide variety of coniferous and deciduous trees clinging to steep limestone bluffs. More than 24 miles of marked hiking trails wind up the hills and into hollows, passing through woods and meadows and pausing at scenic overlooks. Trail heads are at headquarters, which is along a clearly marked side road that lies a little over a mile into the unit.

The forest also contains picnic and camping sites, a maze of scenic, unpaved roads, and trout streams.

At Harpers Ferry the loop meets a section of the Mississippi River that is part of the Upper Mississippi Wild

10. Turbulent water, which once powered gristmills on this site, tumbles down rocks at Dunning's Spring, near Decorah.

Life and Fish Refuge, the longest national wildlife refuge in the United States—284 miles, stretching from Wabasha, Minnesota, to Rock Island, Illinois. The refuge contains an unusual mixture of flora and fauna. Easily spotted during the summer months are great blue herons, egrets, and turkey vultures. In early March, during the spring migration, up to 200 American bald eagles as well as canvasback ducks can be seen. There are many good spots along the river to pull over and watch for wildlife. Binoculars are helpful.

13 Effigy Mounds National Monument is a remarkable place. Ancient Indian burial mounds from the Hopewellian culture—1000 B.C. to A.D. 600—are near the parking lot, which is also near the visitor center. A stop here to see the exhibits and an audiovisual presentation can enrich your understanding of the area before beginning a tour.

The one-hour walk on Fire Point Trail, which climbs to the bluff top, passes many mounds. Of the 191 mounds preserved here, 29 are in the form of bears and birds.

Besides the mounds, wooded bluff-top trails offer spectacular vistas. Trailside exhibits explain the Hopewellian culture and interesting natural phenomena. Guided walks are given by rangers during the summer months.

12. This wind-bent cedar is among the wide variety of trees that cling to the slopes of limestone bluffs in the sprawling Paint Creek Unit of Yellow River State Forest. The area, near Waukon Junction, also harbors deer, wild turkeys, and ruffed grouse.

14 A scenic drive along the Mississippi leads to a 1.7-mile-long bridge built in 1977 that crosses the river between Marquette, Iowa, and Prairie du Chien, Wisconsin. Inconspicuous signs mark the way to the lavish Villa Louis.

Built in 1870 by the son of a wealthy fur trader and speculator, the Villa Louis is one of the most splendid examples of Victorian architecture and furnishings in America. It is a showplace of fine furniture, art objects, crystal chandeliers, paintings, and rare books.

The Prairie du Chien Museum is located in the villa's coach house. Exhibitions and dioramas portray the history of southwestern Wisconsin. A study of fur trading in the upper Mississippi River valley can be seen in a separate fur museum.

sandstone. There are campsites here, and nearby backwaters reachable from McGregor are great for catching panfish and bass.

16 Between Minneapolis and the mouth of the Missouri River at St. Louis, the U.S. Army Corps of Engineers has converted the Mississippi into a series of 29 dam-and-lock combinations, creating a nine-foot-deep channel that is used by barges transporting such cargo as grain, coal, metal, and petroleum. Pleasure craft ranging from houseboats to canoes also use these watery steps.

A good place to watch lock operations is the observation platform at Lock and Dam Number 10 at Guttenberg. From Route 52 turn left onto Goethe Street and go five blocks. At the T-junction at River Park Drive, turn left and go one more block.

To the west of the pleasant city of Cedar Rapids are three state parks, each of which features the limestone cliffs and caves that are prominent in this part of Iowa, and the Eden Valley Refuge, a wild preserve harbored among these limestone bluffs. Historical and cultural highlights dominate the southern part of the tour, which passes Herbert Hoover National Historic Site, the Old Capitol and the territorial governor's home in Iowa City, Amishland around Kalona, and the Amana Colonies.

1 Cedar Rapids, an attractive city on the Cedar River, is a manufacturing center and marketing point for the rich agricultural lands that surround it. The city has 62 parks, with a total of 3,500 acres of land for recreation. One of the most appealing of these is Bever Park, with densely wooded areas and oak trees shading the expanses of green lawns. To reach the park from downtown, follow First Avenue, the main street, and turn right onto 19th Street S.E. From 19th turn left onto Bever Avenue and follow the signs.

The Czeck Village, on the south side of Cedar River between 15th and 16th avenues, is an interesting historic area where Old World influence is still retained. Tours are available.

2 From First Avenue in Cedar Rapids, 10th Street S.E. leads into Mount Vernon Road, which intersects Route 13. A right turn onto Route 13 leads through rolling cornfields to Route 30. Take the East 30 exit to Palisades-Kepler State Park.

The park's entrance leads through oak and maple forests to picnic shelters, campsites, cabins, and a nature study area. The first right turn beyond the ranger housing leads past Indian burial mounds. From the end of this road it is a short walk to limestone cliffs where there is a view of the Cedar River.

3 Where Route 1 meets Route 151, take Route E 34 for 3.4 miles to the Wapsipinicon State Park entrance.

The park offers hiking, fishing, nature study, climbing limestone and sandstone cliffs, and exploring caves that honeycomb the bluffs. Wild flowers, particularly red columbine, color the cliffs and forest floor in spring. During the fall, deciduous

15. *Pikes Peak State Park near McGregor offers a panoramic view of islands and bayous of the Mississippi. The peak rises 485 feet above the river, which makes it considerably lower than Colorado's peak of the same name—but the vista is no less memorable.*

15 The drive to Pikes Peak State Park's 485-foot summit begins at the south end of Main Street in McGregor, Iowa. Offering a spectacular view of the Mississippi and Wisconsin rivers, Pikes Peak is the highest bluff on the Mississippi. The park's heavy forest is ablaze with color in the fall.

Other attractions include two trails leading past river overlooks, waterfalls, effigy mounds, and cliffs of fossiliferous limestone and colored

17 White Pine Hollow State Preserve is a hilly region containing the largest remaining stand of white pine in Iowa. The countryside surrounding the preserve is highlighted by neat farms with red barns trimmed in white. The preserve itself is open only to foot travel. Well-marked gravel roads along Route 52 south of the town of Millville lead to the boundaries of the preserve, where several pathways begin.

4. The corn is green and golden-tasseled in fields of rich, dark soil. Iowa grows more than a billion bushels of this crop a year, making it the leading corn-producing state. Much of it is used to feed hogs, which Iowa raises at the rate of about 20 million annually. Of the two types of storage bins shown above, the more modern ones (on the right) are sheathed with metal.

trees form a golden ceiling over the hiking trails.

Wapsipinicon's other attractions include picnic and camp sites and a nine-hole golf course.

4 Four miles north of Onslow, Route E 17 leaves the flat cornfields that flank Route 136 and winds through more hilly terrain. The road drops to Canton, crosses the Maquoketa River, and passes through the little village of Emeline. A right turn onto a gravel road 2.2 miles beyond Emeline leads to the west entrance of Maquoketa Caves State Park. If you miss this turn, a right turn on Route Y 31 leads to the park's main entrance.

The 192-acre park centers on a steep ravine that contains 13 caves. Pathways and electric lights make passage through the major caves easy, but to explore some of them a good flashlight is needed.

A natural bridge and a balanced 17-ton limestone block are features along the ravine walls. White pine and aspen shade the slopes here, and wild flowers carpet the woods. Tent and trailer facilities are available.

5 In Baldwin, look for Jackson County Maintenance Shed No. 8 as a landmark for the first road south, which turns to gravel on the edge of town. After about a mile you reach the Eden Valley Refuge, 200 acres of wooded hills that are a county bird and wild flower preserve.

About three miles of hiking trails wind through woods and meadows, crossing a swinging bridge over Bear Creek. The one-mile Bear Creek Interpretive Trail loops from a nature center, where trail booklets are available. The center is staffed on week-

ends in summer and on Sunday afternoons in the spring and fall. Semi-modern tent and trailer facilities are available, and there are primitive campgrounds for backpackers.

6 The Herbert Hoover National Historic Site honors the 31st president of the United States, who was born in the village of West Branch in a two-room cottage near his father's blacksmith shop.

The Birthplace Cottage is the center of this late 19th-century village, which has been restored by the National Park Service. The buildings open to the public are the blacksmith shop, a schoolhouse, a visitor center, and the Friends Meetinghouse where Hoover's mother was acknowledged by her fellow Quakers as a "recorded minister".

The Herbert Hoover Presidential Library and Museum is on the outskirts of the village, and the graves of the former president and his wife are also here.

7 Founded in 1839, Iowa City, the former state capital, has two buildings of architectural as well as historic interest.

The Old Capitol is on the University of Iowa campus on Clinton Street and Iowa Avenue. Completed in 1855 in the Greek Revival style, it has been carefully restored and has an unusual reverse spiral staircase.

Plum Grove State Historic Site is located on five acres at Carroll Street and Kirkwood Avenue, in the southern end of town. It was the home of Robert Lucas, Iowa's first territorial governor. Built of red brick in 1844, it has been completely restored and is furnished in the style of that era. The

grounds are shaded by large oaks, the official state tree. It is closed from late fall until early spring.

8 As you approach Kalona, you may see huge workhorses in the fields and horse-drawn black buggies on the road, for this is Amishland.

Settled in 1846, Kalona is the largest Amish–Mennonite community west of the Mississippi. Advertising itself as "not just a one-horse town," Kalona has many hitching posts in the alleys off its main streets. Old Order Amish maintain their religious beliefs: they reject extravagant clothing and modern education. They do not pose for photographs, which they believe to be graven images and thus banned by the Bible.

Although many Amish farmers use modern farm machinery, some do the plowing, fertilizing, and harvesting with horses.

In Kalona the Historical Village relating to Amish–Mennonite life and the Mennonite Museum are in the eastern end of town.

9 The Amana Colonies consist of seven charming villages that were built between 1855 and 1861 by members of the Community of True Inspiration, a Christian sect that originated in Germany, France, and Alsace. Fleeing religious persecution, they came to America and eventually established this community on 26,000 acres of land. Today there are many members of the Amana Society living in these villages. All the members share in the profits of their work.

The colonies are famous for the excellence of their products. The woolen mill, furniture factory, winery, and smokehouse offer tours.

The Country Lincoln Loved

Here, in the state of Illinois, Abraham Lincoln learned the law and first came to the attention of the nation

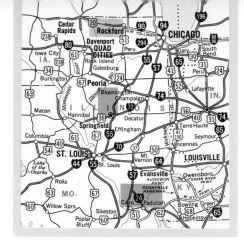

"To this place, and the kindness of these people, I owe everything." So said Illinois' most famous adopted son, Abraham Lincoln, as he left Springfield for the White House some 120 years ago. The mark of Lincoln is still on his beloved state, where his body is entombed on the outskirts of Springfield in one of the nation's most hallowed shrines. New Salem, the little town where Lincoln settled after he arrived from Indiana with the clothes on his back and not much else, has been restored, as has his Springfield home. Other sites associated with Lincoln are plentiful in the state where he lived for more than a quarter of a century, grew to manhood, fought in the Black Hawk War, married, had his children, practiced law, and debated another adopted Illinoisan, Stephen Douglas.

But the "Land of Lincoln" is more than its rich past. The mighty Mississippi River on Illinois' western border throbs with the goods of the nation and of the state, which produces a cornucopia of agricultural and industrial products. The prairies are alive with small towns and bustling cities, but vast areas have been set aside as parks and preserves. Exploring these byways, you can understand why the French explorer Joliet called the vistas of the prairies "the most beautiful" he had ever seen.

Craggy limestone bluffs overlooking the Mississippi, the fertile Rock River valley, the Apple River's deep, twisting limestone gorge, and the nostalgic quiet of somnolent river hamlets await you along this medium-length tour. The route roughly follows a triangle that was cut millions of years ago through Illinois' fertile prairie soil by the three rivers in the state's scenic northwest tip.

1 Residents like to call Galena "the town that time forgot." Named for the rich deposits of lead ore (galena) developed here in the early 1800's, it is one of the most historic and picturesque river towns in the Midwest. The town was laid out in 1826 on the stairsteplike bluffs rising on both sides of the Galena River, some four miles from where the river flows into the Mississippi. The booming lead town prospered and, for a time, was larger than Chicago. But when the shallow lodes played out, Galena's fate was sealed.

You can see how unchanged the town is as you explore the riverfront area along the levee or climb the steps connecting some of the terrace-like streets. You might like to start your tour at the Chamber of Commerce Visitor Center in the old Galena Railroad Depot at Bouthillier Street and Park Avenue. Here you can get information and maps with suggested walking and auto tours of the town. If you like, you can arrange for a professional guide to drive your car to the various sites and explain their significance as only an insider can.

On a stroll along Main Street you can see a variety of old houses and shops with gingerbread trim.
2 The road to Scales Mound (an old stagecoach route) quickly climbs up from the Galena River valley and enters a region many residents call the Black Hawk Hills, after the local Sauk-Fox chief. The road passes limestone bluffs and scenic lookouts, and goes up and down small hills like

1. Historic houses and churches are found on almost every street of the river town of Galena, where Lincoln's most famous general, Ulysses S. Grant, once lived. One of his homes here is now a state memorial.

SPECIAL FEATURES

ROAD GUIDE ▬▬▬	HIGHLIGHT 1
STATE PARKS	
With Campsites ♠ Without Campsites △	SKI AREAS 🎿
RECREATION AREAS	
With Campsites ▲ Without Campsites △	SCHEDULED AIRLINE STOPS ✈
SELECTED REST AREAS ⊼	OTHER AIRPORTS ✈
POINTS OF INTEREST ⊡	BOAT RAMPS

ROAD CLASSIFICATION

CONTROLLED ACCESS HIGHWAYS
Interstate interchange numbers are mileposts.

TOLL HIGHWAYS

OTHER DIVIDED HIGHWAYS

PAVED HIGHWAYS

LOCAL ROADS In unfamiliar areas inquire locally before using these roads

Interchanges   Service Area

Paved   Gravel   Dirt

MILEAGE

MILEAGE BETWEEN TOWNS AND JUNCTIONS 3 / 4

MILEAGE BETWEEN DOTS 35

SCALE

ONE INCH 17 MILES   0   5   10   20

ONE INCH 27 KILOMETERS   0   5 10   15   32

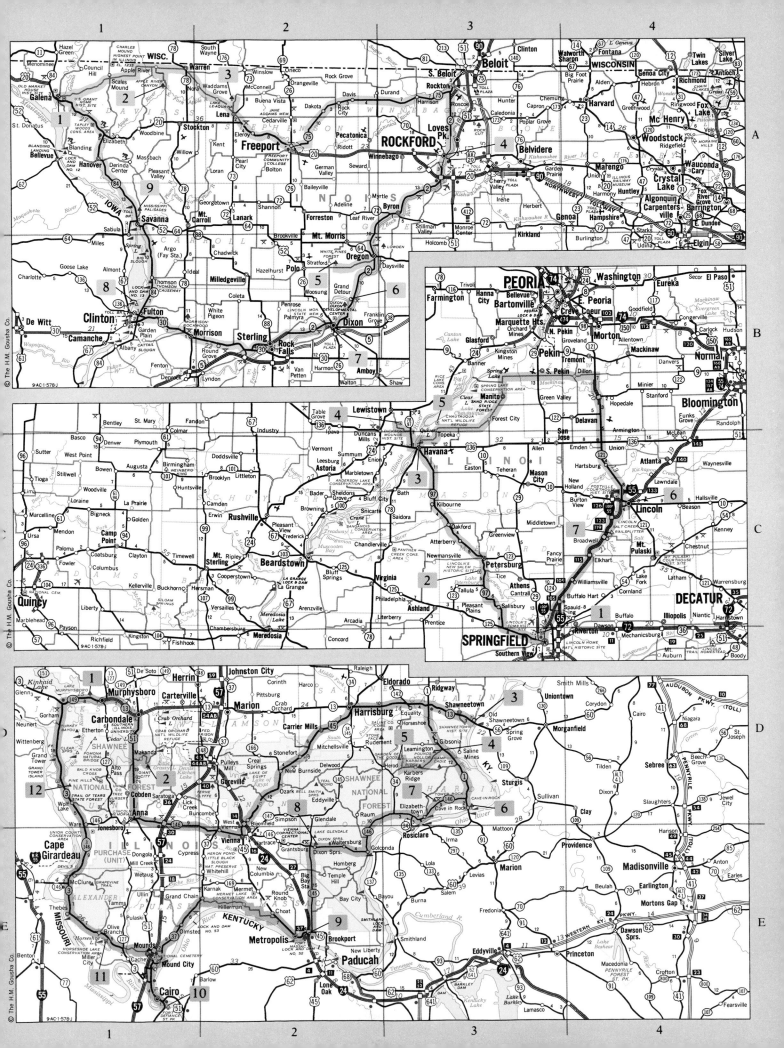

a roller coaster. About 12 miles east of Charles Mound a small sign marks the turnoff south for the Apple River Canyon State Park, a beautiful area with hiking, picnicking, camping, and fishing facilities.

The park is in a section of the Midwest's Driftless Area, the name geologists have given a region of land untouched by the glaciers that scraped across much of the continent, including most of Illinois, during the ice age. Fossils that escaped the glaciers here are still to be found in the ravines and along the cliffs. Since the ice melted, the small Apple River has cut a steep-walled, winding valley in the limestone bedrock. In places the valley resembles a miniature, tree-lined Grand Canyon, with crenellated cliffs, striated bluffs, and pools of deep, cool water where trout and other kinds of fish lurk in the shadows.

3 The route continues through hilly farming country to Lena and the turnoff for Lake Le-Aqua-Na State Park. Embracing a scenic lake on a hill surrounded by woods and mead-

6. An example of the first self-scouring steel plow, complete with its doubletree hitch, is outside the blacksmith shop of its inventor, John Deere. The plow cut a clean furrow, and Deere & Co. became the largest producer of farm implements in the world.

ows, the park is an impressive showground of the natural attractions of the Black Hawk Hills area. There are facilities for canoeing, hiking, picnicking, fishing, boating, horseback riding, and horse camping. During the summer the park rangers present nature programs regularly.

4 East of Freeport, Route 75 follows an old stagecoach trail through rich farmland in the Sugar River valley to Rockford on the Rock River. The second largest city in the state, Rockford straddles the river where stagecoach drivers used to ford it, hence its name. As you explore the city, you may want to visit the riverfront Sinnissippi Park at 1300–1900 North Second Street, a cool, green garden around a small lagoon, with footpaths and a greenhouse; the Burpee Natural History Museum at 813 North Main Street, a Victorian mansion containing extensive displays of native Illinois wildlife, minerals, and Indian artifacts; and the Tinker Swiss Cottage, a replica of a Swiss chalet full of antiques and Lincolniana.

5 Just south of the town of Oregon, a road to the west leads to the state's last stand of white pines, situated in White Pines Forest State Park on the banks of Pine Creek. The park offers a unique look at the tree that provided much of the wood for Lincoln's skillful rail splitting. Trails lead along the winding creek beside moss-covered cliffs and through clusters of hardwoods, including maple, ash,

and white oak (*Quercus alba*), the state tree. In the spring or summer you might also catch sight of the state bird, the cardinal, and the state flower, the violet. The forest also is home for pine finches and pine warblers, raccoons, opossums, chipmunks, and red squirrels. The park has a lodge and cabins and facilities for fishing, camping, and picnicking.

6 Grand Detour, a hamlet on the Rock River, is so named because it lies in an oxbow curve in the river that was frequently traveled by early fur traders. In 1836 a Vermont smithy set up his forge here and during the next few years built what has become known as "the plow that broke the prairies." His name was John Deere.

The rich, black prairie soil that Deere encountered was a boon to farmers of the period, but it stuck like glue to their iron or wooden plows. A plowman, and his span of oxen or hitch of horses, had to stop every few feet to scrape the plow. From a discarded saw blade, Deere built a steel plow that was self-cleaning as it turned the dark earth into even, smooth furrows and made possible the agricultural development of the West. You can visit Deere's restored home and blacksmith shop and take a guided tour of the site where the historic plow first took shape.

7 Just south of Grand Detour, in Dixon, Route 2 crosses the Rock River. At the north end of the bridge is Lincoln Statue Drive. Here a statue

2. A rocky trail at Apple River Canyon State Park is cantilevered over the gentle river, little more than a stream. The park lures fishermen on the lookout for walleyes.

shows Lincoln when he was a beardless young captain in the Black Hawk War. Nearby is the Old Settler's Memorial Log Cabin on the site of Fort Dixon, once an important western outpost in country disputed by the Indians. The cabin was built in 1894 and contains period furnishings.

8   From Dixon, Route 2 follows the scenic Rock River and joins Route 30, which continues west and descends into the Mississippi Valley. You can see the river in action at the U.S. Army Corps of Engineers Lock and Dam No. 13, a few miles north of Fulton. Any time you visit the installation, the chances are you can see a mammoth Mississippi River towboat "locking through" the dam, one of 27 such barriers in the nearly 900 miles of the Upper Mississippi between Minneapolis, Minnesota, and where the river joins the Ohio River at Cairo, Illinois.

No. 13 and the other dams divide the river into a series of long pools with a minimum channel depth of nine feet. The pool created by No. 13 stretches upstream some 30 miles, measures about 4 miles across at its widest point, and is one of the most popular stretches of the river with boaters, fishermen, and sightseers.

The locking through operation is necessary since the 600-by-110-foot lock is too small to hold both the boat and the barges of the usual tow. The captain nudges a section of his tow into the lock, and deckhands scramble to detach some of the barges. The dam operator then closes the gates and lets water pour into or out of the lock to raise or lower the barges to the next level. You can watch the whole show from several observation platforms and learn more about it from the available brochures.

9   Another dramatic perspective of the lordly river is offered at the Mississippi Palisades State Park. The palisades are steep limestone cliffs similar in form to those along the lower Hudson River. The cliffs soar in places to 250 feet above the river. The palisades are a dramatic element in an otherwise gently rolling state park, which offers camping, trail rides, boating, and fishing.

The view from the lookout platform is something not to be missed, especially by photographers. Below is the wide expanse of the river, several wooded islands, and broad bottomlands across the river in Iowa. You might even see the same towboat you saw at Lock and Dam No. 13.

The cities of Petersburg, Lincoln, and Springfield, the state capital, lie near the geographic center of Illinois and at the heart of "Lincoln Land." As a relative newcomer from Indiana, Lincoln lived and worked in New Salem (near present-day Petersburg) for six years. The city of Lincoln is the only community named for him with his knowledge and consent.

Lincoln and several other tall state legislators, known as the "long nine," were instrumental in having the capital moved to Springfield from Vandalia in 1837. Lincoln settled in the capital in the only home he ever owned, and he first achieved national prominence while living there.

The earliest residents of this area were Indians who settled along the river. At Dickson Mounds Museum there is an excavated burial ground, a collection of artifacts, and a reconstructed village revealing how these prehistoric people lived.

In the nearby watery lowlands is a wildlife refuge where vast numbers of waterfowl stop to rest, as they must have done for thousands of years before the white man came.

1   In north Springfield, at the northern end of Monument Boulevard, you come to what is probably one of the most visited Lincoln shrines in the country. Lincoln's Tomb State Historic Site, in Oak Ridge Cemetery, lies not far from the center of the city that launched him on his path to greatness. Lincoln was buried in the cemetery on May 4, 1865, at the request of his wife. You can still see the public vault where the president's body was first interred. Four years later workmen broke ground for a memorial tomb. The marble monument in the burial chamber of the completed memorial does not contain the president's body because of the discovery of a plot to steal it for ransom. The coffin is now below the surface of the floor.

Follow the signs south to the Lincoln Home National Historic Site. At the National Park Service Visitor Center you can get maps and brochures describing sites relating to Lincoln and other historical points in and around Springfield. You will probably want to visit the Lincoln Home, the residence he owned, a

9. Limestone bluffs vie with the broad Mississippi River in majesty, just as the railroad along the rim of the Mississippi competes with its towboats and barges for freight. The islands were carved by the sweeping turn of the meandering river.

block east of the visitor center. The Greek Revival house has been faithfully restored and stocked with period furnishings. Also in the area is the Old State Capitol, on Capitol Plaza, with its museum of Lincolniana and, during summer nights (weather permitting), a sound-and-light program that dramatically describes Lincoln's 25 years in and around Springfield.

2 Lincoln was a gangling youth when he came to New Salem in 1831, and although he stayed in town only six years, he left New Salem a man. During his sojourn here he was a storekeeper, a postmaster, a surveyor, a woodchopper, and a captain in the Black Hawk War, as well as an elected member of the Illinois General Assembly.

Today at the Lincoln's New Salem State Historic Site you can wander the dirt streets of the restored town and see it much as Lincoln did. Houses, shops, stores, industries, a school and church, a tavern, and other structures have been carefully reconstructed according to original maps and archives obtained from the Lincoln family. One building, the Onstot Cooper Shop, built in 1835, is original. If you wish, you can enjoy the illusion that Lincoln himself and his fellow townspeople are your guides by renting a headphone and listening to a tape recording describing the town and its history. There are campgrounds and picnic facilities in the park surrounding the reconstructed village.

3 North of Lincoln's New Salem State Historic Site the route crosses the Sangamon River and meets the Illinois River at Havana. Abraham Lincoln and a friend arrived here in 1832 as they were canoeing home to New Salem from the Black Hawk War. The site is marked by a monument in Riverfront Park between Main and Market streets. The park is an inviting place to stretch your legs and watch the boats plying the Illinois. Lincoln returned to this small river community frequently between 1839 and 1857 during his days as a circuit-riding lawyer. While campaigning for the U.S. Senate in 1858, he spoke for two hours in Rockwell Park, a few blocks north of Riverfront Park.

4 Dickson Mounds Museum commands a tall western bluff of the Illinois River where some 700 to 900 years ago 237 Indians were interred in a burial mound along with their tools, utensils, pottery, and weapons. After years of painstaking excavation, archeologists unearthed these graves, and they remain just as they were found. Although there may be other burial sites nearby, this one provides a good indication of the culture here. In an amphitheater at the site you can see a dramatic sound-and-light program that re-creates the history of the area. Standing in the darkened theater, seeing the skeletons spotlighted where they lie, and hearing of the accomplishments of these people is an unforgettably moving experience.

The museum also has exhibits and displays tracing developments here from prehistoric times to the arrival of the first explorers and settlers. Excavations of the floor patterns of the Eveland Indian Village that flourished here help to explain the everyday life of these people. Closed New Year's, Easter, Thanksgiving, and Christmas days.

5 For uncounted centuries waterfowl and other birds have stopped in the fertile lowlands bordering the Illinois River on their way between

2. On New Salem's main street stands a reconstruction of the double cabin (above) built in 1832 by Joshua Miller, blacksmith, and John A. Kelso, philosopher, who married sisters. Lincoln often came to this cabin to visit Kelso, who introduced him to the classics. A statue of Lincoln carrying a book and his ax (right) stands at the entrance to the village.

3. *The riverboat* Talisman *plies the Sangamon River north of the Lincoln's New Salem State Historic Site near Petersburg. Many of the boat's passengers are vacationers eager to experience the way of life Lincoln was accustomed to when he lived in these parts.*

Although no one is sure why the southern tip of Illinois, bounded on the west by the Mississippi River and on the east by the Ohio River, is called Little Egypt, the name has stuck for generations. Perhaps the custom began in the early 1800's when the founders of Cairo, at the confluence of the two mighty streams, named the settlement because of the resemblance they thought it had to the site of the city on the Nile. Resemblance or not, the pronunciation has changed. In these parts the word is kay-ro. *Many residents also refer to the area as the Illinois Ozarks because of its geological similarity to Missouri's Ozark Mountains on the other side of the Mississippi.*

northern breeding grounds and their winter habitats in the south. During the 1930's, when dam and levee building along the river threatened the natural environment, the area around Chautauqua Lake was set aside as a wildlife refuge. Here in the fall and winter some 100,000 ducks and 40,000 Canada geese pause on their annual migration. Mallards comprise the major part of the duck population. During the summer you can probably sight several species of heron as well as egrets, wood ducks, bobwhites, mourning doves, American goldfinches, and other birds.

If you boat, hike, picnic, or fish within the reserve, or camp in the nearby Sand Ridge State Forest or the Spring Lake Conservation Area, the chances are you may also see many other examples of local wildlife, including deer, opossums, foxes, and perhaps even a muskrat, a beaver, or a mink.

Northeast of Spring Lake you drive by quarries where huge equipment extracts sand and gravel deposited by meltwaters of ice age glaciers. The rich farmland farther west produces some of the state's best crops of corn and soybeans.

6 The small city of Lincoln is the seat of Logan County. Lincoln was surveyed, mapped, and dedicated by Abraham Lincoln in 1833. A marker near the old depot depicts the unique way Lincoln christened the town: he used the juice of a watermelon.

At 914 Fifth Street, not far north of the city's attractive town square, you can visit a replica of the Postville Courthouse where Lincoln practiced his profession as a circuit-riding lawyer. (The original courthouse was purchased by Henry Ford in 1929 and moved to his Greenfield Village at Dearborn, Michigan.) The replica, an Illinois state historic site, has a courtroom that is based on the original one where Lincoln argued many of his cases. Numerous displays depict other facets of Lincoln's life as a frontier lawyer.

7 About three miles southeast of the courthouse on Route 55 you can see another reminder of Lincoln's life at the Railsplitter State Park. The rolling, wooded park, with picnic grounds and playgrounds stretched out along the banks of the meandering Salt Creek, contains several examples of the split rail fences that figured in Lincoln's rise to greatness.

1 Lake Murphysboro State Park, one of the prettiest state parks in Illinois, encompasses some 900 acres of woodland, meadows, and hills surrounding a sprawling man-made lake. The lake was created when a 600-foot dam was built across Indian Creek, a tributary of the Big Muddy River. The park attracts wild flower fanciers in spring and summer when several different species of native orchids spangle the woodland floor. In August and September patches of purple fringeless orchids burst into bloom. There are facilities for campers, hikers, picnickers, archers, and boaters, and the lake is stocked with largemouth bass, sunfish, bluegill, crappies, and channel catfish.

2 South of Carbondale, Route 51 deserts the level prairie and descends into the rugged Illinois Ozarks. Near a deep valley is the entrance to Giant City State Park, named for the house-size blocks of sandstone that appear to have been scattered randomly throughout the lush forest by some colossus. In reality, the force of the weather over millions of years ate away at soft shale layers underlying a deep layer of sandstone that formed tall rock outcrops. Eventually the sandstone shattered into huge blocks, with many of them perched in unlikely positions.

Several hiking trails thread among the most picturesque of these gray stone behemoths. The park also has facilities for canoeing, fishing, and picnicking, and in the summer interpretive programs are presented.

3 From Vienna to Harrisburg, Route 45 cuts across a beautifully wooded section of the Shawnee National Forest. For detailed information about the area, stop at the Forest Headquarters at 317 East Poplar Street in Harrisburg, where maps and brochures are available.

East of Harrisburg you cross Route 1 and continue on a picturesque spur for about nine miles to Shawneetown and into what you may think is a time warp. Old Shawneetown, on the western bank of the muddy Ohio River, is the oldest city in Illinois, or perhaps it is more accurate to say *was* the oldest. Founded in the early 1800's, the community boomed as a gateway for settlers moving to the fertile prairies lying just to the west.

But the river that brought prosperity washed it away. The great Ohio River flood of 1937 came over the levees and virtually destroyed the city, sweeping some buildings off their foundation. Most of the residents rebuilt on higher land in what became New Shawneetown. (This town later dropped the "new", and "old" was added to the other town.)

The flooded-out city is now a virtual ghost town, with only about 400 residents. Some restorations have been done since part of the town was made a state historic site, but most of the streets and buildings remain as they were when the river retreated more than four decades ago. Exploring the town is an eerie experience: a river breeze flaps a rusty screen door, wild flowers bloom between the steps of the Greek Revival Shawneetown Bank, and pigeons explode from beneath the roof of an abandoned house. You can get a walking map at the John Marshall House Bank, which is open for tours.

4 Shawnee National Forest's Pounds Hollow Recreation Area is just west of Route 1 on Karber's Ridge Road. Watch for the sign about nine miles south of the junction of Routes 1 and 13. The area is a sylvan retreat located in a beautiful hollow typical of the Illinois Ozarks. Well-marked nature trails lead around the lake and rugged rock outcroppings. There are facilities for boating, hiking, camping, picnicking, and fishing. You may sight some of the national forest's 500-odd species of mammals,

4. In Pounds Hollow's canyon (left), nonflowering plants include reindeer lichen (top), Cetraria (center), and striped turkey-tail fungus.

birds, reptiles, amphibians, and fish, including drumming grouse, wild turkeys, white-tailed deer, beaver, gray foxes, raccoons, opossums, and squirrels. You can also see magnificent specimens of black, white, red, and scarlet oak trees.

5 If you like the lay of the land around Pounds Hollow, you may want to continue to the Shawnee National Forest's Garden of the Gods Recreational Area, which is even more remote and rugged. Along the way you follow the scenic Karber's Ridge Road through some of the prettiest parts of the Illinois Ozarks. Once you arrive at Garden of the Gods, you can understand its name. Here is some of nature's most fanciful sculpting of the region's outcroppings of native sandstone. Over the centuries weathering and erosion have worn away the softer parts of the rocks and rills more quickly than the harder. The result is a mammoth rock garden of fantastically shaped sandstone towers, overhangs, crevices, and balanced boulders.

Well-marked trails, catwalks, and stairways let you wind among the most picturesque formations.

6 Cave-In-Rock lies just outside the boundary of Shawnee National Forest and overlooks the broad Ohio River a quarter mile east of Route 1. The immense cryptlike, arched cavern, some 55 feet wide, 40 feet high, and 300 feet long, opens in the side of a huge rocky cliff like a grotesque, gaping mouth. The cave is an easy walk down the 60-foot cliff, but visitors who wish may see into the cave from above by looking through a small skylight.

From soon after the Revolutionary War until the 1830's the cave was a natural lair for river pirates, con artists, highway men, and other scoundrels who preyed unmercifully on the pioneers, boatmen, and merchants who used the river as a highway west. Inside the gaping cave, with light reflected from the river playing weirdly on the rock walls and ceiling, you can easily imagine that pirates still lurk just out of sight in the shifting shadows. After you leave the cave, you can relax at the park's picnic grounds or stroll along one of the nature trails.

7 Tower Rock Recreation Area, part of Shawnee National Forest, lies along the Ohio River about five miles west of Cave-In-Rock. The remote, wooded park has facilities for camping, picnicking, boating, and hiking. One of the nature trails climbs steeply to the lookout atop Tower Rock, a limestone bluff about 160 feet above the river's muddy waters. You can see for miles up and down the river and across a broad expanse of floodplains in Kentucky.

8   As the road turns west at Golconda, it follows what was once an old Indian trail to Dixon Springs State Park. The wooded setting is accentuated by the rugged hills of the Illinois Ozarks that in rainstorms become laced with diaphanous waterfalls and cascades. Some of the hill brooks run noisily through tunnellike passageways beneath a canopy of century-old trees. Many of the hillsides and large boulders are covered with startlingly green moss, ferns, and sinuous vines. You can swim in a tree-shaded swimming pool at the park, and picnic, hike, and camp.

9   On the outskirts of Metropolis, Fort Massac State Park overlooks the Ohio River a few miles downsteam from where the Tennessee River enters from Kentucky. The reconstruction of the palisaded wooden-and-earth fort was completed in 1973. Wandering along between buildings and ramparts, you can gct a good idea of what an American fort and trading post looked like on the frontier in the mid-1700's. An interpretive center with displays and a slide-sound program surveys the history of the fort.

Campers and picnickers can enjoy the contemporary beauty of the site from the park adjoining the fort. On a summer night, particularly when fog is rising from the brown waters, campers are treated to a special show: towboats plying the narrow channel light up both banks of the river with stilettolike beams from their searchlights and fill the night air with the melancholy sound of their horns.

10   A short spur south of Mound City leads you to Fort Defiance State Park on Cairo Point at the southernmost tip of Illinois.

Fort Defiance, now long disappeared, was vital to the Union during the Civil War when it guarded the strategic confluence of the two rivers and served as a jumping-off place for some of Gen. Ulysses S. Grant's forays into the Confederate heartland. If you picnic here or stroll beneath the shade trees, you are almost certain to see powerful diesel towboats on both rivers, which are slightly different shades of muddy brown.

11   The Horseshoe Lake Conservation Area is the wintering place of 100,000 to 150,000 Canada geese and numerous bald eagles. In the summer the shallow lake seems a misplaced part of the Deep South. The shores of the horseshoe-shaped lake are crowded with tall bald cypress, tupelo gum, and swamp cottonwood trees, whose branches in many places form a canopy overhead. At several spots along the scenic drive around the lake you can walk out over the water on short fishing piers built between the massive tree trunks.

The actions of some of the anglers may mystify you. The lake requires a shallow-water fishing technique called bucktail fishing, which some experts believe originated here. A bucktailing fisherman uses a fly rod to bounce the lure up and down in the water or move it in a small circle. In spite of the name, the bucktail lure is tied with calf's hair, not that from a deer's tail. The park also attracts campers, picnickers, and boaters.

12   Just north of Wolf Lake, a tiny river valley town, Forest Highway 24 turns east and brings you to the Pine Hills Recreation Area, one of the most scenic areas in the Shawnee National Forest. (The road to the park is well marked, but you may find it helpful to have a detailed map, available at any one of the national forest's offices.)

The Pine Hills Area provides a spectacular look at the state's rugged southern hill country. Seven miles of scenic road run along the top of a high ridge that overlooks the distant Mississippi. The road is flanked with dense woodlands of cherrybark and pin oak, shagbark hickory, and red gum trees. Hikers can follow the three-quarter-mile-long Inspiration Point Forest Trail to a rocky overlook some 350 feet high. Directly below is the La Rue Scenic Area, and on the southwest horizon are the Missouri Ozarks. If you wish, you can return to State Route 3 by continuing along Forest Highway 24.

5. At a point where an Indian hunter or warrior might have stopped to scan his surroundings, a latter-day hiker pauses at the Garden of the Gods in Shawnee National Forest. These fanciful rock formations gave the garden its name.

Land of the Ozarks

Missouri's rolling hills, crystal caves, and winding lakes and rivers make it a delightful state to see

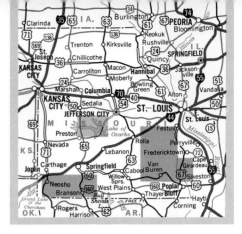

The Ozarks of southern Missouri, built from an isolated dome of igneous sedimentary rock and deeply eroded by streams over the last 380 million years, are less than mountains and more than hills.

Now honeycombed with caves, the region is clothed with oak and hickory forests and is watered by a wondrous profusion of springs.

Almost all of the roads through the Ozarks follow ridgelines along the hilltops, drop down into twisting river valleys, only to climb yet another ridge. Roads such as these invite a leisurely pace because of constantly unfolding vistas of the rolling hills.

The countryside around the Lake of the Ozarks, extending from Eldon in east to the town of Warsaw in the west, is a land of seemingly endless waterways in a setting of wooded hillsides. Dogwood (Cornus florida), the state tree, brightens the spring with drifts of white blossoms and adds its flaming foliage to the autumn scene.

This is the part of the Ozarks that lures thousands of visitors to its resorts, marinas, and miles of beaches, the region of the Show-Me State, as it is called, that is known as the center of Missouri's vacationland.

1 The town of Eldon is a small farm community and a tourist center. Its tree-shaded streets and pleasant residential sections retain the quiet atmosphere of the 1880's, when the town was settled.

2 The Bagnell Dam, a few miles to the south of Eldon, was constructed across the Osage River in 1931 to provide electrical power for some quarter of a million Missourians. The dam's hydroelectric power plant, with its eight huge turbines, is open to visitors. Guided tours are given several times a day.

Perhaps the most important consequence of the dam's construction, other than power, was the creation of the Lake of the Ozarks, Missouri's largest and most popular resort area. Sometimes nicknamed the Missouri Dragon, the lake with its 1,375 miles of shoreline curls and twists westward for 129 miles through the Osage River valley. Year-round residences, summer cottages, marinas, hotels, motels, and various resorts line the lake's wooded shores.

The road crosses the half-mile-long Bagnell Dam to the town of Lake Ozark, a small tourist center whose assortment of shops, motels, restaurants, and amusement arcades comes to life in summer. There are also excursion boats, seaplanes, and helicopters from which to view the lake and its environs.

3 Lake of the Ozarks State Park, with some 17,000 acres on the lake's eastern border, has several campgrounds, swimming beaches, boat-launching ramps, and excellent fishing. Bass, bluegills, catfish, and walleyes flourish in the clear waters. Boats are available for rent. The park is the only one in Missouri with its own airport.

Within the park is the Patterson Hollow Wild Area. A 10-mile hiking trail through the 1,200 acres of wilderness begins at the log cabin that serves as a nature center. Like most of Missouri's forests, the woods here are comprised almost entirely of oak and hickory trees. The great variety of hardwoods that once flourished here has been depleted by years of lumbering and land cultivation.

Pastures long abandoned to the wilderness, several ponds, and a meandering creek bed attract native animals, such as deer and raccoons, and many birds, including the eastern bluebird, the official state bird.

2. Osage Beach, a small resort town that was established in the late 1920's soon after the Bagnell Dam was proposed, stretches along the eastern shores of the Lake of the Ozarks. Vacation homes, each with its own small dock, are nestled in the wooded hillsides.

SPECIAL FEATURES

ROAD GUIDE	HIGHLIGHT
STATE PARKS	POINTS OF INTEREST
With Campsites / Without Campsites	SKI AREAS
RECREATION AREAS	SCHEDULED AIRLINE STOPS
With Campsites / Without Campsites	
SELECTED REST AREAS	OTHER AIRPORTS

ROAD CLASSIFICATION

CONTROLLED ACCESS HIGHWAYS
(Entrance and Exit only at Interchanges)   Interchanges

TOLL HIGHWAYS

OTHER DIVIDED HIGHWAYS

PAVED HIGHWAYS

LOCAL ROADS In unfamiliar areas inquire locally before using these roads   Paved   Gravel   Dirt

MILEAGE

MILEAGE BETWEEN TOWNS AND JUNCTIONS   3 / 4   MILEAGE BETWEEN DOTS   35

SCALE

ONE INCH 18 MILES   0   5   10   20

ONE INCH 29 KILOMETERS   0   5   10   20   32

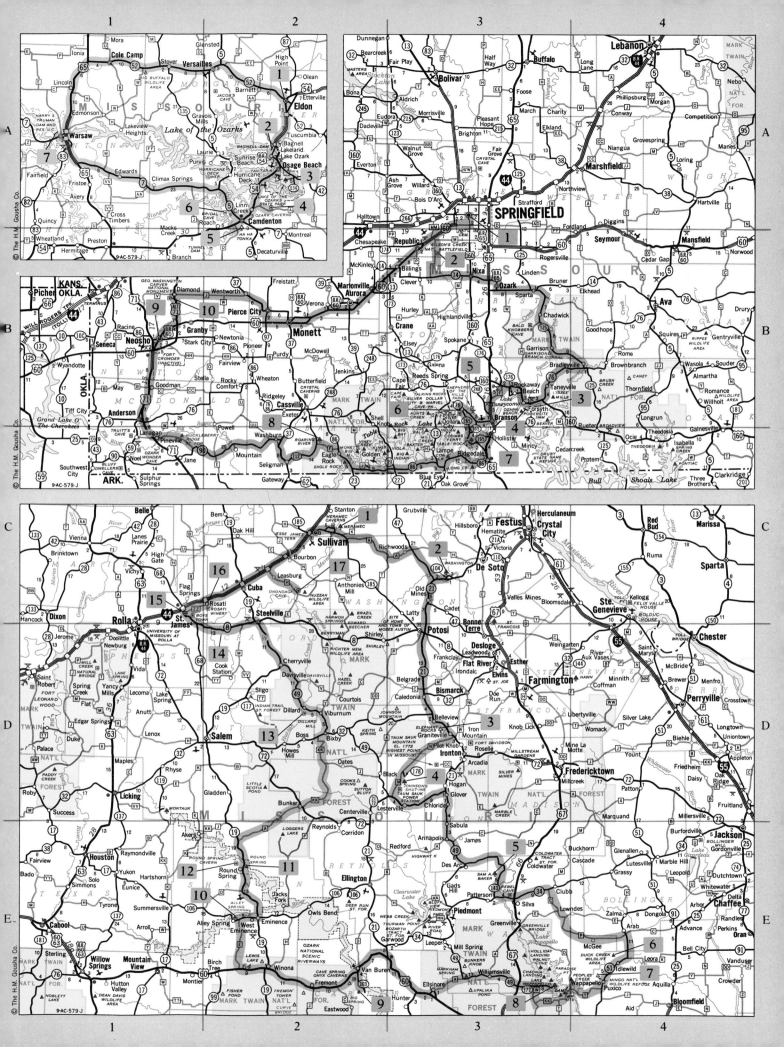

4   The Ozark Caverns have some interesting geologic formations where stalactites and stalagmites are still in the process of being formed. The caverns are best known for the formation called the Angel Shower, a colorful combination of stalactites and waterfalls. Guided tours through the caves are given every day during the summer.

5   Ha Ha Tonka State Park overlooks the forest-bordered Niangua Arm of the lake. Here you can find evidence of collapsed caverns, including a remnant of a cavern ceiling that now forms a natural bridge 70 feet wide and 100 feet high, with a span of 60 feet.

A gravel road within the park leads to Ha Ha Tonka Spring, which discharges an average of 48 million gallons of water a day from the cave system. Rocky bluffs 250 feet high surround the area. As the springwaters flow into the Lake of the Ozarks, they are parted by an island strewn with toppled boulders.

road that cuts through the bluffs, revealing rusty red stains that were formed when iron, which had been leached by water from the rock, was deposited on the surface as the water evaporated.

An elaborate visitor center at Kaysinger Bluff overlooking the dam houses a reconstructed archeological dig spanning about 30,000 years of Ozark prehistory.

The Truman Reservoir, completely surrounded by wooded hills, is almost as large as the Lake of the Ozarks. Truman State Park is a heavily forested area that is alive during the summer with such birds as mourning dove, quail, cardinal, wood thrush, and bluebird.

Northward from Warsaw the road passes through agricultural land that is less rugged than the classic Ozark terrain. Hay, corn, milo, and herds of cattle fill the fields, some of which are bordered by split rail fences. Junipers, which are also called eastern red cedars, grow so close together

The southwest corner of Missouri, where the state adjoins Oklahoma and Arkansas, is known as the Ozark Plateau. Forest-clad mountains rise above the hills to the north, and many waterways, some natural and some man-made, wind through the deep valleys that punctuate the landscape.

Caves and springs, so numerous in all parts of the state, are here intermingled with history. Not far from Springfield one of the fiercest battles of the Civil War was fought, and on a farm near the little town of Diamond was born one of America's best-known native sons, a young black man who so admired Gen. George Washington that he adopted his name.

1   Springfield, on the James River, was settled in the 1830's and soon became a busy dairying community. Today, with several colleges, art museums, and a symphony orchestra, Springfield is both a cultural and commercial center, with many of its industries still related to dairying.

2   Wilson's Creek marks the site of the first big Civil War battle for control of Missouri. Exhibits at the National Park Service Information Center explain the battle. A self-guided auto tour traverses the battlefield and goes to Bloody Hill, where most of the fighting occurred.

Route 125 south of Sparta cuts through the Mark Twain National Forest, which was pieced together in 1933 from land that had been depleted by decades of logging, forest fires, and unsuitable farming. The Forest Service began a restoration program in the 1930's, and the hills of the Ava Ranger District, north of the so-called great lakes of the Ozarks, responded well.

Through this area today there is a scenic, winding drive along ridgetops from which red cedar- and oak-covered hills roll to the horizon, with vines of bittersweet clinging to old split rail fences at the roadsides.

3   Between Taneyville and Forsyth the road comes to the headwaters of Bull Shoals Lake, which was formed on the White River by a dam in Arkansas. Beside a branch of the lake, which looks like a moderately wide, calm river, is Shadow Rock Park, a popular place in summer for boating, fishing, picnicking, and camping.

7. *The Osage-orange tree, which flourishes in poor soil and hot, dry climates, grows so thick when sheared that cattle cannot get through. The fruit, shown above, is orangelike and inedible.*

6   The road to Bridal Cave, just beyond Camdenton, winds through stretches of woodlands and drops down a bluff to the cave entrance.

This cavern has colorful cave onyx and flowstone formations and a so-called Bridal Chapel where weddings are frequently held. In the chapel are flowstone draperies that resound with organlike tones when struck.

7   The Harry S. Truman Dam, the largest of a series of federal projects on the Osage River, is reached by a

along the roadside that they almost hide the fences. The juniper's blueberrylike cones are a favorite food of the native birds. This tree is tough and shallow-rooted, and it leads the advance as forested areas struggle to reclaim the fields.

Also growing along the fences is the Osage-orange, a spiny tree often used for hedgerows because of its ability to thrive in poor soil. The tree is also known as the bowwood, since Indians used it for that purpose.

6. The gristmill at Silver Dollar City has an overshot waterwheel, whose geared shaft turns the grindstones within the mill. The sluice gate regulates the speed of the wheel.

4 Watch for a narrow, inconspicuous road to the south just beyond the bridge near Forsyth. It drops down the limestone cliffs to Powersite Dam, the first of the 12 hydroelectric dams that formed the great lakes of the Ozarks. Powersite, built in 1913, is not impressively large, but it does impound Lake Taneycomo, the lake that was responsible for the tourist industry in the Ozarks. The old site of Forsyth was flooded when the Bull Shoals Lake was formed. New Forsyth, built high on the hills above the lake, provides a bird's-eye view of the waters and the surrounding hills.

5 Shepherd of the Hills Farm, about seven miles beyond the town of Branson, is set in a typically lovely Ozark landscape. The farm is the scene of Harold Bell Wright's popular novel *Shepherd of the Hills*, which tells of the trials and tribulations of the hill folk he met here at the turn of the century.

Wright wrote most of his book at a scenic overlook now known as Inspiration Point, where statues of the novel's main characters stand today. During the summer a pageant reenacting the story is staged nightly at the nearby Old Mill Theater. A grist-

mill grinds corn that is sold at the visitor center, and a motorized tram tours the area.

6 Silver Dollar City is the largest tourist attraction in the Ozarks. The city is a combination craft center and theme park where demonstrations of such various crafts as spinning, weaving, wood carving, glass blowing, and soap-making are given, while musicians perform on typical Ozark instruments—fiddles, guitars, and homemade dulcimers. The park is closed from November to May.

Marvel Cave, beneath Silver Dollar City, is one of the world's largest. The tour of the cavern begins in a room as big as the Houston Astrodome. In the winding passages are huge formations, including a 505-foot "waterfall" of stone. The entrance fee to Silver Dollar City includes admission to Marvel Cave.

7 The School of the Ozarks, a tuition-free college for needy Ozark students, sits on a bluff overlooking Lake Taneycomo. Dress codes are maintained at the school, attendance at chapel is required, and there is a conscious commitment to hard work. The students, who earn their way by working for the college, constructed the parklike campus.

Visitors are taken on a miniature train to the Gothic chapel; the Edwards Mill, which is a replica of an 1850 water-powered mill where corn is ground to be sold at the college gift shop; and the sprawling Ralph Foster Museum, an orderly attic of memorabilia from the Ozarks and other parts of the world.

8 Beyond the limestone cliffs that accent the landscape around Table Rock Lake's headwaters, the road turns northwest at Eagle Rock, follows a roller-coaster route through woods and pastures, and continues to Roaring River State Park.

Here the main feature is Roaring River Spring, which has waters that gush from the base of a high dolomite cliff and drop into the ponds and raceways of a state trout hatchery.

Except for the fast-flowing, sycamore-lined river, which is filled with trout, and the campgrounds bordering its banks, the 3,459-acre park is steep, heavily forested wild land. Five trails climb the hills and drop into the hollows. A naturalist is on duty year-round to lead groups of hikers and to give nature talks.

In Mark Twain National Forest, Sugar Camp Scenic Drive, a well-graded gravel road, heads down the

8. The White River, photographed from a high bluff, meanders westward through its tree-lined banks toward the dam, visible in the distance, that was built to create Table Rock Lake. In the state park surrounding the lake there are facilities for camping and picnicking.

side of the ridge and circles back to Eagle Rock. On the way the road, flanked by outcrops of limestone, rises and descends through a green canopy of oaks and passes a picturesque log cabin. There are several overlooks along the way.

From Eagle Rock westward the road passes through forests and fields as it meanders among Ozark farms that cling to hillsides. Vultures, locally called Ozark eagles, soar on thermal currents above the deep valleys. As you continue beyond the Powell Fire Lookout, which towers above a planted forest of loblolly pine, you enter Huckleberry Ridge State Forest. Ponds along the road provide water for cattle and also retard the runoff that has been eroding the Ozarks for millions of years.

Here in the forest the abundant oaks produce acorns sought by both deer and turkeys, and fill the forest with brilliant foliage in autumn. Flowering dogwood flourishes here too, trimming the woods with large white blossoms in spring and scarlet leaves in fall.

9 Neosho calls itself the City of Springs, thereby capitalizing on a phenomenon common to the Ozarks, where there is one of the greatest concentration of springs in the United States. The springs, formed by the heavy yearly rainfall and the predominance of porous dolomite and limestone rocks, flow through the extensive system of streams and rivers that carve their sinuous courses through the landscape.

There are four springs in Neosho that supply 1,500 gallons of 58°F water a minute to the Neosho National Fish Hatchery, the second oldest federal hatchery in the nation. (The oldest is Craig Brook in Maine.) More than 50,000 pounds of rainbow trout fingerlings and 300,000 to 400,000 smallmouth bass are produced here annually.

The road from Neosho to Diamond passes hayfields, orchards, and open oak woodlots, as the Ozark hills begin to intermix with the prairies.

10 The George Washington Carver National Monument commemorates one of the Ozarks' greatest native sons and one of America's most important scientists. Born in the closing years of the Civil War, George Carver

and his mother, Mary, both slaves that belonged to farmer Moses Carver, were kidnapped by border bandits. The baby was recovered and became the foster son of the Carvers. As a youth he took Washington as his middle name.

George Carver's foster parents encouraged his thirst for knowledge. He attended a black school in Neosho and earned a Master of Science degree at Iowa Agricultural College. From there he went to Tuskegee Institute in Alabama, where he spent the rest of his life teaching efficient farming practices and developing significant advances in agricultural

10. The statue by Robert Amendola of George Washington Carver as a boy is located in the park named for the famous American scientist and educator.

science. He was a major force in encouraging southern farmers to break their dependence on cotton as their primary crop. A bequest of Carver's established the George Washington Carver Foundation, which conducts various kinds of scientific research.

The visitor center at the monument details Carver's life and achievements with displays and literature. Nearby is the start of a ¾-mile nature trail that loops through the fields and forests in which George wandered when a boy.

Caves and springs and the many parks around them, scattered among great stretches of national forest, dominate the landscape in this part of Missouri.

From Sullivan southward almost to the Arkansas border, the route follows the mountains, winding through the woods and along picturesque waterways. The drive circles to the west and north, past Johnson's Shut-Ins State Park, an area of unusual rock clefts enclosed by hills, and on to Duck Creek and Mingo wildlife preserves.

Along the road between St. James and Cuba are the Missouri vineyards, known for their disease-resistant wild grape rootstocks, which have contributed to the productivity of grapes in both America and France since the turn of the century.

1 The small farming community of Sullivan was named for Stephen Sullivan, who donated land through the center of the village for the St. Louis–San Francisco Railway right-of-way. Four miles east of the town is the Meramec State Park, a 7,102-acre recreation area that stretches through the Meramec River valley.

The river cuts through a limestone–dolomite belt that has been eroded by underground streams to resemble a sponge. It is riddled with 70 springs and more caves than any other river system in the world. Twenty caves are found in the park. Fisher Cave, the largest and most popular, offers guided tours that take visitors past bizarre dripstone formations. The cave is closed from October to April.

Trails weave through the woods to other features, such as Copper Hollow Sinkhole and Mud Sink Cave, which are caves for spelunkers. Some of the caverns are closed to visitors for the protection of the Indiana bat, an endangered species that has found refuge here.

The park has a small natural history museum as well as facilities for boating, fishing, and swimming in the Meramec River.

2 At Washington State Park there are several Indian petroglyphs (designs carved on rocks) made 400 to 1,000 years ago. Because of their soft surfaces, dolomite outcrops are ideal for such carvings. The rock is easily destroyed, however, by acid waters,

3. *These huge granite boulders in Elephant Rocks State Park were once covered with sedimentary rock that was removed by exfoliation, a process of expansion and contraction that peels off the outer surface. Through this process, granite always takes on a rounded form. The person at the top of the rock ledge, silhouetted against the horizon, is dwarfed by the enormous boulders.*

and for this reason the petroglyphs at Washington State Park are sheltered by an open pavilion.

A swimming pool, picnic and camp grounds, and hiking trails along the bluffs overlooking the Big River are included in the park.

3 At the town of Graniteville you can see many buildings of the material for which the town was named. Just north of town is the entrance to Elephant Rocks State Park, an area that has some of the most dramatic granite outcroppings in Missouri. The huge boulders, igneous rock more than a billion years old, were eroded into rounded forms by thousands of years of slow weathering.

Basins in the surface of the granite slabs on which the "elephants" rest were caused by chemical reactions between the rock and rainwater. Shallow depressions became enlarged when water accumulated in them and then froze, helping to chip out basins.

From the parking lot a one-mile nature trail, with explanations in both Braille and standard print, follows a route that circles the rocks.

4 At Johnson's Shut-Ins State Park, a pleasant quarter-mile paved path leads along the East Fork of the Black River to the "shut-ins," gorges where rivers have cut their way through overlying sedimentary rock to the old igneous rock underneath. The hard rhyolite (ancient volcanic rock) at Johnson's Shut-Ins restricts the water's flow to narrow rock-bound channels, which were cracks formed when the volcanic rock cooled and the Ozarks were uplifted.

5 In Sam A. Baker State Park trails wind up and down Mudlick Mountain's forested slopes. The swift, clear waters of Big Creek surge through several shut-ins.

Named for a former Missouri governor, the 5,148-acre park contains picnic areas, campgrounds, and cabins for rent.

7. *Wood ducklings look out of their nest at the Mingo Wildlife Refuge. Other local ducks include mallards and gadwalls.*

6 The road winds through the mountains as it approaches Duck Creek Wildlife Management Area, where 6,100 acres of swampland have been set aside for hunting. It includes three large, shallow pools with a cover of water grasses and bald cypress and tupelo trees, forming an area that is ideal for waterfowl and other wildlife.

From the turnoff at Arab, good gravel roads take you through the preserve, a fascinating swampy environment that usually can be seen only from a boat.

7 Adjacent to Duck Creek preserve is the Mingo National Wildlife Refuge. Both areas are part of the dense Mingo Swamp, which formed when the Mississippi River shifted its channel 18,000 years ago. A wide variety of trees grows in this remnant of hardwood swamp.

Local farmers till 700 acres of the land and leave a share of their crops in the fields for the wildlife of the refuge. Wood ducks—among the most beautifully marked of all the waterfowl—are a prime attraction at Mingo. These birds nest in cavities of mature trees. An observation blind at the end of a short boardwalk through the woods provides an excellent view of the ducks.

The visitor center, which overlooks Rockhouse Marsh, contains displays about the history, the geology, and the wildlife of Mingo.

9. The crystal-clear waters of Big Spring, which have a constant temperature of 60°F, bubble forth from an opening in a mountainside, form a rock-edged pond, and join the Current River on its 225-mile course from Montauk Spring to the Black River in Arkansas.

8 The Wappapello Dam across the St. Francis River impounds an 8,600-acre reservoir known as Wappapello Lake. Wooded slopes rise from the water, and marinas line the shore. At the state park, which stretches along the shores of the lake, there are facilities for such water sports as boating, fishing, and swimming, as well as for picnicking and camping. Trails for hiking and backpacking wind through the park's hillsides.

9 Ozark National Scenic Riverways—long, narrow parks adjacent to the wild, unspoiled Jacks Fork and Current rivers—wind to the northwest from the town of Van Buren, a fishing resort on the Current River. The area is known for its numerous springs, including Big Spring, one of the largest in North America. The millions of gallons of water that gush from the spring daily come from a wide area, flowing through passages

dissolved in dolomite bedrock and emerging here at an opening formed by the downcutting of the Current River. While driving along Route 103 to Big Spring, look for the Skyline Drive. On this four-mile loop you can see an excellent wildlife habitat, split rail fences, picnic areas, hiking trails, and unexcelled scenic vistas.

10 A wooded, hilly, winding road goes north from Route 60 to Alley Spring on the Jacks Fork River. The waters of this spring come from as far away as 11 miles, flowing through underground conduits and maintaining a temperature of about 60°F year-round. When the surrounding countryside is all ice and snow, watercress flourishes in the mild springwaters, forming a carpet of fresh green foliage.

Nearby, the red Alley Spring Mill, powered by water from the spring, grinds corn today just as it did in 1894 when it was built.

As the road continues northward, it traverses another part of the Ozark National Scenic Riverways, an area with beautiful vistas of rolling wooded hills all along the way.

11 As you descend into the Current River valley, you come to Round Spring, which is located in a col-

10. A scenic drive, shown here following mountain ridges, takes you through the Ozark National Scenic Riverways, a narrow park along the Jacks Fork and Current rivers. The Jacks Fork (right) winds through a wooded valley. At various points along these two rivers, johnboats—long, narrow, and flat-bottomed—as well as canoes can be rented.

lapsed dolomite cave. The spring-waters bubble up into a deep, almost perfectly round basin and then flow to the river through a natural bridge that was formed by the ceiling of the collapsed cave.

12 A short distance up the valley is the Round Spring Cavern, a cave whose formations are so fragile that tour groups are limited to 10 persons. The two-hour tour of the cave is conducted by lantern light.

The cliffs containing the cave were stained in vertical patterns by dripping water that evaporated, depositing minerals on the bare cliff face.

Continuing north, the rolling, narrow, twisting road suddenly becomes flatter and straighter as it approaches the New Lead Belt, where this valuable material, found in abundance here, is being mined and smelted.

13 As the road approaches Dillard, it passes through a series of pine plantations, indicative of the interest in reforestation where necessary in the Ozarks. At the southern edge of the town is the Dillard Mill State Historic Site, stretching along Huzzah Creek. A short violet-bordered path follows the creek past a millpond to the well-restored barn-red Dillard Mill, which ground grain for the many farmers in the area from 1900, when it was built, to the 1960's.

In the 132 acres of the historic site, where trails wind through the woods, you may see deer, turkeys, beaver, and many kinds of wild flowers.

14 The town of Steelville, known as a fishing and farming center, is located on the Meramec River. Seven miles west of the town, in the forested river valley, is Maramec Spring Park, a preserve where Missouri's first iron furnace was built. An iron-ore deposit in the area was used as a source of paint by the Shawnee Indians, who guided ironmonger Samuel Massey to the spot in 1825. Massey built the furnace in 1826, obtaining power for both the furnace and a nearby mill by constructing seven wooden undershot waterwheels that were turned by the constantly flowing waters of Maramec Spring.

The iron furnace that stands in the park today, no longer in use, was built in 1857. The old mill is gone, but the spring still bubbles from a circular pool at the base of a dolomite bluff

and supplies water to a trout-raising pool. An observation tower in the park provides a fine view of the Meramec River basin and the park's lovely grounds.

Near the towns of St. James and Rosati is a plateau called the Big Prairie, an area known for its abundance of wild grapes. Here in the 1890's domestic grapevines were planted, and winemaking became a Missouri industry. Although it is not an important part of the state's economy today, wine is still made in Missouri, mostly in the Big Prairie area.

17. In the Lily Pad Room of the Onondaga Cave, strange rock formations that resemble the large, round leaves of water lilies seem to float on the cavern's pool. Also rising from the water-covered floor of the cave is a series of cone-shaped stalagmites, formed by the drippings from the large stalactites that hang from the ceiling.

15 The St. James Winery, a new establishment, operates with modern equipment that controls every step of the process. Visitors, who are offered a self-guided tour and a tasting table of 18 different still wines and 3 sparkling wines, can buy cheeses, wines, and equipment for making wine at home at the winery headquarters. Picnic tables have been set up under a canopy of trees for the convenience of visitors to the establishment.

16 Using old-fashioned methods, the Rosati Winery, 4½ miles east on State Route ZZ, operates in a dimly lit brick building where the wine ages in white oak casks well covered with

spiderwebs. A narrow stairway leads up to an observation tower on the roof that looks out over acres of vineyards. Self-guided tours of the winery and its vineyards, and a tasting of about a dozen different kinds of wines, are offered.

Harvesttime, from mid-September to mid-October, is the best time of year for a visit.

17 Onondaga Cave, outstanding in an area where remarkable caves are common, is a huge cavern that displays wonderous formations. It took 60 to 100 million years for the slightly acid rainwater to dissolve the 400-million-year-old dolomite and carry it away via the Meramec River. Meanwhile, the water was dripping down the cave walls, evaporating, and leaving its load of dissolved rock as formations of colorful onyx.

This is a so-called living cave, as the process continues today, with water still dripping and running through the cave. Guided tours along walkways go past such features as the Queen's Canopy and the unique Lily Pad Room.

Nicely landscaped grounds and lawns above the cave form a pleasant park along the Meramec River.

Traveling in Arkansas

Rugged scenery, sparkling waterways, and forested mountain peaks blend with scattered pasturelands

Although Arkansas has many important industrial areas, its great stretches of forest-clad mountains to the west and the bottomlands to the east give this Land of Opportunity, as the state has been nicknamed, a beauty both wild and pastoral.

Two major mountain ranges—the Ozarks, which reach up into Missouri, and the Ouachitas (*wash-y-taws*)—are separated by the Arkansas River, largest of the many sizable streams that cut through the state. With countless lakes, ponds, mountain streams, limestone caves, and mineral springs, this countryside, known as the Interior Highlands, has become a major center for sportsmen and vacationers.

On the Delta and Grand Prairie that extend to the eastern border are plantations whose crops of rice, cotton, and soybeans form an important part of the economy of Arkansas.

One of the world's best known spas, the city of Hot Springs is nestled in the Ouachita Mountains of western Arkansas. Thousands of years ago the thermal waters in this region were sought out by Indians, who recognized that the waters had curative powers.

West and north of the city the Ouachitas stretch to the banks of the Arkansas River. Across this great waterway, one of the nation's longest, are the slopes of the Ozark Mountains. Valleys, ridges, and mountain streams fill the landscape, with an occasional open pastureland and cattle farm among the hills.

1 The cosmopolitan city of Hot Springs, a resort center and health spa located in the foothills of the Ouachita Mountains, was settled in 1808 by pioneers who came to the area because of its thermal springs. Since the 1870's visitors from around the world have come to partake of the waters' supposed curative powers.

The thermal water, which originates as rainwater and sinks slowly to a great depth, is heated by contact with hot rocks. Highly permeable zones collect the heated water in the aquifer and provide avenues for the water to eventually travel up to the surface.

Forty-five of the springs have been capped and the water piped to the town's famous row of bathhouses. Three springs preserved in their original state can be seen. A "tufa trail" climbs a hillside to an area where this mineral from the hot springs has been deposited.

Hot Springs National Park, 4,500 acres of forested hills with hiking trails, campgrounds, picnic groves, and a visitor center, is almost completely surrounded by the city. A drive up West and Hot Springs mountains takes you through dense pine, oak, and hickory woodlands to an area above the city, where pink lady's slippers and sundrops flourish.

2 About six miles south of Bismarck lie De Gray Lake and the adjacent state park, a region ringed by low hills. Campsites, interpretive trails, a golf course, tennis courts, good fishing, a marina, and a 96-room lodge and convention center make this a superior recreation area.

The pleasant city of Arkadelphia, situated on a bluff overlooking the Ouachita River, was an important port in the days when steamboats plied these waters. Today it is an industrial and agricultural center.

1. Although the domed building in Hot Springs' bathhouse row, shown here, is officially known as the Health Services Bathhouse, it is still called Quapaw, the name it was given when it was built in the 1920's. All the bathhouses are on the National Register of Landmark Buildings.

SPECIAL FEATURES

ROAD GUIDE ▬▬▬	HIGHLIGHT **1**
STATE PARKS	SCHEDULED AIRLINE STOPS ✈
With Campsites ▲ Without Campsites △	
RECREATION AREAS	OTHER AIRPORTS ✈
With Campsites ▲ Without Campsites △	
SELECTED REST AREAS ✕	BOAT RAMPS ◢
POINTS OF INTEREST ■	INFORMATION CENTER ✹

ROAD CLASSIFICATION

CONTROLLED ACCESS HIGHWAYS
(Entrance and Exit only at Interchanges)

OTHER DIVIDED HIGHWAYS

PAVED HIGHWAYS

LOCAL ROADS In unfamiliar areas inquire locally before using these roads — Paved — Gravel — — Dirt — —

MILEAGE

MILEAGE BETWEEN TOWNS AND JUNCTIONS

MILEAGE BETWEEN DOTS ●—35—●

SCALE

ONE INCH 22 MILES   0 5 10 15   25

ONE INCH 35 KILOMETERS   0 5 10 20 30 40

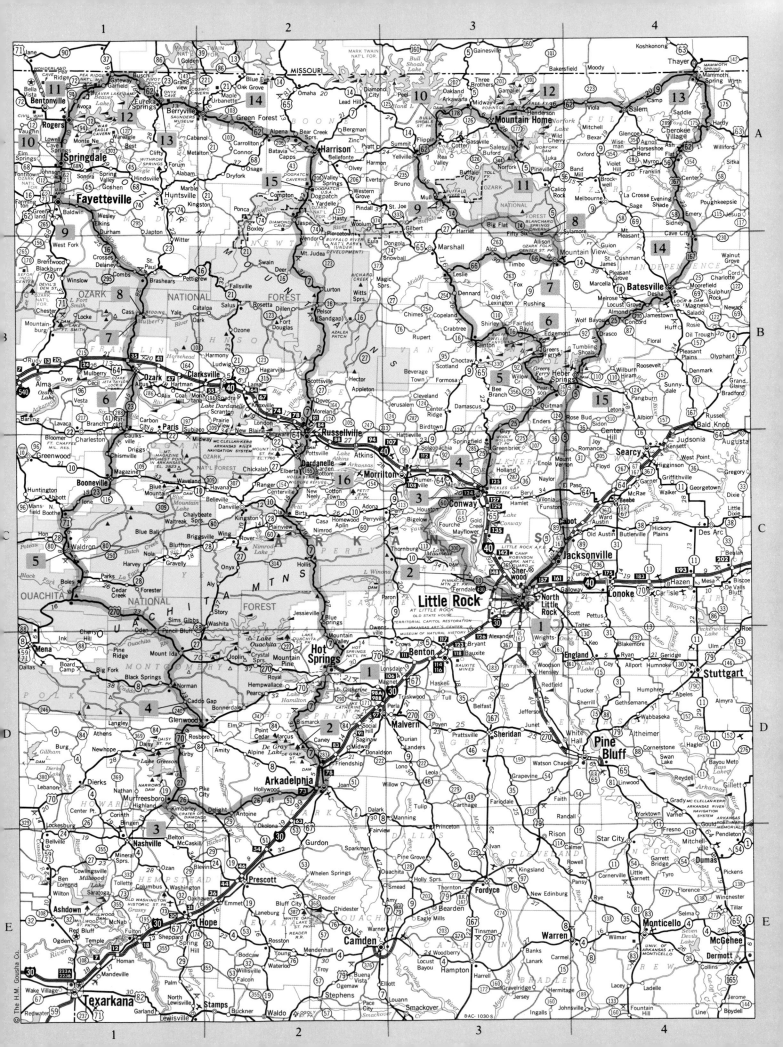

3 The Crater of Diamonds, near the city of Murfreesboro, is the only diamond mine—actually, a field—in the United States. The crater, now known as Crater of Diamonds State Park, draws amateur prospectors, who are allowed to keep whatever stones they find. One such prospector searches only after a rainstorm, another just sits and looks for glints of light. Although most of the specimens found here are small, a 16.37-carat stone was found at the crater in 1975, and a 4.25-carat canary-yellow diamond was picked up on May 15, 1980.

Ka-do-ha, an ancient Indian area on an old channel of the Little Missouri River on the outskirts of Murfreesboro, was the home of mound-building Indians about a thousand years ago. Some of the mounds were used as foundations for homes and temples, others for tombs. Nearby is a small museum with displays of stone, shell, and pottery artifacts. The region is popular with vacationers who come to hunt for arrowheads.

4 The road follows the Caddo River, a clear mountain stream, as it goes through Caddo Gap in the Ouachita National Forest. The town of Caddo Gap, particularly popular with fishermen, is located near the river, and people who live on the opposite side use a high suspension footbridge to get to town when the low vehicular bridge is under water.

Mount Ida, a resort town located at the western end of Lake Ouachita, is known for its several rock shops, which display specimens of novaculite and quartz crystal. Near the city are the crystal mines, and visitors are invited, for a fee, to try their luck at finding interesting pieces.

5 At Waldron, a city with the air of a western town, is Blythe's Museum, open year-round and full of Indian artifacts and such memorabilia as an early Edison phonograph and cylinders in working condition, as well as a good gun collection.

A lush green valley surrounded by deep forests leads to nearby Lake Waldron and the recreation areas of Knoppers Ford and Jack Creek, with East Poteau Mountain to the west and Pilot Knob to the east.

6 Ozark, a small town at the great north bend of the Arkansas River, is the center of a poultry-raising region. The town's main industry is the processing and shipping of turkeys and chickens.

About two miles east of the town are the Ozark Overlook, which offers a panoramic view of the rolling countryside, the Jeta Taylor Dam, and a recreation area where campgrounds and picnic groves are available.

Altus, six miles southeast of Ozark, is the wine capital of Arkansas. It is set in the midst of vineyards that cover the hillsides for miles around. Visitors are welcome at the wineries; at the Wiederkehr's Winery luncheons and dinners are served along with samples of the wine.

As the road continues northward, it leaves the Ouachitas and enters the Boston Mountains and the Ozark National Forest. Cleared patches of private property are scattered along the way, each one surrounded by a dense forest of hickory, oak, and shortleaf pine (*Pinus echinata*), the state tree.

7 Some of the finest white-water canoeing in Arkansas is found on the Mulberry River at Turner Bend, two miles south of Cass. Here canoe rentals are available. Near the town of Cass is a pinnacle known as Bee Rock, a large boulder that provides protection for the nests of millions of honey bees drawn here by the clover carpeting the hillside. Early settlers,

The ingenious beaver

The beaver, an aquatic rodent native to North America, grows to about three feet long and has a wide, flat tail and heavy, brown water-repellent fur. Beavers build their lodge (right) at the edge of a stream, on a platform of sticks, rocks, and mud, providing it with two underwater entrances. Nearby they keep a cache of twigs and branches. By gnawing through trunks and felling such trees as the ash (below left), and adding sticks, stones, and mud (center), they construct a dam (right) to maintain the proper water level. Beavers usually live in colonies of 10 or 12 families, each unit having 2 kits, as the young are called. These animals, if undisturbed, forage and maintain their dams during the day. Otherwise they work at night.

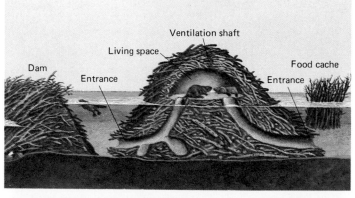

Ventilation shaft
Living space
Dam
Entrance
Food cache
Entrance

who had little actual money, found such an abundance of honey and beeswax in the area that they used these products as currency.

8 The Redding Recreation Area, which stretches along the Mulberry River in the Ozark National Forest, is a wilderness where such wild flowers as trout lilies, mayapples, and trillium bloom in early spring, followed in May by both pink and white wild phlox. Such wildlife as deer and wild turkeys roam the forest. The preserve, with facilities for camping and picnicking, is a popular vacation spot. In spring, when the river is high, there is excellent boating and fishing. The area is three miles east of Cass on Route 1003.

The road follows the upper White River on the way to Fayetteville, winding through farmlands strung along the cool, green valley. The White River, with long quiet pools and unexpected hairpin turns, is ideal for float trips and is popular with vacationers who bring their own craft. Hickory, oak, sweet gum, and cottonwood trees line the river's banks, providing shelter for bluebirds, red-tailed hawks, and kingfishers. In the bordering meadows you may see an occasional Calloway—a cattle that is all black except for a wide, white band around the middle—grazing contentedly.

9 Fayetteville, a hilly town, is dominated by the University of Arkansas and its activities. "Old Main," the red brick 1876 administration building, stands four stories high; its two mansard towers form a familiar landmark on the city's skyline. The University Museum houses a magnificent collection of quartz crystals and other minerals.

The historic Headquarters House, built in 1853, served as both a Union and a Confederate command post during the Civil War. Today it is a museum and open to visitors.

10 In 1839 a group of Cherokees camped at the site of the present town of Springdale on their forced march to Oklahoma. Today Springdale is an important food-growing and processing center and the poultry capital of Arkansas. Here the Shiloh Historic District and its museum present displays that show what pioneer life was like in north-

west Arkansas. The town is the scene of an annual July 1–4 Rodeo of the Ozarks, one of the best known of the many rodeos held in the state during the summer.

As you travel north you come to an apple orchard, a slope full of color when the apple trees and the lavender-flowered paulownias are in bloom.

11 A seven-mile driving trail through the Pea Ridge National Military Park follows historical markers

11. At Pea Ridge National Military Park a Civil War artillery gun stands as a reminder of the battle won by Union forces here in March 1862, ending a campaign begun in Missouri weeks earlier to drive Confederate troops out of that state.

that tell the story of the battle that has been called The Gettysburg of the West, an encounter that saved Missouri for the Union. Within the park is the Elkhorn Tavern, a station on the Butterfield Stagecoach Line. The tavern, which survived the battle but was later destroyed by guerrillas, has been rebuilt around the original chimney, and is now open to visitors.

12 Around Beaver Lake are many excellent recreation areas, with seven nature trails, camping grounds, fishing and boating facilities, and a swimming beach. At the bottom of the cliff at Beaver Lake Dam are several hundred feet of Cotter dolomite with chert, a dark-colored flintlike rock. On top of this are 6 to 12 feet of Powell dolomite, which is wave-patterned and lighter in color. There is

no chert in this layer. The dolomite was laid down by ancient seas 400 million years ago.

Eastward across the top of the state, the surface rock is the St. Joe limestone member of the Boone formation, a limestone with a few chert nodules. Tiny fossil impressions in the rocks can be seen along the road in the cuts through the hills.

At Inspiration Point on the gorge of the White River there is a dramatic view of the wooded Ozarks to the north and of the river as it winds its way into Missouri. Here too is a structure known as the Castle, a mansion built in the early 1900's by a German immigrant who chose this particular hilltop because the scenery reminded him of the Rhineland. The Castle, open to visitors, is furnished as an early-1900's American home.

13 The Victorian town of Eureka Springs has been called the Little Switzerland of America. The city, which clings to the side of a mountain, has a tangle of streets that includes 50 U-turns, 51 V-turns, and 16 S-curves. Forty miles of stone walls hold up a series of earthern terraces. The entire downtown area is listed in the National Register of Historic Places. The town is known for the performances of the Passion Play,

which are put on in a 4,100-seat amphitheater throughout the summer.

There are 63 springs within the city limits, the waters coming from hillsides where St. Joe limestone rests on Chattanooga shale, a junction that can be seen near Little Eureka Springs at an overhanging bluff.

The top of the bluff has a bed of gray-green shale 8 to 12 inches thick, underlaid by dark brown-to-black fissile clay shale.

14 At Berryville, a farming community, the Saunders Museum has an impressive collection of historical weapons, including some that were used by Jesse James, Billy the Kid, and Pancho Villa. Each year during the last weekend of September the Saunders Memorial Muzzleloading Gun Shoot is held in Berryville, an event that is attended by top marksmen from all over the world.

The road continues on cleared hilltops through farming country. Apple orchards line the road, and hot apple pie and apple butter are offered for sale at roadside stands.

15 Dogpatch U.S.A., patterned after the make-believe town of cartoon fame, is built on two levels. On the town's hilltop are Mammy Yokum's Pancake House, a convention center, and a U.S. Post Office (zip code 72648). A funicular carries you downhill to the rest of the village, which has as attractions Mammy Yokum's cabin, an Indian village, and craft workshops. People costumed as Li'l Abner and other Al Capp comic strip characters greet visitors.

The stretch of road from Dogpatch to Russellville is said to be one of the 10 most scenic drives in the nation. It goes through the heavily forested Ozarks, descends to the Buffalo River through stands of sassafras, maple, oak, and hickory, and crosses the riverside meadow.

The road then begins to climb again and reaches the top of Judea Mountain, called Judy, which takes you back into the Boston Mountains. At the summit the scenery opens up for an expansive view of the Buffalo River Canyon. In spring the hills are dotted with the lavender blossoms of the paulownia tree. In summer the turkey vultures, with their brilliant, bare red heads, soar on the canyon's air currents almost at eye level.

Russellville, a thriving city named for a British physician who settled here in 1835, lies on the north bank of the Arkansas River. Although coal mining was important here during the late 1880's, food processing has taken over today as the major industry, and the mines are now flooded with water from nearby Lake Dardanelle.

In 1819 the city of Dardanelle was a Cherokee trading post. At the Council Oaks, two great white oaks on the bank of the Arkansas River, Cherokee chief Black Fox, on May 6, 1820, reluctantly signed away all the rights of the Cherokees to their land south of the river.

16 Holla Bend Wildlife Refuge, a wilderness area on the Arkansas River, offers protection to such wildlife as deer, raccoons, opossums, and

16. Raccoons, always curious, peer from their tree home. These furry mammals, relatives of the bear, can be seen at the Holla Bend Wildlife Refuge.

wildcats. The refuge, on Route 155, has a wintertime population of thousands of snow geese and bald eagles. The drive through the wilderness is open year-round.

South of Jessieville is Blue Springs, the roadside location of a rock shop that sells an unusual brown rock shot with quartz crystals often called Arkansas diamonds. A drive of about 10 miles leads to a mountain of quartz and to Coleman's Mine where, for a fee, visitors may hunt for the crystals.

From the city *of Little Rock north to the Missouri border, the countryside through the Ozarks is a series of mountains, rivers, and resort towns, making this one of the most popular vacation areas in Arkansas.*

Several man-made lakes, created by dams across the White, the North Fork, and other rivers of northern Arkansas, provide bays, inlets, harbors, and beaches with marinas and campgrounds for the many vacationers who come here to enjoy the beauty and wonders of this hilly landscape.

1 According to legend, Little Rock, the state capital, was named by French explorers who came up the Arkansas River in 1722 and camped by what they called a little rock jutting out above the riverbank.

The city, founded in 1822, lies along the south shore of the river and marks the dividing line between the flat coastal plain to the east and the foothills of the Ouachita Mountains to the west.

Although it is the state's largest city and a major industrial and cultural center, Little Rock has retained much of its early atmosphere, particularly in historic Quapaw Quarter, where several stately homes such as Trapnall Hall and Villa Marre have been preserved. The old state capitol, a lovely Greek Revival building, is now a museum. The present capitol is a structure of classical Greek style whose exterior is faced with Batesville marble, a limestone quarried at the nearby city of Batesville.

In Little Rock are several parks, including Allsopp and Boyle. In April and May these garden spots are alive with migrating birds and are carpeted with wild flowers. Burns Park, in North Little Rock, a twin city across the river, has campgrounds and picnic areas.

To the west of Little Rock the banks of the Arkansas River are lined with cottonwood trees. The cottonlike fluff of the trees' seed capsules, for which the tree is named, drifts down like snowflakes in the month of May.

As the road leaves the river, it climbs steeply up the face of massive Jackstone Sandstone Cliff, a hillside covered in spring with flowering kudzu vines, azaleas, redbuds, and dogwoods.

2. Two trails in Pinnacle Mountain State Park lead through the forest to the summit, the elevation seen above, where there is a magnificent view of Lake Maumelle and the surrounding countryside. The lake, part of Little Rock's reservoir system, has many coves, inlets, and harbors, and several marinas. The area is popular with vacationers who enjoy its peace and beauty. For backpackers a special attraction are the spring wild flowers that grow in the woods and fields.

Red trillium

Rue anemone

Bird's-foot violet

Spring beauty

2   Pinnacle Mountain, almost perfectly dome shaped, is surrounded by a state park. At the headquarters an observation platform provides a magnificent view of the distant valleys. Here too is the start of the Ouachita Trail, a 200-mile-long path for backpackers, and the Kingfisher Trail, which follows the Maumelle River. Guided wild flower walks are held in late March and April.

A five-mile drive takes you to Lake Maumelle. In the fall migrating ospreys, herons, and white pelicans can usually be seen on the lake. Eagles come to the area in winter.

As the road continues northward, it goes through stretches of dense pine woods, interspersed with farms and cattle ranches.

Near Conway there is an area of "pimple mounds," slight rises in the earth about 2 feet high and 40 feet in diameter, believed to have been created in the last ice age by wind and water. During an arid phase there was only scattered scrub here on a barren prairie. Drifting soil collected around the vegetation, and later, rainfall in various places helped deepen channels between the heaps of soil. These mounds can be seen only on land that has never been plowed.

3   Conway was settled in 1870 by A. P. Robinson, who named the town in honor of the politically prominent Conway family. It is known today for its three colleges. On the grounds of the Faulkner County Courthouse, in the center of town, is a well-preserved log cabin with a dogtrot, which is a roofed passageway connecting two parts of a house. The structure was once a station on the Butterfield Stagecoach Line to California. This building and others dating from the town's early days are open to visitors.

4   Pickles Gap Creek Crafts Village, a center for craft shops, also includes a farm, a gristmill, a general store, and a covered bridge. Woodworkers and other craftsmen display their skills here and offer their wares for sale.

As you drive through this high, open tornado country, you can see storm cellars at the older homesites. Called "fraidy holes," some of these safe havens are covered with earth; others are made of solid concrete. Statistics prove that there are fewer tornado casualties in regions with these shelters than in places where there are no shelters.

5 Greers Ferry Lake, in the foothills of the heavily wooded Ozarks, is a playground area with superb boating and fishing. Walleyes weighing as much as 22 pounds have been caught in these waters. U.S. Army Corps of Engineers public-use areas at the town of Greers Ferry, on The Narrows section of the lake, have picnic areas and camping sites.

At Sugar Loaf Mountain, an island in the lake reached by boat, a path designated a national recreation trail winds up to the summit, where there are picnic shelters and a spectacular view of the lake.

6 Bluff Dweller Canyon, whose rock formations and caves, according to archeologists, served as dwellings for prehistoric Indians, has picnic facilities in its tree-shaded valley.

As the road climbs through the pine-covered hills, it winds among large outcrops of sandstone. In April the blossoms of shadbush, redbud, and dogwood provide splashes of color against the evergreens.

7 The town of Mountain View is the center for Arkansas folk music. Every Saturday night, year-round, the Mountain View Folklore Society presents traditional mountain music in Courthouse Square. At the Ozark Folk Center on the edge of town, where all kinds of musical instruments are made, craft demonstrations and musical events are held throughout the summer. During the third and fourth weekends of April, the Annual Arkansas Folk Festival is held here.

The center is made up of some 50 stone-and-cedar buildings. Trams carry visitors from the parking lot to the auditorium, which is called the Craft Forum, the hub of the center's activities.

The road cuts through limestone cliffs in this part of the Ozarks. Here the square-tailed cliff swallows build their mud nests in the rocky precipices and share the area with yellow warblers, which make their nests in the nearby willows.

8 Blanchard Springs Caverns, limestone caves in the heart of the Ozark National Forest, are known for their unusual formations of stalactites, stalagmites, and the so-called draperies. Some of the stalagmites form towering columns, such as a

65-foot giant in a room that measures about 1,200 by 180 feet and is called The Cathedral.

Dripstone Trail, the easier of two that wind through the tunnels, is a little more than a half-mile long and takes you into two major rooms in the cave's upper level. The walking areas are paved. Discovery Trail, much more difficult, with some 700 steps to negotiate, begins at a lobby 216 feet below the surface (reached by elevator) and threads through the caverns for more than a mile. This trail is closed from October to May.

8. This giant column, 65 feet tall, is one of the outstanding features of the Dripstone Trail in Blanchard Springs Caverns.

The caverns are surrounded by a recreation area that offers camping, picnicking, swimming, canoeing, fishing, and trail hiking. A walk along Mill Creek leads from the caverns to Blanchard Springs, where the underground stream that runs through the caverns emerges.

9 Buffalo River, the nation's only stream to be designated as a national river, flows through a land of rugged mountains and limestone cliffs. The area known as Buffalo National River is a narrow strip of territory along the

more than 130-mile length of the stream. Buffalo Point has nature trails, campgrounds, picnic groves, a swimming beach, canoe rental services, and overnight cabins.

Canoe trips are available for runs of an hour, all day, or overnight with camping on a gravel bar.

Yellville, once known as Shawneetown because it had been the site of an Indian village, was named for Col. Archibald Yell, who was active in early Arkansas politics. Today Yellville is the commercial center for many recreation areas in the surrounding mountains.

The town has retained the atmosphere of its early days, with many of its old buildings still standing.

Northeast of Yellville the drive takes you through a pastoral countryside, with apple orchards, red barns, and grazing cattle.

10 Bull Shoals Lake, formed by a dam on the White River, is one of the largest in Arkansas. With hundreds of miles of shoreline, the lake provides excellent water sports of all kinds. Fishing for bass, bream, crappies, trout, and stripers attracts anglers from all over the state. Below the dam the White River offers some of the finest trout fishing in the Midsouth. Resorts and fishing outfitters dot the river's banks. On the drive across the dam there is a magnificent view of the cliffs and river valley downstream.

11 A side trip of about 12 miles from the town of Mountain Home, whose principal industry is tourism, takes you to the Wolf House, in the riverside village of Norfork. The house, a two-story log structure with two immense chimneys, an upstairs veranda, and a dogtrot, was built about 1809 by a blacksmith-preacher-fur trader named Jacob Wolf. Through the years the building has served as a county courthouse, a post office, a church, a trading post, and a residence and is now a museum. Furnished with pioneer artifacts, the building tells the story of life in early Arkansas.

12 Norfork Lake, formed by a dam on the North Fork River, is known for its excellent fishing. At Robinson Point Recreation Area on the water's shores, a scenic three-mile hiking trail winds along the limestone cliffs above the lake.

Our National River

The Buffalo River, a free-flowing stream that runs for some 132 miles through northwest Arkansas, was named a national river in 1972 in order to preserve its crystal-clear waters as well as the land through which it travels. It is our only river with the distinction of having been deemed "national."

The river winds through the Ozark Mountains and passes impressive limestone cliffs whose caves were once inhabited by Indians. The several stretches of white water along its course are a constant challenge to sportsmen who come to try their skill at shooting the rapids in canoes.

At Buffalo Point, 17 miles from the town of Yellville, there are facilities for camping, housekeeping cabins, day-use pavilions, picnic grounds, and canoe rentals. And through the surrounding mountains, several nature trails have been established by the National Park Service, the organization that administers the river.

9. *Canoeists on the Buffalo River paddle through a quiet stretch toward the limestone cliff called Roark Bluff, downstream from the Still Creek access point. The river, famous for its rocky, scenic shoreline, is popular with canoe enthusiasts from all over the country.*

The small farming community of Salem is the scene of the Ozark Mountain Music Makers' free concerts, which are held on Saturday nights year-round at the Civic Center just north of the town.

13 According to an Indian legend, Mammoth Spring suddenly gushed forth from the earth as an Indian chief was burying his son, who had been killed while searching for water. The spring, on the Missouri border, has a flow of 150 to 200 million gallons a day, making it by far the largest spring in Arkansas. In the state park that surrounds the spring are the restored depot of the Frisco Railroad, which is now a museum, a national fish hatchery, picnic grounds, and a one-mile walking trail.

The waters of Mammoth Spring join the Spring River, one of the best in the state for float trips and canoeing. Fishing is excellent for rainbow trout in the upper reaches, and for small-mouth bass and walleyes near the town of Hardy.

Hardy is the home of the Arkansas Traveller Folk and Dinner Theatre, an outdoor arena nestled in the Ozark hills where folk plays are performed while meals typical of the area are served. The theater is closed from Labor Day to Memorial Day.

South of Hardy the road goes through Evening Shade, named for the grove of trees that protected the settlers from the hot "evening"—or afternoon—sun.

In this part of the Ozarks the hills are forested with oak, cedar, and sweet gum trees, which flourish in the rocky soil. The Indians sought out the cedars because their shaggy bark was excellent for tinder.

14 The first settler in Batesville, one of the oldest towns in the state, built a house in 1812 at the mouth of Poke Bayou where it joins the White River. During the 1800's there was a button factory in the town that cut blanks for pearl buttons from 16 different species of freshwater mussels, including the elephant-ear, pocket-book, and monkeyface. Today the quarrying of limestone, the production of agricultural lime, and tourism are the important industries, as are farming and poultry raising.

Nearby, on Route 69, is Spring Mill, the last of the 19th-century water-powered mills to operate in Arkansas. Here, in 1976, meal was ground for distribution by the Bicentennial Wagon Train on its journey to Valley Forge, Pennsylvania.

After crossing the White River, the road climbs steeply up Ramsey Hill through stands of oak and cedar to disclose a fine view of the city and the river valley. The grazing cattle, soybean fields, huge bales of hay, and long poultry houses that can be seen give evidence of cattle and farming country. The climb continues up Dean Mountain, taking you back into the Ozark Mountains.

15 The resort city of Heber Springs, named for its seven sources of mineral water, sits at the foot of Round Mountain. Many Arkansas craftsmen live and work in the area and take part in the annual Ozark Frontier Trail Festival and Craft Show, an event that is held in the city in mid-October. A free hootenanny is held in the Spring Park Auditorium every Saturday night from Memorial Day to Labor Day.

The drive crosses several east–west ridges of the Arkansas River valley. In late winter the orange broom that carpets the hillsides catches the afternoon sun as strings of blackbirds stream across the sky, heading toward their overnight roosts.

The Magnolia State

From its alluvial plains to its pine-clad hills Mississippi is a place of beauty and tranquility

There are cotton fields, to be sure, and the state tree, *Magnolia grandiflora*, is so highly thought of that its blossom is also the state flower. But there is much more here than just these symbols of the South. Mississippi also has forests, rolling prairies, and innumerable ponds, rivers, and creeks. The countryside is green most of the year, and the many meadows and farms instill a sense of serenity.

All through the state are gracious towns and cities with antebellum homes that recall the elegant era of the plantation South.

From Jackson, Mississippi's historic capital, this tour takes you through the southwestern part of the state to the river cities famous for their antebellum mansions. North of Vicksburg the Great River Road leads through the Delta, where some of the largest cotton plantations in the world are found and where the great Mississippi River still dominates the scene. Turning eastward, you drive through rolling farmland and then follow the beautiful Natchez Trace Parkway back to Jackson.

1 Jackson, an attractive, cosmopolitan city with a modern skyline, has been the capital of Mississippi since 1821, and its antebellum public buildings are fine examples of Greek Revival architecture. The Old Capitol, built in 1833-40, is now the State Historical Museum, and its elegant interior is filled with colorful exhibits tracing the history of Mississippi.

In the heart of the business district you find the Governor's Mansion, the residence of the state's chief executive since 1842. The white-painted brick structure resembles the White House, and it is a showcase for some of the finest 19th-century American furnishings around. The historic section of the mansion is open for tours.

The Mynelle Gardens are a glory of camellias, azaleas, and roses. A path wanders beneath Chinese jujuba, magnolia, and dogwood trees to a lagoon where arched footbridges are entwined with wisteria.

2 The Mississippi Petrified Forest, 20 miles north of Jackson, is the only forest of its kind east of the Rocky Mountains. The petrified logs are the remains of sequoias, firs, maples, and spurges that were carried down from the north by a great river about 36 million years ago. Stripped of limbs, bark, and roots by the journey, and buried in sand and silt, the logs slowly turned into stone.

A nature trail leads through a fragrant, mossy forest, a landscape of small gullies and ridges, where the petrified logs are strewn. Markers explain features of geological interest, such as the miniature Badlands, and identify the living trees, which include loblolly pines, winged elms, blackjack oaks, and wild plum. The walk takes about 30 minutes and terminates at the visitor center museum. Closed on Christmas Day.

2. The geological past of the Petrified Forest is revealed in the eroded soils of the miniature Badlands beyond this stone log, one of many found here. The bluff's lower layer of reddish sand is where the logs were buried and petrified by silica-rich water. The tan-colored upper layer is silt blown from floodplains and streams at the end of the last ice age.

SPECIAL FEATURES

ROAD GUIDE	HIGHLIGHT	**1**
STATE PARKS — With Campsites / Without Campsites	SCHEDULED AIRLINE STOPS	
RECREATION AREAS — With Campsites / Without Campsites	OTHER AIRPORTS	
SELECTED REST AREAS	BOAT RAMPS	
POINTS OF INTEREST	INFORMATION CENTER	

ROAD CLASSIFICATION

CONTROLLED ACCESS HIGHWAYS (Entrance and Exit only at Interchanges) — **5** Interchanges

OTHER DIVIDED HIGHWAYS

PAVED HIGHWAYS

LOCAL ROADS — In unfamiliar areas inquire locally before using these roads — Paved / Gravel / Dirt

MILEAGE

MILEAGE BETWEEN TOWNS AND JUNCTIONS — 4 4

MILEAGE BETWEEN DOTS — 35

SCALE

ONE INCH 24 MILES — 0 5 10 15 25

ONE INCH 38 KILOMETERS — 0 5 10 20 30 40

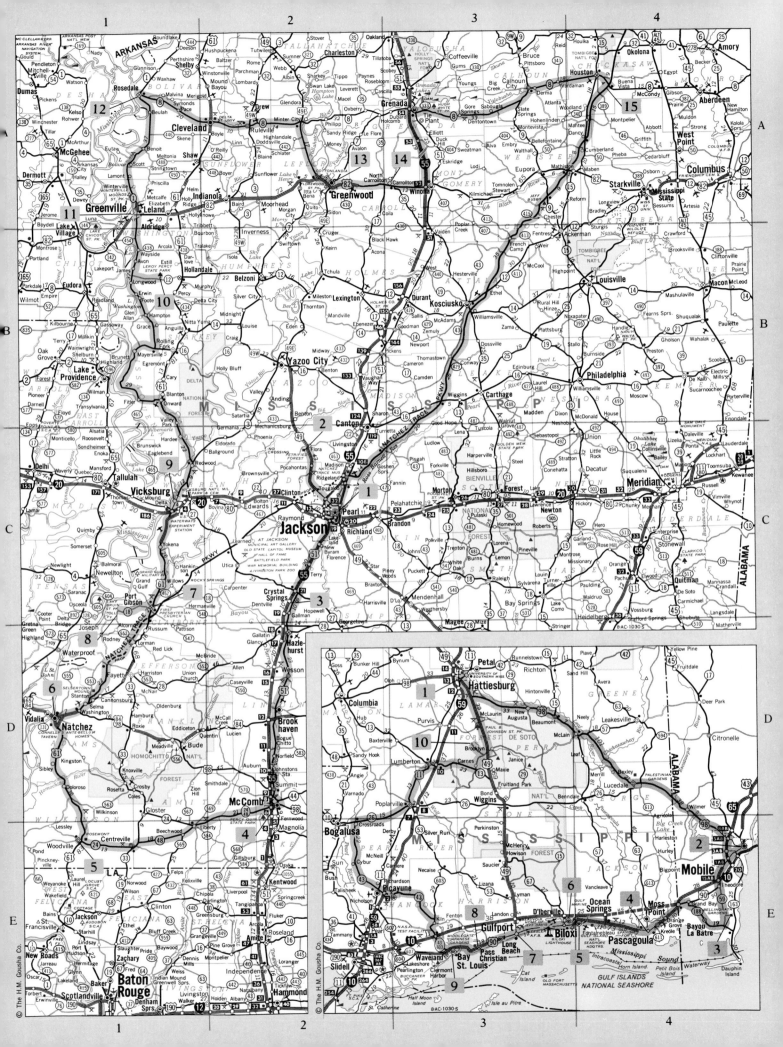

6. One of the most magnificent Greek Revival mansions in Natchez is Stanton Hall, whose double parlors combine to form a 70-foot ballroom. The design of a Natchez architect and the work of local builders and craftsmen, the structure testifies to their skills.

3 South of Jackson, in a region once noted for its production of truck crops, is the town of Crystal Springs, sometimes called Tomatopolis. From the 1870's until recent times, the town had been a major tomato-shipping point. Now the Crystal Springs Experiment Station, which is concerned with vegetable research, has hybridized a tomato that people can grow at home under greenhouse conditions. The state-run station, located south of town on Route 51, is interesting to see and welcomes visitors.

As you continue south, take time to see Hazlehurst, a lovely town with restored 19th-century homes.

4 A bustling business center, McComb is also a place of azaleas and dogwood and antiques shops. A major attraction here is The Ice House. Built in the 1890's when McComb supplied ice to refrigerate railroad cars, the splendid structure has been salvaged and converted into a complex of shops and has an unusually attractive restaurant.

Westward are pine forests and beautiful rolling grasslands where huge herds of well-fed cattle can be seen. There are few towns, the traffic is light, and the roads are excellent.

5 Woodville has been selected as the town "best typifying the antebellum South" by Harvard University. Self-guiding maps are available at the Town Hall's visitor center for seeing this gracious town. The historic churches are open to visitors, and group house tours can be arranged.

About one mile east of Woodville a rural lane leads from Route 24 to Rosemont, the plantation where in the early 1800's Jefferson Davis spent his youth. Rosemont, now restored as a 300-acre working antebellum plantation, is closed from December to March and on weekends the rest of the year.

6 Natchez is a mecca for everyone seeking the grandeur of the Old South. Scattered throughout the city are nearly 50 elegant mansions and hundreds of gracious, smaller houses with architectural features, woodwork, and antique furnishings that are notable for their beauty and craftsmanship.

The oldest city on the Mississippi, Natchez became one of the world's great cotton ports during the steamboat era (1820–60). During that time planters amassed great fortunes, built imposing homes, and collected silverware, china, and other art objects. Most of Natchez' great houses, like D'Evereux and Stanton Hall, are of the Greek Revival style popular then, but some older dwellings, such as Evansview, are of a Spanish and French colonial style that had evolved in the West Indies. Unique among them is Longwood, an Oriental fantasy. The octagonal red brick house with its arabesque trim, arched windows, and pale blue dome stands uncompleted. Work was interrupted by the Civil War and never resumed.

8. These brick-and-plaster columns crowned with iron capitals survived the fire that leveled Windsor. Prior to the Battle of Port Gibson the Confederates used the mansion's cupola to send signals across the river to Louisiana. Later the house became a Union hospital.

In spring and fall 30 to 34 houses are open for tours organized by the Pilgrimage Garden Club (located at Stanton Hall on High Street), the Natchez Garden Club (at Magnolia Hall on Pearl Street), and Deluxe Tours (at the Prentiss Club on Pearl Street). Some 20 houses are open to the public year-round.

Patrician Natchez, situated on bluffs overlooking the river, is known as Natchez-ontop-the-Hill. Below the bluffs is Natchez-under-the-Hill, a remnant of the original river port. Some of the old buildings here have been revamped as restaurants and nightspots.

On the road north from Natchez you pass the small town of Washington, where Aaron Burr, a former vice president of the United States, was arraigned for treason in 1807.

7   Port Gibson began as a rowdy settlement at a flatboat landing on the south fork of Bayou Pierre. It grew to be a quiet, cultivated community, and it is said that in 1863, following the Battle of Port Gibson, Gen. Ulysses S. Grant found the place too beautiful to burn. The town is a harmonious blend of federal and neoclassic architecture. Even the jail is in the Greek Revival style.

You can get a map for a self-guided walking or driving tour of the village at the visitor center on Church Street. Also on Church Street, look for the lovely pink-plastered First Presbyterian Church with its steeple that has a 12-foot golden metal hand pointing heavenward. The original hand was carved of wood and covered with gold leaf, but it was destroyed by woodpeckers.

8   In a desolate expanse of fields 10 miles southwest of Port Gibson, 23 Corinthian columns stand in eerie silence. They are the ruins of Windsor, once the most lavish of Mississippi's antebellum mansions. The 45-foot-tall fluted columns had supported the roof projecting over galleries that encircled the house. The mansion was completed in 1861 at a cost of $175,000; a few weeks later the owner died at the age of 34. Windsor survived the Civil War, but in 1890 a careless houseguest dropped a cigarette. Fire destroyed the entire house except for the columns, sections of balustrade, and the iron stairs.

The drive between Port Gibson and Windsor provides an atmospheric introduction to the view of the ruins. The hillsides and ravines along the way are shrouded with tangles of kudzu vines and gray moss, suggesting attic cobwebs.

9   The past seems only yesterday in Vicksburg, where history is carefully preserved. In 1863 this was a town of about 4,000 people, but its location on bluffs commanding a bend in the Mississippi River made it the focal point of the Union campaign to seize control of the river and divide the Confederacy.

The crescent-shaped Vicksburg National Military Park encompasses the battlefield, a rough terrain where the Blue and the Gray fought for 47

On the well-maintained park grounds are spreading oaks, huge magnolias, and grassy slopes that are almost covered in spring with pale blue violets. The roadsides are studded with monuments and tablets and the imposing memorials erected by 26 states to honor their fallen. Seeing them is a poignant experience.

One of the features in the Vicksburg National Military Park is the U.S.S. *Cairo*. The ironclad gunboat, sunk in 1862, was the first vessel in history to be torpedoed by an electrically detonated mine. The grave of the ship, complete with its armaments, personal gear, and stores, was discovered in the Yazoo River in 1956, all having been preserved by mud and silt for nearly a century. The

9. *Vicksburg National Military Park is a landscape of trenches and breastworks made by the thousands who fought here. The white marble cenotaph rising above emplacements of cannon is Mississippi's tribute of honor to her sons who served in the bitter siege.*

excruciating days. From the entrance a 16-mile-long road through the park follows the progress of the Union forces as they bored their way through ridges and bayous, "foot by foot, yard by yard," toward the Confederate strongpoints. There are 15 stops where you can leave your car to read markers describing the action of both sides. At Fort Hill, where Confederate guns are still trained on the old riverbed, a voice box relates the story of the naval battle in which the ironclad Union gunboats ran the Vicksburg batteries.

gunboat is being restored and a related museum is under way.

Downtown Vicksburg is filled with lovely antebellum churches and houses, some of which show their battle scars. In Cedar Grove, for example, a mansion facing the river, a cannonball fired by a gunboat remains imbedded in the parlor wall, and a second ball has left a hole in the floor. The Old Court House Museum, an imposing structure with classic porticoes on all four sides, gives further insights into the Civil War period and the town's earlier history.

11. *Cowboys herd cattle along the bank of the levee near Greenville. Although the scene is placid, the Mississippi is a constant threat. Following the great flood of 1927, a tremendous control program* *was begun, and massive main levees were built that extend more than 2,000 miles. The levees have severed some towns like Greenville from their riverbanks.*

The Biedenharn Candy Shop on Washington Street is a charming place to see and to enjoy a soda. In 1894 Mr. Biedenharn became the first person to bottle Coca-Cola, and the shop is now a quaint Coca-Cola museum. The shop's restored parlor has the original onyx soda dispenser and an 1890's soda fountain counter.

The Waterways Experiment Station of the U.S. Army Corps of Engineers, two miles south of Route I-20 on Halls Ferry Road, is interesting to children as well as adults. The station has more than 50 miniature models of U.S. rivers and harbors that simulate silting, wave action, and other natural forces. They are used to test designs for proposed waterways projects. The visitor center here offers films and displays showing other work being done in the laboratories. Scheduled guided tours are offered at 10:00 A.M. and 2:00 P.M. weekdays except on major holidays.

10 The Leroy Percy State Park is a paradise for nature lovers. Pileated woodpeckers, robins, grackles, rabbits, and deer are among the wildlife here, and at the end of the park, in an enclosed pond fed by 100°F artesian water, are a number of alligators, some of which were caught in the nearby rice fields and waters. The picnic and camp grounds are in a lovely open grove of moss-hung cypresses. The park also has a play-

ground, a small zoo, a wildlife interpretive center, and a nature trail through a bayou.

Route 1, the Great River Road, takes you through the Delta, a 225-mile-long plain lying between the Mississippi and Yazoo rivers. The state's great cotton plantations are in this area, which has some of the most fertile soil in the world. Here too are miles of rice fields, with channels of water lying like thin strips of mirror between the long, neat rows of green stalks from late spring into autumn.

Along the west side of the Great River Road are marshes, oxbow lakes created by the vagaries of the Mississippi, and, every few miles, the levee, picturesque with cows grazing on its green slope. From the highway a number of access lanes lead to the top of the levee where you can drive along a narrow gravel road. Through the willows and cypresses growing on the margin of land below, you occasionally see the pale coffee-colored river wending its way south.

11 The attractive river town of Greenville is known as the Towboat Capital of the World. Main Street takes you to the top of the levee and a large, cobbled parking area sloping down to Lake Ferguson, which was the bed of the Mississippi before the river was rechanneled. A marina restaurant with houseboats tied alongside juts out into the water. Benches

atop the levee make this a pleasant place from which to survey the scene.

While in Greenville, take a few minutes to explore Washington Street. The town has transformed it into a parklike area, and the traffic lane curves like a garden path around the flower beds.

About five miles north of Greenville the Winterville Mounds rise on the east side of the road. A museum camouflaged by a roof of earth has artifacts and displays presenting the story of the Indian Mound Builders who had lived here for centuries prior to the arrival of the Spanish explorers in 1540.

Continuing northward through Scott, a crossroads, you pass one of the world's largest cotton plantations, the Delta and Pine Land Company.

12 The Great River Road State Park, on the river side of the levee at Rosedale, is an inviting place for picnicking and watching river traffic. A tower overlook in the park has a picnic pavilion and provides magnificent views of the river. The park (which is under water about once every 10 years) offers camping and fishing and also has a nature trail for the handicapped.

13 Turning toward Greenwood, the road cuts a straight course through a sea of cotton with not even a ripple of a hill visible on the horizon.

The ginning, marketing, and shipping of cotton is the primary business of Greenwood. Of special interest in this lively, prosperous town is Cottonlandia, a museum with displays representing the history of Delta cotton. It has a fascinating array of old farm equipment, including a boll weevil catcher, and an outstanding regional collection of Indian artifacts from about 8000 B.C. to A.D. 1800. There is also a lovely outdoor garden with Mississippi wild flowers. The museum is closed on Mondays and on major holidays.

The Florewood River Plantation State Park, just off Route 82 two miles west of Greenwood, is a working re-creation of an 1850's cotton plantation. A tour of the 100-acre farm, with its planter's home, slave quarters, sorghum mill, and other buildings all authentically furnished and equipped, gives you a view of plantation life in those times, and if you visit in autumn you can pick cotton in the fields. The park is closed on Mondays and on major holidays. Craft activities are suspended from December to March.

14 Nestled in the hilly countryside east of Greenwood is Carrollton, an unspoiled 19th-century town. Its main street, courthouse square, and deeply shaded avenues with houses built by an aristocracy who made fortunes in cotton are all lovely to see. Take time to browse in J. J. Gee's, a general store that has been in continual operation for a century.

From Carrollton the road rolls across wooded hills toward Grenada Lake and the Hugh White State Park, where there are swimming beaches, picnic groves, and campgrounds. Look for a turnoff to the park east of the attractive old town of Grenada.

Driving toward Houston you cross flat farmland with fields of soybeans and sweet potatoes. (Vardaman is called the Sweet Potato Capital of the World.) In Houston, stop to visit Horn's Big Star Supermarket. The basement is a museum of intriguing 18th- and 19th-century paraphernalia, all of it found by Mr. Horn "right under his nose."

15 A few miles east of Houston take the Natchez Trace Parkway to return to Jackson. Lined with tall pines and oaks, dogwoods, and flowering shrubs, the parkway is a beautiful drive, and it is highlighted every few miles with nature trails and sites of historical, archeological, and geological interest, each with interpretive markers. There are also places for picnicking. Be sure to have with you the excellent descriptive map of the Trace available at visitor centers.

The Natchez Trace

From Natchez, Mississippi, to Nashville, Tennessee, the Natchez Trace Parkway unrolls its romantic past.

As far back as 8,000 years ago, paths beaten by buffalo along watershed divides in this area were used as trails by the Indians, and in the 1700's the French and the British found a network of these trails running between Natchez and Nashville. Soon numbers of settlers were tramping this wilderness route.

A new phase in the history of the Trace began in 1785 when a flatboat delivered a load of flour at Natchez. The river trade increased rapidly, and so many Tennesseans and Kentuckians who floated the cargo downriver plodded home via the Trace that it became known as the Boatman's Trail.

In the meantime, the national importance of the Trace was recognized, and it was cleared and widened as a public road. Postal service began in 1800, inns were built, and thousands of men and women journeyed the Trace, enduring the hardships and braving the robbers lurking in the woods. The most famous of its travelers was Andrew Jackson.

But following the advent of steamboat transportation in the 1820's, the Trace reverted to a quiet forest lane, and it was nearly forgotten until 1938, when it was made a parkway in the National Park System.

15. *Ten miles east of Port Gibson, where the Natchez Trace Parkway intersects the Old Trace, a 10-foot-wide path through the woods (top), you can park and walk in the footsteps of the pioneers. East of Jackson a boardwalk leads through a hauntingly beautiful swamp (above) with water tupelo and bald cypress trees standing in shadowy green water.*

Here in the southeast corner of the state you find a section of Mississippi's pine belt and the Gulf of Mexico coastline with its white sand beaches, colorful seaports and fishing villages, and lively resort towns. A short swing into Alabama takes you to the historic city of Mobile. Heading back north from the Gulf, you traverse the peaceful Mississippi countryside patched with forests and laced with streams.

1 Hattiesburg, formerly an important lumbering center in Mississippi's longleaf pine belt, is a beautiful turn-of-the-century town with a neat main street, red brick buildings and churches, an imposing county courthouse, and large Victorian houses. If you decide to explore the city, be sure to see the campus of the University of Southern Mississippi, where traditional white-pillared buildings are juxtaposed with handsome structures of modern design.

Route 98 to the east passes through fringes of the De Soto National Forest. The area's original forest was cut down long ago, and the land has been gradually replanted with longleaf, slash, and loblolly pines. Evidence of its harvest are the logs you see piled by the road, on railroad cars, and in lumberyards. As you approach the Alabama border you find numbers of great trees snapped in

The formation and path of a hurricane

A hurricane is an intense, whirling tropical cyclone with an eye—a zone of calm that may be 20 miles wide and 40,000–50,000 feet high—at its center. The mechanics of a hurricane's formation is not completely understood, but it starts as a common, warm-weather storm over the ocean, with hot, moist air moving into a low pressure area. Given a spin by the earth's rotation, the air spirals inward and upward and condenses. As more moisture-laden air is drawn in, the centrifugal force of the wind increases. When this outward force equals the inward pressure of the air, the eye of the storm is established. Hurricanes reaching the Caribbean area originate off west Africa. Some veer northeast and spend themselves over water. Others strike the coast, with winds up to 200 miles per hour, and then break up as they move over land.

A cross-section of a hurricane shows the movement of winds and rainbands (the shaded areas) around the storm's eye—counterclockwise in the Northern Hemisphere and clockwise in the Southern. As the warm, moist air spirals upward, it creates suction that pulls in more moisture-laden air.

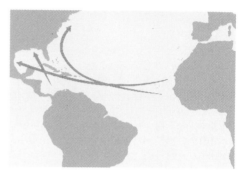

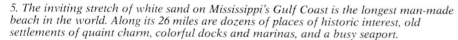

two or uprooted by Hurricane Frederic in September 1979.

2 At Mobile, turn off Route 98 and follow Route 65 south to the second cloverleaf; then turn east onto Route 90, which becomes Government Street, a main artery through the city. With its stately buildings and great oaks, Government Street is an attraction in itself, and it leads to the old

parts of Mobile along the bay and Mobile River. In old Mobile you can stroll along block after block of charming houses and small shops, a number of which are embellished with iron lacework.

At the mouth of Mobile River is Fort Condé Village, a picturesque, early-1700's French settlement with brick streets and quaint shops and houses. The fort, a reconstruction on the original site, is open to visitors.

Moored at the dock near Fort Condé, and also open for tours, is the $200 million battleship U.S.S. *Alabama*, which led the U.S. fleet into Tokyo Bay at the end of World War II.

Not far away is Oakleigh, an elegantly furnished neoclassic antebellum house that is now a museum. To find it, turn south onto Roper Street from Government Street and continue another 2½ blocks.

Mobile is resplendent in March when the azaleas become a floral extravaganza of pink, white, purple, and red. Arching over the avenues and the banks of azaleas are venerable oaks, their boughs luxuriantly hung with Spanish moss.

3 The Bellingrath Gardens are ranked among the most beautiful in the world. In 1979 Hurricane Frederic devastated the 75 acres of gardens that had been developed and per-

5. *The inviting stretch of white sand on Mississippi's Gulf Coast is the longest man-made beach in the world. Along its 26 miles are dozens of places of historic interest, old settlements of quaint charm, colorful docks and marinas, and a busy seaport.*

fected over a period of 48 years, but their restoration was undertaken immediately and the grounds are again lovely. The Bellingrath Home, a charming residence built of old, handmade bricks, with balconies ornamented with black iron lacework, and a richly furnished interior, is another attraction here.

4 Reentering Mississippi, you drive through Pascagoula, a famous shipbuilding center; sophisticated warships are constructed in the yards you can see from the road. Pascagoula's oldest structure is the Old Spanish Fort. The sturdy building, which resembles a farmhouse, was built in 1718 to protect land given to a French duchess by Louis XIV. Later the fort passed into Spanish control; today it is a colorful museum of local history.

5 The Gulf of Mexico spreads before you at Ocean Springs, a village of historic interest. Settled by the French in 1699, it became the first capital of the Louisiana Territory. In the 1850's Ocean Springs became a popular health spa noted for its mineral waters. Many of its houses date from that period, and the village has retained its 19th-century charm.

From the long bridge spanning Biloxi Bay there are beautiful views of water and land, and in the luminous rose of sunrise or sunset the sight is breathtaking. For the next 26 miles the road edges a sparkling strip of white sand beach. Facing the Gulf from the north side of the highway are luxurious private homes.

6 Biloxi hums with activity and interest. Along the beach are docks, shrimp boats, marinas, and children's amusement parks. In the middle of the highway is the gleaming white Biloxi Lighthouse, which has been in continuous operation since 1848, except for an interval during the Civil War. Through the palms and oaks you can see Beauvoir, the Southern Planter-style house where Jefferson Davis spent his last years. Now a museum, it is closed on Christmas Day.

The shrimp season at Biloxi begins in the middle of June with a colorful three-day festival, but tours on a trawler are offered most of the year except on Sundays. Here, from shipboard, you see how the great conical nets are used to harvest shrimp.

10. The nine-banded armadillo is one of the most frequently seen inhabitants of the De Soto National Forest.

7 A few miles to the west is Gulfport with its deep-sea harbor. This was once a major shipping port for lumber, but it is now a popular resort and a great banana terminal where

A Float Trip Down Black Creek

Black Creek is easily navigable by raft or canoe for 33 miles, and the primeval peace and beauty it offers is worth seeking out. The gentle current carries your boat along at an average speed of one mile per hour, leaving you free to bird-watch or fish for bass, catfish, and bream off the tree-shaded banks. In the solitude of this unspoiled wilderness, only the sound of a leaping fish, a deer, or a wild turkey breaks the stillness.

The river's broad sandbars are ideal for picnicking or camping, and there are inviting campgrounds at the four landings downstream, where you can take out. You can also stop along the way for a swim.

Canoes can be rented at Black Creek Canoe Rental in Brooklyn for a few hours or several days. (Canoes should be reserved for weekends.) You can park your car at the rental place and arrange to be picked up at the end of your float trip. A river map showing landings and mileages is also available here. The canoe rental company is closed Mondays and Tuesdays.

Additional information about float trips can be obtained from the District Ranger, Box 248, Wiggins, Mississippi 39577.

nearly 16,000 boxes can be unloaded hourly. A small train takes you on a tour of the port.

8 The small fishing village of Pass Christian was settled in 1699 and has been a vacation spot for more than a century. Presidents Jackson, Taylor, Grant, Theodore Roosevelt, Wilson, and Truman have all found relaxation here. To find the attractive houses with their white picket fences and semitropical gardens, watch for the sign pointing to Scenic Drive as you enter the town. Scenic Drive parallels the beach.

9 As you cross the 1.9-mile-long bridge spanning Bay St. Louis, you can see the fascinating variety of fishing boats, pleasure boats, and barges that ply these waters. To see the old coastal town of Bay St. Louis, turn onto Beach Drive at the west end of the bridge. This drive also leads to Buccaneer State Park, a pleasant place for swimming, camping, and fishing.

Leaving the flat, swampy coastal area and heading north, you traverse gently rolling grasslands that are picturesque with small ponds cupped at the base of slopes, tiny creeks, and hundreds of pastured cattle.

Near Lumberton are long stretches of evenly spaced young pines and extensive pecan orchards. Just north of the village, a road leading east to the plant of the Bass Pecan Company offers a pleasant drive through the orchards. In October you can see mechanical harvesting equipment shaking the tall trees and sweeping up the fallen pecans.

10 Big Creek Landing, on County Route 335 about seven miles west of Brooklyn, is a secluded spot among the pines in De Soto National Forest. The landing has a picnic table and a paved boat ramp, but its main interest is as the starting point for float trips down Black Creek, one of Mississippi's most scenic streams. (See the float-trip information given at the left.) The forest itself is filled with small natural wonders, such as the insect-eating pitcher plant and the exotic armadillo.

From Brooklyn to Hattiesburg the road wends its way over a rolling terrain, cutting through woodlands and farmlands. It is a lovely, gentle countryside typical of Mississippi.

Bayou Country

Louisiana boasts a blend of land and water that gives the state a character all its own

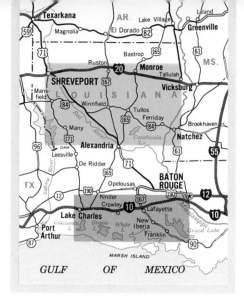

A state rich in such varied resources as rice, sugar, cotton, oil, waterfowl, fish, and game, Louisiana also benefits from the various cultures contributed by its diverse settlers.

In the north are rolling hills, fragrant pine forests, and fertile Delta farmland. The south, with its mysterious marshlands and wildlife refuges fed by coastal waters, is dotted with towns that retain an Old World charm in their architecture, language, and customs.

This tour starts at Shreveport, a town made possible by one man's invention, and continues to an ancient site whose settlers left intriguing ceremonial mounds for us to ponder. Passing through the rich Mississippi Delta, the route loops west into the Red River valley to the state's oldest city and detours for a look at magnificent gardens that are always in bloom.

1 Shreveport, a very pleasant, relaxed city on the banks of the Red River, owes its existence to riverboat captain Henry Miller Shreve. In 1832 the Red River, for about 160 miles, was clogged with wood, debris, and snags, a blockage that became known as the Great Raft. Shreve was hired by the government to break the logjam by means of the snag boat, his own invention. In 1835 part of the river was opened to navigation, and the city named for Shreve began to grow. Subsequently, the river silted up, but it is now being made navigable again for barges going to the Gulf of Mexico.

The visitor center provides maps of the city, brochures, and suggested walking tours. Closed weekends.

A highlight of the East Downtown Walking Tour is the R. S. Barnwell Memorial Garden and Art Center. The spacious domed conservatory houses handsome permanent plantings and seasonal displays.

The Louisiana State Exhibit Museum, a marble rotunda near the State Fairgrounds, contains paintings, historical relics, and a fine series of dioramas showing the state's wildlife and natural resources. Closed Christmas Day.

An excellent collection of paintings and sculptures by Frederic Remington and Charles M. Russell, as well as 16th-century Flemish tapestries and a large collection of Wedgwood pottery, are among the highlights in the Norton Art Gallery. Closed Mondays.

2 The Germantown Colony Museum is a quaint reminder of the communal village founded in 1836 by German pioneers fleeing religious persecution. On display are three original log cabins with their handhewn squared logs, replicas of a blacksmith shop and a smokehouse, and also an assortment of artifacts used by the settlers. Closed Mondays and Tuesdays.

3 At Monroe are the Louisiana Purchase Gardens and Zoo, located on 100 acres of Delta land. The color-splashed formal gardens, winding footpaths, and waterways through live oak groves make a visit here rewarding and memorable.

The delightful zoo has an impressive collection of 750 rare animals in simulated natural habitats. The zoo also provides a history lesson by focusing on events in the Louisiana

The American Rose Center

Pocketed in the piney woods just west of Shreveport is the American Rose Center, an enchanting 118-acre garden administered by the American Rose Society. The society, headquartered here, grows and evaluates new hybrids and officially registers all varieties of roses.

Near the administration building and the parking lot are special beds planted with new varieties submitted by amateur and professional rose hybridizers. Other beds are resplendent with varieties that have won All-American Rose awards. A walk winds through the woods to clearings with more gardens, each different in design; their loveliness can be enjoyed from the invitingly placed gazebos and benches. The roses bloom from April through December in this mild climate; in other months the gardens are exuberant with annuals, bulbs, and flowering shrubs. Open on weekdays, and on weekends when the roses are in bloom.

Territory that led up to its purchase by the United States from the French in 1803. You can explore the gardens and zoo on foot, by boat, or on the miniature Lewis and Clark Railroad. Closed from November through March.

Also in Monroe is the Masur Museum of Art, which has a small but interesting collection of artifacts that were found at the Poverty Point Indian Mounds (see number 4 below). Closed Mondays and in July and August.

4 Route 17 to Poverty Point cuts through cotton fields and small farmsteads with horses and cattle grazing peacefully. This is flat country, lightly wooded with pines and oaks. Here too around the houses you can see the magnolias (*Magnolia grandiflora*) that bear the state flower.

The complex of earthen mounds on the 400-acre site at Poverty Point was made by an Indian people who lived here about 3,000 years ago. The

SPECIAL FEATURES

ROAD GUIDE	HIGHLIGHT	**1**
STATE PARKS — With Campsites ▲ Without Campsites △	SCHEDULED AIRLINE STOPS	✕
RECREATION AREAS — With Campsites ▲ Without Campsites △	OTHER AIRPORTS	✕
SELECTED REST AREAS ⊼	BOAT RAMPS	◢
POINTS OF INTEREST ■	INFORMATION CENTER	⊛

ROAD CLASSIFICATION

CONTROLLED ACCESS HIGHWAYS
(Entrance and Exit only at Interchanges) — Interchanges

OTHER DIVIDED HIGHWAYS

PAVED HIGHWAYS

LOCAL ROADS In unfamiliar areas inquire locally before using these roads   Paved   Gravel   Dirt

MILEAGE

MILEAGE BETWEEN TOWNS AND JUNCTIONS   •4 ↓ 4 •

MILEAGE BETWEEN DOTS   • 35 •

SCALE

ONE INCH 25 MILES   0   5   10   15   25

ONE INCH 40 KILOMETERS   0   5   10   20   30   40

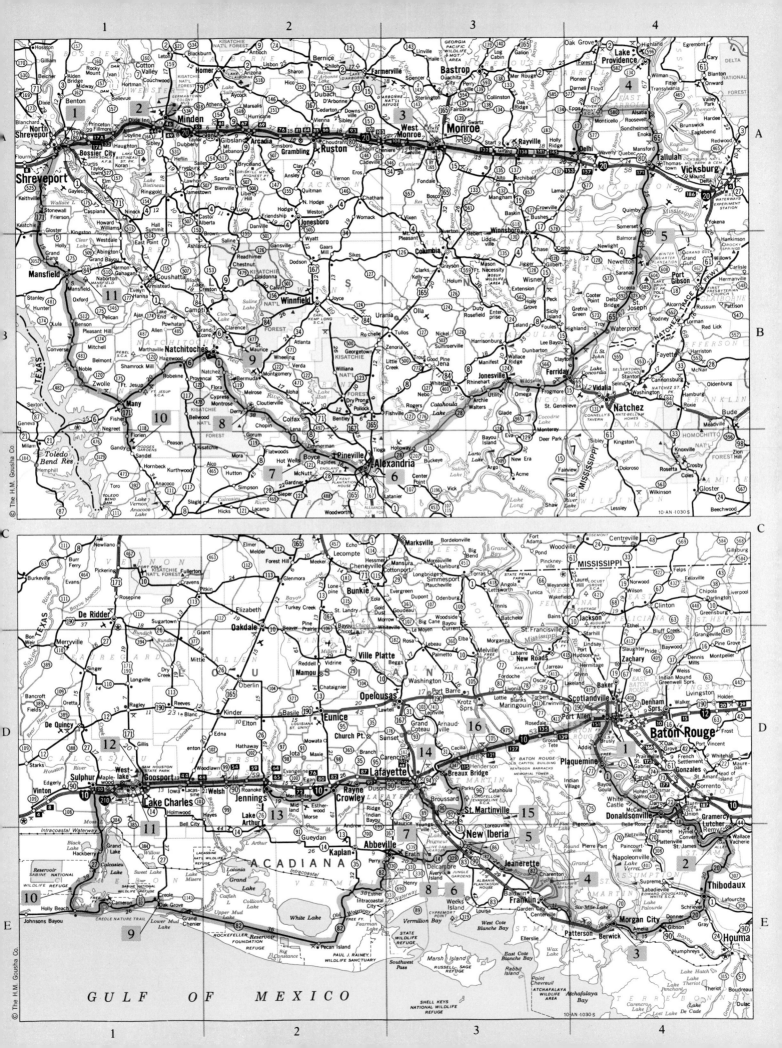

central part of the complex consists of rows of long, octagonal ridges, about 5 to 10 feet high, in a concentric arrangement; it was probably used ceremonially.

An established cooking method of the period was to heat stones and place them into food vessels. The inventive Poverty Point Indians, lacking stones, fashioned balls of clay, dried them in the sun, and used them for the same purpose. These clay balls can be seen along with other artifacts at the visitor center.

5 To the east and south of Poverty Point the farmland is flat, and along the straight roads you can see cattle, cotton gins, sawmills, and groves of pecans. At Newellton take Route 608 to Winter Quarters Plantation. This tin-roofed mansion with a veranda stands in a grove of trees and overlooks Lake St. Joseph. During the siege of Vicksburg in 1862–63, the owner of the mansion is said to have agreed to allow Gen. Ulysses S. Grant's troops to stop there overnight in exchange for sparing the home. Closed Mondays and Tuesdays.

The network of local roads can be confusing, and it is best to return via Newellton to Route 65.

At Ferriday you are only 12 miles from the interesting old town of Natchez, Mississippi. For a description of Natchez, see page 240.

Route 28 west of Ferriday frequently runs along the top of a dike above the flat fields and the lakes, ponds, and waterways. In places the land is so swampy that houses are constructed on short stilts to avoid flooding. The many oaks in this area are festooned with mistletoe and Spanish moss.

6 In Alexandria, Route 28 leads to a traffic circle. Go south on Route 71 for about a mile and turn right on Route 496 to Kent Plantation House. Built about 1795 in the classic Louisiana style, the house has been completely restored and now serves as a museum that colorfully depicts an earlier mode of living.

Route 121 to Hot Wells passes table-flat, rich red-earthed farmland planted mostly with soybeans and cotton. Palm, pine, and magnolia trees grow side by side, creating a pleasing palette as the shades of green vary from light to dark.

7 Hot Wells Resort Area has facilities for picnicking, pool-swimming, and camping, as well as a restaurant, a motel, and a bathhouse. The therapeutic mineral waters are drawn from an underground spring.

Adjacent to Hot Wells is the Cotile Recreation Area, with a large lake, a wooded water area, and a boat-launching ramp. Fishing, camping, swimming, and waterskiing are of-

fered. A road winds along the water, bordered with picturesque oaks and hanging moss. There are inviting picnic tables on a rise in a grove of pines interspersed with dogwood.

Between Boyce and Cloutierville, Route 1 passes through a cypress swamp, piney woods, and the Little Eva Plantation, with its acres of pecan orchards. Local folklore claims that this was the setting for Harriet Beecher Stowe's novel *Uncle Tom's Cabin*.

8 The charming Bayou Folk Museum in Cloutierville is housed in a representative Louisiana building dating from the early 1800's. The lower story is of brick; an outside staircase leads to the upper story, which is made of cypress mortised with wooden pegs.

From 1880 to 1883 this was the home of Kate Chopin, whose best known collection of Creole short stories set in Cane River country is *Bayou Folk*. The house is filled with fascinating memorabilia of the Chopin family, including jewelry, china, glass, a collection of sewing machines, and three early phonographs.

9 Watch for the Aquarium and National Fish Hatchery to the right of Route 1 in Natchitoches. The hatchery produces large quantities of striped and broadmouthed bass as well as channel catfish. Twenty tanks in the aquarium display these fish as well as baby alligators and turtles.

Natchitoches is Louisiana's oldest city and one of its most delightful. Founded in 1714 as a French trading and military post by Louis Juchereau de St. Denis, it is on Cane River Lake. This town is the most French of northern Louisiana, and some of its old homes have the filigreed wrought-iron balconies reminiscent of New Orleans.

A walk through the Historic District is most rewarding for the fine, well-preserved 18th-, 19th-, and turn-of-the-century buildings and the wrought-iron verandas overhanging the sidewalks.

Rogue House, on River Bank Drive beneath Front Street, is now a museum and is a fine example of "bousillage" construction, a mixture of clay or mud, animal hair, and Spanish moss packed in between the cypress beams. River Bank Drive is

6. *The Kent Plantation House in Alexandria, now a museum, has several outbuildings, including a slave cabin, a carriage house, and a barn. The interior of the milk house, shown here, displays a typical assortment of early 19th-century kitchen equipment.*

10. *The Hodges Gardens are vibrant with seasonal displays of color as in spring when tulips, pansies, azaleas, and dogwoods bloom. Along the 10 miles of road that encircles the lake are elk and buffalo pastures, forest, and picnic areas.*

From Baton Rouge, this tour takes you to Acadiana, dominated by the Cajuns with their colorful patois, cuisine, and music. The route winds through a wild and wonderful nature trail; stops at St. Martinville, the resting place of the legendary Evangeline immortalized in Henry Wadsworth Longfellow's poem; and ends with a memorable boat ride through the Atchafalaya Basin.

1 Louisiana's lovely capital on the Mississippi owes its name to a descriptive notation, "baton rouge," written in 1699 by a member of French explorer Pierre Lemoyne, sieur d' Iberville's party when he observed a red pole in an Indian encampment here.

A good place to begin a tour of the nation's seventh largest port is at the visitor center, located in the Old State Capitol on North Boulevard. This Gothic Revival castle, now a national historic landmark, is worth a visit for its large spiral staircase that winds toward a stained-glass dome.

Here brochures are available listing tours to handsome antebellum mansions and to the zoo, which houses more than 400 animals.

An interesting contrast to the old capitol is the new one. Rising 450 feet above the river valley, it is the tallest state capitol in the United States, and

particularly appealing, with its brick paving, magnolia and sycamore trees, and lovely view of Cane River Lake.

10 Hodges Gardens, created by conservationist A. J. Hodges, is a large and spectacular horticultural park and wildlife refuge. In the 1940's Mr. Hodges planted 39,000 acres of pine seedlings in a barren section and started a 4,700-acre arboretum. When a stone quarry was discovered within the area, he and his wife developed a garden, utilizing the rock formations.

A petrified tree believed to be thousands of years old is at the entrance to the main garden area. In spring and summer an excursion boat cruises the lake. Flowers bloom during every season: tulips, azaleas, and dogwoods in spring; lilies and roses in summer; chrysanthemums and berried shrubs in autumn; and narcissus, anemones, and camellias

in winter. There are pebbled concrete walks through the gardens, whose beauty is enhanced by streams and soothing waterfalls cascading gently over steps. Closed from Christmas Day through New Year's Day.

11 In the spring of 1864 the Confederate Army, under Gen. Richard Taylor, won its last major battle of the Civil War by turning back Union forces, led by Gen. Nathaniel P. Banks, at Mansfield. This victory prevented the capture of Shreveport, the Confederate capital of Louisiana, and ended the Red River campaign. The Mansfield Museum commemorates this battle with displays of weapons, uniforms, and other artifacts.

Today the battlefield adjoining the museum is a peaceful, pastoral place with handsome split rail fences, pathways and trails through grassy hills, groves of pine, and a picnic area.

1. *Louisiana's Old State Capitol, framed by its handsome gardens, is situated on a hill overlooking the Mississippi River.*

249

from an observation deck on the 27th floor you can see the 27 acres of formal gardens on the grounds.

The Louisiana State University's Rural Life Museum depicts various aspects of rural life in the 1800's. Here you can see an overseer's house, slave quarters, a plantation commissary, a sugar mill, a blacksmith shop, and a country church. Some of the buildings are original, and others are reconstructions. All are appropriately equipped and furnished. There is also a collection of farm tools and equipment. The museum, which is closed weekends, is on the grounds of the Burden Research Plantation.

Below Donaldsonville, the winding road follows the river between a

2. The double row of live oaks that leads to Oak Alley Plantation was put in, according to one legend, by a settler who built a log cabin on the grounds in the early 1700's. Both the mansion and the trees have been named a national historic landmark.

grass-covered levee and flat farmland. For a glimpse of the river, take one of the ramps that lead to the unpaved road on top of the levee.

2 In steamboat days, passengers looking landward between St. James and Vacherie were impressed by a very beautiful alleyway of live oaks leading from the River Road to a mansion. Built in the 1830's, the house was first called Bon Sejour. However, the river-borne observers referred to the place as Oak Alley, and so it has

remained. The mansion was completely restored in 1925. Guided tours are available daily; closed on Thanksgiving, Christmas, and New Year's days.

The road to Thibodaux leads straight to crawfish country, as evidenced by the signs that appear along the road near town.

3 At Morgan City, an inland port and commercial fishing center, ships are docked right beside the highway.

Swamp Gardens, a natural swamp area once inhabited by Indians, loggers, and fishermen, offers guided tours on raised wooden walks. Wildlife, including deer, squirrels, and bullfrogs, and many kinds of songbirds are found among the cypress

trees, one of which is said to be 800 years old. The bald cypress (*Taxodium distichum*), the state tree, flourishes here. Lifelike figures representing the early settlers are placed among the trees.

4 Toward Franklin you enter sugar country and pass through cane fields where you can see the trailers used to take cane to the mill.

Oaklawn Manor at Franklin, splendidly situated in beautifully landscaped grounds on Bayou Teche, was

built in 1837 as the manor house of a large sugar plantation. The gardens, landscaped by a French architect to resemble those at Versailles, are exquisite. With its white exterior, six massive Doric columns, and opulent furnishings, Oaklawn Manor is the quintessential southern mansion. Closed Thanksgiving, Christmas Eve, Christmas, and New Year's days.

5 As you approach New Iberia, you get closer to Acadiana, or Cajun country. Originally from France, the Acadians lived in Acadia, Nova Scotia, for 150 years, developing their own culture in relative isolation. They became refugees from British rule in Canada, and shortly after the founding of New Iberia in about 1765, many Acadians settled here.

The Shadows-on-the-Teche, one of New Iberia's lovely plantation mansions, was built in 1831 and fully restored in the 1920's by the great-grandson of the builder. Surrounded by enormous live oaks draped with Spanish moss, the 16-room Greek Revival mansion echoes with the romance of the Old South. Closed Thanksgiving, Christmas, and New Year's days.

6 Avery Island, about six miles south of New Iberia, is actually a salt dome. Salt goes with pepper, and at Avery Island hot Mexican peppers are grown in the thick layer of soil covering the core of rock salt. Salt and pepper, blended with vinegar, constitute the famous Tabasco Sauce, which has been made on Avery Island for over 100 years by the McIlhenny family.

In addition to the Tabasco factory, which is open to the public, the stunning Jungle Gardens are not to be missed. You can drive or walk along the roads winding through groves of giant twisted live oaks and 60-foot bamboo canes. Stands of magenta, pink, red, and purple azaleas bloom in the spring along with camellias. There are grassy openings leading to the bayou, peaceful lagoons, and a lily pond. Part of the roadway is arched with foliage, creating cool green tunnels to contrast with the spectacular flowers.

A startling sight is the Chinese Garden with its huge Buddha, which more than 800 years ago sat in a temple near Peking.

6. Bird City at Avery Island is home to a variety of birds, including the great egret (left), which is feeding as an alligator slumbers nearby. The great egrets nest on large "tables" placed in the marsh (above). The Louisiana heron (top, left) prefers a platform of bamboo sticks. A pair of cattle egrets in their breeding plumage (top, center) and the little blue heron (top, right) bristle at sight of the photographer.

Bird City, a heron sanctuary, is a man-made lake surrounded by buttonwood trees. Started by Edward Avery McIlhenny in 1892 with only seven snowy egrets, the sanctuary now hatches and rears 20,000 herons each year, along with egrets and other birds. It is gratifying to watch the white birds ruffling their lovely plumes, the feature that nearly led to their extinction by plume hunters.

7 The entrance to Live Oak Gardens on Jefferson Island is flanked with a two-mile *allée* of live oaks. The 20-acre display here includes a beautifully landscaped series of gardens that are connected by a pathway.

There are formal and informal plantings of foliage and flowering plants, and among the latter are more than 300 varieties of *Camellia japonica*. There is a rose garden, an Elizabethan knot garden, designed so that the plantings interlace, a rock garden, and a Japanese garden with a handsome teahouse.

8 Delcambre, called the Shrimp Capital of Louisiana, is a large port on the Delcambre Canal, which leads to the Gulf of Mexico. A colorful spectacle is the unloading of the shrimp trawlers. A four-day shrimp festival, which includes a blessing of the fleet, is held in August.

8. The fleet of shrimp boats docked at Delcambre indicates the importance of the shrimp industry to the people who live along Louisiana's estuaries. As much as 76 million pounds of these popular crustaceans are caught commercially in Louisiana each year.

West of the Old Waterway the road runs along a dike, with marshy land on both sides. The vista for miles around is a sea of grass with a low horizon. This outer portion of the Gulf Coast Plain is as flat as it looks, never rising more than 20 or 25 feet above sea level.

Although it might appear to be a wasteland, the marshes actually comprise the 84,000-acre Rockefeller Refuge, where annually hundreds of thousands of geese, ducks, and wading birds pass. The refuge is also the home of muskrats, raccoons, otters, and alligators.

Visitors can fish by permit, obtained by writing to the refuge office at Grand Chenier. Closed from October to March.

9 The Creole Nature Trail, which follows the coastline of the Gulf of Mexico from Oak Grove to Holly Beach, is built on old beach ridges called *cheniers*, a name that comes from the Acadian word meaning "a place where oaks grow." The live oaks here are able to withstand the constant salt-water spray from the Gulf as well as the salt water in the ground.

In Cameron, midpoint of the trail, there are many shrimp boats as well as three shrimp-processing plants. Boats can be chartered for deep-sea fishing in the Gulf for marlin, red snapper, and bluefish.

Near Cameron a free 50-car ferry crosses the Calcasieu Ship Channel, a narrow inlet of the Gulf of Mexico, 24 hours a day. If you make the trip in daylight, you may catch a glimpse of jumping, rolling porpoises at play.

10 The Sabine National Wildlife Refuge, part of the Creole Nature Trail, contains 142,846 acres of pools amid low-lying ridges. There are 125 miles of canal that can be traveled by boat. In addition to snow geese and migrating ducks, there are about 9,000 alligators in the refuge. A fascinating creature, the alligator is best observed at a distance. Although it may appear harmless, lazing in the sun, it moves with amazing speed and is very dangerous. Fishing is permitted from March through mid-October. At the refuge headquarters, about 13 miles north of Holly Beach, trail information and leaflets are always available. A one-mile walking trail goes through the marshlands,

with a tower at the end for an excellent overview. In the winter you can see thousands of blue and snow-white geese alongside the road.

In a state that seems fond of calling various towns the "something" capital, Hackberry is not left out. This Crab Capital of the World boasts of its hard-shelled blue crabs, which are abundant in Calcasieu Lake.

North of Hackberry is the Intracoastal Waterway; this portion is 125

feet wide and 12 feet deep. It runs across the Gulf Coast and is principally used for barge transportation. Live oaks abound, as well as hackberry trees, willows, blackberry bushes, and wild roses. At Intracoast Park, on the south bank, there are facilities for boating, picnicking, swimming, and fishing.

11 In 1781 Frenchman Charles Sallier built a house on the shore of a lovely lake. He became so renowned

---

Rice-growing in Louisiana

Rice fields, which must be flooded, require levees to control the water. In the old, highly productive rice-growing region of southern Louisiana, most of the levees are straight and permanent. The fields are usually leveled under water by scrapers mounted on tractors, as illustrated, and then after the water has settled into the ground, presoaked seed is broadcast by airplane. Fertilizing and spraying are also done by plane. When ripe, the golden grain is harvested by large combines.

In the newer rice-growing areas of northeastern Louisiana, the levees frequently wind like meandering streams across the land: the fields there are not so level as those in the south, and thus the levees must follow the contour lines. Most plantations use conventional surveying equipment to establish these lines. But some growers now employ laser devices that detect and transmit elevation variations to receivers mounted on tractors. Thus guided, the tractors trace the course of the new levees on the dry soil. Following the curves of this track, twin-disk plows raise the levees. The fields are then precision-leveled with land planes, drill-planted with dry seed, and flooded.

Underwater leveling

Spotter guiding plane

Young rice plants

Harvesting the grain

Rice plant in flower

Mature rice

for his hospitality that his property was known as Charlie's Lake. As a town grew up in the area, it took the more dignified name of Lake Charles, and it is now the largest city in southwest Louisiana.

Lakeshore Drive curves around the north shore of the lake with its wide expanse of sandy white beach backed with a fringe of palm trees. You can swim here, sail, or just relax in the sun. The visitor center offers brochures for the Creole Nature Trail.

The Imperial Calcasieu Museum, which has displays of local historic interest as well as original Audubon prints, stands on the site of Sallier's original home, shaded by the magnificent 300-year-old Sallier Oak.

12 It is well worth driving 12 miles north to visit Sam Houston State Park, 1,068 acres of unspoiled natural beauty. Wildlife is abundant in the forests of tall trees, through which streams and rivers flow. There are numerous hiking trails as well as picnic and camping areas. Stone cabins are available on the Calcasieu River, where there are boats for rent.

East of Lake Charles, in the heart of Cajun country, it is interesting to tune in to the local radio stations for a sample of the distinctive Cajun dialect and music.

13 In Jennings is the Zigler Museum, where a collection of European and American art is housed. The Louisiana Gallery features local artists, past and present. Particularly absorbing are dioramas of wildlife scenes. The museum is closed on Mondays.

The route to Crowley is flanked by rice fields. Crowley, the Rice Capital of America, hosts a rice festival in October, with rice-eating contests, parades, and a street fair. The Rice Museum contains displays relating to the rice industry, the history of Crowley, and Acadian culture. The museum is closed on weekends and in January.

At Rayne you can see a large aboveground cemetery, a necessity in this wet, low-lying land.

14 Lafayette, founded in 1824, has become the commercial hub and heart of Acadiana, especially since an oil center was established here in 1952. It has a large Acadian population, and every fall there is a weekend festival of food, music, and native crafts. Brochures may be obtained at the visitor center.

Just a short drive from downtown Lafayette is Acadiana Park, which contains an archeological site showing artifacts of at least two Indian cultures some 6,000 years old.

About 5,000 years ago the Mississippi River flowed through the park and carved the land into rolling hills, separating the 117 acres into a prairie terrace and a floodplain. The higher area has facilities for tennis, baseball,

16. Opossums, which are marsupials, inhabit the Atchafalaya Basin, where this baby was found hiding in a clump of Spanish moss.

and basketball, as well as picnic grounds and a meadow for kite-flying. The bottomland, mostly in its natural state, can be explored along the three-mile nature trail. At the entrance to the trail a three-story cypress building serves as an interpretative center. Campsites are set in an area of live oaks and hickories.

The Acadian Village and Tropical Gardens is a re-creation of various aspects of life in a bayou village in the early 1800's. In a setting of about 10 acres of tropical gardens and woodlands, you can see furnished period homes, a chapel, and a general store. The gardens themselves are lush with plants native to this region and to Asia and Latin America.

Lafayette is also a good place to sample such Creole and Cajun dishes as gumbo, crawfish, and jambalaya.

During February and March, when azaleas are at their peak, there is an Azalea Trail in Lafayette encompassing miles of the colorful floral display.

The Lafayette Museum occupies an antebellum town house that was the residence of Alexandre Mouton, who was Louisiana's governor in 1843. In the museum is a colorful display of Mardi Gras costumes. Closed Mondays.

15 St. Martinville, where wrought-iron balconies overhang the sidewalks, is a charming town with interesting French characteristics. St. Martin de Tours Church, built in 1832, still contains some sections of the earlier 18th-century structure, including the pews and altar, as well as a carved marble baptismal font said to be a gift of Louis XVI.

Slightly to the side and rear of the church is the Evangeline Monument. It is believed that Emmeline Labiche, the model for Longfellow's poem, is buried in the church. However, the statue was posed for by Dolores del Rio, who acted the part of Evangeline in a 1929 film.

St. Martinville, formerly a modest trappers' camp, attracted many Acadian refugees. When a number of French aristocrats fled here during the French Revolution, bringing with them their courtly ceremonies and grand balls, St. Martinville became known as Le Petit Paris.

On Port Street, at Bayou Teche, stands the Evangeline Oak. Legend has it that Evangeline's boat docked under the large old tree when she completed her journey from Nova Scotia, only to learn that her fiancé, Gabriel, had married another because he thought her lost.

The Longfellow Evangeline State Commemorative Area is situated on the banks of Bayou Teche and offers boating, swimming, and picnicking. Amid a dense stand of ancient live oaks laden with moss is the Acadian House Museum, once the home of a military commander.

16 Henderson is the gateway to the Atchafalaya Basin, an area of beautiful, largely wild swampland, home of alligators, rabbits, deer, and birds. The waters are well stocked with fish.

A number of boat tours are available. Gliding through swamps and streams, where the glistening waters reflect cypress, willow, and oak, is a thrilling way of experiencing how adventurous life was for those who dwelled in this primitive wilderness.

Dynamic Texas

In discussing the Lone Star State, Texans tend to deal in superlatives—and not without reason

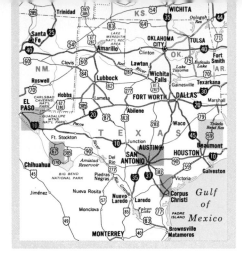

"**The sun is riz.**/The sun is set./And we ain't out of Texas yet!"

This oft-repeated rhyme reflects the dominant impression travelers have of Texas. It is on the huge side of big. The second largest state is 750 miles or more from border to border. It is the only state to have been an independent nation. When Texas was annexed by the United States in 1845, parts of the Lone Star Republic were lopped off to be included later in smaller states.

Texas still is large enough to contain a colossal variety of scenery and natural resources. It is difficult to imagine a sharper contrast than that found among the bleakly beautiful desert of West Texas, the dense forest of the Big Thicket, the pastoral lands, splashed with history, near San Antonio, and the sparkling Gulf Coast.

This loop of contrasts *takes you into the cool darkness of New Mexico's Carlsbad Caverns and through the searing white light of Texan salt flats. Chihuahuan desert abuts oasis woodlands in Guadalupe Mountains National Park, where you find the highest point in Texas, once a reef secreted in an ocean. Territory called the abode of the Devil blends into lush farmland along the Rio Grande.*

1 It seems inappropriate that the largest natural underground chamber in the world is in New Mexico, rather than Texas. The Big Room in Carlsbad Caverns has a floor area as large as 14 football fields. The ceiling is so high that the U.S. Capitol could be tucked in one corner.

Self-guided walking tours of the caverns pass incredible stone splendors, some of which bear fanciful names, such as Totem Pole and King's Palace. The longer tour begins at the natural entrance and covers three paved miles. For the shorter tour of 1½ miles, an elevator takes visitors directly to the level of the Big Room. A lunchroom is located within the caverns. Natural cave temperature is about 56° F.

Views from the park's visitor center extend over 100 miles into Texas along the Guadalupe Mountains and the Delaware Basin. A nearby nature trail winds through hot desert dominated by Torrey yucca and juniper. At the cavern's entrance is an amphitheater devoted to bat-watching. Each evening just before sunset, between late spring and early autumn, thousands of bats swirl from their daytime roosts in an unvisited section of the caverns to venture forth in search of insects.

The access road (Route 7) to Carlsbad Caverns National Park snakes through lower Walnut Canyon in the Guadalupe Mountains. Plants typical of the Chihuahuan desert bloom here; among them are claret cups, yellow prickly pear cacti, pink Wright spiderworts, and thorn-studded ocotillo whips tipped with flame-colored blossoms. As the road climbs the escarpment of Capitan Reef, pause at turnouts for fine views of the rugged scenery of Walnut Canyon.

2 The Guadalupe Mountains constitute the most extensive exposure of the world's largest fossil reef. Formed between 225 and 280 million years ago from the lime secretions of minute algae, Capitan Reef curves 350 miles through Texas and New Mexico like a giant horseshoe. Most of the reef, however, is now buried beneath sediments that form the arid plains of West Texas. Its most prominent feature is El Capitan, a sheer cliff rising 2,000 feet above the desert.

Guadalupe Mountains National Park is primarily for hikers and backpackers. Walking is particularly pop-

2. El Capitan in Guadalupe Mountain National Park served as a landmark for stagecoach drivers, cattle herders, and pioneers heading west. Its imposing escarpment overlooks the high plains and rolling mountains of the Delaware Range.

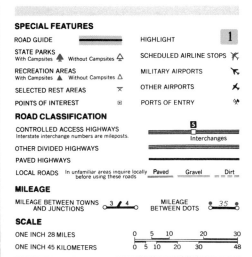

SPECIAL FEATURES

ROAD GUIDE	▬▬▬	HIGHLIGHT	**1**
STATE PARKS With Campsites ▲ Without Campsites △		SCHEDULED AIRLINE STOPS ✈	
RECREATION AREAS With Campsites ▲ Without Campsites △		MILITARY AIRPORTS ✦	
SELECTED REST AREAS ⊼		OTHER AIRPORTS ✈	
POINTS OF INTEREST ⊡		PORTS OF ENTRY ⚓	

ROAD CLASSIFICATION

CONTROLLED ACCESS HIGHWAYS
Interstate interchange numbers are mileposts.

OTHER DIVIDED HIGHWAYS

PAVED HIGHWAYS

LOCAL ROADS   In unfamiliar areas inquire locally before using these roads   Paved   Gravel   Dirt

MILEAGE

MILEAGE BETWEEN TOWNS AND JUNCTIONS   3 / 4   MILEAGE BETWEEN DOTS   • 35 •

SCALE

ONE INCH 28 MILES   0   5   10   20   30

ONE INCH 45 KILOMETERS   0 5 10   20   30   48

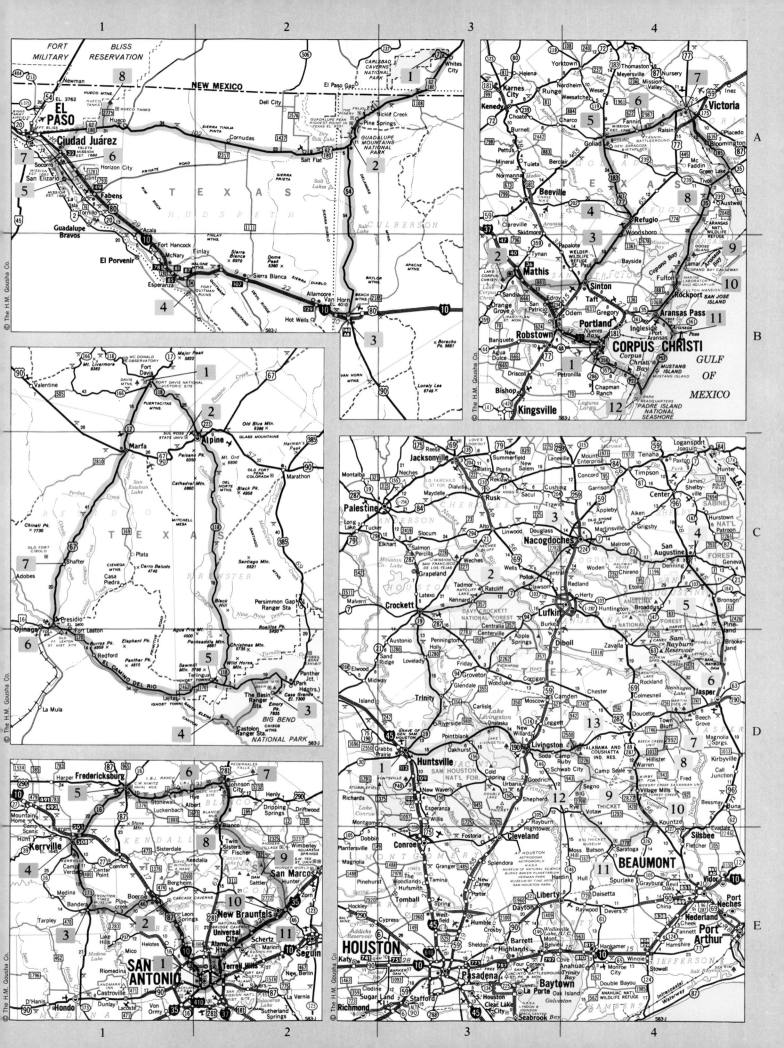

ular in McKittrick Canyon where plants of the desert mix uniquely with plants of the mountains to form a scene of great beauty and scientific interest. To reach McKittrick Canyon, turn north from Route 62/180 at a well-marked intersection 11½ miles south of the Texas–New Mexico border. A gate across the McKittrick Canyon road is unlocked at 8 A.M. and closed at 4:30 P.M.. A visitor center at the trail head familiarizes hikers with the natural wonders of the canyon.

8. In Hueco Tanks State Historical Park the depressions in the volcanically formed mountains serve as natural cisterns for rainwater. Pictographs left on rock walls by prehistoric Indian tribes who settled in the area record their visits to the tanks.

Route 62/180 cuts through the southeast edge of the park, providing good views of the limestone escarpments of the Guadalupe Mountains. The famed Butterfield Overland Mail stage to California followed this path for a time in the late 1850's.

Route 54 runs along the western base of the Delaware and Apache mountains, both a part of the Capitan Reef. Much of the way the highway passes through the large Baylor Mountain Ranch. You may see Texas longhorn cattle grazing here, below the dramatic red shale cliffs of Sierra Diablo, "Mountains of the Devil."

3 Two miles west of Van Horn, Route 10 cuts through the Carrizo Mountains. This is the route of the San Antonio–California Trail. On the

pass a scenic overlook, surrounded by mesquite, displays a historical marker that tells the story of the trail.

4 At the intersection of Routes 10 and 34 is a carefully built adobe replica of old Fort Quitman. Three miles away is the site of the original fort, where between 1858 and 1877 the U.S. Army maintained a post to protect travelers.

On the south side of Route 10 is rich agricultural land irrigated with water from the Rio Grande. Along here are fields of long-staple Egyptian cotton, the main crop, and orchards of pecans (Carya illinoensis), the state tree. Across the river, in Mexico, rise the dramatic peaks of the Sierra Madre.

5 Take the Clint exit from Route 10 and follow signs to the San Elizario Presidio Chapel, built in the 1770's to serve Spanish soldiers stationed at the colonial seat of government. The white chapel, still used, preserves the classic architecture commonly associated with Spanish missions. Across the street is Los Portales ("The Arcade"), widely considered to be the oldest building in Texas. The mood of Spanish colonial life is easy to feel in a stroll around the square bounded by these centuries-old buildings.

6 Five miles north of San Elizario is the town of Socorro, named for the settlement in New Mexico from which Spanish colonists and a few Pueblo Indian friends were driven in the Pueblo Revolt of 1680. Eventually coming here, the refugees established the mission, which still contains its original hand-carved roof beams.

7 Continue three miles to the south edge of El Paso, where you find the Ysleta Mission. Established in 1682, this is the oldest mission in Texas; the church has been restored in its original, charming style. The Ysleta Mission is part of the Tigua Indian Reservation pueblo complex, the oldest community in Texas. The Tiguas offer a fascinating program that explains Pueblo culture.

8 Hueco Tanks State Historical Park has been a welcome stop for desert-weary travelers for centuries. These natural rock basins collect rainwater, algae-laden but nectar to the pioneers who crossed this parched land. Indian pictographs were left here hundreds of years ago. Hiking is permitted among the large, rounded rock outcrops at this site.

East of Hueco Tanks you see why their stored rainwater was so welcome. The Chihuahuan desert is dominated in some stretches by giant soaptree yucca (Yucca elata), in others by creosote, and in still others by cholla cactus. But the desert is lush compared to the salt flats. Shallow lake beds with no outlet, these basins accumulate sediments and salt carried down by flash floods from the Guadalupe Mountains. Recent floods have buried most of the salt with enough silt to allow four-wing saltbushes to dot the wasteland.

Mirages
Driving on a hot day, especially in the desert, you are apt to see a mirage—a lake or a pool of water where none exists. Mirages are caused by the bending of light rays from the sky. Angling down through cool, dense air, and then striking the layer of warmer, lighter air close to the ground, the light rays are refracted, or bent, along your line of vision. The bent rays produce an image of the sky that appears to be a lake. Mirages can be photographed.

"Texas beyond the Pecos," West Texas is the arid land that most non-Texans imagine the state to be, with stark, weirdly eroded peaks more than a mile high, separated by brushy deserts. The scenes are austere, majestic, and romantic with western cowboy lore.

Excellent roads through these very wide and open spaces visit uncrowded canyons and oasislike parks in the ecosystem known as the Chihuahuan desert. Highlighted by historic forts and ghost towns, this loop also passes among the natural wonders of Big Bend National Park.

1 In the midst of the scenic Davis Mountains is Fort Davis National Historic Site. One of the best preserved forts in the Southwest, Davis was built in 1854 for the protection of travelers on the San Antonio–El Paso Road, an important section of the Overland Trail to California. Soldiers garrisoned here in 1857 were given a novel assignment when Secretary of War Jefferson Davis (for whom the fort was named) imported camels from the Mideast to be tested for use by the army in American deserts. The experiment proved a failure.

The National Park Service has preserved some of the 50 stone and adobe buildings that comprised Fort Davis in 1891, when it was finally abandoned by the army. In summer, Park Service personnel in the dress of the 1880's interpret life in the old days at Fort Davis.

2 From Alpine, follow the signs to Sul Ross State University Museum of the Big Bend on Route 90. The displays here include Indian artifacts, reconstructions of a frontier general store and a blacksmith shop, a stagecoach, a buggy, and various pioneer items. Fill up on gas at Alpine.

The road south, through grassland and brushy desert, is accented by a succession of volcanic mountains. Above the relatively lush ranchland along Calamity Creek are cliffs of basaltic lavas, weathered into columnar patterns over 50 millions of years.

Early in the morning, especially in winter, watch out for jackrabbits. They spend nights soaking up heat from the sun-warmed pavement.

3 Dramatic contrast is the dominant feature of 1,106-square-mile Big Bend National Park. A green ribbon

4. *The impressive Santa Elena Canyon stretches for some 10 miles along the western edge of Big Bend National Park. The Rio Grande, which runs through the canyon, reflects the almost vertical walls and separates the United States, on the right, from Mexico, on the left.*

of floodplain traces the 107-mile curve of the Rio Grande that gave the park its name and southern border. Three canyons cutting into limestone walls accent the river's course.

Most of the park is Chihuahuan desert, studded with creosote bush, mesquite, ocotillo, and some 60 species of spiny cacti, most noticeably the prickly pear. But the symbol of Chihuahuan desert is a relatively small, prolific agave called lecheguilla, whose dagger-sharp leaves are a danger to man and beast. Brown volcanic pinnacles and deeply eroded arroyos add a rugged character to the landscape. Above the desert rise the Chisos Mountains with their patches of cool, pleasant woodlands.

Much of the park's activity radiates from the Chisos Basin. A three-mile-wide amphitheater eroded in the hard igneous rock of the Chisos Mountains, The Basin rewards visi-

tors with its lovely, Shangri-la aspect, after the six-mile climb up the twisting road through Panther Pass.

The quarter-mile Window View Trail is an excellent evening walk from The Basin, providing glorious views of the sunset spreading across the desert.

4 Take the Santa Elena Drive through the park for the 43-mile trip from park headquarters to Santa Elena Canyon. With its 1,500-foot-high limestone walls, this is the most awesome of the three canyons along the Big Bend. Early morning is the best time to visit the canyon, for the cool air and for photography.

On your return from Santa Elena Canyon, pause at Castolon, an outpost built by the army in 1919. From the late 1800's until the present, wild and desperate characters have occupied a prominent place in stories of this frontier spot.

257

5. A marvel of highway engineering, El Camino del Rio tackles steep grades as it follows the Rio Grande and offers spectacular scenery, such as this view of the river as it winds among mountains and cliffs crowned by dramatically eroded outcrops of rock.

5   Terlingua is another ghost town, spawned by a mercury-mining boom in the 1890's. Millions of dollars of quicksilver were extracted before the mine closed in 1946. Of the many adobe ruins, the most impressive is that of the mine owner's winter home.

Route 170 north to Presidio is a famous 50-mile scenic drive called El Camino del Rio, "the River Road." It parallels the sinuous bend of the Rio Grande, passing colorful erosional features of limestone and volcanic rock. Cliffs and canyons create romantic western vistas along here.

6   On the River Road just east of Presidio is Fort Leaton State Historic Site. Originally a Spanish frontier settlement, the site was acquired in 1848 by an American settler, Ben Leaton, who established a private fort and trading post here. For the next several decades, stories of evil deeds swirled around the fort and its inhabitants. You can tour about 25 rooms in the restored fort to observe the adobe architecture and a legendary life-style.

7   Fill up on gas at Presidio, for Shafter is practically a ghost town. Its picturesque ruins mark the site of a silver-mining boom in the 1880's. It is said that the campfires of cavalrymen out of Fort Davis melted silver from a vein on the surface. However true the story may be, the area came to be called "the richest acre in Texas," producing $18 million in silver.

North of Shafter is wide-open grassland. The grama grass is sparse

Rafting the Rio Grande

Terlingua is headquarters for Far Flung Adventures, a national park concessionaire for raft trips down the Big Bend of the Rio Grande. The rugged rafts plunge over white-water rapids and carry you through wilderness isolation in the shadows of awesome canyons. These guided trips can last just a day or up to a week. Hearty campfire meals are provided, but you need to bring your own sleeping bags and utensils.

but nourishing, and cattle thrive on it. Ranches here are so vast that airplanes are used to supplement cow ponies to herd cattle. Along here watch for pronghorns, the swiftest runners in the United States.

6. As you drive along the River Road, you may see a band of javelinas seeking edible roots on a mountainside. The javelina (hă-vuh-lee-nah) of the Southwest is the collared peccary, easily recognized by the whitish-gray band around its neck.

Texans get a warm tone in their voice when they speak of the Hill Country. Drier than the lush lands to the east, yet not so parched as the high plains to the west, it is a very pleasant region that abounds with resorts, camps, and dude ranches; it was also the home territory of President Lyndon B. Johnson. Below the Balcones Escarpment, the colorful metropolis of San Antonio and the town of New Braunfels sit on fertile plains.

1   Everyone who visits San Antonio should "Remember the Alamo!" A fortresslike chapel, the Alamo was built in the 1740's at a Spanish mission to Christianize Indians on the Spanish colonial frontier and became the "Cradle of Texas Liberty."

After the Mexican Revolution disposed of Spanish rule in 1821, the Mexican government invited Anglo-Americans to move to Texas. In 1836 the Americans revolted. The Mexican ruler, Santa Anna, counterattacked with 4,000 troops.

With the aim of consolidating the Texan forces, Gen. Sam Houston ordered the San Antonio commander, William Travis, to blow up the indefensible Alamo and join him. Refusing, Travis moved his men (they eventually numbered 188) into the crumbling fort and tried to hold it.

From February 23 to March 6, 1836, Santa Anna lay siege to the fort, killing every defender. On April 21, Houston and his army of 783 men surprised the Mexicans at San Jacinto and totally destroyed their superior force. The battle cry at the fight that won Texas independence was "Remember the Alamo!"

Alamo Plaza, containing the meticulously restored old mission chapel, is in downtown San Antonio, easily reached from Route 37.

Besides the Alamo, four other centuries-old Spanish colonial missions grace the San Antonio scene. All have been carefully restored and are organized into a tour that starts from Mission Road.

Near the Alamo is Paseo del Rio, a lovely showplace of urban redevelopment. This walkway meanders along the San Antonio River. It is shaded by graceful cypresses, oaks, and willows, landscaped with subtropical plants, arched by dramatic bridges, and lined with colorful shops and outdoor restaurants.

Leaving San Antonio, Route 10 climbs the Balcones Escarpment, a line of hills arching north from Del Rio and the Mexican border to the Red River near Denison.

2 From the highway follow Cascade Caverns Road 2.2 miles east to the caverns. About one-third of a mile long, the Cascade Caverns extend 140 feet below the surface and boast a 90-foot underground waterfall. In this wet cave the low, jagged ceiling sparkles in the artificial light, for each of its myriad small stalactites is tipped by a jewellike water droplet.

3 Along the road to Bandera grazing land mixes with forests, clumps of sotol, and wild flowers, including bluebonnets (*Lupinus subcarnosus*), the state flower. This steep-sided country contains many dude ranches. Striving to maintain a frontier atmosphere in the appearance of its buildings, Bandera bills itself as the "Cowboy Capital."

4 Kerrville, widely praised for its pleasant climate, is the center for numerous camps and dude ranches. The surrounding hills are covered by red cedar and live oak, ideal habitat for white-tailed deer and wild turkeys. Hiking is popular at peaceful Kerrville State Recreation Area.

5 Fredericksburg, a neat, attractive town nestled in a green valley, was settled by German families in 1846, and many of their traditions are preserved here. Be sure to notice the tiny "Sunday houses," identified by historical medallions. These were built by early settlers whose farms and ranches were far from town. On weekends they would journey to Fredericksburg to shop on Saturday and attend church on Sunday. Also unusual is the Vereins Kirche, a reconstructed "coffeemill church," which was fort, meetinghouse, and school for the settlers.

6 Well-tended pastures, orchards, and farms dominate the scenery for 17 miles to a well-marked turn into Lyndon B. Johnson National Historical Site and LBJ State Historical Park. A state park visitor center across the Pedernales River from the LBJ ranch contains Johnson memorabilia and shows films about the president. Closed on Christmas Day.

The only way to reach the LBJ Ranch itself is via a free bus from the visitor center. On the 90-minute tour you see the "Texas White House," the small schoolhouse attended by LBJ as a tad, his birthplace, and his grave.

7 At Johnson City, named for the pioneer ancestors of Lyndon Johnson, you can visit another unit of the Lyndon B. Johnson National Historical Site. Across the street from the visitor center, which contains LBJ exhibits, is Johnson's boyhood home, restored to its 1922–25 appearance.

From the visitor center you can walk or ride a horse- or mule-drawn wagon down a pleasant, shaded lane to Johnson settlement, the restored home of the president's grandparents. The collection of old barns, a dogtrot log house, and corrals show how ranching evolved in the Texas Hill Country. Closed Christmas Day.

8 Blanco is a resort community in picturesque ranchland. From the town square, detour west 3.2 miles on Route 1623 to an unmarked, unpaved road that heads downhill to a concrete low-water crossing of the Blanco River. Some 200 yards downstream from the crossing, you can pick up the 120-million-year-old tracks of a *Brontosaurus*, a dinosaur and one of the largest of all land animals. During low water the dinosaur's path is easy to see: a series of grooves in the rock (where its feet dragged) and tubs (where its feet sank into the mud). The big, round footprints are deep enough for a small child's bath. Upstream from the crossing you can find two interesting prints where the animal stood still and where the mud oozed up around its feet.

In season, tall, yellow Maximilian daisies frame the pastoral vistas along Route 32. These flowers were planted for highway beautification at the instigation of Mrs. Lyndon B. Johnson.

9 Canyon Lake, an impoundment designed to control floods, is contained within steep, green hills and is known for its beautiful scenery. Eight parks border the lake.

10 At Sattler, a hamlet about three miles south of Canyon Dam, turn west onto Route 2673. After 1.8 miles turn east onto River Road (unnumbered), a scenic drive along Guadalupe River that brings you to New Braunfels and its suburb, Gruene.

Founded in the late 1840's by German settlers, these towns have something of an Old World atmosphere. Both have restored homes, mills, churches, and commercial establishments from their pioneer period. The highlight of New Braunfels' German heritage is the *Wurstfest*, or "sausage festival," held each year in the early part of November.

11 Natural Bridge Caverns, named for the 60-foot natural limestone bridge that arches its entrance, is one of the largest and most spectacular caves in Texas. Very dramatic formations deck the walls, ceiling, and floor. A tour of this damp cave, which has a constant temperature of 70° F, takes an hour and 20 minutes. Closed Christmas and New Year's days.

11. The natural stone arch for which Natural Bridge Caverns was named spans a shady rock-strewn opening in the wooded landscape. The cave has a depth of some 250 feet; a walk leads down to its entrance beneath one end of the natural arch.

Circling through the Texas coastal plain, this loop traverses farm- and ranchlands, dotted by oil wells. Starting from the harbor of Corpus Christi, you visit a water-sport center at Lake Corpus Christi and stop at a large private wildlife refuge. A series of Texas historical sites, swathed with stories of the Texas Revolution, comprises a substantial portion of the route. As you near the Gulf again, nature takes over as the dominant interest.

1 Corpus Christi began as an obscure trading post. Today, however, this city has a major deepwater port and is the center of a Gulf Coast vacationland. Shoreline Boulevard borders a picturesque yacht basin adjacent to the downtown business district. Fishing and swimming in tropical waters are popular pastimes in the bay.

2 A well-marked road six miles south of Mathis leads off Route 359 to Lake Corpus Christi State Park. Water sports and fishing are featured at this reservoir on the Nueces River.

3 About seven miles north of Sinton on Route 77 is the inconspicuous gate to Welder Wildlife Refuge. The largest private wildlife refuge in the world, with 7,800 acres, it is located on the Robert H. Welder Ranch. Research is an important emphasis at the preserve, whose mammals, birds, reptiles, and amphibians, plus the plants that support them, are de-

scribed in a museum. The refuge gates open to visitors at 3 P.M. on Thursdays.

4 Passing through ranching, farming, and oil-producing country, you reach Refugio, named for a mission established here in 1795. Our Lady of Refuge Church, on the mission site, has a model of the original mission and is open to the public. The largest anaqua tree in the United States spreads its blossom- or fruit-laden branches above the church grounds. There are also several fine old houses to see.

5 Goliad is a shrine of Texas independence almost equal in importance to the Alamo and the San Jacinto Battlefield. Across the San Antonio River from Goliad (two miles south of town along Route 183) is Presidio La Bahia, the best example of a Spanish colonial fort in Texas.

Built in 1749 to protect the nearby Mission Espiritu Santo, the fort was the prison in 1836 of Col. James Fannin and 342 men who had surrendered to Mexican forces. Santa Anna ordered the Mexican commander at Goliad to kill all the prisoners on Palm Sunday, March 27. Their mass grave is marked by a monument a few hundred yards from the fort. On April 21, 1836, at San Jacinto, the battle cry of "Remember Goliad!" joined with "Remember the Alamo!" as Texans surprised the Mexican army and captured Santa Anna.

Goliad State Historical Park, across the river, contains the reconstructed Mission Espiritu Santo. A restored workshop and museum display the story of the mission's work among the Indians. Several shaded campsites and picnic grounds add to the park's attraction.

6 A mile south of Fannin on Park Road 27 is Fannin Battleground State Park. A monument memorializes the Battle of Coleto Creek, which resulted in Fannin's surrender.

7 Victoria, founded in 1824, was one of the first towns incorporated by the Republic of Texas. The chief landmark in the town's Memorial Park is an old wind-driven gristmill built of hand-shaped logs secured by wooden pegs and homemade nails.

Heading southeast through flat coastal prairies with marshes and bayous, the route cuts across the Heysen Oil Field, indicated by refining and pumping station facilities, and skirts Green Lake, aptly named for the color of its water. The best view of the lake, which swarms with water birds, is from the bridge spanning the Victoria Barge Canal.

8 Aransas National Wildlife Refuge is one of the most famous in the national refuge system. Its 55,000 acres are the winter home of the whooping crane, the archetype of endangered species. Altogether, about 350 species of birds are found here. One of the most frequently seen is the mockingbird, the state bird of Texas. Dainty white-tailed deer, fox squirrels, javelinas, and armadillos are particularly in evidence, and wild boars, skunks, nutrias, and raccoons are seen occasionally.

A 16-mile paved road loops through the various wildlife habitats. An observation tower on this road is a favorite place to watch for whooping cranes from mid-October through mid-April. Excellent pamphlets detailing seasonal highlights are available at the refuge headquarters.

9 The access to Goose Island State Park is well marked from Route 35. In addition to the attractions of boating, camping, and fishing, the park features the "Big Tree," one of the two largest live oaks in the United States. This solid giant with massive twisting branches is estimated to be 1,000 years old.

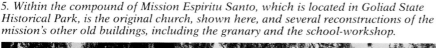

5. *Within the compound of Mission Espiritu Santo, which is located in Goliad State Historical Park, is the original church, shown here, and several reconstructions of the mission's other old buildings, including the granary and the school-workshop.*

8. Numbers of the endangered whooping crane (above) rest at the Aransas National Wildlife Refuge from autumn into spring. From the observation tower, during these months, you can observe the satiny white birds as they swoop down to a tidal marsh to fish, along with other shorebirds. Wild turkeys and smaller birds feed in the open grasslands and find nighttime shelter in the mottoes, clumps of live oaks that punctuate the flats (right).

10   Route 35 spans the mouth of Copano Bay next to an old causeway that now forms a long fishing pier. To see what the fishermen are after, visit the exhibits at the Texas Parks and Wildlife Department Marine Laboratory at the yacht harbor in Rockport. Besides recreational fishing, commercial fishing is an important business here. The fresh oysters and blue crabs are gustatory delights.

One mile south of the Copano Bay causeway turn east onto Fulton Beach Road for the scenic route into town past picturesque live oaks and Fulton Mansion, a state restoration.

Between Rockport and Aransas Pass the route provides views of the Gulf of Mexico, marshes, water birds, and swaying palms. Aransas Pass is named for the seaway from the Gulf into Corpus Christi Bay. Crossing this watery pass via a free state-run ferry, you can view porpoises.

11   Port Aransas is one of the popular vacation spots on the Gulf. Innumerable bait-and-tackle and boat-

12. Flourishing on the dunes of Padre Island National Park are clumps of evening primrose. Because the brilliant blossoms of this night-flowering plant remain open in the morning, it is easily mistaken for its day-flowering relative, the sundrop.

rental shops proclaim that fishing is the main lure of this village. Crabs, shrimp, clams, and fish freshly caught in the Gulf are delicious specialities in local restaurants and are available at very low prices in roadside markets.

12   Built by waves and sculptured by winds, Padre Island is a classic barrier island, stretching along the Gulf Coast for 113 miles. A very popular recreation area, the island presents a wide, clean sand-and-shell beach to the Gulf. Sand dunes as high as 38 feet parallel the beach. Behind the dunes is a zone stabilized by grasses and shrubs. These varied habitats support more than 400 species of birds.

Padre Island National Seashore preserves an undeveloped 70 miles in the middle of the island. Paved roads extend only a few miles from each end of the island. To drive along the soft, sandy beach in between, a four-wheel-drive vehicle is necessary. One can be rented in Corpus Christi.

The pine forests of eastern Texas are the absolute opposite of the popular view of Texas. Not desert, or dry, or even open, this area contains some of the best forest land in the United States. Here is the Big Thicket National Preserve, the crossroads of American plant life and a wilderness of green solitude and mysterious, surprising beauty. East Texas was the gateway to the Texas frontier, and many historic structures are preserved as memorials to its pioneer tradition.

1   Founded in 1836, the year of Texas independence, Huntsville became Sam Houston's home. At Sam Houston Memorial Park are pre-

3. *Among the places of historic interest in Nacogdoches is Millard's Crossing, a cluster of early pioneer homes, such as the one above, and a small Methodist chapel. The buildings have been moved here from nearby, restored, and furnished with antiques.*

served his white frame house, a law office, a carriage house, and the "Steamboat House," where he died in 1863. A museum on the park grounds displays memorabilia of the dynamic character who more than any other created and shaped Texas.

Heading north, you drive through farmland and ranchland, bridge an arm of Lake Livingston, and continue through woodlands broken by pastures dotted with cattle.

2   The entrance to Ratcliff Lake Recreation Area in Davy Crockett National Forest is clearly indicated. Ratcliff Lake is in a lovely forest setting. A scenic Forest Service road provides access to its shores.

3   A town steeped in history, Nacogdoches had long been an Indian settlement before Spanish explorer Hernando de Soto visited it in 1542. Today historic buildings stand as monuments to the community's interesting past. Especially noteworthy is the Old Stone Fort reconstructed on the campus of Steven F. Austin University. The substantial two-story structure was built as a Spanish trading post in 1779, and doubled as a fort during troubles with Indians. From the balcony that extends across the front fly eight flags that symbolize the sovereignty claims of nations and expeditions over the fort. Its museum elaborates on this history.

4   At the roadside midway to San Augustine is Halfway House, an 1840's stagecoach inn. Now privately owned, it is still maintained to appear as it did when Sam Houston and other Texas notables stopped here.

San Augustine, gateway to frontier Texas, has many historic homes and commercial buildings that have been restored. Prominent among them is the Greek Revival-style home built in 1839 by pioneer Texas statesman Ezekial W. Cullen. Today the edifice houses a museum.

5   The terrain on the way to Pineland can be imagined easily from the community's name. East of the intersection of Routes 96 and 83 is the headquarters mill of Temple Industries, one of the largest lumber companies in Texas. On weekday tours of the mill, visitors can see the various steps in making plywood and veneer.

6   South of Pineland the route touches the Sabine National Forest and then crosses the dam that impounds Sam Rayburn Reservoir, the largest body of fresh water wholly within Texas. The open water is popular with boaters, and the flooded forest land lures fishermen. Several parks present roadside views of the lake, and the Letney Creek Recreation Area offers spots for swimming, camping, and picnicking.

7   Martin Dies, Jr. State Park stretches along the eastern shore of Steinhagen Lake, an impoundment of the Neches River. On an old terrace of the river, the 705-acre park contains shallow sloughs lined with picturesque cypress and willow trees. Trails and picnic sites are shaded by beeches, pines, and magnolias. Also popular here are fishing, boating, and swimming. Do not miss the lovely nature trail reached via a bridge to an island in the Walnut Ridge Unit, north of Route 190. Along this trail you are likely to see woodland warblers, pileated woodpeckers, and several kinds of water birds.

8   To the south and west lies the Big Thicket National Preserve, a unique meeting ground for plant species from New England forests, Florida swamps, and Texas desert. The huge preserve consists of 12 separate units of land and water. Three units—Beech Creek, Hickory Creek Savannah, and Turkey Creek—are now open to visitors and are along this loop.

Big Thicket is administered by the National Park Service, which maintains a visitor information station at the south end of the Turkey Creek Unit (for road directions see below). Here you can get free trail guides and current information about the facilities of the units and about naturalist-guided hikes. The station is open daily from spring through autumn and on weekends in winter.

To reach Beech Creek, the first of the Big Thicket units on this drive, follow Route 1746 west of Town Bluff for 6½ miles, and go south on Route 2992 for another 5.3 miles. A mile-

Big Thicket National Preserve

To protect the several ecosystems found in southeastern Texas (see number 8), the Big Thicket National Preserve was established by the National Park Service in 1974 with an authorization to purchase 84,550 acres. So far parcels of land totaling some 73,000 acres have been acquired in a 50-mile-square area spreading into seven counties. The preserve now has eight land units and four river and stream corridors. In 1980 three of these areas were opened for the public's enjoyment. The development of hiking trails and visitor facilities in other units is planned.

long trail starts near the parking lot and loops through a mature remnant of a beech–magnolia forest. This natural mix of trees from the northeast and southeast United States occurs almost exclusively in this part of Texas. These trees form a green roof, blocking out sunshine, and hence reducing the amount of undergrowth. The quiet, cathedrallike woods is a habitat for deer, armadillos, and squirrels.

9   Continue south on Route 2992, then west on Route 1013, and south on Route 69. About 4½ miles below Warren, turn west onto Route 2827, which brings you to the Hickory Creek Savannah Unit. Here you find the contrasting ecosystems of the dry long-leaf pine uplands and the pine savanna wetlands. Along a one-mile trail you may discover any of the seven species of orchids that flourish here, insectivorous sundew, blue flag, and other wild flowers growing among the long-leaf pines. You also come upon sandy knolls that support both dogwood and yucca.

10   The Turkey Creek Unit is a long, narrow strip of preserve paralleling Route 69 to the west, and it has three access roads. The southernmost, Route 420, which turns east off Route 69 just 11 miles below Warren, also brings you to the Park Service's visitor information station.

Of all the units in Big Thicket, Turkey Creek contains the most incredible diversity of plant communities. Trails thread through majestic forests, swamps with stands of cypresses and tupelos, and wet areas called baygalls, named for the plants commonly found here: white bay and gallberry holly.

11   In Saratoga the Big Thicket Association has a museum that presents the area's natural and cultural history. Legends about the Thicket are an interesting part of the museum's story, presented with a slide program, dioramas, plant collections, and photographs. Closed Mondays.

12   At Segno, detour west on Route 943 to the place where the road crosses the stream in the preserve's Menard Creek Corridor. (Watch for yellow blazes and boundary signs on trees along the road.) Menard Creek penetrates the "Tight-eye" region. The name comes from the remarkably dense forest cover, containing a high concentration of swamp cyrilla, or titi bushes, that form impenetrable thickets. It is said that even a canebreak rattler has to back through such places with its eyes shut.

13   The Indians at the Alabama–Coushatta Indian Reservation run an extensive visitor program, including craft demonstrations, Big Thicket tours, and a restaurant featuring traditional Indian food.

Tall pines create an aislelike boulevard of the road on the drive toward Lake Livingstone, with occasional openings for farms and homes. Lake Livingstone is both a reservoir and a recreation area for Houston, and its 452 miles of wooded shores are spangled with parks and marinas.

Marbled salamander

Coral fungus

Green tree frog

Green anole (lizard) on moss

Mushrooms on host vegetation

Upland chorus frog

9. A carpet of ferns (top) borders a stand of pines and dogwoods in the Big Thicket National Preserve near Warren. Among the trees and plants of the thicket can be found an abundance of small creatures and various fungi, such as those shown above.

Oklahoma: The Sooner State

Settlers who jumped the starting gun to stake claims sooner than was legal found a rich and varied land

For many centuries before the coming of the white man, Indians roamed the wilderness that became present-day Oklahoma. This was also the land given to the five Indian tribes who were driven from their homes in the southeastern part of United States during the 1830's.

In 1907 this territory, whose name came from two Choctaw words, *okla* ("people") and *humma* ("red"), became a state.

The state is best known for its prairies and its oil wells. Less well known are its mesa country and its mountains, regions of beauty beyond the flatlands and in opposite corners of the state.

With its panoramas of sand dunes, red rock buttes, and arid, canyon-strewn wastelands, northwestern Oklahoma is so unlike the state's Great Plains area that despite the cattle ranches and wide fields of wheat that crop up here occasionally, the landscape seems a world away from the farmlands to the south.

1 Orienta, a small crossroads hamlet, serves as the entrance to the Cheyenne Valley. Two miles west of the town, on the right, is a turnoff with an information chart giving a description of the desertlike landscape ahead.

Buttes, known as the Glass Mountains because of their coating of selenite crystals, are topped with several feet of gypsum, their strange formations rising up as much as 300 feet above the valley floor.

The buttes were created when water flowed through the area millions of years ago, eroding the clay and shale and leaving the harder gypsum caps with their fantastic shapes.

The valley, which stretches on for some 35 miles, is colored brick red and is almost entirely without vegetation, with no houses, no farms, no signs of civilization—just the straight road in the haunting landscape.

Beyond the Cheyenne Valley the road turns to the north and continues through rolling scrublands covered with sagebrush. Every now and again a clump of tumbleweed, the stringy purplish weed that is blown into balls by the wind, appears along the road.

2 The sand dunes of Little Sahara Recreation Area extend along the west side of the highway for about four miles and stretch back into the countryside for many more. Motor-cycles, jeeps, and dune buggies frequently scale the impressive sandy heights.

On holidays during the summer, races of various kinds are held, attracting thousands of visitors, both participants and spectators.

Campsites and picnic tables are available in the narrow grassy area along the road, and there are several inviting slopes where children delight in stretching out and rolling down sideways.

Waynoka, a small town that has grown from a railroad siding to a farming community, is known for the abundance of rattlesnakes in its environs. An annual event called a rattlesnake roundup, held during April, attracts thousands of snake enthusiasts, who compete for prizes in such categories as the largest number of rattlers collected as well as the smallest and the heaviest. At the end of the day a rattlesnake barbecue is held, when all the hunters and visitors partake of the reputedly delicious fare.

The picturesque little village of Freedom, which was beautified several years ago by the addition of weathered wooden facades on all

2. This is not distant Araby but an arid stretch of Oklahoma aptly named Little Sahara. The view from the ridge is of 1,450 acres of sand sculpted into crescent-shaped mounds by the wind. Like ocean waves in slow motion, these hills move across the land.

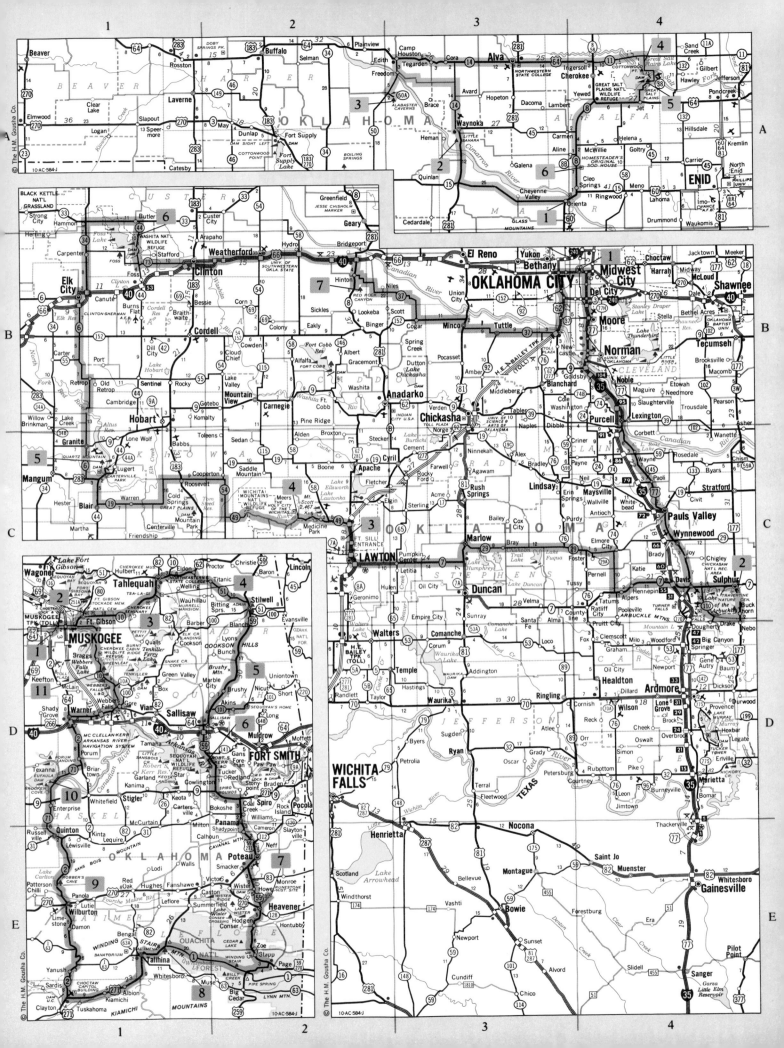

buildings on the two-block-long Main Street, is a trading center for the nearby ranches and wheat farms.

3 Six miles south of Freedom is the Alabaster Caverns State Park. Among its five caves is Alabaster Cavern, one of the largest known gypsum caves in the world. A ¾-mile tour of its accessible part starts at the visitor center and winds down into Cedar Canyon to the entrance, a sinkhole in the canyon wall.

The cavern has three distinct areas: a collapse section, where there are large rooms filled with enormous fallen boulders of gypsum, shale, and selenite; a dome section, whose ceilings have many small domes; and a channel section smoothed and polished by an underground stream. At the exit, another sinkhole, visitors are met and transported back to the center. Near the cave's exit a natural bridge, formed by millions of years of erosion, spans the canyon.

Eight kinds of bats inhabit the caverns, among them the big brown, the big-eared, and, most numerous, the cave myotis bat, which numbers in the thousands here.

Clumps of cottonwoods are used as windbreaks along the route east of Freedom, where crops of wheat fill the fields. These high rolling prairies are dotted with oil wells whose pumps are located in the midst of the cultivated fields.

4 At the Salt Fork of the Arkansas River the farmlands yield to rimy marshes where flocks of ducks paddle about. This is the northern end of the Great Salt Plains National Wildlife Refuge, a 32,324-acre tract of water, desert, and marsh.

The headquarters of the refuge is two miles south of Route 11 on Route 38, a sandy road winding through woods. From the parking area here a nature trail loops through a verdant wilderness that is a haven for waterfowl, shorebirds, deer, raccoons, weasels, and mink.

Southward, the refuge encompasses Great Salt Plains Lake (a res-

Digging for Selenite Crystals

You can dig for selenite crystals at the posted site in the national wildlife refuge on weekends and holidays from April 1 to October 15. All you need is a shovel. Dig a hole about two feet wide and two feet deep, and allow it to fill with groundwater. Then splash the sides of the hole to wash away sand and clay until a crystal is exposed. Gently free it with more water. Since the crystals are soft, let them dry and harden in the sun and then protect them with a wrapping of tissue paper before you carry them away. Additional information about the site is given by the refuge headquarters (see highlight 4 above).

ervoir) and the Great Salt Plains, several square miles of salt-encrusted mud flats devoid of vegetation. The Salt Plains lure rock hounds in search of selenite crystals.

5 Near the dam at the eastern end of the lake is the Great Salt Lake State Park. Within its three units are picnic spots, campsites, boat ramps, and a beach. Sheltered picnic tables are found along the road.

If you wish to investigate the selenite crystal area, take the dirt access road leading north off Route 64 just six miles west of Jet.

6 South of Aline is the Homesteaders Sod House, a turn-of-the-century "soddie," as these makeshift homes were called. The two-room house is preserved within a frame building and furnished in the style of the early settlers. Buffalo-grass sod blocks, cut about 6 inches deep, 16 inches wide, and 36 inches long, were laid in the manner of bricks, with a sod block covering the seam between the blocks beneath. The roof, held up by three ridgepoles and rafters of split blackjack oak, was covered with sod about 12 inches thick. Flour sacks sewed together lined the ceiling of the house to keep out sifting soil, snakes, and insects.

The road southward skirts flatlands dotted with oil wells, wheat fields, and ranches as it approaches Cleo Springs and Orienta.

5. The selenite crystal area is in the southwest corner of the Great Salt Plains. Forming in wet, subsurface soil where gypsum and saline solutions are in heavy concentration, the crystals embrace small particles of sand and clay, which often group in an hourglass configuration unique to this area. Iron oxide in the soil gives them a rich brown color. The clusters, "penetration twins," and single crystals shown here are typical. Crystals seven inches long have been found.

Oklahoma's Great Plains, the part of the state that includes the capital and the wide open landscape to the south and west, is a flat expanse of prairie filled with farmlands and cattle ranches. Crops of soybeans, cotton, peanuts, pecans, and wheat flourish in these fields, where houses are far apart and some towns are little more than a few buildings at a crossroads.

The plains, interrupted here and there by low mountains, are crossed by rivers and accented by lakes where recreational sites have been developed and large wilderness areas have been reserved for wildlife.

The plains—the disastrous Dust Bowl of the 1930's—display today a quiet beauty and a sense of peace and orderly prosperity.

1 Oklahoma City, the state capital, spreads out over 620 square miles of prairie atop an extensive oil field that was not discovered until several years after the city was established. Since its beginnings in 1889, when the land was opened up to homesteaders, the city has grown from a pioneer settlement to an important cultural and commercial metropolis. Its impressive skyline of modern civic and business buildings rises almost like a mirage from the surrounding plains, where flat farmlands and extensive cattle ranches fill the landscape.

Oklahoma's state capitol, one of the few without a dome, is famous for its front lawn, where a working oil well stands, producing petroleum as it attests to the importance of this natural resource in the state's economy.

Guided tours of the imposing white limestone building, whose rotunda serves as a state-run tourist information center, are given daily except on holidays.

The road south from Oklahoma City toward the Lake of the Arbuckles region crosses wide, flat prairies and follows the Canadian River as far as Purcell. This small town, settled in 1887 when the Santa Fe Railroad came through the area, sits on a steep bluff above the river.

Pauls Valley, a town built on the bank of the Washita River, dates back to the 1840's, when a pioneer named Smith Paul established a large farm here on Indian land. The area became known as Smith Paul's Valley,

1. Turner Falls, a spectacular cascade, drops 77 feet to form a natural swimming pool. As long ago as 1868, the scenic vicinity of the falls, not far from the town of Davis, became a popular recreation area where Oklahomans came to escape the summer heat.

which was eventually shortened to Pauls Valley. In 1979 the town was placed on the National Register of Historical Places because of its 19th-century brick buildings.

Today the town is best known for its rose gardens in Wacker Park and for the city lake, where boating, fishing, picnicking, and camping are popular.

From Davis to Sulphur, a city named for the many mineral springs that flow through the area, the road skirts the northern boundaries of the Chickasaw National Recreation Area, a preserve that includes the Lake of the Arbuckles.

2 Situated in the so-called travertine district of Chickasaw is the Travertine Nature Center. Here you find

exhibits of local wildlife, such as a rattlesnake (in a glass cage), two aquariums of native fish, and identification charts of trees and wild flowers found in the region. Here too is the starting point of several self-guided nature trails.

The center is named for a stream that runs through soft carbonate rock called travertine (related to limestone), which is formed from deposits left by mineral waters.

Travertine Creek flows into Rock Creek, a stream that was dammed in 1968, forming the Lake of the Arbuckles and ensuring the surrounding communities of adequate water supplies.

More than eight miles of hilly roads here wind through low mountains, which were formed by an uplift that occurred some 300 million years ago. Once as high as the Rockies, they have been worn down to their present size—some 700 feet above the surrounding plain—by millions of years of erosion.

Along the 36 miles of shoreline of the Lake of the Arbuckles there are three designated recreation areas where boat ramps, camping sites, and picnic grounds are provided. Fishing, swimming, and waterskiing are permitted in these waters, where channel catfish, largemouth bass, bluegill, sunfish, and crappie are native.

To circle the lake, turn west from Route 177 at the sign for the Goddard Youth Camp and follow the winding road back to Routes 110 and 7.

As you cross the treeless prairies toward the town of Lawton, you pass several small communities that serve as centers for both crop and cattle ranchers and for nearby oil-producing companies. The road turns from its arrow-straight course only to go around acres of a rancher's property.

Lawton was created almost overnight by some 10,000 homesteaders in the first days of August 1901, when the U.S. Land Office opened up the region with a lottery for the 160-acre plots. Today the city is well established and prosperous. In its short life it has become Oklahoma's third largest city and an important hub in its economic well-being.

3 Fort Sill, today the U.S. Army Field Artillery Training Center, dates back to 1869 when it was established

In the Event of a Tornado

Tornadoes, the most violent of all storms, occur in all 50 of the United States, but most of them strike in Tornado Alley, a belt extending from Texas northward toward Canada. They happen year-round, but mostly in April, May, and June, and between the hours of 3 and 7 P.M.

Spawned by thunderstorms, tornadoes develop here when warm, moist air from the Gulf of Mexico collides with cold air sweeping across the Rockies. The typical funnel-shaped cloud, visible because of its moisture content, is a column of swirling air with velocities of 170 to 250 miles per hour. Spinning around the core of the funnel are several smaller twisters, or suction spots.

Although the formation of tornadoes is not fully understood, meteorologists are increasingly successful in forecasting them, using Doppler radar. They can now alert people 20 to 30 minutes before a strike.

If you are on the road and in the path of a tornado, stop the car at once, jump out, and lie facedown in a ditch or hollow. If you are in a building, go to the basement, or seek a small, windowless ground-floor room—a bathroom, hall, or closet—in the center or on the side away from the impact of the storm.

to provide protection for settlers. The fort's old post corral and guardhouse are now part of a museum complex that includes MacLain and Hamilton halls, which have displays of military

equipment from colonial times to the present.

Geronimo, the famous Apache chief who led raids into Mexico and in some of the Plains states, was held as a prisoner of war at Fort Sill for many years. He died in 1909 and is buried on the post grounds.

Fort Sill's Key Gate, closest to the museum, is located three miles north of Lawton just off Route 277/281.

4 As you approach the Wichita Mountains Wildlife Refuge, rolling hills begin to appear on the horizon. Route 49 winds through Medicine Park, skirts Lake Lawtonka, enters the refuge at the east gate, and immediately begins to climb up through the round-topped, 500-million-year-old granite mountains. Here are herds of buffalo, Texas longhorns, elk, and wild turkeys, all living contentedly on the open grazing land that is sometimes called a prairie sea with islands of rocks. The peaks rise some 700 feet above this "sea."

On the mountain slopes are scattered short, wind-distorted post and blackjack oaks, while an occasional stray tree dots the prairie.

Mount Scott (2,467 feet), the highest peak in the refuge, was once sacred to the Wichita Indians, who lived on these lands centuries ago. The summit offers a view of the 20 or so lakes within the refuge.

As the road winds through the wilderness, a sudden turn brings you to the prairie dog town, where there is a turnoff and parking space. The little creatures, lured by the sound of foot-

4. Buffaloed by a stray—and stubborn—bison, a car pauses at Wichita Mountains Wildlife Refuge, where animals have the right-of-way. The glassy surface of Rush Lake (right) reflects clouds and sky, with the Wichitas as a dark backdrop.

steps overhead, poke their heads up from their burrows and, if one stays fairly quiet, come out to investigate their visitors.

At the refuge headquarters, just a few hundred yards to the south of the main road, you can obtain a map and information about the areas where camping, picnicking, boating, and fishing are permitted. Route 49 traverses the refuge and leaves it at the west gate, about five miles beyond the headquarters building.

The flat, high plateau between the Wichita refuge and Quartz Mountain State Park appears to be one enormous wheat field. In the spring, when the wheat is only about a foot high, its dark bluish-green color contrasts handsomely with the brilliant red soil of the occasional unplanted plots along the road.

5 Quartz Mountain State Park, whose startling red rocky peaks of granite appear just beyond the park entrance, stretches along Lake Altus Lugert, a reservoir that provides excellent fishing, boating, and swimming. The park road winds through wooded slopes where hackberries, cedars, oaks, and mesquites shelter many kinds of birds, including the cardinal and the quail.

Quartz Mountain Lodge, at the end of a winding drive up through the mountains, overlooks the lake. The lodge offers overnight accommodations and a restaurant, with several tennis courts and a golf course nearby. Cabins are available, and there are camping sites and picnic grounds as well.

The rough, rounded red granite rocks that make up the mountains were formed by weathering along natural joints and formations in the granite bedrock. Rainwater seeping into these cracks over millions of years gradually rotted the minerals and produced rounded blocks and boulders, sometimes called "devil's marbles" or "woolsocks."

One of Oklahoma's richest oil areas surrounds Elk City, whose skyline includes a refinery plant and grain elevators standing almost side by side.

6 On the east side of Foss Lake, just south of Butler, is the entrance to Washita National Wildlife Refuge. Wild turkeys, quail, and deer roam through the wooded wilderness. The

7. Cyclists—one of them with a small passenger—ride past the sandstone walls of Red Rock Canyon. The grade here is not steep, except when entering and leaving.

refuge is a wintering ground for thousands of Canada and northern geese, as well as many other kinds of waterfowl.

7 Red Rock Canyon State Park, a popular recreation area, is a 100-foot-deep ravine whose brilliant red sandstone walls account for its name.

Just inside the park's entrance gate there is a short, very steep road (on which campers and trailers are not allowed without the ranger's assistance) that takes you down to the floor of the canyon. Here are picnic grounds, campsites, a small lake, a swimming pool, and a stream that flows through the wooded ravine.

The only way out of the mile-long canyon is via the steep entrance roadway, whose hairpin turns and steep incline can be intimidating. But the cool green meadow and the tall hardwood trees that flourish in the protected chasm are well worth the drive down and back.

At Minco and Tuttle, small farming communities, the many grain elevators against the skyline are an indication of the importance and extent of the nearby wheat fields that spread out on the never-ending prairies.

From Muskogee and the town of Tahlequah south to the Ouachita National Forest, the scenery varies from farmlands to rolling hills where, scattered among the scrubby growth, herds of Herefords, Black Angus, and Shorthorn cattle graze.

Here are the remnants of early Indian settlements and the outposts of frontier days that have become modern cities and towns. And in these wooded hills is the site of an ancient rune stone whose discovery revived a long-held belief that the Vikings wandered, more than 900 years ago, through these hills and valleys.

1 Muskogee, at the confluence of the Verdigris, Grand, and Arkansas rivers, was settled in 1872 as a trading center for prospectors and homesteaders. Today, with two grain elevators, two glass factories, and a paper-processing plant, the city plays an important part in Oklahoma's economy.

Honor Heights Park, on the western edge of town, is a 124-acre area with azaleas and rose gardens, picnic grounds, and a swimming pool. The park is also the site of the Five Civilized Tribes Museum (Cherokee, Chickasaw, Choctaw, Creek, and Seminole), so named by the U.S. Bureau of Indian Affairs after these people had developed a society that included well-organized forms of government, religion, and education.

Here in the museum the cultural history and traditons of these tribes are preserved. Displays include examples of their arts and crafts, historic costumes, and many artifacts found in this Indian land.

2 Fort Gibson, a large stockaded stronghold dating back to 1824, was once the westernmost of the U.S. outposts, serving to keep the peace between the Indian and the white man. Both Zachary Taylor and Robert E. Lee, officers in the U.S. Army, were stationed here at Fort Gibson, which has today been completely reconstructed.

Within the stockaded area there are quarters for enlisted men and officers, two guardhouses, and two blockhouses. The fort was a safe and popular stopping place for settlers who were heading west and was also the headquarters where peace trea-

3. A Cherokee potter shapes a bowl in the dappled shade of the Village of Tsa-La-Gi near Tahlequah. Finished pots are on display in the foreground.

ties with the Indian tribes were signed. The fort was abandoned in 1890. A visitor center outside the stockade offers information and publications about the fort.

3   Tahlequah, where the Cherokees settled after they had been driven from their native homes in the East, is today the headquarters of the Cherokee Nation. The Village of Tsa-La-Gi, a reconstructed Cherokee settlement, is located 3½ miles south of Tahlequah just off Route 62 on Route 82. Here in an outdoor amphitheater the story of the tribe's march from the East is told in a drama entitled *The Trail of Tears*, the name given to the Indians' tragic exodus. Performances alternate with presentations of *Will Rogers, the Cherokee Kid* and are put on several times a week during the summer.

At the village Cherokees demonstrate pottery making, basket weaving, and other crafts and explain the everyday life of the tribe 300 years ago. Included in the museum complex are the Memorial Prayer Chapel, an arboretum and herb garden, and a small wildlife refuge where half a dozen buffalo and several deer graze in a fenced-off field.

4   About a half-mile from the village is the Murrell Mansion, also on Route 82. This elegant home was built

about 1845 by George Murrell, who married the niece of a Cherokee chief, became a major in the Confederate Army, and fought in the Civil War. The restored mansion, set in old-fashioned gardens and surrounded by a white picket fence, is furnished in Victorian style, with several family pieces included.

About five miles beyond the town of Tahlequah the road crosses the Illinois River. Here, on both sides of the road, are signs offering float trips on the quiet stream whose banks in spring are bedecked with dogwood and redbud (*Cercis canadensis*), the tree that represents the state and is seen in full bloom in April.

Shortly after leaving Tahlequah the road drops down a hillside in the wooded, rolling landscape where grazing lands, interspersed with fields of soybeans, stretch for miles along the road.

5   Near the present-day town of Sallisaw is the one-room log cabin that was home to Sequoyah, inventor of the Cherokee alphabet, from 1830 to 1842. The building is preserved within a stone structure that is set in the midst of a wooded, 10-acre park seven miles east of the town. The park is closed on Mondays and also on holidays.

6   From Sallisaw the road passes through a hilly forest that suddenly opens upon an expansive view of the Robert S. Kerr Reservoir to the west, with a long, high concrete bridge across the Arkansas River straight ahead. The reservoir was created when the Robert S. Kerr Dam was constructed in 1967–70. Locks in the dam, together with several others along the waterway originating in the Port of Catoosh in Tulsa, make it possible for shipping to move between the port of Muskogee and the Gulf of Mexico.

A narrow road turns down a slope, crosses a bank above a sandy beach, and takes you to the dam, where there is a visitor center, a parking area, and an observation tower from which, with luck, you can watch as a barge negotiates the channel through the locks.

7   The busy town of Heavener (pronounced *heev*ener) lies at the foot of a ridge known as Poteau Mountain, which rises to the northeast 1,200 feet above the almost flat plateau. Halfway up this peak is the Heavener Runestone State Park, where in 1912 hikers discovered a great slab of rock 12 feet high, 10 feet wide, and 16 inches thick, its face inscribed with markings that have

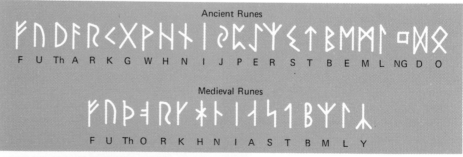

7. The illustration above shows letters from two Scandinavian alphabets that have been translated to the date November 11, 1012, by using the decoding methods of cryptography. The eight characters, cut about a half-inch deep into an upright stone, are purported to be a Norse rune left by Viking visitors to Oklahoma nearly a thousand years ago. Some scholars of Scandinavian history, however, have disputed this claim, doubting that the Norsemen could have strayed so far from home. The slab, pictured at left, was found near a branch of the Arkansas River, which flows into the Mississippi. Voyaging Vikings might have headed up these rivers.

been authenticated as Norse runes—carvings or characters in the runic alphabet. The carving gives the date of A.D. 1012, which revives the theory that the Vikings wandered through here long before Columbus arrived in the Western Hemisphere.

The stone stands on the slope of a deep ravine and is now enclosed in a stone building. A visitor center serves as the entrance to a trail down the side of the ravine to the museum, almost 50 feet below.

The park has picnic grounds and offers a magnificent view of the surrounding countryside from a turnaround on the mountainside. On the hillsides are dogwood, redbud, shortleaf pine, hickory, mockernut, and several kinds of oak, all trees that thrive in poor, dry soil.

To reach the park, cross the railroad tracks in the center of Heavener, take the first turn north, and follow the signs to the entrance, three miles from the railroad. A rustic arch, almost lost in the trees, spans the road that leads up the mountain to the park.

Just beyond Heavener the road enters the Ouachita National Forest, a 300,000-acre expanse of wooded mountains, river valleys, and lakes, with marked hiking trails, campsites, picnic grounds, and waterways that are popular for boating, fishing, and swimming.

Some 40 kinds of trees grow in the forest, with long-needle pine and several kinds of oak the most prevalent. Wild flowers too are abundant and include the state flower, mistletoe (*Phoradendron flavescens*).

8 Just beyond Stapp—only a small roadside sign indicates that the hamlet is nearby—the road intersects the Talimena Skyline Drive, a 55-mile-long highway that runs from Mena, Arkansas, to Talihina, Oklahoma. The spectacular route winds through the forest, climbs to the mountaintops, and drops down again. In dry, hot weather forest fires are a constant threat.

There are several turnoffs along the drive where posters describe the points of interest in the view.

At the end of the drive the road drops down to the Talimena State Park, a 20-acre recreation area in the wooded foothills of the winding Stair

8. *Heaven seems to be your destination as the Talimena Skyline Drive winds sinuously into blue distances. Rhythmically rising and falling, the ribbon of road offers vistas of lakes and woods. The most heady vista is simply all that abounding space.*

Mountains, with facilities for camping and picnicking and hiking.

Talihina, a town whose name is the Choctaw word for "iron road," was established at the time the Santa Fe Railroad was put through the area. Today the town is a center for sportsmen, both hunters and fishermen, because of its location in the wooded valley through which many trout streams flow.

9 Robber's Cave State Park is a 8,500-acre area with streams, canyons, wooded hills, and large rock formations. The park is named for a cave in a sandstone cliff used, according to legend, by outlaws as a hideout. Steps leading up to the cave entrance have been carved in the cliff. The park offers campgrounds and rental cabins, as well as all kinds of water sports, including boating and fishing.

10 Eufaula Lake, nestled among the rolling, wooded hills of Arrowhead State Park, appears along the west side of the road between the towns of Enterprise and Porum. A winding route through the park leads to many lakeside picnic groves and a beach. Some of these narrow roads

become boat ramps as they reach the water's edge.

Eufaula Lake and the extensive recreation area were formed by a dam across the Canadian River, which is traversed by Route 71. At the far end of the dam there is an enormous rock wall stratified with black anthracite intersected by bright orange-red granite, an imposing eminence that forces the road to veer sharply to the east.

At Webbers Falls the road crosses the Arkansas River and turns north through a gentle rural landscape.

11 A short distance beyond Webbers Falls Lake, which appears on the west side of the road, is Greenleaf State Park to the east. Here too is a lake, a long and narrow body of water where fishing is said to be exceptionally good. The wooded park is home to a variety of wildlife, including deer, skunks, raccoons, and rabbits. An 18-mile backpacking trail, which goes through the wilderness and circles the lake, lures serious hikers at all times of the year.

The winding, hilly route back to Muskogee is one of ever-changing vistas of water, woods, and farms.

Discovering Kansas

Traveling these highways and byways reveals this to be a not-so-plain Plains state

Kansas may have the reputation of being a dull, featureless plain, but reality belies the image. Kansas farmers create masterpieces of abstract design with green, gold, and brown bands of crops that stretch across the vast wheatlands. Drillers for petroleum populate the prairies with bobbing pumps that resemble huge prehistoric beasts. Wild flowers, including the sunflower, the most pervasive state symbol, sprinkle every imaginable color along the fencerows bordering Kansas roads. Federal dam builders have created large lakes across the state, providing havens for hordes of migrating waterfowl. Neither here nor elsewhere will you see the jayhawk, which gives Kansas one of its nicknames (the Jayhawk State), for this is a creature of legend rather than of fact.

The cattle country of the Flint Hills remains relatively unchanged since the days of the cowboy. And, as in "Home on the Range" (the state song), antelopes (pronghorns) still play on the plains of Kansas.

On this tour you drive through rich farmlands, passing four U.S. Bureau of Reclamation reservoirs whose waters irrigate milo (grain sorghum), corn, and alfalfa hay. Dryland wheat farming also is intensively practiced here.

The geographical center of the 48 contiguous states, just north of Lebanon, is a point of interest. To the south is Waconda Lake, the largest reservoir in this area. Route 24 follows the south fork of the Solomon River beyond Osborne, a stretch along which cottonwoods interrupt the expected level scenery of Kansas.

Beyond Webster Lake is the town of Nicodemus, settled by former slaves in 1877. Farther along the route, Norton Reservoir, with adjacent Prairie Dog State Park, has a state wildlife area, while a restored stagecoach station can be visited in Norton, to the east.

At the Kirwin National Wildlife Refuge you can see the state's largest flocks of Canada geese during migration periods, as well as many other kinds of wild birds and mammals along the roads of the sanctuary.

1 Smith Center, logically enough, sits square in the center of square Smith County and is the county seat. A picturesque octagonal Dutch-style windmill rises above Wagner Park, not far from Route 36.

German homesteader Charles Schwarz built the mill in Reamsville, north of Smith Center, in 1882. A miller in Europe, Schwarz saw no reason to waste the ever-available wind power that is a persistent presence on the Kansas plains. For many years he ground wheat and corn grown on surrounding farms.

In 1938 the mill, long since abandoned, was dismantled and moved to Smith Center, where it was rebuilt. It no longer grinds grain, but is still a good example of an authentic European-style wind-powered mill.

2 An elaborate intersection 11 miles east of Smith Center directs you north to the geographical center of the nation's 48 contiguous states.

There is no doubt that the geographical center had more significance before Alaska and Hawaii achieved statehood. Increased mobility—better roads and cars, greater use of airplanes—and changing patterns of commerce have also diminished the significance of being equidistant from the boundaries of the country. But, like the summit of a mountain, the center of the nation retains a certain fascination.

3 Near the grain elevator in Glen Elder is a sign proclaiming "Best Little Town by a Dam Site." Earth-filled Glen Elder Dam impounds 12,586-acre Waconda Lake. Built by the U.S. Bureau of Reclamation for flood control and irrigation water storage, the reservoir submerged three springs, the biggest known as Great Spirit, that had made the little town of Waconda Springs a health resort.

The lake has 62 miles of shoreline, but most of the recreational use is at Glen Elder State Park along Route 24 at the dam. Waconda Lake is one of the finest fishing lakes in Kansas, and boating is a primary emphasis at the park. A boat-renting concession operates during the summer, and there are four launching ramps, two docks, and a marina.

4 The Bureau of Reclamation also built Webster Lake for flood control and irrigation. Recreational side benefits are concentrated in Webster State Park, with units on both the north and south shores connected by a road across the earth-filled dam. Fishing is the main attraction here and boat ramps are available.

Nicodemus, situated about 10 miles west of the park, is a reminder that Kansas achieved statehood in 1861 on the verge of the Civil War. During the trying times that followed, Kansas was a haven for runaway slaves. In 1877 blacks from Kentucky founded Nicodemus, which remains the only all-black town in Kansas. These former slaves called themselves "Exodusters," identifying with the Israelite slaves who were led out of Egypt by Moses and confronted the task of scratching out a living from a dusty, inhospitable environment. Nicodemus has been designated a national historic landmark.

An oil derrick along Route 24 at the west edge of Hill City marks an oil museum. Here are displayed various types of old oil-drilling equipment, mineral samples, and other items related to the oil industry in Kansas.

SPECIAL FEATURES

ROAD GUIDE	HIGHLIGHT	**1**
STATE PARKS	POINTS OF INTEREST	
With Campsites ♠ Without Campsites △		
RECREATION AREAS	SCHEDULED AIRLINE STOPS	
With Campsites ▲ Without Campsites △	MILITARY AIRPORTS	
SELECTED REST AREAS	OTHER AIRPORTS	
With Toilets Without Toilets		

ROAD CLASSIFICATION

CONTROLLED ACCESS HIGHWAYS
Interstate interchange numbers are mileposts.   Divided **5** Undivided

TOLL HIGHWAYS   Service Area ■ Interchanges

OTHER DIVIDED HIGHWAYS

PAVED HIGHWAYS

LOCAL ROADS In unfamiliar areas inquire locally before using these roads   Paved   Gravel   Dirt

MILEAGE

MILEAGE BETWEEN TOWNS AND JUNCTIONS 3 / 4   MILEAGE BETWEEN DOTS • 35 •

SCALE

ONE INCH 17 MILES   0   5   10   20

ONE INCH 27 KILOMETERS   0 5 10   20   32

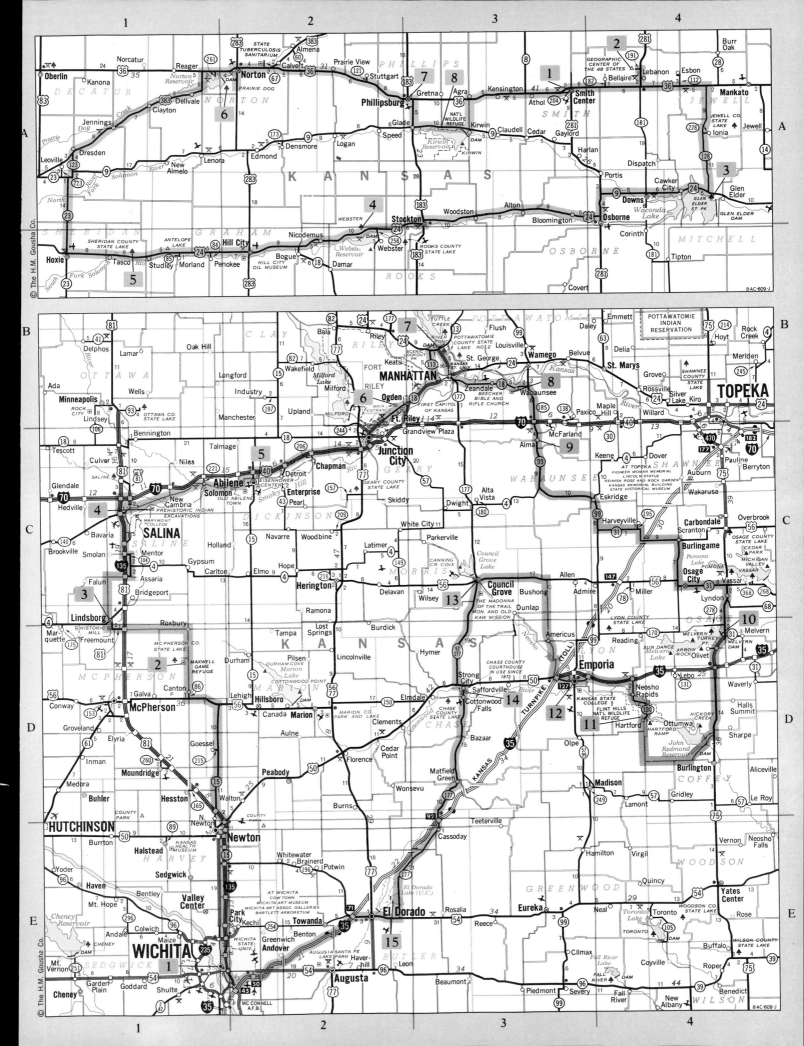

5 The gravel road leading to Sheridan County State Lake leaves Route 24 at a well-marked point four miles west of Studley. As you reach the crest of a hill where the lake appears with surprising suddenness, it seems as though you might be about to drive right into it. The lake, however, is about 100 yards ahead at the bottom of a gulch. A pleasant oasis of water and cottonwoods, the state land uphill from the site is a refuge for native plants among hundreds of square miles of carefully domesticated cropland.

This wild environment is an alternative to the predominant large-scale agricultural artistry of Kansas farmers, who create bold geometric landscapes of green, gold, and brown.

Winding east, past the cottonwoods in the valley of Prairie Dog Creek, you pass lush colorful fields of milo, wheat, and hay where rough stone outcroppings contrast starkly with the cultivated bottomlands.

6 A mile east of Dellvale signs along the north side of the road announce the boundary of Norton Wildlife Area. This is a public hunting land managed by the State Fish and Game Commission specifically for wildlife production. It is a likely place to see roadside wildlife, such as deer or pheasant.

From Prairie Dog State Park you can view the reservoir behind Norton Dam. The Leota Cove Area on the north shore features boat-launching

Growing wheat

Part of the Great Plains, Kansas produces more wheat on its flat and fertile land than any other state. Farmers plant the crop with a drill, which drops seeds into furrows and covers them with earth. When the grain has matured, combines move through the golden crop, cutting it and separating the kernels from the stems and chaff in one operation. The combines then spew the kernels into trucks for the haul to grain elevators.

Drilling (planting) wheat is dusty work.

October-planted wheat is this high in April.

Waves of grain ripen in the Kansas sun as harvesttime nears.

Three combines in formation reap and thresh the grain.

A bounty of golden kernels spouts from a combine into a truck.

Grain elevators keep the wheat dry for its move to the market.

8. On a prairie, farmers pile up stacks of milo, a grain sorghum used, as is corn, to make syrup and to feed the animals. Milo has a compact bearded head and large seeds. Kansas ranks second among the states in the production of this hardy grass.

ramps and picnic facilities. The best view of the lake is from the dam and the south shore.

In nearby Norton is Station 15, a restored cabin of heavy, squared cottonwood timbers that served as a stagecoach stop between Fort Leavenworth and Denver. Inside, behind enlarged windows, costumed mannequins depict scenes from the station's stagecoach-era history.

7 Winding between bottomland trees and wheat fields, the first things you see upon approaching Phillipsburg are likely to be the stacks and towers of the petroleum refinery on the northwest edge of town. Built in 1939, this refinery was the first in the nation to be owned by an agricultural cooperative.

On the west edge of Phillipsburg, Old Fort Bissell sits alongside Route 36. Here the Phillips County Historical Society has reconstructed a palisade on the site of a refuge built in 1872 by local homesteaders as a protection from Indian raids. Although the federal government had nothing to do with the fort, most of the homesteaders were Civil War veterans, well-armed and well-organized. The peaceful benefits of military preparedness were demonstrated at Fort Bissell, which was never used. Its mere presence shielded local settlers.

Two log cabins also built in 1872 have been moved to Fort Bissell. One cabin houses an extensive gun collection; the other contains pioneer artifacts. Various other 19th-century pioneer buildings have been brought to Fort Bissell, where they exhibit objects related to pioneer life.

8 Milo is the popular crop in fields in and surrounding Kirwin National Wildlife Refuge, southeast of Phillipsburg. Corn and winter wheat also are grown on some 2,000 acres cultivated on refuge land. These grains are grown on a sharecrop basis by local farmers, who leave a portion in the fields to feed the 130,000 ducks and 42,000 geese that use the refuge daily during the height of spring and fall migrations.

The refuge is near the 100th meridian, the line that marks a division between birds typical of the West and those of the East. Kirwin therefore has representative species from both areas of the country. Among the most spectacular are white pelicans in warm months, sandhill cranes and their exceedingly rare cousins, the whooping cranes, during spring and fall migrations, and golden and bald eagles during the winter.

Woodlands and grasslands border 5,000 acres of water in Kirwin Reservoir, around which wind 29 miles of gravel road. For the motorist with limited time, the 1½-mile loop road from the headquarters offers a good tour of the refuge. The loop begins in a grassland habitat distinguished by badger burrows, marked by mounds of earth around six-inch semicircular holes. The badgers themselves may be somewhat more difficult to sight.

The gravel road that leads east from the headquarters takes you past overlooks of the reservoir and to the town of Kirwin.

On the south shore the roads provide better views of the lake, and the prairie dog town here is a delight.

The Flint Hills *of eastern Kansas dominate the area. The hills are named for the hard siliceous cherty rocks popularly known as flint, and the shallow, rocky soils here defied the plows of early settlers who toiled to transform the landscape. Instead, the long, rolling slopes remained grassland, and homesteaders used the abundant limestone instead of scarce timber to build barns, fences, and houses. While the Flint Hills were once just 1 percent of North America's 250-million-acre tallgrass prairie, today the hills are among the largest remaining section of that long-since plowed and paved pastureland.*

The drive north of Wichita presents a vista of wheat fields, and in the rolling plains around Canton, elk and bison find sanctuary.

The Smoky River valley brings into view a slice of Scandinavia: Lindsborg, a town that preserves the heritage of its Swedish founders. Near Salina lie excavations of prehistoric Indians, where artifacts and the bones of these ancient farmers rest.

East of the hills are lakes that provide a haven for thousands of migrating water birds. Waterfowl are also plentiful year-round at Peter Pan Park in Emporia, given to the city by its famous newspaperman, William Allen White. Prairie Parkway offers further fine vistas of the Flint Hills and takes you past pioneer buildings to El Dorado Lake.

1 Although Wichita is surrounded by fields of grain in which petroleum pumps rise, the city is known worldwide as a center of aircraft manufacture. The four aircraft companies in this one area produce some 10,000 airplanes every year, and three of them, Cessna, Beech, and Gates Learjet, offer regular tours for the public.

From 1872 until 1880 Wichita was truly a wild and woolly cow town to which cattle were driven from Texas for shipment to eastern markets. This colorful period is preserved at Historic Wichita Cowtown, a collection of restored 19th-century buildings in the center of the downtown area.

In stark architectural contrast to Cowtown is the Wichita Art Museum, which resembles a sculpture of triangular brick prisms. While much of the permanent collection and many of the temporary exhibits reflect a similar contemporary style, the highlight of the collection is a gallery of 19 works by the renowned cowboy artist Charles M. Russell. The museum is closed Mondays and legal holidays.

2 The route north from Wichita follows the historic Chisholm Trail for about 20 miles. About six miles north of Canton is the Maxwell Game Refuge, where you can see protected herds of elk and of bison, the spectacular animals that once dominated the Great Plains until their number was drastically reduced during the heyday of 19th-century hunters and trappers. By 1879 only stragglers were left. Now protected by law, the bison, Kansas's state animal, no longer roam wild on the plains. The 200 bison at the refuge graze peacefully in the open pastures.

Herds of elk, once the second-most abundant grazing animal in Kansas, were also decimated during the 1800's. Reintroduced at Maxwell, about 50 elk roam the refuge today.

The Maxwell Game Refuge contains 2,254 acres and its animals are uncaged, so sightings cannot be guaranteed. The odds, however, favor seeing bison. Elk are fewer in number and tend to take cover among the cottonwoods (*Populus deltoides)*, the official state tree. The best times to spot elk are early morning or early evening.

3 In the 1860's a Chicago group formed the first Swedish Agricultural Company to buy land for homesteading, and 1869 the town of Lindsborg was settled by the Reverend Olof Olsson, who brought his flock from Sweden to the Smoky River valley. He established the community around the Bethany Evangelical Lutheran Church, set up its first school in his house, and founded Bethany College, famous for its 100-year-old Messiah Festival. Swedish is taught in the schools and blends with English on the streets. Other cultural markers, such as Swedish festival costumes, old-country facades on commercial buildings, and a profusion of red Dala horses, the town's symbol, are maintained mostly for appearance's sake.

Preservation of Lindsborg's Swedish and pioneer heritage is focused on the Smoky Valley Roller Mill and on Old Town, both on the banks of the Smoky Hill River. The gristmill has been restored to its turn-of-the-century condition. The adjacent museum houses exhibits of local history and wildlife displays. Both sites are closed on Mondays from November through April and on legal holidays.

Old Town is a reconstruction of a main street in a pioneer village. The Swedish Pavilion, also on the grounds, was part of Sweden's exhibit at the 1904 World's Fair in St. Louis. The pavilion and mill are both on the National Register of Historic Places.

Swedish culture is manifest in Lindsborg, but Swedes were not the first Europeans on the scene. In 1541

2. A 12-point buck elk in the safety of Maxwell Game Refuge. These noble animals were all but eliminated from the state of Kansas by 1900.

the Spanish explorer Francisco Vásquez de Coronado penetrated the Great Plains to this locale, where he at last gave up his well-recorded search for cities of gold. Northwest of Lindsborg, one of the sandstone buttes that form the Smoky Hills is known as Coronado Heights. From here, 300 feet above the plain, the view takes in miles of wheat fields. Golden when ripe, they fulfill, after a fashion, the Spaniard's dream.

4 To the north, at Salina, the skyline is commanded by huge concrete grain elevators, hallmarks of Kansas's thriving agriculture. Nearby, the remains of prehistoric Indian farmers, preserved in a burial pit, testify that agriculture was practiced in the region 800 to 1,000 years ago.

From a clearly marked road off Route 70, a mile's drive through rich bottomland fields of wheat, milo, and soybeans brings you to the excavations and exhibits of artifacts. Discovered in 1936, the burial pit has been skillfully excavated, with 140 skeletal remains left in their original flexed positions on pedestals of dirt.

5 Abilene, at the junction of the Smoky Hill and Chisholm trails, is the site of the Dwight D. Eisenhower Center. Four of the five buildings at the center are of white Kansas limestone. The fifth is the white wood-frame home where the future general and president grew up, preserved as it was in 1946, when Ida Stover Eisenhower, the general's mother, died. The buildings are surrounded by 23 acres of landscaped grounds and large parking lots. Only qualified scholars engaged in research are admitted to the section of the library that holds the Eisenhower papers, but exhibit areas that complement the displays in the adjacent museum are open to the public.

Located near the Eisenhower home is the Place of Meditation, a beautiful white churchlike structure in which President and Mrs. Eisenhower and their first son are buried. The building has an area reserved for meditation and quiet reflection.

The Eisenhower Center was developed with private donations and is managed by the National Archives and Records Service of the General Services Administration. The center conveys the message that the World War II general and 34th president of the United States was very much a product of his Kansas environment.

Old Abilene Town, not far from Eisenhower Center, is a commercial reconstruction depicting the days when Abilene was a rip-roaring cow town infamous for such gunslingers as Wild Bill Hickok.

6 East of Abilene, at the confluence of the Republican and Smoky Hill rivers, stands Fort Riley, an important military installation that was established in the Flint Hills in the early 1850's.

3. *A carpet of gold and green spreads below Coronado Heights, named for the Spanish explorer Francisco Vásquez de Coronado. The castle on the heights adds to the magic of the scene. Here and there among the fields are white farmhouses, picked out by the sun. Dorothy in* The Wizard of Oz *longed to return to just such a Kansas farm, with magic of its own.*

A self-guided tour of the 101,000-acre facility is well-marked and features the limestone quarters where Lt. Col. George Armstrong Custer once lived. A cavalry museum and a herd of bison can also be seen.

7 Winding eastward over the oak- and juniper-dotted Flint Hills, you reach the outskirts of Manhattan, where a turn to the north on Route 113 leads to a scenic overlook of Tuttle Creek Dam and Reservoir.

The 7,500-foot earth-filled dam, situated near the mouth of the Big Blue River, impounds the second largest lake in the state—15,800 acres with 112 miles of shoreline. Like other Army Corps of Engineers dams, it is intended primarily for flood control during periods of heavy precipitation as well as a downstream water supply during dry periods.

A secondary use is for recreation, such as boating, swimming, and fishing. There are 12 public-use areas along the lakeshore.

8 Passing limestone barns on the floodplains of the Kansas River, below the craggy Flint Hills, the route comes to Wabaunsee and the stone Beecher Bible and Rifle Church. Although still used for services today, the church is a reminder of a violent page in Kansas history.

Wabaunsee was settled in 1856 by ardent abolitionists from New Haven, Connecticut, whom the Reverend Henry Ward Beecher—brother of Harriet Beecher Stowe—inspired to carry the fight to Kansas. Beecher himself gave the Beecher Bible and Rifle Colony $625 to buy rifles and sent each colonist a Bible, saying he believed the Sharps rifle to be "a truly moral agency" carrying more moral power to slave owners in Kansas than a hundred Bibles could. As a result, Sharps rifles were known as Beecher's Bibles in Kansas and were even said to be shipped into the territory in boxes marked "Bibles." During this period of violence be-

6. *Hinged windows open wide to catch the breeze, and a partly screened porch stretches the length of the limestone house. These features helped Lt. Col. George Armstrong Custer endure the summer heat here in his quarters at Fort Riley.*

12. A small boy watches ducks ply the placid water in Emporia's Peter Pan Park, named in memory of journalist William Allen White's daughter, Mary. At right from the top: a male wood duck, a male redhead duck, and a blue-winged teal.

tween the pro- and the anti-slavery factions the territory became known as Bleeding Kansas.

9 Following the route southward, the terrain drops somewhat unexpectedly into a creek valley. Nestled here is the town of Alma, which has as fine a collection of 19th-century limestone homes and commercial buildings as any town in the Flint Hills. Here too is the Dwight-Alma Dairy, which offers a morning tour through its cheese factory. Be sure to call ahead to find out whether they will be making cheese on the day you want to visit.

The land south of Alma is widely regarded as an example of Flint Hills scenery at its best.

10 A well-marked intersection on Route 75 directs you to Melvern Lake, created when the earth-filled Melvern Dam impounded the Marais des Cygnes River in 1973. The river was named Marsh of Swans by early French trappers seeking beaver pelts. Today whistling swans are only a memory here, but beaver still gnaw through the cottonwoods that line the river channel below the dam. Thousands of geese, ducks, and pelicans rest on the lake during both the spring and the fall migration periods.

Public-use areas built by the Army Corps of Engineers dot the lakeshore and dam area. These feature picnic and camping sites and boat-launching ramps. Oak, maple, and sycamore are some of the tree species that can be found along a paved nature trail. Below the dam is an historic steel cable bridge that has been relocated and preserved here.

11 Flint Hills National Wildlife Refuge, southwest of Melvern Lake, is not in the Flint Hills, which rise 22 miles farther west. Rather, it sits amid flat and rich fields of wheat, corn, milo, and soybeans. The refuge's 18,500 acres occupy a large part of John Redmond Reservoir, built by the Army Corps of Engineers for flood control.

This marshy habitat is ideal for ducks and geese, nearly 100,000 of which may congregate at the refuge during spring and fall migrations. These include snow, Canada, and white-fronted geese and more than a dozen species of duck. The very conditions of high water and good cover that make the area ideal for waterfowl also hamper human observation of wildlife. Most of the 40 miles of road in the refuge are gravel, and many of these are subject to flooding.

Although parts of the refuge are closed in autumn so that human intrusion does not drive ducks and geese out of their protected haven during hunting season, large areas remain open for observation.

One of the most convenient and likely spots to see waterfowl is outside the refuge boundary at Otter Creek recreation area, near the south end of the dam. Other good viewing sites are the road across the dam and the Hickory Creek recreation area at Ottumwa early in the morning.

12 Emporia, to the northwest on the Neosho River, sits on the edge of the Flint Hills. The excellent pastureland there does much to make Kansas the nation's fourth largest producer of beef. The Emporia area sends more than 100,000 cattle to market annually.

Yet more than for beef, Emporia is known for the eloquent small-town wisdom of editorials written by William Allen White, the late publisher of the Emporia *Gazette*. A memorial to White, who died in 1944, sits on the tree-rimmed shore of a lake in Peter Pan Park. The name of this municipal park derives from an editorial White wrote after the death of his young daughter, Mary, in a riding accident.

"She was a Peter Pan, who refused to grow up," White eulogized, affirming that her enthusiastic spirit remained even after her body was laid to rest. The tribute is contained on two bronze tablets that flank a bust of the editor.

Wild mallards and teals swim in the park's lake. A few yards from the main body of water, a fenced moat surrounds a small island where pintail, redhead, and wood ducks and many other waterfowl congregate.

13 In the heart of the Flint Hills, Council Grove sits at the birthplace of the old Santa Fe Trail. Here, in 1825, Osage Indians and U.S. commissioners negotiated a treaty permitting the trail's passage over Indian land. Preserved under a canopy on Main Street is an oak stump remaining from the grove that sheltered that treaty council. A similar canopy nearby protects the stump of an elm under which, two generations later, Lt. Col. George Custer camped with the 7th Cavalry. On Main Street an oak tree that is still alive served as a mail drop from 1825 to 1847, when letters were deposited at its base by pack and wagon trains.

In addition to historic trees, Council Grove boasts a number of historic buildings, including a particularly grim jail. More appealing in looks and purpose is the old Kaw Mission, built of Flint Hills limestone. In 1847 the federal government moved the Kaw (or Kansa) Indians here from their old reservation near Topeka. In 1849 a Methodist Episcopal mission was established to provide schooling for these Indians. In 1851 it became the first school for white children in Kansas. Today the building is a state museum.

With these and many other historic sites, a corridor through the town of Council Grove has been designated a national historic landmark. Council Grove was also selected as the site for a "Madonna of the Trail," a statue that portrays a pioneer mother facing the rugged life of the trail.

Less than two miles northwest of town, on the Neosho River, is Council Grove Dam. Made of earth, it is 6,500 feet long and impounds a lake that normally covers 2,860 acres. During flood time the area of the lake may increase to 5,340 acres. Projected to serve as a water supply for the towns

of Emporia and Council Grove, the lake has also become a popular recreation area with fishing, boating, and swimming.

The thin, rocky soil of the Flint Hills is apparent in cross-sections opened by road cuts. The hand of man on this inhospitable soil has remained relatively light. A few small stock ponds have been dammed on hillside gullies to store water and to retard soil erosion. Windbreaks of trees are planted to protect building sites and sometimes remain long after the buildings themselves have gone. Because of the scarcity of trees, settlers often built with limestone instead of wood, as at the Z- (Z bar) Ranch, which is 17 miles south of Council Grove.

The Z- (originally called the Spring Hill Ranch) has a three-story house built in 1881 that boasts a mansard roof, quoined corners, and a columned porch. The house, surrounded by trees, is not so easily seen from the road as are the massive stone barn and other outbuildings. The ranch, listed on the National Register of Historic Places, is not open to the public, but can be viewed from the outside.

14. A handsome reminder of the Victorian era's elegance is the Chase County Courthouse in Cottonwood Falls. It was built with an attention to detail that more modern and efficient buildings often lack.

14 Another impressive structure that is also on the National Register is the Chase County Courthouse in Cottonwood Falls. Built in 1873, it is the oldest courthouse still in use in Kansas. Its red mansard roof, trimmed with iron crestings, rises to a clock tower. The building was designed in the French-Renaissance style revived during the Victorian era. The handsome walnut spiral staircase and woodwork inside can be viewed during the day, when county business is being conducted.

Unpretentious but just as interesting in their way are the limestone fences that often line Flint Hills roads. These date from an 1867 law abolishing the open range that favored the cattlemen at the expense of homesteaders. The same law provided state payment of $2 for every 40 rods (a rod is 16½ feet) to landowners to build and maintain stone fences or hedges 4½ feet high. The Flint Hills had an inexhaustible supply of limestone suited to fence-building, and many stone fences still stand.

Gravel roads east of the Kansas Turnpike (Interstate 35) from Matfield Green and Cassoday traverse a part of the proposed Tallgrass Prairie National Park. Here is the largest population of greater prairie chickens in the world, but with such an expanse of wide open prairie into which these grouse can disperse, they are hard to spot from the road. Winter is the best time to see them.

15 El Dorado Lake, the newest in a series of flood-control projects, has created a handsome lake of about 8,000 acres behind a four-mile-long dam that rises 99 feet above the Walnut River.

As a vantage point the Army Corps of Engineers has built an overlook tower, approached by a bridged ramp over the flood level of the lake. The entire structure is made of native stone, some of it salvaged from an 1897 schoolhouse, the site of which was inundated by the lake. The date block over the door of old "School District 94" is embedded in a pillar at the beginning of the ramp. The opposite pillar bears a plaque commemorating the school and the pioneers whose homesteads were destroyed at the time that the dam was built and the entire area was flooded.

Heartland of the Plains

Nebraska roads—through sculptured landscapes and grassy plains—are rich with historic landmarks

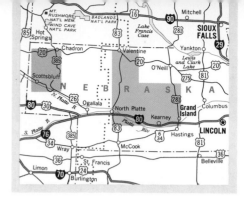

***Nebrathka* is a Siouan word** meaning "flat water," a name the Indians applied to the state's principal river, now called the Platte. Meandering "a mile wide and a foot deep," the Platte on its roundabout way from the Rocky Mountains to the Missouri River has deposited in Nebraska a broad band of rich soil. The level terrain of the Platte Valley made this a natural route for prehistoric Indians, emigrants on the Oregon, Mormon, and California trails, the Pony Express, Overland Stage, Union Pacific Railroad, and Western Union Telegraph—not to mention Interstate 80, which cuts across the state. Against such backdrops as Chimney Rock, Fort Robinson, and the Sand Hills, some of the most colorful events in the history of the nation took place.

The Sand Hills, *which cover some 20,000 square miles, are the dominant feature of this tour. This area has changed little in the 15 to 20 thousand years since winds sweeping across dry riverbeds deposited these rolling ridges of sand. This is the largest dune system in the Western Hemisphere. It is one of very few such areas in the world that gets significant precipitation. Hence this is not a desert. The dunes are held in place by grasses, accented occasionally by planted trees and by windmills. There are also some 1,600 lakes in the area.*

1. The Danish Evangelical Lutheran Church near Railroad Town reveals the details typical of Scandinavian design.

1 Coming from Interstate 80 over rich bottomland now giving way to commercial establishments, Route 281, the American Legion Memorial Highway, leads to the Stuhr Museum of the Prairie Pioneer. The principal building, impressive enough from the highway, is even more striking after you head past a fee station and discover that the templelike structure sits on an island in a round artificial lake. The building, which was designed by the renowned architect Edward Durrell Stone, looks like a national shrine transported from Washington, D.C., and placed squarely on the open plains.

Leo B. Stuhr, the farmer whose bequest of land and money started the museum, wanted to commemorate his parents and other pioneers.

Railroad Town, a restored 19th-century village within the museum complex, is an assembly of buildings brought from as far as 100 miles away and laid out according to plans devised by the Union Pacific for towns it established in the 1860's. Most of the buildings are furnished in turn-of-the-century style.

All during the summer, craftsmen labor in the village and a 1908 steam locomotive pulls a train across the museum's prairieland.

Near Railroad Town is the museum's 200-piece collection of 19th-century farm equipment, antique autos, and tractors. These contrast strikingly with the modern machines you see operating on Nebraska's farms today.

2 Mormon Island State Wayside Area, with its 153 acres, is the largest and one of the most elaborately developed of the 23 roadside state parks in Nebraska. It is one of only two such wayside areas that require a state park entrance permit. The main feature of Mormon Island is a 46-acre lake, popular with sailboaters. The lake, like others along the route, was created when fill material was excavated to build the highway.

Several families who were in the last of the great Mormon migration to Salt Lake City wintered on this island in 1884-85. They left three graves and their name on the land when they resumed their journey in the spring.

Early travelers along the Platte saw few trees from their covered wagons except on islands in the river. Prairie fires, started either by lightning or by

All About Entry Permits

A permit is required for entrance to all major Nebraska state parks, most recreation areas, and two wayside areas. Daily and annual permits are available.

The permits, which must be posted on the windshield, are sold at the Game and Parks Commission offices in Alliance, Bassett, Lincoln, Norfolk, North Platte, and Omaha, and at all manned state park areas. They are also available from conservation officers and all vendors of hunting and fishing permits.

Indians intent on improving the grasslands for buffalo, destroyed the trees. Today, however, because the fires are now controlled, forests again grow along the river and provide a habitat for deer, quail, and other wildlife. The deer are most likely to be seen at the edge of alfalfa fields near the shelter of adjoining woods.

SPECIAL FEATURES

ROAD GUIDE	▬▬▬	HIGHLIGHT	**1**
STATE PARKS With Campsites ▲ Without Campsites △		POINTS OF INTEREST	⊡
RECREATION AREAS With Campsites ▲ Without Campsites △		SCHEDULED AIRLINE STOPS	✹
SELECTED REST AREAS	✕	OTHER AIRPORTS	✈

ROAD CLASSIFICATION

CONTROLLED ACCESS HIGHWAYS
Interstate interchange numbers are mileposts.

OTHER DIVIDED HIGHWAYS

PAVED HIGHWAYS

LOCAL ROADS In unfamiliar areas inquire locally before using these roads   Paved Gravel Dirt

MILEAGE

MILEAGE BETWEEN TOWNS AND JUNCTIONS   3 / 4   MILEAGE BETWEEN DOTS   • 35

SCALE

ONE INCH 19 MILES   0   5   10   15   25

ONE INCH 30 KILOMETERS   0   5   10   20   30   40

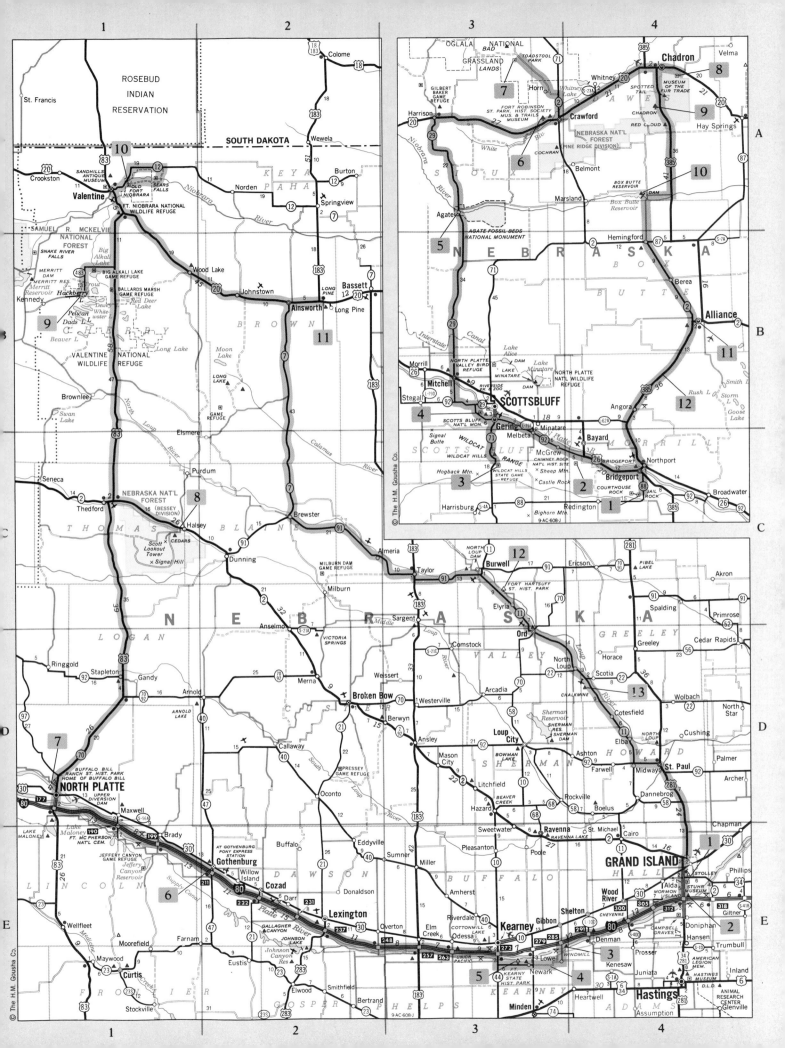

3. *To make use of the incessant winds sweeping across the flat prairies, large windmills like this one were developed to pump life-giving water from the ground.*

3 Windmill State Wayside Area is named for Windmill Crossing, where the Pawnees forded the Platte River on their annual bison hunts. There are three antique windmills here that have been moved from other sites. The largest, 60 feet tall, stands at the entrance to the area. This old-timer, with some 200 blades on a 20-foot wheel, first began pumping water in a Colorado town about 1890.

Beneath more than half the area of Nebraska is an enormous reservoir of groundwater, and the many windmills, old and new, seen on the horizon all across the state indicate how this water is brought to the surface.

4 The National Audubon Society established the 1,800-acre Lillian Annette Rowe Bird Sanctuary along the south channel of the Platte in 1973. The sanctuary is not easy to find. At the Gibbon Interchange of Interstate 80, turn south on a paved road. After crossing the second of two narrow bridges over channels of the Platte, take the first gravel road to the right.

At times, you may see western meadowlarks (the official state bird), red-headed woodpeckers, killdeers, bobolinks, eastern kingbirds, quail, and ring-necked pheasant. Deer are common in early morning or late evening, grazing in the fields and pastures with the horses and cattle. The pheasant, though still fairly common, are becoming less so. The alfalfa fields in which they often nest must be mowed at about hatching time, and the nests are inadvertently destroyed.

The special glory of the Rowe Sanctuary and the reason for its existence is the coming of the cranes in the spring, a wildlife event unique in all the world.

From their wintering grounds in Mexico, Texas, and New Mexico, about 225,000 sandhill cranes assemble along the Platte where the sandbars and shallow water provide an ideal staging ground. During the month of March, this vast assemblage of cranes spend their days in the fields eating waste grain (mostly corn) and in the wet meadowlands along the river eating beetle larvae, earthworms, and green vegetation. They also perform a courting ritual, presumably entertaining to the cranes and certainly of interest to their human audience.

During this month of mating and preparation for the remainder of the migration to Alaska and to Siberia, cranes can be seen along Interstate 80 and the parallel secondary roads between Grand Island and Lexington. As the early sun burns through river fog, silhouetting cranes and leafless cottonwoods (*Populus deltoides*), the official state tree, the birds rise to greet the morning with a bugle chorus. They often fly low over Minden Bridge on Route 10, and you can clearly see them, with their red caps, their long gray necks extended straight ahead, and their long legs extended straight behind.

5 The gravel road through the Audubon Society's crane haven follows the route of the Oregon Trail, which was quite wide here in this immense flat river plain. Not far west, where several feeder trails merge, you see the emigrants' first important landmark, Fort Kearny. Built in 1848 as one of a string of posts protecting the route, Fort Kearny played an important role in the nation's westward expansion. Completion of the trans-continental railroad in 1869 reduced the flow of wagons on the Oregon Trail, and in 1871 the military marched away.

When Lt. Daniel P. Woodbury laid out the fort, he outlined the parade grounds with cottonwood saplings. Although the post's land was opened to homesteading and its buildings torn down, today these trees stand guard over the former parade grounds. There are exhibits in a visitor center, and a blacksmith-carpenter shop can also be seen.

There is a great blue heron rookery in the cottonwoods on the south side of Interstate 80 about six miles west of Interchange 222. The nests might be missed, but in spring and summer the herons themselves are easy to see.

6 The original site of the Pony Express Station at Gothenburg is on a private ranch south of the Platte along the Oregon Trail. Today the station is located at Ehmen Park.

Duck your head as you enter the building. The door was built for the wiry jockeys who for 18 months in 1860-61 carried the mail and telegraph messages across the nearly 2,000 miles of wilderness between St. Joseph, Missouri, and Sacramento, California. Newspaper advertisements called for riders weighing less than 135 pounds who were daring young men, "orphans preferred." The simple, unheated building is closed during the cold weather. When the station is open, you can deposit letters here in saddlebags and they will bear a special postmark to show they were mailed at a Pony Express station. The completion of the overland telegraph in late 1861 put the Pony Express out of business.

Less romantic, but more profitable, are the alfalfa dehydration mills at Gothenburg. Nebraska processes almost half of the dehydrated alfalfa produced in the United States, and Gothenburg is a major center of the industry. You can visit the plants and see green alfalfa converted into pellets for livestock feed.

7 At the Buffalo Bill Ranch State Historical Park you will find part of William Cody's ranch, called Scout's Rest, and, nearby, the Western Heritage Museum and an arena where rodeos are held nightly during most of the summer.

4. *Sandhill cranes are among the many birds that can be seen along the Platte River. The greatest number of cranes stop off here in March on their migration to Alaska and Siberia. On the right are sandhill cranes in the shallows of the Platte near Overton.*

Having acquired 65 of Cody's original 4,000 acres, the Nebraska Game and Parks Commission has done a superb job of restoring Buffalo Bill's Victorian mansion, huge barn, and other ranch buildings. The trees have grown tall since the time when Cody introduced the Hereford bull Earl Horace to this part of the plains, staged the first rodeo in the United States, and wintered his Wild West Show here. Guides will show you through the mansion and barn, and describe the life and legend of one of Nebraska's most colorful characters.

As you leave the North Platte River valley and enter the Sand Hills, there is a striking change from tree-lined river bottoms to rolling expanses of grass. The almost 13 million acres of the Sand Hills comprise the largest expanse of grassland in the United States. Windmills dominate the skyline of this land where water seeps quickly through grass-frozen sand dunes to accumulate below the surface and in the many ponds and marshy meadows.

Farming in the Sand Hills is not practical because plowing the native grasses causes devastating soil erosion from the winds. Instead, the land is used for cattle ranching. Black Angus, Herefords, mixed breeds, and longhorns feed on the rich native grasses here. Barbed-wire fences divide the huge expanse into manageable units. The worn-out boots you see on fence posts serve no purpose. They simply reveal the twinkle-eyed humor of Nebraska ranchers.

In the Sand Hills you will occasionally see belts or clumps of trees that have been planted for shade or as windbreaks. Some of the houses that once stood there are now gone, but the trees still remain.

8 Most of the trees in the windbreaks along the roads started life as seedlings in the Bessey Division nursery of the Nebraska National Forest. When Theodore Roosevelt set aside the area as a national forest preserve in 1902, it was a contradiction in terms, for there were no trees. Those planted since that time demonstrate that University of Nebraska botanist Dr. Charles Bessey was correct in his conviction that such plants could be

6. *It requires a vivid imagination to relate this simple way station where fast-moving Pony Express riders changed horses to the excitement and danger involved in their feats.*

10. *Here, from the top, are some of the animals you may see in Nebraska: elks, pronghorn antelopes, bison, and Texas longhorn cattle. All of these are found at Fort Niobrara National Wildlife Refuge.*

grown on the Great Plains. His name spelled in huge letters by trees on a hillside three miles west of the forest entrance commemorates his vision. The Bessey Division is used to determine which trees will survive on the plains and how to grow them.

You can take a self-guided auto tour of the nurseries and forest. A fire tower provides a panoramic view of the area.

This forested land attracts wildlife not ordinarily seen in the Sand Hills. The most spectacular is the wild turkey. Another is the sharp-tailed grouse, especially fascinating in mid-April during the mating rituals, which can be watched from observation blinds. Mule and white-tailed deer also inhabit the forest.

9 The 36 lakes in the Valentine National Wildlife Refuge are scattered along both sides of Route 83 as it bisects the 71,516-acre preserve. Signboards along the north and south borders of the refuge provide information and detailed maps of the area. Driving the routes marked "public use trails" in a normal passenger car is possible during some times of the year under certain weather conditions, but it is safer to stay on the hard-surfaced roads in the refuge.

The cooler months of spring and fall are best for walking the trails. These are migration times, and wildfowl and wading birds are abundant. As many as 300,000 ducks may stop here. It was primarily for these birds that the sanctuary was established in 1935. Ticks too are a wildlife form commonly found here in spring.

Besides the lakes along Route 83, the best paved road from which to see water birds is near the refuge headquarters at Hackberry Lake. The staff can provide day-to-day information about what kinds of wildlife are likely to be seen and where.

10 Lewis and Clark went past the mouth of the Niobrara River a long way downstream from what is now the Fort Niobrara National Wildlife Refuge. But their vivid descriptions of prairies teeming with wildlife—bison (buffalo), elks, pronghorn antelopes, prairie dogs, and deer—can be applied to the large display pastures at this 19,122-acre refuge. Longhorn cattle add the romantic western touch of yet another era.

Canoeing on the Niobrara

One hundred and twenty miles of the Niobrara River have been nominated for inclusion in the National Wild and Scenic Rivers System. A favorite trip for canoeists begins near the main entrance of Fort Niobrara National Wildlife Refuge, and runs for some 22 miles on the lower part of the proposed wild and scenic river segment.

As the river winds its way past rocky cliffs, steep forested bluffs, and canyon walls you may see bison gazing down from the refuge, great blue heron hunting crayfish along the bank, or deer drinking from the river. About halfway between the launching site and the takeout point at Rocky Ford is a short trail to the 68-foot Smith Falls, the highest in Nebraska. Although it is on private property, the trail is marked by the generous landowner.

The 22 miles can be paddled in six hours or floated leisurely in two days. There are a few commercial campsites along the way. Advice on shorter trips can be had from the Valentine Chamber of Commerce, the staff at the wildlife refuge, or canoe renters in Valentine.

Before driving along the unpaved sanctuary roads, stop at the refuge museum, where a collection of mounted birds and mammals will familiarize you with the animals in the area. Also take time to walk the short path past scenic Fort Falls down to the Niobrara River. Many animals document their visits with footprints on the river's sandy shore.

Driving around the display pastures reveals excellent opportunities for taking pictures of the buffalo wallows and prairie dog towns. Bison and longhorn cattle have uncertain dispositions, and it is a good idea to stay in or near your car.

Canada geese and the great blue herons are easy to spot in the sloughs and ponds. After seeing the pastures, you can continue along unpaved country roads to the Niobrara River bridge, where Sears Falls tumbles into the river, and then take a scenic loop back on Route 12. A worthwhile mile-long detour, marked by a sign on Route 12, takes you to the fish hatchery aquarium in Valentine.

11 Scenic canyons along Long Pine Creek are the highlights of the Long Pine State Recreation Area, a 154-acre oasis on the plains. The "long pines" here are Western yellow pines, (*Pinus ponderosa*). There are highway signs warning of "Hills—Winding Road," but the "winding" is only in comparison to the very string-straight, table-flat prairie roads outside the recreational area.

12 In 1874 construction of Fort Hartsuff began on the North Loup River in the area where Teton Sioux Indians were raiding white farmers and friendly Pawnees. Gravel was readily available here, and nine buildings of the fort were made of concrete. They all survived the passage of a century and are preserved in the Fort Hartsuff State Historical Park. Some of the buildings have been renovated and others are stabi-lized. Guides interpret the historic highlights of this frontier fort.

In the rich, wide river valleys along Route 11 at the southern edge of the Sand Hills, the danger and bitter hardships of farming and ranching are things of the past. The great fields of corn, wheat, and alfalfa, and the herds of quarter horses, beef cattle, and dairy cattle are a tribute to hard work and creative agricultural stewardship. Good examples of this creativity are the huge center-pivot sprinklers that propel themselves in half-mile circles through the fields. Since the 1950's, when these systems were first developed, the state has put more than 5 million acres of land under irrigation.

Summer festivals and the rodeos (especially at Burwell in August) bring together an industrious people proud of their land and heritage.

13 Chalkmine State Wayside Area is one of the most unusual and pleasant of such areas in Nebraska. Here a tree-filled gulch provides respite from the heat of summer driving. Cooler yet are the mine shafts that form a maze under Happy Jack's Peak, a high bluff above the meandering and sandbar-filled North Loup River. In the main shaft, the only one open, the temperature stays about 20 degrees below that of the outside air. There is no electricity in the tunnel and a flashlight is useful.

The route to the top of the peak is rather rough and steep, but the view of the North Loup Valley is worth the climb. In the 1870's Jack Swearengen, a trapper and guide, climbed up here from his dugout below to watch for raiding Sioux. Your view, however, will reveal nothing more threatening than a possible rain cloud.

Why more and more of the plantings you will see will be round instead of rectangular

The center-pivot irrigation system shown here is one of the most important mechanical innovations in agriculture in recent years. Farmers can now automatically water large areas of land with a minimum of labor. A pumping station in the center of the circular planting forces water along pipes mounted with sprinklers and supported by A-shaped frames, called towers. An electric or hydraulic motor in each tower drives the machine in a continuous circle around the center pivot. Flexible couplings at each tower allow the system to adjust to rolling terrain. The speed of the outermost tower sets the rate of the other towers. An alignment device locates the towers that lag behind and moves them ahead to keep the machine in line. The view below shows the sections of pipe supported by the wheeled towers. Note the volume of water that is equally distributed by the sprinklers.

2. Chimney Rock is the remnant of a plain formed by clay, volcanic ash, and sandstone that was swept down from the Rockies by winds and floods some 25 million years ago. These same forces eroded the plain, leaving this landmark capped by hard sandstone.

To drive in this region is to experience firsthand the force of nature as a sculptor and landscape architect. The treeless plains of Nebraska's panhandle rise to meet bluffs, Badlands, and pine-covered buttes. Edging the Wildcat Range are such famous Oregon Trail landmarks as Courthouse and Jail rocks, Chimney Rock, and Scotts Bluff. These features are remnants of ancient plains, formed by rivers as they deposited sediment from the Rockies about 25 million years ago. Also, from time to time volcanic eruptions in the Rockies added windblown dust and ash. The greatest erosion came with the outwash caused by melting ice as the glaciers retreated.

Box Butte Plateau, north of the North Platte Valley, suffered less erosion and remained as a high tableland. Today the area is grass-covered cattle country with few trees.

Pine Ridge, Nebraska's most scenic region, was left even higher than the Box Butte plain. On the canyons and buttes today are mixtures of eastern and western trees that somewhat soften the craggy aspect of the precipitous white cliffs.

1 To the pioneers on the Oregon Trail, the mammoth Courthouse and Jail rocks were exciting to behold. They saw in these rocks a sign that the first (and least difficult) leg of their journey was over. Most of these

Oregon Trail Wagon Train

Entrepreneur Gordon Howard offers many pioneer experiences, all of different degrees of adventurousness. You can ride in a covered wagon with an appropriately costumed driver along the Oregon Trail for an hour or so or for several days. Firsthand experience of the slow pace, rough trail, and the wagon's primitive suspension system can do more to evoke an understanding of the pioneers' fortitude than any number of books, films, or lectures on the subject. A Chimney Rock Covered Wagon Tour takes three hours and gives you a good close look at the rock's formation. For reservations call 308/586-1850 or 586-2440. Other adventures available here include canoeing and float trips on the North Platte.

early-day tourists left the trail for a close-up view of the landmarks. After 500 miles on the trail, this short side trip meant nothing, especially without the wagons. Wagon trains usually camped near the North Platte River while groups of travelers explored the wondrous formations and their hawk and eagle nests.

Someone saw in the taller, 400-foot prominence of Brule clay, capped by a cupola of sturdier Gering sandstone, a resemblance to a courthouse. Wherever there is a courthouse there is sure to be a jail, and thus the adjacent rock was so named.

A mobile museum of the Nebraska State Historical Society is stationed here from Memorial Day through Labor Day. Seybolt Park, in which the rocks are located, is the site of a variety of outdoor functions, such as muzzle-loading and black-powder rifle shooting contests.

2 The pioneers moving slowly westward in their covered wagons could contemplate Chimney Rock for two days before they reached it. This was the most frequently mentioned landmark in pioneer journals. Naming Courthouse Rock required an active imagination, but this rock does look like a chimney.

Many of the emigrants climbed up the sloping base to the final pillar, but the soft Brule clay would not support a higher ascent. Almost all of the pioneers' journals predict the rapid disintegration of the 100-foot spire. But interlayers of Arikaree sandstone provide reinforcement that holds it together, and from its sloping base the column still rises to a height of about 500 feet above the plain.

The closest approach by car begins just west of the intersection of Highways 26 and 92. Turn left on a gravel road and drive for 1½ miles to a T-junction. Turn right and continue to a parking lot at the end of the road.

From this parking area, the base of the rock is about a 10-minute hike across grazing land on trails that climb in and out of the gullies. There are rattlesnakes here, although you are unlikely to see one. Also to be avoided are the sharp-spiked leaves of the yuccas along the path.

If you would rather not walk to the base of Chimney Rock, you will find a good view from Route 92 at a turnout about a half mile west of the intersection with Route 26. The Nebraska State Historical Society maintains a mobile museum here from Memorial Day through Labor Day. A few minutes in the museum will help you further appreciate the significance of Chimney Rock.

3   Bison, elk, and white-tailed and mule deer roam the 385-acre enclosure in Wildcat Hills State Game Refuge, and turkey vultures often soar overhead. There are a few bobcats and wild turkeys here too, but they are elusive and seldom seen.

Ponderosa pines form a striking contrast to the surrounding prairie and the cottonwoods along the North Platte. The view from the parking area next to the highway is fairly good. But the best vistas are from picnic sites farther up the slope. These sites are accessible by gravel roads, which are closed only in bad weather.

Such animals as bison and elk sometimes come close to the fence and can be photographed in a natural-looking setting. The North Platte Valley Museum, just off Route 71 on the outskirts of Gering, is devoted to 19th-century culture in this area and provides a worthwhile insight to another time.

4   Like Courthouse and Chimney rocks, Scotts Bluff is an extension of the Wildcat Range. The bluff rises 800 feet above the North Platte. Hard Arikaree sandstone on top of the bluff has protected the softer rock lower down from the erosion that reduced the surrounding plain to its present level.

The rough terrain between Scotts Bluff and the North Platte forced the Oregon Trail pioneers to leave the river and cut through Mitchell Pass, just as Route 92 does today. The route through the pass was only wide enough for one wagon, and the countless wheels made deep ruts that can still be seen. The museum at the

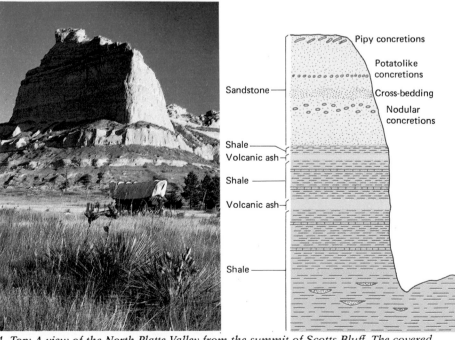

Sandstone —

Pipy concretions

Potatolike concretions

Cross-bedding

Nodular concretions

Shale —
Volcanic ash —

Shale —

Volcanic ash —

Shale —

4. *Top: A view of the North Platte Valley from the summit of Scotts Bluff. The covered wagon (above left) represents the many thousands of similar vehicles that passed the bluff on their way west along the Oregon Trail. Yucca and prairie grass are in the foreground. Geological components of the bluff are shown in the drawing above right.*

Scotts Bluff National Monument explains the history of the monument and has on display a large collection of paintings and photographs by William H. Jackson, the famous frontier photographer who, in 1866, followed the Oregon Trail as a bullwhacker. Visitors can follow a short section of the original trail.

There is also a 1½-mile toll road to the top of the bluff. Here, at an elevation of 4,649 feet, there are superb views of the surrounding countryside and a self-guided nature trail. A high-pitched scream may draw your eye to a red-tailed hawk flying at eye level.

There are no fences to ruin the view or to protect the careless from falling. Stay on the trail and watch your step. There is a rewarding walk down a paved 1½-mile trail from the top of the bluff to the museum. This calls for one generous member of the party to drive down in the car.

5　The relatively new Agate Fossil Beds National Monument protects fossilized remains of ancient mammals underneath the grass-covered Carnegie and University hills. These two hills have long been one of the world's major sources of fossils.

A self-guided nature trail leads from a temporary visitors center to an exposed fossil exhibit on the flanks of the hills. The Park Service plans further excavation and more complete interpretation facilities.

Future development may be considered a mixed blessing by those who enjoy the serenity of the monument just as it is. Prairie grasses are highlighted by the colorful wild flowers. Livestock share the wide open spaces with the great blue herons, mule deer, pronghorns, coyotes, and rattlesnakes. It is not unusual to see prairie rattlers along the nature trail, but they will not bother you if you do not bother them.

6　Fort Robinson State Park, Nebraska's largest state park, is an excellent base from which to explore the delightful Pine Ridge region. The scenery is outstanding, the history of the Indian wars is fascinating, and the choices of things to do are extensive. Everything (including lodging in restored fort buildings) is relatively inexpensive, and many attractions are free. Possibly the best bargain in Nebraska is the "Fort Robinson Ex-

press," a variety of free tours in comfortable vans along the back roads among dramatic buttes covered with ponderosa pine. On the very popular "Early Bird Tours" (you pay about a dollar for homemade sweet rolls, juice, and coffee), the objective is to spot such wildlife as white-tailed and mule deer, pronghorns, wild turkeys, and bison. The success rate is high, and it is a pleasure to let someone else do the driving.

Stagecoach, buckboard, and horse trail rides are also available. Plays, chuckwagon and campfire programs, and rodeos take place on summer evenings. The appropriately costumed park guides perform various functions, including blowing reveille from a platform halfway up a flag-pole erected by the army in the last century. The boom of a cannon accompanies this ceremony at the reasonable hour of 8 A.M.

Fort Robinson also has excellent museums. One run by the state historical society deals with the human history of the fort, including the Indian wars of the 1870's and 1880's. The guardhouse where Crazy Horse was killed while resisting imprisonment is restored. "Fort Rob" was also the lo-

cale of the book *Cheyenne Autumn*, the story of Dull Knife and his determined band in 1879. A natural history museum, complete with the skeleton of an ice age mammoth excavated nearby, emphasizes the geology and archeology of the region.

Fort Robinson State Park plus the nearby state wildlife areas comprise about 40,000 acres of the Pine Ridge, where plants and animals of both East and West merge in one ecosystem. With more than 50 miles of trails, the Pine Ridge has plenty of natural areas for hikers and backpackers who prefer solitude to the bustle of entertainment at the fort.

7　Weird formations have been cut by wind and water in the white and buff clays and rocks in the area of Toadstool Park. It is illegal to take any fossils or artifacts on federal land, but agates, of which there are many, may be gathered.

On your way to and from Toadstool Park, watch for pronghorns and also jackrabbits. The colorful little American kestrel, or sparrow hawk, is a common bird of prey.

Walking along the trails among the toadstool rocks of this classic Badlands, keep an eye out for rattle-

snakes. If you do happen to see one, enjoy watching it from a prudent distance. Under no circumstances should the snake be molested.

You may also see a Burlington Northern coal train, hauling as much as 10,000 tons of "black gold" from Powder River Basin mines in Wyoming. The trains may be 100 cars long, and with luck you will not have to wait for one to clear the crossing into the park.

8 In the Museum of the Fur Trade are the trade goods, weapons, and pelts that red and white men bartered, stole, and died for during America's formative years. Other displays tell the story of the fur trade and portray the lives of the men of various cultures who were involved.

The museum is on the site of the old Bordeaux Trading Post. Built in 1841, it was an American Fur Company post until 1849, and then an independent post until August 1876, when the cavalry confiscated war matériel being sold to Indians from the same tribe as those that had killed Lt. Col. George Custer and his men at the Little Big Horn a few weeks earlier. The trader abandoned the post and went to live with the Sioux.

Archeological digs and research among the trader's descendants still living on the nearby reservation established the location of the trading post and warehouse. Rebuilt on their original foundations, they are now fitted out as they were in the 1870's. Nearby is a garden of Indian crops.

The museum is closed from Labor Day until June; however, a superintendent will open it by appointment (call 308/432-3843).

9 Chadron State Park, an 840-acre recreation complex established in 1921, is the oldest Nebraska state park. Pine Ridge scenery and relatively low humidity and temperature at an altitude of nearly 4,000 feet are the park's chief attractions in summer. In winter, this park usually has the best conditions in Nebraska for cross-country skiing.

A park entrance permit is required for access to the five miles of scenic roads that wind up and down the pine-covered hills in the park. Picnic sites are conveniently placed at scenic overlooks. Camping, swimming, fishing, boating in a lagoon, and trail rides are available during the warm months. These roads are closed only in bad weather.

10 South of Chadron State Park is an area of rich agricultural land. There are occasional stands of cottonwoods growing at the edges of streams and rivers. In the middle of this prairie, at Box Butte State Recreation Area, is the Box Butte Reservoir. Drawn down considerably in summer, the 1,600-acre lake can shrink to 200 acres in very dry years; so boating, waterskiing, and fishing are best early in the season. The reservoir attracts many waterfowl during their migration periods, and the drawdown area at the head of the reservoir is a good place for seeing ducks in the fall.

11 The huge new $45 million Burlington Northern locomotive and car repair facility at Alliance was constructed primarily to help in transporting ever-increasing tonnages of coal from western mines. The complex occupies 110 acres; the roof spans 6½ acres. Twenty locomotives can be repaired here at one time.

Also on the south edge of Alliance is the Prairie States Company feedlot, which proclaims this town as the "Cattle Capital of the West." Visitors who wish to learn about a custom cattle-feeding operation are welcome here if they call in advance.

12 The highway passes through the westernmost arm of the Nebraska Sand Hills, which cover about one quarter of the state. Ice age winds blowing over the beds of dry rivers 15 to 20 thousand years ago lifted vast amounts of sand and formed 20,000 square miles of ridges, mounds, and hills, making this the largest dune area in the Western Hemisphere.

This is one of the few major dune systems in the world that lies in a relatively mild climate with significant precipitation.

Native grasses hold the sand in place against the wind. If the grasses are destroyed, such as by plowing, the result is sudden and complete erosion. To grow crops is to invite disaster, and the Sand Hills are used primarily for grazing cattle and as wildlife preserves.

South Dakota

Where granite spires and pine-clad cliffs of the Black Hills stand above the ageless prairies

The Missouri, the second longest stream in the United States, known simply as The River to South Dakotans, divides the state into what is called "west river" and "east river."

The Missouri River separates the Black Hills, the Badlands, and the vast prairies to the west from the fertile plains to the east, where glaciers once spread rich soil across the landscape.

Rapid City, strategically located within easy range of the Black Hills and the Badlands, has become a popular base for touring the western part of the state.

To the east across wide grasslands is Badlands National Park, a collection of awesome, jagged erosional sculpture where fossils are embedded in the sandy soil.

To the west, the Black Hills are an island of tree-covered uplands surrounded by a sea of grass. Clothed by dark green ponderosa pines, these mountains looked black in contrast to the grassy plains to early explorers.

After crossing into Wyoming to Devils Tower, the first national monument, the route returns to South Dakota and continues on to Spearfish Canyon, Terry Peak, and two towns typical of early gold-mining days.

1 Rapid City, on the eastern slopes of the Black Hills, was settled in 1876 by a group of prospectors searching for gold in the nearby mountains. Mining is still carried on here, along with lumbering and various kinds of manufacturing.

The South Dakota School of Mines and Technology, established here in 1885, has a museum that displays minerals found in the area, fossils from the Badlands, and a reconstructed dinosaur skeleton. On West Boulevard is the Sioux Indian Museum, which has an excellent collection of artifacts as well as displays of modern Indian arts and crafts.

Driving across the almost treeless, undulating plains east of Rapid City, you pass grazing lands and wheat fields laid out in strips to avoid erosion by the incessant wind.

2 Wall, the picturesque little town named for its site at the north wall of the Badlands, is a trading post for farmers and ranchers from the surrounding prairies. The town is famous for its unusually pure water, which comes from wells 3,200 feet deep. The proprietor of the Wall Drugstore started bringing travelers and prosperity to the town in the 1930's by placing signs along the highway advertising free ice water. The signs are now posted for hundreds of miles. Ice water is still served, but the drugstore is now a rambling collection of souvenir shops and luncheonettes, its one small drug counter almost lost in the overwhelming array.

3 Badlands National Park, sometimes called the Big Badlands, is the eroded landscape from which many other such areas take their name. Along the roads through the park are several turnouts where displays explain the geology of the area and identify the fossils from the Oligo-

3. These eroded buttes typical of Badlands National Park offer a glimpse into a world created over millions of years that is still changing as erosion continues. The apt term "badlands" was coined independently by French-Canadian trappers and by Sioux Indians.

SPECIAL FEATURES

ROAD GUIDE	HIGHLIGHT **1**
STATE PARKS With Campsites Without Campsites	SKI AREAS
RECREATION AREAS With Campsites ▲ Without Campsites △	SCHEDULED AIRLINE STOPS
SELECTED REST AREAS	MILITARY AIRPORTS
POINTS OF INTEREST	OTHER AIRPORTS

ROAD CLASSIFICATION

CONTROLLED ACCESS HIGHWAYS
Interstate interchange numbers are mileposts.

Interchanges

OTHER DIVIDED HIGHWAYS

PAVED HIGHWAYS

LOCAL ROADS   In unfamiliar areas inquire locally before using these roads   Paved   Gravel   Dirt

MILEAGE

MILEAGE BETWEEN TOWNS AND JUNCTIONS 3 / 4   MILEAGE BETWEEN DOTS • 35 •

SCALE

ONE INCH 20 MILES   0   5   10   15   25

ONE INCH 32 KILOMETERS   0   5   10   20   30   40

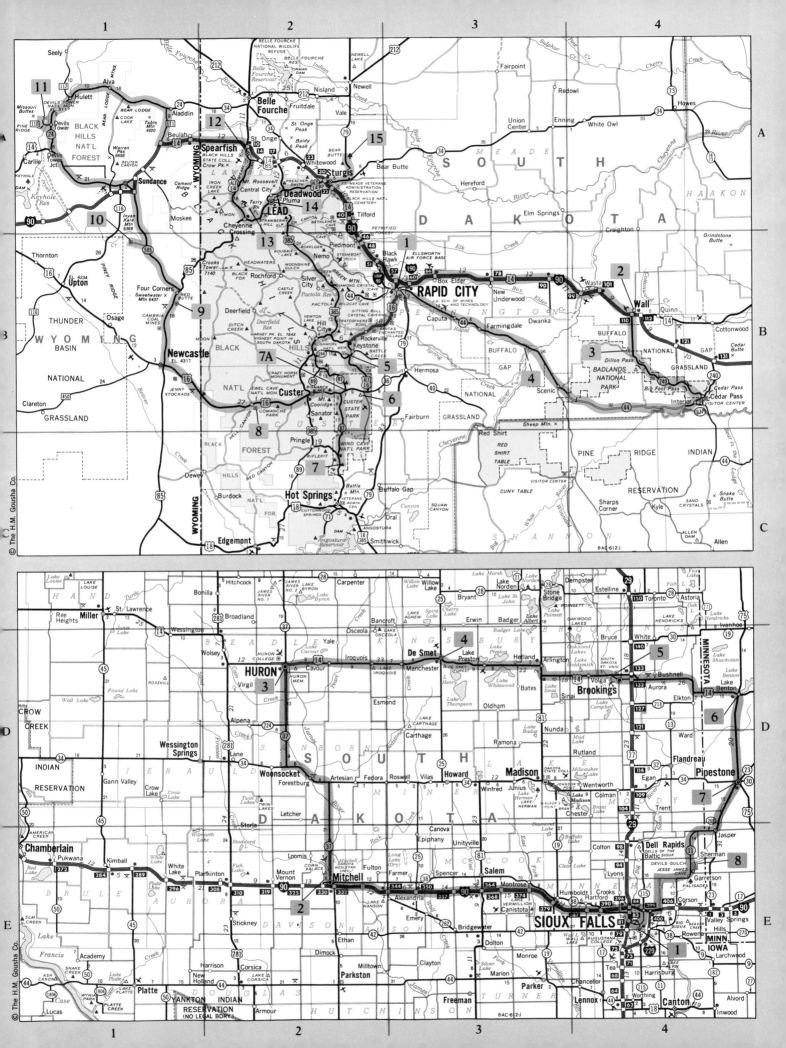

4. *The overgrazing that devastated this golden prairie during the 1930's is no longer allowed on the Buffalo Gap National Grassland. Today this is the site of a vast effort to reverse past abuses and restore the delicate and complex natural ecosystem.*

cene Epoch, buried between 25 and 35 million years ago when the Badlands was flat marshland built of sediment eroded from the Black Hills and volcanic ash blown in from what is now Yellowstone National Park. Today the delicately tinted spires and sharp ridges of the fantastic landscape are crumbling at a rate considered speedy in geological terms.

This erosion has opened one of the world's best treasure troves of fossils, which dates from the time when now-extinct mammals roamed the swamps of South Dakota. A 1½-mile trail winds among the exposed fossils, which have been left in place under clear plastic shields.

Near Cedar Pass is the Badlands Visitor Center. Exhibits of the wildlife in the area are given here, and campgrounds and cabins are available nearby.

4 Buffalo Gap National Grassland is an expanse of almost 600,000 acres managed by the U.S. Forest Service. Plowing and overgrazing of these lands destroyed the natural grass cover, which through the ages had adapted to the area's extremes of temperature, fierce winds, and periodic drought. By controlling the grazing in this area, the land is being restored today.

5 Mount Rushmore National Memorial is the most famous place in South Dakota. When Charles E. Rushmore, a New York lawyer, visited the Black Hills in 1885, he asked a

local prospector the name of that 6,000-foot peak. Since the peak had no name, the facetious answer was "Mount Rushmore." And the name has never been changed.

In 1927 the sculptor Gutzon Borglum, commissioned by the federal government, started the carving of the likenesses of four U.S. presidents—Washington, Jefferson, Theodore Roosevelt, and Lincoln—on the granite face of the mountain. The monument, with its 60-foot-high faces, was brought to its present state in 1941. Sound-and-light programs are given during the summer.

South of Mount Rushmore, on Route 16A, there are spectacular views of the mountains as the road follows the ridges. Tunnels take the road through the highest peaks.

6 Custer State Park, with four lakes and many streams, provides excellent fishing and swimming, and there are also picnic grounds and campsites. Here you can find one of the country's largest herds of bison.

The Wildlife Loop Road, which runs across the park, is an excellent road from which to see such large wild animals as elk, buffalo, deer, antelope, coyote, and bighorn sheep, as well as flocks of wild turkeys.

7 A sharp turn south onto Route 87 takes you to Wind Cave National Park, a prairie wilderness where wildlife thrives. Wind Cave is a large cavern whose passages were dissolved through limestone laid down in warm, shallow seas roughly 300 million years ago. During a massive uplift 60 million years ago, the limestone cracked. Some cracks were enlarged by acidic water, which dissolved the limestone and hollowed out caves. While the humid climate persisted, the lime solutions were carried out. But after a while, drier conditions, at least seasonally, prevailed. The dripping waters in the caves evaporated, and the dissolved limestone was redeposited in the harder crystalline form of calcite. Later the limestone between the cal-

5. *The sculptor worked for 6½ years on this artistic and engineering marvel at Mount Rushmore. It stands as a noble fulfillment of his belief that "A monument's dimensions should be determined by the importance to civilization of the events commemorated."*

cite-filled cracks dissolved, leaving a calcite grid. Networks of these grids are called boxworks, and the world's best displays of a boxwork are in Wind Cave.

7A The road north to Lead (pronounced leed) follows Routes 87 and 385. The first 20 miles or so, after you cross Route 36 on Route 87, is called the Needles Highway. The granite towers along this stretch of hairpin turns and narrow tunnels were intruded among softer metamorphic rocks more than a billion years ago. Erosion left the hard granite spires that form the ragged skyline. The most famous of the spires is the Needle's Eye, a towering monolith with a hole near the pointed top. The road continues northward near Harney Peak (at 7,242 feet, the highest U.S. mountain east of the Rockies), through pine-clad mountains, down the main street of the old mining town of Hill City, and along Sheridan and Pactola lakes to the city of Lead.

8 The route turns westward, through a mile-high green valley, to Jewel Cave National Monument, which has two canyons within its boundaries. Ponderosa pines cover the hillsides, and in spring and early summer wild flowers, including the pasqueflower (*Anemone patens*), the state flower, bloom in the thin soil mixture of sand and clay.

Jewel Cave, located in Hell Canyon, is named for the colorful clusters of aragonite and calcite and the so-called gypsum flowers formed of gypsum crystals that encrust the cavern and sparkle like jewels.

After crossing the state border into Wyoming, you go through the town of Newcastle, known for its oil fields, and continue north to an area of red Spearfish formation of sedimentary rock laid down about 200 million years ago. In some places there are hard white gypsum caps on the soft rock, protecting it from erosion. This capping is particularly evident about 18 miles north of Newcastle, where white rock forms a band above the red slopes along the road.

9 Red Butte, a tower of the red Spearfish rock rising 5,720 feet above the surrounding plain, is kept from erosion by its cap of white gypsum.

10 Inyan Kara Mountain, near the site where Lt. Col. George A. Custer's 1874 expedition camped, is made of hard phonolite porphyry, a volcanic rock that welled up through the flat-lying sedimentary rock about 60 million years ago. (Phonolite is so-called because when struck it rings like a bell.) Water eroded the sedimentary rock, leaving the hard igneous core rising above the plains.

11 Devils Tower, the first site to be declared a national monument (1906), is a fluted, stumplike mountain rising above a ridgetop forest of pines and oaks. The bundle of rock columns that makes up the bulk of the tower was formed beneath a sedimentary rock dome pushed up by magma. As the liquid slowly cooled and solidified, it decreased in volume, causing polygonal cracks to form along the sides of the dome. After the Belle Fourche River stripped away the softer sedimentary cover, the hard phonolite porphyry columns remained. At the visitor center is the start of a trail around the tower.

Shortly after bridging the river in Devils Tower National Monument, the road passes a large prairie dog town full of these appealing members of the squirrel family.

12 The town of Spearfish, South Dakota, is situated at the mouth of Spearfish Canyon, one of the most scenic places in the Black Hills. Colorful cliffs and spires and two lovely waterfalls, Roughlock and Bridal Veil, along with the tumbling, rushing Spearfish Creek and forests of cottonwoods, birches, elms, oaks, and the Black Hills spruce (*Picea glauca densata*), the state tree, make this a popular recreational area.

13 At the Terry Peak Road (Route 194), 2½ miles east of Cheyenne Crossing, you leave the spruce trees and climb through ponderosa pines to the top of 7,071-foot Terry Peak. From the fire lookout on the summit you can see Inyan Kara Mountain to the west, Bear Butte to the northeast, Harney Peak to the southeast, and, all around, ponderosa-covered slopes.

14 (See also 7A above.) A lead (pronounced leed) is a lode or vein of ore, and the town of Lead was named for the famous Homestake lode found here. Today Lead's Homestake Mine produces more gold than any of the other gold mines in the Western Hemisphere.

11. Rising to a height of 1,280 feet above a forested ridge, the rock formation we call Devils Tower was named Bad God's Tower by Indians.

The original mine site is marked by a huge colorful gash in the mountain called the Open Cut, which reveals bands of reddish rhyolite, an ancient volcanic lava formed 2 billion years ago. All mining at Homestake is now carried on underground. There are 200 miles of tunnels, some as much as 8,000 feet deep.

Deadwood, just northeast of Lead, was the center of gold-mining activities in the area until the lode at Lead was discovered. Such colorful historic characters as Calamity Jane, Wild Bill Hickok, and Preacher Henry Weston Smith are buried here.

15 At Sturgis you may wish to take a side trip of about seven miles to Bear Butte State Park, where sacred Indian ceremonial events are still held. Bear Butte is an intrusion of molten rock, formed in the same way and at the same time as Devils Tower.

Rising 1,400 feet above the plains, the butte stands out clearly to the northeast as soon as you leave the elm-lined streets of Sturgis. After turning into the park, you drive through a pasture where you may see a small herd of bison grazing. An easy mile-and-a-half trail to the top of the butte begins at the parking lot behind the visitor center.

From Sioux Falls, a bustling center among farmlands, the road turns west to Mitchell, home of the colorful Corn Palace, and north to Huron, where hunters come every fall in search of pheasants.

The road traverses the landscape made famous by Laura Ingalls Wilder in her *Little House on the Prairie* stories, and goes on to Pipestone, Minnesota, site of the quarry of red stone that was used by Indians for their ceremonial pipes.

At Falls Park there is a scenic drive along a wooded stream and a splendid view of the river and falls.

Sherman Park, at the western edge of the city, has a memorial to the battleship U.S.S. *South Dakota,* a 1,600-year-old Indian mound, and a zoo with some 90 different kinds of animals.

Along Route 90 on the west are rich farmlands and extensive fields of corn, grain sorghum, and hay. The piles of boulders in the fields and the

2. The Corn Palace at Mitchell is decorated with murals created from different colored corn. Grain sorghum and grass help outline the designs and fill in gaps. As many as 3,000 bushels of grain are used to make the new designs every year. The panel of Indians planting corn (right) is one of many on the building's walls. Early each morning the sidewalks below the decorations are swept clean of the grain that has fallen the day before. A week-long Corn Palace Festival is held every September.

1 The waters of the Big Sioux River tumble over rocks of hard Sioux quartzite to create the falls for which the largest city in South Dakota is named. Sioux Falls is an attractive city of colleges, pleasant homes, and wide, tree-shaded streets. It has been a shipping and trading center since it was established in the 1850's and now has a number of meat-packing houses and food-processing plants.

numerous sloughs and pothole ponds indicate that this land was under a continental glacier 12,500 years ago. The ponds today are home to many wading birds, ducks, and geese. You may also see an occasional muskrat house at the water's edge.

2 Mitchell is best known for its Corn Palace, an auditorium designed in Moorish style. The flamboyant building, with multihued towers, domes, and turrets, was built to com-

memorate the area's most important crop. Each year the structure is decorated inside and out with designs created with colorful corn, other grains, and several kinds of grasses.

About two miles north of town, across Mitchell Lake, is the Mitchell Archeological Site, a continuing "dig" at a thousand-year-old Indian village. Guided tours of the grounds here are offered at the visitor center.

3 The ring-necked pheasant, the official South Dakota bird, was introduced to this continent from China in 1881, and nowhere is this colorful game bird more appreciated than in Huron. During the hunting season, from mid-October to early December, hordes of hunters bring lucrative business to the town. The importance of the bird is acknowledged by a 40-foot statue of a pheasant, which is atop a small building near elm-shaded Memorial Park.

4 De Smet is the little prairie town of Laura Ingalls Wilder's *Little House on the Prairie* books. Several sites portrayed in the stories have been preserved and are open to visitors. Guided tours are available in the summer at the "surveyor's house," the white frame building that seemed so magnificent to a little girl who moved here from an unpainted shack on the open prairie.

Mrs. Wilder's readers may remember her vivid descriptions of the South Dakota prairies in the 1880's. The land looks significantly different today, for the tall native grass has been replaced by corn, and there are many more trees than there were a century ago.

5 East of De Smet are glacial sloughs, several lakes, and a series of prosperous farms whose success is due partly to research carried out at the South Dakota State University at Brookings, a town known as the agricultural capital of the state.

At the McCrory Gardens, on the eastern edge of Brookings on Route 14, the university has established trial gardens where both woody and herbaceous plants are tested for their adaptability to the South Dakota climate. Visitors are invited to inspect the more than 200 different species of trees, shrubs, and flowering plants and the 90 kinds of lawn grasses. All the plants are labeled.

7. The Indians still quarry catlinite at Pipestone National Monument. The red stone is used for the bowls of their ceremonial pipes; the pipe stems are wood.

6 The route across the state border to Lake Benton in Minnesota leads through Hole-in-the-Mountain, a pass in the escarpment surrounding Coteau des Prairies, a plateau about 60 miles wide, 200 miles long, and as much as 1,000 feet high.

Fishing for walleyes and pike is popular at Lake Benton, as is boating and swimming. Hole in the Mountain County Park features picnic and camping facilities and such winter sports as skiing, snowmobiling, and snowshoeing. There are also hiking trails through the park.

7 On the north edge of the town of Pipestone, Minnesota, a half-mile road leads to Pipestone National Monument. This place, with its quarries of pipestone, has long been sacred to the Indians. In Sioux legend, the Great Spirit made the first peace pipe from the soft red stone, and called upon all tribes to use the stone to make calumets, which they should smoke to him. The smoke was believed to convey their prayers.

Pipestone—now called catlinite in honor of the artist George Catlin who wrote about the quarries in 1836—is found in thin veins between layers of Sioux quartzite, a harder, pinkish stone. A billion years ago the catlinite was clay, and the quartzite was sand at the bottom of the sea. Becoming deeply buried, the beds of clay and sand metamorphosed. Uplift of the earth's crust and erosion eventually exposed the rock that formed.

The Indians probably discovered catlinite more than 400 years ago. Since then, tribes have traveled as far as 1,000 miles to dig the stone for their sacred pipes, used to solemnize treaties and ceremonies.

In the mid-1800's the Sioux took control of the Pipestone quarry.

Other tribes could obtain the revered stone only by trading with the Sioux. In 1937 the Pipestone National Monument was established, and all Indians were again guaranteed the right to quarry the rock.

The Circle Trail, an easy mile-long loop, takes you across the monument grounds, where you may see Indians quarrying the catlinite. The trail is also a self-guided nature walk, with posted information about the area.

When you leave the monument, turn right onto Hiawatha Avenue and drive through the town of Pipestone to see the buildings of Sioux quartzite that line the historic district on Main Street. Buildings like these handsome pink structures are no longer being constructed, since the expense of shaping quartzite into building stones is prohibitive.

Going south on Route 23 you pass Split Rock Creek State Park, which has camping and picnic sites around a man-made lake. Fishing is popular in the well-stocked lake, and there are several hiking trails.

8 At Garretson, South Dakota, is Devils Gulch, a narrow gap in the quartzite cliffs that tower above both sides of Split Rock Creek. Cedar trees cling to the pink walls, and ferns flourish in the cool deep canyon. Legend maintains that the notorious Jesse James once leapt across this gorge to escape from a pursuing posse. A bridge now spans the gully.

South of Garretson is Palisades State Park, a 110-acre area named for the pink quartzite cliffs that rise up from Split Rock Creek. Pathways along the creek lead to camping facilities and pleasant picnic groves.

8. The sheer walls of pink Sioux quartzite rising up from Split Rock Creek were believed by Indians to have been formed when a tomahawk was thrown from the spirit world by an Indian god. The James boys "holed up" in a cave here after an abortive bank raid, perhaps partly to search for a railroad payroll left in the area and never found.

North Dakota

A last frontier for the glaciers, the great herds of buffalo, and the nomadic Indian tribes

Set in the geographic center of North America, North Dakota may seem to be composed primarily of horizon. However, the perceptive traveler cannot help but notice the significant differences between the water-carved scenery and the land that was shaped by the glaciers.

North and east of the Missouri the glaciers deposited a bouldery clay rich in various minerals on which crops and roadside plants, such as the wild prairie rose (*Rosa setigera*), the official state flower, grow beautifully. The state tree is the American elm (*Ulmus americana*).

The unglaciated lands southwest of the Missouri River are rolling plains, accented by dramatic buttes and Badlands cut by water erosion.

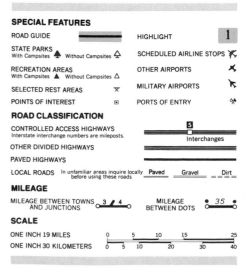

3. These "cedars"—actually junipers—take on this columnar form in the area where lignite burns, but transplanted elsewhere the trees resume their normal shrubby shape. It is thought that smoldering coal somehow leads to this odd growth pattern.

The Badlands country that you see on this tour boasts two of nature's unique phenomena, burning lignite and columnar junipers.

Along the Little Missouri River you can travel leisurely through the colorful eroded scenery, once described as "hell, with the fires out" by a Sioux-chasing general who didn't happen to see the burning coal vein.

Points of interest cluster at the east end of Lake Sakakawea, named for the Shoshone girl who accompanied Lewis and Clark on part of their exploration of the continent.

Inside the humming power plant at Garrison Dam nature seems remote. At the nearby fish hatchery it is carefully controlled, but on an adjacent nature trail it is virtually untouched.

1 Dickinson, the largest town in the southwest quarter of the state, serves as the main marketing area for surrounding farms, ranches, and oil and coal industries.

Edward A. Patterson Recreation Area, which surrounds a lake on the edge of town, is best reached from Exit 12 on Route 94. Patterson Lake is a pleasant place to stop off for picnicking, free camping, and fishing.

2 White Lake National Wildlife Refuge consists mainly of an artificial lake that provides critical nesting and rest areas for ducks and other waterfowl in a region where lakes are few. The U.S. Fish and Wildlife Service, in cooperation with the North Dakota Game and Fish Department, is trying to establish a nesting population of the giant race of Canada geese on the 1,040-acre refuge.

This relatively small area is considered a satellite refuge of Lake Ilo (see entry 11 on page 299) and has no facilities for visitors. However, you might see waterfowl and, in the fall, some deer, if you are observant and do not drive too fast.

3 About 65 million years ago plants growing in humid swamps here died and fell into stagnant water. The partially decomposed plants were covered by blankets of sand and clay, and were in time transformed into lignite, a relatively young, low-heat soft coal. Parts of these coal

deposits were eventually exposed by erosion, and sometimes they were set afire by lightning strikes or prairie fires.

A good example of a burning lignite vein is on Little Missouri National Grasslands. Here a 20-foot-thick seam of lignite lies mostly about 30 feet below the surface. Smoke and steam from the burning vein are easily observable, although the flame is not visible. The heat bakes overlying clay, shale, and sandstone into a red bricklike rock that locally is called scoria. True scoria is volcanic and the correct, but seldom-used, term for the rock here is porcellanite.

As burning consumes the coal, the rocks above lose their support and collapse. This allows more oxygen to reach the vein, which then burns further. This scoria is responsible for much of the striking color of the Badlands and reflects the amount of lignite that has burned here.

At the coal vein you also can see the remarkable columnar junipers. The Rocky Mountain juniper normally is almost shrubby, with a spreading shape. But most of the junipers (locally called cedars) near the burning lignite are narrow and upright. At first thought to be a different species,

SPECIAL FEATURES		
ROAD GUIDE	HIGHLIGHT	1
STATE PARKS With Campsites ⬥ Without Campsites △	SCHEDULED AIRLINE STOPS	✈
RECREATION AREAS With Campsites ▲ Without Campsites △	OTHER AIRPORTS	✖
SELECTED REST AREAS ☒	MILITARY AIRPORTS	✦
POINTS OF INTEREST ⊡	PORTS OF ENTRY	⊗

ROAD CLASSIFICATION

CONTROLLED ACCESS HIGHWAYS
Interstate interchange numbers are mileposts.

OTHER DIVIDED HIGHWAYS

PAVED HIGHWAYS

LOCAL ROADS In unfamiliar areas inquire locally before using these roads   Paved   Gravel   Dirt

MILEAGE

MILEAGE BETWEEN TOWNS AND JUNCTIONS   3   4

MILEAGE BETWEEN DOTS   35

SCALE

ONE INCH 19 MILES   0   5   10   15   25
ONE INCH 30 KILOMETERS   0   5   10   20   30   40

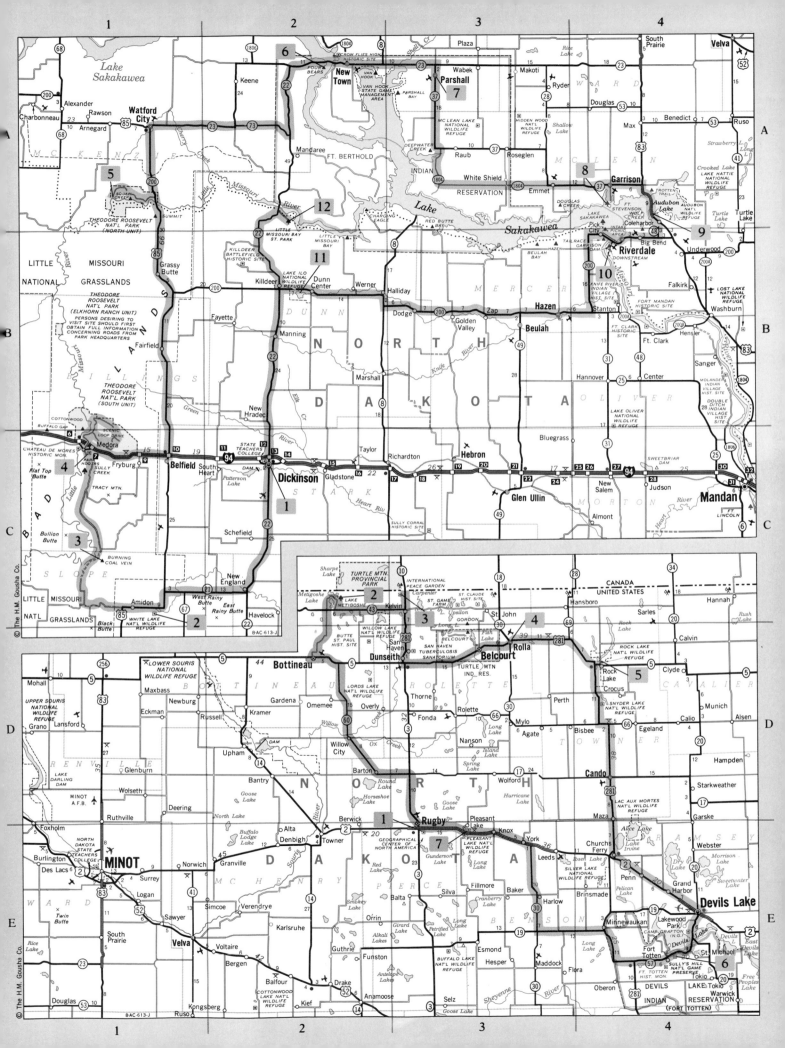

4. *Sculptural forms made of hard sandstone capping a soft clay eroded by wind and water loom along the roads twisting through the Little Missouri National Grasslands and Theodore Roosevelt National Park. Bison once roamed this area.*

these columnar trees resumed their spreading form when transplanted elsewhere. Fumes from the burning lignite are thought to cause the columnar growth, but just how this occurs is not known.

In bad weather it might be wise to inquire in Amidon about the condition of the gravel road that leads to the burning coal vein.

4 The gravel road leading to Medora passes through the rugged landscape of the Badlands, where the big game herds, particularly bison, made their last stand in the 1880's. The little cow town of Medora began to bill itself as a hunting center for eastern sportsmen who were longing for the vanishing frontier. Theodore Roosevelt was one of them; he soon became part-owner of a local cattle ranch where he worked for over a year.

Much of Medora has been restored to look as it did in the 1880's when it was founded by the Marquis de Mores, a French adventurer. He named the new town for his bride and built an elaborate château, which can be seen on conducted tours.

Soon after Roosevelt's death in 1919, North Dakota citizens urged that a park be created in the Badlands to honor him for his love of the country as well as for his conservation policies. The proposal generated little interest at the time. However, years of ignoring the basic principles of conservation led to the Dust Bowl disasters in the 1930's, and much of the parched and barren land reverted to federal ownership and was restored as Little Missouri National Grasslands and Theodore Roosevelt National Park.

The scenic loop road through the South Unit of the park gives access to good hiking trails and spectacular Badlands scenery, and has explanatory roadside signs.

North along Route 85, occasional buttes accent the fields of wheat and sunflowers, and scoria deposits are red details on the prairie.

5 The North Unit of Theodore Roosevelt National Park features a 12-mile scenic drive that ends at Oxbow Overlook; several interesting trails intersect the road.

Two miles east of the junction of Routes 22 and 23 you can first spot Lake Sakakawea lying among the bluffs. This is one of the largest man-made lakes in the country and a prominent landmark in the state.

6 A large portion of Lake Sakakawea is within the Fort Berthold Indian Reservation, which is occupied by the Three Affiliated Tribes—the Mandan, the Hidatsa, and the Arikara. Their history is told in the Three Affiliated Tribes Museum, just west of the lake. Next to the museum is the entrance to Four Bears Recreation Area.

Four Bears was a Mandan chief often portrayed by the explorer–artists George Catlin and Karl Bodmer. The Hidatsas also had a Chief Four Bears, so Four Bears Memorial Bridge, which spans the lake, is named for a Mandan on one end and a Hidatsa on the other. The two tribes felt that other chiefs should be honored, and the Arikaras also wanted to be included, so 19 chiefs are now listed on the structure.

7 When Paul Broste built his castlelike rock museum in Parshall, he used so many glacial erratics that farmers for 20 miles around thought they might be rid of the rocks that interfered with their plowing. Of course the museum did not even come close to using up all the unwanted granite. Inside is an interesting collection of rock specimens from all over the world. The road to the museum turns west from Route 37 on the north edge of town (at the highway maintenance yard).

8 A convenient approach to Lake Sakakawea is from Fort Stevenson State Park. Fort Stevenson was one of a line of picket posts built along the Upper Missouri as a defense against the Sioux. The fort was supposed to defend the friendly Three Affiliated Tribes, but it was too far from their village to do them much good. As it turned out, the three tribes were the protectors of Fort Stevenson, since the Sioux preferred to attack them rather than the fort.

The park is a pleasant, wooded recreation area with camping, picnicking, boating, and fishing. The prairie dog town is a tiny remnant of the plains as they used to be.

From the road atop an embankment between Sakakawea and Audubon lakes you can see part of the 180-foot-high Snake Creek Pumping Station, which is the first step in the immense and controversial Garrison Diversion project to irrigate 250,000 acres of farmland. Conservationists argue that the project damages wildlife habitat.

9 Despite the flooding of the sharp-tailed grouse dancing grounds and the greatly reduced numbers of waterfowl, the 14,776-acre Audubon National Wildlife Refuge is still a worthwhile place to visit. From the eight miles of unpaved sanctuary roads you can see large flocks of ducks, geese, and sandhill cranes, particularly during migration. At refuge headquarters, located at the end of a 0.7-mile-long gravel road leading from the south end of the embankment between Sakakawea and Audubon, you can ask about the most likely places to see interesting birds and mammals.

10 Garrison Dam, one of the largest dams in North America, was built to help control floods on the Missouri River, to generate electricity, and to provide irrigation water. The power plant is an impressive structure, and inside you can feel the place hum and throb as though it were alive.

The Garrison Dam National Fish Hatchery, a half-mile down the road from the power plant, does not hum or throb. The occasional muffled splash is only the result of a cormorant or gull catching a fish before the humans do.

A self-guided tour of the operation takes you through spring and summer production of trout, northern pikes, salmon, and walleyes from eggs to 1½- to 2-inch fingerlings, the stage at which many are distributed to various Dakota fishing sites. Inside the hatchery building is an excellent aquarium display of about 20 fish species native to the area.

A self-guided nature trail of about two miles begins at a campground farther down the road and emphasizes interesting aspects of a well-established riverbottom forest environment. Probably the loudest noise you will hear is the clear, flutelike song of the western meadowlark, the state bird of North Dakota.

11 Created by a dam across Spring Creek, Lake Ilo is an oasis on the rolling semiarid plains and attracts many wild animals, most notably water birds.

After less than half a mile on the road south from Route 200 to the Lake Ilo National Wildlife Refuge, you reach a junction at the 1,250-acre lake. The left branch leads to refuge headquarters on the south shore. The right branch takes you along the north shore to a pleasant park, used extensively in summer for picnicking, swimming, fishing, and boating.

From the park or other points across the lake you can view a wide variety of waterfowl. During fall migration in late October or early November, 50,000 ducks may be resting on the refuge. Mallard, pintail, shoveler, and other nesting ducks usually produce about 700 young per year. The gravel road continues on to rejoin Route 200.

12 Sixteen miles north of the junction of Routes 22 and 200, the Little Missouri Badlands appear beyond farms and ranches east of the Killdeer Mountains.

Little Missouri Bay State Park includes some of the most dramatic and rugged vistas of the North Dakota Badlands. Maintained to offer visitors a wilderness experience, the park provides primitive camping facilities, a corral for horses, and 75 miles of trails for backpacking or riding. A concession adjacent to the park rents horses, but if you cannot explore the Badlands astride a horse, there are good views from a gravel road that heads east from a well-marked point on Route 22. About two miles down the road is the park's picnic shelter, overlooking the Badlands to the north and the rolling farmland to the south. To the northeast the sun glints on the waters of Little Missouri Bay.

Going south toward Dickson, you cross the dry plains where the patterns of planting reveal the need for protection from wind erosion. Crops sturdy enough to resist the wind are planted in alternate rows with crops that are susceptible. The parallel strips are set at right angles to the prevailing wind. Rows of trees planted as shelter belts around the farmsteads provide for the traveler in this open terrain an interesting silhouette against the wide sky.

5. *Oxbow Overlook commands the heights above the floodplain of the Little Missouri River in the North Unit of the Theodore Roosevelt National Park. The water level is low, and the banks of the river are exposed to view. Longhorn cattle (left), which were a part of the West's ranching industry in the 19th century, bask in the sun-dappled park. These sturdy beasts came by way of Texas, descended from breeds of mostly Spanish origin. They are reputed to fight off wolves and even grizzly bears.*

Here in northern North Dakota, in the town of Rugby, you can take your stand in a unique spot in the world—the geographical center of North America. Another interesting location in this glacier-molded landscape is the International Peace Garden, which straddles the border of the United States and Canada and commemorates the more than 150 years of peace between the two countries. Also on this tour is the town of Rolla, a few miles south of the Canadian border, where the federal government has established a plant to manufacture jewel bearings for military guidance systems. The waterfowl, however, that return each year to the thousands of prairie ponds in the Dakotas manage to do so by using internal systems for guidance that are still a mystery to the jewel- and missile-makers.

1 A pillar of granite glacial erratics stands at the intersection of Routes 2 and 3 to indicate the geographical center of North America.

Standing here one realizes that most of the United States is in the southern half of the continent, where the climate is suitable for the production of the agricultural abundance that is evident in the fertile fields of North Dakota. The riches here began with the efforts of pioneers, who are memorialized in the nearby Geographical Center Historical Museum. Here many old buildings have been gathered and restored both inside and out. Also on display are old farm machinery and other artifacts. The museum is closed from October 2 through April 30.

2 Abutting the Canadian border is the inviting Lake Metigoshe State Park, which has a number of ponds and another lake besides the one for which it is named.

Water sports of all types are available on Lake Metigoshe, but School Section Lake is the heart of a wilder section of the park where visitors must be self-propelled by foot or canoe. With their thick forest cover, the Turtle Mountains that roll northwest into Manitoba contrast markedly with most of North Dakota. The Old Oak Trail, a self-guided two-mile path, leads you on an easy walk of about 90 minutes through a haven of woods, water, and wildlife.

Flight patterns of North Dakota's water birds

Geese and ducks, both members of the category of birds called waterfowl, have distinctive flight patterns. Geese—large, noisy, and long necked—usually form a definite V, but sometimes fly in a single-file string. Ducks—smaller, plumper, with shorter necks—fly in great unorganized flocks. Both fly with necks extended.

Other water birds found in North Dakota have characteristic silhouettes in flight. Herons draw their heads between their shoulders; grebes extend their feet as rudders; and cormorants, with short tails, stay close to the water's surface.

Flight of geese
Flight of ducks
Mallard
Black-crowned night heron
Canada goose
American widgeon
Gadwall
Ruddy duck
Blue-winged teal
Pied-billed grebe
Pintail
Double-crested cormorant
Shoveler

3 The entrance to the boundary-spanning International Peace Garden is marked by a gateway that indicates the border, and there is also a pillar flanked by American and Canadian flags. The pillar bears a plaque pledging that the two nations will not take up arms against each other.

Established in 1932 on 2,300 acres donated by Manitoba and North Dakota, the garden reminds visitors that a long peace between neighboring countries is uncommon in the world. The park generates a warm spirit of gratitude that even a Dakota winter cannot chill.

The natural beauty of the Turtle Mountains adds impact to the symbolism of the Peace Garden and the world's longest undefended border. In summer the elaborate formal gardens are also impressive.

Scenic drives winding freely through both countries circle forest-enclosed lakes where waterfowl are common. Deer and other wildlife can be seen in the woods, particularly along hiking trails on the Canadian side. Also in Canada is an arboretum with labeled trees and shrubs.

4 There are many glacially transported granite boulders around Rolla, but the most important "rocks" are minute artificial jewels. On Route 30, one-tenth of a mile north of its intersection with Route 281, is the William Langer Plant, a federal factory where jewel bearings are made for use in guidance systems and other military devices. The jewel bearings are the size of dust grains, and several completed bearings could be lost under a fingernail. Tours can be arranged at the plant.

Many of the employees here are Chippewas from the vicinity of the nearby Indian reservation. A few examples of Indian crafts are on display in the lobby of the plant.

5 Rock Lake National Wildlife Refuge consists of prairie potholes and sloughs that are easily seen from Route 281. Wildlife refuges are common in the prairie pothole country of the Dakotas, and half the ducks in North America are hatched in this habitat. The federal government wants to preserve this prime waterfowl habitat. Some refuges are government-owned, but others are controlled by "easement." For a wetland easement, a farmer is paid one lump sum in return for promising not to drain, burn, fill, or level wetlands. The promise becomes part of the title to the land and obligates each subsequent owner. The 5,507 acres of Rock Lake National Wildlife Refuge are managed under this system. Easements are paid for by the U.S. Fish and Wildlife Service with funds collected from hunters.

Cando is known chiefly for the pioneer independence reflected in its name. During an 1884 county commissioners' meeting an argument raged over the selection of the Towner County seat. Annoyed by the contention that the commissioners lacked authority in the matter, the commission chairman shouted, "We'll show you what we can do. We'll name this county seat 'Cando.'"

6 Sullys Hill National Game Preserve is in the middle of Devils Lake Sioux Tribe Reservation. The refuge has high fences that enclose herds of bison, elk, and white-tailed deer on 700 of its 1,674 acres.

The four-mile loop road is set up as a self-guided auto nature tour through the enclosure. Since the refuge is heavily forested, the wildlife have excellent cover. Overlooks, however, offer fine views of Devils Lake. There also is a self-guided nature trail for hikers that begins and ends at Sweetwater Lake. In the lake you can see such waterfowl as whistling swans, several species of geese, and various ducks. The preserve is reached via a road to Fort Totten, the reservation headquarters.

Fort Totten, built in 1870 as part of a program placing the Sioux on reservations, is the best preserved of the plains' forts. Its buildings surround a parklike area called Cavalry Square. In summer you can visit a pioneer museum and a general store. The Sioux perform traditional dances the last weekend in July.

7 At the junction of Routes 19 and 30 you are in an area of terminal moraines, as illustrated in the photograph below. A parklike roadside rest area on Route 2 is a good place to pull over for a view of the 1,000-acre Pleasant Lake National Wildlife Refuge, 90 percent of which is covered by refuge easements.

Prairie potholes are resting stopover points for waterfowl during migration to and from Canada. On an early autumn morning you may see thousands of snow geese, for instance, rise from the waters on either side of the road to glean grain from harvested fields, the geeses' white plumage contrasting with the dark soil of the glacial prairies. In the early evening the birds return to the potholes in flocks, a thrilling sight as they come honking over the highway.

Potholes are rich, sparkling gems of life, accenting the endless horizon of the prairie. They also hold water on the land until it can sink in.

Without potholes the rain and heavy spring snowmelt cause erosion and downstream flooding.

7. Prairie potholes like this one near Devils Lake make a good breeding place for waterfowl. These potholes were created when retreating glaciers left hunks of ice that made hollows as they melted. The hillside is a terminal moraine, a pile of rock and grit dumped by a glacier at its melting edge. The ridges were pushed up as the ice retreated. Creases are due to gully erosion, which was triggered by man's clearing the vegetation.

Exploring the Western States

A dramatic landscape of snowcapped mountains, magnificent forests, and vast expanses of desert

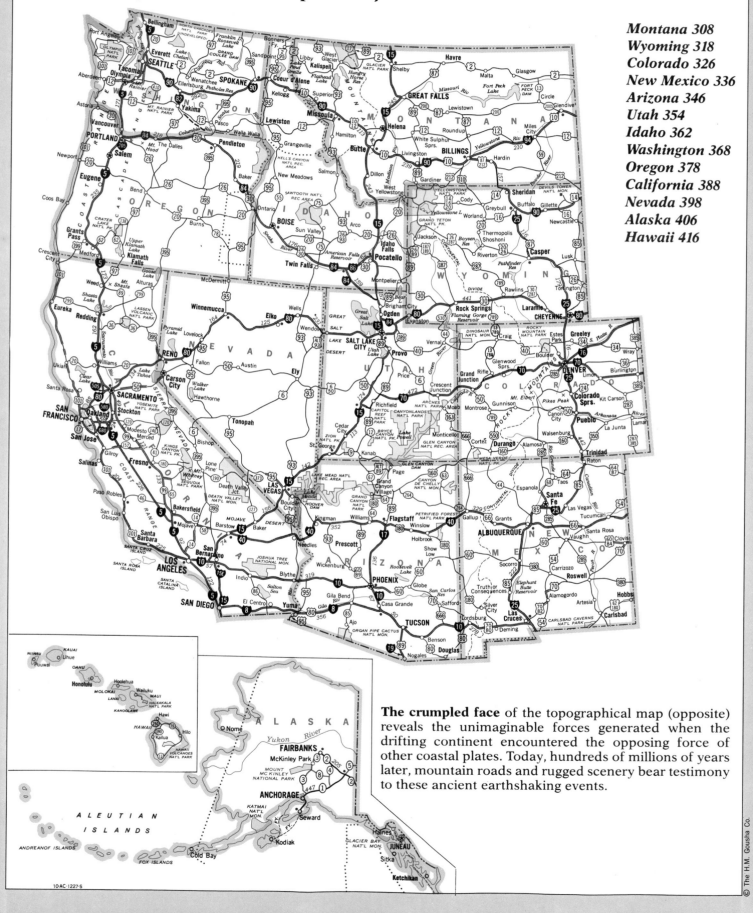

Montana 308
Wyoming 318
Colorado 326
New Mexico 336
Arizona 346
Utah 354
Idaho 362
Washington 368
Oregon 378
California 388
Nevada 398
Alaska 406
Hawaii 416

The crumpled face of the topographical map (opposite) reveals the unimaginable forces generated when the drifting continent encountered the opposing force of other coastal plates. Today, hundreds of millions of years later, mountain roads and rugged scenery bear testimony to these ancient earthshaking events.

10-AC-1227-S

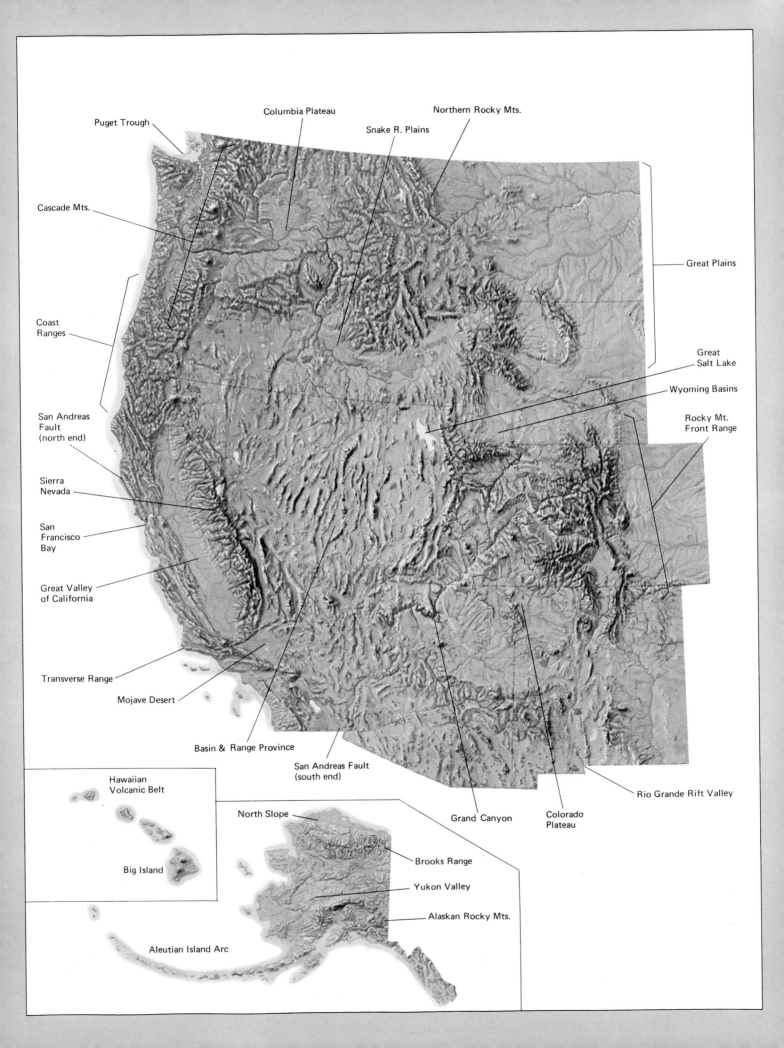

Puget Trough

Columbia Plateau

Northern Rocky Mts.

Snake R. Plains

Cascade Mts.

Great Plains

Coast
Ranges

Great
Salt Lake

Wyoming Basins

San Andreas
Fault
(north end)

Rocky Mt.
Front Range

Sierra
Nevada

San
Francisco
Bay

Great Valley
of California

Transverse Range

Mojave Desert

Basin & Range Province

San Andreas Fault
(south end)

Grand Canyon

Colorado
Plateau

Rio Grande Rift Valley

Hawaiian
Volcanic Belt

North Slope

Big Island

Brooks Range

Yukon Valley

Alaskan Rocky Mts.

Aleutian Island Arc

Plants, Birds, and Animals to Watch For

Some of these, such as redwoods, roadrunners, grizzlies, and Gila monsters, are unique to the West

In the western states are some of the most dramatic natural wonders in America. Here you find the coast redwood that grows to more than 350 feet high, bristlecone pines (not illustrated) that are, at more than 4,000 years of age, the oldest living things, and the many-armed sculptural form of the saguaro cactus in the southwesten desert.

The mountains of the Northwest are literally clothed in dense green forests of fir, hemlock, cedar, and spruce, and in the state of Hawaii is an impressive variety of wonderfully colorful flowers, trees, and shrubs.

Rewarding to see are the Dall sheep that inhabit the craggy slopes of Alaska's mountain reaches; and along the Pacific coast, the sleek seals and sea lions. To be avoided in the desert is the Gila monster, and in the forest the fearsome grizzly is best viewed at a distance through binoculars.

Among the most memorable avian sights in this part of the country are the bald eagle, our national bird, the sprightly roadrunner, the state bird of New Mexico, and the stately trumpeter swan that graces many lakes and marshy ponds.

Trees

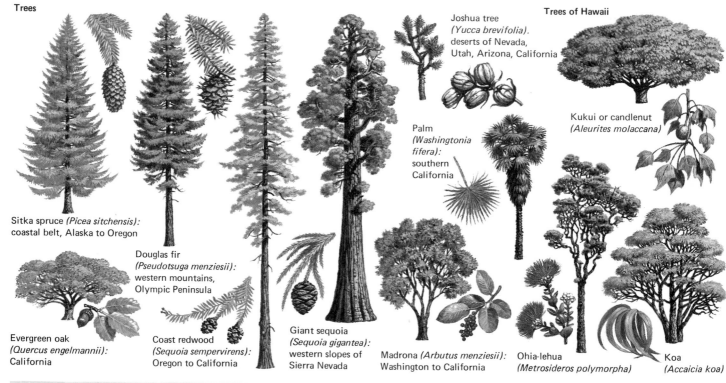

Joshua tree
(*Yucca brevifolia*).
deserts of Nevada,
Utah, Arizona, California

Trees of Hawaii

Palm
(*Washingtonia
fifera*):
southern
California

Kukui or candlenut
(*Aleurites molaccana*)

Sitka spruce *(Picea sitchensis):* coastal belt, Alaska to Oregon

Douglas fir
(*Pseudotsuga menziesii):*
western mountains,
Olympic Peninsula

Evergreen oak
(*Quercus engelmannii):*
California

Coast redwood
(*Sequoia sempervirens):*
Oregon to California

Giant sequoia
(*Sequoia gigantea):*
western slopes of
Sierra Nevada

Madrona *(Arbutus menziesii):*
Washington to California

Ohia-lehua
(*Metrosideros polymorpha*)

Koa
(*Accaicia koa*)

Shrubs

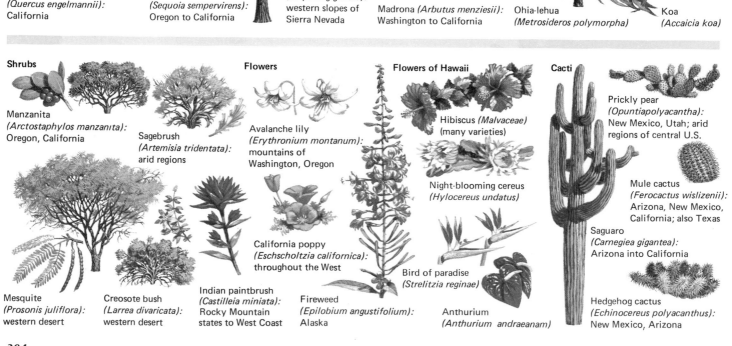

Manzanita
(*Arctostaphylos manzanita):*
Oregon, California

Sagebrush
(*Artemisia tridentata):*
arid regions

Flowers

Avalanche lily
(*Erythronium montanum):*
mountains of
Washington, Oregon

Flowers of Hawaii

Hibiscus *(Malvaceae)*
(many varieties)

Night-blooming cereus
(*Hylocereus undatus*)

Bird of paradise
(*Strelitzia reginae*)

Cacti

Prickly pear
(*Opuntiapolyacantha):*
New Mexico, Utah; arid
regions of central U.S.

Mule cactus
(*Ferocactus wislizenii):*
Arizona, New Mexico,
California; also Texas

Saguaro
(*Carnegiea gigantea):*
Arizona into California

Mesquite
(*Prosonis juliflora):*
western desert

Creosote bush
(*Larrea divaricata):*
western desert

Indian paintbrush
(*Castilleia miniata):*
Rocky Mountain
states to West Coast

Fireweed
(*Epilobium angustifolium):*
Alaska

California poppy
(*Eschscholtzia californica):*
throughout the West

Anthurium
(*Anthurium andraeanam*)

Hedgehog cactus
(*Echinocereus polyacanthus):*
New Mexico, Arizona

Birds

Bald eagle:
coastal belt,
Alaska to Oregon

Dark-eyed junco:
coastal forest
and Montana, Idaho

Wild turkey:
western and
southern U.S.

Dipper:
Alaska,
western U.S.

Trumpeter swan:
marshes, southern Alaska
to Oregon, Idaho, Montana

Elf owl:
southwestern desert

Roadrunner:
southwestern U.S.

Brown pelican:
central California

Cormorant:
California

Nene: Hawaii

Animals

Grizzly bear: Yellowstone,
Grand Teton, Glacier
national parks; Alaska

Dall sheep:
Alaska

Mule deer: Wyoming,
Idaho, Montana

Alaska fur seal:
California coast in winter

Ring-tailed cat:
Nevada, Utah,
Colorado, Arizona,
Oregon, California;
also Texas

Elephant seal:
north California coast

Cougar:
Rocky Mountain states

Ocelot:
southwestern states

Coyote:
throughout the West

Kangaroo rat:
western Nevada,
Arizona, California

Elk/wapiti:
Rocky Mountains

Sea lion:
Pacific Coast

Steller's sea lion:
Pacific Coast

Lizards and Turtles

Gila monster: Utah,
Arizona, southern California

Pacific pond turtle:
Pacific Coast

Banded gecko:
Texas to California

Chuckwalla: Nevada,
Utah, southern California

Desert tortoise:
southwestern desert

305

Equipment as Varied as the Climate

*From hauling logs and shaking trees to the picking of
tomatoes and grapes, you can see machines on the job*

The equipment shown on these pages is adapted to the harvesting of specific crops that are primarily identified with the West. In addition to the specialized machines, there is also a wide range of other interesting equipment that is used on western dairies, cattle ranches, fruit orchards, hopyards, and family farms.

In logging country the equipment used in the woods is not so frequently seen. The sawmills, however, are usually beside a road, and the logging trucks with their great loads of long logs may seem all too visible, especially on a curving, hilly road when you are trying to pass one.

Not all the crops are picked by machine. In the fruit orchards of the Northwest and the vegetable fields of the broad California valleys, much of the picking is still done by migrant workers, whom you can see in the fields as they follow the harvest.

Wherever there are vineyards, there are sure to be wineries nearby. Most of the owners are pleased to show visitors through and explain the exacting process by which the fruit is turned into wine. The wines of California have been constantly improved over the decades and now rank with the world's finest.

Lumber

Loaders such as this pick up logs as if they were matchsticks and position them for the next operation. These logs are on their way to the mill, where they will be cut into boards. The cone-shaped "cyclone" (upper right) collects sawdust, which in less enlightened times was burned.

Instead of the old-time method of setting a "choker" around the logs and dragging them to a loading dock with a long cable on a power-driven drum, these powerful pincers pick up one end of the logs and pull them to where they are needed. This method is faster, and the constant danger of broken cables snapping through the air has been eliminated.

Nuts

In many nut groves and fruit orchards in the West, the tree-shaker has made obsolete the tall, cumbersome (and dangerous) ladders traditionally used at harvesttime. Padded grippers, hydraulically operated, shake the limbs until the crop is safely on the ground.

When the crop is down, the mechanical harvester, equipped with wire tines on a rubber belt, picks up the nuts. Before they emerge from the conveyor at the rear of the machine, the dirt and the grass has been removed.

Grapes

In California's San Joaquin Valley during September and October, you see clusters of hand-picked grapes slowly turning into raisins on paper trays between the rows. Almost half the world's raisin supply is grown here, where it takes only two or three weeks in the hot sun to complete the drying process.

When the raisins are dry, the paper trays are rolled into bundles and "baked" in the sun for a while before the fruit is cleaned and packed. Raisin grapes are planted in rows that run from east to west to provide the sunny southern exposure needed for drying.

Mechanical harvesters straddling a row of grapes lift and shake the vines until the fruit falls off. Belts and bucket elevators move the grapes through the machine, where they are air-cleaned and dropped on a conveyor (at left) that loads them into containers for transport to the winery. One person operates the machine, which can harvest up to two acres an hour.

Vegetables

Because water is so necessary for the production of vegetables, you see in the produce-growing valleys of the West that some remarkable methods have been devised to apply it. The system shown here can spread water, fertilizer, or pesticide over an area up to 3,000 feet wide and a mile long.

Tomato vines, cut at ground level, are conveyed to a shaker that separates fruit from vine and sifts out dirt. Sorting before delivery to the bulk carrier may be done by hand or with an electronic color-sensing device.

This machine is built to eliminate the backbreaking labor of picking beans by hand. A reel of metal fingers flicks the beans off the vine onto conveyor belts that transport them to a hopper as fans remove leaves, stems, and other trash.

Sugarcane

In Hawaii, where about 25 percent of the U.S. produced cane sugar is grown, the machete is pretty much a thing of the past. The vast plantations are mechanized now with machines like this that can cut, clean, and chop up to 90 tons an hour. Speed is vital because the cane begins to lose sugar content as soon as it is cut.

Big Sky Country

The scenic horizons of Montana are assured by the drama of mountain peaks and vast sweeping plains

Although the name *Montana* is derived from the Latin for "mountainous regions," about two-thirds of the state is made up of gently rolling plains that support millions of cattle and sheep and show few signs of human habitation.

With Glacier and Yellowstone national parks on its borders, and watered as it is by rivers and lakes, it is no wonder that nature still dominates the Montana landscape.

Indians wrote the first Montana history on rock, leaving an enigmatic record for archeologists to interpret. Modern history began with expeditions of Lewis and Clark and the fur traders who followed in their wake. Miners followed the fur traders, and soldiers came to protect the miners.

The U.S. Army battling the horse-nomad Indians cleared the way for the cattlemen and the cowboys. Later the sheepmen came to share the range, and the plows of the sodbusters created alternating patterns of wheat, barley, and hay across the vast prairie.

In no other area but Alaska can you see so many animals in the wild as you do on the routes included on these pages.

This tour passes through a smokejumper center in Missoula and heads north into spectacular Flathead Valley to one of the best wildlife loops in the country. Beyond is Flathead Lake, the largest natural freshwater lake west of the Mississippi and one of the most beautiful.

The man-made marvel of Hungry Horse Dam almost pales to insignificance before the wonder of Glacier National Park, and Going-to-the-Sun Road in Glacier is deservedly one of the most famous highways in all of the United States.

The buffalo jump at Ulm Pishkun State Monument offers a good view of the scenery and an interesting aspect of Plains Indian culture. A paved but twisting recreational road follows Lewis and Clark's route along a particularly scenic stretch of the Missouri. The scenery remains spectacular passing through Helena National Forest and over the Continental Divide.

1 Displays at the Smokejumper Visitor Center, off Route 90 just south of the Evaro Interchange, explain the history and work of these fire fighters. As the paratroopers of the U.S. Forest Service, smokejumpers present a romantic image of men who can reach forest fires in remote, roadless areas in a matter of hours to keep small fires from becoming infernos that would consume millions

1. Smokejumpers are trained to parachute to forest fires, where they fight for control until ground forces arrive.

of dollars worth of lumber, wildlife, and watershed.

However, a tour of the facility, especially during the training sessions in June, reveals that the romance of smokejumping rests on a mundane base of very hard, dirty, physical labor.

The Smokejumper Visitor Center is closed from October through May.

Nearby is the Northern Forest Fire Laboratory, where such things as fuels and fire behavior, weather, fire-control techniques, and the use of controlled burns in forest management are investigated. The findings are distributed worldwide to provide foresters with information to help predict the likelihood of fire under various conditions.

One mile after you enter the Flathead Indian Reservation, the Mission

Range rises to the east, a spectacular line of wilderness peaks towering along the edge of the Flathead Valley.

2 Created by glaciers, Lake Missoula once filled the southern end of the Flathead Valley, and rising as an island above the lake was the 4,885-foot high point of what is now the National Bison Range.

Today this wildlife refuge is an island of prairie grassland amid the farmlands that give the valley the character of a beautiful and thoroughly domesticated garden. Heavy woven-wire fences confine and protect bison, elk, pronghorns, white-tailed and mule deer, bighorn sheep, and mountain goats. There is also a wide variety of birds.

The highlight of the refuge is the graveled one-way loop road that begins at the headquarters at Moiese and goes for 19 miles, up and down the steep hills of the 18,452-acre range. A free self-guiding tour brochure is available at headquarters.

At various spots along the road, many within camera range, you are likely to see each of the refuge's big

SPECIAL FEATURES

ROAD GUIDE	HIGHLIGHT **1**
STATE PARKS — With Campsites ▲ Without Campsites △	SCHEDULED AIRLINE STOPS ✠
RECREATION AREAS — With Campsites ▲ Without Campsites △	MILITARY AIRPORTS ⊁
SELECTED REST AREAS ✕	OTHER AIRPORTS ✕
POINTS OF INTEREST ⊡	MAJOR MTN. ROADS
SKI AREAS ⅍	CLOSED IN WINTER Closed in Winter
	INFORMATION CENTER ⊛

ROAD CLASSIFICATION

CONTROLLED ACCESS HIGHWAYS
(Entrance and Exit only at Interchanges) — Divided / Undivided / Interchanges

OTHER DIVIDED HIGHWAYS

PAVED HIGHWAYS

LOCAL ROADS — In unfamiliar areas inquire locally before using these roads — Paved / Gravel / Dirt

MILEAGE

MILEAGE BETWEEN TOWNS AND JUNCTIONS — 3 | 4

MILEAGE BETWEEN DOTS — 35

SCALE

ONE INCH 28 MILES — 0 5 10 20 30

ONE INCH 45 KILOMETERS — 0 5 10 20 30 48

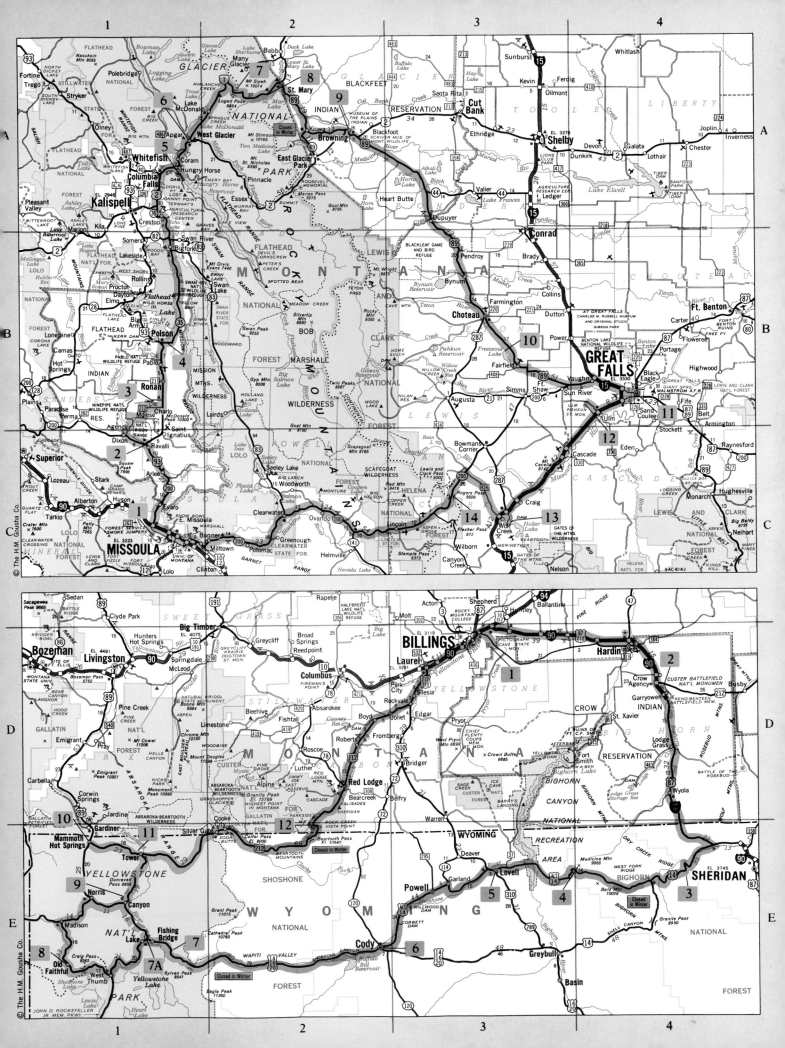

game species. It is inadvisable to get too close. A bull bison can weigh a ton and is unpredictable, especially during rut in August. You are most likely to spot wildlife early in the morning or before the refuge's sundown closings. Allow at least two hours to enjoy this road and more if you have the time.

At the Bison Range Headquarters you can find out about the current road conditions and waterfowl populations at the nearby Ninepipe and

2. At the National Bison Range cowboys round up some of the herd, which is kept between 300 and 500 head. In the early 1800's, at least 30 million of these animals wandered over the prairies. Among other game here are elk, antelope, and deer.

Pablo national wildlife refuges, both of which are superimposed on irrigation water reservoirs. From late March through early May 100,000 migrating ducks and geese may be stopping over here, and in October and November 200,000 may visit on their way south.

The drive from the Bison Range to these wildlife refuges winds through lovely irrigated cropland and pastures that lie in the shadow of the Mission Range.

3 Two miles beyond Charlo is the entrance to 2,000-acre Ninepipe National Wildlife Refuge. From a signboard dispenser, you can pick up a free map of this and the Pablo refuge, as well as a bird checklist. The road traverses the reservoir's dike, which provides the most scenic view of the lake, with the Missions forming the backdrop.

On the south end of the dike the gravel road divides. The left fork degenerates to two parallel tracks through excellent bird habitat. It is

recommended only for high-clearance vehicles in dry weather. The right fork goes to a junction, beyond the refuge, where a left turn leads back to Route 93.

Here turn left to drive through an arm of Ninepipe refuge. The innumerable ponds, usually populated with ducks, are actually potholes that were created when large pockets of glacial ice, insulated by a covering of dirt and rock, melted slowly to create the holes.

4 Just beyond the junction of Routes 93 and 35 is a dramatic hilltop view of Flathead Lake. Below is Polson Bay, a glistening sapphire in a rugged setting of forested mountains. Flathead Lake, 28 miles long and 15 miles wide at its broadest point, stretches north into the haze.

The 35-mile drive along the east shore passes through a wonderful mix of evergreens and orchards. The blossoming fruit trees of spring lead to the appearance in summer of roadside stands offering baskets of cherries, plums, peaches, and apples.

North of Flathead Lake the route passes productive farmland where lush alfalfa crops are rotated with wheat to help keep the soil fertile. Interesting too are the Christmas tree farms along the road. Most of the trees are Scotch pine, each carefully pruned to develop the traditional full and conelike form.

Black cottonwoods line the road as it winds through Flathead National Forest past Lion Lake.

5 Four miles from Route 2 is the Hungry Horse Dam, a classic concrete arch-gravity structure. The dam, as well as the reservoir and the town, was named for two freight horses that wandered away from their sleigh in the fierce Montana winter of 1900-01. The animals wallowed in belly-deep snow for a month and were found just in time to save them from starvation.

Completed in 1953, Hungry Horse is the uppermost of a series of dams built along the Columbia River drainage to generate electricity, control floods, and provide recreation. Rising 564 feet above the South Fork of the Flathead River, the dam created a lake covering 37 square miles to a depth of 500 feet. The awesome pressure of this volume of water is contained by the mass of the arching dam and its thrust against bedrock abutments on the valley walls.

During the summer a visitor center interprets the functioning of the dam, and there is a free self-guiding tour of the dam and power plant. The 30-foot-wide public highway across the top of the dam leads to U.S. Forest Service campgrounds along the 115-mile gravel road that circles the 34-mile-long reservoir. The road is closed in winter.

From the entrance of Glacier National Park to Lake McDonald the road passes through close-growing

3. Far left: The male white-tailed ptarmigan. Left: The female in laying molt. The color of these small grouse changes from brown in summer to white in winter. The bird population at the Ninepipe and Pablo refuges is about 100,000 in spring and peaks to over 200,000 in fall.

7. These high-altitude wild flowers survive in a severe climate where summers are short. Among the plants you can see in the meadows at Glacier National Park are heather, gentian, beargrass, and the yellow glacier lily, shown here.

"dog-hair" stands of lodgepole pine. These trees can grow in burned areas and have successfully taken over from the hemlock–red cedar forest that burned in 1929.

At a T-junction two miles from the park entrance, the famous 50-mile Going-to-the-Sun Road heads east. However, a short detour to the west loops through Apgar Village, a little community that predates the establishment of the park in 1910.

6 From Apgar you have an inspiring view of glacier-formed Lake McDonald, 10 miles long, a mile and a half wide, and 440 feet deep, the largest lake in the park.

The loop through Apgar rejoins Going-to-the-Sun Road and follows the shore of Lake McDonald for nine miles past many scenic turnouts. Mountain peaks are reflected on the surface of the lake, and the colorful cobbles on the bottom are easily seen through the placid, crystal-clear water. These attractive glacier-borne mudstone boulders were colored red and green by the environment in which the mud was laid down over a billion years ago.

The swamp country a mile above McDonald Falls is an ideal habitat for moose, the largest animal in Glacier National Park. You may also see beaver here.

About three miles beyond the swamp area is Avalanche Campground. There is an interesting interpretive trail along Avalanche Creek, as well as a relatively easy two-mile hike up to Avalanche Lake.

The road north gradually climbs out of the red cedar–hemlock forest and into stands of Engelmann spruce and subalpine fir. Rounding a bend, you see the Garden Wall, with the slash of Going-to-the-Sun Road rising across it. The Garden Wall is a broad cliff that forms a knifelike ridge, very narrow on top. Glaciers not only carved this side of the ridge but the opposite side as well, leaving a wedge of rock between two streams of ice.

As the road climbs at a steady 6 percent grade toward Logan Pass, there are many turnouts from which to enjoy the abundant wildlife. You can nearly always pick out white dots, which are either mountain goats or snow patches on the Garden Wall. If the dots move, they are goats. If you see buff-colored animals on the cliffs, they are mountain sheep. Binoculars are a definite asset here.

7 At Logan Pass you cross the Continental Divide. Water that falls on the west side of this line flows toward the Pacific; water on the cast side rolls toward Hudson Bay or the Gulf of Mexico. The pass was formed when glaciers on both sides of the Divide ground away the ridgeline to create this low point.

Of special interest at Logan Pass are the alpine meadows with their brilliant wild-flower colors and the subalpine fir and whitebark pine trees that are stunted and deformed by their winter battles with the elements here at their highest survival elevation.

A difficult problem for park managers is how to keep nature lovers from trampling the objects of their interest. Life is tenuous at best in an environment where the soil is thin, the winter is nine months long, and snowstorms are no surprise on any day of the year. A careless foot can destroy a flower. Thousands of feet destroy a mountain meadow.

For this reason the National Park Service Visitor Center at Logan Pass has constructed an elevated boardwalk through the "Hanging Gardens" to protect the surrounding plants from foot traffic on this delightful mile-and-a-half trail to Hidden Lake Overlook.

The glaciers in the park, all remnants of a minor ice age that occurred about 4,000 years ago, have melted back drastically during this century. No more than 50 are left, and they all are gradually receding.

8. *This view from Wild Goose Island Overlook of glacier-rimmed St. Mary Lake is the most photographed site in Glacier National Park.* *The small rocky island in the foreground is Wild Goose Island, for years the nesting site of a pair of wild geese.*

From Hidden Lake Overlook you can see this typical glacial lake, sitting in a cirque carved by a glacier that plucked away the rock to form a crescent-shaped array of cliffs.

A mile east of Logan Pass a tunnel bores through a limestone spur of Piegan Mountain, and a snowmelt waterfall sparkles down onto the road at the tunnel's lower end. Below the tunnel, if you pause to look back up toward the pass, there is an excellent view of the glacially formed "horn" shape of Reynolds Mountain, with Reynolds Creek dropping via a waterfall into the thousand-foot-deep valley.

About three miles below the sign for Jackson Glacier, a road cut passes through red mudstone called Grinnell Formation. A small turnout provides an opportunity to stop for a closer look at the colorful rock. Here too is a view of Reynolds and Heavy Runner mountains rising above the Engelmann spruce and lodgepole pine forest. Very different from the lush hemlock–red cedar forest on the west slope, these trees reflect a drier climate in the rain shadow east of the mountains.

8 All travelers here look forward to reaching St. Mary Lake. Ten miles long, as much as a mile wide, and 246 feet deep, it is the second largest lake in the park. From a point about 10 miles below Logan Pass is the most popular photographic view in the park and includes Wild Goose Island in the foreground. The distant view is a perfect example of how glaciers straighten a river valley, steepen its sides, broaden its floor, and carve the peaks above into dramatic forms.

At St. Mary the road pulls away from the mountains onto the rolling plains. In the Blackfeet Indian Reservation the open prairies are cut by hollows containing lodgepole pine, aspen, spruce, and fir. Gradually the trees become more and more sparse, and your eye is drawn to the ragged outline of mountains cutting across the western horizon.

The prairie slopes very slightly to the east, and road cuts reveal beds of water-rounded gravel just below the surface. You can easily imagine the whole area as one continuous plain before streams cut the gullies and hollows.

9 In the midst of these wheat- and cattle-producing plains sits Browning, a Blackfoot town and the headquarters of the tribe's reservation and government since 1895.

The clothing, tools, ornaments, and other artifacts made by Plains tribes are well displayed here in a permanent collection at the Museum of the Plains Indian. There are also changing exhibits by contemporary Indian artists and a sales shop with authentic and unusual Indian arts and crafts.

Route 89 winds across wheat- and hay-covered prairies to Choteau, where the culture of white plainsmen is preserved at the Teton Trail Village, a collection of pioneer buildings and artifacts.

10 Freezout Lake Waterfowl Area is a 12,000-acre preserve 15 miles south of Choteau. Here gravel roads wind along marshes that may serve a million waterfowl during migration, including as many as 300,000 snow geese and 10,000 whistling swans.

Wheat and barley are planted in the refuge to keep the hordes of waterfowl from disturbing the crops of nearby farmers. The habitat has been improved with islands for nesting, windbreaks for cover, and dikes to ensure a constant water supply. The most spectacular times to visit are late March and April or September, October, and early November.

11 Among the bluffs and buttes and fields of barley and wheat, Great Falls sits on the Missouri River. Named for a series of five waterfalls and their intervening rapids, this city is one of the largest in Montana. However, its growth has been at the price of the falls, whose grandeur have been diminished by the construction of power plants.

Downstream from Black Eagle Falls is the Giant Springs Heritage State Park and Fish Hatchery. One of the largest springs in the world, Giant Springs pours 134,000 gallons per minute into the Missouri River at a constant temperature of 52°F. A constant spring provides a good source of water for raising trout at the fish hatchery, which is open to visitors. Also scattered about the nicely landscaped grounds of the park are interpretive signs about the expedition of Lewis and Clark, who first described Giant Springs and the Great Falls.

Not to be missed in Great Falls is the attractively designed Charles M. Russell Museum, at 12th Street and 4th Avenue North, which has a large collection of this western artist's paintings and sculpture. Russell lived in Great Falls, and few artists have been so successful at interpreting America's frontier heritage.

In the log studio here where Russell worked, everything, including brushes, paints, and artifacts used as models for his detailed paintings, is much as it was when the artist died in 1926. His home, adjacent to the studio, is also preserved as a memorial.

You can discern that the topography along Route 15 between Great Falls and Ulm is the background for many of Russell's paintings. However, strip cropping to prevent soil erosion has replaced the prairie grasses that Russell used as setting for his bison, Indians, and cowboys.

12 From the Ulm exit, a gravel road leads to the Ulm Pishkun State Monument. *Pishkun* is a Blackfoot word for a "buffalo jump," to which herds of bison were stampeded via lanes with sides of stone that guided them to the top of a cliff. The bison in back pushed those in front over the edge, and the herd was easily dispatched by Indians waiting below.

For thousands of years this was a common hunting technique. The Europeans' introduction of the horse and the gun to the plains established a horse-nomad culture, enabling the Indians to hunt bison effectively from horseback. At the jump site there is an interpretive trail that loops around the cliff.

You may want to see the prairie dog town near the park entrance. Once as common as bison, these amusing rodents have been drastically reduced in number by poisoning because of their competition with cattle and sheep for grass. Also, their burrows were considered to be a nuisance and dangerous to livestock, which could stumble in them and break a leg. Another casualty in the war on prairie dogs is the black-footed ferret, a strikingly marked weasel that preyed on the "dogs." Today the ferret is nearly extinct.

At Cascade, Route 15 adjoins the Missouri River as it meanders from the mountains, and a sign at the Hardy exit indicates the Missouri River–Wolf Creek Canyon Recreation Road. Here the Missouri flows between greatly eroded ridges of ancient lavas that were laid down 100 million years ago. The recreation road follows the river for 33 miles among scenic hills covered by ponderosa pine (*Pinus ponderosa*), the official state tree.

There are many campsites and access points for fishing along the river. Look for California gulls overhead or bobbing on the water.

13 At Holter Lake Recreation Site there is a camping and boating area run by the U.S. Bureau of Land Management. In the early years of this century the lake was built on the Missouri River by a utility company to generate electricity.

The road northwest climbs from the town named for Wolf Creek and up the creek itself, past colorfully layered cliffs of sedimentary rock laid down over 300 million years ago and interspersed occasionally by igneous rock extruded about 100 million years ago. Beyond the ponderosa and cottonwoods of Wolf Creek Canyon, the road rises to attractive open cattle country.

14 Following the Middle Fork of the Dearborn River, Route 200 climbs into conifer woodlands before entering Helena National Forest. A mile and a half inside the forest boundary, at Rogers Pass (elevation 5,609 feet), you again cross over the Continental Divide.

On January 20, 1954, the thermometer dropped to a brisk –70°F at a mining camp near the pass, to set a record low temperature for the lower 48 states.

A sign marks the beginning of Blackfoot Canyon, where colonies of beaver have dammed streams to create swamps filled with quaking aspens and cottonwoods. The canyon's ponderosa pines grow unusually tall and are decked with bright green wolf lichen.

Beyond the canyon the landscape opens to a wide, green bowl of lush pastures, broken here and there by hills and rimmed by low mountains. To the north rise the mountains of Scapegoat Wilderness Area in Helena and Lolo national forests.

Prairie dog towns

Prairie dogs, so called because of their "bark" and their habitat, live in "towns" of several hundred burrows. The crater-shaped entrances, as much as a foot high, often lead to more than one home, all connected by tunnels. Paths to areas of grasses and other herbs on which these rodents feed crisscross the well-worn ground of the towns.

Prairie dogs have an elaborate system of communication, as illustrated at the right.

Grooming   Territorial call   Sentinel

Recognition kiss

On this tour *you see ancient rock*
shelters inscribed with Indian picto-
graphs, the site of Custer's Last Stand,
and the huge reservoir backed up in
deep, dramatic Bighorn Canyon. Here
too is the spectacular Wapiti Valley in
Shoshone National Forest, and Yel-
lowstone, the world's first and most
famous national park. Finally, the
Beartooth Highway takes you up to
new heights and across the alpine tun-
dra and Beartooth Pass in Shoshone
National Forest.

1 Pictograph Cave State Monument, tucked into a sandstone cliff
above Bittercreek Valley near Bill-
ings, is named for rock paintings, or
pictographs, covering the largest
cave's walls. More than 100 pictographs, painted with natural pig-
ments, portray events over the centuries up to the time the white man
appeared on the Montana plains.

Although archeologists removed
all artifacts from the caves in 1937,
paved and dirt paths are equipped
with signs that explain their findings
about the caves' inhabitants.

Taking the Lockwood exit from
Route 90, you turn right at once onto

2. The male sharp-tailed grouse, 17 inches
long, performs the mating dance with tail
raised, wings dropped, and feet stamping as
he makes low cooing sounds

Coburn Road. The final 2½ miles to
the monument are unpaved and im-
passable when wet.

As Route 90 heads east to Hardin
and the Crow Indian Reservation, it
traverses rolling grassland, dotted
here and there by junipers. South of
Hardin, more trees, mostly cottonwoods, line the highway along the
well-watered banks of a famous
river—the Little Bighorn.

The surrounding territory was a
Crow reservation, but in June 1876
the Crows' enemies—Cheyennes and
a few Arapahos and Sioux under the
Sioux warrior Sitting Bull—
trespassed on their land in the biggest
congregation of Indians ever assembled on the plains.

Crow scouts accompanied U.S.
Cavalry units that set out to force the
trespassers back onto their own reservations. The Bureau of Indian Affairs, misjudging the situation, told
the army that only 800 warriors were
involved. The fact was that 10,000 to
12,000 Indians had joined Sitting
Bull's forces, including some 4,000
warriors who were among the best
cavalrymen on earth, many of them
armed with the latest repeating rifles,
which they had obtained from reservation traders.

When an army unit encountered
them on Rosebud Creek, east of the
Little Bighorn, the Indians fought the
army to a standstill, forcing it to
withdraw. Exultant over their success, the Indians moved their camp to
the Little Bighorn Valley.

Lt. Col. George A. Custer, leading
one arm of a pincer movement, and
unaware of the Rosebud battle,
rushed his cavalry into a position
where he could block an expected
Indian retreat as another army unit
advanced.

Custer, realizing that some Sioux
had seen his force of about 600 men,
feared the enemy would escape the
trap. He divided his exhausted column into four units to surround and
attack a superb, eager-to-fight army,
which he was unaware outnumbered
him five or six to one.

2 The result of Custer's attack—
more than 260 U.S. soldiers, scouts,
and helpers killed—is graphically de-
lineated by white marble memorial
slabs on the slopes at Custer Battlefield National Monument. Most of the
victims are buried in a common grave
near where Custer and about 50 men
made a brief last stand amid a breast-
work of dead horses.

Except for the white markers, the
battlefield looks much the same as it
did on that blistering June 25 afternoon. Native grasses and sage cover
the hill. Sharp-tailed grouse still
scurry through the grass. Meadowlarks, now Montana's state bird, still

1. The peaceful Little Bighorn River meanders through the valley where thousands of
Indians once camped, readying to fight the U.S. Cavalry. Mounds in the foreground are
eroded remnants of sediments laid down in a lake that once filled the basin.

sing as sweetly as they did when Custer's men galloped to destruction.

A road connects the hill where Custer died to a hill five miles away, where the rest of his divided force united and, though suffering heavy casualties, managed to hold off the Indians until the afternoon of the next day. The Indians slipped away, and the besieged soldiers were rescued by the other army column, advancing up the Little Bighorn. A paved, self-guiding interpretive trail connects 18 points of interest along the loop of the defense perimeter.

After you cross into Wyoming and head west, you can see the highway switchbacking up the Bighorn Mountains. These mountains rose while the valley sank along a crack in the earth's crust over 60 million years ago. At a road cut where you enter Bighorn National Forest, the bends created in rock layers by movement along this fault are clearly displayed.

3 About three miles inside the forest, Sand Turn Observation Point gives an excellent view of the Tongue River valley below and of the Fallen City, an aptly named jumble of huge boulders a short way above. A likely place to see elk in winter is along Route 14 in the Tongue River Big Game Winter Range, near Dayton, Wyoming.

4 The three-mile gravel road to the Medicine Wheel is good, but it crosses a narrow ridge where the view from each side is either fantastic or frightening, depending on your susceptibility to acrophobia.

The Medicine Wheel, probably about 600 years old, is one of several of these mysterious circles of stone found along the eastern slopes of the Rockies in the United States and Canada.

This circle on Medicine Mountain is the most elaborate, with a diameter of 80 feet. A large cairn sits in the center, and 28 irregularly spaced rock spokes radiate from it to the rim. Smaller cairns are positioned around the rim.

5 Probably more significant as an example of future energy sources than the hydroelectric potential of Bighorn Lake is the National Park Service Visitor Center for Bighorn Canyon National Recreation Area at Lovell, Wyoming. This innovative

dark red brick building utilizes solar collectors to supply about 50 percent of its heat. A small pond increases the efficiency of the solar system by reflecting more energy into the collectors. Inside the center you can see various exhibits as well as motion pictures about the area. Lovell proudly calls itself the "Rose Town of

Wyoming" because of the many rose gardens that decorate two city parks and most homes.

Almost 30 miles before you reach Cody, you can see the jagged square top of its local eminence, Heart Mountain, rising above the productive irrigated alluvial fields of the Shoshone River valley.

6 Cody is named for William F. "Buffalo Bill" Cody, the colorful scout and showman who settled in this area and promoted it as a gateway to Yellowstone National Park. The main attraction of the town is the Buffalo Bill Historical Center, which has four fascinating museums that memorialize the art and culture of the American West.

The Buffalo Bill Museum contains memorabilia of the showman's life, and in the Winchester Museum is a collection of more than 5,000 projectile weapons that outline the complete story of firearm development.

The Whitney Gallery of Western Art has a notable collection of the work of the finest painters and sculptors of the American West, including Charles Russell, Frederic Remington, Albert Bierstadt, Carl Bodmer, and Alfred Miller.

The outstanding Plains Indian Museum displays an extensive treasury

6. At Old Trail Town the singletrees and doubletrees in the foreground, used as part of a wagon hitch, are a dramatic reminder of a slower, simpler way of life. Note the pile of horns at the extreme right and the buildings' false fronts.

of artifacts that explain the Plains Indians' life-style, religion, traditions, and art.

Another attraction at Cody is Old Trail Town, a collection of historic Wyoming buildings and relics, as well as the graves of celebrated frontiersmen who have been reburied here.

Buffalo Bill Dam is located in Shoshone Canyon. Completed in 1910, it was the first concrete arch dam in the world and backs up the Shoshone River to form Buffalo Bill Reservoir, the core of Buffalo Bill State Park.

The dam can best be seen from pull-offs at each end of a series of three tunnels through a buttress of Rattlesnake Mountain, which supports the north end of the dam.

Beyond Buffalo Bill Reservoir, the route follows the North Fork of the Shoshone River through lovely Wapiti Valley with its rather stark, rolling sagebrush hills and lush, irrigated hay pastures.

7 Yellowstone is the world's first and most famous national park—deservedly so. No place on earth has a wider variety of natural wonders.

Yellowstone Lake, 20 miles long and 14 wide, with a shoreline of 110 miles enclosing 137 square miles of water as deep as 320 feet, is like an inland sea. One of the best spots from which to view the lake is Lake Butte, at the end of a one-mile spur that rather suddenly cuts to the right about nine miles west of Sylvan Pass.

Most of Yellowstone Lake is in a basin formed 600,000 years ago, when indescribable eruptions covered thousands of miles with volcanic pumice and ash. After the sudden removal of so much volcanic material, the surface of the ground collapsed, forming a large caldera that is now partially occupied by the lake.

West Thumb Geyser Basin, just west of the lake, has colorful bubbling paint pots and hot springs.

7A An alternate drive takes you to the Hayden Valley, an ancient glacial lake bed that now is a good place to spot such large waterfowl as trumpeter swans and Canada geese, as well as bison and moose. At the upper end of the valley is a collection of dramatic hot-water features.

8 The geyser Old Faithful is the most popular attraction in the park and a national symbol. Yellowstone has the world's largest collection of geysers and hot springs. These indicate that there is still volcanic activity not far below the surface.

Whereas the vast majority of the millions of annual visitors see these wonders in summer by car, the hot springs and geysers of Yellowstone are most spectacular in winter. Most roads are closed to cars but not to snow coaches and snowmobiles. A park concessionaire uses clanky but warm over-the-snow vehicles to haul visitors from the south and west entrances to scenes made dramatic by the contrast of fire and ice.

On the way to the Upper Geyser Basin, which includes Old Faithful, Castle Geyser, Morning Glory Pool, and many other highlights, the road crosses the Continental Divide twice in 17 miles. Down the Firehole River from the Upper Geyser Basin, the road passes through Midway and Lower geyser basins, where boardwalks and side roads lead to all sorts of bubbling, gurgling, hissing sulfurous marvels. The Fountain Paint Pots Trail in Lower Geyser Basin reveals a wider variety of such features than any other trail in the park.

9 At Artist, Inspiration, or Lookout points you can view the sublime spectacle of the upper Grand Canyon of the Yellowstone. Here hot water and steam have discolored the volcanic rock, changing it to the yellow for which the canyon-cutting Yellowstone River is named.

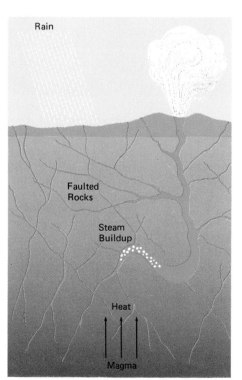

8. *The eruptions of the geyser Old Faithful (left) probably result from water seepage collected in a "gooseneck", created by faulting and fracturing of the bedrock. Heated by molten rock (magma) below, steam is generated to blow out the cooler water above it in the vent. This usually occurs at intervals that average 60 minutes. Shorter intervals between eruptions seem to indicate stresses in the earth's crust and are sometimes used to warn of impending quakes.*

Thermal pool

Fumaroles (steam vents)

Mud pot

9. *From Inspiration Point you can watch the bottle-green Yellowstone River spill up to 60,000 gallons of water a minute over the awesome Lower Falls.*

11 Petrified wood is a relatively common fossil, but it is found in an uncommon form in Yellowstone. Unlike most petrified "forests," those of Yellowstone are still standing upright. Mountain man Jim Bridger, who first reported these fossils, claimed that the petrified forests were populated by petrified birds singing petrified songs. Bridger exaggerated a bit, of course, but when surrounded by a modern forest, the stone tree trunks of Yellowstone are lifelike enough to give the appearance of living trees.

The Yellowstone trees were killed and buried during sporadic volcanic eruptions of breccia, ash, and dust. After the trees were buried, their organic tissue was so exactly replaced by dissolved minerals that many of the petrified trees are identifiable. Here, turned to stone, you will see maple, sycamore, magnolia, and redwood, to name a few. The only petrified tree close to the road is on a well-marked side road about 18 miles east of Mammoth.

12 In the midst of the switchbacks is the large parking lot of Rock Creek Vista Point in Montana. The vista point's railing-enclosed platform is reached by a paved and easy 800-foot walk. A glacially altered valley's distinctive U-shape is clearly seen in Rock Creek Valley to the west.

About a mile south of Artist Point are the Upper Falls of the Yellowstone, which drops 109 feet, and the Lower Falls, which plummets 308 feet—a breathtaking spectacle that makes them one of the most photographed features of the park. Ospreys nest on multicolored pinnacles standing out from eroded canyon walls. These magnificent birds complement the canyon, wheeling and soaring below the rim, looking for fish in the river.

Note that this is the terminus of alternate drive 7A, which is described on page 316.

10 A left turn from Tower Junction takes you on a 16-mile side trip to Mammoth Hot Springs. Hot water dissolves limestone beneath the earth and comes to the surface at Mammoth, where the water cools and deposits the limestone in a series of delicately tinted terraced pools.

Beartooth Pass, about 65 miles east of Tower Junction, is the highest point on the road, 10,940 feet above sea level.

Below Twin Lakes, the Beartooth Highway contorts itself into a series of switchbacks that far out-twist those west of the pass. Five times in 10 miles the highway doubles back on itself, dropping 6,000 feet.

10. *Minerva Terrace at Mammoth Hot Springs was formed by hot water evaporating while seeping through rock rich in calcium carbonate, thus creating travertine terraces.*

Scenic Symbol of the West

Wyoming—storied land of cowboys and Indians where the Great Plains meet the Rockies

The geologic terminology "basin and range" does scant justice to Wyoming's awe-inspiring landscape, but it does help to explain its structure. The area was formerly covered by seas whose sediments were compressed to form thousands of feet of rock. About 60 million years ago the sedimentary rocks laid down by these seas were thrust on edge, folded, and broken in some places. In others the rocks were depressed to form basins. As they pushed upward, the young mountains were eroded by wind and water, a continuing process that has created the spectacular peaks and canyons you see here today.

The treeless basin lands are the realm of cattle and of the cowboy, whose emblem is seen on license plates and road signs. Here too is the pronghorn (often called antelope), the swiftest runner on the continent. Within the basins are large deposits of the fossil fuels: coal, oil, and natural gas; and in the mountains there is timber. But Wyoming's prime asset is its dramatic landscapes and sparkling beauty.

As you follow the Bozeman Trail south of Sheridan, you traverse some fine cattle country and pass many battle sites where the Indians tried in vain to stem the tide of white emigrants. Heading west from Buffalo, the road climbs through the magnificent Bighorn Mountains and then descends through the Tensleep Canyon to the Bighorn Basin. Following the Bighorn River to Greybull, the route then heads east to cross the Bighorns at Granite Pass. The eastern slope is a prime habitat for wildlife, and the Powder River valley is a home on the range for prosperous ranchers.

1 Sheridan is an economic center for surrounding ranching and mining activities. The multigabled Sheridan Inn represents the town's traditional role in these western industries and is a national historic landmark. Built in 1893 by railroad and land interests, the inn boasted such notable guests as Presidents Theodore Roosevelt, William Taft, and Herbert Hoover. Buffalo Bill Cody, the most colorful

guest, purchased a part-interest in the hotel in 1894. From its porch Cody auditioned local cowboys for his Wild West Show.

2 The Bradford Brinton Memorial near the town of Bighorn is typical of the region's more prosperous ranches. The large 20-room ranch house features antique furnishings, ranching artifacts, and Brinton's extensive collection of western art and rare books. Antique wagons and buggies are displayed on the grounds, and cattle and horses graze the pastures. The ranch is located at the end of a road lined with cottonwood (*Populus sargentii*), the official state tree. It is closed from Labor Day to May 15.

3 The State Bird Farm, operated by the Wyoming Game and Fish Commission, is primarily concerned with producing 12,000 Chinese ring-necked pheasants for release each year on Wyoming hunting grounds. The success of this program is evidenced by the pheasants you may often see along the roads. Staff members say that from mid-May to early June is the best time to visit. At that time the most interesting aspects of pheasant production are taking place. To reach the bird farm, turn east onto a gravel road at the northern edge of Bighorn. It is about a three-mile drive through ranchland.

For a few miles Route 87 follows the Bozeman Trail, named for John Bozeman who, in 1863, scouted this shortcut from eastern Wyoming to newly discovered gold diggings in Montana. The trail saved hundreds of miles, but it also cut across hunting grounds with large herds of bison, and the Sioux and Cheyennes opposed its use. Battles ensued, and the trail became known as the Bloody Bozeman. It presented such danger that the U.S. Army allowed no caravans of less than 100 wagons to take the route. The Indians outnumbered the soldiers, knew the land intimately, and were well trained for plains warfare. Only courage and discipline enabled the army to hold the trail, but discipline broke down on December 21, 1866, when an officer named William Fetterman disobeyed orders and led 80 troopers into a trap set by the

Indians. None of the soldiers survived the battle now known as the Fetterman Massacre. A large pillar of cobbles overlooks Route 87 at the battle site.

4 At Fort Phil Kearny National Historic Landmark, not a trace remains of what had been an important fort on the Bozeman Trail. In 1868 it was abandoned by the army and promptly burned by the Indians. The Bozeman Trail was closed. By then, however, its usefulness had already lessened with the completion of rail

3. The showy ring-necked pheasant, which is bred at the State Bird Farm, is a popular target of Wyoming hunters.

SPECIAL FEATURES

ROAD GUIDE	HIGHLIGHT	**1**
STATE PARKS	SKI AREAS	
With Campsites ▲ Without Campsites △	SCHEDULED AIRLINE STOPS	
RECREATION AREAS	OTHER AIRPORTS	
With Campsites ▲ Without Campsites △		
SELECTED REST AREAS	MAJOR MTN. ROADS	
POINTS OF INTEREST	CLOSED IN WINTER	Closed in Winter

ROAD CLASSIFICATION

CONTROLLED ACCESS HIGHWAYS
(Entrance and Exit only at Interchanges) — Interchanges

PAVED HIGHWAYS

LOCAL ROADS In unfamiliar areas inquire locally before using these roads   Paved   Gravel   Dirt

MILEAGE

MILEAGE BETWEEN TOWNS AND JUNCTIONS 3 4   MILEAGE BETWEEN DOTS • 35 •

SCALE

ONE INCH 23 MILES   0   5   10   20   30
ONE INCH 37 KILOMETERS   0   5 10   20   30   48

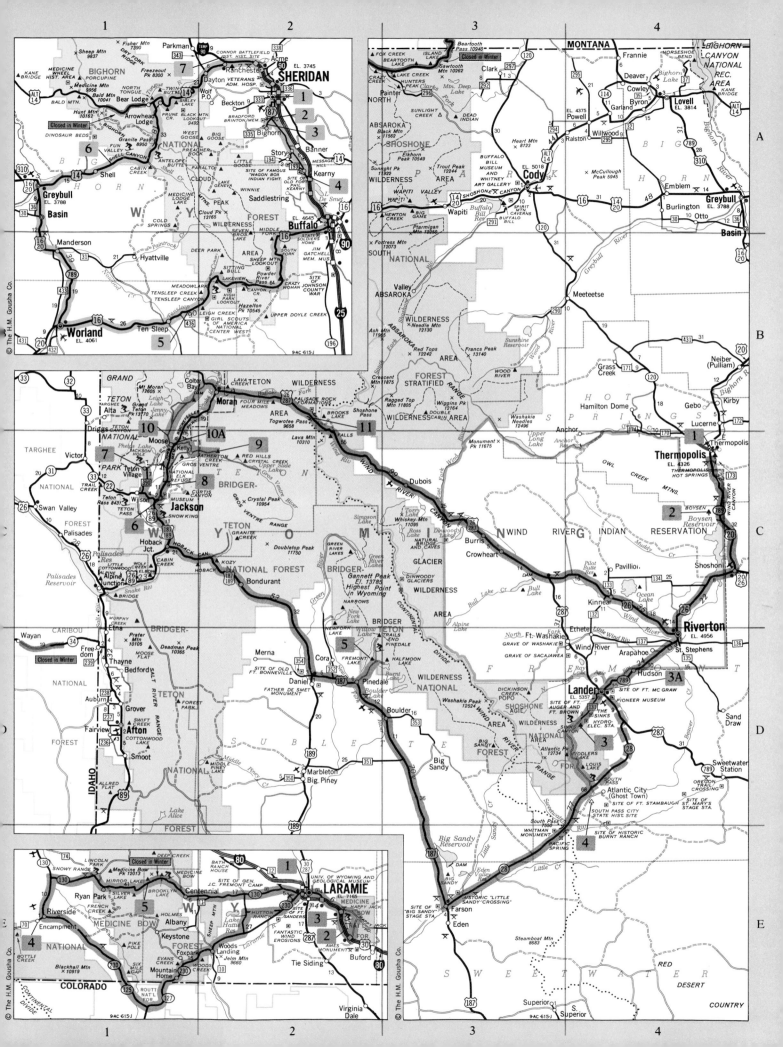

4. *A geologist's delight, the Bighorn Mountains were formed by tremendous forces that distorted once-level layers of rock into enormous bulges called anticlines. This spectacular formation was created over millions of years. Its highest point is Cloud Peak.*

lines farther south. Markers interpret the events that occurred at the fort and the nearby battlefields.

At Buffalo the road begins to ascend the Bighorn Mountains, winding gradually up through ponderosa pine and quaking aspen. Cattle paths crisscross grassy hillsides, and beaver ponds dot the watercourses. Visible always to the north and west are the craggy alpine towers of Cloud Peak Wilderness, named for the 13,165-foot summit of the Bighorns. Lodgepole pine replaces ponderosa by the time you reach 9,666-foot Powder River Pass. Surrounding the pass are the grass-covered hills of an open tableland, bordered by a forest of Engelmann spruce and subalpine fir.

Tensleep Creek cuts a scenic gorge through the Bighorns. Beyond Meadowlark Lake the road descends below pink-and-yellow banded cliffs with overhangs, caves, and natural arches. Formations of brilliantly colored rock border the creek where the canyon opens onto Bighorn Basin.

5 Green lawns surrounding trout ponds and water raceways mark Wigwam Rearing Station, the largest trout-spawning facility in Wyoming. Rimmed by red cliffs on one side, the station's 420 acres are contained on the other by Tensleep Creek, whose waters sometimes supply the ponds. Most of the 3.6 million gallons flowing daily through the raceways comes from two springs and a well that supply water at a constant temperature of 50° F. The temperature is an important factor because trout grow

A Trail Walk in the Bighorns

For a fine walk through this subalpine forest, turn south onto an unpaved road 6.8 miles beyond Powder River Pass. After crossing open pastures of sage, the road skirts a fenced off area called the High Park Range Study Plot. The fence was put up in 1953 to keep out grazing animals to help measure the effects of grazing upon vegetation. Plants within the plot are notably higher. The trail begins at the forest edge 1.3 miles from the highway and leads to the High Park Fire Lookout. Allow about 20 minutes for the hike to enjoy the pleasant woodland. The lookout sits at 9,477 feet and gives excellent views of Bighorn National Forest, the high mountains of the Cloud Peak Wilderness, and, far below, blue Meadowlark Lake.

faster and are more disease resistant in cold water with a high content of dissolved oxygen.

A highway sign five miles east of the town of Ten Sleep indicates the turn onto a short gravel road leading to the station's parklike grounds where visitors are welcome.

Rangeland supporting cattle and sheep alternates with corn- and hayfields along the valley of the Bighorn River between Worland and Greybull. Oil and natural gas fields are visible among the highly eroded Badlands edging the valley. This varied landscape is the setting for the town of Greybull, where the route turns east to follow Shell Creek to Shell Canyon.

6 Shell Canyon was created by stream erosion and mass slumping of water-saturated slopes. Along the canyon walls you can see how layers of sedimentary rocks were bent by the uplift of the Bighorns 60 to 75 million years ago. At the bottom of the canyon, Shell Creek has reached hard granite and is now cutting much more slowly.

Informative signs on this and other aspects of Bighorn natural history are found at the interpretive center overlooking Shell Falls, midway between Shell and Granite Pass. At the overlook, paved walkways lead to the rim of a dramatically deep and narrow gorge where the creek has widened a joint in the granite.

Beyond the open uplands of 8,950-foot Granite Pass, the road descends through excellent wildlife habitat and grazing land. Beaver ponds mirror the evergreen spires of spruce and fir. Deer, elk, and moose browse among the willows along stream courses and at the forest edge. At the Tongue River Big Game Winter Range, 7.3 miles east of Sibley Lake, elk may occasionally be seen.

7 More evidence of the Indian wars lies ahead where the road again touches the Bozeman Trail. The Connor Battlefield site, in a riverside park at Ranchester, was the location of an Arapaho camp. In 1865 a party of 330 soldiers under Gen. Patrick E. Connor surprised the encampment, killing 64 Indians and destroying about 250 lodges. Connor subsequently lost his command for carrying the battle to the women and children.

From Hot Springs State Park in Thermopolis, the tour leads through Wind River Canyon, follows the shore of Boysen Reservoir, and crosses a stretch of typical Wyoming cattle country to Sinks Canyon State Park. Beyond the Sinks lie the Wind River Range, the largest and highest range in the state, and South Pass City, a significant historic site and a restored gold-mining town. The town of Jackson is the gateway to the tour's scenic climax, Grand Teton National Park. East of Togwotee Pass the road descends through the Wind River Range, with dramatic views of volcanic cliffs, and enters the grassy rangeland of the Wind River basin.

1 You are not likely to miss Hot Springs State Park at Thermopolis. On Monument Hill a sign made of large white rocks boldly proclaims: "World's Largest Mineral Hot Springs." The springs pour out millions of gallons of 134°F water daily. Originating in mountains 10 miles away, the hot water flows underground and rises to the surface through a geologic fault at Thermopolis. During its time beneath the ground, the water dissolves minerals from the rocks through which it passes. Since hot water can hold more of this material in solution than can cold water, some of the mineral load must be dumped as the water cools on the ground. The resulting deposits are mounds, cones, and terraces, usually of limestone (calcium carbonate) in the form of travertine.

Though most of the Big Springs water flows to the Bighorn River, some is channeled into cooling pools and then on to bathhouses. The park maintains both indoor and outdoor pools for year-round bathing. There are also boardwalks around the terraces, and a large, tree-shaded picnic area. As an interesting sidelight, the state maintains a herd of bison in a scenic setting on red hills above the springs. The animals can be observed along a three-mile loop drive.

2 Boysen State Park rims the 19,560-acre Boysen Reservoir, which is impounded by an earth-filled dam at the narrow southern end of Wind River Canyon. The road runs along the lake for a mile beyond the dam, then leaves the shoreline except at occasional inlets, and finally leads to a 0.8-mile-long bridge that crosses the lake's waters where they back up against gray cliffs. The park, which has camp and picnic grounds, is popular for water sports and fishing.

3 From Lander you can reach South Pass City either by way of a year-round route (see 3A, described on page 322) or via this route, which takes you to Sinks Canyon State Park and then continues on a mountain road open when weather permits.

The Popo Agie (pō-pō′-shĭa) River rises in the glaciers and snowfields of the Wind River Range, but in Sinks Canyon State Park it disappears into the ground and emerges half a mile down the valley. The Indian name Popo Agie translates as "Beginning of the Waters."

To reach the park and the Popo Agie, take Fifth Street (Sinks Canyon Road) out of Lander, and then turn west and continue for 10 miles on Route 131. Prosperous river-bottom ranches line this stretch of the road. About half a mile inside the park a turnout marks the "Rise of the Sinks," a clear spring about 40 feet below an overlook. The cave into which the Popo Agie disappears is near the state park visitor center a half-mile up the road. At the visitor center, exhibits give not only the geological story of

1. The terrace boardwalks at Hot Springs State Park allow close-up views of the dramatic travertine formations created by the cooling mineral waters (above). The brilliant colors of Rainbow Terrace (right) are due mainly to the presence of algae that grow in the warm water. Without the algae, the travertine would be nearly white. Rainbow Terrace superbly displays the happy combination of living algae and lifeless mineral. Beyond the terraces several cooling pools can be seen.

3A. *From a turnout on Route 28 south of Lander the view sweeps northward along the valley of Red Canyon Creek. The stream, bordered by vegetation, cuts through red beds some 160 million years old. Folding has deformed the cliffs and ridgelines, harder layers in the red beds, into a broad basin. Near the skyline are pink and orange sandstones formed 135 million years ago.*

the Sinks but also the fur trade history of the Wind River Range.

The paved road ends at the edge of Shoshone National Forest, a mile beyond the Sinks, but a scenic gravel road continues, climbing into the Wind River Range. After seven miles and a series of switchbacks, you reach Frye Lake, a reservoir that makes an excellent foreground for 13,400-foot Wind River Peak—if irrigation needs have not reduced the lake to a puddle.

Watch for moose in the marshes around Fiddlers Lake and glacial pothole pools. And for the best views of Louis Lake, go to the Forest Service campground on the south shore. Beyond Louis Lake the route descends along Rock Creek, and then climbs again along switchbacks that offer the best vistas of the entire road. **3A** If you opt for the all-weather route from Lander, you skirt the Wind River Range and pass the valley of Red Canyon Creek, a dramatic red bed area. Red beds are sedimentary rocks laid down 135 to 270 million years ago in tidal flat areas of seas that covered Wyoming. These red beds can be shale, sandstone, or siltstone. Coloration is derived from the oxides of iron-bearing minerals in the rocks. At the turnout on Route 28 about 16 miles south of Lander, a vista of varied geology extends from the head of the valley northward.

4 The gravel road to South Pass City State Historic Site wanders past the shafts, pits, and structures of abandoned gold mines for 2.5 miles until it reaches narrow Willow Creek Valley. Here the gold-mining camp of South Pass City boomed just after the Civil War. The town is now being restored by the Wyoming Recreation Commission to the way it was during its heyday in 1869 when it had 2,000 residents, a population that has not been matched since.

During the mid-1800's a flood of emigrants journeyed westward through South Pass, a 29-mile-wide gap in the mountains. Traveling in thousands of rapidly deteriorating covered wagons, they trekked toward new lives and uncertain futures in the Pacific Northwest. Instead of pausing at the pass, they eagerly pushed on over the Continental Divide to see water flowing westward to the Pacific. They found it at Pacific Spring, a slash of green in the gray sage below the viewing point on Route 28. The viewing point, four miles west of the pass, is easily missed.

5 Fremont Lake, the second largest natural lake in Wyoming, is 12 miles long and a mile across at its widest point. Its western shore marks the farthest advance of a glacier that flowed down the valley of Pine Creek until the ice reached a lower and warmer elevation of about 7,500 feet.

Here the ice melted at the same rate at which it advanced, the snout of the ice remaining stationary. The glacier continued to carry rock debris, which it dumped in a ridge at the melting spot. This terminal moraine acted as a dam when the glacier eventually retreated. Fremont Lake is only one of many in the area to form behind a morainal dam.

At Stinking Springs, in Hoback Canyon, preoccupation with scenery may be briefly interrupted while you cope with the odor of hydrogen sulfide. The rotting-cabbage smell comes from a milky-colored, cold-water spring pouring more than 2,000 gallons of sulfur water per minute into the river. The sulfur is from an underground deposit leached by the springwater.

6 The town of Jackson is a supply center for ranches in the area, but its economy revolves largely around tourism and sports. Though nearby Grand Teton National Park is the goal of most visitors, Jackson has its own attractions, including many fine art galleries.

7 At Teton Village, a 2.4-mile aerial tram takes passengers to the 10,450-foot crest of Rendezvous Peak. From the top, the view encompasses the Teton Range, other mountains, and Jackson Hole basin. A "hole" is fur trade jargon for an open valley surrounded by mountains.

8 The National Elk Refuge is managed by the U.S. Fish and Wildlife Service to provide a wintering ground for elk that migrate south from the Yellowstone area. The 8,000 or so elk (the largest herd in the world) are supported by supplemental winter feeding. Having grown accustomed to the intrusion of wagons or trucks bringing hay pellets, the elk are not frightened when horse-drawn sleighs full of spectators glide through the herd. Seeing majestic bulls so close, with the Tetons rising in the background, is a memorable experience. The sleighs run from December 26 to March 31.

Driving north from Jackson, you are not aware of the vista hidden ahead. The valley that contains Jackson is dropped down along a fault, and the fault scarp blocks the Teton Range from view. Suddenly, as the road tops the scarp, the Tetons leap up before you, with one jagged summit after another cutting across the sky. The rugged grandeur of the Tetons—the highest of which is the 13,766-foot Grand Teton—is an expression of their youth in geologic time and of the mechanics of their creation. Although the rocks are more than a billion years old, the uplift creating these peaks was scarcely 10 million years ago, and so they have not had time to erode as much as older mountains. As tilted blocks in the earth's crust, they rise straight up, with no intervening foothills to reduce the visual impact of their 7,000-foot elevation above the terrain.

9 On June 23, 1925, 50 million cubic yards of dirt, rock, and trees suddenly thundered down Gros Ventre ridge, across a valley, and some 400 feet up the side of another ridge. The debris formed a natural dam, impounding Lower Slide Lake. On May 18, 1927, floodwaters ran over the dam, releasing a flash flood that wiped out the town of Kelly. The Gros Ventre Slide is first visible at an unmarked point on Antelope Flats Road, 1.2 miles from Rockefeller Parkway, as a bare gash on the side of a tree-covered ridge to the southeast. For a close-up view, drive through Kelly and continue for 12 miles.

10 The Teton Park Road between Moose and Jackson Lake Junction, five miles west of Moran, hugs the base of the mountains and provides access to the best scenery in the area, but in winter this route is closed north of the Cottonwood Creek Turnout. If you find it closed, take the Rockefeller Parkway, which is open year-round (see 10A, which is described on page 324).

Just north of Moose Village, a half-mile spur off Teton Park Road leads to the unusual Chapel of the Transfiguration. Built of logs in 1925, it is designed so that the peak of Grand Teton is perfectly framed in a window above its altar. The Episcopalian chapel is probably one of the most photographed houses of worship in the United States.

On Teton Park Road, which follows Cottonwood Creek, the mountains towering above are so commanding that many motorists miss seeing the moose along the creek and, in summer and fall, the fields of red Indian paintbrush (*Castilleja linariaefolia*), the state flower, and other wild flowers.

At South Jenny Lake Junction the western skyline presents a very different and even more imposing arrangement, with Teewinot Mountain,

The building of the Tetons

The Teton Range (below) is a Tertiary fault block about 40 miles long and 10 miles wide, formed some 60 million years ago when stresses beneath the earth's crust created a gash in the surface. The Tetons were built when the fault block was tilted downward toward the west, uplifting the eastern side of the block and giving it a steep slope almost 1½ miles high. The jagged peaks were sculpted by glaciers. The uplifting and a great deal of erosion have uncovered a Precambrian complex of ancient crystalline rocks, including schists, gneisses, and granites. Glacial deposits and lake and stream debris at the base of the eastern face cover the valley floor, which was formed by a depressed fault block east of the Teton fault line.

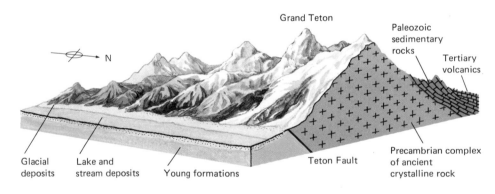

the Grand Teton, and Mount Owen forming a trinity of pointed peaks called the Cathedral Group. For the most classic views of the Cathedral

Togwotee Pass and the Continental Divide at 9,544 feet. To the north the ramparts that form the southern end of the Absaroka Range rise 1,364 feet

A short drive east of Laramie meanders through forested mountains and traverses some unpaved road among the strange Vedauwoo Rocks. West of Laramie the route climbs from rangeland into forest, then dips briefly into rangeland again in Colorado, only to ascend once more through subalpine forests to the tree line in Wyoming's Snowy Range.

1 The name of the city of Laramie commemorates Jacques LaRamie, a French-Canadian fur trader killed by Indians in 1820. Of special interest in the city is the University of Wyoming. The Geology Museum, which has a *Brontosaurus* skeleton and a full-scale model of a *Tyrannosaurus rex*, welcomes visitors, as does the university experimental farm.

Entering the Pole Mountain Division of Medicine Bow National Forest east of Laramie, the highway comes onto crystalline metamorphic rocks 1.4 billion years old and passes between grotesquely eroded masses of pink granite, which are known as the Sherman Mountains. For the best views of this spectacular landscape, take the Happy Jack Road for about 12 miles and then turn southwest onto the Vedauwoo Road, an unpaved six-mile cut through the mountains.

2 The Vedauwoo Picnic Ground, reached by a short spur off Vedauwoo Road, allows you to examine these formations more closely. Huge granite boulders, many larger than a house, balance above picnic tables where families eat secure in the belief that what has stood for so long will continue to stand. The boulders have weathered out of the granite bedrock—erosion having worked inward along natural joints and fractures—and were exposed to view after wind and rain swept away the debris. This area, which offers fishing, ski touring, and camping amid fragrant ponderosa and lodgepole pines, is a year-round attraction.

3 Summit Rest Area, atop 8,640-foot Sherman Hill, is the highest point on Route 80, as it once was on the transcontinental railroad. Above the highway rises a 35-foot pedestal topped by a 13½-foot bust of President Abraham Lincoln, a proponent of transcontinental railways.

Along Route 230 southwest of

11. Five miles east of Togwotee Pass this pinnacled escarpment, banded with white volcanic ash, looms spectacularly above the road. The scarp, which is at the southern end of the Absaroka Range, is being eroded and is slowly receding northward.

Group, especially as reflected in String Lake, turn west at North Jenny Lake Junction and follow the loop drive along String and Jenny lakes back to South Jenny Lake Junction.

The textbook quality of Teton glaciation is seen best from the top of Signal Mountain, reached via a five-mile spur from Teton Park Road.

10A In the event of winter snows, take the Rockefeller Parkway from Moose to Moran. This excellent highway, open year-round, follows the Snake River and crosses sagebrush flats where Park Service turnouts are strategically placed to interpret mountain glaciers, geology, plant life zones, and history. Probably the most popular turnout is Snake River Overlook, where the sinuous line of the river leads your eyes pleasantly up to the classic outline of the Grand Teton.

11 Climbing past beaver ponds and meadows covered with flowers in the summer, the road eastward reaches

above the pass and zigzag across the sky. In the rock walls you see gray layers of volcanic conglomerates and white bands of volcanic ash. Five pine-lined miles down the east side of the pass you round a bend for a startlingly dramatic view of cliffs of the same volcanic rock.

Twelve miles below Togwotee Pass is a white memorial sculpture honoring "tie hacks." Between 1914 and 1946 these loggers, most of whom were Scandinavian, cut and shaped about 10 million railroad ties.

Crowheart Butte appears on the horizon about 30 miles from Dubois. This was the site of a legendary duel in 1857 between chiefs of the Shoshone and the Crow tribes in which the victorious Shoshone took the heart of his victim. Questioned about the truth of the story many years later, the old Shoshone chief would only reply, "A young man does a lot of foolish things."

2. *This unusual granite formation near the Vedauwoo Picnic Ground was originally a massive rock split into blocks by fracture planes. Weather has widened the joints and rounded the corners, creating smooth boulders. Some boulders left "perched" like the one here may wobble in a high wind.*

Laramie, the broad landscape forms a basin bounded on the east by the Laramie Range. The Laramie River, along with numerous tributary lakes, ponds, and streams, drains the basin and makes the highway an excellent drive for viewing waterfowl. Largest of these waterfowl havens is Lake Hattie Reservoir, reached by a short paved road through hayfields.

Occasional logging trucks are encountered as the road climbs through mixed stands of lodgepole pine and quaking aspen in the Snowy Range Division of Medicine Bow National Forest. Crossing the border into Colorado, the road descends through less forested land where cattle can be seen grazing. Swinging northwest and returning to Wyoming, the highway passes ranches that announce their names on large signs above gateways.

The meadowlark, Wyoming's official state bird, can frequently be heard singing a joyful proclamation that the world is beautiful and he is the best bird in it.

4   A copper discovery in 1897 created the town of Encampment, known for years as Grand Encampment because large groups of Indians formerly gathered here. The smelter at this boomtown was fed by a 16-mile-long aerial tramway—at that time the longest tramway in the world. In 1908 Grand Encampment's economic bulwark, the Ferris-Haggarty Mine, was closed. The mining years live on, though, in the Grand Encampment Museum, a reconstructed ghost town with an interpretive center. Guided tours lead through old buildings that have been moved to the site and refurbished.

Special demonstrations, such as arrowhead making, are scheduled. The museum village is closed from Labor Day until the end of May.

5   For more than 40 miles the road climbs from sagebrush flats up long forested slopes with glistening lakes to 10,847-foot Snowy Range Pass and to the Libby Flats Observation Point. Near the pass the forest thins and the few remaining trees sprawl against the rocks. Branches grow only down-wind—an adaptation called "flagging." Above the tree line is arctic-alpine tundra, a life zone where only

5. *Along Snowy Range Road you can see "flagged" trees. One of this trio has not survived the rigors of the climate.*

plants that hug the ground can survive. In the billion-year-old rocks near the road can be seen beautiful examples of stromatolites, some of the world's oldest plant fossils, looking like giant cabbages with their tops truncated by glacial erosion. From the observation point on the pass, the view down past forests to the treeless plains containing Lake Hattie is impressive. Here, within a few road miles, you find the same life zones that you would find by driving several thousand miles from the Wyoming basin country to sea level at the Arctic Circle. The Snowy Range Road is closed during winter.

4. *The reconstructed town of Encampment now has a population of about 700. At the turn of the century a copper strike brought thousands of men into the area seeking riches. Reminders of those days include these buildings.*

Colorful Colorado

Rivers, canyons, plateaus, plains, and soaring mountains create a dramatically varied landscape

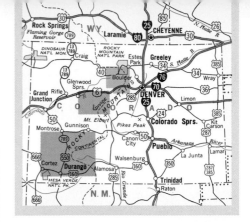

Colorado's lofty landscape, with more than 800 peaks rising above 11,000 feet, has the highest and some of the most spectacular roads in the nation. Seen from these highways are many of the "Fourteeners," as peaks with elevations of more than 14,000 feet are called. When the snows come, many of the mountain passes are closed, and the perpetual snowbanks bordering the roads at the highest elevations can be festooned with additional flakes during any day of the year.

As you gain 5,000 feet of elevation on a few miles of mountain road you pass through the same sequence of plant communities that you would encounter on a drive of thousands of miles north to the Arctic Circle.

The farther north you go, the later the spring, as signaled by the early-blooming flowers.

The gold of the aspens takes over with the arrival of autumn, and as winter, which has been lurking around the summits, finally descends to cover the lower slopes with snow, the color continues. The remarkable cobalt color of the sky caused by the low light dispersion of thin mountain air casts its brilliant blue upon the frosty white, bringing to full circle the year-round beauty for which the state is famous.

From the colorful village of Georgetown, the road westward crosses broad open ranchland below the peaks of Eagles Nest Wilderness. Beyond the lakes of the Arapaho National Recreation Area, you enter Rocky Mountain National Park, a 410-square-mile wildlife sanctuary where among the many spring delights is the blue columbine (Aquilegia caerulea), the state flower.

Trail Ridge, the nation's highest through highway, rises above the tree line to a broad alpine tundra, an area higher than the glaciers that shaped the steep-walled canyons below.

Broad lakes and mountain passes mark the landscape as the route circles southward through some of Colorado's historic mining country, where remnants of more active days are still visible on the flanks of the mountains.

1 Georgetown, known in the gold rush days as Silver Queen of the Rockies, contains prime examples of the western adaptation of elegant Victorian architecture in the styles of classic revival. The well-preserved and restored 19th-century residences of this famous mining center attest to the affluence brought to the area in the late 1800's by the $200 million in silver extracted from the surrounding mountains.

Several of Georgetown's buildings are open as museums. Among them is the Hamill House, a century-old mansion acquired in 1874 by silver baron William A. Hamill, who later enlarged the house and added several outbuildings. Also on view is the restored Hotel de Paris, a bit of old Normandy set down in the Rockies. The hotel was run by one Louis Depuy, who became known for his complete disregard for the interests and feelings of his guests.

The historic Georgetown Loop, a railroad line that opened in 1884 and ran between Silver Plume and Georgetown carrying passengers, ore, and freight, has been restored and is once again making the 2½-mile daily run. Stops are scheduled along the railroad where the old mines can still be seen.

1A The road westward takes you over the scenic 11,992-foot Loveland Pass through 21 miles of superb landscape. However, due to snow this highway is sometimes closed in winter. You can bypass this drive by choosing to go through the Eisenhower Memorial Tunnel, which pierces the Continental Divide almost 1,600 feet below the crest.

2 The old mining town of Dillon now lies under Dillon Reservoir, which was completed in 1964 to provide water for ever-thirsty Denver. New Dillon, a center for skiing, dog racing, and sailing, is a planned resort community set in the midst of spectacular mountain scenery.

The almost two-mile-high reservoir, like all those in Colorado, is drawn down in summer, exposing the shoreline. The lake must wait for the winter snows to melt before it will again be filled.

Confusing Parks

The western custom of calling any open grassy valley surrounded by tree-covered mountains a "park" is often baffling to visitors. Unlike city, state, and national parks, these areas have no specific boundaries and are not reserved for public use.

Some of these so-called parks, like the one through which Colorado's Blue River flows, are several miles long and wide. These were formed by the subsidence of large fault blocks during the uplift of the Rockies 60 million years ago.

Others, such as those that cover only a few acres, were caused by the more recent phenomenon of glaciation or even, perhaps, by siltation of a pond behind a beaver dam.

Because these open meadows, excellent areas for grazing and growing crops, were favored by 19th-century homesteaders, several towns, such as Estes Park, Meeker Park, and Allenspark, have grown up in these areas and have taken their name from the park name, causing confusion for many a visitor to these wide open and lofty places.

SPECIAL FEATURES

ROAD GUIDE	▬▬▬	HIGHLIGHT	**1**
STATE PARKS With Campsites ♠ Without Campsites △		SCHEDULED AIRLINE STOPS	✈
RECREATION AREAS With Campsites ▲ Without Campsites △		MILITARY AIRPORTS	✠
SELECTED REST AREAS	⊼	OTHER AIRPORTS	✦
POINTS OF INTEREST	⊡	MAJOR MTN. ROADS	▬▬▬
SKI AREAS	⚐	CLOSED IN WINTER	Closed in Winter

ROAD CLASSIFICATION

CONTROLLED ACCESS HIGHWAYS
(Interstate interchange numbers are mileposts.)

Interchanges

OTHER DIVIDED HIGHWAYS

PAVED HIGHWAYS

LOCAL ROAD   In unfamiliar areas inquire locally before using these roads   Paved   Gravel   Dirt

MILEAGE

MILEAGE BETWEEN TOWNS AND JUNCTIONS   3 ⁄ 4   MILEAGE BETWEEN DOTS   ● 35 ●

SCALE

ONE INCH 20 MILES   0   5   10   15   25

ONE INCH 32 KILOMETERS   0   5 10   20   30   40

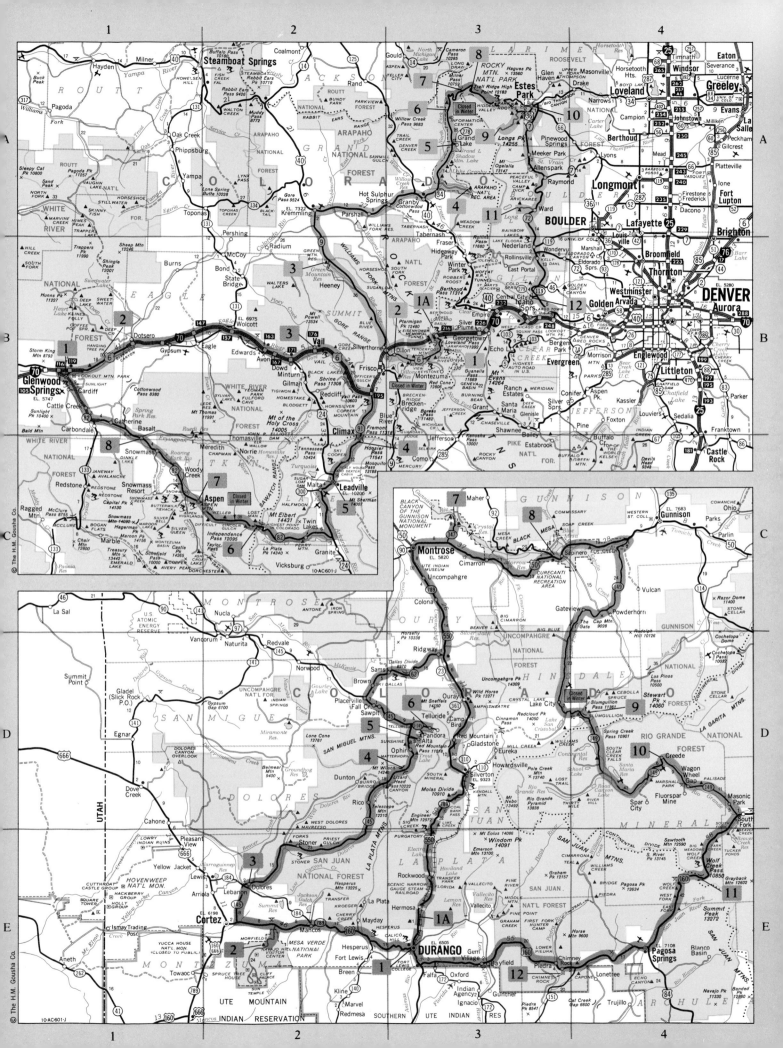

3 The road along the Blue River runs through a scenic park north of Dillon. Towering above the park is the magnificent Gore Range in Eagles Nest Wilderness. These 13,000-foot-high peaks overlook great stretches of pastoral sage and grasslands in the Arapaho National Forest. Green Mountain Reservoir reflects all this magnificence, except when it has been drawn down to a puddle.

4 The Arapaho National Recreational Area, which has five lakes and covers 36,000 acres in a glacier-gouged valley near the headwaters of the Colorado River, was once known as the Shadow Mountain National Recreation Area. Renamed and enlarged in 1978, it is still listed by its old name in some guidebooks to the area. There are conducted nature walks, wilderness hikes, and campfire programs during the summer, when boating, fishing, and picnicking are also available.

Here the rolling terrain is a combination of glacial debris and outwash, covered by lodgepole pine and aspen. Many of the islands in the area's lakes are tops of moraines, glacial deposits left behind when the ice melted. In the distance are the heavily forested mountains in adjacent Rocky Mountain National Park and Indian Peaks Wilderness.

5 Grand Lake, Colorado's largest natural body of water, is a center for water sports. The town of Grand Lake, on the north shore, claims to have the highest yacht club in the world. Although it is part of the state's irrigation system, this lake is never drawn down, its level having been guaranteed before the system was approved and built.

As the road enters Rocky Mountain National Park, just beyond Grand Lake, it climbs among the forests and meadows of the Kawuneeche Valley, offering intermittent views of reddish peaks in the Never Summer Range. Deer and elk are frequently seen here in their favorite habitat of forest-edged meadow.

6 Nine miles north of Grand Lake is the Holtzwarth Homestead, part of the Neversummer Ranch, which the National Park Service operates as a museum. During the summer, park personnel in period costumes give tours of the 1915 dude ranch, explain-

3. Green Mountain Reservoir, a part of the extensive Colorado irrigation system, is overshadowed by the snowcapped peaks of the Gore Range in the Eagles Nest Wilderness. Sagebrush and grasslands border the reservoir. This area of the Arapaho National Forest has some of the finest trails for backpacking in the Rockies.

ing the horse-drawn haying machinery and offering slices of freshly baked bread from the old-fashioned wood-burning oven.

7 At Milner Pass a Park Service sign explains how water on one side of the Continental Divide eventually flows into the Pacific, while that on the other side reaches the Atlantic and the Gulf of Mexico.

7. A bighorn ram feeds on grasses growing in rock crevices. For the protection of these nimble animals, trails through their grazing lands have been closed to visitors.

From the shores of Poudre Lake a steep trail shoots up above the tree line, through magnificent stands of Engelmann spruce and alpine fir, to the Crater Overlook. Although the heavily eroded spires on the western slope of Specimen Mountain do somewhat resemble a volcanic caldera, they are actually remnants of large ash and lava flows from an eroded volcano.

From the overlook you can also see the snow-decked peaks of the Never Summer Range across the Colorado River valley, brilliant carpets of alpine wild flowers, the comical yellow-bellied marmot, and the friendly golden-mantled squirrel. The main attraction here, however, is the bighorn sheep, lured by the mineral licks in the crater and the lush grazing on the tundra slopes. The bighorn sheep is the state animal and the symbol of Rocky Mountain National Park.

8 Alpine tundra is a unique feature of Rocky Mountain National Park. Rarely is tundra so easily reached as along the 11 miles of Trail Ridge Road that extend above the tree line. A Park Service Alpine Visitor Center at Fall River Pass, and a tundra nature trail at the Rock Cut turnout five miles beyond, help to explain this environment. Here you might see the yellow-bellied marmot,

the industrious little pika, which is a round-eared relative of the rabbit, and also Clark's nutcracker—a raucous, entertaining bird that was named for William Clark of Lewis and Clark fame.

Trail Ridge Road, the highest continuous roadway in the nation, reaches its peak elevation of 12,183 feet between Gore Range Overlook and Lava Cliffs turnout, just beyond Fall River Pass.

The forest struggles constantly to overtake the treeless tundra, battling wind and weather for control of the summits. The average elevation of this battle line is 11,500 feet in Rocky Mountain National Park. Trees along this line are called *Krummholz*, German for "elfin" or "crooked wood." Winter winds carry bits of granite and ice that "sandblast" the trees, killing all new growth on the windward side.

As Trail Ridge Road drops down below the tree line it passes two large turnouts—at Rainbow Curve and, five miles farther along, at Many Parks Curve. These are excellent places from which to view traces of the mountain glaciation that occurred a few thousand years ago. Beaver dams and lodges are common sights from a bend of the road a few miles beyond Many Parks Curve.

9 Bear Lake Road, a nine-mile spur that leads through Moraine Park, penetrates some of the most spectacular scenery in Colorado. The road follows Glacier Creek, which is often lined with Colorado blue spruce (*Picea pungens*), the state tree. The Moraine Park Visitor Center offers information on the park's wildlife and the glacial scenery. Rising across the valley floor is the long tree-covered ridge of the lateral moraine that gives the park its name.

Bear Lake itself is circled by a paved nature trail. The lakeshore swarms with wildlife, including an occasional mule deer and elk.

10 "Big T," the Colorado–Big Thompson Project, named for the river and the canyon close to where the headquarters is located, is a series of reservoirs, tunnels, and aqueducts that diverts water from the western slope of the Continental Divide to the thirsty east. The system includes Marys Lake and Lake Estes on the edge of tourist-oriented Estes Park Village. The village is a year-round resort surrounded by icy lakes and streams and snowcapped mountains. There are many campsites and picnic grounds, with excellent skiing and trout fishing available. A tramway up Prospect Mountain offers a view of the Continental Divide.

From Marys Lake the road cuts across the flank of Lily Mountain and descends into Tahosa Valley. The sheer east face of Longs Peak, one of the most dramatic of the so-called Fourteeners, dominates the scene. Easily visible to half the state's population, Longs is among the best-known peaks in Colorado.

11 A three-mile side trip west of the town of Ward to Brainard Lake Recreation Area takes you to the Indian Peaks Wilderness, where you see one of the most startling skylines in Colorado—Navajo, Apache, and Shoshone peaks all in a row.

12 The heart of the Colorado gold rush was located in what is now the Central City–Black Hawk area.

Once called the "richest square mile on earth," Central City, now a national historic district, produced over a half-billion dollars in precious metals during its heyday. While the mines no longer produce commercially profitable quantities of minerals, nearby streams are often lined with amateur gold panners on summer weekends.

Downtown Central City contains the finest collection of 19th-century commercial buildings in Colorado. These include the Opera House, a sturdy structure that still draws packed audiences during summer performances. Central City, with its tours, operas, and crowds of bustling tourists on its narrow, twisting streets, has successfully maintained the mood of a western gold rush boomtown.

8. *The Trail Ridge Road in Rocky Mountain National Park offers spectacular views of craggy rock formations. In this area you can sometimes catch sight of such residents as (from the top) Clark's nutcracker, the curious pika, and the yellow-bellied marmot, related to the prairie dog.*

3. In the center of Vail is the Colorado Ski Museum and Hall of Fame, where displays include the gear of local 19th-century miners, mailmen, preachers, and others, who found that, in this land of snow, skiing was the best way to move about the countryside.

Glenwood Springs, *known for its geothermal pools, is the starting point of a scenic route that traces the cut made by the Colorado River through Glenwood Canyon, whose walls reach up as much as 1,000 feet above the rushing stream.*

Beyond the canyon lie open range-land and irrigated hayfields. As the road continues eastward along Gore Creek, it climbs to Vail, the world-famous ski resort, and continues on to Fremont Pass, the site of the world's largest molybdenum mine.

Mining continues to dominate the scene as you approach Leadville, the highest town in the nation. Across an expanse of grazing lands you can see the outline of Mount Elbert, the highest peak in the state.

From Aspen, a ski and cultural center, there are spur roads that give you access to the much-photographed 14,000-foot Maroon Bells and the ghost town of Ashcroft.

Along the Roaring Fork River is Mount Sopris and a tree nursery named for the peak. Here the U.S. Forest Service raises thousands of seedlings each year to reforest the burned slopes and logged lands of the Rocky Mountains.

1 Glenwood Springs, a year-round resort known as the gateway to the White River National Forest, claims to have the largest hot mineral water pool in the world. The pool, which is visible from the highway, is 600 feet long and has a constant temperature of 85–90° F. It is fed by the waters of nearby Yampah Springs. Also fed by the springs is an outdoor therapy pool, which has a temperature of 102–105° F. Since the springs have a daily flow of 3½ million gallons, the water in both pools changes completely every eight hours.

For generations the Ute Indians soothed their pains at these springs, which years ago flowed in the bed of the Colorado River. At the beginning of the 1880's the main stream of the Colorado was diverted and the hot springwaters channeled to the pools in Glenwood Springs. Both pools are open to visitors year-round.

The town is surrounded by excellent hunting and fishing country, with many campsites and picnic areas. The third weekend in June marks the annual Strawberry Days Festival, when everyone who comes to town is served with a bowl of the fresh berries and cream.

East of Glenwood Springs the road shares with the Colorado River the narrow, 17-mile gorge of Glenwood Canyon. You enter the canyon through a gash cut in the massive layer of gray Leadville limestone laid down on a sea bottom 310–350 million years ago. Today the area is noted for its many marine fossils.

Water by itself would not have cut the gash in the rock, but the Colorado's heavy concentration of silt and gravel works like a rasp. The river's turbulance in spring is awesome, a thundering white-and-brown challenge to rafters shooting the rapids. In fall, however, the wild water becomes calm and reflects in its quiet pools the majestic grandeur of surrounding cliffs.

2 Nine miles into the canyon there is Hanging Tree Park, which has picnic grounds, campsites, and many trails. One trail, 1.2 miles long, leads up to scenic Hanging Lake. The view of Bridal Veil Falls, which drops from the cliff to a 500-foot-wide basin below, is so spectacular that the climb is well worth the effort.

Beyond Glenwood Canyon the road passes through irrigated hayfields and open grazing land and soon follows the Eagle River, a large tributary of the Colorado.

From a scenic overlook 5½ miles east of the town of Eagle you can see snowcapped, glacier-carved Gold Dust Peak and New York Mountain, 12,000-foot summits that tower above typical glacial valleys whose steep sides were created by rivers of ice.

3 Vail is the largest one-mountain ski area in North America and perhaps the most famous. Founded by World War II mountain troops who trained in the area, Vail is a planned community, a pedestrian town where one walks to most of its shops and restaurants. A gondola lift carries skiers and hikers to high-altitude trails with views of the Gore Range and a famous Fourteener, Mountain of the Holy Cross.

The Vail Nature Center, whose headquarters is in a converted farmhouse, is a seven-acre preserve along Gore Creek and well hidden from the highway. Hikers, cross-country skiers, and snowshoers can follow excellent self-guided trails with the help of pamphlets and cassette tapes available at the headquarters, where there are also displays of local plant and animal life as well as a good reference library. Closed Thanksgiving, Christmas, and New Year's days.

4   As you drive over Vail Pass to Copper Mountain's ski complex you wind through magnificent glacier-carved scenery. To the south, close to Fremont Pass, is the AMAX Climax Mine, the largest molybdenum mine in the world. AMAX conducts guided tours of its plant and is doing what it can to minimize the damage to the scenery caused by the removal of this useful ore. The company promises to completely reclaim and replant the site after all the ore is removed, a sizable task that may not be accomplished until the year 2016.

5   Leadville, at 10,152 feet, is the nation's highest incorporated city. The discovery of silver here in the 1870's created a roaring boomtown. More recently, lead, zinc, and molybdenum production have preserved the area's tradition of mining and kept its economy stable.

Leadville looks like a mining town. Well-preserved Victorian homes stand adjacent to commercial structures considerably less attractive. Although never a resort town, Leadville has always drawn visitors. In the 1880's they came to look at the silver barons. Today the lure includes a diverse collection of museums that preserves the memory of the colorful boom times.

Among the best of the museums is Healy House, a substantial Victorian home built in 1878 for one of the silver barons and restored meticulously to its 1899 condition.

Far different from the immaculate grounds and Victorian decor of Healy House is the shack where Baby Doe Tabor died. Baby Doe was a beauty for whom silver baron Horace Tabor left his wife.

The richest of the Tabor mines was the Matchless, which produced as much as $100,000 per month. The silver panic of 1893, however, reduced the Tabors to poverty. In 1899, just before he died, Horace told Baby Doe to hang on to Matchless, saying that it would make millions again.

It never did, but Baby Doe stayed with the diggings until 1935, when she froze to death in a shack, now a museum, at the entrance to the mine that had brought her a fortune.

The two highest peaks in Colorado, Mount Elbert and Mount Massive in the Sawatch Range, are readily visible from Leadville.

6   The road through Independence Pass in the Sawatch Range runs by the large Twin Lakes Reservoir and then crosses the Continental Divide. Through tortuous switchbacks, which are closed from October to mid-June by snow and avalanches, the road brings you with surprising rapidity to the tree line, where there are great expanses of alpine tundra.

A short walk from a parking lot at the pass takes you across a rolling tundra landscape to overlooks, where glacier-carved valleys and peaks can be seen in the distance.

The vertical lanes you see on slopes at either side of the pass are avalanche runs, which generally start on a ridgeline and descend to a fan-shaped base. Everything along these paths is destroyed beneath tons of cascading ice, snow, rock, and debris. A classic avalanche chute is seen on the left of the highway about eight miles down the road from Independence Pass. This chute runs straight down a mountainside to the Roaring Fork River valley.

7   Aspen, in the valley of the Roaring Fork River, was founded by miners from Leadville who went in search of Leadville limestone, a host rock for silver. They found the ore and, with the example of roaring Leadville behind them, set out to establish a more sedate community.

The mines faded from importance in the 1890's, and today the town's economy is based on skiing in winter and artistic endeavors in summer.

6. The ghost town of Independence, named for the pass where it is located in the heart of the Sawatch Range, today has only the remnants of what was once a flourishing 19th-century village of log buildings that served as a center for early prospectors.

Much of the Victorian charm of its early mining days still remains.

Castle Creek Road takes you from Aspen to Ashcroft, a ghost town 11 miles to the south. Along the way there are gabions, wire baskets filled with stones to buttress the road where rock slides occur.

Ashcroft, now a preserved historic

7. *The peaks called Maroon Bells were named for their shapes and for the unusual dark red color of the rock. Known by mountain climbers as the Deadly Bells, the shale and sandstone peaks are so fragile that footholds give way without warning.*

landmark, flourished in 1880, but when the railroads bypassed the town, it quickly declined and eventually became part of White River National Forest.

Maroon Creek Road leads to Maroon Lake, 9½ miles southwest of Aspen, which reflects the splendor of Maroon Bells. These 14,000-foot peaks, located in Maroon Bells–Snowmass Wilderness, are part of the Elk Mountains. Layers of sediments deposited the future mountains here as mud flats 225–270 million years ago. As they were thrust over each other by subsequent mountain building, the formations became severely crumpled. Into their cracks welled molten rock, which carried the minerals sought by miners. Wildlife in these mountains today include coyotes, mountain sheep, deer, moose, and elk.

Beyond Aspen the route follows Roaring Fork River, whose banks are lined with blue spruce and cottonwood. Lush bottomlands give way to forested red sandstone hills.

Although gambel oak turns a striking rusty red in autumn and provides an excellent habitat for wild turkeys and deer, it is considered a weed tree that should be replaced by pines and spruces, which can produce lumber. For this purpose, and for reforesting logged and burned woodlands, the U.S. Forest Service developed Mount Sopris Tree Nursery and named the extensive tree-growing area for the nearby peak.

8 Located near Basalt, the Mount Sopris Tree Nursery grows more than 15 million Engelmann spruce and lodgepole and ponderosa pine seedlings annually.

Although tours are not regularly scheduled, you can arrange with the Forest Service to inspect the nursery.

Southwest Colorado, one of the most scenic and historically interesting sections of America, not only has such awe-inspiring natural wonders as the Black Canyon of Gunnison River but also the man-made Silverton Railroad and the gold-flecked Million Dollar Highway. Here too is Mesa Verde National Park, where hundreds of years ago Indian cave dwellings were built in the cliffs just below the flat tops of the mesas.

In this land of rushing streams, narrow valleys, and 14,000-foot peaks there are vestiges of the last century, when gold and silver drew prospectors from far and near and towns sprang up overnight. Many of these mining centers are now preserved as historic landmarks. Some are still flourishing, and others are but ghostly reminders of their former bustling prosperity.

1 Durango, best known as the southern terminus of the Silverton Railroad, was established in 1880, when the railroad was put through the region. Today Durango is a major shipping center for the farm products grown in the surrounding countryside and for lumber from the San Juan National Forest. It is also popular with fishermen, campers, hunters, skiers, and adventurous rafters who brave the rapids of the Animas River, which was named River of the Souls of Purgatory by Spanish explorers.

1A This alternate drive runs from Durango to Ridgeway through some of the most spectacular scenery in the San Juan Mountains. The route follows the Animas River, passes old mining sites, goes by Electra Lake above Lime Creek Canyon, and crosses the Molas Divide as it approaches Silverton, which is off to the right on a short side road.

Today Silverton, "the mining town that never quit," is still a busy mining center, as it has been ever since the 1860's when the first prospector arrived here.

As the road continues north it becomes what is called the Million Dollar Highway, so named, some say, for the gold-flecked gravel with which it is paved or because its construction cost a million dollars. Others insist that the name comes from the magnificent mountain scenery through which it passes.

As you approach Ouray, another mining town, the road descends along the wall of Uncompahgre Canyon by a series of hairpin turns on narrow ledges that seem to hang directly above the town.

2 West of Durango the road goes through forests of ponderosa pine, juniper, and gambel oak. Aspen groves carpet the flanks of the La Plata Mountains, rising in the distance to the north. The low southern end of this range leads into the Mancos Valley, whose verdant hayfields contrast with the dark oak-green of the mesas.

The rugged, flat-topped prominences here are dominated by an imposing escarpment to the southwest, named Mesa Verde ("green table") by Spanish explorers.

The remarkable ruins of Indian cliff dwellings at Mesa Verde were discovered in the 1870's. In 1906 the Mesa Verde National Park was created to preserve the ruins.

A scenic 21-mile drive takes you from the park entrance at the base of the mesa up to the main ruins at Chapin Mesa.

The Mesa Verde people lived in the cliffs for less than a century. By A.D.

1. The narrow-gauge Durango–Silverton steam railroad runs along the Animas River through the San Juan National Forest.

1300 they had merged with pueblos to the south. The still unanswered question "Why did these people leave?" echos silently among the ruins.

Vantage points along the way offer many fine views of the caves in the

An Historic Railroad

With whistle blasting and steam hissing, the narrow-gauge railroad, which was established in 1883, starts its daily run from Durango to Silverton, chugging out of its quaint depot for a cliff-clinging adventure.

The 44-mile ride runs along narrow cliffside ledges, through deep gorges, along riverbanks, and across trestles, with unexcelled mountain scenery all the way. The trip is especially beautiful in autumn when the yellow of aspens combines with the gaudy shades of the highly mineralized rock of the cliffs.

You can choose the shelter of the original yellow passenger cars (or their look-alikes copied in 1964), or you can opt for a better view by sitting in the open gondola car.

After a two-hour stay in Silverton, a national historic landmark where hard rock mining is still a major industry, the train returns to Durango. If you prefer, you can go back by bus over one of the most scenic roads in America.

The railroad runs daily from June to October. Only by making reservations can you be assured of a seat during the peak summer season.

2. The Cliff Palace, shown here, is the best known of the prehistoric cliff dwellings in Mesa Verde National Park. Recent studies suggest that the tribe left the area because the agricultural methods they had used for hundreds of years had depleted the soil, making it unsuitable for growing adequate food crops.

walls of canyons that cut through the mesa rim.

These canyons began forming 25 million years ago, when sandstone and shale that had been deposited on a shallow sea's floor were heaved up and tilted slightly south. Tributary streams to the Mancos River cut the canyons, leaving the long tablelands or mesas. The rain and melting snow that trickle through the sandstone surface of the mesas emerge along canyon walls as seeps and springs. This water supplied the ancient farmers, but the seeps eventually weakened and undercut the sandstone, leaving alcoves in the cliff faces. Here the Indians built their houses, kivas (underground ceremonial rooms), and storage bins.

As early as the sixth century A.D. farmers worked the top of the mesa, growing corn and squash, raising dogs and turkeys, and hunting deer and bighorn sheep. Some of these game animals are represented by ancient etchings on cliffs at Pictograph Point, which can be easily reached by a short, well-marked trail from the Chapin Mesa Museum.

3 The town of Dolores is long and thin, squeezed between red cliffs that confine the Dolores River valley. Green fields of hay, rustic old barns, and cottonwood trees accent the cliffs, which are covered with deciduous oaks and aspens. Beyond Stoner, blue spruce trees add variety and texture to the hillside scenery.

High peaks of the San Miguel Mountains come into view near Rico, an old mining town of scarred and denuded hillsides and weathered tipples, the structures used for the unloading of ore cars.

4 At Lizard Head Pass you may see sheep grazing on rolling meadows, with Sheep Mountain towering overhead. Immediately beyond the pass is Yellow Mountain, named for the autumn color of the aspens that cover its flanks. In the fall this golden glory, mixed with the cobalt of Colorado skies, is reflected in Trout Lake.

5 The sharp point of Wilson Peak dominates the scenery as you descend the San Miguel Valley through Uncompahgre National Forest. One of the most interesting views of Wilson is from the ghost town of Alta. This much weathered, well-preserved collection of old houses and mining buildings is reached via narrow, unpaved, three-mile Boomerang Road, a spur that leaves the highway a mile beyond Ophir.

6 Dropping down into the canyon of the San Miguel River below red-and-white San Juan peaks, the route continues to Telluride, a town named for tellurium, a gold-bearing element found in the area. Telluride, now a national historic landmark, is surrounded by waterfall-spangled, cloud-piercing peaks. On October 27, 1902, from a platform in front of the Sheridan Hotel, now restored, William Jennings Bryan repeated his famous "Cross of Gold" oration, which was first delivered at the 1896 Democratic National Convention in Chicago. In summer the Telluride Air Force hang gliders soar above the town, riding the thermal currents to altitudes of 19,500 feet.

As the road turns into the valley of Leopard Creek, it climbs steeply toward Dallas Divide, a pass with spectacular scenery in autumn.

7. It took the Gunnison River, seen through the crack of Black Canyon, more than 2 million years to cut through the uplifted metamorphic gneiss. In some places along the river's edge the canyon is no more than 40 feet wide.

12. *In autumn the groves of aspens growing on the slopes of the San Juan Range turn to gold, framing the nearby Chimney Rock and Courthouse Mountain ridge. Below these peaks stretch the dark* *green piñon–juniper woodland. Piñon seeds, commonly known as pine nuts, are used extensively in cooking, and, after they have been roasted, as tasty snacks.*

An alternate drive terminates at the junction of Routes 62 and 361. (See 1A on page 332.)

7 Six miles east of Montrose a spur climbs along eroded hillsides to the entrance of Black Canyon of the Gunnison National Monument. The eight-mile South Rim Drive overlooks the narrow, steep, somber gorge, which was given its name because sunlight shines into the chasm only briefly each day.

8 As the highway climbs from the Gunnison River Canyon to a hilltop, the 20-mile-long Blue Mesa Lake comes into view. The vertical cliffs rising above the lake to the mesa tops are formed of breccia, an easily eroded rock created when old volcanic cones exploded. The lake was created by a dam built across the Gunnison River.

In winter the Blue Mesa area is an important deer and elk habitat. Keep an eye turned skyward to spot golden and bald eagles soaring overhead.

As you turn south into foothills and ponderosa forests you can see The Gate, a pair of high cliffs that pinch off Lake Fork Valley. As the valley widens it reveals the towering Wetterhorn and Uncompahgre peaks.

9 As the road climbs to 11,361 feet at Slumgullion Pass, it offers outstanding views of aspen-covered slopes, beaver ponds, and colorful mineralized peaks.

Spring Creek Pass is in the headwaters of the Rio Grande, which eventually forms the U.S.–Mexico border. The road is unpaved for 6.8 miles as it follows Big Spring Gulch below a long sheer volcanic cliff called Long Ridge.

10 Two monoliths, each 1,000 feet high, at the mouth of Willow Creek Canyon dominate the town of Creede, where rich silver deposits were discovered in 1890. Creede was the wildest of Colorado's mining towns. It attracted such notorious characters as Frank James, Bat Mas-

terson, and Calamity Jane. Today Creede's mines are still being worked.

11 At Wolf Creek Pass the road crosses the Continental Divide from the San Luis Valley on the east to the San Juan Basin on the west. Beset by avalanches, the road passes through a concrete shed designed to let the "white terror" pass overhead. There are escape ramps on the road for cars whose brakes fail on the steep grades.

12 Chimney Rock and the nearby prominence called Courthouse Rock, so named because of their close resemblance to the two famous erosional remnants along the Oregon Trail in Nebraska, look down on a mesa top covered with hundreds of Indian ruins of the Mesa Verde type. These can be visited only on specially conducted tours. Because peregrine falcons, an endangered species, nest on cliffs around Chimney Rock, these limited tours are not given until midsummer, when the birds' breeding season is over.

Land of Enchantment

New Mexico's contrasts in scenery and the remarkably clean dry air make it an inviting destination

New Mexico is indeed a land of enchantment. For the motorist, one magic view after another springs up with vivid contrast in the clear air.

The contrast comes largely from the mountains; 73 separate ranges rise from the desert. Some mountains are islands of vegetation; others, barren rock born of volcanic eruption.

Additional contrast is found on the plains. Through the irrigated Rio Grande valley runs a ribbon of rich, green agricultural land. Even more important to the economy are the herds of livestock that graze on the pasturelands throughout the state.

To these contrasts, people of three distinct cultures add even more diversity. Indian culture includes Pueblo villages. Spanish colonial culture is more evident, particularly in the capital of Santa Fe, oldest seat of government in the United States. The capital's proximity to the U.S. frontier attracted a third culture, that of the Anglo-Americans who came by way of the Santa Fe Trail.

Pueblo Indian ruins in the Four Corners area include Aztec Ruins, Salmon Ruin, and Chaco Canyon. Modern Pueblo culture is displayed in the artistry of Zuni jewelers. Navajo art is evident in rugs and blankets marketed in this region. Geological interest focuses on the San Juan Basin, the Nacimiento Badlands with their energy resources of fossil fuels, and to the south, lava flows and cinder cones only a thousand years old. El Morro National Monument symbolizes the harmony of Indian, Spanish, and Anglo cultures in New Mexico.

1 Indian arts and crafts of most Southwest tribes are available in Gallup, where you can also hear disc jockeys whose patter is in Navajo.

At nearby Red Rock State Park a museum exhibit outlines the story of Navajo "code talkers," recruited for South Pacific duty during World War II because the Japanese, excellent at breaking English code, were unable to translate Navajo. Native plants and their uses, a display (with explanations in Braille) demonstrating the knowledge archeologists gain from studying botany, and arts of North American Indian tribes also are found in the museum.

The park, set beneath dramatic red cliffs of Entrada sandstone, also serves as a convention center and an arena for rodeos and other events. A trail passing Church Rock, eroded from the Entrada, leads past a hogan on Navajo tribal lands just beyond the park's campgrounds.

2 Heading north you pass below the flat-topped, highly eroded Chuska Mountains through the Navajo Indian Reservation, the largest in America. This 25,000 square miles of desert supports only a small number of inhabitants but is nevertheless considered to be overpopulated by both livestock and people.

First visible about 30 miles north of Gallup are isolated volcanic necks, hard black monoliths that were once molten cores which filled the necks of volcanoes 25 million years ago. The first of these is Bennett Peak, followed by Ford Butte and Barber Peak. The last and grandest of all is Ship Rock, rising some 1,700 feet above the Navajo plains. The rock stands as a symbol of the Four Corners, where New Mexico, Colorado, Utah, and Arizona adjoin, the only place in the nation where four state boundaries come together.

2. Ship Rock, the tallest of a series of volcanic towers on the desert floor of the Navajo Indian Reservation, was named by early pioneers for its resemblance to a sailing vessel. To the Navajo Indians it was a legendary giant bird that came to rest as a rock.

SPECIAL FEATURES

ROAD GUIDE	HIGHLIGHT **1**
STATE PARKS	SKI AREAS
With Campsites ▲ Without Campsites △	SCHEDULED AIRLINE STOPS
RECREATION AREAS	MILITARY AIRPORTS
With Campsites ▲ Without Campsites △	
SELECTED REST AREAS	OTHER AIRPORTS
POINTS OF INTEREST	BOAT RAMPS

ROAD CLASSIFICATION

CONTROLLED ACCESS HIGHWAYS
Interstate interchange numbers are mileposts.   Divided **5** Undivided
                                                     Interchanges
OTHER DIVIDED HIGHWAYS

PAVED HIGHWAYS

LOCAL ROADS In unfamiliar areas inquire locally
before using these roads   Paved   Gravel   Dirt

MILEAGE

MILEAGE BETWEEN TOWNS   3   4   MILEAGE   35
AND JUNCTIONS   BETWEEN DOTS

SCALE

ONE INCH 26 MILES   0   5   10   20   30

ONE INCH 42 KILOMETERS   0 5 10   20   30   48

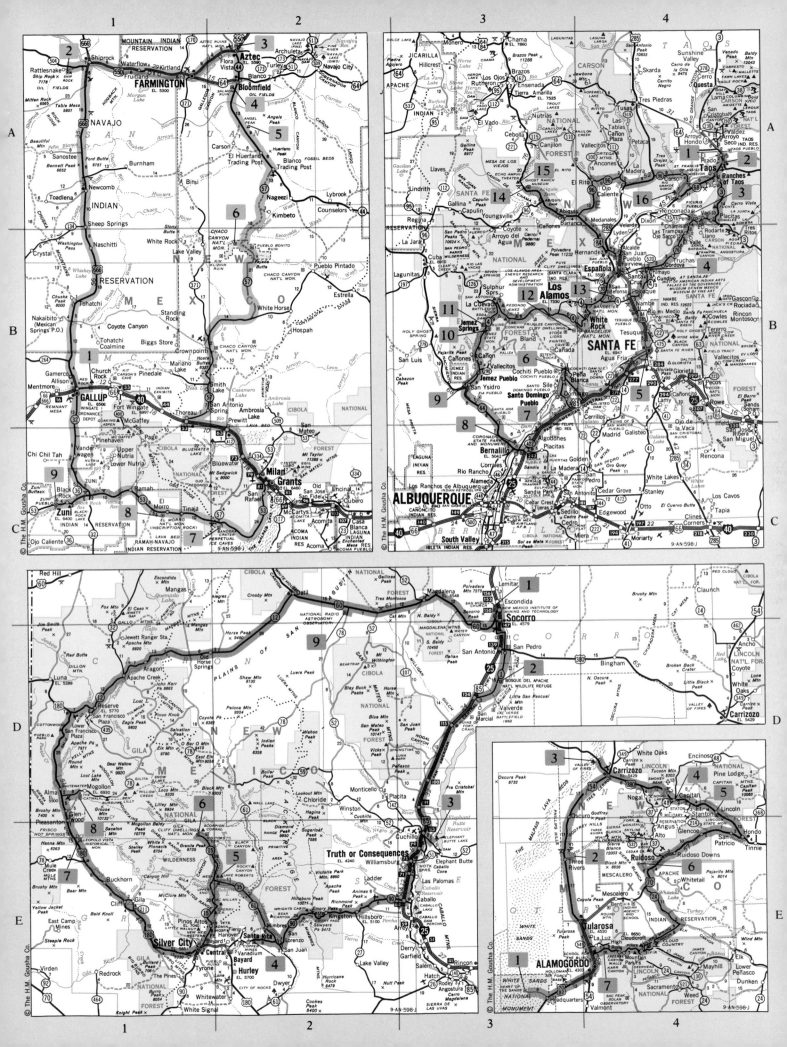

6. Pueblo Bonito—"beautiful village"—in Chaco Canyon National Monument, was an apartment complex of 800 rooms. In the courtyard are 32 kivas, circular buildings used for religious and other ceremonial events. The walls of the E-shaped pueblo were made of cut stones reinforced with stone chips, a combination that produced a mosaiclike effect.

3 At Aztec Ruins National Monument the great kiva—a worship center and the focus of pueblo life—is one of the very few ruins of ancient Indian pueblos restored to its original appearance of 800 years ago. The current popular policy is to merely stabilize ruins by piling back stones that have fallen down and capping them with cement to halt further deterioration. While the rest of Aztec Ruins is stabilized, the great kiva, because of its size and advanced construction techniques, was a worthy choice for the expensive restoration process.

From a visitor center containing artifacts discovered here, a self-guiding trail winds around what was once a 500-room, 3-story apartment building that housed about 450 people. Built as a planned unit, the pueblo represents an extension of the culture that produced the huge complex of pueblos that were developed in this part of the world.

Contrary to what pioneers who settled this land a century ago thought, their Indian predecessors were not Aztecs. They were Anasazis, Navajo for "ancient ones." At their peak, these farmers had a standard of living in some ways higher than that of Europe at the same time, and their population in the Four Corners area may even have surpassed the number of people the area supports today. During the 13th and 14th centuries their culture failed to support them in this land, and they abandoned most of their villages.

4 Salmon Ruin is named for George Salmon, who homesteaded here and protected the ruins from vandals and pothunters. The ancient pueblo has yielded valuable information about its Anasazi builders.

The planned community of 250 rooms was built between A.D. 1088 and 1095, a very short construction period for so large a structure. Salmon Ruin is thought to be a colony of the great Chaco Canyon pueblo, and by the middle of the 12th century both it and Chaco Canyon were abandoned. About a century later the buildings were reoccupied by a people related to the Mesa Verde branch of Anasazis, but they too abandoned the pueblo after a short time.

Conducted tours of the ruins, led by archeologists, are offered for large groups. Self-guided tours are also available.

5 South of Bloomfield, Route 44 runs through high desert grazed by herds of Navajo sheep. Often you see the flocks tended by a gray-haired grandmother in long skirts or by a Navajo teenager astride a trail bike.

Watch for the Nacimiento Badlands, a dozen miles from Bloomfield to the left of the highway. Soon a large sign marks a left turn onto a road to Angel Peak Recreation Area in the heart of the Badlands. Here all of the San José sandstone has eroded away except for the top 100 feet of Angel Peak. Deep beneath the broken landscape are pools of oil and gas and huge reserves of coal, residue from masses of swamp plants that died here millions of years ago.

An aura of mystery and awe has long surrounded this land of many colors. Spanish explorers called the area Nacimiento—a "Christmas nativity scene"—for they imagined the craggy top of Angel Peak (known locally as Rabbit Ears Peak) to resemble outspread angel wings. Navajos saw the land as a dwelling place of "holy ones" and still weave its hues into their wool rugs.

6 Just beyond Blanco Trading Post is a sign that indicates the dirt road to Chaco Canyon National Monument. A superlative collection of ruins, Chaco Canyon is reached only by motorists whose interest in such is sufficient to encourage them to drive

the 29 miles of bumpy, dusty road to experience the canyon's wonders. In stormy weather, it is a good idea to call the staff to check on road conditions (505/786-5384).

Those interested in purchasing Navajo arts and crafts can take a break in the drive by visiting the Brethren in Christ Church Mission, two miles south of Route 44. This boarding school for Navajo children sells rugs and jewelry made by relatives of the students to help pay tuition costs.

By the time you reach the borders of Chaco Canyon National Monument, you are sure you have reached the middle of nowhere. You have arrived nine centuries late. About A.D. 1050 Chaco Canyon was one of the most important cultural centers in North America. In an area eight miles long and two miles wide were 16 towns and hundreds of other dwelling sites. Population estimates range between 5,000 and 7,000 farmers, architects, priests, builders, potters, and jewelers and their families.

Besides impressive buildings as high as five stories, it is believed that these people built miles of water-diversion canals, as evidenced by several uncovered segments. They had roads for foot travel, some as wide as 30 feet. Totaling 300 miles in length, these roads linked population centers within the canyon and connected other pueblos, such as Aztec and Salmon ruins, to Chaco.

A large and complex society is reflected in their ambitious building projects. Newcomers who migrated to Chaco were welcomed. Foreign trade flourished, extending as far as the Meso-American cultures of Mexico and Central America. Yet after A.D. 1200 only the wind and wildlife moved along Chaco's roads and through its buildings.

Every square inch of farmland was needed to grow corn and squash to feed the large population. Constant irrigation made some fields too alkaline for use. Others were washed away in summer storms. Periodic drought took its toll. Entire forests were cut down for building and for fuel for cooking and heating. When the canyon forest was depleted, wood for these necessities was brought in from as much as 50 miles away.

In any case, pressures fell first on the groups and families least able to cope with them, and a few at a time they departed.

From the north boundary it is seven miles to the visitor center at Chaco Canyon. On the way are eight major pueblo ruins, constructed in the fine Chaco Canyon style of masonry, as well as many sites awaiting excavation.

South of Grants, Route 53 passes recent black lava flows called the Malpais—the "Badlands." A mere 1,000 years ago these were red-hot and molten. The fresh basalt is covered here and there by lichens, crusty plants that begin the slow process of turning new rock into living soil.

7 More fresh lava flows 24 miles from Grants, astride the Continental Divide, indicate the approach to 800-foot-deep Bandera Crater. Violent volcanic eruptions some 5,000 years ago created the unusual rock formations in this area, including the Perpetual Ice Caves.

8 The headland of El Morro National Monument rises 200 feet from the valley floor. Travelers over the centuries have camped at a spring beneath these pitted cliffs and have found the Zuni sandstone soft and easy to carve.

The first carvers were Indians, who chiseled petroglyphs of bighorn sheep. Spanish explorer Juan de Oñate, founder of the first European settlement in New Mexico in 1598, was the first European to carve on El Morro. Spanish inscriptions record the story of conquest, conversion, and colonization for the next 169 years. After the United States acquired this area of the Southwest from Mexico in 1848, Anglo names began to mix with Indian and Spanish, making El Morro the symbol of New Mexico's harmonization of three cultures. A museum marks the beginning of a self-guiding trail that loops through the park and past the most significant carvings.

9 Three miles beyond Ramah, through such desert foliage as piñon, juniper, and sage, you enter the Zuni Indian Reservation. Continue along to Zuni Pueblo, the largest in New Mexico. Perhaps the first things you notice here are the *hornos*—beehive-shaped ovens used for baking bread. However, the real staff of life for the Zuni Indians is jewelry making, and in the pueblo there are several stores featuring this famous inlay work of silver and semiprecious stones.

The Shalako ceremony in late fall is a highlight of the Zuni year. Photography is forbidden at the ceremony and at all religious ceremonies and in all religious shrines.

8. El Morro National Monument was established to preserve the 200-foot-high monolith for which the park is named. The rock, roughly triangular in shape, covers some 12 acres. El Morro, meaning "headland," is also called Inscription Rock. Its hard cap has protected the lower areas of soft sandstone, where 17th-century travelers carved messages, as shown above. A deep canyon runs into the center of the rock, where a spring has been found.

Indian farmers of the Southwest who had lived a sedentary existence in permanent villages for many centuries were called Pueblo Indians by the Spanish because the Indian communities outwardly resembled the pueblos, or villages, in Spain. Pueblos in the countryside around the city of Santa Fe are among the oldest continuously inhabited settlements in this country.

Beginning with Taos, this tour includes some of the most interesting pueblos around Santa Fe and the ruins of several others that were abandoned prior to or soon after the Spanish exploration of the Southwest.

Complementing the pueblos are an important modern scientific research center, scenic forests, and fascinating geological formations.

named Popé from the San Juan Pueblo led the way in driving the Spaniards temporarily back to Mexico. The people of Taos joined the rebellion after Popé made his headquarters there. In 1847 the Taos Indians played an active role in attempting to oust the American conquerors.

Taos produces a variety of handicrafts, including drums, moccasins, and baked goods produced in *hornos*, beehive-shaped ovens.

2 The town of Taos was founded in 1615 around a plaza that is still the center of activity for the many artists and craftspeople who now populate the area. About a block away and now preserved as a museum is the home of famous mountain man and Indian fighter Kit Carson. The museum contains relics of the Carson

There is a museum here and partially excavated ruins of churches that were sacked by Comanches.

4 Route 76, part of the colorful High Road to Taos, twists through forests and along ridgetops, passing homes and villages of fine weavers where English is spoken less frequently than Spanish. The woolen goods made here can be purchased at shops in Chimayo.

5 Sante Fe, the state capital, is highest in altitude of any capital in the United States. Founded in 1610 by the Spaniards, it had previously been the site of an Indian pueblo. The Palace of the Governors dates from the founding and was the original seat of government. Indian craftsmen often sell their wares under its portals.

Here at the central plaza ended the Sante Fe Trail, and here Stephen Watts Kearny took control of the Southwest for the United States in 1846. Today the building houses a museum, and in its immediate vicinity are shops and art galleries.

The nearby Cathedral of St. Francis of Assisi, erected in 1717, is the most recent of the fine churches built on the site since 1610. It was remodeled in 1869–84 in Romanesque style under the supervision of French-born Archbishop Jean Baptiste Lamy.

6 Cochiti Dam stretches more than five miles across both the Rio Grande and the Santa Fe River drainages. A visitor center at its north buttress provides information about the area and has exhibits of pottery made by the Cochiti Indians and their predecessors.

Cochiti Pueblo is home to people who trace their ancestry to the Indians who excavated the cave dwellings now preserved in Bandelier National Monument. The Cochitis are well known for their ceremonial drums, and the pueblo's two water towers are painted to resemble them. Photography is not permitted here or at Santo Domingo.

7 You can see the ancient beehive shape of adobe ovens and modern chain-link fences side by side here at Santo Domingo. This is one of the largest and most conservative pueblos. The people are friendly and noted for the quality of the jewelry they make.

1. Indians in Taos Pueblo today live in adobe structures almost exactly like those built hundreds of years ago. The apartment complex shown here stretches along the flat valley floor beneath the snowcapped peaks of the Sangre de Cristo Mountains.

1 The northernmost of the Pueblo people, residents of Taos Pueblo live in multistory adobe apartments, the classic image of the pueblos that were discovered by the Spanish in the 16th century.

Today the people of Taos Pueblo welcome visitors and, for a fee, permit their homes to be photographed. Three centuries ago a Tewa Indian

era and explains his importance in New Mexico's history. Nearby is Kit Carson Memorial Park with its 20 acres of lawn, trees, and flower beds.

3 Picuris, one of the least frequented pueblos, but well worth a visit, is best known for its glittering pottery made from mica-filled clay and intended, unlike most Pueblo pots, for use as cooking vessels.

Potters of the Southwest

The Pueblo Indians of the Southwest have long been known as expert potters. In ancient times they created their pots by rolling pieces of clay into long, slender coils and placing one atop another until the desired shape and size was achieved. The surfaces were smoothed with a stone, and the vessels were dried in the sun.

Not until after A.D. 500 were painted designs used. These decorations varied, as shown in the photographs at right. For background color, a slip (a solution of clay and water) was used. Colors were derived from different kinds of earth and various plants. Designs were applied with a brush made of shredded yucca blossoms.

In the late 1800's a Hopi Indian named Nampeyo began to copy the techniques, designs, and colors used by her early ancestors. During the early 1900's her daughter, Fannie Nampeyo, carried on the practice, and today Fannie's daughter is also making Hopi pottery in the tribe's ancient manner (top, far right).

The 10-inch-tall Anasazi pitcher (left) was found in New Mexico, in an area called Kama-a. It dates from about A.D. 800. The jar (right), 12½ inches tall, comes from Tularosa and dates from about A.D. 1175.

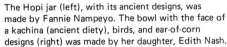

The Hopi jar (left), with its ancient designs, was made by Fannie Nampeyo. The bowl with the face of a kachina (ancient diety), birds, and ear-of-corn designs (right) was made by her daughter, Edith Nash.

Zuni pottery often featured geometric designs, as seen on the jar at the left. The white-rumped deer with a red heart line (right), another favorite design of the Zunis, is popular with collectors today.

The ancient Mimbres, who lived in the Mogollon section of New Mexico, followed a custom of "killing" pots by making holes in them, as in the ones shown here, and burying them with the dead.

---

8 At Coronado State Park and Monument there is a pleasant riverside campground and the site of the excavated ruins of Kuaua. Found among the ruins of this settlement that dates from A.D. 1300 was a collection of murals that represents some of the finest examples of prehistoric art in the United States.

9 Crusty brown loaves of bread baked in the ever-present *hornos* are sold at roadside stores and stands in the area of Jemez Pueblo. Here too you can find fry bread, a flattened circle of dough cooked over a fire while you wait. The pueblo, sited by the red-and-yellow cliffs at the mouth of Jemez Canyon, features pottery of two completely different styles. The brightly colored pottery appeals to some, while the subtler, softer-toned designs are chosen by those of quieter tastes.

10 A scenic drive up Jemez River Canyon brings you to Jemez State Monument, where the ruins of Giusewa Mission and parts of the pueblo are preserved. The mission, one of 10 that was built between here and Jemez, served double-duty as a fortress and has walls 6 to 11 feet thick. The museum and self-guided trail offer information on Pueblo culture, life here in the early 1600's, and details of the mission's colorful history.

11 Soda Dam is a massive wall of natural travertine formed by a hot spring over many centuries. Hot water dissolves limestone beneath the ground, bubbles to the surface, and cools. As it cools, it deposits the lime (calcium carbonate) to form travertine, an elegant variety of limestone. The dam, now 300 feet long, 50 feet wide at the base, and still building, is pierced by the foaming Jemez River. From the resultant natural bridge hang delicate draperies of travertine.

12 Three miles after entering the Bandelier National Monument, the road drops more than 500 feet into spectacular Frijoles Canyon, where in the 14th century Pueblo Indians excavated cliff dwellings in the soft volcanic rock of the canyon walls. The only cutting tools the Indians had at that time were made of harder stone. A museum on the valley floor traces Indian culture from A.D. 1200 to the present. The ruins are connected by a self-guided trail. The monument is named after Adolph F. A. Bandelier, an archeologist who, in the late 1800's, studied Indian culture and encouraged public interest in Pueblo life.

13 San Ildefonso is most famous for its fine pottery, although other arts and crafts are also important to this pueblo. The late Maria Martinez, world famous for her black matte

11. Soda Dam forms a bridge over the torrent of Jemez River. An aroma of sulfur hangs in the air above the hot spring here, which for many years men have used as a curative bath.

pottery creations, made her home here, as do several noted Indian painters.

This pueblo is located on the plains, with far-away mountains providing a beautiful backdrop. It is one of the few Indian villages that permits photography, although a fee is charged for the privilege.

14 The Ghost Ranch Museum, which is combined with a zoo, was designed by the U.S. Forest Service to acquaint visitors with the lore of northern New Mexico's national forests. On a half-hour self-guided tour you see wildlife species and plants native to the area. Along the trail the unusual rock formations of the surrounding mountains can be spotted through mounted viewing scopes.

15 Shouting, usually frowned on in scenic places, is the order of the day at Echo Amphitheater Picnic Area. Natural weathering has sculpted a bowl in the face of a cliff that has superb acoustics and produces amazing echoes.

Short trails with interpretive signs wind through the surrounding forest of juniper and piñon (*Pinus edulis*), the state tree.

Route 96 climbs from the valley of Rio Chama through rolling landscapes used mostly for grazing. The desert plants appear more luxuriant once you cross into Carson National Forest, heading for the town of El Rito. Notice on the map that for a short distance Route 96 merges with Route 285. Continue east and north on Route 285 for nine miles beyond their junction. Then watch for a sign indicating a right turn for Pilar. Not until you have made this turn does a sign confirm that you are continuing on Route 96.

16 Beyond Carson there is a series of switchbacks on a gravel road leading to the bottom of Rio Grande Gorge and the village of Pilar. Rio Grande Gorge State Park, where the gray-green sage suddenly is rent by a black gash more than 500 feet deep, borders the river.

On the way back to Taos the road is somewhat bumpy but poses no significant problems, particularly since everyone tends to drive slowly along this stretch to enjoy the magnificent scenery.

South of Socorro, Interstate 25 follows the green strip watered by the Rio Grande. Along the river is one of America's best known wildlife refuges and the Elephant Butte Reservoir. To the west of the river is Gila (pronounced heela) National Forest, the Santa Rita copper mine, and some ancient Indian cliff dwellings. An elevated trail leads through the narrow gorge of Whitewater Canyon, above the rushing waters of a creek, and across the Continental Divide. On the Plains of San Agustin, the world's largest radio telescope contrasts with an 1885 drovers' trail still in use today.

1 The red-tiled spires of San Miguel Church rising above the town of Socorro pay tribute to the Piro Indians, who gave succor to the Spanish

2. A startled mule deer buck poses in a grassy meadow. These animals, which can often be seen at Bosque del Apache National Wildlife Refuge, are larger than eastern white-tailed deer.

settlers in 1598. Although the original mission fell into ruin, some of its walls were used in building the "new" church when the Spanish resettled in the area in 1819. Inside the neat adobe structure are hand-carved pews, sacred vessels, and antique paintings.

2 Take Exit 139 for San Antonio and follow the signs to the Bosque del Apache National Wildlife Refuge.

Turn east on Route 380 and south on Route 1 for eight miles to the entrance of the refuge. An information booth at the entrance provides brochures to guide you along a 15-mile loop through the winter home of thousands of ducks, geese, and sandhill cranes. The magnificent whooping cranes, now an endangered species, also take shelter here. Mule deer are abundant and are most frequently seen bounding across the fields early in the morning and at dusk.

3 The waters of the 36,000-acre Elephant Butte Reservoir, formed by a dam on the Rio Grande built in 1916, can be seen to the east before you reach the exit for Elephant Butte Lake State Park.

The Rio Grande was dammed to provide irrigation for many miles of valleys stretching through southern New Mexico and into Texas. As a result, rich crops are grown in this area today.

Elephant Butte is one of the state's most popular parks for water sports; marinas, picnic sites, and campgrounds dot the western shore. For landlubbers, the south end of the lake, across the dam, offers the pleasant shade of cottonwoods and is most appealing.

Elephant Butte itself now rises from the lake, an ominous brownish-black neck of a volcano long eroded by the Rio Grande.

Because the narrow road across the dam is one-way, it is best to return to U.S. 85 and take Interstate Business Loop 25 to Truth or Consequences. Here under a pavilion on Main Street are the travertine-sheathed Geronimo Hot Springs. A nearby museum containing artifacts relating to the area's history tells the story of how the town of Hot Springs changed its name to that of a quiz show to draw more people to its mineral baths.

4 From rolling creosote desert, the road skirts Kingston, a ghost mining town dating back to the 1880's that has become an artists' colony, and continues through canyons and orchards along Percha Creek before climbing into Gila National Forest. You top out at Emory Pass with its panoramic viewing point at the end of a short, unpaved spur.

7. *The view from Leopold Vista Point in the Gila Wilderness looks westward to the snowcapped Mogollon Mountains beyond the evergreen-trimmed foothills. The row of scrubby junipers in the foreground borders Little Dry Creek, a stream that is seldom full.*

Descending from the pass through forests and canyon, the road drops down to pastures, and lush, irrigated hayfields line the road to San Lorenzo. Ten miles down the road, the open-pit copper mine at Santa Rita, one of the largest in the nation, is some thousand feet deep and spreads out for more than a mile. It can be viewed from an overlook at its edge. This copper lode was shown to the Spaniards by the Indians in the late 1790's and supplied metal for Mexican coinage until the start of the Mexican rebellion in 1810.

A museum at the overlook includes mining equipment and mineral exhibits. The museum is closed from Labor Day to Memorial Day.

5 The road goes through orchards and irrigated hayfields as it follows the Mimbres River valley into the Gila National Forest. Here Lake Roberts offers campgrounds and nature trails. Upper End Campground is the trail head of two paths. One leads along the lakeshore, with signs along the way describing the plants and other natural features. The other, Pictograph Canyon Trail, leads to a series of rocks on which the centuries-old designs were made by Mogollon Indian farmers.

6 Past the lake is a scenic 19-mile drive to Gila Cliff Dwellings National Monument. The visitor center has information about the Mogollon Indian cliff dwellings and the adjoining areas. A two-mile-long unpaved road along the West Fork of the Gila River leads to a parking lot. A self-guiding interpretive trail loops up a small canyon to ruins of Mogollon homes. Tree rings in the supporting timbers that remain indicate that they were cut no later than the 1280's. The mystery of why the Indians deserted their dwellings here is compounded as you consider the beauty of the place. One theory that archeologists have suggested is that they were forced out by a series of protracted droughts.

7 The road goes through open rangeland surrounded by tree-dotted volcanic mountains. In the Gila Wilderness the Leopold Vista Point honors the vision of one of America's most influential conservationists, Aldo Leopold, who brought about the creation of this first wilderness area in 1924 to protect resources of the spirit that only wilderness contains. An interpretive sign at the vista point identifies prominent features in this 750,000 acres of rugged mountains and deep canyons.

8 On the north edge of Glenwood look for the Trout Hatchery and The Catwalk. The state-run hatchery produces as many as a million rainbow trout annually to stock streams and lakes in southwestern New Mexico.

The Catwalk of Whitewater Canyon is an elevated trail that follows the route of an old water pipeline up an incredibly narrow gorge where volcanic cliffs rise dramatically on each side. Built in 1893 to supply water and generate electricity for a mining camp, the pipeline became obsolete in 1913 when the ore mill closed. All that is left is the mill's ruin, clinging to the hillside near the end of the spur road here.

The Continental Divide is located about nine miles beyond Aragon. There is nothing obvious about the Divide, but it is interesting to consider that water falling west of the line makes its way to the Pacific and what

8. *The Catwalk, hugging the craggy walls of narrow Whitewater Canyon, is seen here before it was damaged by a spring flood in 1979; its restoration is expected by 1983.*

343

falls on the other side flows toward the Atlantic and the Gulf of Mexico. The water that falls right on the line here is absorbed by the stands of ponderosa pines.

9 Beginning 25 miles east of the Continental Divide are the Plains of San Agustin. Ten thousand years ago, at the end of the last great ice age, this treeless expanse was a lake. Water covered 350 square miles to a maximum depth of 164 feet.

White towers east of Datil are part of the National Radio Astronomy Observatory's Very Large Array Telescope (VLA). Set on railroad tracks laid in a Y-pattern, the 27 dish-shaped VLA antennae collect and analyze cosmic radio waves that bombard the earth from outer space. Each arm of the "Y" is 13 miles long, and the 272-ton antennae and transporters move on the track at 5 miles per hour.

The radio telescope feeds the extraterrestrial noise into computers to produce an image of the source of this radiation. Among the subjects studied with this telescope are the structure of the universe, the evolution of stars, and the chemical makeup of gas clouds between stars.

These sensitive instruments are here because they have unique environmental requirements. They must have a large flat area remote from large population centers, subsoil capable of supporting the weight of the antennae without shifting, and low humidity to reduce distortion of incoming waves. The surrounding mountains also help protect the purity of the cosmic radio waves.

Turn south at Route 78 and follow the signs to the National Radio Astronomy Observatory about two miles down the road.

Here the staff provides the visitor with remarkably clear explanatory literature. From the viewing porch, you can look in to see the astronomers at work with computers and other space age hardware.

Route 60, three miles beyond its junction with Route 52, runs along a nearly century-old sheep and cattle trail on the south side of the road, beyond a barbed-wire fence. Although trucks are generally used for transport, about 1,000 cattle and 2,000 sheep are sometimes driven along the trail in April and October.

On the western edge of this varied area is the White Sands National Monument, the ancient rock pictures at Three Rivers Petroglyph Site, and the fascinating Badlands of the Valley of Fires State Park.

To the east, Smokey Bear Historical State Park honors the fire-preventin' bear born on Capitan Mountain in Lincoln National Forest. The village of Lincoln has preserved sites of death and destruction of the Lincoln County War. Mescalero Apaches are leaders among Indian tribes in welcoming tourists to their reservation, an extensive area in the midst of the Sacramento Mountains.

The U.S. Forest Service overlook at Fresnal Canyon is a good transition point from which to view the immense variety, from desert to forest, in this part of New Mexico.

1 White Sands National Monument includes 145,000 acres of unusual gypsum dunes. Legend has it that the snowy wraiths seen swirling across the dunes are Spanish maidens searching for lost lovers. A visitor center at the entrance explains the adaptation of plants and animals to this large gypsum desert and provides a history of the dunes.

You can drive a 16-mile nature trail through this hot sand desert that looks like New England snowdrifts. Along the edge of shifting dunes there is also a mile-long walking trail. Numerous roadside turnoffs provide points from which to ascend the hills for a view of this vast area of very fine white gypsum particles that the persistent winds have deposited in this strange landscape.

2 Creosote bush, an evergreen that is one of the most widespread of American desert plants, borders the road north of Alamogordo and contrasts dramatically with the lush green irrigated fields.

The first farmers in this area were Mogollon Indians, who hunted, farmed, and created enduring artwork between A.D. 900 and 1400. A well-marked road at Three Rivers leads five miles east to an excavation of a Mogollon village. On a nearby ridgetop, volcanic rocks are covered with artistic designs created by these people. The rough trail through this open-air gallery climbs past rocks with crude depictions of local wildlife, hunters, mythical beasts, and renderings of abstract designs. More than 5,000 petroglyphs are spread over 50 acres along the ridge.

1. Ever-changing drifts, rippled by the prevailing southwest winds, form great arcs across the landscape at White Sands National Monument. The road through the park is in constant danger of being buried by blowing sands and must be frequently cleared.

3   To the west of Route 54, about where the White Sands end, is the Malpais (a Spanish term for "badlands"), a bed of dark, basaltic lava some 44 miles long and 5 miles wide.

The best place to explore this old lava flow is Valley of Fires State Park. At the park a self-guided one-mile nature trail winds through an area of collapsed lava tubes. You can get a brochure about the animals and plants that have made a home of this stark environment. Some small creatures, such as cactus mice that stay here all their lives, have darker coloration than their nearby relatives.

4   Crossing grassland dotted with soaptree yucca (*Yucca elata*), New Mexico's state flower, the route climbs into woodlands in Lincoln National Forest. At a vista point just inside the forest boundary a large sign indicates that this forest is the birthplace of Smokey the Bear.

After a 17,000-acre fire in May 1950, a bear cub, badly burned and hungry, was found clinging to a charred fir. Rescued and cared for, he came to be called Smokey. He was sent to the National Zoo in Washington, D.C., and became a living symbol for fire prevention. An interpretive museum in the town of Capitan presents Smokey's history along with the principles of preventing fires in our forests. The famous animal is buried in Smokey Bear Historical State Park in Capitan.

5   Today the sleepy, one-street town of Lincoln, seat of the nation's largest county, belies its stormy past.

In this area once ranged vast cattle herds whose ranchers sold their beef to the federal government to feed reservation Apaches and their soldier guards. Much money changed hands, hoodlums flocked to the area, and theft and murder were more common than law and order.

In this scene of near anarchy, two rival merchants, J. J. Dolan and J. H. Tunstall, emerged as competitors for the business of supplying beef, flour, and hay to nearby federal forts. Dolan & Co., the longer established firm, objected to the loss of its lucrative monopoly and launched a war of personal vilification. Soon the rivals were trading bullets.

The Lincoln County War was waged for five months and ended with the killing of the head partner of Turnstall & Co. and the bankruptcy of Dolan & Co.

Lincoln County purchased the Dolan store and converted it to a courthouse. Here the infamous Billy the Kid, while awaiting execution for murder, escaped imprisonment. A few months later at Old Fort Sumner the Kid was killed by Sheriff Pat Garrett. Today the old courthouse, complete with bullet holes, is a state monument and museum.

The plant that symbolizes the West

Tumbleweed, any of several *Amaranthus* species, is found on prairies and arid western landscapes. The many-branched plants grow about three feet high and have greenish-purple stems and clusters of tiny flowers that appear from June to August. In late summer when these shallow-rooted plants become dry, the constant western wind tears them from the ground, rolls them into tangled balls, and blows them along roadsides and across open fields, scattering seeds along the way. They are often lodged against fences and buildings.

The crown jewel of their tourism industry is Inn of the Mountain Gods, a palatial hostelry designed for luxury and leisure on the shores of man-made Lake Mescalero. Five miles southwest of Ruidoso, turn west from Route 70 at the sign of the hostelry. The activities here include golf, tennis, horseback riding, swimming, boating, and fishing. The tribe also owns the Sierra Blanca Ski Area, noted for downhill skiing.

6   The 460,000-acre Mescalero Apache Reservation, home to more than 2,000 Indians, includes Sierra Blanca, the "White Mountain." This massive volcanic remnant is the highest mountain in the area and is sacred to the Apaches. The road through the reservation penetrates dark forests of pine, spruce, and fir, the basis of the tribe's lumber business. The Mescaleros are also among the state's leading cattle ranchers.

The most noteworthy accomplishment of the Mescaleros is their innovative leadership in opening their reservation to recreational activities.

7   Descending the steep grades from Cloudcroft, the road passes many apple and cherry orchards to approach the only highway tunnel in New Mexico. At its other end is a U.S. Forest Service vista point.

Here interpretive signs explain the sedimentary rock of the Fresnal Canyon walls. Primarily these are limestone and gypsum, formed in ancient seas and lagoons. The creek far below, lined with green cottonwoods, tumbles over sparkling falls into quiet pools. In the distance the White Sands gleam below the purple outline of the San Andres Mountains.

The Grand Canyon State

Arizona, famed for its healthful climate, is a colorful land of canyons, deserts, and Indian cultures

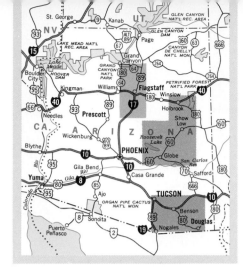

Arizona's license plates proclaim it the "Grand Canyon State," and that celebrated canyon is not only the foremost highlight of Arizona but indeed it is one of the outstanding wonders of the world.

On the northern plateau of the state is the reservation of the Navajo Indians, whose colorful traditions are still maintained. Extending into the reservation is the Painted Desert, an area ribboned with vividly hued shales and sandstones.

The southern edge of the Colorado Plateau is marked by the cliffs of the Mogollon Rim, which runs through broad stretches of national forests. The southern part of Arizona is truly a sun belt. Here is found the saguaro (*Carnegiea gigantea*), a giant branching cactus, sometimes called the Arizona-Giant, that produces the state flower and symbolizes the arid Southwest.

From the Grand Canyon, this route traverses a corner of the Navajo Indian Reservation to ruins of a far older Indian culture at Wupatki National Monument. The eruption of nearby Sunset Crater in A.D. 1065 set into motion a unique sequence of events in the history of pre-Columbian Indians about which you can learn at Walnut Canyon, Montezuma Castle and Well, and Tuzigoot national monuments. Fort Verde and Jerome state historic parks commemorate the pioneers who came to settle this part of the country in the late 1800's.

The Supai sandstone towers of Oak Creek Canyon almost rival the fame of the Grand Canyon. In Flagstaff, the Museum of Northern Arizona explains the area's anthropology, biology, and geology. A dramatic butte dominates the scene in Kaibab National Forest as you once more approach Grand Canyon National Park.

1 A mile deep and 10 miles wide where the road runs along the South Rim, the Grand Canyon in size and form is, indeed, the essence of grandeur. Its hugeness is unaffected by the teeming thousands of people who come to see it. From the lookout points along the rims it is possible to experience a sense of wilderness that is seldom so easily attained.

What is more difficult to experience is a real sense of the canyon's size and the vast time scale it represents. From Hopi Point, west from Canyon Village, as from other observation turnouts along the road, you can look down to the dark Vishnu schist in the Inner Gorge, below the broad Tonto Plateau. This hard rock originated 2 billion years ago. The Kaibab limestone on the rims was laid down in a sea 250 million years ago. But the canyon itself began forming only about 6 million years ago, so it is geologically youthful.

Hopi Point is one of the canyon overlooks along West Rim Drive, a

1. From Hopi Point on Grand Canyon's South Rim you can see the Colorado River as it cuts through a bed of schist half as old as the earth itself. Capping the rosy sandstone walls are bands of gray limestone packed with marine fossils from an ancient sea.

SPECIAL FEATURES

ROAD GUIDE	HIGHLIGHT **1**
STATE PARKS	SKI AREAS
With Campsites ▲ Without Campsites ⌂	SCHEDULED AIRLINE STOPS
RECREATION AREAS	MILITARY AIRPORTS
With Campsites ▲ Without Campsites △	OTHER AIRPORTS
RECREATION AREAS	BOAT RAMPS
With Toilets ✗ Without Toilets ✗	PORTS OF ENTRY
POINTS OF INTEREST ⊡	

ROAD CLASSIFICATION

CONTROLLED ACCESS HIGHWAYS
(Interstate interchange numbers are mileposts.)   Interchanges

OTHER DIVIDED HIGHWAYS

PAVED HIGHWAYS

LOCAL ROAD   In unfamiliar areas inquire locally
before using these roads   Paved   Gravel   Dirt

MILEAGE

MILEAGE BETWEEN TOWNS   3 ⌿ 4   MILEAGE   ● 35 ●
AND JUNCTIONS   BETWEEN DOTS

SCALE

ONE INCH 24 MILES   0   5   10   15   25

ONE INCH 38 KILOMETERS   0   5 10   20   30   40

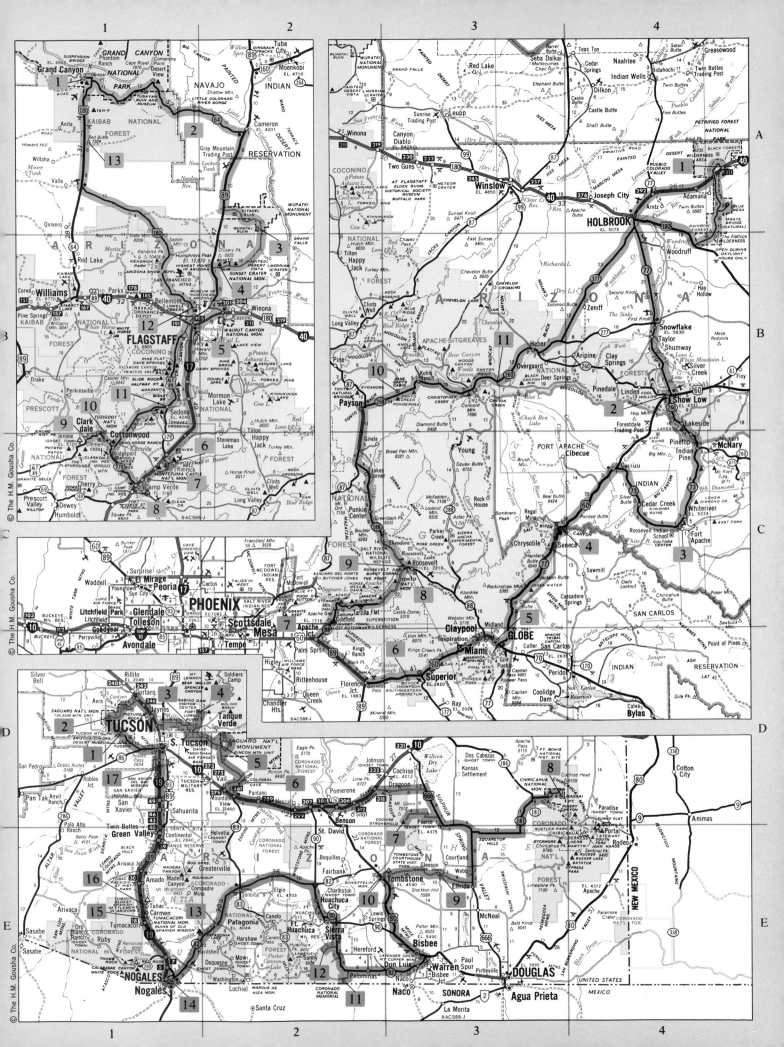

7½-mile road that is closed to private vehicles from May to September, when a free public shuttle departs every 12 to 15 minutes for convenient viewpoints.

The 25-mile East Rim Drive, open throughout the year, winds through piñon and ponderosa pines past many popular overlooks and a museum. Early morning and late afternoon are considered the best times for viewing the canyon's gorges, mesas, and pinnacles. Early dawn is best for photography.

There are other things to see besides awesome depth and color. Erosion forms, such as the fancifully named Duck on a Rock, occur along the rim. Such wildlife as chipmunks, Abert squirrels, and mule deer are common. And the remains of an ancient pueblo, Tusayan Ruin, is the focus of the National Park Service's explanation of prehistory in this area.

2 Route 64 crosses into the Navajo Indian Reservation some eight miles from Grand Canyon National Park. As you enter the reservation, note to the north the steep-walled gorge of the Little Colorado River. There are three roadside overlooks of the gorge. The last of these is deservedly the favorite, with its fine view that drops many hundreds of feet straight down from your toes to the muddy Little Colorado.

Navajos sell their crafts, primarily jewelry, at many stands circling the large parking lot at the third overlook. The prices are low compared to area shops. Bargaining is not the usual custom here. The Navajos are a friendly, open people, but in this part of their reservation they do not care to be photographed.

3 A well-marked turn off Route 89 leads through Wupatki National Monument, where ruins of ancient Indian structures are protected. Indian homes were not protected in A.D. 1065, when the violent eruption of lava, cinders, and ash that formed Sunset Crater probably turned Sinagua farmers into gasping refugees.

When nature's pyrotechnics had ceased, the Sinaguas began to venture back into the cooled area of devastation. They found 800 square miles of desert covered by a thin layer of ash and cinders, which acted as a water-retaining mulch. Soon the area

was dotted with cornfields and pueblos in a prehistoric real estate boom.

But too many people came and the land was overfarmed. In 1215 a long cycle of severe droughts began, eventually driving away the Sinaguas. Today a National Park Service visitor

7. Montezuma Castle, built between 1100 and 1300 into the side of a limestone cliff, was a 20-room "apartment house" that could accommodate about 50 people.

center at Wupatki Ruin contains displays explaining the rise and fall of Sinagua culture.

4 The route continues through 18 miles of cinder-covered hills to Sunset Crater National Monument. Rising 1,000 feet above ponderosa pines, black sand dunes, and fields of black lava is the classic cinder cone of Sunset Crater. Hot springs and vapors threw out mineral-laden sprays as the volcano cooled, painting the crater rim with a perpetual sunset.

The road circles the crater to the Lava Flow Nature Trail. Beyond is a visitor center with exhibits about volcanism and its ways.

5 In the real estate boom that followed the ancient ash falls near Sunset Crater, it is believed that some Sinagua people were pushed out and found their way to Walnut Canyon.

The 400-foot-deep canyon must have been a trial for its industrious residents. Water probably had to be hauled up steep paths from Walnut Creek. Equally steep is the three-quarter mile Island Trail, a self-guiding interpretive loop past Sinagua cliff ruins.

The Sinaguas left Walnut Canyon after building more than 300 rooms in the cliffs during 150 years of occupation. Their departure was the beginning of a general collapse of Indian agriculture in the Southwest.

6 Montezuma Well is a limestone sink 470 feet wide, 125 feet deep, and half-filled by water from a spring. This active spring dissolved a cave from layers of limestone originally deposited on a large, ancient lake bed behind a dam of lava. Eventually, the roof of the cave collapsed, forming a circular sink.

It is believed that about A.D. 1100, Sinagua Indians, forced perhaps by overpopulation from Sunset Crater, entered this region, which had been farmed by Hohokam Indians since A.D. 700. The two peoples blended their cultures, which included irrigation of fields.

During the 1200's the Indian population, relying on these irrigated fields, probably swelled with refugees from the ruined farmlands around Sunset Crater. Conflict developed, as documented by various artifacts found in excavations at Montezuma Castle National Monument, of which the Well is a detached unit. By 1450 all the pueblos in the Verde Valley were deserted because of what geologists believe to be catastrophic droughts.

7 The well-preserved cliff dwellings of Montezuma Castle are visible beyond the visitor center. Early settlers wrongly assumed that these pueblos had been built by Aztec refugees from Spanish conquest.

Built by Indians far more primitive than those of Montezuma's nation, Montezuma Castle was deserted several generations before Hernando Cortes landed in Mexico. Settlers also assumed the dwellings were defensive, hence the term "castle."

8 In 1865 white farmers built a dam to divert water in the Verde Valley and began irrigating crops. This put them in conflict with Yavapai-Apache Indians, who had used the

11. The drive along Schnebly Hill Road in Oak Creek Canyon offers impressive views, as shown here, of the great sandstone ramparts. Patches of scrub pine and oak cling to life in the crevices along the cliffs and share the desert floor with wild flowers.

Slide Rock is a popular roadside swimming area. At the top of the canyon, Oak Creek Canyon viewpoint provides excellent vistas of this 1,200-foot rent in the Colorado Plateau. The easy-access cliffs below the viewpoint are popular with rock climbers.

12 On the north edge of Flagstaff along Route 180 is the Pioneers' Historical Society, which displays a 100-year-old doctor's office, old buggies, and period clothing. A mile farther on is the Museum of Northern Arizona. In addition to permanent displays of Indian arts and crafts, there are special shows and demonstrations by Hopi and Navajo artists in July.

The road to the north provides excellent views of San Francisco Peaks, young volcanic mountains, some of which were built 18 million years ago and others 400,000 years ago. The tallest crag, glaciated Humphreys Peak, is 12,670 feet above sea level.

13 Just inside the boundary of Kaibab National Forest, a Forest Service sign explains the geology of Red Butte, visible to the east. At 7,324 feet, the butte is a remnant of sedimentary rocks formed of stream and river deposits 180 to 225 million years old. Once covering the entire area, these deposits were washed away except where a hard basalt layer from a lava flow during the last 70 million years capped the sedimentary rock, protecting it from erosion.

area for hunting. So the whites called in the army.

Fort Verde was established in 1871–73, the third military post to be built in the valley. Today, Fort Verde State Historic Park preserves four buildings of this post.

9 The copper community of Jerome was a boomtown of 15,000 people in the 1920's but shrank to less than 100 when the ore gave out in 1953. Developing now as an art colony, Jerome has raised its population to about 550.

10 On a ridgetop overlooking the Verde River is another Sinagua ruin, Tuzigoot National Monument. Tuzigoot largely escaped vandalism and raids by white pothunters before it was excavated by professional archeologists. Their finds of shell jewelry, pots, and textile remnants are preserved in a museum nearby.

11 Sedona, situated at the southern entrance to Oak Creek Canyon, has built its commercial establishments in typical frontier style.

North of Sedona, Route 89A climbs up the narrowing canyon. Bold red spires are replaced by close-set walls of younger sedimentary and igneous rock. In cool, dark woods are the U.S. Forest Service campgrounds and many private resorts and lodges.

12. Humphreys Peak, mantled in snow in early autumn, gleams in the sunlight above a grove of golden aspens. The summit is part of the San Francisco Peaks, a series of extinct volcanoes named in the early 1600's by a group of Franciscan monks.

1. Tepees (left) are eroded layered clay deposits in the Petrified Forest National Park; fallen petrified logs (above) lie in the soft eroded soil along a trail through the area.

The forces of erosion in this part of Arizona reveal various geological highlights. They include Petrified Forest National Park and the Mogollon Rim.

A delightful by-product of the wealth derived from the copper mines near the town of Globe is the Boyce Thompson Southwestern Arboretum, founded by a mining magnate.

As this route follows three sides of the Superstition Mountains, you pass reservoirs of the Salt River Project and the ancient cliff dwellings of Indian farmers who also used these waters for irrigation. The road traverses two contrasting woodlands. The goal of one is to protect the watershed of metropolitan Phoenix; in the other, it is to limit tree growth so that forage plants can also flourish.

1 The visitor center at Petrified Forest National Park, located at the entrance, shows a film explaining the formation of petrified wood.

Fallen trees toppled into backwaters, where they were covered by silt. This kept oxygen away from the wood and prevented it from rotting. Silica carried in groundwater filled the wood cells. Eventually, one of the world's greatest accumulations of petrified wood was formed.

Looping past scenic overlooks of the Painted Desert, the park road heads five miles south to structures of Indians who lived here about 600 years ago. At Puerco Indian Ruin, walls of a 125-room village stand on the banks of the Puerco River. A short spur to the right about a mile farther leads to Newspaper Rock, a large block of sandstone on which Indians carved petroglyphs.

Blue Mesa marks the start of the feature for which Petrified Forest National Park is named. Wayside exhibits explain interesting aspects of the petrified logs. On either side of Long Logs Trail the few living trees are shrublike, and the fallen stone trees are giants of multicolored agate. Agate House is a partially restored pueblo built by ancient Indians with chunks of petrified wood. The visitor center at Rainbow Forest has displays about the park.

2 Show Low received its odd name when a card game once settled ownership of a ranch on which the town now stands. Route 260 southeast of Show Low is a highly developed recreational area in the ponderosa pine-shadowed lake country atop the Mogollon Rim. Popular for fishing, these lakes all were created by streams dammed up to store water.

A self-guided U.S. Forest Service nature trail leads past Mogollon Rim Overlook. This easy mile-long path begins at an obscurely marked turnoff six miles from Show Low and loops through ponderosa woods.

3 Dropping into White Mountain Apache Indian Reservation through forests along the drainage of the North Fork of the White River, Route 73 passes through the tribal headquarters town of Whiteriver. A few miles farther is a well-marked turn to Fort Apache.

Founded in 1870 to help subdue the rash of outlaws, Fort Apache still contains many of the original buildings. The log house that served as quarters for the famous Indian fighter Gen. Gerald Crook now houses an Apache arts and crafts store. When it became Theodore Roosevelt Indian School, the old fort gained some massive pink sandstone buildings in the 1930's.

4 South of Carrizo you soon begin a descent into Salt River Canyon. Passing several turnouts, Route 60 switchbacks down 2,000 feet to bridge the river and climbs back out on the other side.

The Salt River is named for salt springs about seven miles downstream from the bridge. Fairly near the bottom of the canyon, a large turnout decorated by alien-looking palm trees provides a good view of waterfalls a half-mile upstream from the bridge. The falls can be reached via a short walk from the end of a narrow unpaved road just before Route 60 reaches the river. Swimming is unsafe here.

5 Long hills of mine tailings are visible between the copper towns of Globe and Miami. The light-colored rubble is waste rock from the mill, while the black rock is burned slag from the smelter. Tours of Inspiration Consolidated Copper Company are available.

6 Copper mining provided the money for the Boyce Thompson Southwestern Arboretum, named for the first president of Inspiration Consolidated. Realizing that plants of arid lands had received little study, Thompson, in 1927, established and endowed an arboretum in a desert below Picket Post Mountain.

Plants from arid and semiarid regions all over the world were brought here to be studied. The arboretum also serves as a state park where the beauty of both exotic and native desert plants can be enjoyed. More than 6,000 species are found here.

7 Lost Dutchman State Park serves as a 300-acre Sonoran desert foreground for the Superstition Mountains. The park is named for the legendary Lost Dutchman Mine, where prospector Jacob Waltz supposedly exploited rich gold diggings in the 1880's. There are many gory tales about the search for gold in the Superstitions, but geologists say gold veins there are unlikely.

About seven miles from Lost Dutchman Park, Route 88 reaches an overlook of Canyon Lake. Water sports are popular here, and camping and picnic sites dot the lakeshore.

About five miles from Tortilla Flat the pavement ends. The road winds down some 800 feet to the bottom of Fish Creek Canyon. Ascending again, through Salt River Canyon, you come upon the impressive sight of Roosevelt Dam as it blocks a narrow gorge and backs up the waters of Salt River and Tonto Creek.

8 Centuries before the dam was built, the Salado Indians (who were similar in many ways to other Southwest pueblo farmers) were diverting the water from Salt River to irrigate their fields of corn, squash, beans, cotton, and other crops. Their canals patterned the river's floodplain until it was inundated in 1911. The Salados had moved into Tonto Basin about 1100, living at first along the river's edge. Eventually they chose more de-

fensible sites, and about 1300 they moved into caves in the cliffs. A century later they left the area.

The visitor center at Tonto National Monument has many Salado artifacts, including beautifully woven

4. The roadrunner, the state bird, can be seen almost anywhere in Arizona, including here in Salt River Canyon. It feeds on snakes, nests in thorny shrubs, rarely flies, and races through cactus fields and along roadsides at up to 15 miles per hour.

cotton textiles, tools, and both plain and elaborately painted pottery. The discovery of some of the decorated pieces in other archeological sites suggests that they were popular trade items. A half-mile paved nature trail leads up to one of their cliff villages, the ruins of which have been protected from weather by their limestone umbrella.

9 Roosevelt Dam, named for Theodore Roosevelt, a fervent advocate of water storage and conservation in the arid West, was the first of

several constructed in the Salt River Project. Completed in 1911, it remains the tallest masonry dam in the world. Driving across the dam, you have fine views to the north of Theodore Roosevelt Lake, formed by the dam, and to the south, of Salt River Canyon. Leaving the lake, Route 188 climbs amid saguaros to welcome pavement.

10 Route 87 winds up through the transition zone south of the Mogollon Rim to magnificent stands of ponderosa pines near Payson.

Many of Zane Grey's well-known western novels, including *Under the Tonto Rim*, were set in this country, where he built a cabin in which to work. You can park at a wooden gate bearing a sign that casts a Z-G shadow on the short path to the cabin. Now restored and filled with Zane Grey memorabilia, the building evokes the exciting mood of Grey's stories.

11 A dozen miles beyond the turn-off to Zane Grey's cabin, the road begins to climb the cliffs of Mogollon Rim. Vistas stretch out to the hazy south over illimitable acres of dark green pines. The fault line that cuts across Arizona forms a dramatic escarpment where Tonto Basin becomes Apache–Sitgreaves National Forests. Wide road shoulders allow you to pull over and walk along the edge of the rim above the treetops.

The 7,600-foot highlands along the Mogollon Rim intercept moist air from the Pacific and support the growth of the worlds' largest unbroken stretch of ponderosa pines.

6. The Boyce Thompson Southwestern Arboretum, which is well known for its extensive cactus collection, has in its gardens the favorites shown here. From the left, with close-ups of their blossoms just below, are the claret hedgehog, the teddy bear cholla, the beaver tail, and the yellow-flowered barrel cactus, which is a species of Ferocactus.

Beginning in the Sonoran desert, this drive passes through Sabino Canyon Recreation Area and continues to Saguaro National Monument and Colossal Cave. A striking change in cultures is evident as you cross the border into Mexico. Spanish colonial culture is preserved in part at Tumacacori National Monument, Tubac, and San Xavier del Bac.

1 The Arizona–Sonora Desert Museum stands amid giant saguaro forests in Tucson Mountain Park; the route from Tucson is well marked. A minimum of two hours should be allowed for this zoo, botanical garden, nature center, and research facility. Its displays, including a walk-in bird enclosure containing 35 species, all concern the Sonoran desert.

2 Two miles ahead is the Tucson Mountain Unit of Saguaro National Monument. Stop first at the Park Service information center to view exhibits about the monument and to check the water hole for wildlife. A nature trail a mile beyond the center leads through a cactus forest averaging 15,000 to 20,000 saguaros per square mile. Listen for the single-pitch chortle of the huge cactus wren, the state bird.

The monument's dirt roads wind among dramatic desert scenes. Take the Bajada Loop Drive 1½ miles beyond the information center. A little more than 2 miles farther along, turn onto another unpaved road, which winds through magnificent desert vistas for 12 miles to pavement and the way back to Tucson.

3 Arizona's main fort a century ago, Fort Lowell, surrounded by its own park, today is a scattering of adobe walls, some of which are incorporated in picnic shelters. A museum interpreting the fort's history is in a reconstruction of the 1885 commanding officer's quarters. Closed Sundays and Mondays.

4 Head north on Craycroft Road for almost three miles to Sunrise Drive, which takes you to the visitor center at Sabino Canyon Recreation Area in Coronado National Forest.

The center features exhibits about local geology and history. Private cars are banned to protect the environment. A convenient tram shuttles visitors into the canyon.

2. In Saguaro National Monument the giant cacti stand like sentinels above the desert scrub. The Gila woodpecker (upper right), which drills a hole in the pulpy trunk for a nest, lets the sap dry to form a hard lining. Clusters of white flowers (right) appear at the ends of the cactus branches in May and June.

5 Classic stands of giant saguaro cactus are preserved in Saguaro National Monument's Rincon Mountain Unit. A saguaro survives its first tender years in the harsh desert under the shade of some other plant, often green-trunked paloverde (*Cercidium torreyanum*), Arizona's state tree. Not until saguaros are about 75 years old do they reach approximately 20 feet in height, when they begin to assume their familiar branching shape.

At the visitor center pick up a self-guiding tour leaflet for the nine-mile Cactus Forest Drive.

6 Continue on Old Spanish Trail to Colossal Cave, a large and only partially explored cavern dissolved from a layer of Escabrosa limestone. Guides lead visitors past indirectly lighted calcite cave formations, such as Crystal Forest. Several exhibits depict the cave's history.

7 A well-marked turn off Route 666 follows 10½ miles of unpaved road to Stronghold Canyon, the fortresslike hideout a century ago of the famous Chiricahua Apache chief Co-

chise. Rimmed by granite crags and supplied with springs, the canyon sheltered his raiders, who virtually depopulated the surrounding area of white settlers. When Cochise died in 1874, members of his tribe buried him in this beautiful spot, in a grave that has never been found.

At a U.S. Forest Service campground is a nature trail that takes you amid the plants and boulders of the canyon.

8 Stop at the visitor center two miles inside the boundary of Chiricahua National Monument to view exhibits about the natural and human history of the Chiricahua Mountains.

Six-and-a-half-mile Massai Point Drive climbs up Bonita Canyon, lined with grotesque natural sculpture. The road cuts through a bright red layer of ancient lake beds, hugs a cliff, and tops out at Massai Point, which offers a wide view of the monument and of grasslands to the east and west. An exhibit building here has explanations of the geology of the area, and a half-mile self-guided nature trail loops above the fantastic landscape.

9 The dusty road from Elfrida to Tombstone cuts across the southern flank of the Dragoon Mountains, an area thoroughly exploited at the turn of the century for its copper, lead, zinc, silver, and gold. The town of Gleeson flourished with the mines, but now only multihued tailings on the hillsides and brown adobe ruins along the road remind you that Gleeson was once much more than the ghost town you see today.

10 Tombstone is a monument to boldness inspired by silver. In 1877 prospector Ed Scheffelin traveled with a military detachment to Fort Huachuca. When he left the soldiers to look for silver, it was assumed that Apaches would kill him. Rather than silver, soldiers told him, he would find his tombstone.

When the prospector found his first strike, he called it Tombstone. Whatever grim humor the name possessed vanished as word of rich silver deposits created a boomtown. Scoundrels flocked in, and the town became the scene of lawless incidents, one of which was the famous gunfight between the Clanton gang and Wyatt Earp's law enforcers.

After seven wild years, rising underground water that flooded the mines and a drop in the price of silver put an end to the boom. Today Tombstone lives on its reputation of past death and destruction. The town is a national historic site and contains a state historic park at a century-old Victorian courthouse, now a museum.

11 Coronado National Memorial sits on the U.S.–Mexican border within sight of the San Pedro Valley, which was the route into present-day United States of the Spanish explorer Francisco Vásquez de Coronado in the mid-16th century. Pause at the visitor center to see exhibits that tell the story of the first major exploration of the Southwest by Europeans. Montezuma Pass, 3½ miles beyond the center, provides a vast panorama of Mexico from Coronado Peak.

12 Returning to Route 92, continue north for another seven miles and then take Ramsey Canyon Road to the Nature Conservancy's Ramsey Canyon Preserve. This was formerly the Mile-Hi Ranch, known as the Hummingbird Capital of the United States.

Hummingbirds of 14 species swarm around dozens of sugar water feeders here from March through October. They begin migrating into Ramsey Canyon in March and reach a peak in late summer.

13 In Patagonia, just 0.3 of a mile beyond the bridge over Sonoita Creek, turn onto North Fourth Avenue. After 0.2 of a mile turn onto an unpaved road that leads to the Nature Conservancy's Patagonia–Sonoita Creek Sanctuary.

This 312 acres of cottonwoods along a 1½-mile stretch of the creek is preserved as one of the best remaining types of this habitat in the state of Arizona. The sanctuary attracts a wide variety of birds and birdwatchers. The most prominent of the former is the striking black-and-red vermilion flycatcher.

Access to the sanctuary trails, which weave through idyllic woods and meadows along Sonoita Creek, is via one of the four gateways that are spaced along the road. The road fords the creek beyond the sanctuary and rejoins Route 82.

14 Nogales in Arizona adjoins Nogales in Mexico. The neighboring cities form a popular border crossing rich in Spanish colonial history dating from 1539. No passport is necessary for U.S. citizens to cross over to the Mexican side for shopping in colorful markets. Native crafts include ceramics, baskets, and items of leather, silver, glass, and tin.

15 There is the ruin of a stately old church at Tumacacori National Monument. Begun in 1795, it was intended to be a magnificent church for its Indian congregation, but this dream was hampered by the anarchy that beset the area after the Mexican Revolution of 1821. Then Apache raiders made life tenuous, and the last Indian converts fled Tumacacori in 1848, leaving the church to gradually fall into ruins. A museum explains Indian and Spanish colonial history.

16 Heading north on Interstate 19, you may be interested in stopping off at the charming old village of Tubac, now an art center. A museum interprets its colorful history.

17 A few miles south of Tucson look to the west over miles of saguaro to the white, double-towered Mission San Xavier del Bac, reached via San Xavier Road exit. Founded by Father Kino in 1700, San Xavier is situated in a Papago Indian settlement called Bac, meaning a "place where water appears." The water is the Santa Cruz River, a stream that flows underground (when it flows at all) before surfacing here. Erected between 1783 and 1797, San Xavier del Bac is a blend of Spanish, Moorish, and Mexican styles.

17. The Mission San Xavier del Bac catches the morning sun on its eastern wall. Why one tower was left unfinished remains a mystery. In the distance to the left is the Mortuary Chapel, whose bells hang in an arched tower.

Highlights in Utah

Sculptured canyons, a salty lake, and the rugged Rockies create memorable scenery on every side

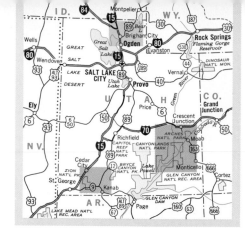

The range of rewarding drives in Utah is remarkable. In the south are broad deserts split by deep, colorful canyons, wild and scenic rivers, and natural bridges and other erosional sculptures.

Northeastern Utah, however, is a territory of high peaks adjacent to broad basins. Most of the state's people live here along the foot of the Wasatch Mountains, on rich soils deposited along the edge of prehistoric Lake Bonneville, which covered much of Utah 12,000 to 75,000 years ago. Great Salt Lake, a remnant of Lake Bonneville, is still the largest lake west of the Mississippi.

The western leg of this loop provides distant views of Great Salt Lake and near views of Willard Reservoir. The road then passes through mountains spangled with maples and fertile valleys with irrigated fields. Climbing over the terraced shoreline of now evaporated Lake Bonneville, you enter beautiful Logan Canyon in Wasatch-Cache National Forest. After 30 scenic miles the highway emerges at Bear Lake Summit. From Bear Lake the road then climbs through the forest before descending to the Ogden Valley, Pineview Reservoir, and the narrow confines of Ogden Canyon.

1 The 68,000 inhabitants of Ogden, Utah's fourth largest city, frequently use the letters LDS in everyday conversation. Employed as either a noun or an adjective, LDS means Church of Jesus Christ of Latter-day Saints, the Mormons. Utah was settled primarily by Mormons, now 65 percent of the population.

Ogden's Mormon temple is on a square in the middle of town. The circular temple's spire looms 180 feet above Temple Square's elaborate landscaping. Also on the square is the Daughters of Utah Pioneers Museum, which displays clothing, crafts, and furniture of earlier days.

2 From the elevated section of Route 15 you can see the Promontory Mountains rising above Bear River Bay of Great Salt Lake, the largest saline lake in the Western Hemisphere. Its water is much saltier than the oceans,' since it has no outlet.

Water sports are popular at Willard Bay State Recreation Area, a freshwater reservoir covering 9,900 acres on Great Salt Lake's floodplain.

3 From Route 15 take the exit marked Brigham City for Bear River Migratory Bird Refuge. The route leads through the center of town along Forest Street and is well marked. Less obvious signs lead you along paved roads through 15 miles of cropland and marshes to refuge headquarters. All visitors must register at the headquarters, where there is a small natural history exhibit. Staff at the headquarters can tell you the best places to spot spectacular waterfowl along the 12-mile self-guided auto tour through the refuge.

This spot, where the Bear River flows into Great Salt Lake, has been a bird haven for thousands of years. Today it is one of the top dozen places in the United States for seeing birds

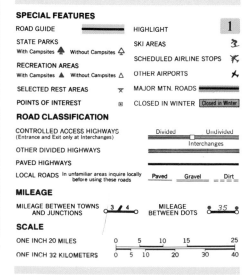

3. The barren Promontory Mountains brood above the marshes of the Bear River Migratory Bird Refuge, where more than 200 species of birds have been sighted. Among them, at right from the top, are the avocet, the white pelican, and the western grebe.

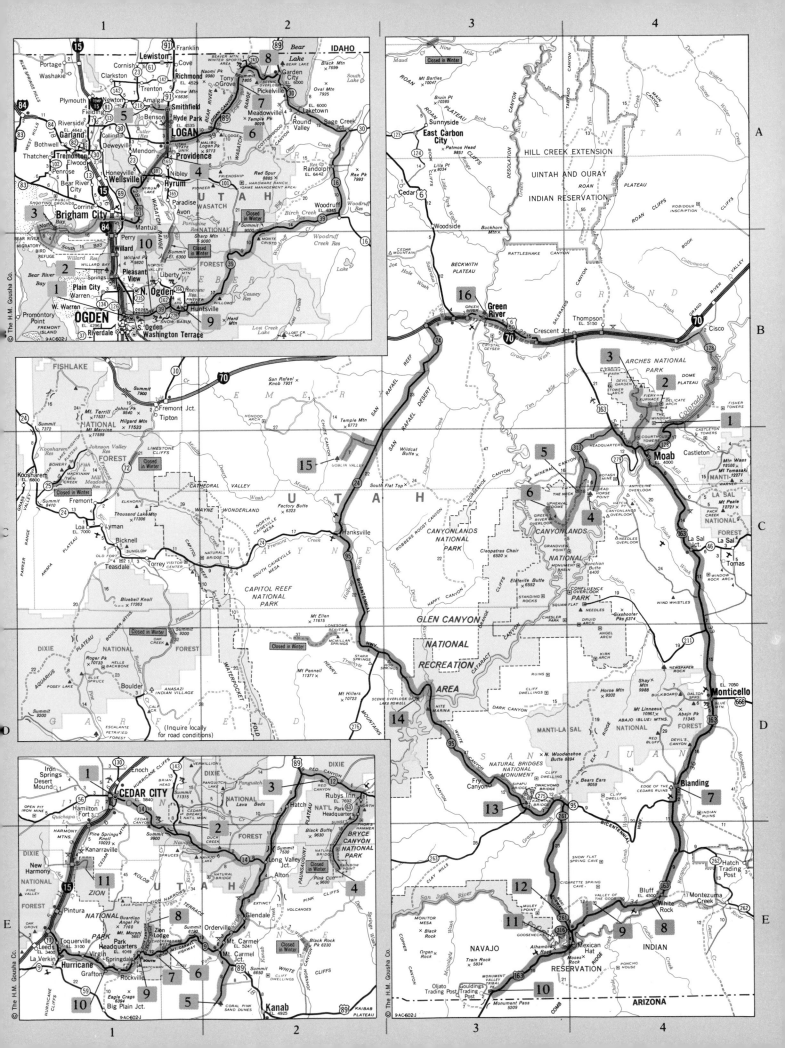

and one of the very few places where waterfowl concentrations approach the fabled numbers described by the first explorers. At the height of the fall migration there may be 25,000 whistling swans, a half-million ducks, and a quarter of a million swallows here.

Another common bird at the refuge is the California gull, chosen the state bird of Utah because it saved the Mormon pioneers from starvation. Huge colonies of California gulls nesting around Great Salt Lake consumed overwhelming swarms of crickets that threatened the vital first harvest of the Mormons in 1848.

4 Along Route 89/91 bigtooth maples on the Wellsville Mountains make a showy backdrop for the 120-acre Ronald V. Jensen Living Historical Farm and the Man and His Bread Museum. Situated on the left side of the highway, this facility of Utah State University is an engrossing presentation of 19th-century farming in the arid West. The museum houses many artifacts of pioneer agriculture, and a variety of farm implements is displayed outdoors.

5 Cache Valley was so named because mountain men kept their caches of beaver pelts here. The val-

8. *Bear Lake, a remnant of ancient Lake Bonneville, stretches between mountains and the flatlands irrigated by its waters. The Idaho–Utah border bisects the lake. Beaver skins once provided income in this area, but raspberries are now the cash crop.*

ley has become Utah's dairy district, and the inhabitants claim their cows are not only contented but slightly conceited. Visitors are welcome at five cheese factories. Of these, the Cache Valley Dairy Association at Amalga is large and clearly signposted from Logan. A self-guided tour of the dairy leads past the various operations involved in turning out more than 100,000 pounds of cheese a day.

6 You can see sedimentary rocks in Logan Canyon that were stacked in horizontal layers some 565 million years ago. After that, about 135 million years ago, the land began to warp and fold, turning the horizontal rock upward. This folding can be seen in rocks along the canyon walls.

The rock layers reveal fossils of creatures that existed when the material forming the rocks was first deposited. Laid out in an orderly manner, the fossils tell us about the development of life from primitive algae to complex mammals that roamed Lake Bonneville's shore.

About 10 miles into the canyon a U.S. Forest Service sign indicates a block of stone containing a remarkable pattern of squiggles and ridges.

These markings, made by marine worms, are cemented in the sand of a beach deposited about 400 million years ago.

7 Five miles beyond the marking display, Logan Canyon twists through curves resembling those of a river winding lazily across a flat landscape. When the land was first revealed by the receding ocean, a waterway meandered across flat terrain. Renewed uplifting increased the downcutting power of the river, deepening the valley, but not enough to cut through the meanders. Today the river flows fast and cuts relatively quickly, but it is trapped in its ever-deepening meanders by limestone cliffs.

Near the end of the curviest part of the canyon is Ricks Spring, which flows from limestone that was formed about 425 million years ago. Snowmelt from surrounding high peaks trickles into cracks and flows along a fault to emerge from a cave along the north side of the road. You can see the fault, a vertical crack at the back of the cave.

As the road climbs higher, short-needled trees are replaced by quaking aspen, sage, and limber pine. This

6. *Bicyclists carrying camping gear enjoy one of the less hilly stretches of Logan Canyon. Autumn has tinted the foliage along the winding highway.*

is prime habitat for elk, the state animal. Crossing over the Bear Lake Summit at 7,800 feet, you leave the canyon behind. If you are reluctant to depart from such a lovely place, you may wish to pause for a 30-minute walk along the mile-long Limber Pine Trail.

8   About a mile beyond Bear Lake Summit is a scenic overlook of the 20-mile-long, 7-mile-wide Bear Lake. Unlike Great Salt Lake, Bear Lake has an outlet at the northern end and thus contains fresh water used to irrigate surrounding fields. The area is well known for its raspberries, harvested in late July and the first two weeks of August.

Beyond Bear Lake the road crosses austere rolling red uplands to the Bear River valley, where irrigated hay fields support a large cattle industry. Route 39 takes you along Birch Creek and Walton Canyon. The road climbs into Wasatch National Forest (officially called Wasatch-Cache National Forest), where ridgetop turnouts provide good views of the Uinta Mountains, 100 miles to the southeast, one of the very few major ranges in America to run east and west.

9   Below a line of cottonwood-shaded Forest Service campgrounds strung along the canyon of the South Fork of the Ogden River, the Ogden Valley widens into a rich expanse of irrigated farmland. Numerous irrigation canals crisscross the valley, diverting water from and to Pineview Reservoir.

This water-recreation mecca has a more complex storage system than its blue surface reveals. Water is stored not only in the reservoir but beneath it. A seal of clay separates reservoir water from a thick layer of sand and gravel resting on limestone bedrock. The sand and gravel hold water that is pumped via wells and a conduit to the city of Ogden.

10   Ogden Canyon is twisting, narrow, and steep-walled. Oaks, cottonwoods, maples, and evergreens line the Ogden River. Layers of sedimentary rock that were upended millions of years ago rake across the skyline. Fishermen step out into the river in waders where there is no room to stand between water and canyon wall, casting their lures for the state fish, rainbow trout.

From Cedar City and the Iron Mission *State Historical Monument, this route traverses the Markagunt Plateau, climbing to Cedar Breaks National Monument, a preview of the sculptured cliffs of Red Canyon and Bryce Canyon National Park. Beyond is the glory of Coral Pink Sand Dunes State Reserve and Zion National Park.*

1   Cedar City was founded in 1851 by English, Scottish, and Welsh miners, who opened nearby coal and iron deposits. The beginnings of Cedar City's iron industry are commemorated at Iron Mission State Historical Monument. The monument is on Main Street, 0.7 of a mile from the Route 14 turnoff.

Route 14 climbs the Markagunt Plateau via colorful Cedar Canyon. Outstanding views present themselves in Dixie National Forest, especially from the turnout at Zion Overlook, which provides a vista of Zion National Park. Missing, however, are cedars. Mormon pioneers thought the abundant, scaly-needled trees with fragrant red heartwood were cedars, but they are really junipers. True cedars are not native to North America.

2   Winter snows close the road to Cedar Breaks National Monument to all but snowmobilers, cross-country skiers, and snowshoers. But during the warm months a three-mile drive brings you to the monument boundary, and another mile to a visitor center at Point Supreme, one of four main overlooks on the rim of the breaks.

"Breaks" is a pioneer term for the escarpment, or "breakaway," of an amphitheater eroded in an explosion of color on the side of a plateau. Dozens of hues of red, gold, violet, and white glow from these cliffs. Nature trails in Cedar Breaks are supplemented by guided walks and talks in the summer, when the color of the wild flower display rivals the year-round color in the cliffs.

3   Most people reach Bryce Canyon National Park via Red Canyon in Dixie National Forest. Indeed, many travelers think they have arrived at Bryce when they see Red Canyon's

2. The pinnacles of limestone in this natural amphitheater at Cedar Breaks National Monument are baroque in character. The forms were sculpted over a period of 13 million years by frost and trickling water. The cliffs glow with a dozen different hues.

5. *The yellow light of the setting sun denies the name of this vast sand pile: Coral Pink Sand Dunes State Reserve. But the color of the sand changes as the light changes, just as the dunes shift their contours under the constant probing of the wind. Dune buggies also leave their marks briefly on these sinuous hills.*

spires and cliffs. But Red Canyon deserves recognition for its own geology. At its western end, black lava flows contrast with pinnacles of red siltstone. The volcanic rock is not found in the national park.

Route 12 passes through two arches blasted in fins of rock in Red Canyon. Signs warn motorists to stop and admire the canyon only at designated turnouts, of which there are many. A U.S. Forest Service nature trail, the Pink Ledges Trail, leads among fanciful rock forms.

4 Bryce Canyon National Park is not really a canyon. Its 36,010 acres contain a 20-mile-long escarpment, part of the Pink Cliffs. This eastern edge of the Paunsaugunt Plateau is indented by a dozen dramatic amphitheaters whose wild variety of brilliant colors is greatly understated by calling them "pink." Bryce has been carved by erosion into "hoodoos"—spires, walls, arches, and other monuments—and is painted shades of red, yellow, white, and purple by iron and manganese. Hoodoos are so called because by twilight or moonlight they have the ghostly look of hooded figures.

Bryce's 20-mile-long main road climbs along the top of the Pink Cliffs. In summer, sego lily (*Calochortus nuttallii*), Utah's state flower, waves its three-petaled white blooms in sunny open spaces amid forests along the rim.

Beyond the park entrance station is a visitor center with displays and Park Service staff to explain local natural history and geology. The park's most remarkable geological formation is Bryce Canyon Amphitheater—called by an early cattleman "a helluva place to lose a cow." Today's visitors are more likely to be awed by the colorful maze of rocks among which dart violet-green swallows and white-throated swifts in summer. From Sunset Point there is a 1½-mile walk, Navajo Loop Trail, which leads through narrow defiles

and such fancifully named forms as Thor's Hammer and Temple of Osiris. Bryce Point is a good spot from which to view the Wall of Windows, which extend out from the main cliff. Peekaboo Loop Trail affords even better views.

Winter snows close the road south of the main amphitheater. Warm-weather travelers can drive on through forests that include blue spruce (*Picea pungens*), Utah's state tree. Turnouts look down on natural bridges and arches and various other sculptures.

5 A clearly posted turn off Route 89 leads to Coral Pink Sand Dunes State Reserve. Pines and sage try to encroach on the edges of the reserve, but expanses of lifeless sand undulate to the flanks of surrounding sandstone hills.

Rain erodes sand grains from the loosely cemented Navajo sandstone. Wind then dumps the pink sand on the dunes. Ironically, Navajo sandstone was formed by the same sort of wind process 150 to 170 million years ago. As the sand became rock and then sand again, perhaps one day it may again be rock.

6 After passing the Zion National Park entrance station, you are surrounded by petrified sand dunes. Navajo sandstone is the most prominent rock in Zion. Winds deposited this sand during a retreat of the sea, piling

up layers 2,000 feet thick. The patterns in which varying winds arranged beds of sand are revealed by erosion cutting through the sandstone. These slanted patterns are called cross-bedding.

The most spectacular example of cross-bedding along the highway is Checkerboard Mesa, about a half-mile inside the park boundary. A well-marked turnout provides a good view of the mesa, crosshatched by erosion along points of stress.

7 Zion–Mount Carmel Highway, considered a marvel of engineering, winds among pines and junipers growing from cracks in the rock. The most spectacular engineering feat on the highway is the Zion–Mount Carmel Tunnel, a bore of 1.1 miles through Navajo sandstone at the face of Pine Creek Canyon. The tunnel reduced road-building scars, which are limited to ventilation arches in the cliff. From switchbacks that descend 700 feet into the canyon, you have views of the Great Arch of Zion.

This arch is more then 700 feet wide at the base and nearly 600 feet high. Like the other arches in the canyon, it was formed by the breaking away of a slab of rock along a crack parallel to the canyon wall. The cracks appeared during the area's uplift. If the slab is undercut by erosion, its unsupported weight causes internal stresses that weaken the

Some of the most magnificent and *awe-inspiring scenes in America are in Canyonlands and Arches national parks, Monument and Goblin valleys, and in other highly sculptured landscapes carved by the Green, Colorado, and San Juan rivers.*

1 The many arches in the 114 square miles of Arches National Park are the largest concentration of such features in the world.

It is worthwhile to stop at the visitor center just inside the park to pick up a map and descriptive material. About 10 miles from the center watch for the spur to the Windows, a collection of eight large arches and miscellaneous holes, gaps, spires, and balanced boulders. A short stroll from the end of the spur brings you to North and South Windows, Turret Arch, and the famous Double Arch.

Double Arch is a combination of the usual fin with a hole in it and a pothole arch. Pothole arches are formed horizontally when flowing water dissolves a depression near the edge of a cliff. Meanwhile, erosion undercutting from the face of the cliff works its way toward the pothole. When a passage finally perforates the lip of the cliff, water flows through the opening, greatly increasing the erosion. The larger of the openings in magnificent Double Arch is 163 by 157 feet.

2 Two-and-a-half miles beyond the turnoff to the Windows, a sign indicates an unpaved road to the path leading up to Delicate Arch. Here erosion has worn away most of the fin, leaving only the pink stone arch standing grandly on the rim of a sandstone bowl. The 1½-mile path to the arch rises 500 feet and can be a hot and tiring walk. There is a distant view of Delicate Arch 1.3 miles beyond the trail head, at the end of the unpaved road.

3 The paved road passes an area called Fiery Furnace, a labyrinth of red sandstone fins named for its color at sunset, not for its temperature at noon in July. At Devils Garden, Skyline Arch rises to the right a half-mile from the end of the pavement as a reminder that arch creation is an ongoing process. In 1940 a large wedge dropped from beneath the span, in an instant more than doubling its size.

rock. The lower part of the weakened rock falls away, but the upper part is prevented from falling because it has greater mass than the width of the opening below it. This keystone effect holds the slab in place, forming a strong arch.

8 A turn to the north off the highway leads along Zion Canyon Scenic Drive, six magnificent miles through the most marvelous of Zion's scenery. The canyon inspires a religious reverence that has resulted in such names as East Temple, Three Patriarchs, and Angels Landing for its prominent pinnacles. The most famous of the monoliths is Great White Throne, best viewed from a parking area 4.7 miles up the scenic drive.

Walks increase your appreciation of the scenic grandeur. Probably the easiest is a quarter-mile path to Weeping Rock from a well-marked parking area 4½ miles up the scenic drive. On the other extreme, the path to Angels Landing is 2½ steep miles to the top of a rock where early explorers predicted only winged angels ever could set foot.

9 The scenery between the Zion–Mount Carmel Highway and the park's south entrance is almost as awesome as along the scenic drive. West Temple, the highest tower, is 3,805 feet above the canyon floor. Nearby Altar of Sacrifice gains its gory name from the streaks of bright red iron oxide that have leached down to stain its white cliffs. Appropriately, the Watchman looms 2,600 feet above the South Entrance Station. The visitor center has exhibits on Zion's archeology.

10 Perhaps the most photogenic ghost town in Utah, Grafton is reached via a bumpy road from Rockville. Three-tenths of a mile inside the eastern edge of Rockville, the town's first street to the south leads over a one-lane iron bridge. Thereafter, bear right each time the road forks, except at a rutted driveway two miles beyond the bridge. Pavement ends at a cattle guard 0.7 of a mile from the bridge, and unpaved road proceeds for 2.6 dusty miles to Grafton. Remember that ghost towns seldom are on main thoroughfares.

Begun in the 1850's, Grafton was an unsuccessful effort of the Mormons to establish a cotton plantation in this part of Utah. Today only several buildings remain.

11 A 5.2-mile spur road that is closed in winter penetrates the high desert scenery of the northern section of Zion National Park. Red sandstone monoliths tower above deep and narrow box canyons, the Finger Canyons. These are viewed from turnouts, trails, and a picnic area along a road that climbs from Taylor Creek Canyon over Lee Pass and up the side of Timber Creek Canyon.

Normally, arch enlargement is a grain-by-grain process.

Arch destruction also proceeds in Devils Garden. The next one to fall will probably be Landscape Arch, a 20-minute walk beyond the pavement's end. A graceful 291-foot band of stone, Landscape Arch is the longest natural arch in the world. No one knows how long it will last, but it seems much more delicate than Delicate Arch.

4 From Route 163 a well-marked spur penetrates the canyon lands of the Colorado and Green rivers to Dead Horse Point State Park, an arrowhead-shaped promontory 2,000 feet above the Colorado River. Junipers growing from red sandstone at the point frame a stupendous 5,000-square-mile vista.

5 The road into Canyonlands National Park leads to The Neck, a 60-foot-wide isthmus to Island in the Sky. Cliffs dropping 1,000 feet along the sides of this peninsula once made

4. *The muddy waters of the Colorado River are seen below Dead Horse Point. The point got its name from some wild mustangs that hunters left fenced in on this mesa top, where the animals died of thirst.*

Island in the Sky a 25,000-acre cattle pasture that could be enclosed with a 60-foot length of fence at the neck.

About six miles from The Neck is a worthwhile half-mile walk to Mesa Arch, which is made of Navajo sandstone and hangs on the edge of a cliff. A self-guiding trail leads to fine views into the canyons below the arch.

6 Upheaval Dome looks like a crater, but it was a dome 40 million years ago. At that time a huge salt deposit far below the sandstone bulged upward and warped the surface in some areas, including Upheaval Dome where six layers of rock were tilted on end. The force of water has since eroded the dome to the bulls-eyelike basin you see here.

You can view Upheaval Dome from Whale Rock, a prominence of Navajo sandstone on the crater rim. The viewpoint is a 15-minute walk from a well-marked trail head.

East of Route 163 is Church Rock, a Byzantinelike monolith marking where Route 211 cuts west 36 miles to four-wheel drive roads that explore Canyonlands National Park. South of Church Rock, Route 163 passes through fields of hardy rye alternating with desert grazing land and piñon pine–juniper forests. Dominating the view to the right are the Abajo, or Blue, Mountains.

7 One of the highest peaks in this range is Mount Linnaeus, at 10,959 feet a striking backdrop for fascinating Edge of the Cedars State Historical Monument on the west side of Blanding. This ruin of an Anasazi Indian pueblo is explained by a self-guiding trail that includes entry into a kiva. Anasazi life focused on these round, partially subterranean rooms, used for men's social clubs, temporary homes, and religious ceremonies. Next to the ruin is a museum that explains the cultures of Anasazi, Navajo, and Ute Indians and early white settlers in the region.

Route 163 north of Bluff runs through a picturesque canyon guarded at its southern portal by the Navajo Twins. These locally famous columns are shale protected from erosion by a hard cap of sandstone.

8 Less than 2½ miles south of Bluff on Route 163 a sign marks a turn to the south onto an unpaved road to Sand Island Campground on

the banks of the San Juan River. Where the road forks left to the Bureau of Land Management campground, continue right to a sandstone cliff covered with petroglyphs. The sandstone is coated by desert varnish, a dark film of iron and manganese oxide leached from the rock and deposited on the surface by evaporating moisture. Indians created rock art by pecking designs out of the varnish, exposing the lighter rock that lay underneath.

The Sand Island petroglyphs reveal Indian efforts extending over a thousand years. Some designs are easily identified as desert bighorn sheep, one being shot by a hunter with a bow. Others are undecipherable to whites but easily recognized by Hopi Indians from Arizona as symbols of their clans, such as a tadpole or a flute player.

9 Ten miles beyond Sand Island is Valley of the Gods, a showcase of erosional sculpture. The mysterious structures are made of relatively soft red siltstone and clay. The road continues to Mexican Hat Rock, which is shaped like an inverted sombrero, and is also formed of red siltstone and clay. Rising behind the rock are colorful synclines and anticlines. These surface rocks are wrinkled as if the parallel layers were pushed from the sides. The tops of these undulations are anticlines; the troughs in between them are synclines.

10 The dramatic buttes and spires of the Navajos' 29,817-acre Monument Valley Tribal Park may constitute the most famous scenery in the world. It has been the location for innumerable television commercials and motion pictures. The Navajo people maintain their culture here more conservatively than on most of their huge reservation.

At the entrance to the park is a visitor center where Navajos present displays and sell their handiwork.

11 A "gooseneck" is the local term for what geologists call an incised meander, and here at Goosenecks State Park are the world's most spectacular examples.

The San Juan River's outline was established millions of years ago when this area was a broad plain. As the land rose, the cutting power of the river was increased but not enough to

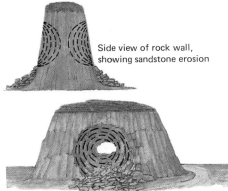

Side view of rock wall, showing sandstone erosion

Opening in center, with stream flowing around wall

Stream flows through bridge

13. *Sipapu Natural Bridge (left), in Natural Bridges National Monument, was originally a solid wall of sandstone crowned by rock of greater density. The sandstone was eroded on both sides by the effects of heating and cooling, until a hole appeared through the center of the wall. As the erosion process continued, the opening grew larger. Finally, a stream, which had previously been diverted by the wall, passed through the opening, leaving the old riverbed around the bridge.*

break through the curves of the meanders. Thus the river has entrenched itself in a narrow, winding canyon some 1,500 feet deep. In one section, where the river doubles back on itself seven times, it flows for five or six miles to cover a straight-line distance of one mile.

12 From the San Juan Reserve, Route 261 continues over a red-soiled desert along the west edge of Valley of the Gods and then heads directly into a buff-and-red-banded 1,110-foot cliff of Cedar Mesa sandstone. You may wonder where the highway is going. It is going up that cliff.

A mile beyond a rough dirt access road that goes into the Valley of the Gods, you reach the end of pavement and come to a series of tortuous switchbacks up the cliff that was invisible from the desert below. This is Moki Dugway. "Dugway" is a pioneer Mormon term for roads carved from remarkably steep terrain. There are several turnouts at which to stop and enjoy the view.

13 A well-marked spur from Route 95 leads to Natural Bridges National Monument, where three huge bridges show three different phases of natural bridge building. Streams cutting through their entrenched meanders produced these spans. Using silt as abrasive, the streams bored holes through narrow necks of the meanders. Once the hole was punched through, the stream could flow through it, greatly increasing the rate of erosion.

Beyond the visitor center, which features a museum and a native plants walkway, a one-way circle drive of eight miles connects trail heads for short paths to each bridge. The first is Sipapu, a mature bridge, now little affected by its stream and enlarged only by weathering. A 268-foot span, Sipapu is the second-longest natural bridge in the world, surpassed only by Rainbow Bridge in Glen Canyon National Recreation Area. The bridge is almost perfectly symmetrical.

The second bridge is Kachina, massive and still being cut by floodwaters in White Canyon. The third is Owachomo, a delicate-looking span of 180 feet, worn to a 9-foot thickness over the last 10 million years.

14 Spanning three dramatic canyons—White, Colorado, and Dirty Devil—Route 95 passes through Glen Canyon National Recreation Area to a scenic overlook of Lake Powell. Like a dragon lying across red rocks, Lake Powell backs up behind Glen Canyon Dam, far downstream. Many canyon lovers claim that Glen Canyon was the Colorado River's biggest and best achievement in Utah before it was inundated by Lake Powell. The controversial Glen Canyon Dam has become a symbol to its opponents of a tragic mistake that must never be repeated.

15 Route 95 rolls through North Wash, a deeply carved red canyon. After taking Route 24 beyond Hanksville, you come to Goblin Valley State Reserve with its stone demons—goblins and other features eroded from Entrada sandstone.

16 Main tributary of the Colorado, the Green River is a significant waterway in its own right. Popular with canoe and raft river runners, the Green offers both placid stretches and white-water thrills amid towering red canyon walls.

Land of Contrasts

Idaho's rich farmland is set off by dense forests, rugged mountains, canyons, lakes, and lava flows

As a state best known for the excellence of its potatoes, Idaho can be full of surprises for the first-time visitor. Hells Canyon, the deepest in North America, and the Ketchum–Sun Valley ski resorts have been well publicized; but the myriad lakes, the gold rush country, lava beds, sand dunes, and ice caves are, for most people, unexpected delights.

There are some 2,000 lakes in Idaho, and here in the northern part of the state, home of the Coeur d'Alene Indians, you can see many of the most beautiful ones. The route begins with Coeur d'Alene Lake and touches Rose, Kilarney, Medicine, Chatcolet, Round, Benewah, Twin, Spirit, Pend Oreille, and Priest lakes. This is also timber country, blanketed with evergreen forests and laced with hiking trails.

1 Coeur d'Alene is located in timber country, and a steady supply of logs from the surrounding forests is harvested to keep the town's sawmills running. The U.S. Forest Service plays an important role in reforestation, and for a look at their program, you can visit the U.S. Forest Service Nursery from June through August. The nursery has an annual capacity of 38 million trees.

To promote an understanding of Idaho's pioneer background, the Museum of North Idaho, on Northwest Boulevard, has a photographic exhibit featuring pictures of early miners and mines, Indians, steamboats, and loggers. Other exhibits include a turn-of-the-century kitchen, a blacksmith shop, mineral samples, and logging equipment.

Also in the town is Tubbs Hill, which offers the pleasures of a natural lakeshore wilderness on city property. Nature trails lead to beaches and lookout points. There are small caves to explore at the base of the hill.

The annual Lake Coeur d'Alene Days Festival in mid-May includes logging events, a boat parade, and various games.

Coeur d'Alene Lake, extending for some 30 miles south of the town with which it shares the name, has more than a hundred miles of shoreline, with good sandy beaches, marinas, launching ramps, and resorts. The lake is a favorite with fishermen who vie for cutthroat trout and kokanee salmon. In winter when the lake freezes over, die-hard fishermen remain undaunted, trying their luck at fishing through the ice while skaters glide on the frozen surface.

One of the best ways to enjoy the beauty of the surrounding countryside is by water. Boat rentals are available and tours, from a short lake cruise to a day-long backcountry trip, depart from the First Street and City Docks in town. A favorite outing here is the 48-mile trip down Coeur d'Alene Lake and up the St. Joe River to St. Maries. The lake, like most others in Idaho, fills a long trough scoured out of the mountains by the ice age glaciers, and this region, like so much of the rest of the state, is one of primitive beauty. It is lovely in fall when the gold of the tamaracks is seen with the dark green firs and pines. Among the latter is white pine (*Pinus strobus*), the state tree.

Route 90 follows the lake for about 11 miles before entering the Coeur d'Alene National Forest. In Fourth of July Canyon, about five miles into the forest, you can see a large tree stump bearing the date July 4, 1861, and the name of Capt. John Mullan, who blazed the trail that is now part of Route 90.

2 In Old Mission State Park is the graceful Coeur d'Alene Mission of the Sacred Heart, Idaho's oldest standing building. It was designed and built by Father Anthony Ravalli, a Jesuit

1. This view of Lake Coeur d'Alene looks north toward the community of Coeur d'Alene, with Tubbs Hill on the right. Notice how the forests of evergreens push right down to the edge of the water all around the shoreline.

SPECIAL FEATURES

ROAD GUIDE	HIGHLIGHT **1**
STATE PARKS With Campsites / Without Campsites	SCHEDULED AIRLINE STOPS
RECREATION AREAS With Campsites / Without Campsites	MILITARY AIRPORTS
SELECTED REST AREAS	OTHER AIRPORTS
POINTS OF INTEREST	MAJOR MTN. ROADS
SKI AREAS	CLOSED IN WINTER

ROAD CLASSIFICATION

CONTROLLED ACCESS HIGHWAYS
Interstate interchange numbers are mileposts.

OTHER DIVIDED HIGHWAYS

PAVED HIGHWAYS

LOCAL ROADS   In unfamiliar areas inquire locally before using these roads   Paved   Gravel   Dirt

MILEAGE

MILEAGE BETWEEN TOWNS AND JUNCTIONS   3 / 4   MILEAGE BETWEEN DOTS   35

SCALE

ONE INCH 22 MILES   0   5   10   15   25

ONE INCH 35 KILOMETERS   0 5 10   20   30   40

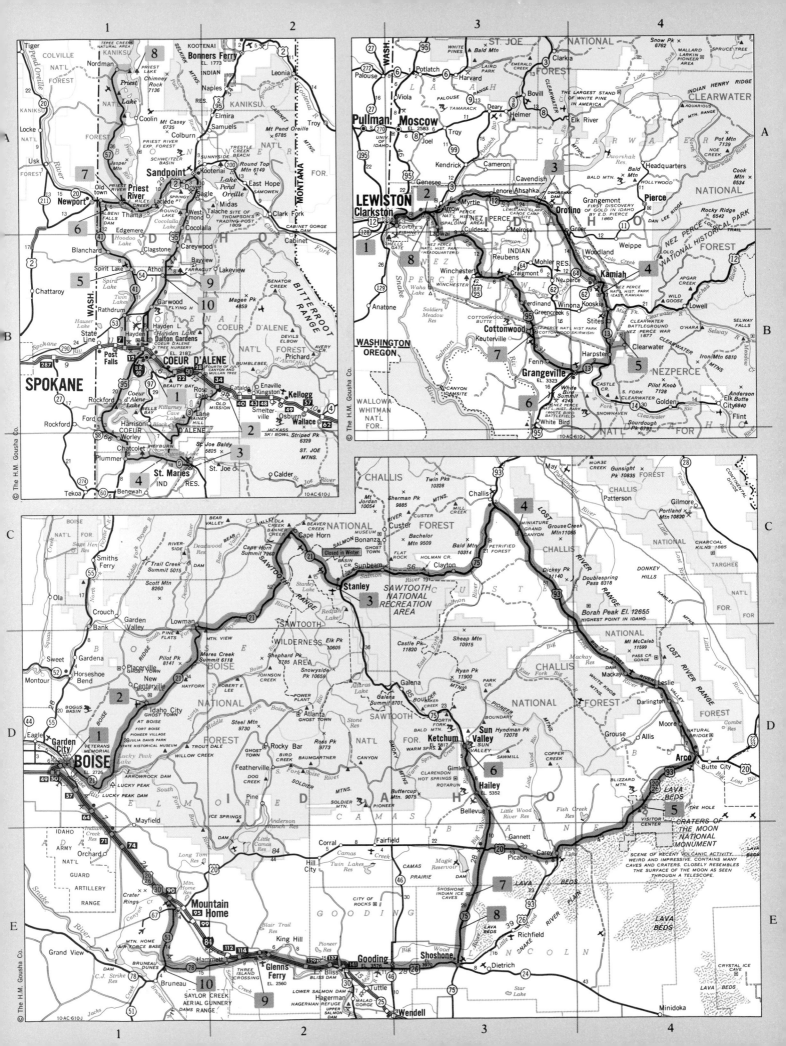

missionary, and the Coeur d'Alene Indians. Begun in 1846, the timber-and-mud building was not completed until 1853. Interior walls, carvings, and ceiling panels were added later. Only primitive tools were used, and the entire structure was assembled with wooden pegs. You can still see some of the original pegs in the floor.

A half-mile trail leads to the sites of the mission's original parish house, barn, gristmill, cabin for brothers and travelers, and cemetery.

The route winds its way through a farmland valley and wooded foothills, passing Rose, Kilarney, and Medicine lakes, all fine spots for trout fishing. The Coeur d'Alene River is especially good for rainbow and cutthroat in summer and fall.

3   St. Maries is a lumber center and the starting point for trips along the St. Joe, the world's highest navigable river. A favorite backcountry camping trip of canoe enthusiasts is the 12-mile stretch of river, some of it white water, to the ghost town of St. Joe, once a booming mining camp.

4   Heyburn State Park, which has more than 6,000 acres of gentle hills and rich forest, is along the shores of Chatcolet Lake. The park offers campsites, nature trails, swimming, picnicking, boat rentals, and a general store. In winter there is cross-country skiing, snowmobiling, and ice fishing. The waters here are among the best in these parts for bass fishing.

2. The columns of the Coeur d'Alene Mission are reminiscent of the Greek Revival style of the mid-1800's.

From a viewpoint on Route 5 about two miles inside the park you can see the St. Joe as it flows between Chatcolet and Round lakes. From here it is easy to understand why Idahoans call this the "shadowy St. Joe." The reflection of the leaves of hillside trees create moving patterns of light and dark on the clear waters.

5   The tiny country town of Spirit Lake with its spruced-up storefronts has an inviting air of individuality. The lake, 2,440 feet high in a lovely mountain setting, is part of what once was an immense ice age lake called Clearwater. The name Spirit Lake evolved from an Indian legend.

6   The workings of the Albeni Falls Dam on the Pend Oreille River can be seen on a self-guided tour. Closed from October through April. There is a picnic area and a scenic overlook at the dam. Camping facilities and a boat ramp are available at Albeni Cove, on the south end of the dam.

7   The town of Priest River is the starting point for boaters making trips upriver to Lake Pend Oreille, one of the largest freshwater lakes in the United States. Camping facilities and boat launches are located at Priest River Park. Priest River's annual Loggers Celebration is held the third weekend in July and features lumberjack contests, raft races, a horse show, and a fireworks display. The river is famous for its trout, and it is also on a major flyway for migrating ducks and geese.

8   Over 20 miles long, Priest Lake is actually two lakes in one, Upper Priest and Priest, connected by the scenic Priest River Thorofare. The natural beauty of the lake is enhanced by its dramatic backdrop, the Selkirk Mountains, and the surrounding dense forest of Douglas fir, white and lodgepole pine, spruce, and cedar. There are sandy beaches for swimming, safe boat launchings and landings, and some of the finest trout fishing in the country. For rock climbers, a jagged, 200-foot promontory called Chimney Rock provides a challenge to their skills.

9   Bordering the southern end of Lake Pend Oreille, at the foothills of the Bitterroot Mountains, is Farragut State Park, the unlikely site of a former naval station. The park now offers picnicking, swimming, boating,

8. The 200-foot height of Chimney Rock, on the east shore of Priest Lake, is a favorite of climbers, some of whom can be seen scaling and atop the granite spire.

and excellent fishing. Hiking trails wind through the surrounding forest, where white-tailed deer are often spotted. Mountain goats may be seen on the cliffs opposite Eagle Marina. Among the birds to be seen here are ducks, red-tailed hawks, and bald eagles. A museum features exhibits of the history of the area and its native wildlife, as well as old naval station records and photographs.

10   In addition to Henley Aerodrome's usual business of charter flights, this tiny airport in Athol has a display of antique planes and offers hot-air balloon rides as well as sightseeing flights in open-cockpit biplanes. There are also air shows with stunt flying.

Should you be driving along this route during the first weekend in September, you may want to spend some time at the Kootenai County Fairgrounds to enjoy some of the local food and festivities.

Hells Canyon, carved over millions of years by the Snake River, is the deepest in North America. This awesome gorge played an important role in American history, sheltering Indians and settlers, and providing for each (at separate times) food and safety from enemies. This land of the Nez Perce tribe is rich in Indian and pioneer legend and history.

1 Lewiston, at the confluence of the Snake and Clearwater rivers, is the starting point for boat, float, and canoe trips along the Snake River to Hells Canyon, between Idaho and Oregon. Check with the Chamber of Commerce for a list of outfitters and guides in the area.

A park road and a bicycle path follow the Snake River for four miles from downtown Lewiston to Hells Gate State Park, where excursion boats leave for the 180-mile round trip to Hells Canyon, the deepest gorge in North America. Cut over a period of 4 million years by the Snake River, this mile-deep canyon is bordered by Seven Devils Mountain on one side and a steep wall of basaltic rock on the other. Hells Gate State Park has a swimming area, a playground, picnic facilities, a horse corral, and water-ski docks. There are hiking and horseback riding trails and a campground.

Lewiston is also the starting point for an auto tour of country that had once been the homeland of the Nez Perce Indians. At historic sites signs document the culture of the Indians and also their fateful contacts with the settlers and others who came here.

Winding along the Clearwater River, and at times hugging the base of high, jagged canyon walls, the highway retraces the route taken through this area by Meriwether Lewis and William Clark on their trek to the Pacific coast in 1804–05.

2 From a pulloff on the south side of the highway six miles east of Lewiston, you can see on the rocky slope a natural formation that suggested to the Nez Perces the fishnet used by Coyote, a supernatural being in their mythology.

Three miles away, just east of the junction of Routes 95 and 12, is a rock formation known to the Indians as Ant and Yellowjacket. According to legend, Coyote was so angered by the fighting between these two that he turned them into stone.

3 Canoe Camp, a tiny park on the Clearwater River, is the place where Lewis and Clark camped in the autumn of 1805 and, before proceeding downriver, learned from the amiable Nez Perces how to build dugout canoes. A dam and a fish hatchery here have altered the scene since their time.

4 Close by the river in the East Kamiah site of the Nez Perce National Historic Park is a 30-foot-high volcanic rock outcropping known as the Heart of the Monster. In Nez Perce legend, the monster was slain by Coyote, and the Indian peoples rose from its flesh and blood.

A half-mile down the road you pass the MacBeth Schoolhouse, named after Sue and Kate MacBeth, who served as missionary-teachers among the Nez Perces from 1873 to 1893. The wood-frame building is privately owned and not open to the public. Close by stands the First Indian Presbyterian Church, which opened its doors in 1871.

5 In 1877 the formerly peaceful Nez Perces repeatedly fought the U.S. Army over rights to their rich reservation land. The clash at Clearwater Battlefield was a turning point: although neither side won, the Indians lost heart and decided to abandon their land to avoid further bloodshed.

6 Grangeville is surrounded by gently rolling plains, much of which is planted with wheat. Several miles southwest is the Camas Prairie, where the Nez Perces gathered each summer to dig the camas roots, edible wild tubers that were an essential part of their food supply. Some camas still grows here. A mining town back in the 1890's, Grangeville hosts the annual Border Days celebration in July, which features a rodeo.

7 At an attractive wayside area 2½ miles southeast of Cottonwood, you can picnic and enjoy the lovely, rolling wheat fields. Here, in July 1877, a party of U.S. Army volunteers skirmished with Nez Perces led by Chief Joseph. Afterward the Indians set out for Canada. They were stopped in Montana where Joseph surrendered, ending the war.

8 Upon meeting Lewis and Clark in 1805, the Nez Perces had wanted to learn more of the white man's ways, and years later they requested teachers. In 1836 Henry R. Spalding, a Presbyterian minister, was sent out, and in 1838 he and his wife estab-

3. Clearwater River, shown near Orofino, was one of the routes used by Lewis and Clark to cross Idaho.

lished a mission at Lapwai (now Spalding), with the first printing press, school, and church in Idaho. Only two piles of rocks remain.

The visitor center at Spalding, the headquarters of the Nez Perce National Historic Park, has a museum featuring artifacts of early missionary life and exhibits on the Nez Perce culture.

3. *Mount Regan dominates the mountains rimming Sawtooth Lake in the Sawtooth Wilderness Area. To see this view requires a demanding nine-mile round-trip hike from the trail head at the end of Iron Creek Road, off Route 21 two miles west of Stanley.*

This area, rich in contrasts, *offers the bustle of Boise and its historic district of turn-of-the-century buildings, a look at the Oregon Trail, and Grimes Creek, where the Idaho gold rush began. Here too is the luxury of the Ketchum–Sun Valley resorts, the natural beauty of the Sawtooth Wilderness Area, and the dramatic forms of ice caves and sand dunes.*

1 Boise, the capital and largest city in Idaho, is a growing trade center for agriculture, livestock, mining, wool, and lumber interests. Originally the area was named Les Bois by French fur trappers and explorers. The present spelling and pronunciation was established by the early settlers. Pioneer life is recalled in several authentic interiors of early-day buildings at the Idaho State Historical Society Museum in Julia Davis Park, where there is also a pioneer village and a zoo.

The Old Boise National Historic District includes various handsome brick and native sandstone buildings built at the turn of the century to replace the wooden structures of the 1860's. A booklet is available that contains maps of walking tours of Boise.

On Route 21 to Idaho City you may want to stop off at the Boise National Forest Ranger Station for information about the Boise National Forest and the Sawtooth Wilderness Area, including their hunting and fishing regulations. At a vantage point about a mile and a half from the ranger station you can see part of the Oregon Trail sloping from the rimrock down to the flatlands below.

A pleasant place to stop is Warm Springs, just south of Idaho City. Here there is a picnic ground and camping area and also a pool fed by a hot spring for comfortable year-round swimming.

2 Founded only 10 weeks after gold was discovered here by George Grimes and his party of miners in August 1862, Idaho City quickly became the largest town in the Northwest. In one year the gold rush swelled the population to 6,275 people—5,691 of whom were men. More gold was reportedly taken from the Boise Basin than from all of Alaska. As the gold diggings were depleted, so was the town, and in 1942 World War II brought gold production to a halt. But the boomtown lore and legend still remain. Leaving Idaho City the winding road climbs into the Sawtooth Mountains. Winter comes early here and snow closes some sections of the road. In the fall it is a good idea to check locally to determine road conditions.

3 Once a gold-mining camp and supply point, now a ranching center, Stanley is a rustic town with log buildings and unpaved streets. Situated on the Salmon River, at the north end of the Sawtooth Basin, this is a popular starting point for expeditions into the Sawtooth Wilderness Area and the Sawtooth National Recreation Area. White-water float trips originate near Stanley and travel the Salmon River, called the "river of no return" because in earlier times its currents and rapids made upstream navigation impossible.

Along the Salmon River, in the Sawtooth National Recreation Area, watch for the roadside signs that describe the spawning beds and the life cycle of the salmon.

4 The walls of Grandview Canyon, Idaho's "Grand Canyon in Miniature," rise 2,000 feet. One of the formations here is Grandview dolomite, a white hard-textured rock formed when the ocean covered this region about 380 million years ago. The most interesting time to be here is late in the day when the canyon walls reflect the changing hues of the setting sun. The road south passes the Mount Borah viewing point, where the natural history of the area is explained. The 12,662-foot peak was named for William Borah, who served as a U.S. senator from Idaho from 1907 to 1940.

A few miles south, amid a treeless expanse of desert, the Mackay Reservoir is a welcome oasis, offering picnic grounds and a splendid view of the mountains.

5 At Craters of the Moon National Monument you can walk across the once-molten lava, now hardened into globular blobs, twisting ribbons, and cinder cones. The 83 square miles of basaltic lava fields have large depressions, or craters, which resemble the moon's pitted surface. This strange landscape was the training site for the first astronauts to land on the moon. The visitor center shows an excellent film on volcanic action as it may have occurred here and has exhibits of lava formations.

Well-marked trails across the lava flows offer a chance to examine the different kinds of lava. A seven-mile auto loop winds around major points of interest. A campground, kept open from May to September, is located near the entrance.

On the side trip to Ketchum and Sun Valley you might be interested in the Blaine County Historical Museum on Main Street in Hailey. At the Hailey Airport ask about sight-seeing flights over this scenic area.

6 Ketchum, once a booming mining town named for fur trapper and prospector Dave Ketchum, came upon hard times after the crash of the silver market in 1893. The Ketchum–Sun Valley area, which is a beautiful terrain located among the Boulder and Pioneer mountains of Sawtooth National Forest, now offers some of the finest skiing in the country as well as golf, tennis, horseback riding, swimming, float trips, and ballooning over Wood River valley and Bald Mountain. In summer Sun Valley holds the Basque Festival, with music, folk dancing, athletic exhibitions, and a Basque feast.

7 The Shoshone Ice Caves are a series of ruggedly sculptured craters with walls of lava and a constant temperature of 30° to 33°F (–1° to 1°C). In autumn water seeping into the caves freezes, covering ceilings and walls with sparkling ice crystals. Closed October 16 through April 30.

8 Mammoth Cave is a mile-long volcanic lava tube with walls of varied colors and interesting shapes. The self-guided tour takes about 20 minutes. A log cabin houses a large taxidermic exhibit of local wildlife and birds. Closed Christmas and New Year's days and in bad weather.

9 The Three Island Crossing State Park, one mile west of Glenns Ferry, commemorates the pioneers of the Oregon Trail. It was here they found that the Snake River could be forded without having to swim. An authentic Conestoga wagon near the visitor center entrance helps you see how rough the ride must have been with iron-shod wheels and no springs.

10 Bruneau Dunes State Park is a sweeping desert composed of hills of sand. Four miles of road, not all paved, extend through the active dunes. There are picnic grounds, campsites, nature trails, and, unexpectedly, a small lake.

5. Trees are beginning to take hold in the lava at the Craters of the Moon National Monument. The twisted tree in the foreground at left was probably killed by lack of moisture. The closeup above is of pahoehoe *(Hawaiian for "smooth lava"). Rough lava, called* aa, *is also found in the area. These lavas are composed of an iron-rich basalt. The brilliant flower growing in this forbidding environment is cushion eriogonum.*

The Northwest Corner

An incomparable panorama of snowcapped mountains, island-studded waters, and sandy beaches

Washington, the Evergreen State, has an abundance of spectacular and varied scenery that is readily accessible by automobile.

The three tours here take you through the San Juan Archipelago, around the Olympic Peninsula, along the Puyallup Valley, and then high across a massive flank of majestic Mount Rainier.

The Northwest was Indian country when the Europeans first came here seeking furs. Many of the tribes are gone, but their language still remains in place-names on the map. On the road keep an eye out for such signs as Duckabush, Queets, Lilliwaup, Tulalip, and Humptulips, as well as Skokomish, Puyallup, Dosewallips, and Quillayute.

With only a few hours of driving and a few days to spare, this island-hopping tour will reveal the watery splendors of the San Juan Islands. You will also dip into Canada on Vancouver Island and enjoy the Old World charm of Victoria, British Columbia.

1 Anacortes, at the northern tip of Fidalgo Island, is a logical point of departure for this circular tour. It is also a popular gateway for day trips to the nearby San Juan Islands. Washington State Ferries run daily from Ship Harbor through the San Juans and on to Vancouver Island in Canada. Anacortes is also the home of numerous charter fleets. If you wish to explore or fish the waters of the San Juans, you can rent a sailboat or a motorboat, large or small, skippered or not, for a day or an overnight cruise.

2 The 2,339-acre state park at Deception Pass, with 13 miles of water frontage, offers a fine setting for camping, hiking, swimming, and fishing. At Rosario Beach you can enjoy a picnic and a view of the surf rolling in past the jutting cliffs.

Continue south over the Deception Pass Bridge, which connects Fidalgo and Whidbey islands. Deception Pass is an ancient river channel created as the earth's crust rose after the melting of the last glacial ice. Sea level has since risen here and the earth has been sinking, so the old channel is now submerged.

3 From Deception Pass to Coupeville the road goes through a gently rolling land of hills, farms, and pastures that are edged by thick woods. Coupeville, founded in 1853, is one of the oldest towns in the state. Front Street, which sweeps around Penn Cove, is lined with restaurants and shops in restored 19th-century buildings. Original blockhouses and churches are open to visitors. Two miles west of Coupeville is The Captain Whidbey Inn, built in 1907 of Madrona logs. The Madrona (*Arbutus menziesii*) is a remarkably handsome tree with red flaking bark. An evergreen native to the Northwest, its sinuous growth makes it unsuitable for logs or lumber, and it is rare to see it used for building. The trees used for the inn, however, came from a crowded grove, and their environment forced them to grow straight.

4 Cars and campers line up early to get on board the little Keystone–Port Townsend Ferry across Puget Sound. The ferry carries vehicles, and

2. A graceful steel bridge, built in 1935, spans Deception Pass between Fidalgo and Whidbey islands. The strong, swift current of Puget Sound rushing through the narrow pass often prevents small boats from navigating these waters.

SPECIAL FEATURES

ROAD GUIDE		HIGHLIGHT	**1**
STATE PARKS With Campsites ▲ Without Campsites △		MILITARY AIRPORTS	
RECREATION AREAS With Campsites ▲ Without Campsites △		OTHER AIRPORTS	
SELECTED REST AREAS	ⅹ	PORTS OF ENTRY	
POINTS OF INTEREST		MAJOR MTN. ROADS	
SKI AREAS		CLOSED IN WINTER	Closed in Winter
SCHEDULED AIRLINE STOPS		BOAT RAMPS	
		COVERED BRIDGES	

ROAD CLASSIFICATION

CONTROLLED ACCESS HIGHWAYS
Interstate interchange numbers are mileposts.

OTHER DIVIDED HIGHWAYS

PAVED HIGHWAYS

LOCAL ROADS In unfamiliar areas inquire locally before using these roads   Paved   Gravel   Dirt

MILEAGE

MILEAGE BETWEEN TOWNS AND JUNCTIONS   3 ∕ 4   MILEAGE BETWEEN DOTS   • 35 •

SCALE

ONE INCH 17 MILES   0   5   10   20

ONE INCH 27 KILOMETERS   0   5   10   20   32

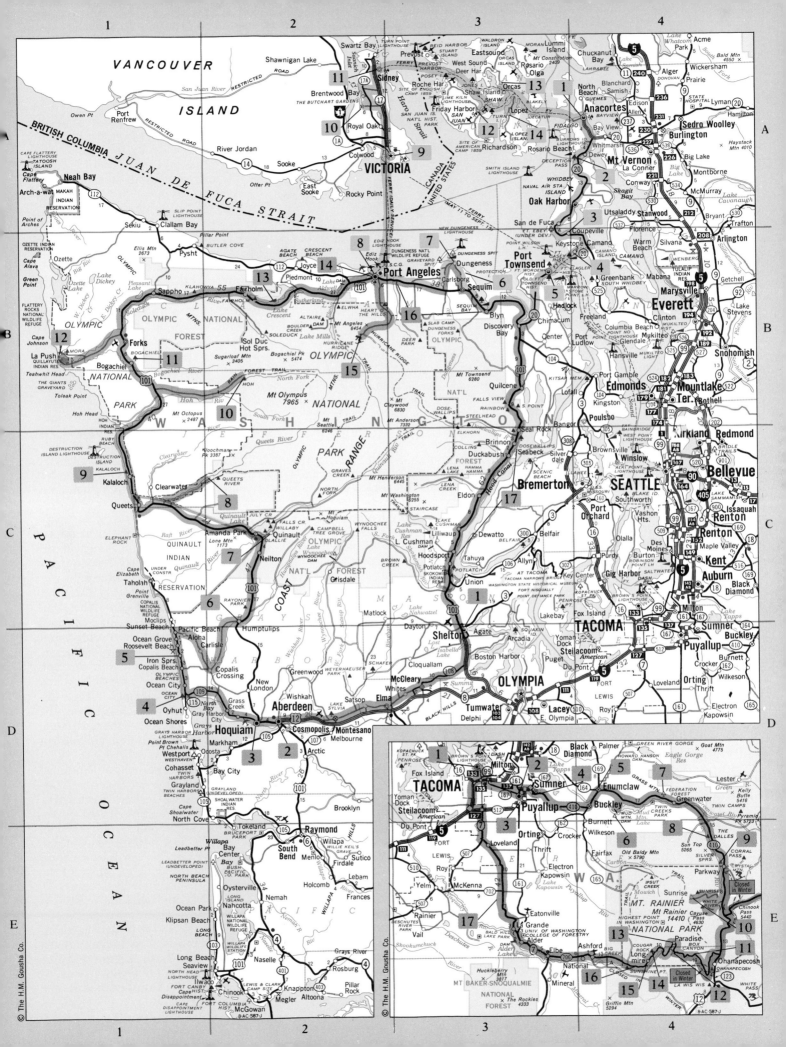

in the summer, especially on weekends, you may be forced to wait several hours.

5   First settled in 1851, Port Townsend rapidly developed into a typical Wild West boomtown. It became the gateway to Puget Sound as sailing vessels and steamers of many nations steered into its harbor.

With a land boom came wealth, and dozens of Victorian mansions with widow's walks, towers, and turrets were erected and trimmed in the fashion of the day with the ornate decoration known as gingerbread. Falling into financial collapse after the crash of the 1890's, Port Townsend was restored to economic stability when the Crown Zellerbach Corporation began construction of a paper mill here in 1927.

Today visitors come to Port Townsend to stroll by the spruced-up brick and stone buildings of historic Water Street, sample the local seafood at its waterfront cafés, and browse through antiques shops and art galleries. Tours of the old Victorian homes are held twice annually—the first weekend in May and the third weekend in September. The town honors Washington's official flower, *Rhododendron macrophyllum*, with a festival each spring.

The route from Port Townsend around Discovery Bay and west to Port Angeles takes you through the "banana belt" of the Northwest. This area is in the so-called rain shadow of the Olympic Peninsula. Precipitation here averages 17 inches a year, while the average for the state is about 40 inches, and the Hoh Rain Forest, some 40 miles away, has more than 140 inches annually.

6   Six miles north of Sequim (pronounced skwim), you come upon the Olympic Game Farm, home to many four-legged movie stars. Most of them wander free and even walk up to your car looking for a snack. From the car you may photograph donkeys, bison, guanacos, zebras, elk, deer, and numerous fowl. Bears are contained behind fencing and may put on quite a show for a tossed marshmallow or two. Olympic Game Farm animals have appeared in more than 80 wildlife features, including films made by Paramount, Walt Disney, and other studios.

5. *The 1889 Starrett House is typical of the Victorian-style mansions built in Port Townsend when it was one of the most prosperous harbors on the west coast.*

7   A loop road north of Sequim leads to Dungeness, place-name of the succulent Dungeness crab. At low tide, armed with wading boots and a garden rake with covered prongs or a long-handled dip net, you can go crabbing on the public beach. Walk slowly through the water, watching for dark patches of eelgrass. Gently sweep across the grass until rake meets crab. Scoop it up carefully (it is unlawful to puncture the shell) and drop the crab in a bucket or a burlap bag. Only males that measure at least six inches across the back may be kept. Females and soft-shelled or

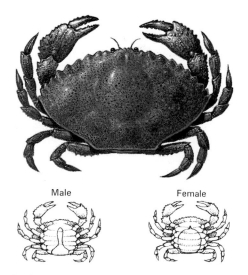

Male   Female

7. *The Dungeness, most popular crab on the west coast, can weigh up to four pounds.*

moulting crabs must be returned to the water. The narrow, triangular abdominal plate on the male is about one-half as wide as it is long. The female's plate is rounder and wider. To identify your crab as a bona fide Dungeness, look for brown, gray, or red points on its claws. The smaller rock crab that inhabits the same waters has black points.

8   Crossing time on the Port Angeles–Victoria Ferry is an hour and 35 minutes. This is a large ferry, but it is not possible to make advance reservations. When traffic is heavy during summer weekends, it is wise to arrive 1½ to 2 hours early to ensure getting aboard. There is a comfortable glassed-in deck and coffee shop, and an open deck that provides splendid views of the Olympic Mountains.

For more about Port Angeles, and a side trip to Hurricane Ridge, see numbers 14 and 15 on page 374.

9   The first thing to do after disembarking at Victoria is to stop at the Greater Victoria Visitors' Information Centre, opposite the Empress Hotel on the Inner Harbor Causeway, to pick up sight-seeing information and a map of the city. Free walking tours of Victoria's Old Towne originate here during the summer.

This picturesque old city is ideal to explore on foot. You can visit an art gallery featuring Canadian crafts and Eskimo carvings, department stores, a fine American Indian museum, British woolen, linen, china, and toffee shops, and finish up at the Empress in time for an English high tea.

Sight-seeing vessels leave from the dock in front of the Empress Hotel several times a day to tour the harbor and Gorge Waterway.

10   From Victoria take Route 17 north to the famous Butchart Gardens. Created by the late Mr. and Mrs. Robert Pim Butchart in an abandoned limestone quarry on their 130-acre estate, and developed over the years, the extensive gardens are kept open to the public by members of the family. There are always flowers in bloom, no matter what the season, as you walk past sunken gardens, fountains, Japanese and Italian gardens, and in the Show Greenhouse of exotic plants. The coffee shop and restaurants are also filled with plants. At night during the summer months the

10. Butchart Gardens, ranked among the most beautiful in the world, are interesting the year-round and have a remarkable variety of flowers, shrubs, and trees. Among the flowers in this sunken garden area are ageratums, begonias, snapdragons, and marigolds.

aware of the unhurried pace that is characteristic of this wooded archipelago. As you drive your car off the ferry at Friday Harbor and follow the shore road, there is little traffic to contend with. You may wish to examine the local marine life on display at the University of Washington's Oceanographic Laboratory (open only on Wednesdays and Saturdays) or perhaps visit the San Juan Island Historical Park.

13 Orcas is the hilliest of the San Juans. Mount Constitution, in Moran State Park on the eastern side, is 2,409 feet high. You can climb the stone tower at its crest for an unobstructed 360-degree view of the San Juan and Gulf islands, the stunning, snow-capped Olympics, Vancouver Island, the Strait of Georgia, Bellingham, and Mount Baker.

14 In the summer the Sidney–Anacortes Ferry stops at Lopez Island on its evening run only. In winter it stops on every run. Fairly flat, with acres of pasture, agriculture, and little traffic, Lopez remains a favorite with bicyclists for its gentle terrain and unspoiled beauty.

If staying overnight on any of the islands, be sure to reserve a room well in advance. The limited number of hotel accommodations fills up quickly, especially in summer, and some are booked months ahead.

gardens are illuminated, and on weekends there are spectacular fireworks displays coordinated with a musical accompaniment.

11 Sidney, near the north end of the Saanich Peninsula, is a busy city convenient to year-round golf, a quiet rural countryside, and an international airport. You can take a day flight on a seaplane, stopping at lakes and beaches for a picnic lunch and swim, or you can charter a boat and try the excellent salmon fishing off Canada's Gulf Islands.

In the summer, reservations for the Sidney–Anacortes Ferry can be made a day in advance. You may board either the morning or evening boat for your return to Anacortes via the San Juan Islands. Remember that you pass through customs at Anacortes. Also, if you wish to disembark at any of the island stops, you must make your decision at Sidney, since special boarding procedures are followed for those who plan to travel interisland.

12 The group of islands clustered here is known as the San Juans. Their climate, tempered by the water, is mild. The average summer temperature is in the mid-seventies and the annual rainfall is about 20 inches. San Juan itself is the most populated of the islands, but even here one is

13. A soft carpet of moss covers this peaceful area atop Mount Constitution on the eastern side of Orcas Island. The first island in the background is Lopez. Other islands of the San Juan group can also be seen in the distance.

9. Forested, rocky headlands between Kalaloch's Beaches 2 and 3 merge dramatically with the sea. A day of mist and rain like the one shown is not unusual on the northwest coast. Note the piles of driftwood along the shore.

The Olympic Peninsula of Washington, the site of Olympic National Park and National Forest, embraces four Indian reservations. Laced with streams, it is the natural environment of rare species of plant and animal life. Its juxtaposition of rain forest and snowcapped mountains is unique on the North American continent.

1 The logging community of Shelton bills itself as the Christmas Tree Capital of the World, in honor of one of its major exports, Christmas trees. For a glimpse of the timber industry from tree to finished product, free tours start daily in the summer from the main gate of the Simpson Timber Company, downtown, and include visits to two sawmills, a veneer plant, and a manufacturing plant.

Route 108 winds past Christmas tree farms through a valley that is surrounded by timberland. There is considerable evidence of "clear cutting" where you can see large areas of land stripped bare of trees. Tiny new trees are then planted to create another crop that will be harvested in 30 years or so.

2 As you enter Aberdeen, busy Grays Harbor is to the south. Here you may stop along the waterfront to watch logging trucks deposit their heavy loads and oceangoing freighters take on their cargoes.

3 An unexpected treasure, and a national historic site, is Hoquiam's Castle, in the town for which it is

named. This 20-room mansion, built in 1897 by lumber tycoon Robert Lytle, was restored in 1971 by the Robert Watson family, who now use it as their home. From its hilltop site, this turreted Victorian extravaganza has a sweeping view of Grays Harbor and the Pacific. Its interior is embellished with elegant crystal chandeliers, Tiffany-style lamps, stained glass, hand-carved woodwork, and authentic turn-of-the century furniture. Closed in winter, but open by appointment.

4 Ocean City State Park on the edge of the Pacific is a delightful spot, with picnic and camping sites arranged among groves of small shore pine. Ocean swimming, surf fishing, and clamming are available. Digging for the succulent razor clam is one of the most popular activities along the Washington seashore. Grocery stores and sporting goods shops sell or rent the narrow-bladed shovels called clam guns, and often offer helpful advice. Digging near the surf line at low tide is the most rewarding. Walk slowly, looking for a "show," a small depression or dimple, in the wet sand. Dig straight down, keeping the blade vertical and about four inches on the ocean side of the hole. Remove one or two scoops of sand, then start digging with your hands and grab the clam before it gets away. There are also tubular devices that can be centered over the hole and pushed down and pulled up to remove a core of sand.

Dig with care. Razor clams have thin, sharp-edged shells that are easily broken. You must have a license. The number of clams you may legally possess is usually 15, but this can change and should be checked. All holes in the sand should be filled in by the diggers to ensure proper growth conditions for young clams. There is good clamming on most of the wide flat beaches between Ocean Shores to the south and Moclips to the north. The season is closed from July through September.

5 From Copalis Beach the road climbs for 2½ miles to a splendid viewing point at Iron Springs. Park your car and walk through hemlocks, firs, and cedars to the edge of the cliff. Looking outward you see spectacular coastal views. Looking down you see the surf smashing on the rocky shore 100 feet below.

6 In a clearing in the woods near the banks of the Humptulips River is the Humptulips Salmon Hatchery. Here you can observe several different species of young salmon in large outdoor tanks. As part of a statewide conservation program, these fish are released in the Humptulips River when they reach the proper age for ocean migration.

7 Some 17 miles past the hatchery is the turnoff for Lake Quinault. Surrounded by lush rain forest, the lake, which is about four miles long and two miles wide, is contained by a terminal moraine. On its south shore

Lake Quinault Lodge provides overnight accommodations and is the starting point for one-day raft trips. Inquire also about horseback riding and hikes through the rain forest. Also located on the south shore is the Quinault Forest Station, where you can park and take a short nature trail through the forest. Since boating and fishing regulations are issued, in part, by the Quinault Indians, who retain certain tribal rights to the lake here, it is advisable to check with the ranger for information concerning these activities.

8 An unpaved road leads from the highway through 14 miles of dense, lush rain forest along the Queets River. You do not have to leave the car to see the luxuriant carpets of ferns, the maples and hemlocks hung with club moss, and the Sitka spruces, Douglas firs, and red alders covered with pale green lichen. Nor is it necessary to travel the length of the road to experience the unique character of its beauty. But if you drive the full distance to the campground, park, and then hike an additional 2½ miles, you can see the world's reputedly largest Douglas fir, 221 feet tall and 14 feet 6 inches in diameter.

9 At Kalaloch there is a campground on a bluff 50 feet above the beach; Kalaloch Lodge provides overnight accommodations and rents out clam shovels. At the ranger station you can pick up information about beach hiking, surf fishing, clamming, and smelting.

The beaches numbered 1 to 6 and Ruby Beach along the highway are in the Olympic National Park. These beaches are protected from commercial encroachment. The short trails leading down to them are steep, but once on the sandy shores you can take a long, leisurely walk. At the water's edge the ebbing tide leaves many tide pools. Here at close range you can study starfish, limpets, periwinkles, turban snails, and sea anemones, and see the hermit crabs that make their homes in the former dwellings of snails.

The offshore sea stacks—striking rock formations that are the remnants of headlands that have been weathered and washed away by the pounding surf—are home to the puffins, murres, auklets, coromorants,

gulls, and other birds that you see and hear along this coastal strip.

10 The Hoh Rain Forest, with its paved entrance road and well-marked trails, is the most accessible of the three rain forests along this route. Although it is 19 miles off the highway, a tour of the Olympic Peninsula would be incomplete without seeing this fascinating phenomenon.

Short loop trails begin at the visitor center, which is also the place where backpackers register for longer hikes along the Hoh River Trail into the fastness of the Olympics. About 12 miles of the trail is in the rain forest, but after walking for just a short distance you can experience the unique impact of this place.

The shortest trail here, which is about three-quarters of a mile long, reveals most of the striking examples of rain forest vegetation. At one point the trees, heavily enveloped in club

moss, form a towering tent of greenery—the "Hall of Mosses" for which the trail is named. The light filtering through the pervasive green of the giant trees has an almost mystically luminous glow, especially on cloudy days.

The nurse logs are an interesting aspect of this forest. When a tree falls and begins to decay, it provides a favorable rooting medium for seedlings. You find rows of small trees with all their shallow roots wrapped around the same fallen log, as well as mature trees in straight lines established by nurse trees that have long since decayed completely. Given the average annual rainfall of 142 inches, roots do not have to dig deep for water. The shallow-rooted trees frequently fall in winter storms.

In autumn, leaves of red adler, vine, and big leaf maple turn red and yellow, creating a vibrant patchwork

10. Moss-covered maples dominate this scene in the remarkable Hoh Rain Forest, where almost every square inch of the forest floor is utilized by plants. From the top, above: a young sword fern unfolding, a variety of mushroom, and moss.

14. *Ediz Hook, a natural three-mile-long sandspit jutting into the Juan de Fuca Strait, forms a splendid protective arm around Port Angeles. The booms—logs connected from end to end—are used to contain logs until they are taken to the mill.*

of color among the evergreens. The largest known herd (about 6,000) of Roosevelt elk, a northwestern native of the American deer family, browse in the lush mountain meadows here, but they can also be seen at lower elevations, especially in winter.

11 Bogachiel State Park, a campground on the banks of the Bogachiel River, is a popular fishing spot in fall when the seagoing steelhead trout travel upstream to spawn. Peaceful short trails wind through the densely forested valley, a transitional mixture of moss-draped rain forest trees and ferns and the stately hemlocks, firs, and spruces of the more typical northwestern forest.

12 This side trip to the ocean is highly recommended. Here, by the Indian village of La Push, the beach with its piles of driftwood and dramatic sea stacks just offshore must be counted among the most scenic places on the entire Pacific coast. If your visit here requires an overnight stay, accommodations are available.

13 Lake Crescent—11 miles long and 615 feet deep—was left to us as a legacy of the late stages of the Pleistocene Age about 11,000 years ago by the same retreating glacial system that carved out the Hood Canal (which is actually a natural channel, not a man-made canal), Puget Sound, and Juan de Fuca Strait.

Two resorts and several cabins rim the lake, and boats and fishing supplies are available. In the summer at the National Park Visitor Center you can pick up information and listen to informal talks by park rangers. A three-quarter-mile trail through the forest starts at the center and leads to the 90-foot Marymere waterfall.

14 Port Angeles is the logging and shipping center of the north peninsula. To watch giant logs being made into lumber, plywood, or newsprint, you can visit the Crown Zellerbach Paper Mill, the Peninsula Plywood Mill, or the Rayonier Cellulose Mill.

For information about the Port Angeles–Victoria Ferry, see number 8 on page 370.

15 Before going up to Hurricane Ridge, it is a good idea to stop at the visitor center a mile south of Port Angeles, on Race Street. Among the offerings here is a bird list including more than 240 species, most of which have been seen in the park.

It is a spectacular 18-mile drive up a mountain road flanked by Douglas firs, hemlocks, western red cedars, alders, and leafy ferns to the ridge (elevation 5,500 feet). About halfway up is Lookout Rock, where there are fine views of the strait and Mount Baker. As you continue upward, the snow-covered Olympic crags offer an icy contrast to the green-forested valleys below. At the end of this road there is a lodge where park rangers give lectures and organize nature walks through the great displays of wild flowers found on Big Meadow, or lead hikes up to Hurricane Hill for views over Port Angeles to the Juan de Fuca Strait and Canada.

For the finest roadside view of Mount Olympus, take the narrow dirt road at Hurricane Ridge for nine miles to Obstruction Point. In winter the slopes attract skiers. There are intermediate downhill runs, ski touring, and snowshoeing trails.

16 The road between Port Angeles and Discovery Bay is described on page 370 (numbers 6 and 7) of the San Juan Islands tour.

17 From Seal Rock to Tahuya, Route 101 hugs the banks of the IIood Canal. On beaches along the way clamming and oyster-gathering are permitted in season. Stores and roadside stands sell fresh crabs, clams, and oysters. Here, beside their home waters, these delicacies are dependably fresh and worthy of attention.

In late spring the blooming rhododendrons and dogwoods brighten the roadsides along the canal.

15. *In this view from Mount Angeles, which is noted for its profusion of wild flowers, the road snakes its way through virgin timber toward awe-inspiring Hurricane Ridge. Mount Olympus and the Bailey Range are in the background.*

Mount Rainier's massive snowcapped dome, rising to a height of 14,410 feet, is a dominant feature on the landscape of the Northwest. To the hundreds of thousands of people within viewing distance, it is simply "The Mountain," and in this misty climate the days when "The Mountain is out" are infrequent enough to be looked upon as special. As a beacon that verifies the heart-lifting quality of a clear day, Mount Rainier has become a presence viewed with a fondness that transcends the vastness of its towering, majestic form.

In driving this loop you see the mountain from all sides (weather permitting). And along the way there is a variety of other highlights to enjoy.

1 The city of Tacoma, a little more than a century and a quarter old, is one of the largest industrial and shipping centers of the Pacific Northwest, with foundries, lumber and flour mills, and food- and chemical-processing plants. One of the highlights here is the Washington State Historical Society Museum, which displays a large collection of pioneer, Eskimo, and Indian art and artifacts, as well as tools and furnishings representative of pioneer life in the Northwest. At Fireman's Park is a superb 105-foot totem pole carved by Alaskan Indians. The 638-acre Point Defiance Park at the northwest tip of the city, between The Narrows and Commencement Bay, includes a zoo, an aquarium, rose gardens, Camp Six (a realistic logging museum), and a reconstruction of Fort Nisqually, an old trading post.

2 From Tacoma to Puyallup, Route 410 follows the Puyallup River through a fertile valley, past small truck farms. On clear days Mount Rainier can be seen across the fields, an imposing, iridescent backdrop some 50 miles away.

During summer and early fall, roadside stands sell corn, cucumbers, strawberries, and raspberries fresh from the fields.

Puyallup is a bustling small city, with canneries, fruit-packing plants, and sawmills. There are two museums in the town and a national historic site, the Meeker Mansion. The mansion was built in 1890 by Ezra Meeker, a pioneer from Iowa who

crossed the plains with his oxen and covered wagon on the Oregon Trail in 1852, accompanied by his brother, his wife, and his infant son. The trip to Oregon took five months of hard and often dangerous travel. Meeker helped lay out the town of Puyallup, which is named for a local Indian tribe, and became its first mayor. The restoration and the refurnishing of the 17-room mansion was begun in the late 1970's. It boasts six tiled Victorian fireplaces, many leaded stained-glass windows, and an extensive widow's walk with the original ironwork. It is open for tours.

3 On the outskirts of Puyallup, at the intersection of Routes 161 and 512, is the Western Washington Fairgrounds, where late in September the town hosts the largest country fair in this part of the state. Featured in the exhibition halls are homecrafts and baking contests, artistic displays of

3. Many varieties of choice tulips are grown for their bulbs in large, fertile fields like this one near Puyallup, Washington. The weathered barn and split rail fences are typical of the farm structures seen throughout Washington and Oregon.

farm produce, and livestock and poultry ribbon-winners.

The Puyallup River valley is the center of an annual $4 million bulb industry. For a look at the dazzling floral displays in early spring, turn south at Sumner onto Route 162 toward Orting. The road is bordered for miles with colorful rows of daffodil and tulip blooms.

To continue the loop tour, turn back to Route 410 and head east.

4 One mile beyond Sumner is the Manfred Vierthaler Winery, named for the owner who learned the art of winemaking in his homeland, Germany. The main building, which resembles a Bavarian chalet, is an appropriate setting for the production of wines made by the traditional methods of German vintners. Some of the grapes are grown in California and others come from the promising vineyards of the white Riesling and Müller-Thurgau grapes that Vierthaler has established here in the Puyallup River valley. The winery's informal tasting room commands sweeping views of the valley below. Visitors are welcome daily, and during the harvest in October and November are invited to watch the process of pressing the grapes.

5 For the next 10 miles or so the road passes through timberland, crossing the White River at Buckley.

As you near Enumclaw the rugged terrain gives way to farmland. This area is a major milk supplier for the entire state, and many herds of Holstein cattle can be seen peacefully grazing in the lush green pastures.

On the first Sunday of every month horse traders, cowboys, equipment dealers, and meat-packers from all over the Pacific Northwest and from Texas and Montana gather at the Sales Pavilion to buy and sell horses and equipment. The auctioning of tack starts at noon and is followed by the bidding for horses. Prices are reported to range from as low as $20 for a horse that is considered too small by the packers to as much as $1,800 for a good saddle horse.

For an unexpected roadside treat, stop at Farman's Brothers Pickle Company, one mile east of town on Route 410. Tours are arranged in advance; phone 206/825-2481. The factory is normally open five days a week, and six or seven days during the peak pickle-production time in August and September.

6   Mud Mountain Dam on White River is a federal flood-control project built in a narrow canyon where rock cliffs rise more than 200 feet above the river channel. Originally the river here flowed on the surface but eventually broke through the hard basalt formation, leaving vertical walls. There is an inviting quarter-mile nature trail, playground and picnic areas, and sweeping views of surrounding forests.

7   Route 410 winds between stands of towering Douglas firs, western hemlocks (*Tsuga heterophylla*), the official state tree, and cedars, beyond which are occasional glimpses of the rushing White River.

Largely through the efforts of the Washington State Federation of Women's Clubs, 612 acres of virgin timber in this area have been acquired for the state and designated as the Federation Forest State Park. The beautiful surroundings provide walks ranging in length from less than a half-mile to a mile or so in the natural forest habitat. Guided hikes cover such subjects as wild flowers, wildlife, edible wild plants, and plants and their uses.

At the Catherine Montgomery Interpretative Center exhibits of growing plants, text, and photographs depict the seven general life zones found in the state. These zones, of which there are 10 in the United States, are characterized by variations in altitude and climate and the plant life that thrives in each. In Washington there are the Coast forest, Mountain forest, sub-Alpine, Alpine, and, in the eastern part of the state, the Yellow Pine forest, Bunchgrass, and Sagebrush zones.

9. *Mount Rainier, capped with 27 glaciers, is one of the outstanding scenic wonders in the Pacific Northwest. The wild alpine flowers near the timberline in Paradise Valley Park are Indian paintbrush (red), bear grass (white), and lupine (purple).*

8   For some distance the road skirts the Mount Baker–Snoqualmie National Forest. As it bears to the south in its great circle of Mount Rainier, you may choose to stop at The Dalles campground for a cookout lunch or an overnight rest. Here you can see a giant Douglas fir that is 9.6 feet in diameter, over 250 feet in height, and more than 450 years old.

9   Near Silver Springs the road begins to climb noticeably. At Silver Springs there are camping and picnicking facilities, and the turnoff to the five-mile winding drive up to the Crystal Mountain Ski Area. If you are here in summer, be sure to take the chair-lift ride to the summit for a dazzling, unobstructed view of Mount Rainier and its glaciers.

Entering Mount Rainier National Park, you drive through forest whose awesome silence imparts a sense of remoteness. Each mile of the drive is a highlight. As the road twists and climbs, the giant peak is framed again and again by towering firs, red cedars, and hemlocks. Waterfalls cascade down moss-covered rocks that bank the road; alpine meadows, with their summer carpets of wild flowers, and clear mountain lakes, rivers, and creeks can be seen from the car, as can the numerous trails and the in-and-out views of the canyons below. You also see many of the mountain's 27 glaciers.

The mountain is volcanic in origin, and its two craters are still mildly active. The geologic foundations of Mount Rainier are basalt lavas (similar to those that built Hawaii) that erupted about 20 million years ago. The massive cone of the mountain was created by explosive eruptions during the past million years. The lava is andesitic and noted for its explosive characteristics. Another such volcano of the Cascades was Mount Mazama, which blew up about 7,000 years ago, leaving the 20-square-mile hole of Crater Lake and spreading ash into six states.

Note: Most of the park roads are closed from late November to June or July. When warranted, park authorities may require that your car be equipped with traction devices appropriate for the prevailing weather conditions. During cloudy or rainy weather, thick mists in the canyons limit visibility. For weather information, telephone the Mount Rainier Ranger Station, 206/569-2211.

10 About six miles into the park, veer west onto the access road to Sunrise, the highest point (6,400 feet) you can reach by car on Mount Rainier. A short distance up the road is the park's White River Entrance, where you can get a park map. The magnificent mountain road continues for 16 miles, passing the walk-in White River Campground, and clinging to ridges in giant switchbacks as it makes its way up the slopes. At Sunrise, a subalpine meadowland, there are superb views of Mount Rainier and other peaks in the Cascade Range and of the 1½-mile expanse of Emmons Glacier. You may also see mountain goats on Goat Island Mountain. The Sunrise Visitor Center, open only in summer, offers food and information.

Returning to the highway, continue south on Routes 410 and 123, and then turn west onto Stevens Canyon Road (Route 706). Ascending the canyon walls, this road offers vistas of lava formations and of the creek below. About five miles along, at Backbone Ridge, the road makes a sensational hairpin turn to the north, revealing a vast panorama of mountain peaks and deep valleys molded and etched by the weather and the glaciers.

11 Four miles farther along, at Box Canyon, is a picnic area that offers a 180-degree-wide vista sweeping over the Cowlitz River as it cuts through the narrow canyon below and toward Mount Rainier.

12 At Inspiration Point, which gives a classic view of the mountain, is a plaque inscribed with the words of John Muir, a 19th-century American explorer and naturalist: ". . . there stood the mountain, wholly unveiled, awful in bulk and majesty, filling all the view like a separate newborn world, yet . . . so fine and beautiful it might well fire the dullest observer to desperate enthusiasm."

13 Paradise (5,400 feet), the spectacular park overlooking Paradise River valley, is easily the most popular place on Mount Rainier—partly because of its year-round accessibility by road from the Nisqually Entrance on the west, but also for the beautiful subalpine meadows reaching up the slopes. In April there can be much as 30 feet of snow here, but as the snow recedes, myriads of wild flowers pop up. They are at their best in midsummer. Easy walks and advanced hiking trails begin at the visitor center, where you may meet strollers or serious backpackers en route to the receding snowfields or to the summit.

From any of the trails you might spy a mountain goat or a mule deer.

13. The mountain goat, actually a type of antelope, can often be seen at close range along the mountain ridges here.

However, you are more likely to run into a furry little marmot, taunting you with its high-pitched whistle as it poses for your camera.

The visitor center, open all year, is a large, circular building that offers a 360-degree vista of the majestic peak and the lower terrain. Food and information are also available here. The comfortable, rustic Paradise Inn is open from June 15 to Labor Day. (For reservations write: Mount Rainier Hospitality Service, 4820 South Washington, Tacoma, Washington 98409.)

14 From Paradise to Cougar Rock the dramatic switchbacks of the road provide a startling sequence of spectacular views. Eight miles farther is Ricksecker Point, a breathtaking overlook down to deeply etched canyons and across to Rampart Ridge.

Two miles farther on, Christine Falls is easily visible as its clear waters cascade down the mountain. Soon afterward you may smell the cooking fires at Cougar Rock, one of three major campgrounds in the park.

15 Longmire Entrance has a visitor center, a cafeteria, and a gas station that are open all year, as is the National Park Inn, a hostel with limited overnight accommodations.

Opposite the inn is the start of the Trail of the Shadows, a half-mile nature walk through tall forest and open meadow, passing mineral springs and a pioneer cabin. The trail is at its most beautiful during the period of brilliant autumn foliage.

16 As the road winds down to its exit from the park, you suddenly come upon the shattering sight of Kautz Creek Mud Flow. Like avalanches of snow, mud flows are a product of the glaciers. As the temperature rises, large quantities of earth, rock, and water trapped behind the ice can suddenly break loose and gush downslope, dislodging and carrying away everything in their path. In 1947 a slide on Kautz Creek buried the road under 30 feet of mud and debris. A roadside exhibit explains the devastation caused by a flow and the means by which a forest rebuilds itself.

From here it is just two miles to Sunshine Point, a smaller campground than Cougar Rock but noteworthy as the only one in the park that is open every day of the year.

Leaving the park via the Nisqually Park Entrance and driving toward Elbe, you pass restaurants that feature such delectable seasonal and regional specialities as lake trout and wild blackberry pie, and local craftsmen who display and sell their wares. Alder Lake is a recreation area popular with boating and fishing enthusiasts. Campsites are available.

17 Nine miles north of the lake is the Pioneer Farm Museum, a replica of a functioning homestead of 1887, complete with a barn and hayloft, a smithy, a woodworking shop, a smokehouse, a root cellar, a tannery, a garden, and farm animals. The museum is planned with children in mind, and visitors are invited to explore and to touch the exhibits. There is an area for picnics.

A Realm of Many Splendors

The coastline, river valleys, mountains, and high plains give Oregon an abundance of scenic wonders

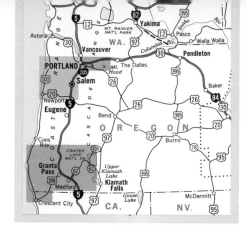

To explore their state is to see why Oregonians consider it to be the most varied and interesting landscape in America. A remarkable aspect is the proximity of mountains to the ocean and of snowy peaks to the Columbia River.

From the verdant farmlands *of the Willamette Valley the route crosses a heavily wooded mountain range and descends to the spectacular scenery of the Oregon coast.*

2 Oregon City, the former site of an Indian fishing village, was the capital of Oregon Territory in the 1840's. The 41-foot-high Willamette Falls has been harnessed for hydro-electric power and made navigable by a series of locks. For an excellent view of the falls, take the free elevator ride at Railroad Avenue and Seventh Street to the observation area. Like the Indians before them, Oregon City fishermen still catch the migrating salmon near the base of the falls.

well as philosophical pursuits. Examples of their finely crafted furniture and other pioneer artifacts can be seen in some of the restored buildings and in the Ox Barn Museum.

5 Salem, the capital of Oregon, lies in the heartland of the fertile Willamette River valley. The surrounding area produces more than a hundred different marketable crops and is a nationwide supplier of snap beans, grass seed, hops, and such cane crops as raspberries, blackberries, and loganberries.

The handsome white marble capitol, crowned with a golden statue honoring the pioneers, dominates the downtown area. Several buildings belonging to Salem's early history have been relocated and restored at the Mission Mill Museum.

6 In summertime the refreshingly pungent fragrance of mint fills the air around Albany. Besides growing a large share of the nation's mint supply, this area is the center of a vast seed industry, with ryegrass as its major export. The community was formally established in 1848 by the

1. In the Japanese Gardens in Portland, azaleas and Japanese maple trees border the series of miniature waterfalls splashing gently down a terraced slope. A serene teahouse garden and a beautiful pond garden are among the other features to be enjoyed here.

1 The city of Portland is fortunate to have so many fine museums, restaurants, and hotels, surrounded by so much natural beauty. An outstanding highlight is Washington Park, which includes nine miles of winding trails through the Hoyt Arboretum, the International Rose Test Garden (where you can examine 400 varieties of roses), and the Japanese Gardens. Here too is the Washington Park Zoo, with one of the largest colonies of chimpanzees in America as well as hundreds of other exotic animals. The Oregon Museum of Science and Industry has a wonderful variety of natural and physical science exhibits.

3 For a closer, more leisurely look at the Willamette, you can board the diminutive Canby Ferry and cross over in minutes to a county park for a picnic lunch. Canby is a horticultural center, and in the spring the surrounding fields are bright with daffodils and irises, and in the fall, with dahlias. In August is the Clackamas County Fair.

4 Aurora is a small peaceful town now given over to antiques shops and restaurants in refurbished old buildings. It was once the site of the Aurora Colony, a religious community founded in 1857. Devoted to the ideals of brotherhood, the colony's members were given to artistic as

SPECIAL FEATURES

ROAD GUIDE	HIGHLIGHT
STATE PARKS	OTHER AIRPORTS
With Campsites ♠ Without Campsites ♤	
RECREATION AREAS	MAJOR MTN. ROADS
With Campsites ▲ Without Campsites △	CLOSED IN WINTER Closed in Winter
SELECTED REST AREAS	BOAT RAMPS
POINTS OF INTEREST	INFORMATION CENTER
SKI AREAS	COVERED BRIDGES
SCHEDULED AIRLINE STOPS	

ROAD CLASSIFICATION

CONTROLLED ACCESS HIGHWAYS
Interstate interchange numbers are mileposts.

OTHER DIVIDED HIGHWAYS

PAVED HIGHWAYS

LOCAL ROADS In unfamiliar areas inquire locally before using these roads

Divided · Undivided · Interchanges · Paved · Gravel · Dirt

MILEAGE

MILEAGE BETWEEN TOWNS AND JUNCTIONS 3 4

MILEAGE BETWEEN DOTS 35

SCALE

ONE INCH 21 MILES 0 5 10 20 30

ONE INCH 34 KILOMETERS 0 5 10 20 30 48

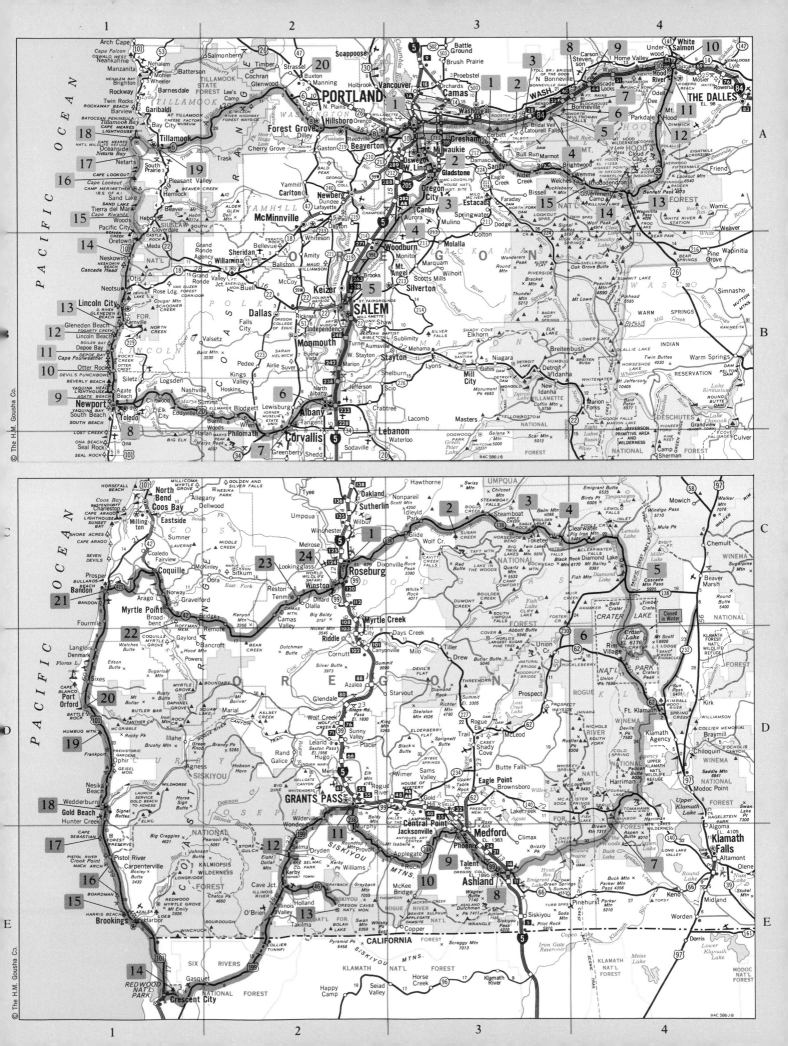

Oregon's tide-pool creatures

An unusually varied assortment of sea creatures inhabits the intertidal areas of Oregon's rocky coast. Some of the kinds most often seen are shown at the right.

The population of these invertebrates is being diminished by collectors, such as beachcombers, scientists, students, and commercial hunters. In specific areas there are legal limits to the number of specimens that any one person can take per day.

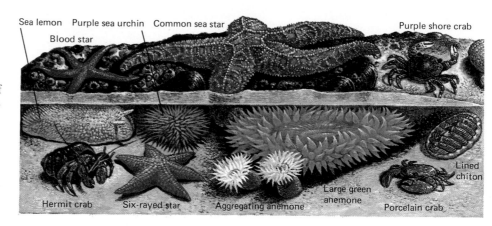

Sea lemon Purple sea urchin Common sea star Purple shore crab
Blood star
Lined chiton
Hermit crab Six-rayed star Aggregating anemone Large green anemone Porcelain crab

---

Monteith brothers, who named it after their hometown in New York.

The town prospered in the last half of the 19th century, and many fine homes were built in the varied elaborate styles favored in the Victorian era. A descriptive pamphlet with a map showing the location of 29 of the most interesting houses is available at the Chamber of Commerce.

For a look at 10 well-preserved covered bridges, a vanishing species of 1930's and 1940's architecture in this area, there is a 2½-hour self-guided driving tour. A folder with maps, directions, drawings, and a brief history of each bridge can be picked up at the Albany Chamber of Commerce.

7 Corvallis is the home of Oregon State University. On the campus the Horner Museum, located in Gill Coliseum, houses a fine collection of pioneer artifacts, Indian handicrafts, and examples of the minerals and fossils found in Oregon. The route to the Pacific winds through the gentle hills of the Coast Range past miles of Oregon blackberry bushes and dense stands of giant Douglas fir (*Pseudotsuga taxifolia*), the state tree, and other conifers.

8 On Yaquina Bay, Newport is a deepwater port for lumber and fishery products, as well as commercial and charter fishing boats. You can stroll along the bayfront, visit the waterfront cafés, bars, and shops, poke about in an old sailing vessel and a maritime museum, and view a cannery or the Undersea Gardens, a submerged aquarium where you literally enter the environment of the marine creatures on display. You can also take a short scenic excursion by boat,

or simply watch, preferably with a cup of fresh chowder in hand, as the fishermen unload their catch. Do not fail to sample the Dungeness crab.

A favorite picnicking spot is the Yaquina Bay State Park, situated on a bluff at the north end of the Yaquina Bay Bridge. Picnic tables are nestled here among trees that have been twisted and trimmed by the constantly blowing ocean winds into shapes that look like Japanese bonsai on a giant scale. The Yaquina Bay Lighthouse, built in 1871, is now a museum. It is closed from October through April.

9 As implied by its name, Agate Beach, long, flat, and wide, offers a treasure trove for the eagle-eyed and persistent collector of water-washed agates. A good time to look is in the early morning when the tide goes out, and the best time is after a storm.

10 North of Newport watch for the Otter Rock turnoff to Devils Punchbowl State Park. A pleasant picnic area overlooks the Pacific, and from the parking lot you can look down into the Devils Punchbowl. This gaping hole in the sandstone terrace was revealed when the roof of two sea caves collapsed. Incoming tides surge

10. From Otter Crest, a promontory on Cape Foulweather north of Newport, you can see how the ocean has chopped away at the coast, pounding around resistant rock cliffs and creating beaches where the land slopes away. Wild flowers cover the banks by the road.

through the "bowl." When the weather is stormy, the churning sea waters resemble a boiling cauldron. A short trail down the slopes of the bluff leads to the Marine Gardens Ocean Shore Reserve and the tide-pool creatures that can be seen in their natural habitat.

11 Depoe Bay, the smallest and most picturesque of the few safe harbors on the Oregon coast, is a haven for commercial and charter fishing boats and for pleasure craft. From the handsome arched bridge over the narrow inlet to the bay you can watch the fishing boats make their careful passage to and from the harbor. The Depoe Bay chowders are a point of local pride. The area is a favorite place for watching whales as they migrate north during March and April and return in October and November.

12 Fogarty Creek State Park, on the east side of the highway, offers picnic sites sheltered from the coastal winds, and has a path leading under the road to a wide, flat beach where the creek winds its way to the rocky outcrop at the ocean's edge. The annual Indian Style Fish Bake is held at the park on the second Saturday of September. Fresh-caught ocean fish, spitted on green branches, are cooked in long rows over open fires and served at the beach.

13 Gleneden Beach is the site of Salishan Lodge, a luxury resort complex that overlooks Siletz Bay and features a championship golf course. For more informal beachcombing, a state park is nearby. On weekends during the summer the Siletz Bay airport offers sight-seeing flights over coastal landmarks, and gives the passengers the choice of heading either north or south.

14 Neskowin, a favorite with golfers, offers a choice of two good courses. There is also a state park for bathing, beachcombing, or picnicking. Horses are available here for riding on winding trails or on the beach.

15 When seas run high at Cape Kiwanda, the pounding of the surf against the steep cliffs is truly an awesome sight to behold. Even in fair weather this is a place for the adventurous. Climbers test their skills on the cape's rocky ledges, and hang-gliding enthusiasts soar over the high dunes and offshore rocks.

12. At Fogarty Creek State Park a roiling sea covers the flat sandy beach with seafoam. The foam was created miles offshore by storm winds that churned the salty waters.

16 Cape Lookout is an ancient lava flow that projects into the ocean for about two miles. You can drive to the summit and then hike a 2½-mile trail through a rugged forest of hemlocks, cedars, and spruces to the point with its spectacular views of the coastline. Sea birds nest in the cliffs here, and deer and raccoons are frequently seen in the forest. Cape Lookout State Park offers a wide, silvery beach and overnight camping.

17 Netarts Bay is one of the finest clamming areas in Oregon. Blue, cockle, quahog, littleneck, soft-shell, and razor clams are found here in abundance. Their beds are well exposed at low tide. Except for the northernmost beach areas, a boat is needed to reach the best clamming places. Boat rentals and information on clamming techniques are available locally.

18 High on a ragged bluff overlooking the Pacific is Cape Meares State Park. A gentle trail leads across the grassy slopes to the Cape Meares Light, built in 1890 and now an historic site. Another trail, through the forest, leads to a lookout point. Do not miss the Cape Meares Octopus Tree, an enormous old Sitka spruce whose massive horizontal branches stretch out, in seeming defiance of the laws of gravity and logic, for nearly 60 feet before turning upward.

18. Oregon's beaches, like this one at Cape Meares, are splendid places for collecting driftwood. Branches and roots left by logging in the Coast Range forests are carried out to sea by the many flooding rivers and then washed ashore by the tides.

20. *Tualatin Valley was one of the first parts of Oregon to be settled. Trappers coming here 150 years ago for beaver noted the rich soil and later returned to farm. In the distance is the snowy cone of Mount St. Helens as it appeared before it erupted in 1980.*

The Tillamook Burn

It was extremely hot and dry around Tillamook on August 14, 1933, and when the humidity dropped below the level considered safe for logging, a man was sent to the woods to tell the workers to quit for the day. But the messenger stopped off for what may have been the world's most expensive cup of coffee. By the time he got to the woods a fire that was started by the friction of one log being pulled across another had been raging through the tinder-dry underbrush for 15 minutes. There was no stopping it, and the fire burned until the end of August. It destroyed 240,000 acres of prime timber, and later fires took another 100,000 acres. In all, 13.1 billion board feet of timber were lost, making this the most destructive forest fire in Oregon's history.

Reforestation, financed by a state bond issue, was begun at once. Seedlings were planted by hand where possible, and on the steeper slopes seed was dropped from planes and helicopters. The job of turning this barren and desolate expanse into a thriving part of the Tillamook State Forest was the largest reforestation project ever carried out by a state agency and took almost 40 years to complete.

19 The lush, verdant pastureland around Tillamook supports the herds of dairy cows that supply the milk for the famous regional cheese. At the creamery, just north of town on Route 101, you can see how Tillamook cheese is made. Leaving the town, Route 6 takes you through a peaceful valley of dairy farms and into the heavily wooded hills of the Tillamook State Forest.

20 The Glenwood Electric Railway comes as a pleasant surprise for travelers in this area. It is a small station museum run by the Oregon Electric Railway Historical Society. An antique trolley car, part of a complete 1910 tramway, clatters its way through a delightful forest setting, an inviting place for picnicking, camping, swimming, and, of course, trolley rides. Closed on weekdays.

Between Glenwood and Portland is the Tualatin River valley. With its temperate climate and fertile soil, it has become the location of a growing number of vineyards that are producing wines of steadily improving quality. Most of the Oregon wineries and their tasting rooms are informal places, geared for casual tours and leisurely sipping and chatting, often with the owners and winemakers themselves.

In this drive of less than 170 miles you see some of Oregon's most appealing scenery. Here the Columbia River wends its way through the majestic gorge that it has carved in basaltic lava flows. Flanking the river is a series of dramatic waterfalls that can vary in character (depending on the season) from windblown gossamer curtains to roaring cataracts.

The route circles Mount Hood and affords unsurpassed views of all sides of this ancient lava cone whose symmetrical slopes rise gracefully from a forested base to the snowcapped peak. The lush, cultivated fields and the large dairy herds seen on the rolling land between Sandy and Portland reveal this to be among the more productive farming areas in the state.

1 On November 3, 1805, Lewis and Clark made camp near the Sandy River. That spot, in Troutdale, is now a pleasantly wooded state park where fishermen, equipped with dip nets, gather for the annual smelt run in late March and early April. The park offers campsites, picnic tables, and a boat launch.

In town, you can arrange for a leisurely, self-guided boat trip from Oxbow Park down the Sandy River. This is a calm and beautiful three-hour drift past tree-lined banks, box canyons, waterfalls, and clear, bubbling springs. In the spring more experienced rafters, seeking white-water thrills, can choose a longer ride from Dodge Park through several rapids.

2 Crown Point State Park, which is perched on a 725-foot-high overhanging bluff, offers a superb view of the Columbia River. Vista House, an ornate mock Tudor structure here, has a gift shop and snack bar.

3 Latourell Falls, one of many beautiful falls in the Columbia Gorge area, drops over a 250-foot basalt cliff into a lovely pool. The area includes picnic facilities and a short trail leading to an excellent view of the falls.

4 Wahkeena Falls derives its name from an Indian word meaning "most beautiful." The falls, with its graceful series of cascades, easily lives up to its name. You can picnic at tables near the falls, or take a moderately steep trail for a rewarding view of nearby Multnomah Falls.

5. Multnomah Falls is perhaps the most popular of the falls along the Columbia River escarpment. Mosses, ferns, and vines have established themselves on the wet cliff.

5 Multnomah Falls, the highest waterfall along the Columbia Gorge, is the focus of a legend that tells of a time when a terrible illness threatened to destroy the Multnomah Indians. The chief's daughter sacrificed herself to save her people and her gravely ill lover by leaping from the top of the 620-foot precipice. Now when the wind blows through the waterfall, it is said that the Great Spirit honors the courage and love of the princess by creating her likeness in a single stream of the upper falls.

The massive, stone Multnomah Falls Lodge, built in 1925, includes a restaurant and a gift shop. A half-mile trail from the parking lot leads up and across a footbridge for a view about midpoint along the falls.

6 Oneonta Gorge is the home of a remarkable variety of aquatic, woodland, and rock-dwelling plants, which grow almost from the river level to high on the bluffs. Botanists have estimated that about half the plants found in the higher elevations grow nowhere else in the world. In addition to the ferns, mosses, and lichens that cover the basalt cliffs, fossilized remains of trees killed by volcanic eruptions are visible at several places along an 800-foot trail through the gorge.

7 Horsetail Falls is a 176-foot cascade of water, which does, indeed, look like a horse's tail. A 1½-mile trail leads to a viewing point.

8 The Bonneville Dam stretches 1,450 feet across the Columbia River and is divided by Bradford Island. The visitor center here has under-

water windows that allow a close-up view of migrating fish. Between the island and the Oregon shore is a huge hydroelectric powerhouse, and on the Oregon shore itself is the Bonneville Fish Hatchery. In summer a boat leaves from the Bradford Island Visitor Center three times a day for a leisurely two-hour river cruise.

9 One of the stops of the sightseeing boat from Bradford Island is the Cascade Locks. Now obsolete, the locks were built at the turn of the century, extending the Columbia River shipping route farther inland and relieving travelers of a long and hazardous portage.

The Cascade Locks Visitor Center houses the Northwest's only sternwheeler museum, which is filled with memorabilia from the days of the big paddle-wheel steamboats that carried freight and passengers up and down the Columbia.

10 The town of Hood River is the hub of business, government, and industrial activity for the fertile Hood River valley, Oregon's largest apple-producing region. From August to

December local fruit packers and processing plants offer guided tours of their facilities.

Favorite times to visit the Hood River valley are in April for the Blossom Festival, when miles of orchards are in full bloom, and in autumn, during the apple and pear harvest, when oaks and vine maples show off their bright fall colors.

11 Panorama Point offers a magnificent view of the valley, with Mount Hood in the background. Vast orchards are crisscrossed by miles of irrigation canals, fields of alfalfa, and rows of berries.

One of Oregon's most scenic drives, Route 35 is graced with several roadside stands that sell local produce in season. Fresh vegetables, spring berries, summer peaches and apricots, autumn pears, apples, and apple cider are irresistible temptations. As you drive south, snowcapped Mount Hood is nearly always in sight.

12 The Mount Hood Winery transforms the cherries, apples, pears, and berries of the Hood River valley into semidry natural wines that are quite

11. Mount Hood, Oregon's highest and favorite peak, is perpetually snowcapped. Since it is isolated from other high mountains, it is visible from long distances. Here it is seen from Route 84 in the Hood River valley at the end of April when the orchards are in bloom.

unlike the artificially colored and flavored fruit wines. The tasting room overlooks the East Fork of the Hood River. Closed Mondays year-round and on weekdays in winter.

South of the town of Hood River, the orchards give way to the deep, tall woods of the Mount Hood National Forest. Polallie, Sherwood, and Robinhood campgrounds all lie close to the East Fork of the Hood River, which parallels the road. Route 35 crosses the Pacific Crest National Scenic Trail, a 2,500-mile pack trail and hiking route that runs along the mountain ranges of the West Coast from Canada to Mexico.

13 Trillium Lake stands in the shadow of Mount Hood, its crystal clear waters surrounded by lush forest. It is ideal for family outings. There are picnicking and camping facilities. Children enjoy feeding the many ducks here, and fishermen are drawn by the prospect of catching the summer steelheads.

14 A six-mile winding drive up Mount Hood past cascading waterfalls leads to Timberline Lodge, an impressive wood-and-stone ski lodge built during the 1930's with funds provided by the Works Progress Administration (WPA). It stands as a testament to the skill of the more than 500 men and women who built and decorated it, and is now a national historic landmark.

Using regional materials, workers shaped fir and pine beams by hand, chiseled volcanic rock into buttresses and a fireplace, wove wool into upholstery fabric, hooked rugs, appliquéd bedspreads and curtains, hand-wrought iron gates and furniture, and created glass mosaics, marquetry, paintings, and wood sculptures. The lodge offers a dining room, a cafeteria, a snack bar, overnight accommodations, an outdoor swimming pool, and a variety of sports, gift, and specialty shops.

Timberline is noted for fine, year-round day and night skiing. In summer the upper slopes are used, and during that season you can take a

14. Nature is the theme of Timberline Lodge, whose roofline echoes the forms of the mountain and the trees. Animals indigenous to the area, such as cougar, deer, and bear, are depicted in carvings, door knockers, and mosaics.

Timberline Flora and Fauna

The natural environment of the timberline is stark. Above the line of dwarfed trees, the bare land is relentlessly exposed to snow, wind, and sun. The alpine vegetation has adapted to timberline conditions by growing close to the ground in small, compacted shapes that minimize the effects of wind and cold. Shrubs, such as red heather and dwarf juniper, hug the ground and send roots down to six feet or so to find moisture. The subalpine fir, white bark pine, and mountain hemlock, which struggle to grow at 6,000 to 7,000 feet, form protective groupings called ribbon forests. The few solitary trees are stunted and twisted by the wind.

Small animals near the timberline either hibernate or migrate in the cold weather. Chipmunks, ground squirrels, pikas, and marmots have small noses and feet, and fur-covered ears and tails as protection against the harsh winds and below-freezing temperatures.

From mid-July to late August many varieties of wild flowers bloom profusely in the alpine meadows. Blue Jacob's ladder, yellow sunflowers and desert parsley, purple cascade aster, white yarrow, and crimson Indian paintbrush and bright red newberry knotweed create a patchwork of mountainside color.

chair-lift ride to Palmer Snowfield, 8,520 feet above sea level, for a breathtaking aerial view of the Cascades. Warmer clothing is usually needed at the higher elevations.

15 The Barlow Road, an 80-mile overland route from The Dalles to Oregon City cleared by Samuel K. Barlow in 1846, gave emigrants an alternate to the risky Columbia River passage. The U.S. Forest Service maintains a replica of Barlow's tollgate. A half-mile west is the Tollgate Campground.

6. The blueness of Crater Lake, as it reflects a bright sky and the volcanic rock walls that rise from its depths, has an intensity that has to be seen to be believed. Off a point of land is the Phantom Ship, the smaller of the lake's two islands.

This route, cutting twice across both the Coast Range and the Cascade Range, highlights the coastline, the forests, and the high desert to exemplify further the remarkable scope of Oregon's scenery.

Outstanding features are Crater Lake, the Oregon Caves, and the great redwoods you see on the short dip into California.

1 Considering the extent of the surrounding timberlands it is not surprising that Roseburg is a lumbering center. Less obvious, until you see the sheep on the hillsides, is the fact that this is also a wool-producing area. An even more recent industry here is winemaking, and in September there is the Oregon Wine Festival, featuring wine tasting and entertainment at the Douglas County Fairgrounds.

Route 138 winds, in part, along the North Umpqua River, where you may see fly fishermen practicing their art.

There are a number of small state parks along this route where you may picnic or go fishing for trout and striped bass.

2 At Susan Creek State Park you can try fly fishing in the Umpqua, camp, go for a short hike to a waterfall, or have a picnic on one of the inviting rocky ledges along the clear, rushing river.

3 Toketee Lake, formed by the damming of the North Umpqua River, features boating and fishing. A half-mile trail to Toketee Falls winds along the river, through forest, past ferns, moss-covered rocks, and fallen logs. The falls flows into two picturesque pools, one above the other.

4 Running parallel to the Clearwater River, Route 138 passes a number of small waterfalls, each with a campground and a picnic area. The most spectacular of these is Watson Falls, 272 feet high and partially visible from the car. There is a pleasant half-mile hiking trail through the forest for a closer view.

5 Diamond Lake was scooped out by glacial action and appeared in its present form approximately 10,000 years ago. Nearly a mile above sea level, it covers an area of 3,000 acres. A number of hiking trails begin near the lake. Some are short and gentle, others are moderately steep with views of the high Cascade Range. Some trails are suitable for horses, which can be rented nearby. At the marina, boat and fishing gear rentals come with free advice. The lake is plentifully stocked with rainbow trout. Overnight accommodations, meals, and bicycle rentals can be had at the lodge.

As you enter Crater Lake National Park, you cross the Pacific Crest National Scenic Trail. You can pick up printed information about the trail when you pay your park fee.

6 Crater Lake is surrounded by contrasting areas of coniferous forest and barren pumice caldera. Between these extremes are the high mountain meadows where, during the short summer season, the wild flowers show off their vivid colors. The lake itself was formed more than 6,000 years ago by volcanic activity. Previously Mount Mazama had been a giant volcanic cone here, higher than the present Mount Rainier. A series of earthquakes released the enormous pressures that built up in its foundations. Suddenly there was a colossal explosion, a hundred times greater than an atomic bomb, leaving behind this wide chasm and covering all of northwestern America with a layer of ash and the immediate area with a layer of pumice. In the centuries that followed, the resulting caldera filled up with rain and snow until the lake achieved the form it has today.

15. At Harris Beach State Park the pounding sea has isolated a rocky promontory, and it now stands as an island with a small, wave-worn beach. The offshore islands along this stretch of coast are rookeries for gulls, petrels, cormorants, and many other birds.

A 1.7-mile trail from Crater Lake Lodge leads east along the rim to Garfield Peak for a spectacular view from 1,900 feet above the lake. From Rim Village, an easy walk along the Discovery Point Trail takes you to the spot from where the lake was first seen, in 1853, by prospector John Wesley Hillman. Travel north from Rim Village to complete the 33-mile Rim Drive around the lake's rugged walls. Several picnic sites along the route offer unobstructed views of distant volcanic peaks reflected in the clear, dark blue waters of the lake.

7　Lake of the Woods offers camping, boating, and fishing, along with a lodge for overnight accommodations. A special section of the lake is set aside for swimming.

8　Ashland is attractively perched in the foothills of the Siskiyou Mountains. Like many towns in the area, it has its share of lumber mills, but its principal industry is tourism. Each year almost a quarter of a million visitors come here to watch the performances of the Oregon Shakespearean Festival. The season opens in February and runs through October. For tickets and information write: Shakespeare, Ashland, Oregon 97520; or phone: 503/482-4331.

In the town the 100-acre Lithia Park is full of flowers, picnic sites, and playgrounds.

9　Medford, the largest city in southern Oregon, is surrounded by the vast pear orchards that cover the valley and the nearby foothills. In April a Pear Blossom Festival celebrates the lovely blooms of thousands of trees.

10　Jacksonville became a prosperous city almost overnight when gold was discovered in the Applegate Valley in the early 1850's. When the gold boom was over, the town continued to expand as an agricultural center, but hard times fell in 1883, when Jacksonville was bypassed by the Southern Pacific Railroad. Today it is a national historic landmark town. A museum, art galleries, antiques shops, and other businesses are housed in restored and refurbished buildings, allowing visitors a fascinating peek into the 19th-century life of a small western town.

Jacksonville is ideal for exploring by foot. Worth seeing are the old U.S. Hotel; the Beekman Bank, built in 1863; the Miller Gunsmith Shop; and the original Rogue River Valley Railway Depot.

Route 238 winds through the farmlands of the Applegate Valley between Jacksonville and Grants Pass. Small roadside stands offer fresh eggs and produce in season.

11　Grants Pass, situated on the Rogue River, is a starting point for many white-water boat trips. Jet boat excursions, from two to five hours long, take you comfortably through Hellgate Canyon. Longer trips by raft through the national wild and scenic section of the Rogue stop for hearty country-style lunches at one of the numerous riverside lodges. Arrangements can be made beforehand to spend a night or two at these rustic accommodations, with the return trip by automobile.

There are also one-day raft trips from Hog Creek to Grave Creek, and kayaks can be rented by those who wish to go it alone.

12　Lake Selmac features campgrounds, horseback riding, bicycle and boat rentals, and fishing. The giant slide in a swimming section of the lake is a favorite with children.

13　Twenty miles east of Route 199 on Route 46 is the Oregon Caves National Monument. Tours through the cavern take over an hour and are conducted year-round. Warm clothing is advised, even in summer, as are sturdy shoes. Some passages require stooping or climbing, but the fantastic beauty of the subtly lit formations is well worth the effort. Children under six and anyone who is unsound of wind or limb are not admitted to the cavern.

Outside, on the canyon floor, is the Château, a six-story timbered lodge surrounded by virgin forest. It has overnight accommodations and perhaps the only dining room in the world with a mountain stream running through it.

14　From May to December the Hiouchi Ranger Station of the Redwood National Park in California offers exhibits and information about the area, famous for its magnificent towering redwoods. You can camp, picnic, hike, fish, swim, or take a float trip down the Smith River at Jedediah Smith Redwoods State Park.

Walker Road, an unpaved road for hiking, will take you down to the Smith River through idyllic groves of awesome redwoods.

Returning to Oregon, Route 101 winds its way north along the coastline, with sweeping views of the Pacific from the road.

15　Just north of Brookings, Harris Beach State Park is a charming place that attracts beachcombers and surf fishermen. A hiking trail leads over a grassy knoll to a beautiful small cove.

16　Samuel H. Boardman State Park is, in fact, a series of parks stretching for about 11 miles along the scenic coast.

Lone Ranch offers picnic tables set on the grassy hills overlooking the shore. From here you can see Twin Rocks, a part of the Oregon Islands National Wildlife Refuge system, just offshore. There is some clamming in season, and both surf and rock fishing are popular here.

At Cape Ferrelo and House Rock points, trails lead to breathtaking vistas of ocean and the surrounding countryside.

There are picnic settings at Whaleshead Cove among the groves of twisted, windswept trees, as well as others near the driftwood-covered beach.

Natural Bridge Cove features a 50-yard trail to a natural arch carved out of solid rock by the pounding of the surf. All of the hillslopes here formerly reached farther out to sea, but the storms regularly sweeping in from the Pacific have eroded the coastline into cliffs, bluffs, and offshore islets. The natural bridge was formed by erosion working under a resistant formation from two sides.

17 At Cape Sebastian State Park a steep, narrow road leads up along the ridge of a bluff overlooking the ocean. From the parking lot, a footpath takes you to a splendid point from which you can see ocean, beach, and wooded hills.

18 Gold Beach, at the mouth of the Rogue River, is the starting point for fishing, sight-seeing, and mail boat trips upriver. Fishermen come year-round for runs of Chinook salmon, coho salmon, and steelhead trout.

Do not miss the jet boat trips up the Rogue. There is a choice of a 32-mile trip to Agness or a 52-mile ride through white-water rapids, with the option of arranging to spend the night at a peaceful lodge beside the unspoiled river before returning to Gold Beach.

19 Humbug Mountain State Park is nestled in the foothills of the coastal mountains. Only a mile or so from the shore, its canyon setting offers a pleasant change of scenery for picnicking and camping.

20 A commercial fishing village, Port Orford also attracts sports fishermen who seek migrating salmon and steelhead trout in the fall. You can buy fresh fish near the harbor, and the restaurants here feature local seafood and fresh wild-blackberry pie in season.

21 Bandon is the producer of Oregon's largest cranberry crop, and a festival honoring that bounty is held in September.

South of town a beach loop road leads from and to Route 101 along a rocky bluff. Several trails lead down to a secluded beach with a view of the rugged offshore rocks. The grassy, windswept knolls of Bandon State Park have an untamed beauty, but the picnic sites are sheltered.

22 Myrtle Point is named for the Oregon myrtle (*Umbellularia californica*), which grows in abundance around the town. Two and a half miles southeast of town is Hoffman Wayside, where you can visit a grove of these rather rare, broad-leaved evergreen trees growing near the Coquille River.

23 The Bejelland Winery, a modest little vineyard, is just 2.4 miles off the highway on Reston Road. Local experts attribute the excellent grapes grown here to the long summer days and the cool nights of the Umpqua Valley, a climate not unlike that of Germany's wine-growing regions. A variety of their wines is offered for tasting.

24 World Wildlife Safari, a half-mile outside the town of Winston, is a drive-through animal and bird preserve. The park's 600 acres resemble a vast African plain, especially in summer, and a three-mile drive takes you past such exotic animals as cheetahs, tigers, mouflon, elephants, wildebeestes, fringe-eared oryxes, and yaks, as well as many others. All are free to roam within the park.

17. Testimony to the power of the sea, remnants of Oregon's headlands stand in the bay below Cape Sebastian. Beyond the spit of land in the distance, a half-mile offshore, rises Mack Arch. Such features characterize Oregon's rugged coastline.

In the Golden West

California, land of extremes, boasts the sparkling Pacific, broad valleys, mountain peaks, and deserts

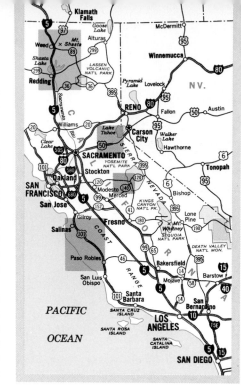

California's countryside, with massive, granite peaks, volcanoes, fertile fields, salt flats, deep canyons, sandy sun-drenched beaches, and more than 8,000 lakes, displays a geological mixture found in no other state.

To the north are the Klamath Ranges and the volcanic Cascades. In the middle, the Coast Ranges are separated from the mighty Sierra Nevada by the 400-mile-long Great Valley. And then to the south are further ranges and intervening desert lands— hot, dry, and sparsely populated.

From the north end of the Sacramento Valley, this route takes you into the Cascade Mountains where remnants of gold rush days bring to mind that historic era. The road then winds through the great Lassen volcanic wilderness, a landscape of snow-trimmed cones rising above forests and lava flows.

1 The thriving community of Red Bluff, stretched along the low, reddish bluffs that border the Sacramento River, has been a shipping center since the 1850's when steamboats carried cargo on these waters.

With tree-lined streets, elegant Victorian houses, and red brick business buildings, the town has retained its pre-1900 charm. The important industry here today is agriculture, as it has been for the last hundred years.

The Willian B. Ide Adobe State Historic Park, named for a member of an 1846 move for Californian independence, is on the city's outskirts. Ide's restored adobe house, complete with household furnishings of the 1840's, is open to visitors. Near the house is an inviting picnic grove.

North of Red Bluff there are flat, open farmlands and pastures, with Mount Shasta soaring high above the countryside.

The city of Redding at the north end of the Sacramento Valley is a popular takeoff point for fishermen and hunters who come to enjoy the nearby mountainous wilderness, where cougars, bobcats, and an occasional black bear roam the forests and fish fill the snow-fed lakes and streams.

2 As you leave Redding you begin to climb into the majestic Cascade Mountains, whose precipitous slopes were once rich with gold. The old mining town of Shasta, situated in Shasta State Historical Park, was a booming center of activity in the 1850's and is now a ghostly reminder of the past. A museum illustrates life here in the gold rush days.

3 West of Shasta the road crosses the Shasta Divide, a forested ridge that separates the watersheds of the Sacramento and Trinity rivers. On the western slope is Whiskeytown National Recreation Area and Reservoir, where boating, fishing, and camping are available.

4 The charming village of French Gulch, once a colorful mining town and still an active community with a church, a general store, and one small hotel, has remained quite unchanged, a living relic of the last century. It is now on the National Register of Historic Places.

5 Weaverville, the center of the state's northern gold-mining area, has become a favorite vacation town. Throughout the wooded mountains nearby, both summer and winter sports facilities are available.

Here too is the Weaverville Joss House State Historic Park, where a temple, built in 1874 by the Chinese who came to work in the mines, displays priceless tapestries, carvings, and other works of art. Guided tours are available. Closed on Thanksgiving, Christmas, and New Year's days.

The road northward skirts Trinity Lake and the Trinity National Recreation Area, where rugged peaks of granite rise from alpine meadows nestled among the high valleys.

6 A narrow, winding, wooded road with many switchbacks takes you to the summit of 5,400-foot-high Scott Mountain, a peak that towers above the gentle valleys below. This drive is often closed in winter because of heavy snows.

7 Yreka, near the Oregon border, is encircled by slopes covered with the ponderosa pines, stately redwoods, and Douglas firs that serve to make lumbering the main industry in this area.

Along the residential streets in the restored section of the town, just west of Route 5, you can see a number of the finest Victorian houses in the state.

From the town of Weed, which offers superb views of majestic Mount Shasta, the route climbs into the foothills at the base of that famous snowcapped peak and levels off as it enters a high plateau.

8 A scenic drive meanders through the wooded terrain at McArthur–Burney Falls Memorial State Park, where there is a one-mile trail to Burney Falls, a sparkling double cascade that drops 129 feet through a wooded gorge into Burney Creek. Campgrounds are nearby.

SPECIAL FEATURES

ROAD GUIDE	HIGHLIGHT	**1**
STATE PARKS	SCHEDULED AIRLINE STOPS	✹
With Campsites △ Without Campsites △	MILITARY AIRPORTS	✈
RECREATION AREAS	OTHER AIRPORTS	✈
With Campsites ▲ Without Campsites △	MAJOR MTN. ROADS	
SELECTED REST AREAS ✕	CLOSED IN WINTER Closed in Winter	
POINTS OF INTEREST ⊡		
SKI AREAS 🎿	BOAT RAMPS	

ROAD CLASSIFICATION

CONTROLLED ACCESS HIGHWAYS
Interstate interchange numbers are mileposts.

Interchanges

OTHER DIVIDED HIGHWAYS

PAVED HIGHWAYS

LOCAL ROADS In unfamiliar areas inquire locally before using these roads   Paved   Gravel   Dirt

MILEAGE

MILEAGE BETWEEN TOWNS AND JUNCTIONS   3 ⌐ 4   MILEAGE BETWEEN DOTS • 35 •

SCALE

ONE INCH 25 MILES   0   5   10   15   25

ONE INCH 40 KILOMETERS   0 5 10   20   30   40

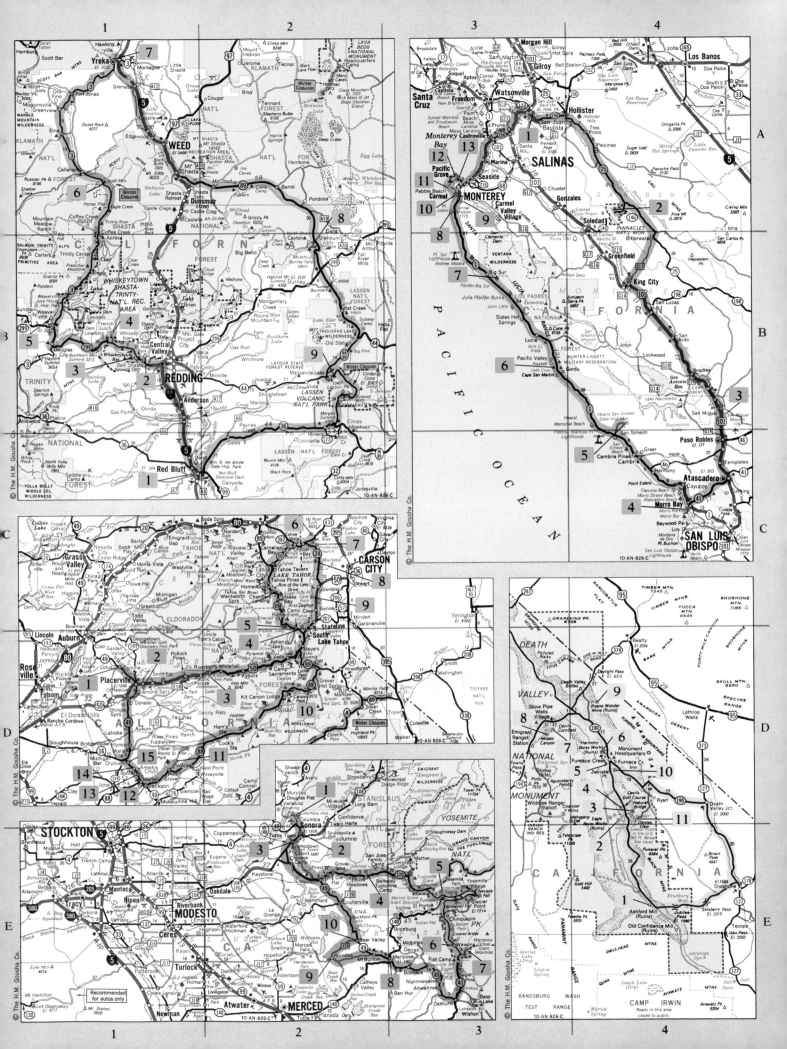

The formation of a volcano

The massive dome of Lassen Peak was formed by lava (fluid rock) as it was forced upward through a vent on the slope of a larger, now extinct volcano. The new dome plugged the vent, and Lassen Peak remained calm for a long time. Below is an idealized profile of one of the Cascade Range volcanoes, illustrating their development. The nose of the descending plate (formerly part of the Pacific Ocean crust) melts, generating magma (melted rock), which rises to a shallow magma chamber that in turn feeds the volcano with its lava.

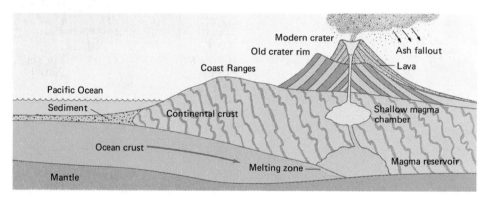

Modern crater
Old crater rim
Ash fallout
Coast Ranges
Lava
Pacific Ocean
Sediment
Continental crust
Shallow magma chamber
Ocean crust
Mantle
Melting zone
Magma reservoir

9 Lassen Volcanic National Park, with 50 glacial lakes and almost as many mountain peaks, is an untamed wilderness of lava flows mingled with meadows, forests, snow-fed streams, and active hot springs.

A 29-mile winding drive leads toward the summit of Lassen Peak, a plug-dome volcano that, after a long quiescence, erupted repeatedly between 1914 and 1917. The peak, which dominates the park, was named for Peter Lassen, a Danish pioneer who used it as a landmark when guiding settlers to the Sacramento Valley.

At an elevation of 8,000 feet there is a parking lot, surrounded by snow even in August. From here you can begin a hike to the 10,453-foot summit, a rugged climb rewarded by a series of breathtaking views from what seems to be the top of the world.

As the road descends, it winds through Bumpass Hell, where steam and the distinctive smell of sulfur confirm that this is an area of active hot springs.

The park includes picnic groves, seven campgrounds, and many hiking trails, as well as waters for fishing and boating. In winter, downhill and cross-country skiing is permitted on weekends, except when heavy snows bring the threat of avalanches.

You leave the forests and the windy mountain roads along a fingerlike ridgetop that gradually drops down through stretches of scrub oak, and reach the treeless, sunny prairies on the way to Red Bluff.

Strung like a chain through the beautiful western foothills of the Sierra Nevada are California's colorful gold-mining towns. Route 49 (numbered in honor of the forty-niners), which links these towns, takes you through a countryside luxuriant most of the year with greenery and wild flowers. Crossing the Sierra Nevada along routes traversed by pioneers, you savor the beauty of Lake Tahoe from a drive that takes you into Nevada.

1 So peaceful is the setting of Sutter's Mill at Coloma that it is hard to believe this was where the world's most frenzied gold rush began.

In 1848 John Marshall, a carpenter building the mill, spotted in the water a bit of placer gold, as alluvial deposits of the metal are called. The stampede began. In 1851 the name "Mother Lode" was given to the 120 miles of gold-bearing source veins prospectors found along the western slopes of the Sierra Nevada.

At the Marshall Gold Discovery State Historic Park, which encompasses most of rustic old Coloma, a self-guiding trail leads from a replica of the original mill to the gold discovery site on a riverbank.

The soft beauty of the countryside between Coloma and Placerville seems to spell contentment. As the road winds around the loaf-shaped hills there are views into small valleys with ponds and rich grass. In late spring flowering vines and California poppies bank the road, in places overhung with trees—feathery digger pines, locusts, silver wattles, huge-leafed western catalpas, black oaks, sycamores, and poplars.

2 Nestled among hills covered with apple orchards, Placerville is a lovely town with colorful old stores, Victorian houses, and cascades of roses. Placerville became prosperous as a depot and outfitting point during the rush eastward to the mines of the Comstock Lode in Nevada.

Among the historic places to see are the Gold Bug Mine in Bedford Park, the City Hall, the Justice Court, and the museum at the El Dorado County fairgrounds.

Climbing steadily but gently from Placerville, Route 50 takes you across the Sierra Nevada through forests of tall pines, cedars, Douglas firs, and dogwoods, with views of deep valleys, soaring granite peaks covered with snow, waterfalls, and white-water streams. The road cuts into a route used in the early days by stage-coaches and the Pony Express.

3 About 19 miles east of Placerville, you hear Bridal Veil Falls before you see it, unless the highway traffic is too heavy and noisy. A turnout at its base gives you a splendid view of the falls hurtling down the steep pine-clad mountainside and into the South Fork of the American River.

4 Lake Tahoe is one of the fairest lakes in the world, and the 71-mile drive around its rim is beautiful at any time of the year. But keep in mind that summer traffic is congested. At the start of your drive, take time to visit the U.S. Forest Service's Lake Tahoe Visitor Center on Route 89, about three miles northwest of the junction with Route 50, for information about things to see and do.

5 Emerald Bay, one of the most celebrated spots on the lake, is a registered natural landmark. The road rounding its western end is notched out of a high cliff, a glacial moraine, and gives a full view of the large, pendant-shaped inlet and Fannette Island, which rests like a small green jewel on the bay's shining surface.

6 At the northern end of the lake, the most spectacular vista is from an overlook on Mount Rose Highway. The overlook, which is at an elevation of 7,597 feet, is three miles from the intersection with Route 28.

7 Ponderosa Ranch, world-famous as the setting for the television serial *Bonanza*, sprawls on the mountainside 500 feet above Lake Tahoe. The ranch has become a living museum of the West, with a collection of antique carriages, farm and ranch equipment, and thousands of other items. There are also barnyard animals, hayrides, and horseback riding. Even if you have never been on a horse, you can take the guided trail ride up through ponderosa pines and enjoy the views of the lake below. Closed January through April.

8 Sand Harbor State Park, about three miles south of Ponderosa Ranch, has one of the best public swimming beaches on the lake as well as picnic areas and nature trails. Ramps and other facilities are provided for the handicapped.

9 South of the tunnel through Cave Rock, a massive granite peak that juts out into Lake Tahoe, a sharp turnoff leads down to a parking area at the water's edge for views of the lake, the snowcaps, and Cave Rock.

10 Discovered by Kit Carson and John Frémont in 1843–44, Carson Pass (8,573 feet) was used by thousands of gold seekers. Looking back from the vista point at the route you have just traversed, you try to imagine the pluck and endurance of the pioneers who crossed this way.

There are several vista points along Route 88 where you can stop to take in the wild beauty of the Sierra Nevada country. Descending the western slopes, you enter a quiet forest of pines and deciduous trees.

11 The small town of Volcano (so named because it lies in a bowl-shaped valley that resembles a crater) was once one of the richest towns along the Mother Lode. The old

4. The rim drive around Lake Tahoe provides nonstop beauty in all seasons. In May and June yellow-blooming wyethia, or mules-ears, splashes the slopes overlooking the lake's north shore while the mountains remain crusted with snow. The fair lake, whose basin was formed 25 million years ago, is one of the highest (6,225 feet) and deepest (1,644 feet) lakes in North America.

buildings are the originals, and the fine St. George Hotel has remained in business all these years. If you visit in April or May, drive northeast on Ram's Horn Grade to Daffodil Hill. The first daffodil bulbs were brought here by Dutch settlers to remind them of home.

12 Jackson, a charming old town with hilly, narrow streets, is the site of the famed Kennedy mine, which had a vertical shaft of 5,912 feet, one of the deepest in American gold-mining history. Its landmark is the Kennedy tailing wheel, visible from the highway. Resembling a large Ferris wheel with its diameter of 58 feet, it has 208 stationary buckets around its rim. The wheel was part of a system of four wheels and connecting flumes that lifted tailings over two hills to an impounding dam, in compliance with the state's antipollution legislation of 1912. A short drive out North Main Street brings you to Kennedy Tailing Wheels Park. The upright wheel, the ruins of another, and the flume are on an oak-shaded hill about 200 feet from the parking lot.

Northward from Jackson are lovely views of luxuriant green hills, ravines, and meadows.

13 Unusually well preserved, Sutter Creek has a storybook charm, with neat, white-painted buildings, flower beds, and shade trees. On Main Street (Route 49), picturesque shops with second-story porches line the high-curbed sidewalks. To see Knight's Foundry, turn east onto Eureka Street. Built in 1873, this is the only water-powered foundry in the United States and it is now included in the National Register of Historic Places.

14 In Amador City (population 185), a picturesque cluster of old buildings, you find the headquarters of the Keystone Mine, now an inn with rooms furnished in the style of the gold rush times.

15 Drytown, which boasted 26 saloons in its heyday, took its name from the diggings at Dry Creek, not from a shortage of liquor. Among the interesting buildings to see here are the old schoolhouse, the butcher shop, and the post office.

Rolling north to a high ridge overlooking Placerville, the road makes a scenic descent into the village.

5. Yosemite Falls, whose upper and lower tiers are linked by cascades hidden in this scene, plunges nearly half a mile to the valley floor. A small footbridge, discernible at the base, affords spectacular close-up views through the spray. Spring is the best time to see the falls, since it is fed by snowmelt and is often dry in summer.

Among the southern mining centers *of the Mother Lode is the village of Columbia, whose streets take you back to the era of the gold rush.*

The road with its formidable switchbacks into the ever-changing scenery of the Sierra Nevada leads to Yosemite Valley, one of the world's most inspiring geological wonders.

1 Columbia, known in Mother Lode country as the gem of the southern mines, looks much as it did in the 1850's and is now a state historical park. Along its sidewalks, shaded by upper porches and projecting roofs, are the old specialty stores, repair shops, a church, a jail, a firehouse, hotels, and entertainment halls, all stocked, equipped, or furnished much as they had been. You can browse in the stores, watch a blacksmith at work, see the theater where Lola Montez performed, and visit the restored schoolhouse. A walking tour, following the self-guiding map available at the park office, takes two hours or so. Tickets are sold for a stagecoach ride.

2 Sonora is a lively business center with colorful reminders of the past, among them Servente's grocery store, one-half of which is still a barroom. There are fine old buildings to see, especially the red frame Episcopal Church (1860) at the north end of Washington Street and the Victorian house across the street. Sonora holds its annual rodeo the second weekend in May.

3 Jamestown, another quaint gold-mining town, has a number of attractively restored buildings, including the two hotels.

If you are a railroad buff, be sure to visit Rail Town 1897, on the edge of Jamestown. The yards of the Sierra Railroad Company, the great roundhouse, and cars and steam engines dating from 1897 are included in the complex preserved here.

Veering west at Moccasin Creek, you leave the rolling green countryside typical of the Mother Lode and head into convoluted brown mountains fissured with deep ravines. The steep switchbacks require caution and low speeds. This route is not recommended for trailers.

Near Groveland the environment changes dramatically. Here are high meadows brilliantly splashed in spring with purple lupine and orange poppies. The road winds pleasantly through stands of Douglas firs and sugar pines and offers views of snow-capped mountains.

4 Again the scenery changes. East of Buck Meadows is the Rim of the World Vista Point. From this appropriately named spot are awesome views across mountains and canyons and down to the Tuolumne River 1,700 feet below you.

After dropping down to the South Fork of the Tuolumne River, the road ascends again, winding through a canyon of evergreens where sun filters through their tall spires to the dogwood and manzanita at their base. From several spots you can glimpse the San Joaquin Valley and California's Coast Range.

Winding down from Crane Flat, the road dips into a long tunnel. As you emerge, Yosemite Valley is suddenly revealed, and its splendor takes your breath away.

5 Sheltered from the world like Shangri-la, Yosemite Valley lies serenely at the base of jagged 3,000-foot-high rock cliffs, spires, and domes. Streaking down the cliffs are several waterfalls, and flowing and cascading through the valley's meadows and groves of dogwoods, incense cedars, pines, firs, and black oaks is the lovely Merced River.

Yosemite Valley is only seven miles long and about a half-mile wide, but few places in the world can match Yosemite's grandeur. It is easy to explore even without a car. There are free shuttle buses at the eastern end and excellent bus tours that show you its celebrated features, including El Capitan, a 3,000-foot-high sheer granite cliff; Half Dome, a rock formation that rises nearly a mile above the

valley floor; and Bridalveil Fall with its lovely gossamer veil. The most accessible of all is the thundering Yosemite Falls: the short paved walk from a parking lot to the base of the falls gives superb views of the upper and lower falls and the cascades, which have a total drop of 2,425 feet.

An intimate and pleasurable way to see the valley is to walk, whether by yourself or on one of the available guided outings. There are also bicycle rentals and stables. There is very little likelihood of seeing a bear, but you are apt to see deer and perhaps a coyote at twilight, as well as smaller creatures and brilliant birds.

Each season has its special beauty in Yosemite, but in summer the waterfalls diminish or dry, and the valley is crowded with visitors. Lodgings or campsites should be reserved two months in advance.

6 The drive leaving the valley on Route 41 is as beautiful and dramatic as the one approaching it. At Wawona, stop at the Pioneer Yosemite History Center. Its furnished pioneer cabins, horse-drawn vehicles, and other exhibits give an interesting view of Yosemite before the first automobile arrived there in 1900.

7. *These ancient sequoias are in Mariposa Grove. The giant trees have massive but surprisingly shallow roots.*

7 The Mariposa Grove of Giant Sequoias (*Sequoia sempervirens*), the state tree, is the home of the Grizzly Giant, the largest sequoia in the park (its girth is 96.5 feet), and at about 2,700 years, one of the oldest. The Grizzly Giant is a 15-minute uphill walk from the parking lot; the grade is gentle but it may prove tiring at the mile-high altitude. A shuttle bus usually operates here.

8 In Mariposa, a small but substantial Mother Lode town, the outstanding landmark from gold rush days is the lovely white frame New England-style courthouse, completed in 1854 and in continuous use ever since.

The Mariposa County History Center has an assemblage of everyday items of the mid-1800's that provides a colorful sampler of life in the gold rush period. Threading the exhibits together are descriptive passages from letters to "Dear Charlie," written by a young settler to his friend back home in Massachusetts.

9 The road to Hornitos from Mount Bullion is narrow and twisting and in marginal condition, but the trip is worth it for a view of one of the nation's most famous ghost towns. (If you have a large vehicle, such as a camper, continue on Route 49 to Bear Valley.) Only a few people now live in Hornitos, a half-collapsed adobe town that once had a population of 15,000 and a fierce reputation. Facing the small dirt square are a Wells Fargo office, a saloon, a jail, and the ruins of the store built by Domingo Ghirardelli, the "chocolate king."

The road from Hornitos to Bear Valley is also marginal, and you have to watch out for straying cattle. The hilly countryside is attractive, however, and abounds with wild flowers.

10 From Bear Valley there are stupendous views of desolate ranges rolling to the horizon. Before you are miles of switchbacks sawing down the rocky slopes of Hell Hollow. Far below are Lake McClure and the Merced River.

Descending, and passing old mine shafts and rustic Coulterville with its sagging, tin-roofed buildings, you eventually reach Moccasin Creek with a sense of relief at being once again in the gentler countryside of the Mother Lode.

This tour of about 300 miles reveals a remarkable variety of scenic, historic, and fascinating places. The scenery includes the rocky volcanic peaks of the Pinnacles National Monument, a peaceful valley of orchards and vineyards, and some of the most spectacular oceanside roads and hiking trails to be found. Three historic missions are reminders of California's early days, and the pre-Depression era is represented by the storybook setting created by William Randolph Hearst at San Simeon. Among other delightful places, unique in character, are the towns of Carmel and Monterey.

1 The mission at San Juan Bautista, the largest of the California missions, was founded in 1797 when the influence of Army and Church extended from Mexico along the Camino Real, or "Royal Way," to the

headquarters is in a restored adobe house owned by descendants of the Breen family, who came west with the ill-starred Donner Party.

The town of San Juan Bautista itself has a quaint, western look, with old-fashioned street lamps, houses with false fronts, and second-story balconies over the sidewalks.

The highway from San Juan Bautista leads through lettuce fields and apricot orchards. South of Hollister you may want to stop at Bolado Park to picnic, swim, or roller skate. Around Paicines, grapes cover the hills for as far as you can see, replaced farther along by orange California poppies and yellow lupine.

2 Pinnacles and spires of volcanic rock, chiseled by the elements, give Pinnacles National Monument its name. Their formation began millions of years ago when lava and

vides a rugged setting for hiking and rock climbing, the only way to explore the pinnacles and canyons.

Chapparal, an ecological community of shrubby plants, grows along the steep, dry hillsides, preventing erosion and providing food and shelter for wildlife.

3 Route 101 parallels the Salinas River valley, which was chosen by the Spaniards as their road to the north. At one time green markers in the shape of a bishop's crosier hung with a mission bell indicated this route.

Mission San Miguel Arcángel was the 16th of the 21 missions founded in California. The best preserved of the missions, it is now a Franciscan museum displaying the habits, the books, and the artwork of the founding monastic order.

Six wineries, most of them with tasting rooms, are located between San Miguel and Atascadero. Brochures giving the names and addresses of the various wineries are available at the Pasa Robles Chamber of Commerce.

4 The road from San Miguel to Morro Bay takes you through vineyards interspersed with almond and fruit orchards and, as you near Morro Bay, prune-plum orchards. Billboards advertise wine-tasting rooms.

At Morro Bay you see the huge, dome-shaped Morro Rock, a monolith that has been called the Gibralter of the Pacific.

5 Set in gardens and terraces of masterful landscaping, with furnishings and art treasures collected from all over the world, the legendary Hearst castle at San Simeon is one of the premier showcases on earth.

La Casa Grande, the twin-towered mansion that was the family residence, is the centerpiece of the 123-acre La Cuesta Encantada—"The Enchanted Hill." It has 100 rooms, including 38 bedrooms, a movie theater, 2 libraries, a billiard room, and a vast medieval dining hall with carvings of saints on the ceiling.

The guesthouses also are mansions in themselves, with marble balustrades, ornate fountains, and gardens studded with classical statuary. Other highlights include the outdoor Neptune Pool flanked by a Greco-Roman temple facade with Etruscan-style colonnades and the indoor Roman

2. Only experienced climbers, or those with a trained guide, should hazard climbing among the spires of Pinnacles National Monument. Although the rocks appear stable, their surface may flake off beneath you. Hiking trails are provided for safety.

frontier of New Spain. The San Andreas Fault passes through the mission grounds; a seismograph records earthquakes, several of which have severely damaged the mission.

The mission and San Juan Bautista State Historical Park are at the far end of town. The historical park's

rocks spewed through cracks in the earth's crust. Later, the shifting of tectonite plates created a rift, the San Andreas Fault, through these rocks. Gradually sliding northward, one of the plates has carried this section of volcanic rock 195 miles from its original location. The park's terrain pro-

5. San Simeon, which has been designated a state historical monument, was built in the 1920's by William Randolph Hearst.

Pool inspired by a fifth-century Roman mausoleum. In the surrounding hills you can see imported wildlife that includes zebras, Barbary sheep, and tahr goats.

Reservations are recommended; for tickets, available eight weeks in advance, write to Department of Parks and Recreation, P.O. Box 2390, Sacramento, California 95811.

Soon after leaving San Simeon you enter Los Padres National Forest and Big Sur, the rugged and beautiful stretch of coast that extends north to Carmel. Along much of this route the highway hugs the shore and provides breathtaking views as it sweeps around the Santa Lucia Mountains.

6 Jade Cove was named for the Pacific blue jade, found nowhere else in the world, and the blue-green nephrite jade that come from this rocky beach. Even though collectors have combed the area for years, it is still possible to find small stones.

7 The best way to see Pfeiffer–Big Sur State Park is to hike its trails. One trail leaving the small park climbs 4½ miles up Mount Manuel (elevation 3,300 feet) for a view of the coast on one side and Ventana Wilderness on the other. Other trails take you to falls, groves, gorges, and sandpiper-filled sea caves and lagoons. Bobcats, deer, peccaries (wild pigs) and, occasionally, mountain lions and black bears can be seen here. You may also see the American peregrine falcon.

This park provides one of many entrances to the 400,000-acre Monterey District of Los Padres National Forest. Others are at the Big Sur and Pacific Valley stations.

Alternately dipping and climbing, Route 1 gives views of the old Point Sur Lighthouse, built in 1889 after two ships had grounded on the point during a dense fog. Six miles farther, Bixby Creek Bridge makes an impressive sight as it arches 285 feet above the canyon with a single, 714-foot concrete span.

8 Because of the wild, primitive beauty of its rock, surf, and groves of Monterey cypress, Point Lobos has been described as "the greatest meeting of land and water in the world." The point, now a state reserve, takes its name from the colonies of California and Steller sea lions that live here—*lobo marino* is Spanish for "sea wolf." Sea otters and seals are also highlights, as well as killer whales that occasionally come here to hunt.

Along the south shore you may notice underfoot a pebbly rock conglomerate known as the Carmelo formation. The sediments in it accumulated at a time when this coastline was sinking, about 60 million years ago.

9 Mission San Carlos Borromeo del Rio Carmelo, founded in 1770 by Father Junípero Serra, includes a museum, a section of which shows the restored cell and kitchen of Serra, the guest rooms, and the mess hall for mission visitors.

10 Under the influence of the writers, artists, and musicians who settled here at the turn of the century, a bohemian life-style developed in Carmel-by-the-Sea, and the community grew into a cozy village noted as much for its civic independence as for the literati who came here; it has no courthouse and no parking meters.

Visit Ocean Avenue with its shops and art galleries and a beach at the end of the street. You should also drive along Scenic Road, which twists along the shore, alternately displaying vistas of the beach and of beautiful homes.

8. The view from Sea Lion Point Trail in Point Lobos State Reserve (right) looks toward a rock known as The Pinnacle. In the foreground is a Monterey cypress. A group of sea lions with their young (above) sun themselves on the shore.

11. *The Seventeen-Mile Drive follows the coastline of the Monterey Peninsula from Carmel to Pacific Grove. One of the features of this scenic route is ice plant, the ground cover shown here. This succulent gets its name from icelike points on the foliage.*

11 Seventeen-Mile Drive passes through exclusive Pebble Beach and Del Monte Forest. This private community is famous for its stately mansions, scenic coastline, golf links, and its strict regulations protecting native plants and wildlife. At Carmel Gate you can get a sight-seeing map with 26 highlights marked.

Both Cypress Point Lookout and the Seal and Bird Rocks picnic area are excellent places for watching herds of leopard and harbor seals and sea lions.

12 When you come to the Pacific Grove Gate, ask for directions to Ocean View Boulevard and Point Pinos. This route along Monterey Bay continues your coast tour through an area as beautiful as Seventeen-Mile Drive. At Lovers Point you can picnic, swim, skin dive, or fish. Past Lovers Point you find "The Magic Carpet of Mesembryanthemum," otherwise known as ice plant. This pink-and-lavender garden blooms from April through August.

Pacific Grove calls itself Butterfly Town U.S.A. because thousands of orange-and-black monarch butterflies migrate here for the winter. The Pacific Grove Museum of Natural History has an exhibit of this migratory phenomenon. The city is also known for its Victorian architecture.

13 At Monterey, one of the highlights is Fisherman's Wharf, a pier with shops, restaurants, fish stores, and facilities for deep-sea sport fishing. John Steinbeck made Cannery Row famous with his novel of the same name describing the sardine-canning industry. Due to overfishing, the sardines gave out in the 1940's, and today the old cannery buildings are restaurants, boutiques, and galleries. The Path of History is a series of walking tours to Monterey's historic buildings and houses.

North of Monterey you drive through Castroville, the self-proclaimed "Artichoke Capital of the World." For 10 miles you see nothing but artichokes growing in neat, well-irrigated rows.

12. *Monarch butterflies cluster and use their wings to warm and shelter each other when it is cool or rainy.*

This drive takes you through Death Valley, an awesome, desolate, but fascinating terrain where very few plants or animals can survive. Within the area are some of California's highest mountain peaks as well as the lowest spot on the continent.

1 In 1914 two men, known as the Ashford brothers, built a mill in Death Valley to process ore from the gold mines scattered in the Black Mountains to the east.

Today, all that remains of the place that came to be called Ashford Mill are the ruins of an adobe office and the cement and timbers from a dumping chute—reminders of the grand era of gold mining in Death Valley, a time of prosperity that lasted from the mid-1870's to the mid-1920's.

The road leading up the valley floor winds through awesome wastes, with the multicolored mountains of the Panamint Range off to the west and the darker, nearer mountains of the Amargosa Range to the east. Thousands of years ago these mountains trapped the runoff of the last great ice age, creating a lake in what is now the dry floor of the valley.

The lake eventually receded, leaving behind the chemicals and mineral deposits that make up the Death Valley Salt Pan. The road skirts this salt pan, which appears as a glittering white sheet extending far into the distance.

2 Near the lowest point on the American continent—282 feet below sea level—is a pool called Badwater, so named because the concentration of salt and other minerals in its waters make it undrinkable.

3 Turning east from the main road, a narrow, dirt, two-mile track leads to a natural bridge that spans a weird and colorful canyon. According to geologists, the bridge was created by the erosional forces of an underground stream. Water trickling down the mountains through the centuries ate away the gravel from beneath the solid rock formation, lowering the canyon floor and exposing the bridge. The road is closed during the summer.

4 A couple of miles to the north, a short spur leads west from the main road to the Devils Golf Course, a hellish-looking field of jagged salt crystals, some as much as two feet high. These strange, broken shapes were caused by underlying beds of salt and water-bearing gravel that extend to depths of more than a thousand feet. The water leaches out the salt and generates the growth of crystals that push upward in columns.

The forty-niners who stumbled into Death Valley on their way to the California goldfields had to cross this obstacle in their covered wagons.

Just past the turnoff to the Devils Golf Course, look on the east side of the main road for the entrance to Artists Drive. This is a one-way road that bypasses a short stretch of the main road and goes through part of the Black Mountain foothills.

The bands of color in the hillsides are formed by shale and gravel in sedimentary layers, separated by volcanic material and eroded by wind and rain over hundreds of centuries. The reds, pinks, and yellows are created by iron salts, the greens by mica, and the purples by manganese.

5   Furnace Creek is an oasis. The creek itself originates in a canyon at Travertine Springs and flows down to form a pool in the valley. Here is the elegant Furnace Creek Inn and Ranch Resort. The ranch was started in the 1880's as Greenland Ranch, northern terminus for the 20-mule teams that hauled borax from nearby Harmony Borax Works to Mojave. After the 20-day round trip, both men and animals needed rest and the wagons needed repairs. Furnace Creek was the ideal spot.

The inn, built in 1926–27 to accommodate visitors to the borax works and to attract tourists to the area, has now been combined with the ranch and expanded into a modern resort with swimming pools, tennis courts, riding trails, a golf course, and a date palm grove of 1,600 trees.

Also here are the National Park Service Visitor Center, the Death Valley Museum, and the Borax Museum. The resort and park are closed in summer.

6   The Harmony Borax Works was built after the discovery of borax here in 1881. The "white gold" was not so much mined as gathered. Chinese laborers simply picked up the soft, fibrous "cotton-balls" of the mineral directly from the salt flats.

4. The Devils Golf Course in Death Valley is a forbidding maze of jagged salt pinnacles up to two feet in height.

This borate was dumped into vats filled with water from nearby Texas Spring, mixed with crude carbonated soda, and fired with wood. A residue of lime and dirt sank to the bottom, and the hot liquid remaining was drawn off into cooling vats. The borax crystalized on rods dipped in the vats and was dried and stored for shipment to Mojave.

7   The Devils Cornfield is a bare, sandy plain punctuated by what appear to be cornstalks. Actually, these are arrowwood plants, which can survive only where the water table is close to the surface, giving the roots moisture year-round.

8   From Stove Pipe Wells Village a 2½-mile dirt road leads into Mosaic Canyon, whose walls are composed of marble fragments from Tucki Mountain cemented into a natural mosaic by pressure and seeping lime water and worn smooth by erosion.

9   The Keane Wonder Mine is tucked away at the end of a dirt road in the foothills of the Funeral Mountains. The ruins include a red house, some rusting pipes, stone masonry at the base of a small canyon, and an old water tank. The area is hot, desolate, and completely isolated.

10   Zabriskie Point was named in honor of a veteran borax miner who pioneered in Death Valley. From the overlook, just off Route 190, you can see for miles. In the distance are the Panamint Mountains and the salt pan; closer up are the Badlands of the Furnace Creek Wash.

11   Dantes View offers the most spectacular panorama of Death Valley. From some 5,000 feet, you can look directly down on Badwater and the immense salt pan.

The road from Route 190 to Dantes View is 13.5 miles long, but it is paved and scenic. About halfway along, you can see Ryan, an old borax-mining town perched high on a mountainside. The town, abandoned in 1928, is closed to the public, but it remains a reminder of earlier and more lively times in Death Valley.

10. Zabriskie Point, one of the starkly beautiful features of Death Valley, has a ridgelike summit crowned with black rock. Ribbonlike channels run from the top to the desert floor, showing the patterns of erosion created by streams of water for millions of years.

Nevada: The Silver State

Once it was Nevada's silver and gold that lured people to its mountains; today the scenery is the attraction

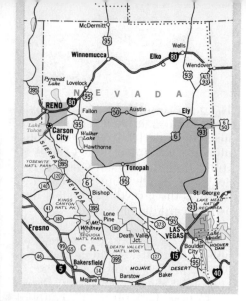

More than a century ago prospectors struck rich lodes of silver and gold in Nevada's mountains and canyons, and hundreds of mining camps and boomtowns dotted the land. Some of these have long since been overtaken by sagebrush and sand, but a number of abandoned mine shafts and ghost towns remain, recalling an adventurous and colorful past. Also reminders of the past, when millionaires were created overnight in the saloons and gambling dens, are the glittering casinos and gambling strips found today in Las Vegas and Reno.

But Nevada's greatest drawing card today is the beauty of its vast, open spaces, mountains fantastically sculpted by erosion, valleys splashed with wild flowers from spring until autumn, and deserts tinted with the subtle greens and yellows of sagebrush and cactus. Here, in the ever-changing light of the wide Nevada sky, the play of colors across the land is spectacularly beautiful.

In the desert north of Reno are the blue waters of Pyramid Lake, a remnant of huge prehistoric Lake Lahontan. High in the mountains to the south are towns steeped in the romance of the old mining days. Here you find Virginia City, which became the largest and most famous of the mining towns, and Carson City, Nevada's lovely capital.

tufa slowly built up, the material assumed these remarkable shapes. Rising 600 feet from the water is the island of tufa for which John C. Frémont named the lake in 1844, since it reminded him of the Pyramid of Cheops. The island can be viewed from the village of Sutcliffe. It is advisable to avoid the side roads approaching the lake because of the danger of getting stuck in the sand.

2. *The beauty of Pyramid Lake is enhanced by the strange tufa formations along the shore and by dramatic Pyramid Rock. The lake lies in the deepest hollow of immense, prehistoric Lake Lahontan, whose old beaches and terraces are still visible on the mountain slopes.*

1 Nestled in a green valley at the base of the Sierra Nevada, Reno is a lively resort town and gateway to the western part of the state. Among the city's features are the Mackay School of Mines' exhibit of early mining materials (closed weekends) and the Nevada State Historical Society, which has displays recording some 10,000 years of history here.

2 The highway north of Reno runs through desert long enough for the blueness of Pyramid Lake to seem like a mirage. Along the lake you see bluffs, pinnacles, and fanciful figures of tufa. A porous rock, tufa is formed where the water is rich in calcium carbonate; plants growing in the water cause the lime to precipitate in seasonal layers. As masses of

Anaho Island in Pyramid Lake is the home of the largest nesting colony of white pelicans in North America. It is a bird sanctuary and cannot be closely approached; a special permit is needed to visit it.

Near Sutcliffe is a solar-energy assisted fish hatchery run by the Paiute Indians, on whose reservation Pyramid Lake lies. Visitors are welcome to see the young cutthroat trout and the cui-ui fish at the hatchery. The prehistoric cui-ui is an endangered species unique (in the New World) to Pyramid and Walker lakes.

Below the big bend in the Truckee River the road rolls through open rangeland and then descends to Silver Springs, a small town in a flat strip of desert. Store signs at the

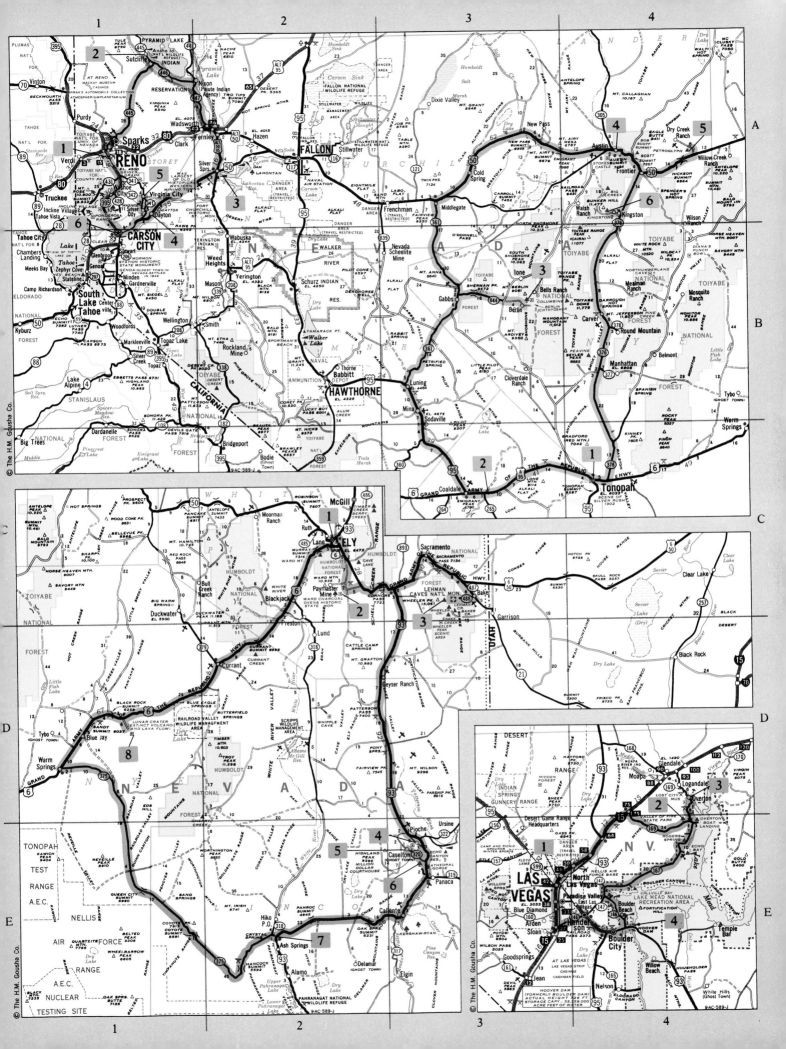

crossroads advertise "Fishworms and Beer," "Saloon and Bait," clues to the excellent fishing in nearby Lahontan Reservoir.

3   The Lahontan State Recreation Area, which encompasses the reservoir and its 72 miles of sandy, tree-fringed shoreline, is a popular place for water sports. The recreation area is reached by a marked, paved access road off Route Alt. 95 three miles south of Silver Springs.

Driving toward Virginia City, you pass through a desert landscape that is perhaps at its loveliest in early May. Mingling with the sagebrush (*Artemisia tridentata*), the state flower, are clumps of greasewood that have become puffs of mauve-pink bloom, filling the air with a sweet fragrance. Paintbrush, buttercups, and other wild flowers add daubs of bright color, and an occasional blossoming tamarisk forms a feathery cloud of soft rose. Rising from the desert floor are rounded golden-green hills set off by the violet of distant ranges. As the road ascends, the snow-mantled Sierra Nevada comes into view.

As you near Dayton, look for a pull-off on the north side of the road where a marker directs you to the mouth of the Sutro drainage tunnel, dug through the mountains to the Comstock Lode in the 1870's.

Mining the Comstock Lode

About 750 miles of tunnels were dug beneath Virginia City to mine the Comstock Lode, a vein of ore about four miles long. Day and night the sound of blasting reverberated in the town and the ground often trembled. Mine cave-ins were frequent. In 1860 Philipp Deidesheimer, an engineer summoned from California, developed a way to support tunnel roofs with a simple square-set timbering system that revolutionized deep mining techniques.

As shafts deepened (a few mines went down 3,200 to 4,200 feet), temperatures rose above 120°F. Air was pumped through pipes to the miners and was cooled with tons of ice lowered by high-speed cages. Candles of a special heat-resistant tallow were imported from England and rationed, one for every two men.

Underground water, often steaming hot, gushed into the mines and caused a number of deaths. To drain the mines Adolph Sutro cut a four-mile-long tunnel through the mountains to the lode in 1869–78, but by the time it was completed, the Comstock was nearly played out.

4   Dayton, a rustic community of great charm with masses of lilacs as well as swinging-door saloons and old

country stores, began as a trading post in 1849 and later became a Pony Express station. The little ghost town now jumps with life, having been revived in 1960 when Clark Gable and Marilyn Monroe arrived to film scenes for *The Misfits*. The village has a small frontier museum, and the Dayton State Park on the eastern edge of town offers historic exhibits related to mining. Picnic sites, campgrounds, and a nature trail are also found in the park.

From Dayton the road climbs steadily. After four miles, turn onto Comstock Highway (Route 17/341), which heads north to Virginia City. About three miles from the turnoff, the Comstock Highway passes the Comstock Bonanza Mine and comes to the small community of Silver City. Here the road forks. Branching to the west is Route 342, the historic roadway up Gold Canyon to Virginia City. This interesting route cuts through Devil's Gate, site of an old toll station, and makes a steep, twisting ascent past a number of old mines.

If you are driving a large vehicle, however, it is advisable to stay on Route 17/341, which is serpentine but not so steep. The two roads, both of which offer splendid scenery, merge on the high slopes of Mount Davidson at the edge of Virginia City.

5   The most famous of Nevada's boomtowns, Virginia City got its start in 1859 with the discovery of the Comstock Lode, a rich vein of gold and silver ore in the mountain. Other strikes followed, and soon there were about 9,000 people living in tents, lean-tos, and dugouts along a 4½-mile stretch of nearby Gold Canyon. Capping all the finds was the Big Bonanza, struck in 1873, which produced ore with probably the greatest concentration of gold and silver ever found in the world. In the next two or three years the population of Virginia City swelled to 25,000. Today the city has fewer than a thousand people.

Frenetic and brashly opulent in its heyday, the place has retained much of its color and authenticity, with buildings that date from the late 1870's and the 1880's. (The Great Fire of 1875 destroyed most of the earlier structures.) Strolling along the boardwalks past picturesque shops and saloons, you can imagine the

5. A shaft headframe and a dump of tailings (foreground) mark the location of one of the deepest shafts sunk at Virginia City. During the feverish mining days the hillside city literally trembled from the constant blasting beneath the streets.

times when the streets were packed with wagons, mule teams, stages, and buggies, and when the doorknobs of many of the town's mansions were made of local silver.

Among the many places to see are "The Way It Was" mining museum, Grant's General Store, and the Chollar Mine. The Chollar, one of the greatest of the old mines, is the only place where you can see the original Deidesheimer timber construction.

As an orientation for sight-seeing, the Visitor's Bureau on C Street shows a 15-minute narrated film on points of interest. There is also a map for self-guided tours of the town.

In the days of the Comstock, the route over Geiger Grade, just north of Virginia City, was the most direct connection between the city and Washoe Valley. Stagecoaches and mule-team freighters frequently carried gold and silver, and the road was the scene of countless robberies and holdups. From the overlook at Geiger Summit (6,799 feet) on Route 17 you can see the old toll road, Dead Man's Point, and Robbers Roost. The scenery from the summit and from Geiger Lookout, farther down the road, is breathtaking.

6 Carson City lies in Eagle Valley, rimmed by the foothills of the Sierra Nevada whose snow-clad peaks loom to the west. The capital of Nevada since 1864, the town is noted for its 19th-century architecture. The handsome residences and public buildings, including the capitol, can be seen on a short walking tour; self-guiding maps are available at the Chamber of Commerce.

Of special interest is the Nevada State Museum, housed in the old U.S. Mint. Here you can see the first of the five coin presses that stamped nearly 14 million silver dollars with the now coveted CC mint mark. In the basement of the building there are full-scale dioramas of mine scenes and a model of a mine tunnel showing the Deidesheimer square-set timber construction. Closed on Thanksgiving, Christmas, and New Year's days.

Leaving Carson City the highway crosses the low mountains to the north and then drops into Washoe Valley, a medley of greens with farms, ranches, and orchards, flanked by the magnificent Sierras.

2. The Gabbs Valley Range presents a striking variety of sedimentary rock that has been tilted up to near-vertical formations from its original, almost-horizontal bedding on an ancient sea floor. What was once sand has become quartzite, now weathered into rugged blocks, while the silts and clays have eroded into rounded patterns.

Here is a loop that traverses pasturelands, salt flats, river valleys, mountain ranges, and canyons. Scattered in this varied landscape are ranches, ghost towns, and defunct silver and gold mines, many of which are being reevaluated as the prices of those metals soar. And in one canyon are the fossils of huge marine animals that lived 180 millions years ago.

1 The stampede to Tonopah followed the discovery of silver there in 1900. By 1907 it boasted several thousand people, two-storied balconied hotels with steam heat, newspapers, and a stock exchange. As a crossroads in prospecting country, Tonopah has survived several booms and busts, and once again mining companies are headquartered here. Some of the town's colorful past remains, including the Mizpah Hotel.

2 To the west of Tonopah lies arid desert with sparse and stunted vegetation and several salt flats. In the midst of this region are the few remains of the Silver Peak mine camp. Discovered in 1864, Silver Peak was one of the oldest and largest mines in Nevada. By 1917 the mine camp had nearly disappeared; today only the shaft timbers and debris can be seen.

The landscape becomes much more varied as the road turns north, climbing progressively hillier country with outcrops of red rock. North of Luning the road ascends the Gabbs Valley Range to a high tableland and then makes a long descent to Gabbs.

3 A side trip of 23 miles to the Berlin-Ichthyosaur State Park is worthwhile for the unusual opportunity to see the fossil remains of six ichthyosaurs, marine reptiles that lived in western Nevada 70 to 180 million years ago when the area was covered by a warm ocean. Ranging from 40 to 70 feet in length, these are the world's largest known ichthyosaurs, which were in turn the largest sea animals of their time. It is believed that they were stranded on shores by receding tides; down through millions of years their bones were covered by 3,000 feet of mud and became petrified. Geological changes in the earth's crust have exposed the hardened shale mass in which they were preserved.

Scheduled guided tours of the exhibit shelter, where the remains of the six sea serpents can be clearly seen, and other fossil sites are given in the summer season. The park also offers a picnic area, campgrounds, and a nature trail. Maps are available at the park headquarters in Berlin, a colorful little ghost town preserved by the state park system.

The drive to Berlin, crossing Paradise Range whose slopes are covered with juniper and piñon (Pinus monophylla), the state tree, offers splendid scenery. From Berlin it is another two miles to the fossil site in West Union Canyon in the Shoshone foothills. The paved road ends seven miles west of the park and a good gravel road continues.

From Gabbs, Route 361 arrows north through rangeland to Middlegate and then makes a steady climb over the Desatoya Mountains to Mount Airy. From the summit there are high, wide, and handsome vistas of the ridges that form north–south ribs across the center of Nevada. After making a long descent into sage-studded Reese River valley, the road winds its way up to Austin in the Toiyabe Range.

4   Boom times in Austin followed the discovery of silver in 1862. Within three years a population of 10,000 made it Nevada's second largest city. About 1880 the mines began to decline in productivity, and by 1887 they were depleted. Today Austin has only about 400 people. The town offers brochures for self-guided tours of the Lander County Court House, the Bank of Austin (now the Austin Public Library), and other landmarks.

At the western edge of the town, near the Pony Canyon silver mines, a graveyard with tall white tombstones poignantly commemorates the many Irish, Scottish, and Cornish mineworkers who came here with their families during the boom.

Stokes Castle, on the south side of Austin, is an austere, three-storied

4. Standing aloof from a mine shaft is fortlike Stokes Castle. Roof-high walls once surrounded the house and its courtyard.

square tower built in 1897 to be a summer home. From the castle there are fine views of Reese River valley.

The road out of Austin climbs steeply, with sharp curves, ascending 1,000 feet to Austin Summit, and then descends more gently through the green and wooded hills of the Toiyabe Range to Big Smoky Valley.

5   A marked and graded dirt road leads from Route 50 to the Hickison Petroglyph Recreation Site, a half-mile off the highway. A short walk from the campground brings you to the gap where the Indian rock carv-

ings are found. Archeologists speculate that the hoof-shaped symbols were made as a form of magic connected with deer hunts—the gap was apparently on the route of an annual deer migration. The recreation site, which offers picnic tables but no drinking water, is best visited between April and October.

6   Many gravel roads run from Big Smoky Valley into the canyons that notch the mountains. Kingston Canyon is the most celebrated because of its great beauty, and it is especially lovely in autumn. From the edge of Groves Lake, a man-made reservoir in the canyon, green-mantled peaks thrust upward into a sky that is usually a deep blue and dotted with white clouds. The road into the canyon leads through meadows with trout streams edged with aspens, cottonwoods, and cattails, and passes the ruins of an old mining camp.

Southward, the road traverses the length of Big Smoky Valley. This valley exemplifies some of the finest qualities of the Nevada landscape—the spaciousness, the changeable and dramatic vistas of cloud and light, the geological variety of the not-too-distant mountains, and the subtle variations of plant life.

6. A brooding sky plays upon the ever-varying landscape of Big Smoky Valley, flanked by the Toiyabe and Toquima ranges whose slopes are patched by dense stands of juniper. From spring until late fall the valley subtly changes as rabbit brush, sagebrush, and samphire take their turn to bloom. You may find nestled among them a flowering prickly poppy, thistle, or primrose.

2. *Sentinels of another era, the Ward Charcoal Ovens once produced fuel for the smelters of the famed Ward Mining District. To meet the demand for charcoal (about 30 bushels were needed to smelt a ton of crude ore), the valley was quickly denuded of trees.*

In the uplands *a few miles from Ely, a former copper-mining town, are the curious Ward Charcoal Ovens, where fuel was produced for smelters. To the east, near the Utah border, is Wheeler Peak Scenic Area, where you find alpine lakes and ancient bristlecone pines beneath Nevada's second highest mountain. Close by are the lovely Lehman Caves.*

On the road south you see another historic mining area and the strikingly beautiful Cathedral Gorge. Turning west and then north, the road crosses mountain passes and desert valleys and leads to Crystal Spring, a lovely oasis, and to a stark, moonlike landscape formed by volcanoes long ago.

1 Ely, picturesquely situated at the entrance of a canyon, was a gold-mining camp originally, but at the turn of the century it became the hub of Nevada's great copper-mining industry. Of the metals that have been mined in Nevada, the yield of copper was the most valuable, and the great Kennecott copper pit, five miles from Ely, was once the largest open mine in the world. The mine was closed in 1978, and it is no longer possible to visit this spectacular site. But you can see a display about it at the White Pine Public Museum in Ely. The museum also has a fine labeled collection of mineral specimens and relics of old mining camps.

2 A gravel road leads from the highway to the Ward Charcoal Ovens State Historical Monument. The 30-foot-high stone kilns, shaped like beehives, were built in 1876 to supply fuel for silver and lead ore smelters at Ward. It took 35 cords of wood (five or six acres of trees) to fill one oven and produce 1,750 bushels of charcoal, and the mountains for miles around were stripped of timber. Eventually charcoal was replaced by coke, which was brought in by rail.

Route 50 winds around deeply fissured mountains that are streaked with purple, rose, and salmon pink and that turn a fiery red as the sun lowers. After making a long descent through a wooded canyon from Connors Pass to Spring Valley, the road climbs the Snake Range to Sacramento Pass, where the land seems to reach endlessly around you, vast and desolate.

3 Entering the Wheeler Peak Scenic Area from Baker, the Asilo Verde Drive climbs Wheeler Peak to an elevation of 10,000 feet. Although care is required on a few sharp bends, the road is not difficult, and it affords magnificent views of both the mountain and the plain below.

From the picnic grounds at the end of the road, a steep and rocky seven-mile trail to the 13,063-foot summit leads through three plant and animal life zones. (Hikers unused to high altitudes should allow plenty of time for rest stops.) Another trail makes a gentle, mile-long ascent to Teresa Lake, one of four alpine lakes in the Wheeler Peak Scenic Area. A fork of the trail leads to the Bristlecone Pine Forest. Gnarled and knotted and bleached by the sun, the bristlecone pines *(Pinus longaeva)* are the oldest living things in the world. One, felled on Wheeler Peak for study, was found to be about 4,900 years old, the oldest discovered so far. Exposed to a harsh environment and deprived of nutrition and moisture, the bristlecones grow very slowly and develop a dense, strong wood. This wood may last, without decaying, for 4,000 years after the death of the tree. The longevity of these pines, their sensitivity to climate, as revealed by their narrow growth rings, and the overlapping of ring patterns of living and long-dead specimens have made possible a chronology of climatic history extending back 8,200 years. Bristlecone pine chronology is used now to correct radiocarbon dates.

At the entrance to the Wheeler Peak Scenic Area is the Lehman Caves National Monument. The limestone caverns are noted for the beauty of their richly colored ribbons, combs, and other delicate formations. An illuminated path winds for about two-thirds of a mile through the chambers.

South of Connors Pass the highway skirts the Shell Creek Range, crosses a divide, and runs through Lake Valley, passing ranches, rich pastures, and expanses of sagebrush, piñon,

3. *Gnarled and weathered, and polished by windblown sand and ice, the bristlecone pines are living links with the ancient past.*

and juniper. Eroded hillsides with brightly banded tipped strata border the valley and create a jagged skyline.

4 Pioche sprang into being after the opening of silver mines here in 1869. Mine owners brought in gangs of toughs to fight off encroachers, and the raw, new town soon had the reputation of being the wildest place in the West.

Pioche still has a frontier flavor. One of the places to see here is the

6 At Cathedral Gorge cliffs of a mellow, buff-colored bentonite clay rise vertically from the valley floor. Thin caps of rock have protected the tops of the cliffs, but over a period of several hundred thousand years wind and rain have eroded the vertical surfaces, creating a fantasy of cathedrallike fluted spires, domes, and arches. The park, which is traversed by a paved road, has picnic areas and walking trails. In wet weather visitors

site of a Paiute village, Crystal Spring became a principal rest stop for California-bound travelers in the mid-19th century.

To the south on Route 93, which divides the desert from the green valley like a knife, is Pahranagat Lake, a wildlife refuge that provides yet another reed-fringed contrast to the desert.

West of Crystal Spring several varieties of cactus and extensive stands of the spikey Mohave yucca and the Joshua tree appear. As you continue, you find many horses and cattle wandering the open range, and across the great, flat stretches you are apt to see a mirage in which distant hills seem to float on the horizon.

8 Cinder cones and deposits of black volcanic rock can be seen in the flat, arid land northeast of Warm Springs. Seven miles off the highway is Lunar Crater, a great, volcanically formed basin. Such a crater, known as a maar, occurs when the lava cone created by a volcanic explosion collapses into the chimney, or neck, of the volcano. Some of the low hills in this dramatic landscape are partial maars, with half-collapsed slopes and peaks. Many are several thousand years old, but they look younger because they are well preserved by the arid climate.

The dirt road to the crater is usually in good condition, but watch out for some 200 yards of soft sand where a vehicle must proceed at a steady pace, nonstop, to avoid getting stuck.

From Currant, a crossroads in ranch country, the road edges Currant Creek through an attractive gorge and ascends to Currant Summit, traversing part of the Humboldt National Forest. Although the area is called a forest, few of the trees and bushes grow more than six feet tall. Here, as in the desert, you notice that the climatic conditions create an orderly, parklike effect, with each plant or shrub tending to stand uncrowded in its own patch of ground. The forest is thus a pleasant place to walk; each piece of vegetation is easily admired, as if it had been placed by a landscape gardener.

Continuing northward, the road emerges from the forest into rolling countryside dramatically accented by flat-topped hills.

6. Fluted by erosion, this golden-hued rock formation suggests medieval architecture as it stands in the narrow valley at Cathedral Gorge. Wind and water, which carved out these striking shapes, slowly continue to sculpt their soft surfaces.

locally famous million-dollar Lincoln County Courthouse. The courthouse, a two-story brick-and-stone building, was completed in 1872 at a cost of $88,000. By the time the debt was paid off in 1937, graft, refinancing, and interest charges brought the cost up to nearly a million dollars. Located in the courthouse is the old jail. A small museum has photographs of Pioche's roistering days.

5 A paved side road leads to Caselton, a ghost town where a few dilapidated buildings patched with rusted sheets of corrugated iron and a mine entrance posted against trespassers are all that remain of its past.

should stay away from muddy paths.

From Cathedral Gorge the road descends steadily to Caliente, a small town with a mission-style yellow railway station and tracks that run along its main street. Heading west across the Hyko Range and descending from Pahroc Summit, you see Pahranagat Valley and Crystal Spring as a brilliant patch of blue and green in the vast brown-and-yellow desert.

7 Crystal Spring is a fairy-tale oasis of green water and shady cottonwoods. Flowering yerba mansa covers the banks of the pond, which is inhabited by small, tropical-looking fish, the desert striped dace. Once the

For all the neon fantasy of Las Vegas *and the overwhelming scale of Hoover Dam, it is the impact and drama of the natural scene that prevails in the southern tip of Nevada. In the Valley of Fire State Park, millions of years of wind and water erosion have carved the colorful sandstone into fantastic shapes that seem to be the very bones of the earth. Here too are hundreds of petroglyphs and pictographs made by the Anasazi Indians, a people who vanished a thousand years ago.*

1 An oasis of gushing springs and verdant meadows in the middle of the desert, Las Vegas was a resting place for frontier traders in the early 1800's. Today it is Nevada's largest city and the world's casino and nightclub capital. The chief attractions are the Strip, a three-mile stretch of glamorous hotels with nightclubs, and the downtown Casino Center, a three-block area on Frémont Street that is said to have 43 miles of neon tubing and 2 million light bulbs in its signs. Seen at night, the Strip and the Casino Center stun the senses.

2 The Valley of Fire State Park offers 50,000 acres of magnificent scenery, with fiery red and soft white sandstone sculpted by millions of years of erosion into domes, arches, and the semblances of grotesque creatures and flowers. Among the park's remarkable sights are Rainbow Vista, a sweep of rock forma-

4. *The waters of the Colorado River, impounded by Hoover Dam and backed up for more than a hundred miles, form Lake Mead. The lake, which extends through Boulder Canyon (above), has altered the desert environment and submerged some remarkable scenery.*

tions streaked with white, lavender, ocher, salmon, and vivid reds, and Silica Dome, a huge deposit of pure quartz—its whiteness unstained by iron—rising among the vivid, rust-red peaks of Fire Canyon.

Also of interest is Mouse's Tank. Mouse was a renegade Paiute who robbed and harassed local Indians and whites alike, and hid in the Valley of Fire. His tank is a declivity in the stone that traps and holds a vital store of rainfall during part of the dry season, there being no springs or streams in this area.

A worthwhile walk in the park is the quarter-mile trail to Mouse's Tank. It goes through a miniature canyon, the walls of which are decorated with hundreds of petroglyphs pecked into the stone by the Anasazi Indians about 1,500 years ago. The petroglyphs, depicting horned men, snakes, suns, and other figures, are more easily seen here than in other areas of the park.

The park's picnic areas and campsites are open year-round, but keep in mind the fact that summer temperatures often reach 120°F.

3 At Overton, the Lost City Museum has a fine collection of artifacts from an archeological digging at an Anasazi village now partly covered by the waters of Lake Mead. The Anasazis, who had irrigated and farmed

the surrounding valley, vanished from the area about A.D. 1000. At the museum there are open-air reconstructions of adobe houses similar to those of the original pueblo.

Southward from Valley of Fire State Park the landscape continues to be dramatic, with delicately colored dry washes and intricately eroded bluffs of multihued sandstone. Visible from the road is the Bowl of Fire, a hollow in the mountains filled with a jumbled mass of great, pitted red rocks that glow in the sunlight like burning coals. Gradually this extraordinary landscape yields to arid desert, and in this setting Lake Mead appears startlingly blue.

4 Hoover Dam, which rises 726.4 feet from bedrock, was the highest concrete dam in the world at the time of its construction in 1931–35; today it is the fifth highest in the Western Hemisphere.

A two-lane highway crossing the 1,244-foot-long crest of the dam gives dramatic views of the project. Tours of the site begin at 8:30 A.M., and the earlier the better because afternoon temperatures frequently reach 110°F, although it is only 65°F inside the dam. A museum at the top of the dam on the Nevada side has a model of the Colorado River and its system of dams that regulates the water supply of much of the Southwest.

3. *Route 167 winds along a dry wash beneath pastel-hued bluffs herringboned by the steep uptilting of the rock formations.*

Nature's Prodigal Display

Alaska is grand and varied, from its sparkling blue-white icescapes to its glacially carved shores

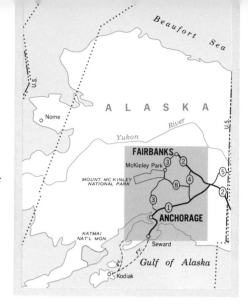

The name Alaska in Aleut means "The Great Country," and it is just that: the landscapes are vast, and the scenery is superlative. It offers icy wildernesses sculptured by glaciers, green-skirted snowcapped mountains, canyons with pounding waterfalls, stark tundra, valleys with lakes and salmon streams, and a coast slashed with inlets and fjords. As winter yields to summer, the valleys shimmer with the pale green of leafing birches and aspens, and wild flowers grow rampant in the fields.

More than twice the size of Texas, Alaska is overwhelmingly large, and only a small part of it is penetrated by roads. This loop covers most of the state's paved, year-round highways. Because the roads to Valdez and Homer terminate at those ports, some backtracking is required.

The tour takes you through the glacier-wrapped Chugach Mountains, often compared with the Swiss Alps; the Matanuska Valley, a lush, green corridor dramatically walled on the north by the Talkeetna Range; the beautiful Kenai Peninsula, called Alaska's Riviera; and Mount McKinley National Park. An alternate summer route provides handsome vistas as it traverses high tundra and crosses the state's highest mountain pass open to cars.

Along the way are unique opportunities (depending upon the time of year) to inspect glaciers at close range, see the calving of icebergs, observe big-game animals and marine life, watch sled dog races, visit old Russian settlements, explore Yukon backcountry, and, possibly, witness the aurora borealis.

There are several ways to reach Alaska for your road tour: you can follow the Alaska Highway to Tok, traversing the Canadian provinces of British Columbia and Yukon. Or take an auto-passenger ferry up the Inside Passage from Seattle to Haines or Skagway in southeastern Alaska; from either town it is about a four-hour drive to Haines Junction, where you pick up the Alaska Highway. Or you can fly to Anchorage or Fairbanks, where you can rent a car.

A word of caution if you decide to drive—the overland distance from Seattle to Tok is 2,156 miles. Most of the highway through Canada is unpaved, and although it is well maintained, it is hard going. Dust can cut visibility to a few feet, and the high twisting road is dangerously slippery when wet.

1 The annual championship dog races held at Tok draw many visitors in late March. But year-round this small town makes a specialty of meeting the needs of the traveler, with lodgings, a clinic, service stations, Laundromats, and stores selling camping equipment. At the helpful visitor center you can get not only quantities of information but fishing and hunting licenses and free coffee. A striking sight at the center is a 150-pound mounted wolf.

Route 1, a paved highway with moderate grades, unfolds one magnificent panorama after another of mountains, streams, and lakes. South of Tok it crosses the Mentasta Mountains, a low range pleasantly wooded with birch, aspen, and white spruce. At intervals you see extensive stands of dead spruce, the result of forest fires. Although the dominant vegetation in this environment is coniferous, birch and aspen often become established in areas cleared by fire. The resulting mixture of trees is more favorable to moose and other big game than purely coniferous cover. Recognizing that some forest fires are natural occurrences and are ecologically beneficial in many ways, resource officials now allow them to burn.

About 36 miles below Tok are attractive views of the Mineral Lakes, set off by a fringe of spruce and the backdrop of the lofty, 100-mile-long Wrangell Range. The shallow, marshy lakes, fed by springs, are a nesting place for geese, ducks, and trumpeter swans. Moose and caribou also come here, the moose to feed on the willow brush and water plants and the caribou to eat the mosses and lichens found in the spongy carpet of grasses. The nomadic caribou, however, are only seasonal visitors.

A few miles south of Mentasta Pass (2,280 feet), the road follows alongside Copper River, a turbulent glacial stream that flows down a broad plain. Crossing the valley are many wandering watercourses created by the spring meltoff; how full or dry they are depends upon the time of the year.

2 The panorama from a viewpoint just south of Porcupine Creek State Campground is magnificent. From the Copper River, which eddies over mud and gravel flats immediately below the road, the broad valley with its dense cover of spruce sweeps toward the snow-clad peaks of the Wrangell Mountains. Dominating the horizon is Mount Sanford, which rises to 16,237 feet.

Unlike neighboring mountain ranges, the Wrangell Mountains are of volcanic origin, and Mount Wrangell is still occasionally wreathed with steam. This volcano is just one of a row that can be followed down the Alaskan Peninsula and along the chain of the Aleutian Islands that stretches across the North Pacific almost to the shores of Asia.

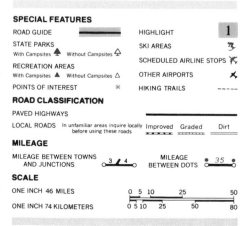

SPECIAL FEATURES			
ROAD GUIDE	▬▬▬	HIGHLIGHT	**1**
STATE PARKS		SKI AREAS	⅔
With Campsites ▲ Without Campsites △		SCHEDULED AIRLINE STOPS	✠
RECREATION AREAS		OTHER AIRPORTS	✠
With Campsites ▲ Without Campsites △			
POINTS OF INTEREST	◉	HIKING TRAILS	- - - - -

ROAD CLASSIFICATION

PAVED HIGHWAYS ▬▬▬

LOCAL ROADS   In unfamiliar areas inquire locally before using these roads   Improved   Graded   Dirt

MILEAGE

MILEAGE BETWEEN TOWNS AND JUNCTIONS   3 ⌐ 4   MILEAGE BETWEEN DOTS   • 35 •

SCALE

ONE INCH 46 MILES   0 5 10   25   50

ONE INCH 74 KILOMETERS   0 5 10   25   50   80

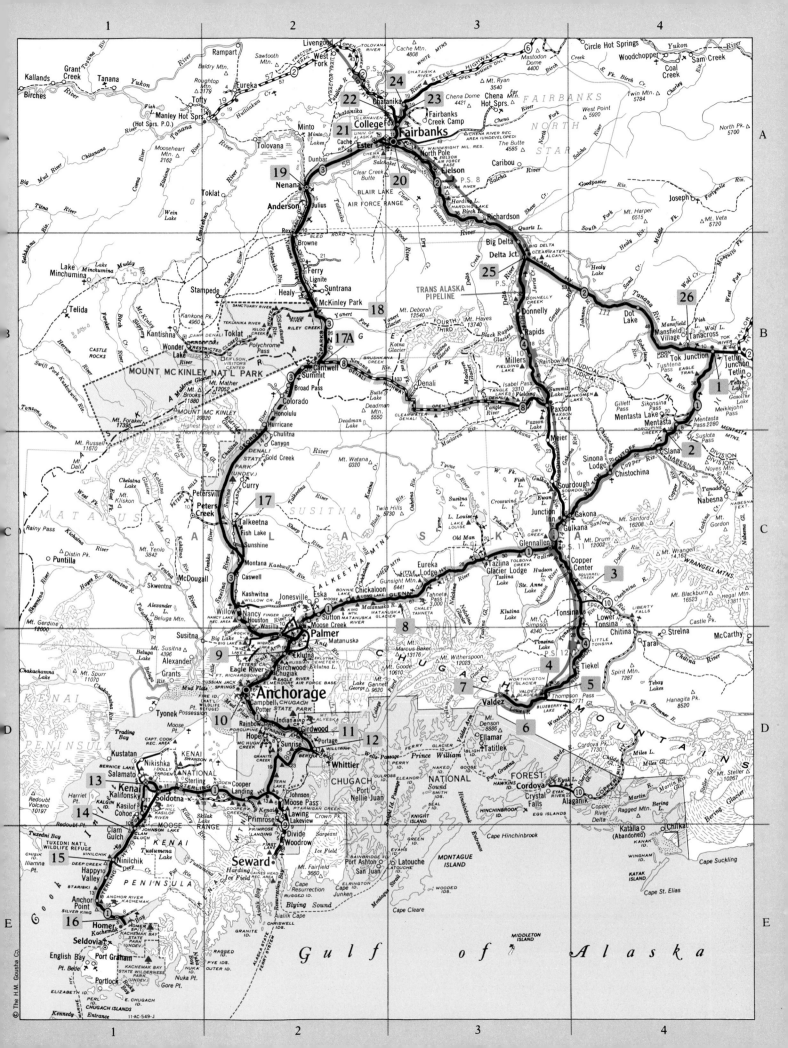

About 1½ miles above the North Junction of the Glenn and Richardson highways, the Copper and Gakona rivers meet. From a hilltop turnout just north of the Gakona River bridge there are good views of the confluence in a semiwooded plain flanked by mountains.

For 14 miles the two highways merge; this stretch of road is relatively built up with hotels, shops, and gas stations. But between the South Junction of the two highways and Valdez, the road offers some of the most spectacular highway scenery in Alaska. Following a gold rush trail staked out more than 80 years ago, the Richardson Highway winds its way through the low terrain of the Copper River valley, and from the road the prospects are wide and open across the valley to the Wrangell Range.

3   About 12 miles south of Copper Center lies Willow Lake. The blue alpine lake, fringed with greenery, perfectly captures the soaring, white silhouettes of Mounts Drum, Wrangell, and Sanford. From the Willow Lake Rest Area, a roadside picnic spot two miles farther along, there are dramatic views across the wide

5. On the road at Thompson Pass, the craggy peaks of the Chugach Range confront you at eye level. The range is actually an uplifted plain formed of both volcanic and sedimentary rocks that became consolidated and then pushed up over a period of millions of years.

valley to the Wrangell Mountains. Seen at sunset, their glistening, frosted peaks resemble mounds of peach sherbet.

Continuing south, the road climbs into the Chugach Mountains; the views become higher and narrower, and you begin to look upward to extraordinarily jagged snow-covered peaks and ridges.

4   Reaching a 2,700-foot-high valley, the highway passes within a few hundred yards of the Worthington Glacier. A short spur brings you right up to it. You can park here and walk across the blackish glacial gravel strewn about for a close-up look into the dark caves and chasms under the glacier's thick, blue overhanging snout. Remember that glaciers are treacherous, and it is foolish to walk on one without an expert guide.

From the small state campground at Worthington Glacier there are also excellent views of neighboring, smaller glaciers in the surrounding mountains. Half of the glaciers in North America are found in the 650-mile-long arc of Alaska's Gulf Coast, many of them slowly grinding their way to the coast where they calve the icebergs of the northern Pacific, as lumps of ice break off.

The summer scenery in this icy wilderness is spectacular. Small pools of melted ice on the glacier's surface capture the blue of the sky, and grass-edged alpine ponds reflect the blue-white tongues of ice on the rocky slopes.

5   As the road climbs through Thompson Pass (2,771 feet), you begin to be on more equal terms with the mountains; they no longer tower above, but are (like the glacier) more or less at your own level. At the bald and exposed summit the Chugach Range and the Sawtooth Mountains sweep around you, and in the green

2. The Gakona River winds around a wayside hotel near its confluence with the Copper River in Copper River valley, seen here in summer greenery. Looming in the distance are Mounts Sanford (left) and Drum, in the Wrangell Range, blanketed with snow year-round.

valley far below, you see the Lowe River racing toward the town of Valdez and the coast. Bald eagles are frequently seen circling at the summit, and in summer a colorful and fascinating variety of small wild flowers, including fireweed and blue forget-me-nots (*Myosotis alpestris*), the state flower, are to be found not far from the road.

West of Thompson Pass the highway descends dramatically, dropping more than 2,000 feet in a few miles and passing through a landscape often compared to the Swiss Alps, with tall, jagged mountain peaks, small, sparkling lakes, turbulent streams, and high waterfalls.

6 Continuing to descend, the road enters Keystone Canyon, whose walls are almost perpendicular. In the canyon are Bridal Veil Falls and Horsetail Falls, which plunge and cascade more than 300 feet and which are crowned, when the sun shines, with perpetual rainbows.

Leaving the narrow canyon, the road follows the Lowe River toward Valdez (which, you are told, rhymes with please), passing the site of Old Valdez, which was destroyed by the Good Friday earthquake in 1964. The small new town is built on bedrock four miles away.

7 Situated on the coast and bordered by soaring mountains channeled with glaciers and canyons, Valdez is a splendid sight-seeing center as well as being the ocean terminal for the trans-Alaska pipeline.

Between Memorial Day and Labor Day there are organized bus tours of the pipeline's facility on the south shore of Valdez Arm, an inlet of Prince William Sound. The access road to the terminal offers good views of the inlet and a chance to observe sea otters.

Another, rather rough road leads a few miles up Mineral Creek, passing numerous waterfalls and old mining sites. In late August and September you can see silver salmon struggling up the creek—and up other streams in the area—to spawn, and in season wild flowers, blueberries, and cranberries are thick along the roadside.

Be sure, if you visit Valdez in summer, to take one of the daily boat tours to Columbia Glacier a few miles away. The glacier, 41 miles long, 3

miles wide, and 300 feet high at the face, flows at the rapid rate of 13 to 19 feet a day. The tour boat comes within a quarter-mile of the glacier, which presents itself at the bay as a pinnacled blue-white cliff, its crystal face rising vertically from the water and reflecting sunlight like myriads of prisms. Because of the speed with which the glacier approaches the bay, there is a chance of your seeing it calve a berg with a thunderous roar as portions of its tip break off. On the cruise you may also observe porpoises, whales, and seals.

Backtracking to Glennallen, you head southwest on the Glenn High-

around Eureka Summit plant life is sparse and dwarfed, corresponding to what you might find at an altitude of around 15,000 feet near the Equator. Compounding the northerly impression, as you continue and the mountains begin to close in on you, are views at close range of Tazlina Glacier and snowy peaks. Especially scenic is Tahneta Pass (3,000 feet), where the road, following Caribou Creek, skirts the base of Sheep Mountain, which rises another 3,300 feet above you.

From a turnout farther along is a spectacular view of the Matanuska Glacier and the valley it blocks.

Why the ice is blue

From a boat you can see the sparkling blue-white face of Columbia Glacier and its many bergs. Glacial ice shows its true color on a fresh surface, as where a berg breaks off, and in open crevasses. A glacial ice crystal acts as a prism, refracting the blue light, which you see, and absorbing the other colors. The blue is most intense on overcast days because more blue than other colors passes through the clouds. Exposed ice soon becomes white as air penetrates the surface and forms bubbles between the crystals. All colors of light are then refracted from the surface, and what you see is white.

way. The road crosses a large plateau and climbs steadily to its highest point at Eureka Summit (3,327 feet), offering fine views of distant ranges and lakes. Occasionally herds of caribou, black bears, and Dall sheep are seen along here.

As the road climbs, you notice how quickly a small change in altitude at this latitude affects the vegetation:

8 At Matanuska Glacier State Wayside you can follow a trail along a bluff overlook for fine views of the glacier. About 27 miles long, it is one of the largest glaciers visible from the road. Wind and melt have fluted its face and sculptured its back into an exotic landscape of hills, pinnacles, crevasses, and caves. Below it, rivulets of ice water stray across the val-

8. *More than half of Alaska's produce is grown in Matanuska Valley. Driving along beneath snow-veined mountains in summer, you pass great fields of lettuce (shown here) and other vegetables, and dairy farms with herds of Holsteins pasturing in green meadows.*

ley floor in summer, and above it, snow-crusted peaks thrust upward into the clouds that frequently drift by. From the wayside to Anchorage, the landscape becomes lusher and, eventually, agricultural.

Matanuska Valley, a 50-mile-long patchwork of farms, lakes, and forests bordered by steep, rugged mountains, was settled by a group of homesteaders in the Great Depression year 1935 and is considered to be Alaska's agricultural heartland. Although the growing season is only about 115 days, it has long hours of daylight, fertile soil, and mild summers modified by the warm coastal waters nearby. The valley is celebrated for its 50- to 70-pound cabbages, but 3-pound ones are actually the norm. The huge prizewinning vegetables shown at the Alaska State Fair in Palmer are usually grown from special seeds. The fair, held annually from late August into September, is interesting to attend.

The valley, increasingly developed as a recreation area, is dotted with campgrounds, fishing lodges, and resorts and is crisscrossed by roads.

9 About 15 miles below Palmer, look for the short side road to old Eklutna, an Indian village that has an old log cabin Russian Orthodox Church and a cemetery noteworthy for its Athabascan Indian graves. The graves are covered by small, colorfully painted spirit houses containing the personal belongings of the de-

ceased. The miniature houses blend Indian and Russian motifs and bear the Russian Orthodox cross.

Nearby is the Eklutna Lake Recreation Area. The campground is in a lovely, wooded mountain setting on Eklutna Lake, with streams, waterfalls, and a glacier in the vicinity.

10 In Anchorage the frontier and modern urban development still jostle each other, though not quite so obviously as is sometimes suggested. Nearly half of Alaska's population

lives in or near this city, which sprawls on a coastal plain at the base of the Chugach Mountains.

Anchorage was almost devastated by the great earthquake of 1964. The city has preserved 135 acres of land crazily heaved and tilted by the quake as a testimonial to its destructive power. Earthquake Park, which is currently overgrown, is located at the western end of Northern Lights Boulevard.

Both Earthquake Park and Resolution Park are excellent spots for observing the dramatic tides that rush into the arms of Cook Inlet, especially in June, and for watching late sunsets. A bronze statue of Capt. James Cook faces the water in Resolution Park, which is named for the vessel sailed by the great explorer when he visited Cook Inlet in 1778.

Southward from Anchorage the road follows the twisting shore of the Turnagain Arm of Cook Inlet for 50 miles. The peaks of the Chugach Range are on your left, and across the arm of the inlet, behind clifflike mountains, is the Kenai Peninsula. The views are splendid.

The tides in Turnagain Arm, second only to those at the Bay of Fundy in Nova Scotia, have a range of 37 feet, and 6-foot tidal bores can be seen. When the tide is low, vast mud flats

9. *Some of the Athabascan spirit houses in the graveyard at Eklutna have two or three stories and tiny glass windows. Such differences in size and elaboration may reflect differences in the status of the deceased. Half hidden by trees is the old log cabin church.*

12. *The bergs drifting and nudging each other in Portage Lake present a frosty scene, even in midsummer. Across the lake is their parent glacier. Other attractions in Portage Lake Recreation Area are beaver ponds and creeks where thousands of salmon spawn.*

are exposed. At sunset during low tide the inlet seems to be speckled with gold as the dying sun is reflected in thousands of pools left behind on the flats by the retreating tide.

11 At Girdwood, about 40 miles south of Anchorage, stop to visit Alyeska Village, Alaska's largest year-round resort and a winter ski center. Winter or summer, be sure to take the chair lift that carries you 2,000 feet up the side of Mount Alyeska. The 1¼-mile ride carries you above timbered slopes, jagged cliffs, waterfalls, and alpine meadows. From the mountaintop are sweeping views of Turnagain Arm, the Kenai Peninsula, and as many as eight glaciers sprawled among the mountains around you.

In Alyeska Village a 22-ton boulder of nephrite jade, mined at Jade Mountain in Kobuk Valley above the Arctic Circle, stands before a shop where you can watch the stone being worked into gift items.

12 From Portage a six-mile side road takes you to Portage Glacier. Winding around mountains, the road edges Portage Creek and a pond dammed by beaver. Beaver dams are frequent sights in Alaska, but along here you have an excellent chance of seeing the beaver themselves, as well as the opportunity in summer to enjoy the variety of wild flowers that grow in profusion.

The road passes three Forest Service campgrounds, near Portage Glacier, and ends at a large overlook at the edge of Portage Lake. Here you can park your car and get a close-up view of the icebergs the glacier has calved, as they float in the silvery blue-green water. It is hard to guess the size of these bergs, since most of their bulk is hidden below the surface of the 600-foot-deep lake, but some are said to weigh millions of tons. By moonlight the scene is rewardingly eerie: the icebergs loom white out of the black water, creaking and groaning like living things.

Portage lies at the entrance to the Kenai Peninsula, a huge, beautiful wilderness punctuated by some of the pleasantest small towns in Alaska. The peninsula, which extends 150 miles into the Gulf of Alaska and has a climate less rigorous than that of New England, is sometimes described as Alaska's Riviera, and in the summer one is aware of entering a more fertile landscape than those to the north and east of Anchorage, with much variety of mountain, lake, stream, woodland, grassy plain, and coastal inlet.

Some 2,700 square miles of Kenai Peninsula form the Kenai National Moose Range, set aside in 1941 to protect the habitat of approximately 3,000 giant Kenai moose as well as Dall sheep and other wildlife. Both moose and sheep are frequently seen from Sterling Highway and in the vicinity of the Forest Service campgrounds that are spaced along, or just off, the road, so have both your camera and your binoculars ready.

Most of the campgrounds are on lakes that offer good fishing for rainbow and Dolly Varden trout, with excellent salmon streams nearby. The campgrounds have foot trails and two or three also have canoe trails and a swimming beach. But if you are camping out or hiking, beware of bears, and follow all the advice of the U.S. Forest Service about how to be safe in bear country.

About 7½ miles west of the junction of Sterling Highway and the road to Seward is an observation point for viewing Dall sheep, with an interpretative sign at the roadside pullover. Farther along you cross the Kenai River and enter the Moose Range.

13 An 11-mile spur from Soldotna takes you to the interesting old town of Kenai, a native village where the Russians established a fur-trading post in 1791. Several weathered hewn-log buildings still stand in Old Kenai, but the most colorful reminder of Kenai's Russian heritage is the charming white frame Russian Orthodox Church. Capping its three turrets are sky-blue onion domes, each mounted with a golden Russian Orthodox cross. Built about 1906 and still attended, it is the oldest of Alaska's Russian Orthodox churches.

Near the church is Fort Kenay, a reconstructed log barracks built by the U.S. Army following our purchase of Alaska in 1867. An upstairs museum in the barracks has a display of Russian artifacts and other items related to local history.

Close by is Mount Redoubt Lookout, an ocean bluff near the mouth of the Kenai River. From the lookout in spring and early summer, you are likely to see white Beluga whales that feed on the salmon here. There is also a fine view of Cook Inlet, and across it, the Aleutian Range whose volcanic peaks Mount Redoubt and Mount Iliamna rise imposingly more than 10,000 feet above the sea. Both peaks are still sometimes active.

Because of the discovery of offshore oil in 1957, Kenai has grown rapidly into a lively, modern town with shopping malls, hotels, oil refineries, and other industrial complexes. The Chamber of Commerce has a centrally located visitor information center happy to direct you to places to see. You can also rent tour tapes here. Closed weekends.

Turning south from Kenai, follow the Kalifonsky Beach Road, a scenic route edging Cook Inlet for 13 miles and passing through Kasilof, an old Indian settlement that became a Russian outpost in 1768. The road then joins Sterling Highway.

14 Seven miles or so south of this junction look for the Clam Gulch Wayside, which has a campground, picnic grills, and well water. The spot is high above the sea, and the scenery is excellent. The beach below, reached by a steep road (too precipitous for trailers), is noted for clamming in late spring and summer, but a sport-fishing license is required.

15 Seventeen miles south of Clam Gulch Road is a short side road to Ninilchik, a fishing village on a bleak stretch of shoreline. It is worth seeing for two points of interest—the old wooden fishermen's shacks down by the harbor and the Russian Orthodox Church, with its onion domes, on the hill. The village was colonized by Russian fur traders in 1820, and their descendants continue to live here.

Driving through the tiny community of Anchor Point, you pass a road marker that informs you that this is the most westerly point you can reach on the continuous system of highways in North America.

Along the coast you may notice a spruce that is taller and more conical than the narrow, spirelike white spruce that dominates the interior forests: this is the Sitka spruce (*Picea sitchensis*), Alaska's state tree.

16 As you approach Homer, a pull-off on a high point gives you a magnificent view of the town spread below 1,000-foot-high bluffs on the shore of Kachemak Bay. Reaching into the wide bay is Homer Spit, a narrow, five-mile-long gravel bar, and on the far side rise the snow-clad Kenai Mountains, ribboned with blue-white glaciers. In summer lupine and fireweed (which turns from magenta to a flaming red in autumn) and other wild flowers spread over the fields and hillsides, and wild berries abound. (Check the Alaska State Park pamphlets for edible varieties.) The splendid scenery, the mild, sunny climate, and the excellent fishing in the bay have made Homer a popular spot for artists and for vacationers from Anchorage, 227 miles away. Weekend traffic is often heavy. The town has a pleasingly relaxed atmosphere and lacks the slightly raw, frontier quality of other places.

Campgrounds and a hotel are found at the end of Homer Spit, where you can fish, beachcomb, or just simply enjoy watching the activity at the small, colorful harbor and docks. The ferry to Kodiak Island, bay excursions boats, and flight-seeing tours give you a chance to observe the island rookeries of seabirds and to spot whales, porpoises, and seals. Be sure also to take the Skyline Drive, which runs for several miles along the bluffs above the town. There are also art galleries in town and an interesting museum of natural history.

Between Anchorage and Willow, as you head north, you pass through rolling farm country whose many lakes have made it a popular recreation area. Leaving Willow, which has been designated as the new site for Alaska's capital, the road climbs through gradually wilder country, with many high bridges spanning creeks and canyons.

17 The small town of Talkeetna, 14 miles down a paved road from the highway, is pleasantly sleepy and still retains a small part of the atmosphere it must have had during its pioneer days. The town, which has been declared an historic site, still has dirt streets and old clapboard buildings, among them the Fairview Inn, a square, two-story structure that, with its bar, remains much as it was originally. Today, Talkeetna is a take-off point for climbers flying to their starting base on Mount McKinley.

The George Parks Highway traverses Denali State Park for 36 miles. Although nature trails are being cleared, there is no easy access to the park at this time, and so it remains a true wilderness, not easily appreciated from the highway. An upland of ridges, lakes, tundra, forests, and swampy meadows, the park is a big-game refuge, but the animals are rarely seen from the road in summer.

If the weather is clear, you may want to stop at a pullout a quarter-mile north of Mountain Haus, a lodge in Denali State Park, to enjoy what is said to be the best roadside view of Mount McKinley.

17A If you are touring Alaska in summer and decide to bypass the northern part of this loop, you can take the Denali Highway from Cantwell to Paxson (135 miles) and then proceed northward to Delta Junction on the Richardson Highway, a total of 213 miles.

16. Homer, sprawled along the southern tip of the Kenai Peninsula, enjoys balmy summers with long, sunny days. Curving five miles into Kachemak Bay, toward the Kenai Mountains, Homer Spit is a haven for fishermen, bird-watchers, and beachcombers.

17. *Turning scarlet as August slides into September, wild blueberry bushes glow on the bronzing floor and slopes of the Susitna River valley north of Talkeetna. For a week or two shrubs and small trees flare brilliantly before succumbing to frost. The George Parks Highway (Route 3), which traverses the valley, is hidden from view by the rows of spruce in the foreground.*

The Denali Highway is a wilderness road open only in summer, and except for the 20-mile paved stretch out of Paxson, it has a rough and dusty gravel surface. But it offers some fine high tundra scenery and grand views of the Alaska Range to the north.

Five miles east of Cantwell Junction, the Denali Highway offers on a clear day a view of Mount McKinley that is hardly equaled from the roads within the national park. The next dozen miles provide handsome views of the Nenana River valley where the steel-blue river, its banks and islands edged with spruce, wanders among golden fields. In the distance, beyond a low forested wall of mountains, the snow-streaked Alaska Range is seen.

As the road climbs and the mountains become closer and higher, you notice that the vegetation is meager; in early summer shelves of ice project over the river as it eddies between banks of snow, and pools of snowmelt spangle the vast expanse of tundra. At 35 miles west of Paxson you cross MacLaren Summit (4,086 feet), the highest pass for automobiles in Alaska. Here the flat, snow-covered land almost meets the sky, interrupted only by the low profile of the Alaska Range to the north.

From Paxson the Richardson Highway ascends along Gulkana River to Summit Lake. The lake is long and very blue and seems—not being towered over by the surrounding peaks—very close to the sky. Crossing Isabel Pass (3,320 feet), the road then begins a long, steady descent toward the lusher landscape around Delta Junction. A few miles beyond Isabel Pass are views of pastel-hued Rainbow Mountain and of Gulkana Glacier.

Along here you are in the heart of big-game country, so have your binoculars at hand. The mountains are full of Dall sheep, moose, and brown bears. To the west are views of the Delta Game Reserve, and if you are lucky, you may spot a herd of bison. 18 The route north from Cantwell soon brings you to Mount McKinley National Park. The visitor center is three miles within the park and is closed only when weather dictates. Registration for campsites is on a first-come, first-served basis.

The highest mountain in North America, Mount McKinley rises abruptly to an elevation of 20,320 feet from a terrain only 3,000 feet above sea level. Possibly no other mountain in the world soars so monumentally from its base. With most of its surface perpetually mantled with snow, the mountain gleams against the sky and is visible for more than 150 miles on a clear day. In summer, however, its peak is often obscured by clouds.

Of the 85 miles of road in Mount McKinley National Park (which is 110 miles long), only the first 14 are paved and, when weather permits, that is as far as you are allowed to go in your own vehicle unless you registered at the visitor center to stay at one of the interior campgrounds, the most distant of which is at Wonder Lake. The surface of the dirt road to Wonder Lake is mostly good, but with some washboarding. Through Polychrome Pass (so named because of the varied coloration of the rocky slopes) the roadway is narrow, with precipitous drops on one side, some sharp bends, and steep gradients, but it is not too forbidding.

18. Mount McKinley (top), seen in the pink glow of early morning, is mirrored by a glacial pool near Wonder Lake. Spreading toward the lower slopes is a colorful mat of tiny plants, such as the spikey green cassiope with its red berries, the low, waxy-leafed bearberry, and reindeer lichen, a lacework of delicate, antler-shaped branches (above left). Deep cushions of feathery spring moss (above right) form on wet calcareous soil.

Visitors are encouraged to use the park's free shuttle buses that depart regularly from the visitor center for 10-hour round-trip tours to Wonder Lake, the classic viewing point for Mount McKinley. Along the route the buses make scheduled stops at a number of scenic points where you can get on or off as you please.

The park landscapes are spectacular, and the floral detail of the tundra is fascinating. There is surprisingly little forest; most of the trees that survive are dwarfed, and some lean tipsily. The drunken-forest effect is caused by the thawing and shifting of the thin layer of ground above the permafrost and the consequent disruption of shallow tree roots.

Found in the park are 37 species of animals, large and small, and about 140 species of birds, most of which are year-round residents, but some of which migrate here from Hawaii,

Japan, and New Zealand, making the park an international community. Among the permanent inhabitants is the willow ptarmigan, the state bird of Alaska. Although you cannot be sure of seeing wildlife, the chances that you will are excellent.

Interesting and informative demonstrations of dog mushing are a regular feature in the summer months. You can also see the sled dogs in their kennels at the park headquarters. In winter the dogs are given the task of hauling stockpiled garbage out of the campgrounds, moving park maintenance equipment, and patrolling.

Other attractions are the flight-seeing tours of Mount McKinley and raft trips on the Nenana River. The park visitor center can tell you where to make arrangements.

19 Leaving Mount McKinley National Park, the road twists through narrow and scenic Nenana Canyon

and drops down the northern slopes of the Alaska Range to Nenana, some of whose 500 people hunt, fish, and trap for part of their livelihood. In summer the river docks throb with activity as freight carried to Nenana by rail is loaded onto barges and tugs to be transported to outposts in the river-laced Yukon Basin.

The town is known for its log watchtower and clock built in 1940 for the Nenana Ice Classic, an annual competition to guess the day, hour, and minute that the ice on the Tanana River begins to break up, which is usually between April 26 and May 15. The precise moment is determined by a sensing device placed on the ice and wired to the clock in the watchtower. The prize for a $2 sweepstake ticket can amount to $132,000, but only residents of Alaska and the Yukon may compete.

From Nenana to Fairbanks the landscape's main attractions are the panoramas of rolling spruce forest, punctuated, near the highway, by stands of wonderfully tall, straight birch.

20 Fairbanks, Alaska's second largest city and the hub of its Interior, lies only 120 miles below the Arctic Circle, and in summer the nights are only short intervals between sunset and sunrise.

A gold rush town born in 1902, Fairbanks began to grow rapidly in 1970 with the rush for jobs on the new Alaska oil pipeline. Today the frontier is still much in evidence, with log cabins and rustic old bars mingling with sleek modern buildings.

For family sight-seeing, a major attraction is Alaskaland, a 44-acre park that is open all year. Among its notable sights are the Goldrush Town, with relocated old log cabins and houses, the old stern-wheeler Nenana, an Athabascan village with a few fine totem poles, and a miniature train that carries passengers around the park. In summer there is a nightly salmon bake.

You can also arrange stern-wheeler cruises, flight-seeing tours to off-beat destinations, and white-water raft adventures. At the log cabin visitor center on First Avenue you can get all the information you need, and also a walking tour booklet on the town's historical past.

If you are visiting Fairbanks or thereabouts in late March or late September, you have in store a rare treat: a view of the aurora borealis. Streaking darkened skies, the northern lights display pulsating bands and arcs of brilliant, luminous colors. The origin of the phenomenon is being studied at the Institute of Arctic Studies at the University of Alaska at Fairbanks.

The first 30 miles of the Steese Highway north of Fairbanks makes an interesting spur, with much evidence of Fairbanks' gold rush and views of the trans-Alaska pipeline.

21 For a close view of the pipeline, look for the turnoff onto Goldstream Road about nine miles above Fairbanks. Along Goldstream Road you can see the huge, silvery pipeline on its sinuous path across the mountains. The pipeline, 48 inches in diameter and 800 miles long, is capable of carrying some 1.5 million barrels of crude oil daily from the oil field at Prudhoe Bay down to Valdez. It is alternately buried and elevated according to climatic and soil conditions along the way.

22 By Pedro Creek, 17 miles from Fairbanks, stands a monument to Felix Pedro, who made the first discovery of gold in this area back in 1902. People still come here for the fun of panning for gold, occasionally with some small success. Gold pans can be bought in Fairbanks.

23 From Cleary Summit (2,300 feet), at Mile 21, you can watch the midnight sun on June 21. Instead of setting in the west, the sun slowly swings across the horizon, in a softly illuminated sky, reaching a due north position at midnight. Then a new day begins as the sun moves clockwise to the east.

A mile down the north side of this mountain is the Cleary Mine, a small gold mine that is still being worked. You can see the encampment, half hidden by a stand of white birch.

24 At Chatanika, about 27 miles north of Fairbanks, huge piles of tailings and an abandoned dredge are the memorial of a field that yielded millions of dollars of gold between 1928 and 1959. The gold dredge is enormous and eerily atmospheric, standing in deep green water like a rusty, creaking *Diplodocus*. White birches have now taken hold on the waves of gravel and rock dumped by the dredges.

From Fairbanks to Tok the highway almost hugs the course of the Tanana River, bridging tributary streams and passing a few lakes with picnic spots. The most notable of the scenic turnouts along the road is at Shaw Creek, which offers impressive views of the Alaska Range to the south.

The first town after leaving Fairbanks is North Pole, where the great attraction is Santa Claus House, a gaily decorated toy and gift shop. Also along the road is Eielson Air Force Base, a reminder of the military's economic importance to Alaska.

At 88.7 miles from Fairbanks both the road and the trans-Alaska pipeline cross the Tanana River. The 1,200-foot span of the pipeline crossing here is second in length only to the pipeline's Yukon River crossing north of Fairbanks.

25 (See also 17A.) Near Delta Junction the world's most northerly herds of bison may sometimes be seen roaming the vast plains and hills of the Delta Bison Range. These majestic creatures had inhabited the upland plains of Alaska from the last ice age to the 15th century, when they disappeared for some unknown reason. In 1927 the Alaska legislature appropriated funds for their reintroduction, and about 20 animals were brought in from the National Bison Range in Montana. The present population is estimated at 300 head.

Delta Junction has become a busy town of 3,500 people, largely because of the permanent maintenance station here for the oil pipeline and the nearby presence of Fort Greely, an army Arctic training center.

20. The aurora borealis is caused by streams of electrons from the sun passing through earth's magnetic field and colliding with and ionizing molecules in the stratosphere. The result is a crackling explosion of pulsating color. The peak viewing times are near sunspot maxima, roughly every 11 years: 1957, 1969, 1980.

26 At Tanacross Junction, 11 miles west of Tok, take the side road to the old Athabascan village of Tanacross. In the graveyard are spirit houses similar to the ones at Eklutna. Also in Tanacross is St. Timothy's Mission.

As you drive through the village you see dog teams that belong to local mushers. The winter is fierce hereabouts, with temperatures sometimes hovering at -70° F, and the dog teams continue to serve a vitally useful function when automobiles are out of commission.

The Alluring Islands

Hawaii, the Aloha State, fulfills the lovely promise of the word, despite growing pressures

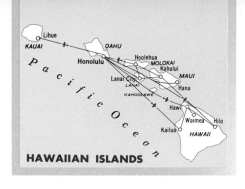

HAWAIIAN ISLANDS

You hear "aloha" in greetings and good-byes and, in most places, sense the spirit of friendship for which it stands. The mildness of the climate and the inviting year-round temperature of the water may tend to soothe the tensions. Even in bustling Honolulu an atmosphere of ease prevails.

For all the sameness of the temperature, there are remarkable scenic contrasts to be enjoyed. Table-flat plantations are flanked by steep cliffs and ravines, and lush jungle growth stands near desolate wastelands. Snowcapped mountains are in view of beaches fringed with palms.

Of the eight islands in this archipelago of volcanic peaks, one is privately owned, another is a pineapple plantation, and one is a military preserve. Each of the others welcomes you with the inviting and varied characteristics described on the following pages.

Oahu, "The Gathering Place," has about 80 percent of the state's population, although it is only the third largest of the Hawaiian Islands. Ringed with sandy swimming beaches, where the high, pounding waves attract surfers, Oahu also has a re-creation of traditional Polynesian life on several of the Pacific islands, an aquarium where visitors can have nose-to-nose encounters with exotic creatures of the sea, and the only royal palace in America.

1 Honolulu, the capital of Hawaii, is an enticing mixture of old and new, Orient and Occident, and presents a relaxed tropical ambiance in spite of its tall buildings and large population. Downtown on King and Richards streets stands Iolani Palace, a handsome ornate Victorian building with white cast-iron railings and fluted columns. Completed in 1882, the palace was the residence of Queen Liliuokalani until the monarchy was deposed in 1893.

Slightly to the east of Honolulu is the community of Waikiki, with its famous beach dominated by Diamond Head, the best-known landform in Hawaii. An ancient crater, Diamond Head came by its name

when sailors a century ago mistook crystals glittering in the volcanic rock for diamonds.

2 In the Bishop Museum, 1355 Kalihi Street, is the Pacific's most impressive collection of Hawaiian and Polynesian antiquities. Hawaiian Hall, whose attractive interior is trimmed with koa wood, has three levels of wooden balconies with wrought-iron embellishments. On view are such rare items as brilliantly colored feather cloaks, superb wood carvings, ancient surfboards, and exquisite jewelry. The most dramatic of the museum's exhibits is a model of a 55-foot sperm whale suspended from the ceiling.

3 Likelike Highway (Route 63) traverses ridged steep hills covered with many textures and shades of greenery. Take Kamehameha Highway (Route 83) south to Route 61 and then follow a narrow blacktop road to Nuuanu Pali State Wayside. The wayside's viewing terrace overlooks the Nuuanu Valley, which is studded with small rounded buttes, and in the distance is the white-fringed Pacific, ranging in color from aquamarine along the reefs to deepest blue far

offshore. The view here is truly spectacular. Continue on Route 61 back to Honolulu and Route H1.

4 The events at Pearl Harbor on December 7, 1941, are well remembered at the U.S.S. *Arizona* Memorial. The building, with its open pavilion decorated with palms and fountains, has a dignity befitting its purpose. Except on Mondays, boats take visitors from the dock to the 184-foot memorial spanning the hulk of the *Arizona*. The names of the 1,177 servicemen who were killed are engraved on the memorial's wall.

4. *Textured rows of densely planted pineapples (some 20,000 plants per acre) contrasting with the red volcanic soil are a treat to the eye as is the fruit to the palate. The fresh pineapple served throughout the Islands is a memorable part of a visit here.*

SPECIAL FEATURES

ROAD GUIDE	━━━━	HIGHLIGHT	**1**
STATE PARKS		POINTS OF INTEREST	▪
With Campsites ▲ Without Campsites △		SCHEDULED AIRLINE STOPS	✕
RECREATION AREAS		MILITARY AIRPORTS	✕
With Campsites ▲ Without Campsites △			

ROAD CLASSIFICATION

PAVED HIGHWAYS

LOCAL ROADS In unfamiliar areas inquire locally before using these roads   Improved ——— Dirt ———

MILEAGE

MILEAGE BETWEEN DOTS ●—— 35 ——●

SCALE (See the individual maps)

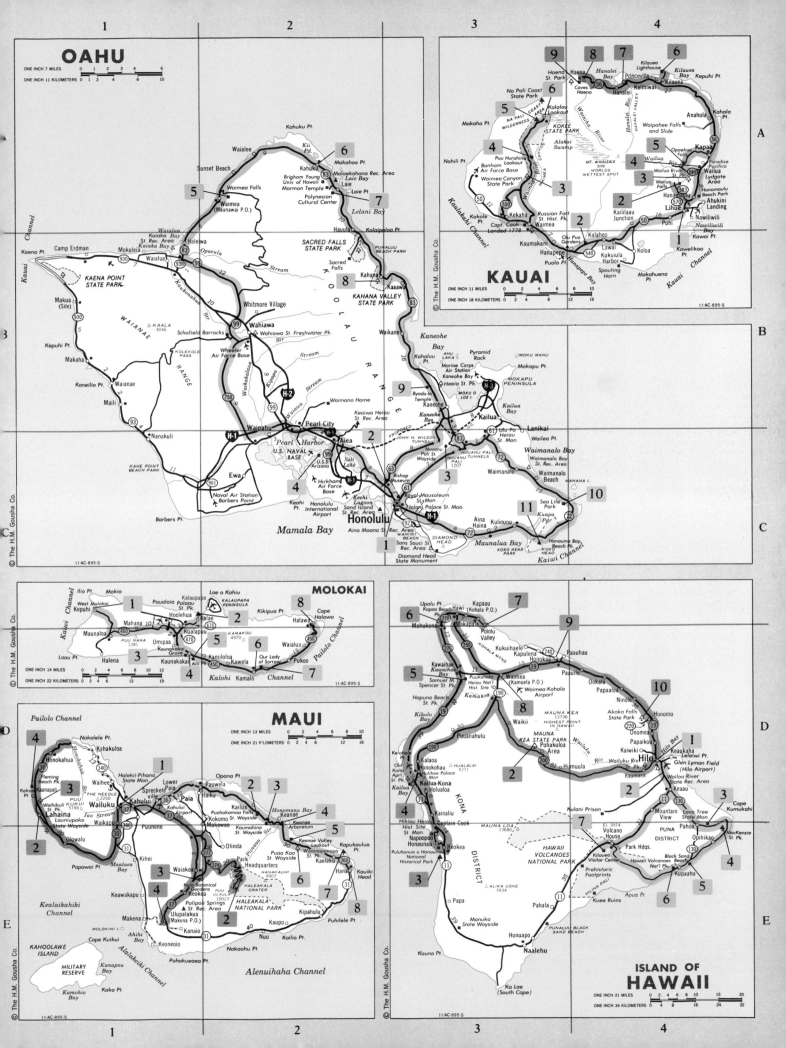

7. *The Fiji village is one of seven communities in the Polynesian Cultural Center. The Village House in the foreground is typical of structures in some of the Fiji Islands. The walls are layered reed, and the roof is made of sugarcane leaves.*

sculptures in a little garden of ginger, plumeria (known as frangipani in the Islands), hibiscus, ti plants, and pineapples. Visitors can walk through parts of the mill without charge, or pay for a more extensive guided tour and learn all about the complex process of extracting sugar from the cane.

7   In Laie is one of the largest Mormon temples west of Utah, a white, modern building at the end of formal gardens flanked by a row of palms.

Nearby and not to be missed is the Polynesian Cultural Center, where one could easily spend a day and evening. Villages typical of those of ancient Samoa, New Zealand, Fiji, Marquesas, Tonga, Tahiti, and Hawaii have been authentically re-created in lush tropical settings. A number of tours are offered, including some with meals and entertainment. The most spectacular show is the evening "Invitation to Paradise".

Most visitors first get the lay of the land by climbing into long outrigger canoes for an absorbing trip on a canal that snakes through all the villages. But you may wander on foot from one village to another, where friendly Islanders are waiting to explain and demonstrate the skills and life-style of their island. You can taste

Turn north through the sugar fields, which soon give way to pineapple plantations. From afar the olive-green tops of these low-growing plants resemble a carpet of spiny grasses. At a road junction about two miles north of Schofield Barracks (a U.S. Army installation), a demonstration garden shows how pineapple is grown. Follow the signs to Haleiwa, where you find a pretty beach and picnic spot. This is the beginning of the high surf area, where you might see experts riding the big waves in the winter months.

5   Waimea Falls Park is reached through a lovely canyon where palm trees line the road. The 1,800-acre park, once the site of a populous Hawaiian village, is today a fascinating mixture of archeological remains and an outstanding natural landscape. Guided tours include a bird sanctuary and arboretum. There are seven miles of hiking trails in this lush green valley as well as a scenic tram ride to the 45-foot falls.

6   At the entrance to the defunct Kahuku Sugar Mill are a converted 1880 steam locomotive that was used to haul sugarcane from the fields and

a large painted sculpture of steam pipes that also functions as a charming birdhouse and weather vane. Bits of machinery, such as pinion gears and plunger pumps, are displayed as

9. *The lovely proportions and lines of the Byodo-In Temple and the surrounding gardens are immediately apparent. Not so obvious, but no less satisfying, are the temple's beautiful materials, delicate craftsmanship, and intricate construction.*

freshly pounded poi, made from taro root, and learn how to dance the hula, to make a fire by rubbing two sticks together, to crack a coconut, and to weave a mat or make a hat from coconut palm fronds.

Heading south from the Cultural Center, the road runs right beside the sea. In some places there are only a few hundred yards of land between the Pacific and the steep volcanic mountains to the west.

8 Kahana Valley State Park, with its grove of tall palms and a little refreshing stream at the base of a steep mountain, is a particularly pleasant stopping place for a picnic. A little farther on you see, rising from the bay, Mokolii Island, locally called Chinaman's Hat, decorated jauntily with a scattering of palms on its rocky top.

9 Kahekili Highway (Route 83) is lined with palms and curves around to Byodo-In Temple. Behind the temple is a dramatic backdrop of steep, deeply fluted green mountains. The Buddhist temple is a replica of a 900-year-old Japanese one. Visitors are invited to ring the five-foot, three-ton brass bell, drawing forth a distinctive tone meant to create a feeling of peace. In the temple is a nine-foot Buddha covered with gold and lacquer. Amid a beautifully landscaped garden is a two-acre pond stocked with more than 10,000 brilliantly colored carp, which to the Japanese symbolize order and perseverance.

10 Sea Life Park presents Hawaiian marine life in an appealing manner. The park's Reef Tank aquarium contains 2,000 specimens, including sharks, stingrays, and moray eels. During shows the high-leaping, trained false killer whales and dolphins demonstrate their intelligence and graceful strength.

11 The road hugs the edge of volcanic cliffs, with scenic overlooks and wind-sculpted trees. At Hanauma Bay Beach Park a shuttle bus runs from the overlook, with its grove of trees and grassy picnic area, to the palm-fringed beach below, in a cove protected by two encircling lava arms. You can also walk down to the beach. There is a reef with natural, calm pools for swimming and coral formations where snorkelers can view the colorful fish.

2. This view from the road looks up the Hanapepe Valley toward the area of Mount Waialeale, which has an average of 460 inches of rainfall per year, one of the heaviest in the world. The cloudscape in the distance is not unusual here.

On Kauai many of the deeply sculptured ridges and valleys for which this island is famous can be enjoyed from the roadside lookouts. The country is so rugged, however, that some areas are the domain only of wild pigs, mountain goats, deer, birds, and the helicopter.

The sugar industry started here in 1835, and you see the waving fields of cane wherever the land is flat enough to cultivate.

The small towns with their weather-beaten buildings and the waterfalls, caves, and rivers give Kauai a peaceful side that contrasts with the raging forces of nature that created the spectacular shapes of the land.

The geological displays at the museum in Lihue are a useful background for appreciation of the dramatic mountains you see on this drive.

A stop at the botanical garden can be of help in plant identification. As the road climbs upward, the views from the lookouts are ever more spectacular, and at the end of the road is a scene that surpasses them all.

1 The Kauai Museum occupies two buildings on Rice Street in the small busy town of Lihue. Its varied and fascinating displays explain the geological and cultural history of Kauai and enhance your appreciation of the dramatic mountains seen on this drive.

The handsome Albert Spencer Wilcox Building has excellent examples of Hawaiian quilts, wooden calabashes, pottery, koa-wood furniture, and the famous featherwork. In the adjacent William Hyde Rice Building are models and dioramas showing interesting aspects of geology, climate, and natural history.

2 Driving west on Route 50, you are soon in a rather flat bowl seemingly surrounded by the jagged tops of gullied green hills. The road dips and rises, flanked by fields of waving sugarcane.

Just west of Kalaheo watch for the sign to Olu Pua Botanical Gardens and plantation. On a pleasant walk through this horticultural preserve you see the understory of ferns, shrubs, and small trees, and the canopy of tall trees typical of tropical forests. This jungle garden has more than 2,000 species of plants, and the foliage is of every imaginable shape, texture, and shade of green. Many of the plants are labeled.

At Hanapepe Valley Lookout a couple of miles west of the garden you see the Hanapepe River winding its way through the green-mantled valley, past cliffs of red rock.

About six miles farther along on Route 50 are the ruins of the Old Russian Fort (1817), mute testimony to the Russians' ill-fated attempt to establish a foothold here. It has been renamed Fort Elizabeth.

3. The variety of lavas and plant growth in the Waimea Canyon creates a remarkably wide range of textures and colors. The narrow river wends its way to the sea, which from this viewpoint (on a clear day) is just visible in the distance.

3 Route 550 out of Kekaha is a narrow blacktop road that works its way up through narrow gullies to the cane fields on the plateaus.

From a lookout at Waimea Canyon State Park, at an elevation of 3,600 feet, you first experience the visual impact of the canyon with its steep, gullied slopes.

4 At Puu Hinahina Lookout (3,500 feet), the view is down the length of the canyon. You can see the thin, bright line of the Waimea River at the bottom and its outlet to the sea in the distance.

5 Kokee State Park has a heavily forested picnic area, cabins, a store, and a restaurant. The small museum has displays of shells and local birds and a scale model of the island.

6 Where the road ends there are two lookouts, Kalalau and Pu'u o Kila, with breathtaking views of the Kalalau Valley. Looking down the valley from one, you can see how Kalalua River works its way to the surf-fringed cove on the sea.

In serried ranks, the ridges on both sides of the canyon drop steeply to the bottom some 4,000 feet below. The ridged escarpments are beautifully patterned and textured with trees, shrubs, and ground covers. Toward the base of the cliffs the outcrops of lava and soil create contrasting patches of deep red.

On the drive back to Route 50, take the east fork down Waimea Canyon Drive for some superb, long views of the cane fields and for an appreciation of the smallness of the island in the vastness of the Pacific.

On this side of the island you can enjoy waterfalls, a lighthouse, a high view of watery taro fields, and some caves and beaches.

Outstanding highlights on this drive are the Fern Grotto trip from Wailua River Marina State Park and the gardens in Paradise Pacifica.

1 For information about Lihue, see number 1 on page 419.

2 On leaving Lihue for a drive along the northern coast of Kauai, make a short detour onto Route 583 to see Wailua Falls. The falls are a double cataract that plunge from an overhanging platform of lava and fall free into the bowllike pool far below. In sunlight, the clouds of spray and mist are shot through with the colors of the rainbow.

3 From the dock at Wailua River Marina State Park you can take a boat trip up a river to the Fern Grotto. The banks of the quiet river are clothed with foliage; on the horizon are verdant mountains where 450 to 500 inches of rain may fall in a year.

A short walk from the boat leads to the grotto, a shallow cave festooned with long, slender fronds of fern. A

2. Typical of the beaches in Hawaii is this palm-fringed crescent of sand and surf at Wailua. Most remarkable in the Islands is that the water maintains a temperature between 75°F (24°C) and 82°F (28°C) year-round.

5. Opaekaa is a cluster of falls, as adjacent flows of water cascade down the steplike layers of Koloa lava.

ribbon of water falls from the cave's rocky overhang. Hawaiians with ukuleles and guitars serenade visitors, and the softness of their music seems appropriate in the lulling calm of this beautiful setting.

4 Adjacent to the dock at Wailua Marina is Paradise Pacifica, a charming series of lagoons, groves, and gardens featuring trees, flowers, and shrubs of the Pacific islands. Many of the plants along the pathways are labeled. Among the trees is the kukui, or candlenut (*Aleurites moluccana*), the state tree. And found in profusion is the lovely hibiscus (*Hibiscus rosa-sinensis*), Hawaii's state flower.

5 Opaekaa Falls is a lacy cascade created by a series of channels reaching the upper rim of the lava cliff. Below, the splash pool is set in a crescent of verdure.

When Route 580 seems to come to a dead end, turn north to again join Route 56 at the town of Kapaa.

About six miles north of Kapaa is a scenic overlook from which you can see the Hole-in-the-Mountain in the Anahola Mountains off to the west. According to legend, the warrior Kawelo hurled his spear at the giant of Hanalei with such force that it tore through the mountain and scattered rocks into the sea. It must be so, for the hole is clearly visible, as are the rocks offshore.

6 Turn into the town of Kilauea and follow Kilauea Road to the lighthouse at the point. From the point you can watch the blue-green surf pounding into a narrow cave, and you may see such birds as red-footed boobies, shearwaters, and frigates. Closed Sundays.

Princeville Plantation was so named for the son of Kamehameha IV and Queen Emma. The community of Princeville is now a resort area with the usual amenities.

7 The road beyond Princeville crosses a series of single-lane bridges over rivers flowing to the nearby sea. On the low headlands there are frequent overlooks of bays and inlets. Of particular interest is the Hanalei Lookout. In the small valley below are taro patches that are designated as a national wildlife refuge for waterbirds, some of which are endangered species. Continuing, the road is narrow and winding.

8 The epitome of a Pacific isle paradise with palms swaying on curving beaches beneath luxuriantly green mountains, Haena was the setting for the Bali Hai scene in the film *South Pacific*. There is an attractive spot for picnicking.

9 The Caves of Haena have a different fascination. The Dry Cave, an opening high on a cliff facing the beach, is actually the large end of a lava tube whose small end is on top of the cliff. Up the road are the Wet Caves, where pools of still water disappear eerily into the caverns.

Not far from here the road ends at palm-studded Ke'e Beach.

Incomparable Perspective

The most dramatic aspects of Kauai's spectacular scenery can best be seen by helicopter, and the service is available through Princeville Airport in Hanalei.

The ascent is sudden, and before you know it, the world appears flat and beautifully patterned with fields, streams, and roads. As your flying carpet approaches the Na Pali coast, the landscape seems to turn on edge and the spectacle of mountainsides dropping precipitously to the sea is incredible, as shown at right.

Leaving the coast and flying down Waimea Canyon, you see slender waterfalls in the distance. On the south side of the island are lava flows and fields of sugarcane. The range of colors, the sculptural shapes, and the scale of the whole are marvelously dramatic.

8. This view from a turnoff on the narrow twisting route reveals the destination at the end of the road, Halawa Beach Park and Halawa Bay. The beauty of the beach and its setting at the end of a valley make this an inviting place for a picnic.

Molokai, the smallest of the islands visited by tourists, has two unique adventures to offer. The Molokai mule ride is memorialized by bumper stickers, T-shirts, and a tropical drink; and the recently established wildlife park is gaining in popularity, particularly among photographers.

1 The climate and terrain at the west end of Molokai is said to be somewhat like that of Kenya and Tanzania. Here on the land of the vast Molokai Ranch, some 800 acres have been set aside as a wildlife preserve for more than 200 animals, including Barbary sheep, giraffes, ostriches, and various kinds of antelopes. Safari tours through the refuge by van are available. The tours are planned in particular to make it easy for photographers to get dramatic pictures of the animals. Private cars are not allowed in the area. Arrangements for tours through the preserve, which is called the Molokai Ranch Wildlife Park, can be made at the airport, at hotels, or through your travel agent.

2 On the way to Palaau State Park, Route 470 rises through a succession of pineapple fields and passes a neat and orderly company town where the pineapple workers live. In the park a short, needle-carpeted trail through a dense stand of ironwood brings you to an overlook where you see the wave-washed Kalaupapa spread out some 2,000 feet below. The surf is far away, but the wind through

the ironwoods creates the same sibilant sound.

Another walk, longer and uphill through the forest, leads to the Phallic Stone and a sign recounting the legend of this unusual outcrop, which was once thought to enhance fertility.

3 Just west of the town of Kaunakakai is a large grove of coconut palms said to have been planted by King Kamehameha V about 1858. The fringed palm fronds are carried high

Riding a Molokai Mule

The adventure for which Molokai is best known is the mule ride down a steep path with some 26 switchbacks, from the heights of Palaau State Park to the Kalaupapa Peninsula. On the peninsula is a settlement established by Father Joseph Damien de Veuster, a Belgian missionary who came here in 1873 to administer to lepers long isolated in this remote region. After years of service, he himself succumbed to the disease. (Today the affliction, Hansen's disease, is controlled by drugs.)

Although the path is narrow and the cliffs steep, the mules are trained and are dependably surefooted on the trail as it zigzags from the high plateau down to the sea. The ride takes about 90 minutes each way; there is also a guided tour of the settlement at Kalaupapa. Reservations for the excursion can be made at your hotel.

above the ground on long, curved, leaning trunks that etch a fascinating crisscross of dark lines against the blue of the sea and sky. The coconuts are carried high too, and signs warn people walking in the grove of the danger of falling nuts.

4 Kaunakakai is a weathered trading center with wooden false-fronted buildings whose overhangs shade the sidewalk. Fishing boats can be chartered at the long wharf.

5 O Ne Alii Beach Park is a pleasant place for a picnic or rest stop. Most of the tables have windbreaks and some have overhead shelters. The rock-strewn beach and muddy water make the spot unsuitable for swimming.

6 Route 450 east runs right by the water at some points. On the inland side are grassy patches of ranchland as the road gradually twists upward toward the steep mountains.

The small, beautifully proportioned St. Joseph's Catholic Church at Kamalo is attributed to Father Damien, the famed priest of Kalaupapa.

7 Built in 1874, the church of Our Lady of Sorrows, just east of the town of Kamalo on Route 450, is also attributed to Father Damien. The edifice was rebuilt in 1966 as a memorial to this priest.

8 To continue on to the end of the road at Halawa can be considered something of a driving adventure. In several places the shoulders of the narrow blacktop are eroded, leaving a jagged edge of pavement, and the surface is pitted and rough. The road twists its way upward, sometimes in blind curves around the lava headlands and sometimes through narrow cuts in the rock. There are no guard rails, and you can pass other cars only at the frequent turnouts.

On the highlands of Cape Halawa the wind has reduced the mighty ironwood tree to the status of a shrub.

Near the end of the road there are views of the distant Moaula Falls and of the crescent-shaped beach far below at Halawa Beach Park. There is a pretty, little church here and a trail that leads to the falls.

Contemplating the beach from the turnaround at the end of the road, one has the definite sense of being in a lovely place that is truly off the beaten path.

Maui is the second youngest and second largest of the Hawaiian Islands. The "Valley Isle" is made up of East Maui and West Maui. The island was formed by two volcanic mountains that were eventually joined together by new lava flows that met in a valley between them. Maui is a place of surprising contrasts, from barren black lava flows to lush, green sea level valleys and high volcanic peaks.

Some poor stretches of road make a circular tour of the island risky, and so the following drives fanning out from Wailuku are suggested.

This drive starts at the edge of a peaceful green valley that was the site of a fierce battle when King Kamehameha conquered the island in 1790. The road snakes through some 50 miles of stunningly beautiful wilderness, dotted with wayside rests, dramatic headlands, and shimmering waterfalls, and ends in a charming quiet town—or for hardy drivers, with a final scenic delight at Seven Pools.

1 Wailuku stands in a dramatic setting on the slopes of the West Maui Mountains at the mouth of the Iao Valley. As you enter the town, driving west from the airport on Route 32, you see a steep, jagged, green-mantled mountain on either side and one in the distance straight ahead. The Iao Valley Road twists through gullied mountains that rise vertically on each side as the valley narrows and leads to the Iao Valley State Park. Here there is a boulder-strewn stream and the Iao Needle, a green-clad peak rising majestically 1,200 feet from the ground. In this valley where rain falls almost constantly, the Needle is often shrouded in mist and clouds.

The 58-mile trip to Hana begins on a broad, gentle plain at the base of a mountain, continues past sugarcane fields, with no indication as yet of the rough, twisting route it becomes. It passes through the charming town of Lower Paia, with its painted, false-fronted wooden buildings. After 19 miles the road becomes narrow, twisting, and bumpy, with a series of S-curves and single-lane bridges across ravines, and you begin to see why this round trip takes from four to six hours of adventurous driving.

1. Iao Needle is a remnant of basalt that has resisted erosion in this rainy place. The moisture has helped establish the plants that now cushion the impact of the precipitation. The figure on the bridge gives an idea of the size of this monolith.

However, the spectacular, unspoiled scenery is worth the bumpy ride.

Since there are no gas stations, restaurants, or telephones until you reach Hana, it is advisable to set out from Wailuku with a full tank and perhaps a picnic lunch.

2 At Puohokamoa Falls State Wayside a path takes you to a sheltered picnic area with a fireplace. The falls cascades over steep stairsteps into a round, rock-bound pool suitable for swimming.

3 A delightful place to lunch is at Kaumahina State Wayside, which has a lovely picnic area in a grassy setting shaded by eucalyptus and palm trees.

4 An interesting place to stop and stretch your legs is the Keanae Arboretum. A pleasant trail alongside a rocky stream winds among dense clumps of tall bamboo, breadfruit, papaya, and guava trees, with a luxuriance of tropical plants and drifts of pink and fuchsia impatiens in the dappled shade. Most of the plants are identified.

5 From Keanae Valley State Wayside Lookout you can view the Keanae Peninsula as well as a patchwork of taro fields and dikes. In this area the Hawaiians live much as their ancestors did when taro root was one of their staple foods.

The road dips down to the sea, climbs a headland, and slopes to the water once again, so quickly that the change can make your ears pop.

6 At Puaa Kaa State Wayside there are picnic tables, pleasant paths along a bubbling brook, lava potholes filled with water, and a swimming pool in a grotto with a fern-edged waterfall.

7 Waianapanapa State Park is situated in a grove of trees on a promontory. From the point you can watch the surf splashing high above the rocks. Within the park is an ancient burial site, a temple site (*heiau*), and a cove with a black sand beach.

8 Hana, an unspoiled Hawaiian village, looks more like a residential community than the sort of town you anticipate at the end of such a difficult road. There are only a couple of stores and restaurants. A fascinating half-hour can be spent in Hasegawa's General Store, which has been in business for nearly 70 years and has a dizzying array of merchandise. At Hana Bay Beach Park the fishing boats at anchor make a colorful picture. You can also picnic here.

If you are ready for another 10-mile stretch of rugged road, head south from Hana to the Kipahulu area of Haleakala National Park. After six miles you reach the striking Wailua waterfalls. Another four miles brings you to the famous Seven Pools, now known as Oheo. There are, in fact, more than seven of these scenic catch basins stairstepping down the slope, as you can see from the bridge across Oheo Gulch.

2. *The remarkable range of subtle colors in the lava adds interest to the dramatic form of the rugged rim and rounded cinder cones of Haleakala Crater. The silversword (*Argyroxiphium macrocephalum*), shown at the right, grows only here and on the Big Island. Between 4 and 20 years of age it develops flowering stalks up to 9 feet high, sets seed, and dies.*

You will find this a breathtaking zig-zag route from sea level to the summit of Mount Haleakala at more than 10,000 feet. Haleakala means "house of the sun," but the eerie desolation found here seems more related to the surface of the moon.

1 For information about Wailuku, see number 1 on page 423.
2 Driving from Wailuku to Mount Haleakala, you cross fields of sugarcane and pineapples and verdant pastureland, and then begin a zigzag climb into the clouds. The road climbs through groves of eucalyptus and over cactus-strewn hills, and as the way grows steeper, there are long views of the coast. In Maui legend, Mount Haleakala is the "house of the sun," but the vast crater at its crest is much more like the moon in its eerie silence and barrenness.

The House of the Sun Visitor Center, 10 miles beyond the headquarters of Haleakala National Park, gives you an orientation about the volcanic history and the predicted future of the region. Leaving the headquarters, the road continues to climb, and if the day is clear you have a panoramic view of the valley, sea,

and mountains. The road, flanked by lava, passes two overlooks and reaches the visitor center of Mount Haleakala at 9,800 feet. From the center the road continues upward for another half-mile to the summit.

The great crater, a gullied valley 3,000 feet deep and 21 miles around, is an incredible spectacle, a lunar landscape studded with cinder cones and streaked with yellow, red, gray, and black lava ash. The peaks of Mauna Loa and Mauna Kea on Hawaii are visible in the distance.

In the park are self-guided nature trails for hardy hikers. It is advisable to bring warm clothing, especially if you plan to hike.
3 Descending from the park, turn left on Route 377 to Kula Botanical Gardens. In a natural setting, paths wind through a garden of tropical and Hawaiian plants, with arbor-shaded benches where you can rest and enjoy the beauty around you.
4 At the Tedeschi Winery, located on Ulupalakua Ranch, one of the largest cattle ranches in Hawaii, wine is made from pineapples. You may sample Maui Blanc, which is very pleasant and dry and only slightly redolent of pineapple.

Route 30 to the west heads for a quaint and charming town that was a busy whaling port in the 1800's and the residence of Hawaiian kings. Visitors here have included New England missionaries and Herman Melville, the author of Moby Dick. The road continues north to a placid beach setting, where the only sounds are made by huge waves crashing on the beach.

1 For information on Wailuku, see number 1 on page 423.
2 Lahaina is one of the Islands' most historic towns. From 1795 to 1843 it was the capital of Hawaii, and in the mid-1800's it became a whaling center; as many as 50 whaling vessels were sometimes anchored offshore at one time. The old town, well maintained, looks much as it did then, when it was visited by Herman Melville, author of the famous novel *Moby Dick*. Near the courthouse a 106-year-old banyan tree spreads its branches over a small park.

The waterfront is a teeming blend of sailing and fishing boats, restaurants, and shops selling crafts. Glass-bottomed boats leave the wharf at frequent intervals for one-hour tours of the nearby coral reefs. From December to May you may see humpback whales in their breeding grounds here.

At the north end of town is the station of the Lahaina Kaanapali & Pacific Railroad, where you can board the Sugar Cane Train for a pleasant 12-mile round trip aboard 1880's-style cars pulled by a handsome little steam engine. Portions of narrow-gauge track paralleling Route 30 are on the original right-of-way where the old-time trains hauled cane from the plantation to the mill.
3 Waihikuli State Wayside, just off the road, is an inviting place to stop for a picnic lunch or for a swim. From the long sandy beach you can see the silhouette of Lanai, the pineapple island, on the western horizon.
4 North of Kaanapali and the many large hotels along its excellent beach, the road becomes rougher and the surf stronger. At Fleming Beach Park, in a delightful setting of ironwoods and palms, there are picnic tables and a curving beach that is favored by surfers. It is not, however, recommended for swimming.

1. *The view from Hilo looks across the fields of sugarcane toward Mauna Loa, the volcano that dominates the skyline on the Big Island. This is the world's largest active volcano and the most volatile on the island, although the eruptions in recent years have been minor.*

The island of Hawaii, *to avoid confusion with the state's name and to describe its size in relation to the rest of the chain, is known as the Big Island. The island may also be the upper part of the world's largest mountains, Mauna Kea and Mauna Loa, which rise some 30,000 feet from their base on the floor of the sea but actually 13,677 and 13,796 feet above sea level.*

The varied climate of Hawaii, which has the driest spot in the state, creates interesting changes of scenery.

Heading south from Hilo, *you can see a dead forest of lava trees and swim at a beach of black sand. In Hawaii Volcanoes National Park the road crosses expanses of smooth black lava and then heads toward the craters at Kilauea's summit, where steaming vents are a reminder that Pele, the volcano goddess, is still in residence.*

1 The town of Hilo, originally shaped by the bay for which it was named, has been altered by the tidal waves that occasionally buffeted this side of the island. The city is known for its stately banyan trees and the delightful 30-acre Japanese Yedo-style Liliuokalani Gardens, where you can stroll among the ponds, topiary plantings, and pagodas.

Nearby, where the Wailoa River, the shortest in the state, flows into the bay, is a market where fishermen auction their catch.

A Hilo highlight is Rainbow Falls. Go west on Wainuenue Avenue and watch for the sign. The falls flows over a lip of lava into a basin. In early morning, when the sun plays on the falls, there are rainbows in the spray.

2 The macadamia nut, a native of Australia, is grown commercially in Hawaii. The Mauna Loa Macadamia Nuts Corporation is the world's largest producer, and here at their factory, you can see how the nuts are processed and packaged.

3 The town of Pahoa, with its wood buildings, false fronts, and tin roofs, is a reminder of the leisurely pace of Old Hawaii. Near the edge of town is Lava Tree State Monument, an eerie landscape of cracked lava flows and upright black formations, dramatic evidence of the original fluidity of the material of which the entire state of Hawaii is composed.

About 1790 an eruption of Kilauea sent molten lava down through a forest of large ohia trees. As the lava flowed around a tree, the moisture in the trunk was sufficient to chill and harden the lava into a cast of the tree, while the unchilled lava between the trees flowed on. These standing shells are the "lava trees" you see in the park. Ferns and other plants are once more establishing themselves here, and the surrounding area has again become a lovely forest of tall trees, in which there is a picnic area.

4 Route 137 to Pohoiki is a narrow red-top pavement that faithfully follows the ups and downs of the rolling land that leads to Mackenzie State Park by the sea.

Beyond the picnic area, which is carpeted with needles from a grove of ironwoods, rugged jettylike fingers of lava create a series of small bays where the surf pounds against the cliffs and sends up great fountains of spray.

3. *Since about 1790, when these lava trees were formed, the casts have weathered into fascinating sculptural forms. Plants of various kinds have taken hold and again bring life to the area of Lava Tree State Monument.*

5. *The stark and unusual contrast of white surf breaking on a black sand beach is one of the memorable sights on the Big Island.*

5 Kaimu Black Sand Beach, fringed with swaying coconut palms, has sand as black as coal—or black as the lava of which it is composed. Both the grainy sand at the water's edge and the porous pebbles farther from the shore are the same black color.

Because of the strong undertow, this beach is not recommended for swimming. At adjacent Harry K. Brown Beach there is a swimming area.

A few miles south of the park you see one of the two painted churches on the island. The church, called the Star of the Sea, has charming proportions, and on the inside every surface is covered with naive paintings.

6 The Hawaii Volcanoes National Park Visitors Center at Wahaula is the starting point of a paved nature trail with many plants clearly identified. Here too is a partial reconstruction of an important religious temple (*heiau*) dating from the 13th century.

The road through this section of the park traverses a sea of black lava that flowed to the Pacific, where jagged cliffs now mark the explosive meeting of melted rock and the surging sea. In some areas the lava has solidified as small rough chunks called *aa*. The smooth, shiny lava is called *pahoehoe*.

All along this route the vast bulk of Mauna Loa, the world's largest active volcano, cuts a rounded arc against the western sky. This is the classic shape of a shield volcano, which has very fluid lava that simply erupts as compared to the more viscous type of lava that creates the explosive pressures that build up under cone-shaped volcanoes like Mount St. Helens.

On the Chain of Crater's Road up to Kilauea Caldera there are turnouts with views of various volcanic phenomena. The path to the lookout at Halemaumau Crater is bordered by steaming vents and hot rocks. Feeling these rocks, which are heated by molten magma that is not very deep within the earth here, gives one a strange sense of being in touch with a primary source of creation.

7 The Kilauea Visitor Center has an interesting 10-minute film about this volcano and some of its recent eruptions.

The short walk from the parking area to the Thurston Lava Tube is fascinating. The steps and path wind down through a jungle of ferns, ohia trees, and other tropical growth to a cool grotto and the tunnel, which is typical of those created when a crust forms over flowing lava.

Shield volcanoes

Volcanoes that rise from midocean have a rounded profile, while cone-shaped volcanoes, such as Mount St. Helens, rise in back of the continental margins. Shield volcanoes do not plug up and blow explosively. They simply erupt. The rate of flow and cooling determines whether the lava will be *aa* or *pahoehoe*.

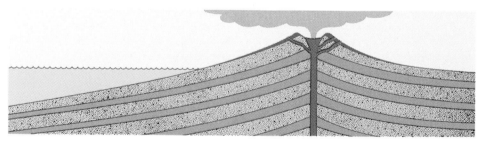

Pahoehoe (smooth) lava

Aa (rough) lava

Kilauea iki (little Kilauea). Kilauea steaming in background

3. Fearsome figures, such as these on display here at the Place of Refuge representing ancient Hawaiian gods, were placed on sacred ground to warn intruders. The frightening carvings were justified, for to ignore the warnings meant death.

A drive west from Hilo circles the dormant mass of Mauna Kea, largest of the five volcanoes that formed the island. Along the route are inviting, palm-fringed beaches and many reminders of the ancient culture of the Hawaiians. In Waimea you find a marvelously eclectic museum, and farther on you discover one of the most beautiful waterfalls in all the Islands.

1 For information about Hilo, see number 1 on page 425.

On the way from Hilo to the Big Island's largest volcano, you drive through residential areas to a high plateau of green fields, ohia trees, tree ferns, and patches of lava. To the northeast is the brooding presence of the dormant volcano, Mauna Kea, which at 13,796 feet is the highest point in Hawaii. Surrounding the base of the mountain is a desolate gray landscape of broken lava.

2 Near a great jagged rift in Mauna Kea's western flank is Mauna Kea State Park, a small oasis and picnic area.

Along Route 190, pastureland edges the plateau and rows of eucalyptus trees parallel the road; in the distance lies the endless expanse of the blue Pacific.

3 Pu'uhonua O Honaunau ("Place of Refuge") is a national historical park. Until the early 1800's, when the ancient Hawaiian religion was abolished, there were many sacred laws that, if broken, were punishable by death. If, however, law breakers could reach an official place of refuge such as this one, they would be safe. An audiovisual presentation in an open pavilion explains the function of the refuge.

The old coast road going north to Napoopoo is narrow and rough for a few miles, but it improves and leads to the Royal Kona Coffee Mill and Museum. Here you can learn about the locally grown coffee and have a sample of this famous brew.

Route 11 north twists its way up and over a headland and follows the Kona coast where, in December, January, and February, tree-sized poinsettias contrast their brilliant red with the cool colors of the sky and sea.

4 Kailua-Kona (so called to avoid confusion with the town of Kailua on Oahu) is a remarkably attractive place on a bay where sports-fishing boats are moored. Here you find the Hulihee Palace, a two-storied house that was the royal summer palace throughout the 1800's. It is now a museum with furnishings of the mid-1800's and a collection of Hawaiian artifacts.

5 Puukohola Heiau is the last of the open stone temples erected on Hawaii. It was rebuilt in 1790-91 of lava blocks without mortar for King Kamehameha I.

6 In Lapakahi State Historical Park, south of Kapaa Beach Park, is an on-going archeological dig; several old foundations have been uncovered and an original Hawaiian grass dwelling reconstructed. The grass, called pili, used for these shelters contains an oily substance that sheds water.

7 The narrow, twisting road to Popolu Valley leads through verdant rolling pasturelands to a vista of distant green-mantled headlands. A trail leads down the nearby cliff to a beach with surf breaking on the sand.

8 The Kamuela Museum in Waimea has an incredible variety of arts and artifacts, including poi pounders, tapa beaters, and fine furnishings and paintings, many of them possessions of the former Hawaiian royal family.

Also in Waimea is the Parker Ranch Center and Museum. Here are artifacts related to the history of the ranch started in 1847 by John Palmer Parker, who worked for Kamehameha the Great and married an Hawaiian before establishing a ranch of his own.

9 In the town of Honokaa is the Hawaiian Holiday macadamia nut factory. There is a gift shop with nut products in every conceivable variety, and the sample tastes make sales resistance difficult. The factory operation in the same building can be viewed through windows.

10 Akaka Falls State Park, in a delightful junglelike setting, provides a steep, paved pathway leading down to Kahuna Falls and then back up again to Akaka Falls, a spectacular cascade that drops 420 feet into a semicircular pond at the base of moss-covered cliffs. There are rainbows here when the sun hits the clouds of mist.

10. The silvery strand of Akaka Falls varies in width with the flow of Kolekole Stream, but the height is dramatic in any season.

INDEX

*Page numbers in **bold** type refer to illustrations and captions. The numbers in brackets [ ] indicate tour highlights.*

*Page numbers in **bold** type refer to illustrations and captions. The numbers in brackets [ ] indicate tour highlights.*

*Page numbers in **bold** type refer to illustrations and captions. The numbers in brackets [ ] indicate tour highlights.*

*Page numbers in **bold** type refer to illustrations and captions. The numbers in brackets [ ] indicate tour highlights.*

*Page numbers in **bold** type refer to illustrations and captions. The numbers in brackets [ ] indicate tour highlights.*

CITY INDEX

Towns and cities that are on or near the recommended tours are indicated here with their alphanumeric coordinates.

Picture Credits

Cover David Muench Photography, Inc. 1 Johnny Johnson. 2–3 Jim Amos/H. Armstrong Roberts. 24 *bottom* Paul A. Knaut, Jr. 26 Paul A. Knaut, Jr. 27 *top* Mary R. Calvert. 28 Henry A. Harding. 29 *top* Bob Clemenz Photography. 30 Fred Sieb Photography. 31 © 1975 Michael Philip Manheim. 32 Clyde H. Smith. 33 *top* Fred Sieb Photography; *bottom* Gilbert Nielsen. 36 Clyde H. Smith. 37 Fred Clauss. 38 *top* Fred Sieb Photography; *bottom* Dick Rowan. 39 Lester A. Sebel. 41 *top* Bullaty-Lomeo; *bottom* Dick Hamilton. 42 *bottom* Angelo Lomeo. 44 Winston Pote/Shostal Associates. 45 *top* Clyde H. Smith; *lower right & bottom* Vermont Travel Division. 46 *right* Dmitri Kessel, *Life*, © 1957 Time Inc. 48 *top* Sonja Bullaty; *bottom* Robert J. Alzner. 49 Hanson Carroll. 52 Massachusetts Department of Commerce and Development Photo. 53 *top* Hans Wendler; *bottom* B. Cory Kilvert/The Stock Shop. 54 Jack Spratt/Picture Group. 55 *top* Rhode Island Department of Economic Development; *bottom* John T. Hopf. 56 *bottom* Jack Spratt/Picture Group. 57 *top* Jack Zehrt; *bottom* John F. Urwiller/Picture Group. 60 Clyde H. Smith. 61 Clyde H. Smith. 62 *top* Judy Skorpil; *bottom* Walter Grishkot/Courtesy of Warren County Public Information & Tourism. 63 Clyde H. Smith. 64 *top* Michael J. Wakefield; *bottom* Edgar E. Webber. 65 *left* Zig Leszczynski/Animals Animals; *right* John Goerg/New York State Department of Environmental Conservation. 68 Paul Rocheleau. 69 *upper* Massachusetts Department of Commerce and Development Photo; *bottom* © 1980 Cecile Brunswick. 71 Walter J. Choroszewski/The Stock Shop. 72 Hank Morgan/Rainbow. 73 *top* Paul Rocheleau; *bottom* Clemens Kalischer. 74 *center* Paul G. Wiegman/Western Pennsylvania Conservancy. 76 Clyde H. Smith. 77 Ed Cooper/H. Armstrong Roberts. 78 *bottom* Grant Heilman Photography. 79 Al Koster/Pocono Scenicards. 80 *top* Camerique. 81 *top & middle right* Jane Latta; *middle left* Edward Lettau/The Stock Shop; *bottom* Courtesy Pennsylvania Historical and Museum Commission. 82 Photo by Brinker Associates, Inc. 83 *left* Donald S. Heintzelman; *right* Alexander C. Nagy/Hawk Mountain Sanctuary Asssociation. 84 *bottom* Ralph Gates. 86 *left* David M. Campione; *top center* (bluebird) Thase Daniel/Bruce Coleman Inc.; *remainder* Leonard Lee Rue III. 87 Ralph Gates. 88 *top right* E. R. Degginger/Bruce Coleman Inc.; *middle right* Richard Kolar/Earth Scenes; *remainder* Zig Leszczynski/Earth Scenes. 89 *top* Alexander Limont/Bruce Coleman Inc.; *bottom right* Dick Hanley/Photo Researchers; *remainder* Anne Heiman. 90 Ralph Gates. 91 *top* Leonard Lee Rue III; *bottom* Ralph Gates. 92 *bottom* M. E. Warren. 94 Orlando Wootten. 95 *top* M. Woodbridge Williams; *bottom* Eric G. Carle/Shostal Associates. 96 *left* Virginia State Travel Service Photo; *right* M. E. Warren. 97 Doris Gehrig Barker. 98 *top* Thomas Peters Lake; *middle* Ralph Krubner/H. Armstrong Roberts; *bottom* Colonial Williamsburg Photograph. 100 *bottom* Arnout Hyde, Jr. 102 *top* Ed Cooper/H. Armstrong Roberts. 103 Howard A. Miller. 104 David Muench/H. Armstrong Roberts. 105 David Muench/H. Armstrong Roberts. 106 *bottom* David Muench/H. Armstrong Roberts. 108 Carroll C. Calkins. 109 *top* Osbra L. Eye; *bottom* Arnout Hyde, Jr. 110 Arnout Hyde, Jr. 111 Richard Berenson. 112 *top left* Governor's Office of Economic and Community Development; *top middle* (sundew) Kim Taylor/Bruce Coleman Inc.; *top right* (pitcher plant) Jack Dermid/Bruce Coleman Inc.; *lower left* (butterwort) Hans Reinhard/Bruce Coleman Inc.; *remainder* William C. Blizzard. 113 Arnout Hyde, Jr. 114 *bottom* Robert Walch. 116-17 *top* Arnout Hyde, Jr.; *bottom* Hugh Morton. 118 Zig Leszczynski/Animals Animals. 119 William A. Bake. 120 *top right* (blossom) Anne Shelton/*The Flue Cured Tobacco Farmer*; *lower right* (leaves) Bruce Roberts; *middle left* (plant bed) *The Flue Cured Tobacco Farmer*; *middle right* (field) Jim Knight/*The Flue Cured Tobacco Farmer*; *bottom left & right* Courtesy of Taylor Manufacturing Co., Elizabethtown, North Carolina. 121 *top* Jean Anderson; *bottom* Hugh Morton. 122 Jay Lurie. 123 Clyde H. Smith. 124 *bottom* Ted Borg. 126 *top* Jack Dermid; *bottom* Ernest Ferguson/Photo Arts. 127 Ken Dequaine. 128 Bruce Roberts/The Phelps Agency. 129 *top* Ted Borg; *bottom* Jean Anderson. 130 *center* Thase Daniel. 132 *top* Wendell D. Metzen; *lower middle* Grant Heilman Photography; *remainder* Leonard Lee Rue III. 133 William A. Bake. 134 Joseph Fire. 135 John Earl. 136 *top* Wendell D. Metzen; *bottom* Carroll C. Calkins. 137 *upper* Fred Zimmerman/The Phelps Agency; *lower* Carroll C. Calkins. 138 *bottom* Jim Tuten/Alpha Photo Associates. 140 Grant Heilman Photography. 141 William Hamilton/Shostal Associates. 142 *bottom* W. Metzen/H. Armstrong Roberts. 143 *top* Helen Cruickshank; *bottom* Robert Motzkin/The Stock Shop. 144 *top* Phil Brodatz; *lower left to right:* Thomas & Karen Metcalf, Zig Leszczynski/Earth Scenes, Kenneth W. Fink/Bruce Colemnan Inc., K. Altie Hodson, R. F. Head/Earth Scenes. 145 *top left* Jim Beck; *bottom left to right:* Barry E. Parker/Bruce Coleman Inc., Thomas & Karen Metcalf, James H. Carmichael, Jr./Bruce Coleman Inc.; *remainder* Burton McNeely. 146 *left* Wendell D. Metzen; *right* R. F. Head/Earth Scenes. 147 *left* Grant Heilman Photography; *right* John Colwell/Grant Heilman Photography. 148 *bottom* Alabama Bureau of Publicity and Information. 150 *top* Lisa Simonton/The Phelps Agency; *bottom* Alabama Space and Rocket Center. 151 Harriet H. Wright. 152 Alabama Bureau of Publicity and Information. 153 *top* Clyde H. Smith; *lower right* Alabama State Council on the Arts and Humanities. 154 *top right & lower right* Clyde H. Smith; *remainder* Grant Heilman Photography. 155 Terry M. Hill. 156 *bottom* © 1980 *Southern Living*. 158 Wesley F. Walden. 159 Van Chaplin © 1980 *Southern Living*. 160 *top* Ken Dequaine; *bottom* Glenn D. Chambers. 161 Kentucky Department of Tourism. 162 © 1980 *Southern Living*. 163 O. Done/Shostal Associates. 164 *top* Shaker Village of Pleasant Hill; *remainder* Bill Strode/Black Star. 165 Midwest Film Studios. 168 Kent & Donna Dannen. 169 Alvin E. Staffan. 170 *top* Kent & Donna Dannen; *lower left* Leonard Lee Rue III; *lower right* Thase Daniel. 171 Kent & Donna Dannen. 174 Kathy & Alan Linn. 175 *top* Ruth Chin; *bottom* Howard A. Leistner. 176 *top* Ken Dequaine; *bottom* Gene C. Frazier. 177 J. C. Allen & Son, Inc. 178 Richard L. Powell. 179 *top* Ruth Chin; *lower left* Photo courtesy Indiana Limestone Institute, Bedford, Indiana. 182 *upper left* Robert P. Carr; *bottom* Leonard Lee Rue III. 184 *top* Tom Algire. 184 Robert P. Carr. 185 *top* Ila Bromberg; *bottom* Robert P. Carr. 194 Les Blacklock. 195 *top left* Stephen J. Krasemann/DRK Photo; *top right* John Mathisen. 196 Joseph Fire. 197 Joseph Fire. 198 *center* Joy Spurr/Bruce Coleman Inc.; *lower* John M. Burnley/Bruce Coleman Inc. 199 Ken Dequaine. 202 Ken Dequaine. 203 *top* Tom Algire; *remainder* Bruce Fritz. 204 Ken Dequaine. 205 *bottom right* Vern Arendt. 206 Ken Dequaine. 207 *top* Kathy & Alan Linn; *middle left & right* Little Norway; *bottom* Ken Dequaine. 208 *bottom* Bert Vogel/H. Armstrong Roberts. 210 Kent & Donna Dannen. 211 Ken Dequaine. 212 Ken Dequaine. 213 *left* Grant Heilman Photography; *right* John Colwell/Grant Heilman Photography. 214 *bottom* James P. Rowan/The Marilyn Gartman Agency. 216 *top* James P. Rowan/The Marilyn Gartman Agency; *bottom* Hedrich-Blessing. 217 Kathy & Alan Linn. 218 *left* Al Levy/Midwest Film Studios; *right* Bob & Miriam Francis/Tom Stack & Associates. 219 James P. Rowan/The Marilyn Gartman Agency. 220 John H. Gerard. 221 James P. Rowan/The Marilyn Gartman Agency. 222 *bottom* Rich Grosko/Photography Diversified. 224 *left* Grant Heilman Photography; *right* Richard Parker/National Audubon Society/Photo Researchers. 225 Richard F. Raber. 226 Kent & Donna Dannen. 227 *top* Jim Day; *bottom* Glenn D. Chambers. 228 *top* Jim Day; *bottom* Jack Zehrt. 229 Kent & Donna Dannen. 230 *bottom* Stephen Green-Armytage. 232 *bottom left to right:* Leonard Lee Rue III, Len Rue, Jr., Jen & Des Bartlett/Bruce Coleman Inc. 233 Wes Lyle/Photography Diversified. 234 Leonard Lee Rue III. 235 *top* Randy Johnson; *lower left to right:* Barbara K. Deans/DPI,

Richard Kolar/Earth Scenes, Perry D. Slocum/Earth Scenes, Joe McDonald/Earth Scenes. 236 Kent & Donna Dannen. 237 Kenneth L. Smith. 238 *bottom* Dan Guravich. 240 *top left* Mitchel L. Osborne; *top right* A. C. Shelton/H. Armstrong Roberts; *bottom* Mississippi Department of Economic Development. 241 J. Fire/Shostal Associates. 242 Dan Guravich. 243 *upper* Mitchel L. Osborne; *bottom* Dan Guravich. 244 *bottom* E. Carle/Shostal Associates. 245 Jen & Des Bartlett/Bruce Coleman Inc. 248 Mitchel L. Osborne. 249 *top* Al Godoy/Louisiana Office of Tourism; *bottom* C. C. Lockwood. 250 Ralph Krubner/H. Armstrong Roberts. 251 *top right* Thase Daniel; *bottom* Jeffrey Milstein; *remainder* Thase Daniel/Courtesy of Avery Island. 252 *upper middle right* (spotter guiding plane) Grant Heilman Photography; *lower middle right* (young rice plants) J. C. Allen & Son, Inc.; *remainder* William E. Barksdale. 253 Dan Guravich. 254 *bottom* David Muench Photography, Inc. 256 Kent & Donna Dannen. 257 David Muench Photography, Inc. 258 *top* Kent & Donna Dannen; *bottom* Stephen J. Krasemann/DRK Photo. 259 Kent & Donna Dannen. 260 David Muench Photography, Inc. 261 *top left* E. R. Degginger/Bruce Coleman Inc.; *top right* David Muench Photography, Inc.; *bottom* Robert P. Carr. 262 David Muench Photography, Inc. 263 *upper* David Muench Photography, Inc.; *middle left to right:* Jack Dermid, Robert W. Mitchell/Earth Scenes, Jack Dermid; *bottom left to right:* Jack Dermid, Robert W. Mitchell/Earth Scenes, Robert W. Mitchell/Animals Animals. 264 *bottom* Bob Taylor. 266 *bottom left* Oklahoma Tourism and Recreation Department; *bottom right* Morris Karol/Courtesy of Great Salt Plains State Park. 267 Oklahoma Tourism and Recreation Department. 268 *left* Oklahoma Tourism and Recreation Department; *right* Bob Taylor. 269 Oklahoma Tourism and Recreation Department. 270 *top* Bob Taylor; *bottom* Scott Farley. 271 Bob Taylor. 274 Grant Heilman Photography. 275 Kent & Donna Dannen. 276 Kent & Donna Dannen. 277 *top* Jim Turner/Photography Diversified; *bottom* Dick Herpich. 278 *left* Kent & Donna Dannen; *middle right* Len Rue, Jr./Bruce Coleman Inc.; *remainder* Alan G. Nelson/Animals Animals. 279 Kent & Donna Dannen. 280 *bottom* Kent & Donna Dannen. 282 Kent & Donna Dannen. 283 *left* Larry R. Ditto/Bruce Coleman Inc.; *right* Nebraska Game and Parks Commission Photo. 284 *top to bottom:* Nebraska Game and Parks Commission Photo, M.P.L. Fogden/Bruce Coleman Inc., Grant Heilman Photography, Len Rue, Jr./Bruce Coleman Inc. 285 *left* Grant Heilman Photography; *right* Kent & Donna Dannen. 286 K. W. Fink/Bruce Coleman Inc. 287 *upper & bottom left* Kent & Donna Dannen. 288–89 Nebraska Game and Parks Commission Photo. 290 *bottom* David Muench Photography, Inc. 292 David Muench Photography, Inc. 293 David Muench Photography, Inc. 294 Clyde John/Courtesy of the Corn Palace. 295 *top right* Morris Karol/Courtesy of Pipestone Indian Shrine Association; *remainder* Kent & Donna Dannen. 296 *bottom* Kent & Donna Dannen. 298 David Muench Photography, Inc. 299 *upper* Robert C. Fields; *bottom* Photo furnished courtesy of North Dakota Tourism Promotion. 301 Kent & Donna Dannen. 308 *center* Robert C. Larsson. 310 *upper* Ross Hall; *bottom left* Charles Summers/Tom Stack & Associates; *bottom right* Charles Summers, Jr./Amwest. 311 Manuel A. Rodriguez. 312 Pat O'Hara. 314 *top* Bob & Clara Calhoun/Bruce Coleman Inc.; *bottom* Donald Young. 315 Jim Elder. 316 Kent & Donna Dannen; *upper right* Lester A. Sebel; *remainder* Manuel A. Rodriguez. 317 *top* Stephen E. Pike/The Stockmarket; *lower right* H. Reinhard/Bruce Coleman Inc. 318 *lower right* Harry Engels. 318 *lower left* Kent & Donna Dannen. 320 Wyoming Travel Commission. 321 Wyoming Travel Commission. 322 David Muench Photography, Inc. 323 *bottom* Pat O'Hara. 324 Kent & Donna Dannen. 325 Kent & Donna Dannen. 328 *top* David Muench Photography, Inc.; *bottom* Charles Summers, Jr./Amwest. 329 *right* David Muench/The Image Bank; *upper left* K. W. Fink/Bruce Coleman Inc.; *remainder* Ted & Lois Matthews. 330 Peter Runyon. 331 Ralph Krubner/H. Armstrong Roberts. 332 David Muench Photography, Inc. 333 *top* L. Sapp/Amwest; *bottom left* Richard Berenson; *bottom right* David Muench Photography, Inc. 334 David Muench Photography, Inc. 335 David Sumner. 336 *bottom* Ray Manley/Shostal Associates. 338 David Muench Photography, Inc. 339 David Muench Photography, Inc. 340 David Muench Photography, Inc. 341 *top* Jerry D. Jacka; *middle* Jerry D. Jacka/Courtesy of the Heard Museum, Phoenix, Arizona; *bottom* David Muench Photography, Inc. 342 Buddy Mays. 343 Kent & Donna Dannen. 344 David Muench Photography, Inc. 345 *upper right* Jerry D. Jacka; *lower* Michael & Barbara Reed/Earth Scenes. 346 *bottom* Bob Clemenz Photography. 348 David Muench Photography, Inc. 349 David Muench Photography, Inc. 350 *left* Harvey-Jane Kowal; *right* David Muench Photography, Inc. 351 *top* M.P.L. Fogden/Bruce Coleman Inc.; *lower left to right:* Brian Milne/Earth Scenes, Don W. Fawcett/Earth Scenes, J. C. Stevenson/Earth Scenes, Robert W. Mitchell/Earth Scenes; *bottom left to right:* Manuel A. Rodriguez, Brian Milne/Earth Scenes, Kenneth R. Morgan/Earth Scenes, Leonard Lee Rue III/Earth Scenes. 352 *left* Courtesy of the Arizona-Sonora Desert Museum; *top right* Jen & Des Bartlett/Bruce Coleman Inc.; *lower right* Terrence Moore. 353 Thomas Peters Lake. 354 *bottom left* David Muench Photography, Inc.; *lower right top to bottom:* Charles G. Summers/Bruce Coleman Inc., Leonard Lee Rue III/Bruce Coleman Inc., M. P. Kahl/Bruce Coleman Inc. 356 *top* David Muench Photography, Inc.; *bottom* John S. Flannery. 357 Dick Dietrich. 358–59 David Muench Photography, Inc. 360 Clyde H. Smith. 361 *left* David Muench Photography, Inc. 362 *bottom* Duane D. Davis. 364 *top* Will Hawkins; *bottom* Duane D. Davis. 365 David Muench Photography, Inc. 366 Pat O'Hara. 367 *left* Pat O'Hara; *right* Bob & Ira Spring. 368 Ray Atkeson. 370 *top* Stephen J. Krasemann/DRK Photo. 371 *top* Ray Atkeson; *bottom* David Muench Photography, Inc. 372 Charlotte Casey/West Stock Inc. 373 Pat O'Hara. 374 *top* Ray Atkeson; *bottom* Bob & Ira Spring. 375 Ray Atkeson. 376 David Muench Photography, Inc. 377 Duane D. Davis. 378 *bottom* Ray Atkeson. 380 *bottom* Ray Atkeson. 381 *top* Ray Atkeson; *bottom* David Muench Photography, Inc. 382 Ray Atkeson. 383 *top* Ray Atkeson; *bottom* Oregon Department of Transportation Photo. 384 *upper* Ray Atkeson; *bottom* D. C. Lowe. 385 Ray Atkeson. 386 Oregon Department of Transportation Photo. 387 Ray Atkeson. 390 David Muench Photography, Inc. 391 David Muench Photography, Inc. 392 Bob Clemenz Photography. 393 David Muench Photography, Inc. 394 David Muench Photography, Inc. 395 *top* Lester A. Sebel; *bottom left* David Cavagnaro; *bottom right* Pat O'Hara. 396 *top* Clyde H. Smith; *bottom* E. S. Ross. 397 *top* David Muench Photography, Inc.; *bottom* Carolee Campbell/Shanti Productions, Inc. 398 *center* David Muench Photography, Inc. 400 A. Atwater/Shostal Associates. 401 Richard Marshall. 402 David Muench Photography, Inc. 403 David Muench Photography, Inc. 404 David Muench Photography, Inc. 405 *top* David Muench Photography, Inc.; *bottom* Richard Marshall. 408 *top* Richard Marshall; *bottom* Bob & Ira Spring. 409 Columbia Glacier Tours. 410 *top* Grant Heilman Photography; *bottom* Bob & Ira Spring. 411 Dennis L. Hellawell. 412 Bob & Ira Spring. 413 Richard Pardo. 414 *top* Bob & Ira Spring; *lower* Manuel A. Rodriguez. 415 Bob & Clara Calhoun/Bruce Coleman Inc. 416 *center* Castle & Cooke, Inc. 418 *top* Carroll C. Calkins; *bottom* Camera Hawaii. 419 Camera Hawaii. 420 Werner Stoy/Camera Hawaii. 421 *top* Bob Clemenz Photography; *bottom* Carroll C. Calkins. 422 Carroll C. Calkins. 423 Lester A. Sebel. 424 *top* Werner Stoy/Camera Hawaii; *inset* Ken Bates. 425 David Muench Photography, Inc. 426 *top* David Muench Photography, Inc.; *bottom right* Bob Clemenz Photography; *remainder* Carroll C. Calkins. 427 *top* David Muench Photography, Inc.; *bottom* Camera Hawaii.